The Collectors' Encyclopedia of
ANTIQUES

Associate Editors
David Coombs GREAT BRITAIN
Joseph Butler UNITED STATES OF AMERICA

Drawings by Christopher Evans

The Collectors' Encyclopedia of
ANTIQUES

Edited by Phoebe Phillips

BONANZA BOOKS · NEW YORK

Copyright © MCMLXXIII by Walter Parrish International Limited

All rights reserved.

This edition is published by Bonanza Books,
a division of Crown Publishers, Inc.

a b c d e f g h

Created by Walter Parrish International Limited,
London, England.

Designed by Hardy / Escasany / Lodwick
Printed in U.S.A.

Bonanza 1978 Printing

Library of Congress Cataloging in Publication Data

Phillips, Phoebe.
    The collectors' encyclopedia of antiques.

    Includes index.
    1. Antiques—Dictionaries.   I. Title.
NK28.P494 1978   745.1   78-14752
ISBN 0-517-26725-X

Contents

Contents

Introduction

There are many different crafts shown in the Collectors' Encyclopedia of Antiques but there is one which is demonstrated throughout the book and on every page—the craft of collecting.

The growth and development of a fine collection is, in a very real sense, a creative art. Beginning with an appreciation of beauty in its decorative and functional forms it leads to an apprenticeship in the study of history, techniques, style and the individual work of artisans and workshops. New research and discoveries ensure that the process of learning is never completely finished. Such knowledge adds immeasurably to the discrimination and pleasure which collectors gain for themselves and may pass on to others.

Freed from the immediate concerns of actual production, a collector may also understand the wider aspects of apparently unrelated crafts, for it has become increasingly clear that they did not exist in separate worlds but shared contemporary influences and even specific designs to a sometimes surprising extent.

Collecting is thus an education as well as a delight for those who achieve even the most modest display. And it is for collectors that this book has been produced.

Our purpose has been to provide a survey of the main collecting fields, together with some of the more important minor crafts. The editorial arrangement has been devised and constructed to be of the greatest practical use to collectors, using a new system which combines the largest possible number of illustrations in the space available with an authoritative text, to give comprehensive reviews of the most important periods.

Each of the sixteen subjects covered in the book has its own section, beginning with a table of contents, introduction, historical and technical aspects of the craft involved, and ending with a glossary, information on maintenance and repair, a list of books for further reading, major museum collections in Great Britain and the United States, and a short index. There is also a main index at the end of the book.

The majority of the subjects have been divided geographically and these geographical groups have been arranged in chronological sequence, according to the date of their most important and most influential periods. For example, the development of Chinese ceramics was followed by Korean ware. In the Western world, there was a greater division between pottery and porcelain, with pottery developing on the Continent in the fifteenth, sixteenth and seventeenth centuries, in England in the seventeenth, eighteenth and nineteenth centuries and in the United States in the eighteenth and nineteenth centuries. Porcelain developed in very much the same way.

This sequence has been followed in most of the sections to enable the reader to understand the evolution of the various crafts, which often spread from one area to another and from one century to the next.

In some minor subjects, there are a few exceptions to the geographical divisions, where a smaller number of illustrations has made it more practical to adhere to the classifications usually followed by collectors; Bottles have been grouped according to use, Boxes by date; Paperweights have been divided into types, as have both Musical and Scientific Instruments, and Toys and Automata.

The geographical terms are generally self-evident; *America* indicates the United States of America, *Continental* the mainland of Europe; and *European* is used for the entire European continent, including Great Britain. *British* generally includes all the British Isles and where appropriate, Ireland.

The subjects themselves, or categories of collecting, have been chosen carefully; the term 'antiques' is generally understood to mean products of the Applied Arts, rather than the Fine Arts, made by craftsmen before the growth of mass-produced factory wares. We have also included objects which show the historical background of each craft, since their traditional skills often extend back into antiquity; in a few cases, we have included modern pieces where innovations have occured which still use the old skills.

However, the main emphasis throughout the book has been concentrated on the eighteenth and nineteenth centuries, where the examples illustrated will be of greatest value to collectors in identification.

The black and white photographs have been marked *a, b,* etc. according to their position on the page. This has been done so that cross-references may be found immediately— these give the page number followed by the letter. In addition, there are subject headings in the margins of almost every page, so that while thumbing through the book, not only the main subject, but the country and usually the date, may be pinpointed at once.

In the long and often complicated task of compiling this book, our thanks are due especially to our contributors. Biographical notes will be found on page 13, but no mere list can convey the gratitude we feel for their hard work and enthusiastic response.

To Roger Barrett in London and Herbert Michelman in New York, our thanks are due for their early and continuing encouragement and support. To David Coombs and Joseph T. Butler, our thanks for their valued contribution as Advisory Editors.

We should also like to acknowledge the help we have received from the many individuals, museums and institutions all over the world in providing the illustrations; and especially the work of Rod Shone in London and Ray Errett at Corning who took the majority of the many photographs commissioned especially for this book. A full list of photographic credits is provided on page 10. We should also like to thank Christopher Evans, whose drawings add much to the detail and design and Mrs. Lloyd, whose drawings ornament the embroidery section.

Last but by no means least, my own very real thanks to our editorial and production staff, particularly, Timothy Auger, Frances McFadyen and Jane Maitland Hudson, who have all worked tirelessly in making this book possible.

Phoebe Phillips, London

Acknowledgements

Acknowledgements are due to the following for permission to reproduce photographs. Thanks are also due to the numerous private collectors whom it has been impossible to acknowledge in detail. Page numbers of colour plates are printed bold.

ARMS AND ARMOUR
Messrs. Sotheby & Co.: 16, 20*a, b, c, d*, 21*a, b, c, d*, 22*b, c, d*, 23*a, b, c*, 24*a right*, 24*a left*, 24*b*, 25*b, c, d*, 26*a, b, c, d*, 28*a, d*, 29*a, b, c, d*, 30*a, b, c, d*, 31*a, c*, 32*b*, 35*d*, 36*a, c*. The Dove Collection: 22*a*. The Durrant Collection: 23*d*. Formerly the Mungean Collection: 25*a*, 28*c*. Formerly the Gyngell Collection: 31*b*. Private Collections; photographs Michael Dyer Associates, London: **33, 34.** Messrs. Christie, Manson & Woods, London: 35*a, b, c*. Private Collection; photographs Bluford Muir: 38*a, b, c*. National Museum of History and Technology, the Smithsonian Institution, Washington: 38*d*, 39*a, b, c, d*, 40*b, c, d*, 41*a, b, c, d*, 42*a, b, c, d*, 43*a, b, c, d*. The Connecticut State Library, Hartford: 39*d*, 40*a*.

BOTTLES
Collection J. M., London; photographs Imitor: 48, **51,** 54*a*, 55*c*, 59*c*, 60*b, c, d*. Collection J. M., London: 59*a, d*, 60*a*. Leslie Scott: 59*b*. The Wellcome Trustees, London: 54*b, d*, 55*a*. The O'Brien Collection, Liverpool: 55*d*, 56*b, d*. Harveys Wine Museum, Bristol: 57*a, c, d*, 58*b*. The Pilkington Museum of Glass, St Helens: 57*b*, 58*a, c, d*. The Corning Museum of Glass, New York: 54*c*, 55*b*, 56*a, c*.

BOXES
Courtesy of Wartski, London, and Private Collections: **52.** The Metropolitan Museum of Art, New York: 62*a, c, d*, 64*a, d*, 65*a, d*, 66*a, b, c*, 67*a*, 68*b, c*, 69*a, b, c*. Collection Haags Gemeentemuseum, The Hague: 62*b*. The Colonial Williamsburg Collection, Williamsburg: 63*a, b*. The Victoria and Albert Museum, Crown Copyright, London: 63*c, d*, 65*b*, 67*b, d*. Trustees of the Wallace Collection, London: 64*b, c*. The Wrightsman Collection; photograph Taylor & Dull, New York: 65*c*. The Art Institution of Chicago, Chicago: 66*d*, 68*d*. The Henry Francis du Pont Winterthur Museum, Delaware: 67*c*. The City of Norwich Museums, Norwich: 68*a*, 69*d*.

CARPETS AND RUGS
Perez (London) Ltd., London: 74, 78*a, b, c*, 79*a, b, c*, 80*a, b, c*, 81*a, b*, 82*a, b*, 83*a, b, c*, 84*a, b, c*, **85, 86, 87,** 89*a, b, c*, 90*a, b, c*, 91*a, b, c*, 92*a, b*, 93*a, b, c*, 94*a, b*, 95*a, b*, 97*a*, 98*b*, 99*a, b*. Ibrahim Beyhum Esq.: **88** *top*. D. C. Dron Esq.: **88** *bottom*, **105, 106** *top & bottom*. Lindfield Galleries: **107.** Messrs. Sotheby & Co., London: 97*b*. The Vigo-Sternberg Galleries, London: 98*a*, 100*a, b* drawing (Christopher Evans). The Victoria and Albert Museum, Crown Copyright, London: 100*c*.

CERAMICS
The Victoria and Albert Museum, London; photographs by C. H. Cannings: **108, 126, 179, 180, 197, 198.** Ostasiatiska Museet, Stockholm: 113*a*. The Smithsonian Institution, Freer Gallery of Art, Washington: 113*b*, 128*c*. The William Rockhill Nelson Gallery of Art, Kansas City: 113*c*. The Ashmolean Museum, Oxford: 113*d*. The Victoria and Albert Museum, Crown Copyright, London: 114*a*, 116*c*, 117*b, e*, 119*c*, 122*b, d*, 123*d*, 124*a*, 131*c, d*, 132*a, b, c, d*, 133*a, b, c, d*, 134*a, b, c, d*, 135*a, c, d*, 136*b*, 137*b*, 138*c*, 139*a, b, c, d*, 145*a, d*, 146*b, d*, 147*a, b, d*, 148*a, c*, entries 170*a*–186*d*, and 188*a*–204*d* inclusive. The Arts Council of Great Britain, The Seligman Collection: 114*b*, 120*b*. The Tokyo National Museum; photograph provided by The Arts Council: 116*b*. The National Trust, Ascott House: 114*c*. Mrs Alfred Clark: 114*d*, 119*b*. Mrs Brodie Lodge: 115*a*. The Percival David Foundation of Chinese Art, London: 115*b, c, d*, 117*d*, 118*a, c*, 119*b*, 120*a*, 121*a, c*, 123*b, c*, 124*c, d*, **125.** The Trustees of the British Museum, London: 116*a*, 121*d*, 124*e*. Sir Harry and Lady Garner: 116*d*, 122*a* (on display at the Leicester Art Gallery). The Bristol City Art Gallery: 117*a*. The Trustees of the Barlow Collection, The University of Sussex: 118*b*. Mrs Otto Harriman: 118*d*. The Burrell Collection, Glasgow Art Gallery and Museum: 119*a*. Spink & Son Ltd., London: 120*d*. The Avery Brundage Collection, San Francisco: 121*b*. Foundation Alfred & Eugenie Baur-Duret, Geneva: 122*c*, 124*b*. The Brooklyn Museum, New York: 128*a*. Faber & Faber Ltd.: 128*b*, 129*a*. The Gompertz Collection: 129*b, c, d*. Musée Jacques Audibert, Lodève: 131*a*. Maidstone Museum: 131*b*, 141*b*. Hastings Museum: 135*b*, 137*c*, 138*d*, 146*c*. Courtesy of Gerald Reitlinger: 136*a, c, d*, 137*a, d*, 138*a, b*, 140*d*, **143, 144,** 145*b*. The Boymans van Beuningen Museum, Rotterdam: 140*a, b*. Collection Haags Gemeentemuseum, The Hague: 140*c*, 141*a, d*. The Rijksmuseum, Delft: 142*a*. Musées Royaux d'art et d'histoire; photographs A.C.L., Brussels: 142*c, d*. Gemeente Museum, Arnhem: 141*c*, 142*b*. Musée de Saumur; photograph J. Decker: 145*c*, 146*a*, 147*c*. Historisches Museum, Basel: 148*b, d*. Nationalmuseum, Stockholm: 149*a, b*. Kunstindustrimuseet, Copenhagen: 149*c, d*. The City Museum and Art Gallery, Stoke-on-Trent: 151*a, c*, 152*b, c, d*, 153*b, d*, 154*a, b, c, d*, 155*d*, 156*c, d*, 157*a, b, c, d*, 158*a, d*, 159*a, b, c*, 160*a*, **161, 162,** 163*c, d*, 164*a, b, c*. The City of Manchester Art Galleries, The Thomas Greg Collection: 151*b, d*, 152*a*, 153*a, c, e*, 155*a, b, c*, 156*a, b*, 158*b, c*. The Haggar Collection: 159*d*, 160*b, c, d*, 163*a, b*. Mrs Frank Nagington's Collection: 164*d*. The National Museum of History and Technology, the Smithsonian Institution, Washington: 165, 166*a, b, d, e*, 167*a, b, c, d, e*, 168*a, b, c, d, e*, 206*b, c*, 207*a, b, c, d*, 208*a, b, c, d*, **215.** Old Salem Inc., Winston-Salem: 166*c*. The Philadelphia Museum of Art: 205. The Yale University Art Gallery, New Haven: 206*a*.

CLOCKS AND WATCHES
Private Collection: **216, 265.** The Kellenberger Museum, Winterthur: 220*a left*, 220*a right*, 220*b, c*, 223*a left*, 223*a right*, 223*c*. Crown copyright, Science Museum, London: 221*a right*, 221*a left*, 224*c*, 226*b*, 230*a*, 232*a*, 236*d right*, 236*d left*, 255*a*, 256*a*, 261*c*, 262*a*, 263*c, d*. Lent to the Science Museum, London by Dr E. G. Manton, London, Warren Polloch Esq., London and Messrs. Negretti & Zambra Ltd., London: 231*d*, 258*a left*, 258*a right*. The Science Museum, London: 262*d*, 263*b*. The Victoria and Albert Museum, Crown Copyright, London: 221*b*, 225*a*, 228*a*, 230*d*, 231*b*, 232*c, d*, 233*b*, 234*a, c, d*, 235*a*, 236*c*, 243*b*, 246*b*, 251*a, b, c, d*, 252*a*, 252*a right*, 252*b, c*, 253*a left*, 253*a right*, 253*c left*, 253*d right*, 256*d*, 257*b, c*, 261*a, b, d*, 262*b, c*, 263*a*, 264*a, b, c*. Musée International d'Horlogerie, La Chaux de Fonds: 221*c*, 222*a, b, c, d*, 223*b*, 224*a, b*. Museo Nazionale della Scienza e della Technica Leonardo da Vinci, Milan: 224*d left*, 224*d right*, 225*b, c*, 228*b*. The Trustees of the British Museum, London: 226*a*, 256*c*, 257*a*. The Trustees of the Wallace Collection, London: 226*c*, 227*a, b, c, d*, 264*d*. Messrs. Christie, Manson & Woods, London: 226*d*. Marouf, Düsseldorf: 228*c left*, 228*c centre*. Strike One, London: 228*d*, 229*b*. R. J. Street: 229*c, d*, 232*b*, 236*a*, 238*a, b, c, d*, 240*a, b*, 246*a*, 247*c*, 249*a*. Kingston Antiques: 230*b, c*, 231*a*, 233*d*, 236*b*, 256*b*, 259*c left*, 259*c right*. Aubrey Brocklehurst: 231*c*. Leicester Museum and Art Gallery: 233*a*. Adrian Burchall Antique Clocks, Bristol: 233*c*, 235*b*. Bayerisches Nationalmuseum, Munich: 237*a, b, c, d*. A. J. White: 239*a*. Heimat Uhrenmuseum, Schwenningen: 239*b*, 242*a, b*. G. Gunning: 239*c*. H. L. Burrows: 239*d*. J. H. Ingall: 240*c*. F. A. van Weijom Claterbos: 240*d*, 241*a, b, c, d, e*. G. Grunsell: 242*c*. Aarhus Kunstmuseum: 242*d*, 259*a, b*. The American Clock and Watch Museum, Bristol: 243*a, c, d*, 244*a left and right*, 244*b, c*, 245*b*, 246*c, d*, 247*a*, 248*b, c, d*, 249*b*. M. J. Tatham: 245*a*. A. W. Fayle: 247*b*. Brian Pearson: 247*d, e*, 249*c*. L. Cheetham: 248*a*. C. S. Jagger: 253*b*, 254*a*, 254*a right*, 254*b, c*, 255*b, c left*, 255*c right*, 257*d*, 258*b left*, 258*b right*. N. Bloom & Son, London: **266.**

EMBROIDERY AND NEEDLEWORK
Messrs. Sotheby & Co., London: 272. City of Norwich Museums *(top)*, Private Collection *(bottom)*; photographs by Coe of Norwich: **283.** On loan to the Maritime Museum, Great Yarmouth: 279*d*. Courtesy of the City of Norwich Museums: 276*e right*, 277*a, c, d*, 278*a, c, d, e*. A.C.L., Brussels: 281*a*. The Victoria and Albert Museum, Crown Copyright, London: 281*b, c, d*, 286*a, b*. The Needlework Development Scheme, Glasgow: 282*a, b, c, d*, 285*b*, 286*c, d*. The Rijksmuseum, Amsterdam: 285*a*. The Kunstindustrimuseet, Oslo: 285*c, d*. The John Judkyn Memorial, Bath: 288*a*, 289*a*. The American Museum in Britain, Bath: **284,** 288*b, c*, 289*b, c*, 290*b, c, d*, 291*a, b, c, d*, 292*a, b, c, d*, 293*c*. The Metropolitan Museum of Art, New York: 290*a*. Historic Deerfield: 293*a*. The Pocumtuck Valley Memorial Association: 293*b*.

FURNITURE

Country Life, London: 298. The Victoria and Albert Museum, London: **301, 302, 320.** The Victoria and Albert Museum, Crown Copyright, London: 305*a*, *b*, *c*, 306*a*, 314*c*, 373*b*, 377*a*, *c*, 378*a*, 379*b*, 381*c*, 322*a*, *b*, *c*, 323*c*, 324*c*, 325*a*, *b*, 326*b*, 327*b*, *c*, 328*a*, *c*, 329*b*, *c*, 330*a*, *b*, 331*a*, 333*c*, 334*a*, *b*, *c*, *d*, 335*b*, 336*b*, 337*a*, *b*, 337 *left*, 337*c right*, 339*b*, *c*, *d*, 340*b*, 341*b*, *c*, 342*a*, *c*, 343*b*, *c*, 345*a*, *b*, *c*, 346*a*, 347*c*, 348*a left*, 349*a right*, 353*b*, 355*c*, 357*c*, 358*b*, 359*a*, 360*a*, *b*, 361*a*, 362*a*, *c*, *d*, 363*c*, 364*a*, *c*, 365*b*, *c*, 366*c*. The National Trust, Attingham Park: 306*b*, *c*, *d*. Courtesy of Ronald A. Lee, London: 307*a*. Museu Esola de Artes Decorativas, Lisbon; print loaned by the Hamlyn Publishing Group: 307*b*. Palacio Nationale, Madrid; print loaned by the Hamlyn Publishing Group: 307*c*. The Rijksmuseum, Amsterdam: 308*a*, *b*, 309*a*, *b*, 310*a*, *b*, 311*a*, *b*, *c*, 313*c*. The Centraal Museum, Utrecht: 308*c*. Castle Amerongen, Amerongen: 308*d*. The Fries Museum, Leeuwarden: 310*c*. The Schleswig-Holstein Landesmuseum, Schleswig: 312*b*. Staatliche Kunstsammlungen, Dresden: 312*a*. Sansouci, Potsdam; print supplied by Deutsche Fotothek, Dresden: 312*c*. Schloss Moritzburg; print supplied by Deutsche Fotothek, Dresden: 313*a*. Braunschweig Museum; print supplied by C. H. Beck'sche Verlagsbuchhandlung, Munich: 312*d*. Museum für Kunst und Gewerbe, Hamburg: 313*b*. Museum für Kunsthandwerk, Frankfurt-am-Main; prints loaned by the Hamlyn Publishing Group: 314*a*, *b*. Nationalhistoriske Museum, Frederiksborg: 315*a*, *b*, *d*, 316*a*. Rosenborg Castle, Copenhagen: 315*c*, 316*b*. Kunstindustrimuseet, Copenhagen: 316*c*. The Royal Collection, Stockholm: 317*a*, *b*, *c*, 318*a*, *b*. Courtesy of William H. Stokes, Rutland: 322*d*. Algernon Asprey Ltd., London: 323*a*, 329*b*. William Job Ltd., London: 323*b*. Messrs. Christie, Manson & Woods, London: 324*a*, *b*, 331*b*, 333*b*, 338*c right*, 342*b*, 344*b*, 348*c*, 351*d*, 361*d*. Barling of Mount Street Ltd., London: 326*a* (2 prints). Biggs of Maidenhead: 326*c*, 330*c*, 344*c*. Phillips of Hitchin Ltd.: 327*a*. John Keil Ltd., London: 328*b*. Mallett & Son Ltd., London: **319,** 331*d*, 333*a*, 336*a*, 346*b*, 350*a*, 360*c*, 363*d*. Frank Partridge & Sons, London: 332*b*, 347*a*. Phillips the Auctioneers, London: 335*a*, 338*b left*, 343*a*, 345*d*, 351*b*, 354*c left*, 354*c right*, 359*c*, 363*b*, 366*b*. Hotspur Ltd., London: 339*a*. Prides of London: 340*a*, 356*b*. John Bell of Aberdeen: 340*d*, 359*d*. Doveridge House Antiques, Tong: 341*a*, 359*b*. Glaishen & Nash Ltd.: 344*a*. Cecil Davis Ltd., London: 346*c*. M. Harris & Sons, London: 347*b*. Ayer & Co., London: 348*a right*, 350*b*, 351*c*, 358*a*. Private Collection; photographs by John Harrison: 348*b*, 353*a*, 364*b*. Gloria Antica, London: 349*b*. Charles Toller, Eton: 349*c*. Redburn Antiques: 350*c*. The Dower House Ltd.: 350*d*. Norman Adams Ltd., London: 352*a*, 355*b*. Woburn Antique Galleries; photographs by John Harrison: 353*c*, 354*b*, 362*b*. David Pettifer, London, 353*d*, 356*c*, *d*, 357*b*. Stair & Co. Ltd., London: 355*a*. The author's collection: 356*a*, 364*d*, 365*a*. Temple Newsam House, Leeds; print provided by *Collector's Guide:* 357*a*. The Beauchamp Galleries, London: 361*b*. Trevor, London: 361*c*. Aldric Young Antiques, Edinburgh: 363*a*. Photographie Giraudon, Paris: 367*a*. Musée de Cluny, Paris: 367*b*, *c*, 368*c*, 374*b*. Musées des Arts Décoratifs, Paris: 368*a*, *b*, 372*b*, 374*c*, 375*a*, 376*b*, 386*b*, *c*. The Philadelphia Museum of Art: 371*b*. Musée Rolin, Autun: 372*a*. Musée du Louvre, Paris: 371*a*, 373*a*, 374*a*, 375*b*, *c*. Connaissance des Arts, Paris: 373*c*, 378*b*, 382*c*, 385*a*. Courtesy of Messrs. Sotheby & Co., London: **369** *top*, 376*a*, 378*c*, 381*a*. The Wrightsman Collection; photographs supplied by the Metropolitan Museum of Art, New York: 376*c*, 378*b*, 379*a*. The Chateau de Fontainebleau: **369** *bottom*, **370,** 379*c*, 382*a*, *b*, 383*c*, 384*b*. The Trustees of the Wallace Collection, London: 380*a*, *b*. Caisse Nationale des Monuments Historiques, Paris: 380*c*. Napoleonmuseum, Arenenberg: 383. Musée National de Malmaison: 384*a*. Chateau de Valençay: 384*c*, *d*, 385*c*. Editions J. Delmas & Cie, Paris: 386*a*. The American Museum in Britain; photograph by D. Balmer: 387. The Angelo Hornak Picture Library, London: **388.** The Wadsworth Atheneum, Hartford: 390*a*, *b*, 400*d*. The Museum of Fine Arts, Boston: 390*c*, 392*a*, 393*a*, *d*, 395*a*, *b*, 399*a*, *b*, *c*, 400*a*, 401*b*, *c*, *d*, 402*b*, *c*. The Metropolitan Museum of Art, New York: 391*a*, 392*c*, 395*c*, 397*c*, 400*c*, 403*a*, *b*, *c*, *d*, 404*a*, *b*, *c*, *d*. The Bayou Bend Collection, The Museum of Fine Arts, Houston: 391*c*, 392*b*, 393*a*, 394*a*, *b*. Sotheby

Parke-Bernet, New York: 391*b*, 393*c*, 394*d*, 396*c*, 397*a*, 398*c*, 400*b*, 401*a*, 402*a*. Sleepy Hollow Restorations, Van Cortlandt Manor, Tarrytown: 391*d*. The Henry Francis du Pont Winterthur Museum, Delaware: 393*b*, 394*c*, 396*d*, 397*b*, *d*, 398*a*, *b*. The Philadelphia Museum of Art: 396*a*, *b*.

GLASS

Cecil Davis Ltd., London: 412, 419*d*, 420*b right*, **421** *right*, 424*b right*, 424*d*, 425*b*, 426*a*, *c*, *d*, 427*a*, *b*, *c*, 428*a*, *b*, *c*, *d*, 429*b*, *c*, 430*a*, *c*, 431*b*, *c*, *d*, 432*a*, *c*, *d*, 433*a*, *b*, *c*, 434*a*, *b*, 435*b*, 436*a*, *b*, 437*b*, *c*, *d*, 438*a*, *d*, 441*b*, *c*, 442*a*, *c*, 443*b*, *c*, *d*, 444*a*, *b*, *d*, 445*a*, *b*, 446*a*, *c*, *d*, 447*a*, *b*, *c*, 448*a*, *b*, *c*, 449*a*, *c*, 450*a*, *b*, *c*. The Trustees of the British Museum, London: 416*a*, *b*, *c*, 417*a*, *b*, *c*, 418*a*, *b*, *c*, *d*, 419*a*, *b*, *c*. The Victoria and Albert Museum, Crown Copyright, London: 420*a*, **421** *left*, 433*d*, 449*b*, 485*c*. Messrs. Sotheby & Co., London: 420*b left*, 424*a left*, 424*c*, 425*a*, 429*a*, 430*b*, 432*b*, 435*a centre*, 438*b*, *c*, 442*b*, 444*c*, 452*a*, *b*, *c*, *d*, 453*a*, *b*, *c*, *d*, 454*a*, *b*, 455*a*, *b*, *c*, 485*a*, 486*d*, 487*a left*, 496*a*, 498*d*, 499*a*, 501*d*. Alan Tillman (Antiques) Ltd., London: **422.** Philip Richardson's Collection: 425*c*, 427*e right*, 443*a*. K. A. Alexander: 426*b*. Private Collection: **439.** The Corning Museum of Glass; photograph by A. Hornak: 440. Richard Butterworth's Collection: 441*d*. Courtesy of the Worshipful Company of Grocers, from the collection of the late Col. W. Churchill Hale: 441*a*. By courtesy of Richard Dennis Antiques: 454*c*, *d*, 456*b*, 485*b*, 486*a*, 487*a centre*. Private Collections: photograph by A. Hornak: **457.** Corning Museum of Glass, New York; photographs Raymond Errett: **458,** 460*a*, *b*, *c*, 461*a*, *b*, 462*a*, *b*, *c*, 463*a*, *b*, *c*, 464*a*, *b*, *c*, *d*, 465*a*, *b*, *c*, 466*a*, *b*, *c*, *d*, 467*a*, *b*, *c*, *d*, 468*a*, *c*, 469*a*, *b*, 470*a*, *b*, *c*, 471*a right*, 471*b*, *c*, 472*a*, *b*, *c*, 474, **475, 476,** 477*a*, *b*, 478*a*, *b* (decanters), 478*c*, 481*a*, *c left*, 482*a*, 483*a*, 498*c*. The Corning Public Library: 481*b*. The National Museum of History and Technology, the Smithsonian Institution, Washington: 461*c left*, 461*c right*, 468*b*, 473*a*, *b*, 477*c*, 478*d*, 479*a*, 479*b left*, 479*b centre*, 480*a*, *b*, 481*c right*. The Metropolitan Museum of Art, New York: 471*a centre*. Oglebay Mansion Museum, Wheeling: 473*c*. Mrs Kenneth M. Wilson: 478*b* (jug). By kind permission of H.M. the Queen: 482*b*. Andre G. Billeci: 483*b*. Harvey K. Littleton: 483*b right*. Private Collection; Corning Museum photograph: 483*b left*. Musée du Verre, Liège: 488*d*. Private Collection; photographs A. C. Cooper Ltd.: 487*b right*, 488*c*. Private Collections; photographs by Taylor & Dull, New York: 491*a*, *b*, *c*, *d*, *e*, 492*a*, *b*, *d*, 495*a*, *b*, *c*, 496*b*, *c*, *d*, *e*, 497*a*, *b*, *c*, *d*, *e*, 498*a*, *b*, *e*, 499*c*, *d*, 500*a*, *c*, *d*, 501*a*, *c*, *e*. Spink & Son Ltd., London: 492*c*, **494,** 495*d*, *e*, 499*b*, *e*, 501*b*. Delomosne & Son, London (vase), and Private Collection (candle holder); photograph by A. Hornak: **493.** Sotheby Parke-Bernet, New York: 500*b*. Messrs. Christie, Manson & Woods, London: 500*e*.

JEWELLERY

N. Bloom & Son, London: 508, 514*c*, 516*b centre*, 517*c*. S. J. Phillips, London: 514*a*. The Rijksmuseum, Amsterdam: 514*b left*, 514*b right*. The Greater London Council as Trustees of the Iveagh Bequest, Kenwood House, London: 515*a*. The Victoria and Albert Museum, Crown Copyright, London: 515*b*, *c*, 517*a*, *b*, 518*a*, 519*a*, 521*c*. Messrs. Christie, Manson & Woods, London: 516*a left*, 518*c*. Van Cleet and Arpels Inc.: 514*d*. Wartski, London: 516*c*. The Lady Lever Collection, Port Sunlight: 516*d*. Connaissance des Arts, Paris: 518*b*. The City of Birmingham Museum and Art Gallery: 519*b*. Cameo Corner, London: **511,** 519*c*. Arthur C. Collinge, Halifax: **512** *top*. The American Museum in Britain; photograph by D. Balmer, Bristol: **512** *bottom*. The Metropolitan Museum of Art, New York: 519*d*, 522*d*, 523*c*, *d*. Sleepy Hollow Restorations; Van Cortlandt Manor, Tarrytown: 521*a*, *b*. The New York Public Library, Astor, Lenox and Tilden Foundation: 521*d*. The White House Collection, Washington: 522*a*. The National Museum of History and Technology, the Smithsonian Institution, Washington: 522*c*. The Cooper-Hewitt Museum of Decorative Arts and Design, the Smithsonian Institution, New York: 523*a*, *b*.

METALWORK

Raymond's News Agency, Derby: 526. The Victoria and Albert Museum, Crown Copyright, London: 530*a*, *b*, 531*c*, 532*c*, 533*b*, 538*d*, 539*a*, *b*, 540*a*.

Acknowledgements

The Royal Pavilion, Art Gallery & Museums, Brighton: 530c. Edward Leigh: 530d, 532b. The Trustees of the British Museum, London: 530e. The Castle Museum, York: 531a, 535a. Crown copyright, permission the Controller of H.M. Stationery Office: 531b. Michael R. Dudley: 531d. Thomas Photos, Oxford: 532a. Gwyneth Pennethorne: 532d. Mrs. V. H. Fairbairn-Eyton: 533a. The City of London Guildhall Museum, London: 533c. Edwin Smith: 533d, 534d, 536a. Peter Hunt: 534a. The Pharmaceutical Society of Great Britain: 535b. Private Collection; photographs Edward Leigh: 535c, 540c, d. Glasgow Museum & Art Gallery: 536b. Original photograph in *Old French Ironwork* by Edgar Frank; line drawing by Christopher Evans: 538a. Courtesy of Roger-Viollet, Paris; photograph provided by the Cooper-Bridgeman Library, London: 538b. Original photograph in *The Encyclopaedia of Metalwork* by Otto Hover; line drawing by Christopher Evans: 538c. First reproduced in the *Gates of Veneto* by John Preece; photograph loaned by the Garnstone Press: 539c. The Syndics of the Fitzwilliam Museum, Cambridge: 540b. Leonard Lassalle, Tunbridge Wells; photograph by A. Hornak: **545.**

MUSICAL INSTRUMENTS

The Victoria and Albert Museum, London: **546.** The Victoria and Albert Museum, Crown Copyright, London: 550a, c, 552d. The Victoria and Albert Museum, London; photograph by R. Shone: 552c. Castello Sforzesco, Museo degli strumenti Musicali, Milan: 550b. The Colt Clavier Collection: 550d. Kunsthistorisches Museum, Vienna: 551a. The Ashmolean Museum, Oxford: 551b. The Royal College of Music, London: 551c. Museo Civico, Bologna: 551d. W. H. Hill Ltd.: 552a. Musée André-Jacquemart, Paris: 552b *left*. The Horniman Museum, London: 553a, b, 554c *right*. The Grosvenor Museum, Chester: 553c. Pyramid Photographic, Nottingham: 553d. Musée Instrumental du Conservatoire National de Musique, Paris: 554a. Germanisches Nationalmuseum, Nürnberg: 554b *centre*, 555a. National Army Museum, London: 554d. The F. F. Hill Collection: 555b. Keith Harding Antiques, London: 555c, d.

NETSUKE AND INRO

The Victoria and Albert Museum, Crown Copyright, London: 560. Mr Raymond Bushell: **563, 564,** 566a–570d and 572c–574d. Collection of Lee Yu-kuan, Tokyo: 572a, b.

PEWTER

Dr and Mrs R. Mallory's Collection: 578, 592a *left*, 593b *left*, 593c. Trustees of the British Museum, London: 582a. The City of London Guildhall Museum, London: 582b. The City of Birmingham Museum & Art Gallery: 582c. John Pinkus: 582d. The Victoria and Albert Museum, Crown Copyright, London: 583c. The Worshipful Company of Pewterers, London: 583d. Art Gallery of New South Wales, Sydney: 584b, 585d. Messrs. Sotheby & Co., London: 585c, 587a, b, 588b, d, 589a, b. The Richard Mundey Collection: 586d, 587 *top*. The Rijksmuseum, Amsterdam: 588a. Mr and Mrs Thomas Williams: 591a, 592c *right*, 592d *left*, 593d. The Henry Francis du Pont Winterthur Museum, Delaware: 591b, 593a. The National Museum of History and Technology, the Smithsonian Institution, Washington: 591c. The New Haven Historical Society, New Haven: 591d. Greenfield Village and Henry Ford Museum, Dearborn: 592d *right*. Mr and Mrs Harvey Muehlenbeck: 592e. The Museum of Early Decorative Arts: 593b *right*.

SCIENTIFIC INSTRUMENTS

The Whipple Museum of the History of Science, Cambridge; photographs by P. A. L. Brunney: **598, 615.** Whipple Museum of the History of Science, Cambridge: 602a, 603b, 604c, 605b, 607a, 609a, d, 611a. Whipple Museum of the History of Science, Cambridge; photographs Edward Leigh: 604b, 606b, c, 609c. The Royal Scottish Museum, Edinburgh; photographs Tom Scott: 602b, c, 603a, d, 604a, d, 605d, 611b. The Rijksmuseum, Leiden: 602d. The Museum of the History of Science, Oxford: 603c, 608b, 610a, b, c, 611c. The Peabody Museum, Salem: 605a, 607b, 608a, 609b. Deutches

Museum, Munich: 605c. The Metropolitan Museum of Art, New York: 606a, d. The National Maritime Museum, Greenwich: 607c, d. Universiteitsmuseum, Utrecht: 608c, d. Crown copyright, Science Museum, London: 610d, 611d.

SILVER

The Victoria and Albert Museum, Crown Copyright, London: **616, 652.** The Metropolitan Museum of Art, New York: 620a, b, d, 621a, 622a, c, 623a, b, c, 624a, b, c, 625b, c, 626a, b, c, d, 627a, b, c, 628a, b, 629a, b, c, d, 630a, b, c, 631a, b, c, d, 632c, 635a, b, c, 636b, c. The Hispanic Society of America, New York: 620c. Musée des Arts Décoratifs, Strasbourg: 625a, 632b. Museu National de Arte Antiga, Lisbon: 632a. Messrs. Christie, Manson & Woods, London: **634,** 638d, 640b, c, 641c, d, 642c, d, 643b, c, 644a, b, c, 645c, d, 646b, 647c, d, 648b, c, 649a, b, d, 650a, d, 653e, 654b, 655a, 655c, 658a, b, d, 659a, b, d, 660a, c, d, 661b, c, d, e, 662c, 667d. The Victoria and Albert Museum, Crown Copyright, London: 636a, 660b. The Worshipful Company of Goldsmiths, London: 638a, b, c, 639a, b, c, 646a, 663a, d. Messrs. Sotheby & Co., London: 639d, 642a, 644d, 645b, 648a, 653a, c, 656d, 657d, 659c, 661a, 662a, b, d. H. R. Jessop Ltd.: 640a. The Worshipful Company of Mercers', London: 640d. Garrard & Co., London: 641a, 646c, 647a, 663e. Spink & Son Ltd., London: 642d, 655d. Bracher & Sydenham, Reading: 643a, 656c. The Worshipful Company of Vintners, London: 643d. J. H. Bourdon-Smith Ltd., London: 650b, 658c. Private Collection: **651.** S. J. Shrubsole Corp., New York: 653d, 673c, 676b. Bearnes Salerooms, Torquay: 654c. Thomas Lumley Ltd.: 654d, 656b. David Udy: 655b. Asprey & Co., London: 656a. Simon Kaye Ltd.: 657b, 663b, 664a, b. Hennells Ltd.: 657c. Gerald Benney: 663c. Courtesy of the Museum of Fine Arts, Boston: 666a, d, 672c, 673d, 675c, d. Firestone & Parson Inc., Boston: 666b, 671b, 672a, 674b, c, d, 676a. The Henry Francis du Pont Winterthur Museum, Delaware: 666c, 667c. The Yale University Art Gallery, New Haven: 667a, 668c, d, 671d. The Fogg Art Museum, Harvard University, Cambridge, Mass.: 667b. Israel Sack Inc., New York: 668a, 672b. Ginsburg & Levy, New York: 668b. The American Museum in Britain; photographs by D. Balmer, Bristol: **669, 670.** Courtesy of the Department of State, Washington: 671a, 673b. The Dartmouth College Collection, Hanover: 671c, 672d. Harry Arons, Bridgeport: 673a. Collection of the Albany Institute of History of Art, New York: 674a. Courtesy of Sotheby, Parke-Bernet, New York: 675a, 676c. The Virginia Historical Society, Richmond: 675b. Hobart House, Haddam: 676d. Gebelein Silversmiths, Boston: 677a, c, d. R. T. Trump Inc., Philadelphia: 677b.

TOYS

Courtesy of Messrs. Christie, Manson & Woods, London: 682, 695b, 696a *left*, 696a *right*, 696c. The Syndics of the Fitzwilliam Museum, Cambridge: 686a *left*, 686a *right*, 689d. The Huntly House Museum, on display at Lady Stair's House, Edinburgh: 686b. The Victoria and Albert Museum, Crown Copyright, London (items on display at the Bethnal Green Museum): 686c *left*, 686c *right*, 689a. The Farncombe Community: **687.** The New York Historical Society: **688.** The Victoria and Albert Museum, London (items on display at the Bethnal Green Museum): 689b, 691c, 692c, 693a *left*, 693b, 694b, 696b, d. Mrs Margot Siesbye, Copenhagen: 696d. Greenfield Village and Henry Ford Museum, Dearborn: 689c, 695d. Courtesy of the Ilfracombe Museum, Ilfracombe: 690a. The Liverpool City Museum: 690b. Courtesy of Messrs. Sotheby & Co., London: 690c. The Museum and Art Gallery, Wardown Park, Luton: 690d. The Misses Boyd: 691a. The City of Birmingham Museum and Art Gallery: 691b. The City Museum, St. Albans: 691d. Collection of Mrs Linda Hannas: 692a. City Museum, Bristol, on display at Blaise Castle House Museum, Henbury: 692b, 694c, 695c. Peterborough City Museum and Art Gallery: 692d, 695a. Collection of Robert Schiffman: 693a *right*, 693c *left*, 693c *right*. Museum of the City of New York: 693d. Courtesy, Essex Institute, Salem: 694a. Collection of Mrs Estrid Faurholt: 694d. Mrs Betty Cadbury: 696a.

Contributors

FREDERICK WILKINSON is one of Britain's leading authorities on the subject of arms and armour. He is well known as a collector and as the author of an impressive number of books.

HAROLD L. PETERSON is widely known as an expert and writer on American arms and armour, serving as adviser to organizations such as Colonial Williamsburg, and holding office in the International Association of Museums of Arms and Military History, among others.

WENDY EVANS worked in the British glass industry for many years, scripting and arranging many exhibitions. A member of the Committee and Editorial Sub-committee of the Glass Circle, she is now with the City of Liverpool Museum.

CLARE LE CORBEILLER, an Assistant Curator of Western European Arts in the Metropolitan Museum of Art, New York, has written on boxes, European goldsmiths' work, and China trade porcelain.

ROY E. G. MACEY is Deputy Editor of Carpet Review, the leading international trade paper, and has been their authority on Oriental carpets for eighteen years. Prior to that, he was with the world's largest specialist Oriental carpet dealers.

LT. COL. W. B. R. NEAVE-HILL is the Oriental Ceramic Society's Honorary Secretary, serving on various exhibition committees—notably for the Sung and Ching dynasty exhibitions, 1960 and 1965, and the Ceramic Art of China exhibition, 1972, at the Victoria and Albert Museum, London.

DIANA IMBER DOLAN is English, and has worked with many leading museum authorities, writing, and doing research and translations in the field of applied art and art history. She is also very interested in Romanesque architecture and pre-history.

REGINALD G. HAGGAR was Art Director of Mintons, Ltd., Head of Stoke Art School, and then of Burslem Art School. Consultant to the Tile and Pottery industry since 1935, he has lectured and written extensively on English pottery.

JOHN P. CUSHION is the Senior Research Assistant in the Department of Ceramics of the Victoria and Albert Museum, London. His lectures on pottery and porcelain, and his books, are well known both in Britain and America. He is an honorary member of the English Ceramic Circle.

C. MALCOLM WATKINS has been Chairman of the Smithsonian Institution's Department of Cultural History since 1968. One of his primary interests has been American traditional pottery, and the Smithsonian's collections have grown considerably under his direction.

E. J. TYLER, a member of both British and American Horological Societies, was an organiser of the 1956 Exhibition at the Science Museum, London, commemorating the invention of the pendulum clock. He devotes much time to study, and experimenting with old methods of clockmaking.

PAMELA CLABBURN has worked as a lingère, dressmaker, embroiderer, conservator of textiles, and teacher of all these subjects. She is Assistant Keeper of Social History at the City of Norwich Museum, England, with special responsibility for textiles.

MARY EIRWEN JONES is an active member of many needlework societies, and has published books on needlework and related subjects. Four of her books have been in her native Welsh language.

EILEEN GONIN has worked in journalism, and has travelled widely, as well as living on the Continent for a time. She was a guide with the National Trust, and has been at the American Museum in Britain since 1968, becoming Associate Curator there in 1970.

LINDSAY BOYNTON was formerly at Leeds University, and is now at Westfield College, University of London. A Fellow of the Royal Historical Society, and of the Society of Antiquaries, he was a founder of the Furniture History Society.

COLOMBE SAMOYAULT-VERLET is a paleographer, and lectures at the Ecole du Louvre. She is the Curator of the French National Museum, the Château de Fontainebleau, and an acknowledged expert on French Furniture.

ANTHONY BIRD is a specialist in antique English furniture, and clocks in particular; in 1938 he set up an antique business in London's old Caledonian market. After five years as a chair-borne soldier, he returned to antiques in 1949.

JOSEPH T. BUTLER is Curator of Sleepy Hollow Restorations in Tarrytown, New York, Adjunct Associate Professor of Architecture at Columbia University, and American Editor of The Connoisseur. He has published numerous books on various aspects of American decorative arts.

Contributors

GABRIELLA GROS-GALLINER lives in London, and is a collector with a scholar's attitude to the subject of antique glass. She is a member of the International Association for the History of Glass, and of the Circle of Glass Collectors.

DEREK C. DAVIS, F.R.S.A., inherited the antique business he still runs from his father. His particular interest is in English and Irish glass, on which he lectures frequently, and his books are well known to collectors everywhere. He is a Fellow of the Royal Society of Art.

PAUL V. GARDNER has been Curator of Ceramics and Glass in the National Museum of History and Technology, at the Smithsonian Institution, Washington D.C., since 1957. He was previously associated with Steuben Glass, and Corning Glass Works, as designer and assistant to Frederick Carder.

KENNETH M. WILSON is Assistant Director-Curator of the Corning Museum of Glass, New York State, and in addition to his work at the Museum, has written widely on his subject, particularly on American glass and its history.

PAUL HOLLISTER, writer and artist, has been exhibiting since 1947 at galleries in America and Britain. He lives in New York City, and has written extensively on glass paperweights, lecturing at museum seminars, and to various glass clubs.

CHARLOTTEE GERE has a comprehensive knowledge of antique jewellery and its design. Her first book on the subject was published in 1972 (Chicago 1973) and she is now working on two forthcoming books. She lives in London.

RAYMOND LISTER has been Vice-President of the Architectural Metal Craftsmen's Association since 1968, and was appointed Governor of the Federation of British Artists in 1972. He is also a Liveryman of the Worshipful Company of Blacksmiths.

MADEAU STEWART is a British Broadcasting Corporation producer and musicologist. For many years she has encouraged museums and private collectors to restore early instruments, so that their sound could be recorded for the B.B.C. Sound Archives.

RAYMOND BUSHELL has practised law in Tokyo since 1948. His initial interest in netsuke was engaged by F. M. Jonas, author of the first book in English on the subject. He was further encouraged by Kichijiro Tanaka, former manager of New York's Yamanaka shop.

The late RONALD F. MICHAELIS was a collector and specialist in antique pewterware for over thirty years. He was a Freeman of the Worshipful Company of Pewterers of London, a member and President of the Pewter Society, and Honorary Member of the Pewter Collectors' Club of America.

THOMAS D. WILLIAMS has catalogued and appraised many important pewter collections, and has served as consultant on American pewter to various museums. He is on the Board of Governors of the Pewter Collectors' Club of America, and was President from 1965 to 1967.

DAVID BRYDEN was for four years on the staff of the Royal Scottish Museum, Edinburgh, and is now Curator of the Whipple Museum of the History of Science in the University of Cambridge.

JESSIE MCNAB DENNIS, formerly with the Victoria and Albert Museum, London, is now Assistant Curator of Western European Arts in the Metropolitan Museum of Art, New York. Her particular interest is in English and Continental silver.

JUDITH BANISTER was Assistant Editor of *Watchmaker, Jeweller and Silversmith* for twelve years, and now freelances as a writer, and designer. Her books on English silver are well known to collectors in America as well as in her native Great Britain.

KATHRYN C. BUHLER was Assistant Curator in the Department of Decorative Arts and Sculpture of the Museum of Fine Arts, Boston, and was later appointed Fellow for Research in American Silver. Since retirement, she has been cataloguing the silver in the Campbell Museum collection.

GWEN WHITE's first book was published when she was still a student, and she has written numerous books on dolls and toys. She also writes for children, and does her own illustrations.

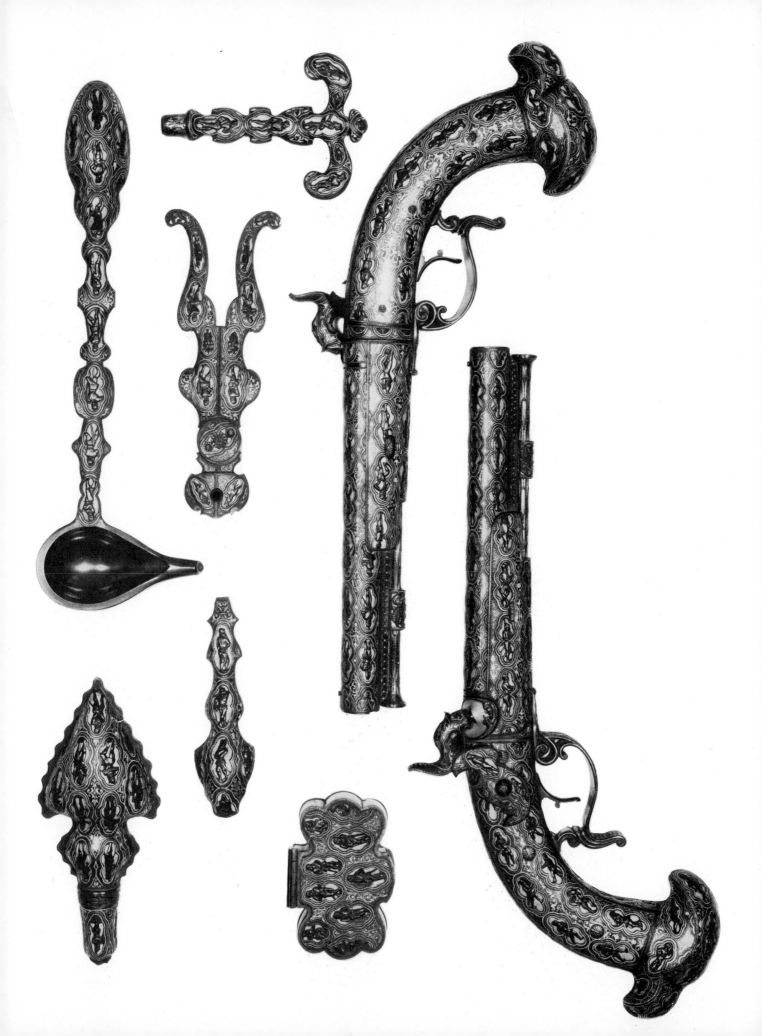

Arms and Armour

In his attempt to defeat his enemies Man has probably used more time and energy than in any other pursuit and his well-known desire to make objects not only functional but also attractive has thus applied to arms and armour. On swords and firearms he has applied his decorative talents, engraving, etching and embellishing with many skills, as well as constantly seeking after improved design and means of production.

There is a fairly clear, discernible line of development in all branches of arms and armour, and the skill devoted to their production, the mechanical ingenuity, and their aesthetic appeal, have all played their part in attracting collectors, who see them, perhaps mistakenly, as collectable items in their own right, entirely divorced from their prime functions of war and injury. The collector has a tremendously wide choice—indeed the only limiting factors are those of personal fancy and financial resources. The number of collections has steadily increased over the last few years, and this increased demand, together with vagaries in the world's economy, has caused an astonishing increase in value. Regrettably, the possibility of large profits has encouraged the production of fakes and forgeries of very high quality, and today it is more important than ever to know one's subject.

Firearms can for all practical purposes be regarded as a fourteenth century innovation; for the collector there is little hope of acquiring anything pre-dating the second half of the sixteenth century, and the chances of these are pretty remote. There are some good quality pieces from the late sixteenth and seventeenth centuries, and for the average collector the period from the mid-eighteenth to the mid-nineteenth century is likely to prove stimulating and worthwhile.

Swords offer wider scope for it is possible to obtain examples, albeit in excavated and somewhat deteriorated condition, of swords dating back to the Bronze Age. In good condition swords from the fifteenth century to the present day are comparatively common.

Armour is less certain and demand varies; however, the field is one offering the collector good opportunities for varied acquisitions and perhaps more unusual objects to display in a modern setting.

Opposite:
Percussion pistols, by Easebio Zuloaga of Eibar; Spain, 19th century.

Arms and Armour
The Craft

The earliest references to firearms in Europe occur early in the fourteenth century but it was not until the fifteenth century that they were produced in sufficient quantity to have a serious effect on military strategy and tactics. The matchlock was the earliest form of ignition and was to remain standard issue for large armies where expense was a big consideration until well into the middle of the seventeenth century. However, for simplicity and ease of handling, the appearance of the wheel-lock was of great importance. Wheel-locks first appeared early in the sixteenth century and were probably of Italian origin. This mechanism produced sparks by means of friction between a piece of pyrites and the grooved edge of a steel wheel; it was effective although very expensive to produce, and was replaced early in the seventeenth century by the much simpler and cheaper flintlock.

This lock also produced sparks by friction but used a much simpler system whereby a piece of common flint was scraped along the surface of a steel plate. The flintlock was to remain the prime means of ignition for firearms until the first quarter of the nineteenth century when research, headed by a Scottish cleric, Alexander Forsythe, led to the introduction of chemical means of ignition. Various compounds were struck by a metal hammer to produce a very small explosion, the flash of which could be used to ignite the main charge of gunpowder. The appearance of the percussion cap which utilized these chemicals in a simple, practical form, changed the face of the firearms industry for it enabled the production of efficient revolvers and later the first effective breech-loading and repeating rifles using a metallic cartridge.

Edged weapons are as old as man himself and range from simple flint hand-axes through to the elaborate swords worn today on ceremonial occasions. For the collector, the earliest to be found are likely to be the Bronze Age swords of which a number have survived. Apart from these, very few swords pre-dating the sixteenth century have survived. During the Middle Ages swords usually comprised a broad cutting blade with a simple cross hilt, but from the fifteenth century onwards there was a growing complexity of hand-guards or bars, loops and plates. There was also a change in technique from the rather crude cutting and slashing to a more extensive use of the point. During the sixteenth century swordsmiths produced the light, long-bladed rapier with its complex hand-guard. During the seventeenth century, there appeared the cup-hilt rapier and, from the middle of the century there was a general trend towards lighter, smaller weapons. Towards the end of the seventeenth century and during the first half of the eighteenth century the most popular sword for civilian wear was that known as the small sword which, although very light and decorative, was nevertheless an efficient means of defence and attack. The production of large quantities of efficient repeating firearms largely rendered the sword obsolete and during the nineteenth century, swords were commonly carried only by officers and cavalry. During the twentieth century the sword was relegated from a fighting weapon to an object of ceremony and ritual.

Armour dates back also to the ancient civilizations and has been fashioned from padded materials, leather, small overlapping plates (scale armour, interlocking metal rings, mail) and combinations of all types. During the Middle Ages, improved and more efficient swords made it necessary to supply increased protection which was achieved by the introduction of larger metal plates. The number of plates fitted to mail gradually increased until, by the early fifteenth century, the entire body was covered with plates, with mail forming a secondary defence. The increasing use of more powerful firearms reduced the defensive quality of armour and from the seventeenth century onwards there was a gradual abandoning of body defences until, by the early nineteenth century, only a few cavalry units in Europe retained a breast- and back-plate, although in Asia, armour continued in use until well into this century.

Continental Arms and Armour Introduction

On the Continent of Europe it was unusual to have long periods without wars; consequently, the demand for arms and armour was constant and heavy. It is hardly surprising therefore, that certain towns came to specialize in their production. Each country—indeed most towns—had its craftsmen capable of producing weapons and armour but during the Middle Ages two countries, Germany and Italy, emerged as the main source of supply. In Italy it was Milan in the north that acquired a great reputation for the amount and quality of armour which it could supply at very short notice. Italian armour was well made, and differed in style from that of German origin, tending to have a more rounded outline and shape. From Germany came much armour which was superb and the so-called Gothic armour, with its graceful shape and skilful design, was the finest ever produced. In the sixteenth century German smiths developed the Maximilian style with its characteristic fluting. The skill of German armourers was recognized by all and their services were often sought by rulers of other countries.

Swords were another speciality of the Germans with the town of Solingen producing blades in large quantities, a tradition which continued until this century, for it was from the workshops of Solingen that the daggers and swords of the Third Reich came.

With the appearance of firearms, Germany rather lost her prime position and gradually France and Belgium took over the market. Liège became one of the main centres of firearms production, especially of the commonplace varieties, including very cheap percussion pistols and revolvers.

France developed quite an extensive arms industry which reached a peak during the Napoleonic era when her factories supplied huge quantities of weapons and armour. There were a number of top quality craftsmen working at this period and some of the most decorative of weapons were produced by Nicolas-Noël Boutet who worked for a period at Versailles. During the nineteenth century the French firearms industry expanded and, in particular, produced numbers of cased sets of percussion duelling pistols. The continental makers fitted their weapons in cases with contoured divisions, each weapon and accessories slotted into its own specially shaped division.

Spain was also famed for the quality of its swords and those from Toledo were especially valued, so much so that some German blades were even stamped Toledo in order to impress the buyer. Spain appears to have had a rather conservative outlook, for bladed weapons, long discarded by the rest of Europe, continued in use in Spain. The left-hand dagger was used by Spanish fencers well into the eighteenth century and the plug bayonet, abandoned by most of Europe in the seventeenth century, continued to be produced until the 1880s. Spanish gunmakers were especially renowned for their gun barrels and it was not uncommon for sportsmen to have a Spanish barrel mounted in a French or English stock. Spanish gunmakers also made extensive use of special locks on their firearms and, in general, did not use the French-type flintlock as did most of Europe, but preferred the Miguelet which differed in manner of construction although not in operation.

Arms and armour from eastern Europe, Poland, Hungary and the Balkans exhibits strong traces of Turkish influence since, for many years, these countries were part of the Ottoman Empire. Balkan flintlock pistols were far more elaborately decorated than those from other parts of Europe.

If it is at all possible to generalize on European firearms, it might be said that they are more decorative than their equivalent British model. On the longarms the stocks were frequently carved and inlaid, a practice not favoured by British makers. The mounts too were often far more elaborate than those on British weapons.

Identification of European weapons is not always easy although many of the makers are known and listed.

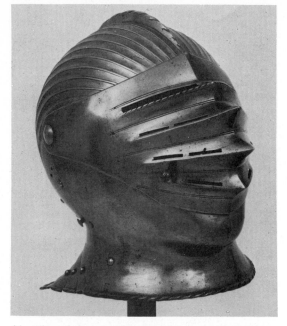

a) Breast-plate and fauld; probably Germany, c. 1450–1500.

The throat and shoulder edges of this plain breast-plate are turned over and there is a central ridge. Attached to the bottom is a skirt, the fauld, consisting of three lames, with straps for the attachment of further strips. The thickness of the various plates was graduated according to the vulnerability of the area protected and the breast-plate was normally the thickest and heaviest of all pieces with maximum thickness at the centre and tapering off towards the edges; back-plates were normally comparatively thin.

b) Close helmet with pivoted visor; Nuremberg, Germany; c. 1520.

During the early part of the 16th century, a style of armour was developed in Germany, its distinguishing feature the use of fluting. The only pieces of the armour which did not carry the fluting were the greaves which protected the shin. This close helmet exhibits the characteristic ridging on the skull whilst the pivoted visor is of the so-called bellows type. Sight and breathing slots pierce the visor which has a bar fitted to the side to facilitate raising and lowering. On the chin piece is stamped the name and mark of Nuremberg.

---

c) Three 16th century swords; Germany, 16th century; lgths. left 42" (107 cm.), centre 55" (140 cm.), right 45" (114 cm.)

Left: The grip on this sword is of a shape often found on swords of the time; the flat quillons are slightly recurved, a feature found on swords used by the Landsknechts—a group of 16th century mercenaries.

Centre: Two-handed swords enjoyed a great popularity during the 16th century, although they were in use long before this. This plain specimen has long, straight quillons and a broad, double-edged blade.

Right: Designed so that it could be used either in a one- or two-handed grip, this type of sword is known as a hand and a half.

d) Chamfron (armour for the head of a horse); Germany, c. 1520–40.

Since the horse was vital to transport men and material, it was frequently protected by some form of armour. In ancient times, this was often of padded material although mail was also used, but following the collapse of the Roman Empire, horse armour seems to have disappeared until the 12th century. Plate armour was most commonly worn during the 15th and 16th centuries and odd pieces are still to be found. Most common are those intended to guard the front of the horse's head, known as the chamfron. This one has the fluting associated with armour of the Emperor Maximilian.

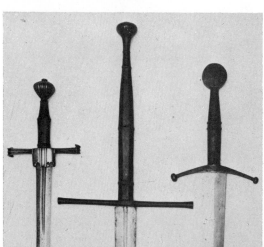

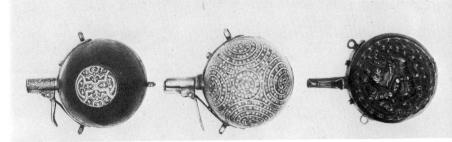

a) Sallet (helmet) with side-pivoted visor; Missaglia workshop, Milan, Italy, c. 1550.

Helmets dating from the 15th century are extremely rare and the fine condition of this one makes it a most desirable piece. Known as a sallet, the type was commonly worn by both foot and mounted troops. The visor is pivoted at the side so that it could be raised clear of the face whilst a slot cut in the crown would have held a crest. The rivet heads which can be seen on the outside originally secured the lining in place. In common with most good quality armour this sallet bears an armourer's mark, that of the Missaglia workshop.

b) Three powder flasks; Germany, late 16th century; dia. 3¼″ (8.25 cm.).

Most early firearms were loaded by pouring powder down the barrel, then placing a pinch of finer grained powder—the priming—in the pan situated by the touch-hole. The priming powder was carried in a small flask fitted with some form of pourer which might also serve as a measure. These flasks were frequently decorated, as here:

Left is wood with a silver medallion set in the side, a spring operated pourer and three carrying rings.

Centre is similar but overlaid with horn engraved with rings and flowerheads.

Right is overlaid with thin iron sheet and embossed with the figure of a mounted man.

c) Two rapiers and a dagger; Germany, c. 1575–1600; lgths. 48″ (122 cm.), 19¼″ (49 cm.), 47″ (119 cm.).

Left: This rapier has a characteristic swept hilt comprising bars, counterguards and a rear, down-curving quillon. The pommel is mushroom-shaped and the entire hilt retains its original blue colouring.

Centre: A style of sword play which enjoyed a long period of popularity taught the parrying of an opponent's blade with a dagger held in the left hand; both weapons were often decorated en suite.

Right: This swept hilt rapier is very similar in style to the other.

d) Crossbow with wooden stock, decorated with plaques of engraved horn; Germany, c. 1600.

Whilst the longbow was faster and required great skill in its use, the crossbow was the more powerful weapon. Though by the 17th century it was largely obsolete, some were used for hunting until the 19th century. Originally the bow was of wood but greater power was obtained by using steel or composite staves until the bow was so powerful that mechanical means were required to pull back the cord. This example fitted with a steel bow has a cranequin or ratchet which was hooked on to the shaft and then used to wind back the cord.

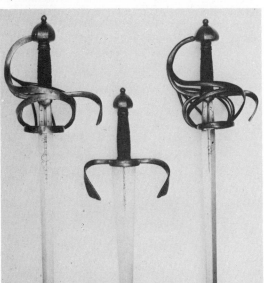

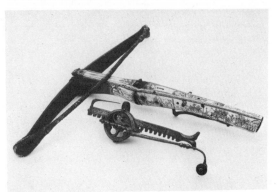

21

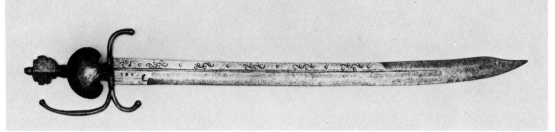

a) *Falchion with leather grip; probably Germany; early 17th century; lgth. 31" (78.7 cm.).*

This type of sword, with slightly curved blade and clipped point, is known as a falchion. The hilt has a leather covered grip and a simple guard comprising a knuckle bow, two down-curving quillons and a simple shell guard. The blade has a single groove—the fuller—running along its length and there is a ricasso just below the quillon. There is some simple scroll decoration and the letters 'I H S' are stamped just below the quillons.

b) *'Tschinke' (wheel-lock) rifle; Silesia, Bohemia, c. 1620; overall lgth. 44" (111.7 cm.).*

Light, very decorative wheel-lock rifles of this type are known as tschinke and are characterized by the particular shape of the butt. The design of the wheel-lock differs from most in that the spring is fitted outside the stock. The trigger guard is so shaped that the butt of the tschinke could be held against the cheek when aiming. As usual for the type, this example is decorated with inlaid panels of staghorn and a large medallion of mother-of-pearl which is engraved with a scene showing ships anchored by a town. Tschinke are ascribed to Silesia.

c) *Horseman's hammer of steel with wire grip; Germany, c. 1600-1650; lgth. 21" (53.3 cm.).*

As the armourer's skill developed, the design and construction of armour were greatly improved so that it could resist or deflect most weapons. Efforts were then made to produce weapons which delivered maximum power on a minimum area and one such weapon, very efficient at piercing armour, was the horseman's hammer. The majority of these date from the first half of the 17th century although in Eastern Europe they were used until much later. This German example is quite typical with wire bound grip and long strip at the top which forms a hook for suspending it from the belt.

d) *Two swords; left and right, 1650, with a rapier, (centre) Germany, late 16th century; lgths. left 37¾" (95.9 cm.), centre 46½" (118 cm.), right 39" (94 cm.).*

The very elaborate hilt of the rapier was simplified during the 17th century and the number of bars, guards and counterguards reduced. Shells often replaced the earlier bars. The centre example is a fine quality rapier with wide quillons, a simple ring guard, and hilt embellished with silver.

Left is a basket hilted sword with hilt made up of shells, a small rear quillon and a few curved bars. The grip is of wood and is bound with wire to afford a firm hold. The blade is single-edged. The other sword is very similar and also dated 1650 on the blade.

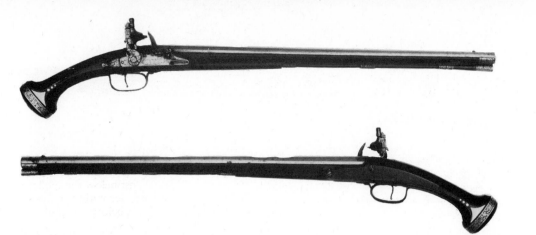

a) Pair of flintlock pistols; marked: Jan Aerts and Mastrecht; *Holland, late 17th century; lgth. 28¾″ (73 cm.).*

Pistols of the late 17th century have a number of features which can be seen on this pair of Dutch flintlocks. Lockplate and cock are both flat and the frizzen is secured by a single screw in place of the later bridle. The barrels, octagonal at the breech and changing to circular section, are long as on most pistols of this period. Cock and lockplate have been etched with a floral pattern and the names Jan Aerts and Mastrecht have been engraved on the lockplate. The ebony stocks are fitted with engraved silver furniture.

b) Flintlock holster pistol; by Heinrich Kapell; Copenhagen, Denmark, c. 1680–90; lgth. 20″ (50.8 cm.).

Although there were differences in detail in the construction, design and decoration of pistols from various countries, the general appearance was not markedly different. Sometimes the only certain way of pinpointing the country of origin is by examining the marks and signatures on the various parts. This flintlock holster pistol resembles those produced in England about the same period, in the simple carving on the stock, and the shape of the lock and butt. The lock is signed by Kapell, who was at one time gunmaker for two of Denmark's Kings, Christian V and Frederick IV.

c) Snaphaunce holster pistol; Italy, early 18th century; overall lgth. 9½″ (24.1 cm.).

The snaphaunce system of ignition appeared around the middle of the 16th century and differed from the later flintlock in that the steel and pan cover were separate. A more sophisticated form was evolved in Italy and pistols using this type of cock were manufactured by Italian craftsmen long after the rest of Europe had abandoned it. This holster pistol has the typical appearance of Italian snaphaunce pistols of the early 18th century. The flat lockplate and cock resemble those found on 17th century weapons. The walnut stock has some simple carving around the lockplate.

d) Flintlock fowling piece; Northern Italy, c. 1700–1725; overall lgth. 44″ (111.7 cm.), barrel 30″ (76.2 cm.).

This piece is fitted with furniture of chiselled steel. The barrel is octagonal in section at the breech, becoming circular. An unusual feature of the construction of the lock is that the frizzen is secured to the lockplate by a screw fitted on the inside of the lockplate unlike the great majority which have the screw on the outside. General appearance with the forward-curving tip of the frizzen, backward-curving tip of the trigger and slight banana shape to the lock are features found on many firearms of this period.

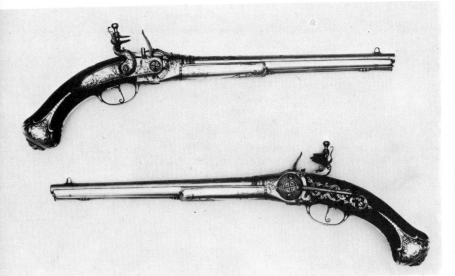

a) left: Pair of breech-loading repeating flintlock pistols; Michele Lorenzoni; Florence, Italy, early 18th century; lgth. 20″ (50.8 cm.); right: detail of trigger.

Many attempts were made to produce repeating flintlock weapons but none was ever really successful as mechanical and safety problems usually proved too difficult. In these examples, a quantity of powder was poured into a reservoir and a number of balls placed in a magazine, both contained in the butt; the loading action was operated by the lever fitted at the side. The walnut stock is inlaid with silver wire and plates, the locks engraved with various battle scenes. Typical of this period are the long spurs extending from the butt cap: as the century progressed, the tendency was to fit shorter ones.

Arms and Armour

Continental

EARLY 18TH CENTURY

b) Detail of lock from a pair of flintlock holster pistols; F. Bigoni, Brescia, Italy, c. 1700–1750.

This is the lock from one of a superb pair of flintlock holster pistols. The stock is of burr walnut carved with foliage and scrolls. The furniture is of gilt bronze and has applied plaques of silver which are chased with cherubs, busts and military trophies. Cocks and frizzen are chiselled and the trigger is finely pierced. F. Bigoni was a gunmaker recorded in Brescia, Northern Italy, an area noted for the quality of its metalwork during the first half of the 18th century. Although a pair, the decoration on the two pistols is not identical.

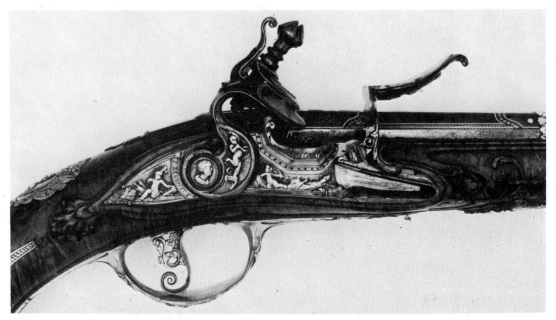

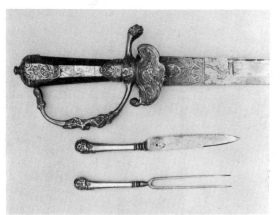

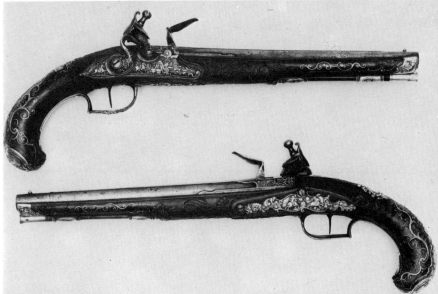

a) *Hunting sword with fork and knife; Germany, c. 1735; lgth. 27⅝″ (69.2 cm.).*

General purpose swords with short blades and simple hilts were popular during the 17th century. During the 18th century they were commonly used as hunting swords and some quite ornate examples were manufactured. This one has the grip covered in tortoiseshell, mother-of-pearl and strips of brass. The blade has an appropriate hunting motif etched at the top. The sheath is so designed that pockets near the top hold a small two-pronged fork and a knife, a feature found in Scottish dirks.

b) *Pair of pistols, highly decorated; by Leopold Becher; Carlsbad, Bohemia, c. 1750; lgth. 17″ (43.2 cm.).*

During the 18th century Prague, in present-day Czechoslovakia, was noted for high standards of craftsmanship. Pistols from Bohemia, particularly Carlsbad, were specially decorative. This pair are very fine, their walnut stocks inlaid with silver wire and carved. The lockplates are chiselled with various figures and the cast silver furniture is also embellished with military motifs. The shaped trigger guard and the rather beak-like shape to the butts are often found on continental pistols.

Arms and Armour
Continental
MID-18TH CENTURY

c) *Flintlock pistol combined with fork; Germany, probably mid-18th century; overall lgth. 8⅛″ (20.6 cm.). (20.6 cm.).*

Combination weapons have long been popular and pistols have been fitted to swords, axes, even crossbows. Pistol-swords were most common but it is debatable as to how practical such weapons were. It is especially difficult to see the value of a combined fork and flintlock pistol. The brass hilt is fitted on the outside with a cock, frizzen and a brass pan, the mainspring being on the opposite side; the barrel is enclosed in the hilt itself. The hilt bears the words 'Schar', 'Aims' and 'F. Richter'.

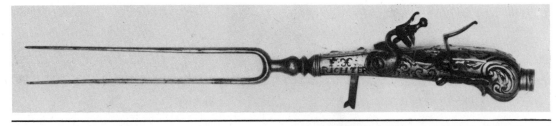

d) *Pair of pistols; by Diego Albarez, Madrid, Spain, 1792; lgth. 16″ (40.6 cm.).*

Spanish gunmakers were especially famed for the quality of their barrels and generally high standard of their decorative skills. Most Spanish guns were fitted with a type of lock known as the Miguelet which was constructed with the mainspring on the outside of the lockplate. Another feature of many Spanish locks was the ring on the screw of the top jaw. These pistols exhibit this feature but have the so-called Madrid lock which has an internal mainspring. The pans are gold lined to overcome the corrosive effect of the burning powder.

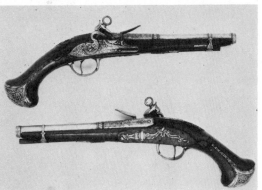

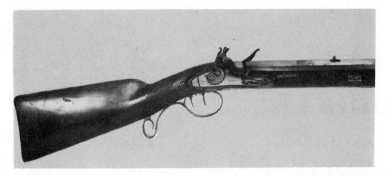

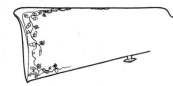

Fine decorated stock inlaid with silver acorns and leaves; maker: C. Koerber.

a) Sporting or target pistol; engraved Delcomyn Kjøbenhavn; *Copenhagen, Denmark, c. 1800.*

Intended for sporting or target use, this rifle has a heavy, octagonal barrel to which are fitted both fore and rear sights. The stock is rather sturdier than that of an equivalent English weapon but is quite plain. The lock is of conventional design including a small roller fitted at the tip of the frizzen spring. The voluted trigger guard was intended to provide a good steady grip and the lock mechanism is fitted with two triggers, one of which set the action so that only the lightest touch was required to fire the rifle.

b) Fowling piece, the barrel inscribed Chretien Koerber a Ingelfingen; *Germany, c. 1820; lgth. 46" (117 cm.). (117 cm.).*

This fine piece has a large, octagonal barrel which is blued and inlaid with silver leaves. Like those of so many continental longarms, the stock is carved and inlaid with filigree and silver studs. On the other side of the butt, the cheek piece is inlaid with mother-of-pearl and ebony. It is not usual for British weapons to have the extension grip behind the trigger although it is a common feature on European weapons. To reduce fouling, the touch-hole is fitted with a plug of platinum, the metal least affected by corrosion.

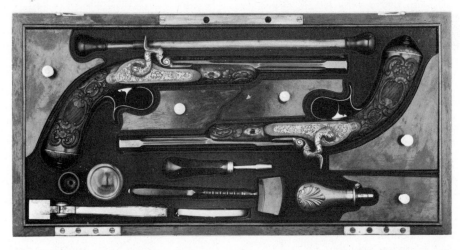

c) Pair of percussion duelling pistols; marked: Anton Vineaz Lebeda; *Prague, Czechoslovakia, c. 1850.*

Duelling pistols were frequently supplied in pairs complete with sundry tools and a powder flask. This fine pair of pistols are rifled, a practice rather frowned on by British duellists. The octagonal barrels are blued and fluted and the locks are etched with foliage whilst the walnut stock is carved with typical rococo ornament. In common with continental practice the pistols and accessories are fitted into recessed compartments in the case which is of rosewood and lined with green baize; it contains cleaning rods, bullet moulds, nipple key and small mallet.

British Arms and Armour Introduction

Little is known about the production of arms and armour in Britain prior to the later Middle Ages, for there are only passing mentions in various records. It is known that much of the good quality arms and armour used by the nobility was imported from Italy and Germany. Armour depicted on various church brasses and in illuminated manuscripts can be attributed to these countries on stylistic grounds and there are references to the purchase of such items. Some armour and weapons must have been made in this country, for the Armourers Company was founded in the fourteenth century and there was a flourishing Cutlers Company in London.

Details become a little clearer in the sixteenth century when a Royal Workshop was established at Greenwich, just outside London, by Henry VIII. A number of foreign armourers were invited to work there and they produced fine quality armour for the King and his noble friends. Henry is known to have purchased large quantities of common 'munition' armour from abroad.

It was in the seventeenth century, due perhaps to the demand created by the Civil Wars (1642–49) that production of arms and armour really expanded. London seems to have been the main supply centre and there was a sword factory at Hounslow, and another was established at Shotley Bridge. However, Birmingham, in the Midlands was, even at this stage, beginning to take over some of the market. Many English swords of the seventeenth century have a characteristic type of decoration which consists of applied silver patterns of dots or floral systems. In Scotland two characteristic weapons were developed: the claymore or broadsword, and the dirk, which had evolved from the old ballock dagger. During the eighteenth century both London and Birmingham produced some very good quality smallswords and makers such as Gill, acquired a well-deserved reputation for good quality blades. In the nineteenth century two names, Wilkinson and Mole, dominated the market for the production of swords and bayonets.

The earliest reference to firearms in Britain occurs early in the fourteenth century and there is little firm evidence concerning the manufacture of guns in this country. However, by the seventeenth century there was quite a flourishing gunmaking colony in London, situated in the area near the Tower of London. In 1637 the London Gunmakers' Company of London was granted its charter and for the next two hundred years London was to be the centre of the British firearms trade.

During the eighteenth century there were a number of very fine makers whose names became synonymous with quality. Manton, Wogden, Parker, Mortimer, Barbar and many others. A number of the makers moved further west out of the old City area, and several set up their shops in the Piccadilly and Regent Street area. Some, like Wogden, specialized in duelling pistols whilst others, i.e. Parker, produced every type of firearm and accessory. Many of their pistols were sold in cases complete with all tools and accessories. British makers differed from those of the Continent in their method of fitting these cases. Instead of using contoured recesses they used simple, straight fences to form the various compartments.

During the nineteenth century the introduction of the percussion system together with the adoption of modern production methods, caused a gradual shift of emphasis and Birmingham began to dominate the firearms market. A few makers kept their London premises and produced custom built sporting guns, but the majority of military weapons were then being produced in Birmingham or at the Enfield Small Arms Factory. Birmingham also produced a quantity of 'cheap and nasty' percussion pistols and revolvers.

In general, British weapons are well made, if somewhat plain in comparison with many elaborately decorated examples produced on the Continent. Above all, they had a reputation for reliability and fine craftsmanship.

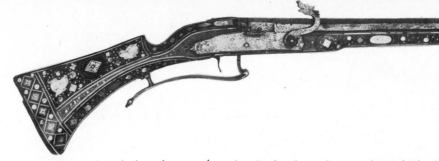

a) Matchlock musket with inlaid walnut stock; c. 1500–1600; lgth. 49″ (124 cm.).

The matchlock musket, usually simple and quite plain in design, was used in quantity by most armies of the 16th and 17th centuries. This example possibly belonged to a member of one of the trained bands, for the walnut stock is inlaid with mother-of-pearl and staghorn. Pressure on the trigger caused the curved arm, or serpentine, to swing forward and press the smouldering end of a piece of burning cord into the pan to ignite the main charge.

b) Straight-bladed cavalry sword; mid-17th century; overall lgth. 36″ (91.4 cm.), blade 31″ (78.7 cm.).

During the 17th century, there was a general simplification in the design of swords and during the English Civil Wars, 1642-49, most of the cavalry were armed with swords of this type. This straight-bladed example has a number of grooves, fullers, intended to lighten it without sacrificing rigidity. The guard was often in the form of a complete basket rather than bars as on this example. Most weapons of this type are described as mortuary swords from the belief that the embossed heads so often included in the pattern represented the martyred King Charles I.

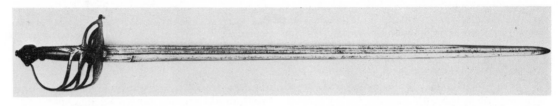

c) Carbine pistol, signed on backstrap E. Trulocke fecit; c. 1660; lgth. 38½″ (97.8 cm.).

Most horsemen carried one or two pistols but some preferred to carry a slightly more powerful weapon, known as a carbine. Originally the name referred to the bore but common usage transferred it to the weapon itself. This is an extremely rare example for it is rifled. The barrel unscrews for loading and a bar and loop are fixed to barrel and breech to prevent accidental loss. The carving on the butt is an unusual feature on English weapons. Samuel Pepys' diary makes mention of the gunsmith E. Trulocke.

d) Detail of rapier hilt; c. 1640; overall length of rapier 51½″ (130.8 cm.).

This is the hilt of an English rapier—it is also known as a tuck. The straight, single-edged blade bears some simple engraving. Two pierced shells replace the earlier counterguards whilst from the knuckle bow, spring seven small loops as well as forward and rear quillons. The top of the knuckle bow is secured to the ovoid pommel by a screw—a feature commonly found on swords of this period. The trip is wire bound and is finished with Turk's head binding at top and bottom.

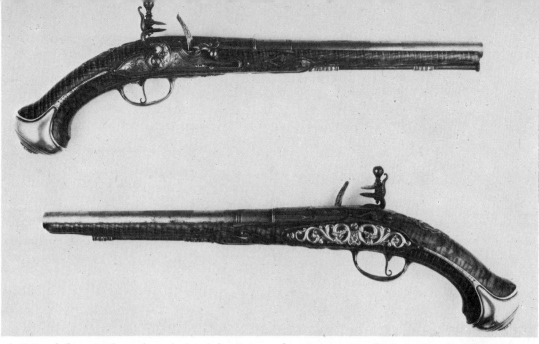

a) Pair of fine pistols made and signed by James Cosens; c. 1670; lgth. 18¾" (47.6 cm.).

James Cosens' name is engraved on the barrels and the lockplates, which are chiselled with scrolls, grotesque heads and figures. Although exceptionally fine, the pistols exhibit a number of features common to other pistols of this period—the trigger with a backward curling tip, the large butt cap and long side spurs reaching almost to the lockplate; the stepped barrel and the slight banana-shape to the lock. Many pistols had some slight carving on the stock, a feature that disappears from pistols about the middle of the 18th century.

b) Blunderbuss; late 17th century; lgth. 30¼" (76.8 cm.).

This blunderbuss of the late 17th century clearly exhibits many typical features of such weapons. The stock has a rather 'chunky' appearance and the simple, almost crude furniture is held in place by nails rather than screws. The lockplate and cock are flat and an essentially British feature is the little hook fitted behind the cock. This safety device was known as the dog and engaged with the slot cut into the back of the cock to hold it secure and safe. The brass barrel bells slightly at the muzzle and bears London marks on the octagonal breech.

---

c) Pocket pistol by John Drew; early 18th century; overall lgth. 7" (17.7 cm.).

Small weapons to be carried in the pocket for self defence were always in demand. Basically, this example is similar to larger pistols of the period but it differs in having no trigger guard and a straight 'pillar' trigger. The barrel unscrews for purposes of loading and the stock is quite plain. On the base of the lock is engraved the maker's name. Although the design changed, small pocket pistols like this were produced right up to the mid-19th century when small percussion revolvers ousted them as personal weapons.

d) Pistol by John Williams, London; c. 1710–20; overall lgth. 12" (30.4 cm.).

Queen Anne pistols of which this is one type were, in fact, made long after the reign of this queen. They have a barrel that unscrews for loading which was effected with a spanner-like key that slipped over the barrel and engaged with the small lug. The breech, pan and housing for the lock mechanism are all incorporated into one metal block. The butt bears a silver escutcheon and a lion's head butt mask. Such pistols were produced in a variety of sizes and were made until the last quarter of the 18th century.

British

EARLY–MID-18TH CENTURY

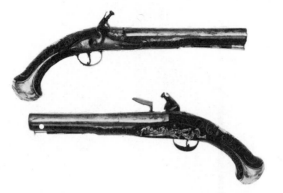

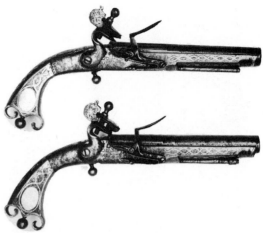

a) Pair of holster pistols; by H. Delany; London, c. 1730; lgth. 15¼" (38.7 cm.).

The walnut stocks of these examples have some carving around the locks and breech but the main decoration is of silver wire inlay, a common feature of pistols of the mid-18th century. All furniture is of silver and the side plate (on lower pistol) is of an unusual design, composed of two bearded heads, a scarf and a sword. The touch-holes are of gold; the barrels and locks are signed. The ramrods retain their original silver tips. An unusual feature of these pistols is the push-on safety catch fitted behind each cock.

b) Pair of all-steel pistols; by D. L. Walker; Dumbarton, Scotland; c. 1725–50; lgth. 11" (27.9 cm.).

Scotland's gunmakers evolved a distinctive type of pistol. Over the centuries it varied in style but the most common variety is easily recognized by its all-steel body and ball trigger. This pair by D. L. Walker have the typical ramshorn butt. The small ball situated between the two curling tips to the butt unscrews and has a pin which can be used to clear the touch-hole. The stocks are inlaid with some silver scrollwork and have belt hooks attached.

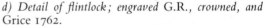

c) Pair of Queen Anne pistols by James Low; c. 1745; lgth. 13¼" (33.7 cm.).

Here, the walnut stocks have some carving in the form of scallops around the barrel breech. The side plates and butt caps are of silver as is the escutcheon plate which bears the crest of Murray of Peebles. Like those of most pistols of this type, the barrels unscrew for loading. They bear London proof marks. The frizzen springs on these pistols are of typical shape rising high and then sweeping down below the pan to engage with the toe of the frizzen.

d) Detail of flintlock; engraved G.R., crowned, and Grice 1762.

Weapons purchased by the Board of Ordnance for supply to the British army had to be of a certain standard: when accepted, they were marked like this lockplate with the crowned 'G.R.', the name of the supplier and the date of acceptance. The practice of dating the lock was abandoned in 1764. William Grice was a big supplier to the Ordnance and many examples of the issue musket called the Brown Bess survive with locks bearing his name. The small hole at the front of the trigger guard was for the attachment of a swivel to hold the sling.

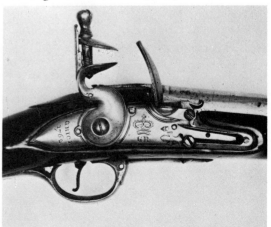

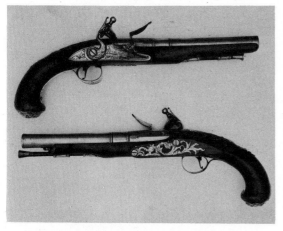

a) Pair of holster pistols; by Joiner of London, silver furniture hall-marked 1778; lgth. 13½″ (34.3 cm.).

Joiner's name is engraved on both barrel and locks. The general appearance is typical of pistols of this period with the plain butt fitted only with a small butt cap fashioned in the form of a grotesque face. The silver furniture bears Birmingham hall-marks. On the octagonal breech of the barrel can be seen the two small impressed ovals which enclose the proof marks showing the barrel has been tested for strength. The side plate visible on the lower pistol is of silver and fashioned in the form of a floral motif.

b) Three-barrel pistol; by Gill of London; c. 1780; overall lgth. 12″ (30.4 cm.).

Each barrel of this pistol was fired in turn, being selected by means of a rotating 'tap' on the left-hand side of the lock. The indentations at the muzzle are for the insertion of a key which was used to unscrew the barrels for loading: powder and ball were placed directly into the breech. Multi-barrel weapons were not produced in large numbers and although two-barrelled examples are not rare, pistols such as this are scarce.

c) Duelling pistols by Joseph Manton; c. 1780; lgth. 15½″ (39.4 cm.).

The Manton Brothers were regarded by many as the finest of London gunmakers although there was some dispute as to whether John or Joseph was the better.

The butts of these examples by Joseph are hatched to afford a firm grip for the duellist but there is very little other decoration at all. Later duelling pistols had a spur fitted to the trigger guard and this was held by the second finger and was thought to improve both aim and grip. There are no safety catches on these pistols. When originally sold, it is likely that they were cased.

d) Flintlock pocket pistol; by John Jones & Co., London, 1790; overall lgth. 6″ (15.2 cm.).

This boxlock flintlock pistol of the late 18th century is absolutely typical. The butt is slab sided and quite plain whilst the short barrel fits directly into the breech section enclosing the lock mechanism; as it unscrews for reloading, there is no need for a ramrod. A sliding safety catch fitted on top of the butt moves forward to engage the cock, and at the same time a projection locks the frizzen. This meant that the pistol could be loaded, primed, set at half cock and safely carried in the pocket. The side of the breech is engraved 'Jnᵒ Jones & Co.'

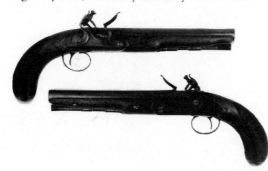

Arms and Armour

British

a) *Blunderbuss; by Wiggin, late 18th century; overall lgth. 27" (68.5 cm.), barrel 11¾" (29.8 cm.).*

From the late 17th century until the early 19th century the blunderbuss enjoyed great popularity. It was believed that the widening at the muzzle spread the load which consisted of a number of lead balls although, in fact, it had little effect. This example has a brass barrel fitted with a spring-operated bayonet which, when not required, is folded back and locked above the barrel. Blunderbusses were occasionally used by the military and were carried for many years by the guards on mail coaches.

b) *Pair of duelling pistols by Wogdon; London, c. 1790; lgth. 14¼" (36.2 cm.).*

Wogdon was one London gunmaker to gain a reputation for the quality of his duelling pistols: at least one poem was composed in his honour. These examples have many features common to duelling weapons of the period; a marked lack of decoration gives them a clean, functional appearance. The barrels bear London marks and have a flattened rib with a foresight. The stocks are quite plain and the iron furniture minimal. One extra feature is a sliding bolt safety catch fitted behind the cock. Many such pistols have some means of setting the trigger to activate the action with minimum pressure.

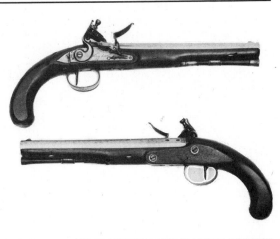

c) *Detail of hilt of military sword; late 18th or early 19th century.*

This hilt, typical of an English military sword of the period has the grip of ivory and the knuckle bow, pommel and small rear quillon gilded. The single-edged blade is slightly curved, and is engraved with various symbols such as the moon and stars, a motif found on swords of many periods. The small ring attached to the top of the knuckle bow is for the fitting of a sword knot which was a loop slipped over the wrist to prevent accidental loss of the sword. This type of sword is often described as a spadroon.

d) *Detail of military sword; by Woolley & Co., Birmingham; c. 1803.*

During the latter part of the 18th century some standardization of military swords was introduced and this hilt is basically that of a pattern 1803 sword. The urn-shaped pommel, knuckle bow and shell guards are gilded, and the grip bound with silver wire. This specimen differs from the usual in having one of the shells hinged so that it could be folded down to prevent discomfort which might be caused by the edge banging against the wearer's hip. The locket on the scabbard bears the engraved name of the manufacturer. The scabbard is of black leather with gilded fittings.

Opposite:
Left: Infantry officer's sword, 1796.
Centre: Swept hilt rapier, c. 1600.
Right: Prussian officer's sword, 1878.

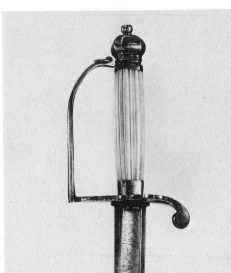

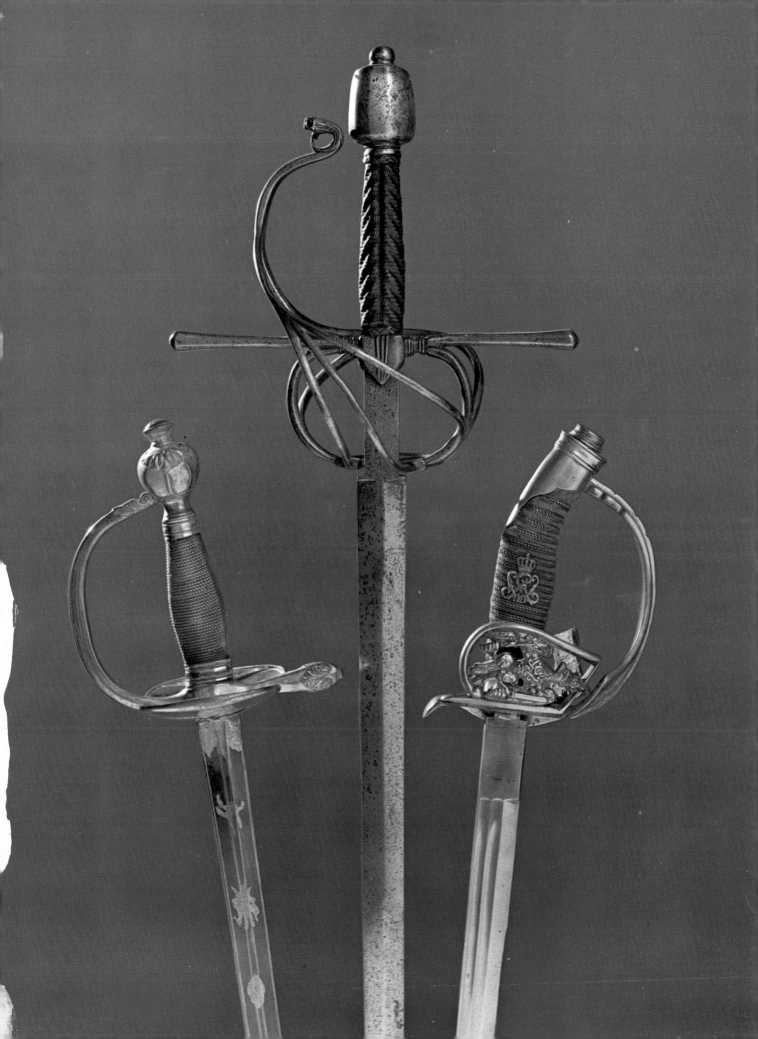

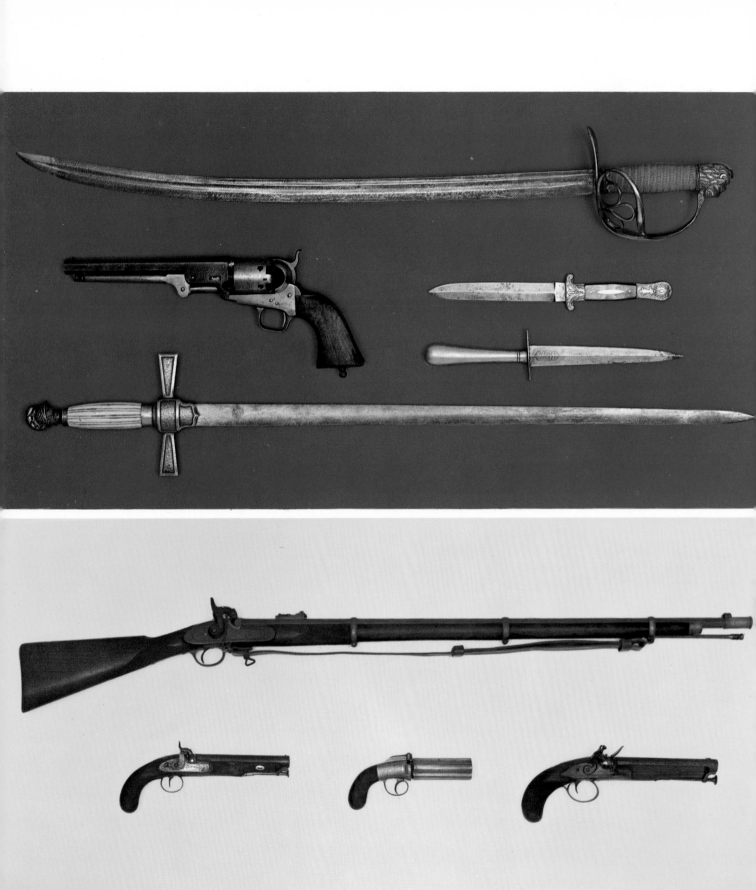

Upper photograph:
Top: Sword hilt with lion's head pommel; U.S.A.
Left: Colt Navy .36 percussion revolver; U.S.A., 1851.
Right: Small daggers with metal hilt and blade; New York,
U.S.A., mid-19th century.
Bottom: Militia N.C.O.'s sword; U.S.A., 1840.

Lower photograph:
Top: Enfield percussion rifle; England, c. 1861.
Bottom, left to right: Percussion holster; England, c. 1820.
Percussion pepperbox pistol; England, c. 1840.
Officer's flintlock pistol; England, c. 1810.
All three pistols were made by William Parker of London.

a) Commemorative Navy sword; 1809; blade lgth. 30" (76.2 cm.).

During the Napoleonic Wars, the Lloyds Patriotic Fund selected acts of bravery by members of the Royal Navy and presented the hero with a commemorative sword; the quality of the sword depended on the deed. This is an example of the £50 sword and was presented to Lt. Pye of the Royal Marines for an action on the Isle of Bourbon in September 1809. The details of the presentation are etched on the blade which is blued and gilt. Both sword and scabbard are ornate with classical themes figured on the hilt and scabbard mounts. These weapons are seldom seen.

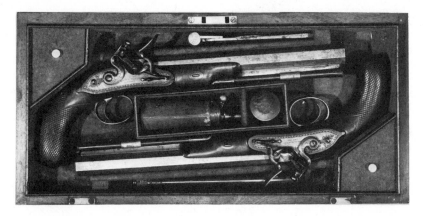

b) Cased pair of flintlock duelling pistols; by Joseph Manton, London, c. 1810; overall lgth. 15¼" (38.7 cm.).

These heavy, octagonal barrels have a recessed rib set underneath to accommodate the ramrod. The locks, engraved 'Joseph Manton, London', are fitted with sliding safety catches and have some engraved decoration. The original case contains a powder flask, bullet mould, rods, container for greased wads and compartments to hold bullets. The sections are divided by simple fences and the whole is lined with green baize. Continental cases usually have the compartments shaped and recessed. English cases are most often of oak although mahogany was occasionally used.

c) Rifled carbine; made in John Manton's workshop; London, c. 1810; lgth. 32" (81.3 cm.).

This example was made by one of John Manton's master craftsmen. It is so constructed that a single barrel, as shown, can be fitted and then the right-hand lock is used. Alternatively a pair of over and under barrels could be fitted, in which case both left- and right-hand locks were utilized. Both locks and barrels bear the name Staudenmayer in gold. The barrel is browned and is rifled whilst the ramrod is connected by a swivel fitting at the muzzle. The walnut stock with its carved cheek-piece has an escutcheon plate bearing the crest of a duke.

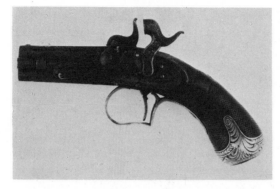

'Hatched' pistol butts afforded a better grip; maker: R. Clarke, London c. 1820.

a) Double-barrelled percussion pistol; by Joseph Egg, London, c. 1820; lgth. 5⅝" (14.3 cm.).

This tiny, well-made double-barrelled percussion pistol was intended to be carried in the pocket for personal protection. The barrels bear, in gold, the legends 'J. Egg London' and 'No. 1. Piccadilly'. A small metal ramrod is fitted at the side of the barrels. The lock mechanism is a little unusual in that the mainsprings are fitted on the outside of the lockplate. The butt is of walnut and the weapon is fitted with silver furniture. At the top of the butt is a small gold escutcheon bearing the initials 'R.G.'.

b) Beaumont-Adams percussion revolver; by Robert Adams, mid-19th century; barrel lgth. 6" (15.2 cm.).

Around the middle of the 19th century there was a tremendous increase in interest and production of revolvers. In the U.S.A., Colt was supreme but in England a number of gunmakers competed for the market. One of the best known of English makers was Robert Adams who produced a number of different models. This one is a five shot Beaumont-Adams percussion revolver, and so called because it incorporated an action patented by a Lt. Beaumont which allowed the weapon to be cocked by the thumb or by pressure on the trigger. This specimen has more engraving than is usual for the type.

c) Revolving rifle by G. William Tranter; mid-19th century; lgth. 41½" (105 cm.).

When the production of percussion revolvers was simplified by the introduction of machines, a number of gunmakers experimented with revolving rifles. This example was made by G. William Tranter, a famous English gunmaker, and

is number 12334. Essentially it is his revolver action fitted with a butt and a long barrel. On pressing the lower trigger the five shot cylinder was rotated and the action cocked. On pressing the top trigger, inside the trigger guard, the shot was fired. This specimen was sold in an oak case complete with accessories.

d) Cutlass bayonet; 1875; lgth. 31" (78.7 cm.).

Weapons which were once thought uninteresting are now sought after. This is particularly so with bayonets and later military swords. This cutlass bayonet was designed to serve either as a bayonet or separately as a sword. In order to have

any use as a sword, it required a good length of blade but when clipped on to the end of the Martini Henry rifle (see Glossary, p. 44) it made the weapon top heavy. It was carried in a black leather scabbard with steel fittings.

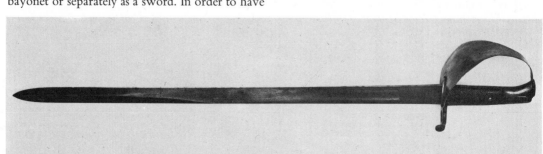

American Arms and Armour Introduction

During the past few centuries, arms and armour have been, perhaps, more important to the average American citizen than they have to his European counterpart. The need to conquer a wild continent with a frontier that did not disappear until almost the beginning of this century made weapons a necessity for a significant proportion of the populace, and the availability of open land has made hunting a sport for greater numbers of people than would be possible in more fully developed lands. And all of this has been in addition to the military activities that have been common to almost all nations. As a result of these factors, the weapons industry has been unusually large and innovative, and the student or collector of American antique arms has a wide field for study despite the short history of the United States.

This is especially true of the firearms field. At first, colonists from all nations relied primarily on guns and pistols produced in their homeland, but armourers were needed to repair and modify these arms. Before 1625, the English colonists at Jamestown in Virginia had established a workshop for arms repair, and archaeological evidence indicates that they were converting matchlocks to flint ignition on an extensive scale. Soon American gunsmiths began to produce complete weapons of their own manufacture. The earliest such gunsmith so far identified is James Phips who worked in Massachusetts about 1650.

Thereafter the industry expanded gradually until by 1748 Hugh Orr of Bridgewater, Massachusetts, found himself in a position to contract to provide 500 muskets for the defence of the colony.

American gunsmiths were especially responsive to the special needs of the new country. First, they quickly switched from the clumsy matchlock to the faster and more reliable flint arms. Then the German and Swiss gunsmiths in Pennsylvania developed the long American rifle from the shorter jaeger rifles of their native lands in an attempt to conserve precious lead and powder. In 1817 John H. Hall invented the first breech-loading rifle to be manufactured on a large scale and then developed the machines, jigs and gauges necessary to make it the first military firearm with completely interchangeable parts. Gunmaking machinery, in fact, became an American speciality. When the rifled musket was developed, an American firm made the machinery to produce the arm at the Enfield Armoury in England, and an American, James H. Burton of the Harpers Ferry Armory, went to Enfield in 1855 as Chief Engineer to supervise production. Later, Burton supervised the manufacture of machinery for a new Russian armoury.

Breech-loading and repeating arms also became a special field of interest. The first American repeaters were made early in the eighteenth century, but it was the middle nineteenth century that brought them forth in abundance. Ethan Allen's self-cocking pepper-box pistol and Samuel Colt's revolver both achieved financial success in the second quarter of the century. Then the Civil War produced a host of inventions, some very poor, though others, such as the Sharps, Spencer and Winchester, attained fame. The Snider and Peabody, which failed in the U.S. became standard in other countries, and the Remington rolling block system became the most widely produced military firearm in the world.

In the field of edged weapons, the United States was never a leader except perhaps with the Bowie knife. Swords generally followed either British or French patterns exactly, and many of them were actually manufactured abroad. Nathan Starr produced the first official enlisted men's swords, and he made a few officers' weapons. Only one firm, the Ames Manufacturing Company, made high quality swords in any number before the Civil War. Even today, most officers' swords are imported.

Armour has been worn in America in almost every conflict since the founding of the colonies, though little was of American make until the Civil War, when bulletproof breast-plates achieved brief popularity. Then armour disappeared until the wars of the twentieth century revived interest in protective devices.

a) Colonial long fowler; Hudson Valley, 1690–1710; lgth. overall, 7' (213 cm.), barrel 6' 6¾" (169 cm.).

The first truly specialized sporting firearms in the world were probably the long fowlers. Their design arose from the belief that the longer the bore, the greater the possible range. Both British and European sportsmen subscribed to this theory and designed firearms, often 7 feet long or more,

accordingly. The first long fowlers in America were English made, but a truly native design developed along the Hudson-Mohawk River fly-way. It featured a fat-bellied stock with some raised carving in the Dutch tradition. Some, like the specimen illustrated, even had Dutch barrels well after England had captured New Netherlands.

b) Kentucky rifle, from 1750; lgth. overall, 52". (132 cm.), barrel 38" (96.5 cm.).

Soon after their arrival, the Swiss and German immigrants in Pennsylvania began to modify their traditional hunting rifles. They lengthened the barrels and reduced the calibre to conserve lead and powder which were scarce along the frontier, and created the hinged brass cover for the butt trap

which they called a patch-box: it was used to carry the greased linen or thin leather patches in which they customarily wrapped the bullet. The Pennsylvania rifle, usually called the Kentucky rifle or the American long rifle, reached its typical form about 1750, continuing well into the 19th century before decadence set in.

c) Committee of Safety musket, c. 1775; lgth. overall 58" (147 cm.), barrel 42" (107 cm.).

At the beginning of the War for Independence in 1775, the local committees or councils of safety in the various colonies contracted with local gun-smiths to produce muskets for their troops. Universally they followed the design of the British new land pattern with a 42-inch barrel and a

calibre of .75. This was the arm with which Americans were most familiar from military service in the wars against the French. After 1777, with the arrival of French muskets in quantity and the formation of new state governments the Committee of Safety muskets were replaced with muskets of the French model of 1763.

d) North and Cheney pistol, c. 1799–1802; lgth. overall 14½" (36.8 cm.), barrel 8½" (21.6 cm.).

After the War for Independence, America continued to follow French designs in firearms, and although muskets copied the 1763 French model, the first official U.S. pistol was an almost exact copy of the 1777 model. American changes provided for a 7½" barrel, one inch longer than the original, and an extra screw for a more secure barrel attachment. Simeon North and his brother-in-law Elisha Cheney produced 2,000 of these pistols under a contract of 1799 and a supplemental contract of 1800, completing them before the end of 1802. Today they are the rarest of all American martial pistols.

a) Model 1802 Harpers Ferry rifle, pre-1807; lgth. overall 47" (190 cm.), barrel 33" (84 cm.).

The Model 1803 was the first military rifle to be manufactured at a Federal armoury, although a few military rifles had earlier been produced by contractors. It owed much to the Kentucky rifle but was shorter with a 33" barrel of .54 calibre— octagonal at the breech, then round for the rest of its length. All mounts were brass. A total of 4023 were made before production ceased in 1807, but the War of 1812 brought renewed manufacture with barrels 3½" longer. Their historical significance is in their probable use on the Lewis and Clark Expedition and other Western explorations.

b) Hall breech-loading rifle, Model 1819; 1817-c. 1845; lgth. overall 52¾" (134 cm.), barrel 32¾" (83 cm.).

In 1811 John Hancock Hall of Maine, with help from William Thornton, patented a breech-loading flint-lock arm that became the first breech-loader adopted and issued on a wide scale by any nation. It was also the first firearm to be manu- factured with completely interchangeable parts. The United States adopted the rifle in 1817, designating it the Model 1819, and Hall moved to the Harpers Ferry Armory to supervise its manu- facture. In all, Hall arms both flint and percussion, rifle and carbine in pattern, were made at Harpers Ferry and by contractors for more than 25 years.

c) Allen and Thurber pepper-box pistol, c. 1837-c. 1847; lgth. overall 7" (17.8 cm.), barrel 3¼" (8.25 cm.).

In common parlance, firearms with a revolving cluster of barrels that fire singly as they pass under the cock or detonator are known as pepper-boxes. They appeared early in Europe, but it was Ethan Allen who brought the form to its height in America. His first patent, granted in 1837, covered the raising and releasing of a hammer with a single pull of the trigger—a characteristic of all Allen pepper-boxes. The same action also rotated the barrels. For more than a decade, these were the fastest firing pistols in America and much more popular than the Colt.

d) Colt Paterson revolver; c. 1836-1842; lgth. overall 15½" (39.4 cm.), barrel 9" (22.9 cm.).

The revolving pistols and long arms made at Paterson, New Jersey, were the first of the long line of Colt firearms and thus are highly prized by collectors despite the comparatively large number that survive. As soon as Colt obtained his American patent in 1836 he founded the Patent Arms Manufactury and started the factory at Paterson. From then until lack of commercial success and military sales forced him into bankruptcy in 1842, he produced his firearms there. His pistols in general were 5-shot and characterized by a folding trigger and the lack of a loading lever.

American

a) Elgin cutlass pistol; c. 1838; lgth. overall 14½″ (36.8 cm.), barrel 4″ (10.2 cm.).

George Elgin patented a combination single-shot percussion pistol and bowie knife in 1837. Three principal firms manufactured these colourful arms in a number of variations and in calibres ranging from .35 to .54, though the total made was very small. The most desirable, such as this example, were those .54 calibre specimens with a full knuckle-guard, and 150 of these were purchased by the U.S. Navy and used on the South Seas Exploring Expedition of 1838-43. They were the only combination weapons ever officially issued by the U.S Government. No civilian market developed and when the expedition returned, manufacture had ceased.

b) Deringer pistol; c. 1845; lgth. overall 4½″ (11.4 cm.), barrel 1½″ (3.8 cm.).

Henry Deringer, Jr. of Philadelphia was perhaps the only gunmaker to design a weapon which attained such popularity that his name became a common noun in American usage. The pistols for which he became famous appeared late in his life, in the 1840s, and were all primarily pocket pistols of large calibre. He made them only in percussion cap ignition. Because he held no patent, there were many imitators, some using his name exactly, others using close variants such as Beringer. One of his pistols was used by John Wilkes Booth to assassinate Abraham Lincoln in 1865.

c) Colt Walker revolver; c. 1847, lgth. overall 15½″ (39.4 cm.), barrel 9″ (22.9 cm.).

Colt Paterson revolvers were highly regarded by soldiers and such units as the Texas Rangers who used them. Pressure was put upon the Ordnance Department to buy and issue them. Maj. William A. Thornton, other American officers and some British officers suggested improvements, including the addition of a trigger guard and a loading lever. Capt. Samuel Walker worked with Colt on these improvements; the first new revolver which Colt named the Walker Model, appeared in 1847. He sent two to Walker who received them just before his death in the Mexican War. With their appearance, Colt returned to business and became successful.

d) Smith and Wesson revolver, Model No. 1, Second Issue; c. 1860.

The Smith and Wesson No. 1 was one of the most important of all American revolvers from the standpoint of arms development. It was the first American revolver firing metal-cased ammunition and one of the first successful rim-fire revolvers produced anywhere in the world. Production began in 1857 with the .22 calibre first model and, in all, some 11,000 to 12,000 specimens of the 7-shot first issue were made before a variation on the model appeared in mid-1860. In all there were three variations of the first model which continued in production until 1879.

a) *John Brown Model Sharps carbine; 1852, 1853; lgth. overall 37½″ (95 cm.), barrel 21½″ (54.6 cm.).*

Christian Sharps, who had worked under John Hall at Harpers Ferry, patented a strong breech-loading action in 1848. The breech-block moved vertically in a mortise when the trigger guard was moved forward and back. Over a period of 20 years, some nine models were produced and perhaps 100,000 saw action in the Civil War. Yet the most desirable to collectors is the 'John Brown Model', a designation covering the almost identical models of 1852 and 1853. John Brown and his men carried Sharpses of these models when they seized the Federal Armory at Harpers Ferry just before the Civil War.

b) *Henry rifle; presented to Abraham Lincoln; early 1860s; lgth. overall 43½″ (110 cm.), barrel 24″ (61 cm.).*

Oliver F. Winchester purchased the Volcanic Arms Company when it went bankrupt and hired B. Tyler Henry to supervise production of the arm. Henry did far more; he perfected a .44 rim-fire cartridge for the rifle making it much more powerful and devised other improvements to make it stronger and more reliable, obtaining patents on these changes in 1860. The Henry went into production in time to see service before the Civil War ended. It continued to be made until an improvement produced a new rifle named the Winchester Model 1866, the first of a long line that continues today.

c) *Spencer carbine; early 1860s; lgth. overall 39″ (99 cm.), barrel 22″ (55.8 cm.).*

Christopher M. Spencer patented a 7-shot metal cased cartridge repeater in 1860. It had a tubular magazine in the butt stock and operated on the lever-action principle. It was the first successful cartridge repeater in the world. A trained soldier could fire 7 shots in 9 seconds and maintain a steady rate of 14 or 15 shots a minute—about five times better than the best men with conventional muzzle-loaders. They began to reach the battle-fields in quantity early in 1863, with considerable impact, though Spencer lost the civilian market to the lighter Winchester after the Civil War.

a) Remington rolling block rifle; Model 1870; lgth. overall 51¾" (131 cm.), barrel 34½" (88 cm.).

This rifle, developed by Leonard Geiger and Joseph Rider, was perhaps the most widely used breech-loader in the world. It was exceptionally strong and simple, and no rolling block breech was ever known to blow out. The Paris Imperial Exposition of 1867 awarded it a medal, pronounc-ing it the finest rifle in the world. Denmark, Norway, Sweden, Spain, Egypt and Argentina adopted it as an official military weapon; China, Austria, Italy and several South American nations purchased quantities; almost every other country experimented with it. Well into the present century, it was also made in a variety of sporting arms.

b) Colt single-action revolver; 1873 onwards; lgth. overall 13" (33.0 cm.), barrel 7½" (19.1 cm.).

The Colt single-action cartridge revolver was known officially at the factory as the Model P when production began in 1873. Since then, its myriad variations have acquired dozens of names including 'Peacemaker', 'Frontier', 'Storekeeper', 'Bisley', 'Buntline Special', 'Thumbuster', 'Plow-handle', and others, some official, some informal. Calibres ranged from .22 to .476. It was the most popular revolver Colt ever made, with both a military and a civilian market, especially in the West. Production continued until 1941 when war-time necessities caused the Colt Company to drop it. Following the War, however, there was such demand that it once again entered production.

c) Trap door Springfield rifle; Model 1873, lgth. overall 49" (124 cm.), barrel 32" (81 cm.).

At the close of the Civil War, Erskine S. Allin, Master Armourer at the Springfield Armory, devised a system for converting the vast stocks of muzzle-loading arms into breech-loaders: a hinged trap door that could be flipped up with a thumb-piece, automatically extracting the spent cartridge. In 1873, an Army Ordnance Board chose an improved version as the official shoulder arm. With official models of 1873, 1879, 1880, 1884 and 1889, this .45 calibre single-shot arm remained the standard infantry weapon for the Indian Wars of the West, and many saw service in the Spanish-American War.

d) Hawken plains rifle; mid-19th century; lgth. overall 53½" (136 cm.), barrel 36¾" (93 cm.).

'Plains rifle' is a collector's term designating the short heavy rifle favoured by fur traders and moun-tain men in the American West from about 1820 to 1860. In the country they travelled, the game was big and the distances great, so that they needed a more powerful weapon than the East's Kentucky rifle. And they travelled much of the time on horseback, thus preferring a short weapon. Jacob and Samuel Hawken of St. Louis were the most famous makers but there were many others who specialized in these rifles, all concentrating on strength and durability, excluding grace and beauty.

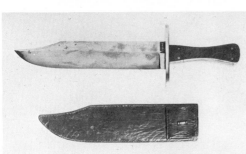

a) Bowie knife from Perryville Battlefield; 1862; lgth. overall 18" (45.7 cm.), blade 12⅞" (32.7 cm.).

James Bowie became a legend in American history as a knife fighter. After a nearly disastrous duel, his brother Rezin gave him a knife: in 1830 Bowie refined it. No one knows exactly what these original knives looked like, but in common parlance before 1840, any big fighting and all-purpose knife was known as a 'Bowie Knife'. Many were made in America, but perhaps the greatest number came from Sheffield, England, especially from the Wostenholme firm whose IXL trademark stood for quality. Bowie knives, like this specimen, were carried in the Civil War as personal arms, especially by Confederates.

b) Sabre with eagle head pommel; 1821–1840; lgth. overall 38½" (95 cm.), blade 32⅞" (84 cm.).

Prior to about 1840 there were very few specific models of officers' swords. The branch of service was indicated by the colour of the metal, and blades were specified from time to time as sabre, cut-and-thrust or straight, with those for foot officers being shorter than 30 inches. Otherwise the decoration was the owner's choice. Classical urn pommels were an early vogue, and there were helmets, Indian heads, horse heads and others, but the eagle head was undoubtedly the most popular decoration. There were· literally hundreds of different varieties; some collectors today specialize in this type alone.

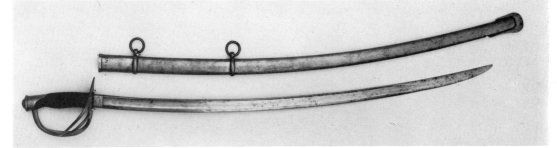

c) Model 1860 light cavalry sabre; lgth. overall 41" (104 cm.), blade 34½" (88 cm.).

The Model 1860 was a lighter version of the Model 1840 dragoon sabre, copied from the French light cavalry model of 1822. Actually the designation 'Model 1860' is a collector's convenience. No document so specifying it has yet been located, and at least two specimens are known dated 1859. It made its primary appearance in 1860, however, and was the principal cavalry sabre of the American Civil War. It was issued but seldom used in the Indian Wars of the West. The Model 1860 had a brass guard; an iron version appeared in a small quantity in 1906.

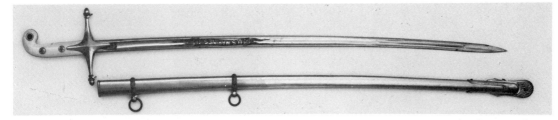

d) Marine Corps officer's sabre, pattern of 1875; lgth. overall 37" (94 cm.)., blade 31½" (80 cm.).

The Marine Corps was the only United States service ever to adopt officially a sabre with a mameluke hilt. Traditionally, this derived from its actions in the campaign against the Barbary Pirates (1801–1805). The type only became mandatory in 1825, but a portrait and surviving specimens indicate that it was used at least as early as 1819. From 1825 (except between 1859 and 1875), the slightly curved sabre with mameluke hilt has been required for officers of the Corps. Swords were abolished for U.S. officers in 1942, but returned after the War with the Marine Corps continuing its traditional pattern.

Arms and Armour Glossary

BLUEING: Many sword blades and metal parts of pistols were heat treated to produce a deep blue colour which was often combined with gilding to produce a surface both decorative and rust resistant.

BORE: Internal diameter of a barrel of a firearm.

BRIDLE: Metal support fitted on the lockplate to which the frizzen was secured.

BROWN BESS: Smooth bore, flintlock musket used by the British Army between c. 1720–c. 1840.

BROWNING: Controlled rusting process similar to blueing, used almost exclusively for firearm barrels.

BURGONET: Light form of helmet normally without any visor, worn in the late 16th and early 17th centuries.

CALIBRE: Diameter of missile fired by a firearm.

COCK: Metal arm of the flintlock fitted with jaws which hold the piece of flint.

CUTLASS: Term derived from the mediaeval cutlace but often loosely used to describe broad-bladed naval weapons.

DUELLING PISTOL: Introduced late 18th century, these plain pistols came easily and accurately to the aim; often in pairs complete with case and accessories.

FLINTLOCK: Simple mechanism the essential feature of which was a jaw which grasped a piece of flint which, when swung forward, scraped down a movable, L-shaped piece of steel, the frizzen, to produce sparks which fell into the pan to ignite the main charge.

FRIZZEN: Piece of metal pivotted above the pan of a flintlock.

FURNITURE: Metal fittings, ramrod, pipes, butt cap, etc. attached to the stock of a firearm.

GILDING: Process of decoration mostly used on sword blades, whereby an amalgam of gold and mercury was placed on the metal and then heated to drive off the mercury leaving the gold deposited in a very thin covering.

GREAVE: Protection for the shin.

HILT: That portion of a sword grasped by the hand; most early hilts were cruciform, but from the 14th century the use of bars, and later, from the 16th century, small plates, afforded extra protection for the hand.

MAIL: Very ancient form of defence dating from at least the third century B.C. and used until well into the 17th century and reintroduced during World War I. It comprised a series of small interlocking metal rings.

MARTINI HENRY RIFLE: Between 1871–91, the official rifle of the British Army was a breech-loading weapon firing a .45 bullet. Access to the breech was by means of a falling block which was actuated by moving the trigger guard. This action was designed by Friedrich von Martini. The barrel used a rifling of seven grooves patented by Alexander Henry.

MATCHLOCK: Earliest firearm ignition; a piece of impregnated cord, the match, was ignited; the glowing end fitted into a movable arm, the serpentine, which on pressure from the trigger, swung forward to ignite the priming powder and then the main charge.

MUSKET: Smooth-bored longarm.

NIPPLE: Small metal pillar with a small hole drilled through the centre and then screwed into the breech of a barrel.

PERCUSSION CAP: The first practical percussion system was introduced by Dr. Alexander Forsythe; early in the 19th century the small copper cap, with a deposit of explosive compound on the inside, often mercury fulminate, was introduced. This was placed over the nipple and struck by the metal hammer of the lock.

POMMEL: Weight fitted at the top of the tang of the sword blade, usually to counterbalance the weight of the blade.

QUILLON: Cross bar guard at the top of a sword blade.

RAPIER: Sword, introduced late in the 15th century, with a long blade and mainly designed so that the point and edge might be used. They were often fitted with a guard comprising a number of bars, in which case it is described as a swept hilt rapier, or with a metal cup, the cup hilt rapier.

RICASSO: Blunted section of the blade situated just below the cross bar of the quillon and intended to permit a finger to be looped over the bars to afford a firmer grip on the hilt.

RIFLING: Series of grooves cut on the inside surface of the barrel and designed to give a spin to the bullet in flight in an attempt to even out deviations from the central axis to increase accuracy.

SEAR: Small metal arm usually designed to engage with a slot or recess in the internal mechanism of a lock.

SMALLSWORD: Light, decorative, but functional sword introduced, probably from France, during the late 1600s; part of civilian costume in Britain until the 1770/80s.

SNAPHAUNCE: Form of flintlock in which the steel and pan cover were separate.

STOCK: Wooden body of a pistol or longarm.

TANG: Last three or four inches of a blade which passed through the quillon and centre of the grip. Blade and hilt were secured by hammering the tip of the tang over the pommel.

TOUCH-HOLE: Small hole piercing the barrel and connecting the pan to the breech.

TUMBLER: Small metal block, usually cut with slots or grooves, and forming part of the mechanism of a gunlock.

Repairs and Maintenance

Rust is the most serious problem facing the collector of any arms and armour and there is no simple, totally effective method of dealing with it. Often it demands a decision of some importance for where rust has developed on a decorated metal surface a choice has to be made as to whether the rust should be removed, thus damaging the decoration, or just minimized and left 'in situ'.

The majority of swords have blades and hilts which are plain and consequently present little difficulty, apart from the physical labour involved in cleaning. The most efficient way to remove rust is by using some form of abrasive, but it must be emphasized that all cleaning removes a small amount of the surface. Even proprietary liquid rust removers etch the surface and must always be treated with care. Even if a very fine jeweller's emery, steel wool, or one of the patent paste abrasives is used, care should always be taken to use only the minimum required. Buffing with a wire or stone wheel should only be used as a last resort and certainly *never* on any weapon of quality.

In the matter of repairs the collector must make his own decision as to the amount of restoration he is prepared to accept. Small repairs such as rebrazing a hammer, replacing a broken spring, substituting a new ramrod for a broken fragment are probably acceptable to the collector; whether a new stock, new barrel, or a completely rebuilt lock are acceptable is very much a personal choice, but a useful guide line is probably, 'the least is best'.

Once the weapon has been cleaned it will probably require no more maintenance than periodic inspections to ensure that fresh rusting has not developed. Dust, particularly when adhering to old oil, should be removed and in the case of firearms it must not be forgotten that lock mechanisms also require a periodic drop of oil.

Fakes and Forgeries

Unfortunately the increased demand for all types of arms and armour has stimulated the market to such an extent that faking has become more common. During the late nineteenth and early twentieth centuries some superb replicas were produced by makers such as Conrad and Schmidt, both of Germany. These were mostly copies of items from famous museums and are consequently unlikely to be handled by the small collector. One of the biggest problems has become that of deciding how much restoration is acceptable before it becomes faking; the largest number of suspect pieces are firearms. It is very difficult to offer general, overall advice in distinguishing between genuine and imitation pieces; the only protection for the collector is knowledge, which comes only from reading and experience in handling as many items as possible.

Some guidance may be obtained by examining the degree of pitting or rust which normally would be expected to be uniform overall, unless there seems to be some specific reason for a variation. The fit of the lock and barrel into the wooden stock should be closely examined since the normal high standard of workmanship produced a very good fit. Signs of recent shaping around the lock plate should always be viewed with suspicion. A number of very good quality replacement parts for antique firearms are available, and if suitably aged, it is very difficult to detect them unless the gun is stripped down to its components.

With swords the problem is a little more difficult since some interchanging of hilts and blades took place during the period of their use. The tip of the tang where it meets the pommel button should not show any signs of recent filing, and the fit of the shoulder of the blade against the base of the hilt or guard was normally very good; any gaps may indicate that at some time the blade was changed.

Generally, armour is easier to assess since most reproduction pieces are too light and of poor shape. The inside surface should be examined for in most original pieces the inside surface was left rough from the hammer and items with smooth, pressed surfaces are almost invariably nineteenth century reproductions.

Arms and Armour Further Reading

General

BAXTER, D. *Blunderbusses*. Harrisburg, 1970.
   Superimposed Loaded Firearms 1360-1860. Hong Kong, 1966.
BLACKMORE, H. *Arms and Armour*. New York, 1965.
   Hunting Weapons. London, 1971.
   Guns and Rifles of the World. London and New York, 1965.
BLAIR, C. *European and American Arms*. London and New York, 1962.
   European Armour. London, 1972.
   Pistols of the World. London, 1969.
BOOTHROYD, G. *The Handgun*. London, 1970.
DIXON, N. *Georgian Pistols: The Art & Craft of the Flintlock Pistol 1715-1840*. York (U.S.A.), 1971.
DOWELL, W. C. *The Webley Story*. Leeds, 1962.
DUNLAP, J. *American British and Continental Pepperbox Firearms*. Palo Alto, Calif., 1967.
HAYWARD, J. F. *Art of the Gunmaker*, 2 vols. London, rev. ed. London, 1964.
HELD, R. *The Age of Firearms*. London, 1959; 2nd ed. Chicago, 1970.
KARR, C. L. and C. P. *Remington Handguns*, 2nd rev. ed. New York, 1952.
LENK, T. *The Flintlock*, ed. by J. T. Hayward. Tr. Urquart. New York, 1965.
LOGAN, H. *Underhammer Guns*. Harrisburg, Pa. and Toronto, 1960.
MAY, W. R. and ANNIS, P. G. *Naval Swords: British and American Naval Edged Weapons 1660-1815*. London, 1970.
NEAL, W. K. and BLACK, D. H. L. *The Mantons, Gunmakers*. New York and London, 1967.
NICKEL, H. *Arms and Armour Through the Ages*. London, 1971.
NORMAN, V. *Arms and Armour*. London, 1964.
   Small Swords and Military Swords. London, 1967.
OAKESHOTT, R. E. *The Archaeology of Weapons*. London, 1960.
PAYNE GALLWAY, R. *The Crossbow*. London, 1958.
PETERSON, H. L. *Daggers and Fighting Knives of the Western World; from the Stone Age till 1900*. London, 1968.
   Encyclopaedia of Firearms. London, 1964.
RILING, R. *Guns and Shooting—A Select Chronological Bibliography Of*. New York, 1951.
STEPHENS, F. J. *The Collectors Pictorial Book of Bayonets*. London, 1971.
TAYLERSON, A. *Revolving Arms*. London, 1967.
   The Revolver 1818-1865, 1865-1888, 1889-1914, 3 vols. New York, 1966-70.
VALENTINE, E. *Rapiers*. Harrisburg, Pa. and London, 1968.
WAGNER, E. *Cut and Thrust Weapons*. Trans. by Jean Layton, New York and London, 1967.
WESLEY, L. *Air-Guns and Air-Pistols*. London, 1955.

WINANT, K. *Early Percussion Firearms*. London and New York, 1961.
WILKINSON, F. *Antique Firearms*. New York and London, 1969.
   British and American Flintlocks. London, 1971.
   Flintlock Pistols. New York, 1968.
   Flintlock Guns and Rifles. London, 1971.
   Guns. London, 1970.
   Small Arms. London, 1966.
   Arms and Armour. New York and London, 1971.
   Edged Weapons. Enfield, 1970.
   Swords and Daggers. London, 1967.

Continental

BLAIR, C. *European Armour*. London, 1972.
BOUDRIOT, J. *Armes à feu françaises modèles réglementaires*, 4 vols. Paris, 1961-67.
HEWITT, J. *Ancient Armour in Europe*. London, 1860 (reprint 1967).
LAVIN, J. D. *History of Spanish Firearms*. New York and London, 1965.
MØLLER, T. *Gamle Danske Militer Vaben*. Copenhagen, 1963.
MOLLO, E. *Russian Military Swords 1801-1917*. London, 1969.

British

AYLWARD, J. *The Small Sword in England*, rev. ed. London, 1960.
BAILEY, D. W. *British Military Longarms 1775-1815*. London, 1971.
   British Military Longarms 1815-1865. London, 1972.
BLACKMORE, H. *British Military Firearms 1650-1850*. London and New York, 1961.
CAREY, A. M. *English, Irish and Scottish Firearms Makers*. New York, 1967.
ROADS, C. H. *The British Soldier's Firearm 1850-1864*. New York, 1964.

American

ABELS, R. *Classic Bowie Knives*. New York, 1967.
ALBAUGH, W. *Confederate Handguns*. York (U.S.A.), 1963 (rev. ed. 1969).
CHAPEL, C. E. *Guns of the Old West*. New York, 1961.
HANSON, C. *The Plains Rifle*. Harrisburg, Pa. and Toronto, 1960.
KAUFFMAN, H. J. *Early American Gunsmiths, 1650-1850*. Harrisburg, Pa. and Toronto, 1952.
   The Pennsylvania-Kentucky Rifle. New York, 1960.
PETERSON, H. L. *American Indian Tomahawks*. New York, 1965.
   Arms and Armor in Colonial America. New York, 1956.
   American Silver Mounted Swords. Washington, 1955.

Museum Collections

Great Britain

BIRMINGHAM: Museum of Science and Industry.

LINCOLNSHIRE: City and County Museum and Usher Gallery, Lincoln.

LONDON: The Armouries, The Tower of London; The Wallace Collection; The Victoria and Albert Museum.

SCOTLAND: The National Museum of Antiquities of Scotland, The Royal Scottish Museum, Scottish United Services Museum, Edinburgh; Glasgow Art Galleries and Museum, Glasgow.

U.S.A.

CONNECTICUT: Wadsworth Atheneum, Hartford; The Winchester Gun Museum, New Haven.

ILLINOIS: The George F. Harding Museum, Chicago.

MARYLAND: Walters Art Gallery, Baltimore.

MASSACHUSETTS: The Springfield Armory Museum, The National Park Service, Springfield; The John Woodman Higgins Armory, Worcester.

MISSOURI: The City Art Museum of St. Louis.

NEW YORK: The Metropolitan Museum of Art, New York City; Fort Ticonderoga Museum; The West Point Museum.

OHIO: The Cleveland Museum of Art.

WASHINGTON D.C.: The National Armed Forces Historical Museum.

Index

Right: Commercial smelling bottle in dark green glass with ground glass stopper, set in open-work silver base; England.
Left: Box, painted enamel on copper, inscribed on the inside Sar^h Watton 1755; Birmingham, England, 1755.

Bottles and Boxes

Glass has been used to make containers certainly since the second millennium B.C. Narrow-necked containers are generally known as bottles: those with wide mouths as jars. Specialized shapes of bottles sometimes have generic names, e.g. vial or phial (small narrow bottles for pharmaceuticals or perfumery), or flask, which is used to describe a number of bottles but is often used for one with a wide flattened body and narrow neck. At certain periods other materials, especially clay and leather have been used for particular kinds of container (e.g. black-jacks and stoneware wine jugs) but they have not achieved the lasting universality of glass, which has been used for scent and toilet preparations, pharmaceutical products, food, wines, spirits and all kinds of beverage.

Boxes are another field with a wide choice of material—everything from tin and wood to precious metals set with stones. They often exhibit miniature versions of the jeweller's arts, enamelling, the use of hardstone plaques, incredibly detailed painting, and finely-worked gold or silver. But other examples, of boxwood, pewter, or horn are found, and the loving care that went into the making of these often simple boxes transformed them into beautifully-fashioned objects, and well worth the time and trouble spent in building up a collection.

Both bottles and boxes are a fruitful source of pleasure, and of historical as well as aesthetic interest to the collector.

The Craft

Bottles

Glass containers are usually formed from hot glass, though the cold carving technique has been used, especially for finishing small costly items, from the eighth century B.C. Later, in the eighteenth and nineteenth centuries, scent bottles were decorated by various forms of cutting, which again added to their cost.

The earliest known glass containers were made by the core winding technique. Very high temperatures are required to melt any glass from the basic mixture of raw materials; such temperatures were difficult to attain in early times and so melting was done in small amounts in successive stages. Then a core of mud was covered with the molten glass by constant twisting so that toffee-like threads were wound around the core which was later gouged out. As glass has to be kept hot enough to be soft while being formed, this process restricted the size of the object created.

Glass blowing, by means of a long hollow blowing iron, probably developed in the first century B.C. Used with moulds, it enabled a wide variety of glass objects to be made quickly, efficiently and with considerable uniformity. Glass factories were set up all over the Roman Empire and glass-makers began marking moulds with their names. Hence 'FRONTINUS' and 'FELIX FECIT' appear on barrel-shaped cylindrical bottles and jugs. Glass bottle manufacturers did not begin marking their wares again until the nineteenth century. Mould-blown bottles were produced in exotic shapes like fish, horns, bunches of grapes and shells, as well as utilitarian shapes—rounds, squares and round-bottomed, long-necked flasks with a protective cover of straw—practical forerunners of the wanded flask and the chianti bottle.

Figured moulds began to be used again during the eighteenth century, especially for small patent medicine bottles. In 1821, Henry Ricketts of Bristol patented a mould-blowing method using a foot-operated open and shut mould and the products bore the firm's name on the base. At the same time, methods for automatic blowing were being explored.

Bottles continued to be mouth-blown by teams of glass-blowers for most of the nineteenth century, although elementary mechanical blowing devices were being patented towards the end of the century. The Ashley post machine (1887)—the most successful—was eventually adapted and used by several companies. The Owens machine, the first successful fully automatic glass-blowing machine, was introduced into Europe in 1906.

Boxes

The distinction between boxes with hinged covers and those without is inconsistent, seemingly based more on size or local tradition than on the type. While English tobacco boxes invariably have loose covers, the lids of Dutch and German ones are hinged. At least from c. 1690, snuff-boxes had attached covers, but after c. 1770 papier mâché, composition and wood snuff-boxes had detachable lids. Without a straight edge for a hinge, small oval and circular boxes, whatever their purpose, had lift-off lids.

Two types of hinge were employed. The simpler, earlier form, sometimes called a stand-away hinge, had three or five cylinders soldered in alternation to two strips of metal, which were then riveted directly into the box or soldered to the metal rims of the body and cover. This did not fit tightly and broke the line of profile and decoration. Gradually the integral hinge developed, used in Paris by 1730. A typical Parisian box, $3\frac{1}{4}''$ (8.2 cm.) long had fifteen beautifully fitted cylinders set alternately along the top edge of the base, and the underside of the cover, held in place by a transverse pin planished to an invisible smoothness. This basic construction was refined in England, c. 1790, to a hinge set in on the top, with only three or five cylinders completely concealed inside.

The presence or absence of marks on a box is a somewhat erratic indicator of its age or provenance. Only France used a strict marking system. Many continental silver boxes, c. 1700-1725, are unmarked. With rare exceptions German boxes of all kinds are never marked; the same is true of English gold boxes until c. 1800. Nor, except in France, were they required to mark the gold or silver mounts of tortoise-shell, hardstone and porcelain boxes. It is thus often necessary to turn to reliably marked French examples for stylistic dating or find other criteria on which to base attributions, a task complicated by interchanging styles and decorative motifs. As English law (until 1798) required a gold standard of 22 carats, while 18-carat gold was acceptable in Dresden, more definitive attributions might be made by assaying the mounts of these boxes.

By contrast, some boxes apparently have too many or conflicting marks. Many Parisian gold boxes bear two different, complete sets of marks. Far from being suspicious, however, they may usually be taken as representing a high rate of repair and alteration during the eighteenth century.

Opposite:
Far left: 'Oxford lavender' rare bottle with deep blue glass gilded neck; early 19th century.
Far right: 'Oxford Lavender' crudely cut gilt and embellished with painted flowers and glass 'gems'; early 19th century.
Top row, left to right: Small flacon in latticinio glass; possibly England (Stourbridge), second half 19th century.
Millefiori bottle with inserted millefiori portrait; Venice, c. 1850.
Small scent bottle in hyalith glass, silver-gilt hinged cap, chain and finger ring; c. 1850.
Centre left: Shell-shaped scent bottle with trail work in opaque white glass; Orléans, France, c. 1675.
Centre right: Scent bottle in lithyaline glass; Bohemia, c. 1840.
Bottom: Double scent bottle, deeply cut, with light blue overlay on clear glass; England, second half 19th century.

Bottles
Introduction

Although probably more glass containers have been produced than any other potential antique, considerably less is known about them than about far rarer objects and the serious bottle collector has to do much basic background research. Most bottles have been discarded, without a thought, broken or whole, somewhere. The minute proportion which have been valued for their antiquity, rarity or workmanship—for instance, Near Eastern core-wound pieces or early blown containers from Roman, Islamic or mediaeval times, have been collected with other contemporary objects. Only comparatively recently have bottles of all periods and kinds become objects for serious collectors and scholars.

In spite of the tremendous variety of objects, in quality, rarity, usage and age coming under the heading 'Bottle', the following general points are useful when considering any bottle or glass container:

1) What was the method of the manufacture and were there any restrictions—perhaps of size, colour or shape, imposed by it?

2) What was the purpose of the object: utility, ornament or, quite often, a combination of the two? What was the nature of the contents: their consistency, value, etc?

3) How scarce was the container or its contents at the time it was made?

4) What were the customs of the time? How were things sold or used?

One of the recurrent problems of the bottle collector is finding out the purpose for which the container was made. The type of glass—green, ordinary and bubbly, or clear and formed with care, the way it is finished, the cost of the materials and the labour and any after-working, help to indicate if its purpose was purely utilitarian and the worth of its contents at the time. Contents with a thick consistency must be in a wide-mouthed container for both filling and removal; costly liquids, especially those subject to evaporation, need a small opening that can be firmly sealed. Contemporary illustrations of all kinds are very useful guides for seeing how domestic and commonplace things

were used or regarded.

Containers in Roman times were probably used for oil, wine, cosmetics and food. Some larger ones had an 'after-use' as cinerary urns. Small spherical pots and jars with rolled lips are also common. Most glass containers of this period are pale to darkish green and transparent and surprisingly light in weight. (The greenish tinge apparent in so much 'ordinary' glass comes from the iron oxide content of the sand. The chemical content of the earliest glass had caused it to be opaque or translucent and strongly coloured.)

Surviving bottles and flasks from the Middle East and Persia of the Sassanian and Islamic periods are well made, solid and often decorated with stylish shallow cutting. The simple onion-shaped bottle is a very distinctive type in mediaeval European manuscripts and fragments are often found in excavations. A lot of utilitarian glass containers must have been produced in the mediaeval forest glass-houses of northern Europe but it was also a period in which many other materials were used.

The sixteenth and seventeenth centuries were particularly important for the British glass industry. Monopoly policy led to a strong, relatively concentrated industry, and the introduction of coal-fired furnaces (partly to preserve timber for ship-building) was significant in the emergence of the bottle glass industry. Quantities of sturdy dark green glass bottles were made and were often shipped packed in amongst coal. By 1696, nearly three million bottles were produced annually in about thirty-nine glass-houses in Britain. Bottles (often containing cider, ale or mineral water) were exported all over the world. Many British-made eighteenth century bottles have been excavated on the Atlantic coast of North America.

In Britain, all sections of the glass industry were affected by the Excise Acts in force 1745–1845. Besides onerous duties and burdensome regulations involving Excise officers in every legal glass-house, the field of manufacture was strictly regulated: bottle houses were not allowed to make bottles of less than six ounces or to use cullet (waste glass) from Crown window glass-houses. Small bottles of all kinds were supposed to be made in flint houses. Decoration, both cutting and enamelling, was usually done by specialist outside firms. To experiment was difficult as duty was paid on the amount of glass *melted*.

From 1800–1900 Great Britain and America showed a steady increase in the use of glass containers for mineral waters and carbonated beverages, food of all kinds, ink and numerous domestic and pharmaceutical products. Not only the maker's name appeared on each bottle (usually on the base) but also the packer's, embossed on the bottle and on the elaborately printed paper label as well.

a) Medicine vials; 17th-18th centuries; hts. $1\frac{3}{8}''$ (3.5 cm.) to $2\frac{3}{16}''$ (5.6 cm.).

Made of light but sturdy—usually greenish—glass, these little bottles were used extensively from the 16th to the early 19th centuries to hold single doses of various potions or medicines. In the 18th century proprietary medicines became popular: the *Gentleman's Magazine* of 1748 mentions 202 types. Many had distinctive bottles: the steeple shape used for 'Dalby's Carminitive' or the mould-blown embossed 'Turlington's Balsam of Life' bottle.

Notice the sharp conical push-up base of the three bottles on the right and the asymmetrical pouring lip of the round bottle (left). The third from the left is an unusual form.

Bottles

Medicinal and general

BRITISH
AMERICAN

b) Wide-mouthed cylindrical specie jars with painted polychrome decoration and labels; probably c. 1783; ht. 15'' (38 cm.).

These jars are mouth-blown in clear glass. The tinned iron caps are cut into 8-pointed 'cannibal crowns' painted red and line-edged with black. The left jar has the label 'Fol. Rosarum' with a pineapple and two dolphins or fishes. The other has 'Rad. Sarsaparil' with a phoenix in gilt, green and black. Another in the same series was recorded with '1783' and 'Ireland' on it, and if the date is correct, it is worth noting that it was just after Ireland was exempt from the Excise duties and regulations which were severely restricting the glass industry in the United Kingdom.

c) Barber's bottle of Mary Gregory-type glass; dark blue with painted white enamel decoration; U.S.A., late 19th century; ht. 9'' (22.8 cm.).

These decorative pieces are usually in Victorian style painted with white enamel designs particularly of children holding racquets, chasing birds or butterflies in a floral setting—thought to have been done in the 1870s and '80s by Mary Gregory, a Boston & Sandwich decorator. Although that factory made enamelled glass then, and perhaps earlier, there is considerable doubt as to whether all—or any—of these pieces actually were painted by Mary Gregory. Similar glass was made in Europe and America and with much made after the Boston & Sandwich Glass Company closed, the 'Mary Gregory-type' designation is applied to undocumented wares.

d) Wide-mouthed cylindrical specie jar, opaque blue glass, gilded glass-domed lid; ht. $15\frac{7}{8}''$ (40.5 cm.).

This mouth-blown jar was for shop display. The term 'specie jar' in the 19th century was always used for a cylindrical jar. Often, clear glass jars were filled with coloured liquids for attractive display, or sometimes with gilded wooden balls, presumably representing pills. After the 1830s, as the window panes in shop fronts got progressively larger, jars up to 31'' (78.7 cm.) high were made and elaborately decorated.

In earlier years, the window had been just an extension of the shop, with jars of opaque glass used to disguise the more unpleasant contents.

a) 'Shop round': Walton Patent, wide mouth with ground glass stopper, glass fronted labelling; 1860s; ht. 7⅛" (20 cm.).

The height of shop rounds was as important as the capacity (from 5 to 60 fl. oz.) since they were often on display. There were many kinds of elegant labelling and stoppering, well-illustrated in old catalogues of glass manufacturers, chemists' suppliers and journals such as *Chemist and Druggist*.

The base of this jar is marked 'W. N. Walton Patd. Sept: 28th 1862'. William N. Walton of New York patented the glass recessed label and though bottles similar to his were sold in England by the York Glass Company, the lettering was reproduced photographically, hence the name 'patent phototype labels'.

b) Pattern moulded flasks and a globular bottle of olive amber and amber glass; produced in unidentified Mid-western glass factories between c. 1815–35; ht. of tallest 8 13/16" (22.4 cm.).

In 1797 Major Isaac Craig and Colonel James O'Hara established the Pittsburgh Glass Works—the first coal-fired American glass-house. Their products were primarily bottles and window glass, the two basic necessities much in demand by the settlers streaming westward. Of the 40-odd glass-houses in Pittsburgh, only 14 produced flint glass-wares.

Open moulds bearing designs of simple vertical ribs or diamonds were extensively used by Mid-western glass-houses to decorate not only bottles, but many forms of table-wares. This type of mould produced decorations derived from English glass, especially from the Bristol area.

American bellows bottle, loop decorated glass, applied trailed and flowered motifs.

c) Baby's feeding bottle of flat oval shape; mid-19th century; lgth. 7½" (19 cm.).

Note the narrow nipple end and filling hole in one side—the shape probably first made in pottery in the late 18th century. The glass ones date from the 1840s and were considered more hygienic. This one has a glass stopper but corks were also used.

There were also conical shapes adapted from a typical German form and later, flattened rounded flask shapes, often with proprietary embossed labelling, a bent neck and internal screw thread into which a special stopper holding a long tube attached to a rubber nipple was fitted; of transparent glass, they were made well into the 20th century.

d) Internal screw stopper bottle with J K & S on the base; by John Kilner & Sons, Yorkshire, England; late 19th century; ht. 8" (20 cm.).

The internal screw stopper was patented in 1872 by Henry Barrett and used, like the swing stopper (1875) on heavy glass bottles for beer, cider and other carbonated beverages.

Kilners were making glass in Yorkshire from 1832 until 1937, when Kilner Brothers Ltd. closed and the rights to the 'Kilner Jar' (for home preserving) were sold. Although there were a number of named food jars, 'Kilner' is the one best known in Britain (cf. 'Mason Jar'—invented U.S.A. 1858—and now a generic name for preserving jar). John Kilner also made signed paperweights from 1844–47 and perhaps later.

a) *Ink bottles; late 19th or early 20th century; hts. $2\frac{1}{4}''$ and $2\frac{3}{8}''$ (5.5 and 5.75 cm.).*

This kind of bottle, crudely fashioned in pale green or bluish glass, often of rather poor quality, was known as 'Burst-off Penny Green Work' (see Glossary). Shapes listed in catalogues include 'Small House', 'Small Fluted', 'Octagon' and 'Bell Gum'. A number of other kinds of bottles could have this finish including 'Blackings', 'Apple Jellies', and 'Sauces'. People are inclined to date this type of bottle too early because of its crude form. They were still listed in the *London Glass Blowers Trade Society Catalogue of Numbers* for 1912.

b) *'Pitkin' pocket bottles, or flasks, and bottles; U.S.A. c. 1790–1840; ht. of stoppered bottle 6'' (15.2 cm.).*

These finely ribbed bottles made with a second gather of glass to strengthen the body, from a process known as the German half post method, have taken on the generic term 'Pitkin' flasks from the Pitkin Glass Works which was established in East Hartford, Connecticut in 1783 and continued in operation, according to tradition, until about 1830. However, such flasks were produced in numerous other American bottle glass-houses.

c) *Figured flasks; U.S.A.—eastern and Midwestern glass-houses, c. 1812–70; ht. of sunburst flask $7\frac{1}{8}''$ (18.1 cm.).*

Figured flasks (often termed by collectors today historical or pictorial flasks) bore purely decorative ornaments such as sunburst, cornucopia, etc. as well as 'portraits' of prominent political figures, heroes, steamboats, railroads and other indications of the developing social and economic way of life. These flasks were very popular between c. 1812–70; unlike many art forms, the quality and design degenerated as time passed. They were produced mostly in olive green, olive amber and aquamarine-coloured bottle glass in New England, New Jersey, Pennsylvania and the Midwest.

d) *Egg-shaped bottle, pale green glass embossed J. SCHWEPPE & CO.; 1832–50; lgth. $8\frac{1}{2}''$ (21.5 cm.).*

The earthenware bottles first used by Jacob Schweppe for his mineral waters did not satisfactorily resist the internal gas pressure so he turned to glass. The straight-sided dump shape with a wired-on cork used during the 19th century for seltzer water leaked when the cork got dry. In 1814, William Hamilton patented the egg-shaped bottle for mineral waters. It had to be laid on its side, keeping the cork moist, and became popular in the 1840s, continuing to be made until 1916.

a) Wine bottle; early to mid-17th century; ht. 9¼″ (23.5 cm.).

One of the earliest types of glass wine bottles: long neck, a comparatively small basic bubble for the body and a small 'kick-up' to form the base. The pronounced 'string ring' was to enable the wedge-shaped cork to be tied down.

The common dark green bottle was used for short term storage between cask and table, and for service. Wine was imported in casks and bottled for the owner. Among the properties of glass listed in Merrett's *The Art of Glass* (1662) was that 'Wine Beer nor other liquors will make them musty nor change their colours nor rust them.'

b) Wine bottle; c. 1670; ht. 8 6/10″ (22 cm.).

Early 'shaft and globe' or 'onion' shape bottles were relatively unstable: thus, necks were shortened while the body became more cup-shaped, with sloping shoulders and a larger base 'kick-up'. This example is very similar to one with the seal 'REP' (Richard Punt, landlord of The Three Tuns, Oxford, 1666–71). One of the earliest dated 'sealed bottles' found is marked 1657 with a King's head and the initials 'RMP'. However, there is a reference in 1571 in the diary of Armand Colinet, a glass-maker from the Low Countries, to providing glass bottles with a blank lozenge for a wax seal.

---

c) Wine bottle; c. 1690; ht. 4¾″ (12.1 cm.).

Between 1680 and about 1715, wine bottles were at their widest and dumpiest with a wide high kick-up base, short neck and still a pronounced string ring. The recent adoption of the corkscrew meant that corks could be pushed right into the neck of the bottle to form a complete seal, allowing wines to mature in the bottle. This development led to the straight-sided bottle suitable for binning —a gradual evolution since some of these wide flat bottles were used until the mid-18th century.

d) Handled bottle jug with seal of 1703; ht. 8½″ (21.6 cm.).

This large very unusual handled serving bottle has the seal 'Rice Wight 1703'. The kick-up is domed, the string ring of the early type and the handle, presumably an optional extra, practical in form.

There are many different types of wine bottle seal, including coats of arms, initials, tavern signs and college bottles. The dated ones do not necessarily show the date of manufacture. There are also the European spa water seals.

1703 was the date of the Methuen Treaty with Portugal which symbolically marked the waning taste of the British for light young wines and the preference for stronger drink including Portuguese wines specially fortified for the English market.

Bottles

British
WINE

a) Wine bottle with seal of 1760, browny-green glass; ht. 7 3/10″ (18.5 cm.).

This bottle with the seal 'EP 1760' illustrates the problem of dating bottles without additional information. Its dumpy shape was current from about the second decade of the 18th century and frequently appears in contemporary illustrations as obviously symbolic of a common 'black' (or dark green) bottle. Without the seal, it would probably have been dated earlier. Other sealed bottles of similar date have straighter sides and a slightly longer neck. This one was found at Cromer, on the Norfolk coast of England.

b) Wine bottle with seal In. Williams 1774, dark green glass; ht. 9½″ (24.1 cm.).

This was the type of bottle that evolved during the mid-18th century and proved most suitable for binning. The neck 'finish' is made by a double application of glass over the end, when it has been broken off the blowing iron and reheated. The slight belling out of the shoulder indicates possible use of a crude mould for initial form. Moulds were used commonly in the 18th century for small proprietary medicine bottles but are thought to have been first used for Bristol-made wine bottles—many exported to the eastern seaboard of North America, often with contents of cider, ale etc.

c & d) Wine bottles made by H. Ricketts, Bristol, England; early 19th century; ht. of 'c' 9 3/10″ (23 cm.), ht. of 'd' 11″ (28 cm.).

The patent granted to Henry Ricketts in 1821 was for an improved method of blowing bottles in an open-and-shut mould. This firm's bottles are marked on the outer ring of the base (the centre is slightly concave) with H RICKETTS & CO: GLASS WORKS BRISTOL and have a distinctive mould mark round the bottle just below the shoulder and the word PATENT above this on the opposite side to the seal (if there is one).

Example *c)* illustrates the danger of dating just by the seal: 'W. Leman, Chard. 1771' was fifty years *before* the patent was obtained.

a) Moulded scent bottle, amber-coloured with silver cap; France, 17th century; lgth. 3½″ (9.0 cm.).

This style is attributable to the Orleans glass-house of Bernard Perrot (see p. 485 *b*), a member of a celebrated family of glass-makers. He became the most eminent French glass-maker of his time (working 1649–1709) and developed a transparent red glass, opaque glass in imitation of porcelain and various flat glass processes.

The stylized decoration flanking the three fleurs-de-lis and crown motif is typical of the mould-blown style of Perrot's glass-house as are three flowering hearts on the same shape, or shell-shaped bottles with opaque 'trailing'. The caps are often of pewter.

b) Lithyalin bottles; Bohemia, probably 19th century; hts. 2½″ (6.3 cm.), and 2⅞″ (7.3 cm.).

This type of opaque marbled glass was developed by Friedrich Egermann (1777–1864), a Bohemian glass manufacturer who had trained as a chemist. Finished by over-cutting, it was produced in red, grey-green and bluish green and was imitated in Bohemia and France. Used for beakers and vases, lithyalin glass was also ideal for scent and toilet waters as it protected the contents from the light.

The red and black example (*left*) may well be by an imitator, but the brick-red bottle (*right*) is by Egermann. It has a silver cap over a ground glass stopper.

---

c) Scent bottles; early to mid-19th century; lgth. of tallest 7¼″ (18.5 cm.).

This type of tall narrow faceted block scent bottle is usually in colourless flint glass. Red is also found, while blue is rare. The faceted shallow cutting and 'cold' gold decoration is characteristic. Quite often the gilded stoppers have traces of sealing wax used to close them, though often stoppers are not the originals. Imported into England in the early and mid-19th century, they probably contained attar of roses, from eastern Europe, and were sold at fairs. They are known to collectors as 'Oxford Lavenders', though glass-makers' catalogues of the time use this name for a standard bottle of another shape.

d) Chained scent bottles; left: cut overlay, centre: colour twist, right: flashed and cut; early to mid-19th century; lgth. of 2 longer 2⅜″ (6.0 cm.).

Small scent bottles were often attached to chains for carrying on a *châtelaine*, bracelet or finger ring.
left: This bottle of pink over white opaque and clear glass was probably made in the early 1900s in Bohemia or Germany.
centre: This was made by assembling fine white opaque and transparent red canes in a mould and then 'picking them up' on a gather of clear glass, probably drawn out to form tubing, cut up and manipulated as required.
right: The annealed clear glass bottle has had a transparent red stain fired in; it was then cut. The caps are all of brass.

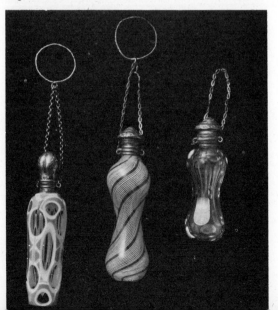

a) Millefiori scent bottles; 19th century; hts. $2\frac{3}{8}''$ (6.0 cm.), and $2\frac{3}{16}''$ (5.5 cm.).

The use of multi-coloured cane has a long history. The basic canes are formed by gathering successive colours or by picking up canes arranged in a pattern (e.g. the head, *left*) on the gather; the lump of hot glass is then drawn out to form a rod, pieces of which are assembled in a pattern, reheated, usually incorporated with a clear glass, then shaped.

Here, metallic particles applied to the hot glass give an 'aventurine' effect. The example, *left*, has a brass cap to hang from a chain and is probably Italian, c. 1845–50. The round screw-top bottle may well be English.

b) Double scent bottles; left: ruby glass with engraved silver cap, right: blue glass; c. 1840–85; lgth. $4\frac{3}{4}''$ (12.0 cm.).

This type of 'compartment bottle' was very popular in Victorian England. They were made to hold scent at one end (with a metal screw cap often protecting a ground glass stopper) and smelling salts at the other. The latter end often had a spring-fitted hinged lid, observable on both these specimens.

Both have characteristic facet cutting: one in panels, the other in flat diamonds, and are considered particularly to English taste. Many colours of glass are found including various reds, blue, green and brown. Caps are usually of silver or gilded brass.

Bottles

European
SCENT

c) Cameo smelling or cologne bottle, light blue background; by Thos. Webb & Son, Stourbridge (England), c. 1887; ht. $3\ 15/16''$ (10.0 cm.).

Cameo was another ancient decorative technique revived in the late 19th century. It is done on 'cased' glass, opaque over colour, worked together and then carefully annealed. The opaque outer layer is then reduced or removed so that only a white pattern appears on the coloured background. 19th century craftsmen used acid to remove most of the opaque layer and hand carved the final design.

The cameo scent bottles created by David Pearce and his son Lionel, who worked for Webbs, were inspired by Chinese snuff bottles and are in a rare class of their own. Here, the hinged silver lid covers a ground glass stopper.

d) Octagonal plunger-operated perfume spray bottle marked R. Lalique on the base and on the silver-gilt top; France, early 20th century; ht. $6\frac{1}{8}''$ (15.5 cm.).

Four panels have moulded dancing figures acid-etched to give a 'satin' finish which contrasts with the four left clear. This use of an obscured finish, often in contrast to clear areas, is very characteristic of the work of René Lalique (1860–1945) in glass (see p. 488 *c* and 519 *d*). It is well described by Janneau as the 'ethereal brilliance of Arctic ice'. Originally a goldsmith, Lalique came to glass via enamel jewellery. The perfumer, François Coty, commissioned him to produce special bottles for different perfumes in the early 1900s, the use of an artist to design packaging revolutionizing the perfume industry.

Boxes
Introduction

The term boxes is used here to denote those offshoots of the European jeweller's art, the small covered containers for such socially necessary items as perfume, rouge, patches, snuff, tobacco and sweetmeats. As costume accessories they enhanced individual countenance in a society of ephemeral tastes; and whereas boxes for sugar, tea, sponges and ink bottles were designed to offset their utilitarian aspect, 'boxes' in the present sense had often, in order to legitimize their appearance, to *acquire* a purpose.

In form as well as function some types of boxes are traceable to Egyptian antiquity, but the modern evolution of the simple container into an object of *bijouterie,* or at least of whimsy, began only in the late mediaeval period with jewelled and enamelled coffrets. Of possible, though lesser, influence, were the *châsses* and pyxes of ecclesiastical origin.

The earliest type is the cosmetic or toilet box: powder boxes are recorded by 1380; perfume boxes are mentioned in 1409 and both the Duc de Berry (c. 1416) and Catharine de Medici (1589) owned civet boxes. Boxes for sweetmeats were among Anne of Brittany's jewels and plate (1490); Elizabeth I had her 'cumfitt' boxes. Boxes for patches, rouge, toothpicks, tobacco and snuff made their appearance in the seventeenth century. The last major innovative form, albeit derived in principal from the Elizabethan pouncet-box, was the eighteenth century vinaigrette. There were, in addition, boxes for games and pills, boxes made to accommodate local customs or manufactures and, simply, boxes. The term was for a long time a general one: as late as 1745 mention is made of '*boîtes ou tabatières*' as if it were unimportant to distinguish between them; equally unspecific is the reference (1772) to boxes 'for the pocket or toilet'. Of greater concern to its owner than the use of a box (gold snuff-boxes were as likely to contain the freedom of a city, or gifts of money or jewels, as snuff) was its value or the fashionableness of its design. It is evident from the historical record that the function of a box was generally subservient to its form and decoration which, in turn, were adaptable to boxes of differing use. Thus a fourteenth century powder box and seventeenth century snuff-boxes were pear-shaped. Meissen porcelain apples served as snuff-boxes, Chelsea porcelain lemons as toilet boxes. Among figural boxes the range was wider. The Orléans perfume boxes (1409) were composed of cagework gold birds filled with perfumed sachets; Queen Elizabeth's sweetmeat box (1574) was tortoise-shaped; Madame de Pompadour bought a patch box in the form of an enamelled swan (1752) and a lacquer snuff-box modelled as a cat (1757). Variety in shape and material was essential. Louis XIV's boxes (1673) were polygonal of five, six and eight sides, round, oval, heart-shaped, triangular, trefoil and star-shaped. Boxes modelled as boats, shells, sedan chairs and books were in evidence by 1730, shortly followed by the popular barrel, basket and globe (or onion) forms and, with the rise of the porcelain and enamel manufactories, such sculptural fantasies as swans, shepherds, camels, Moors' heads, doves and sphinxes.

The variety of materials was as considerable. Until the dominance of gold in the eighteenth century the more usual materials were horn, ivory, tortoiseshell, silver and the base metals. It was not beneath Cardinal Mazarin's dignity to possess six copper gilt boxes (1653), and all but a few of Louis XIV's were of silver. Hardstones, mother-of-pearl and shell were all in use by 1700, and the first quarter of the century saw the growing production of boxes in enamel and porcelain. Tortoiseshell piqué boxes were popular c. 1690-1720, their designs reflecting a repertoire of baroque ornament shared by England, Holland and Germany during that period; and the gold mounted hardstone boxes characteristic of German work were almost as common in Hanoverian England.

The virtuosity of the Parisian goldsmiths and the ingenuity of the *marchand merciers* in combining materials set a technical and aesthetic standard that rather eclipsed less costly material, and admiration for the quality of French gold boxes is demonstrated by the emulatory pseudo-Parisian marks struck on Swiss gold boxes late in the eighteenth century. But from about 1775 gold boxes forfeited their stylistic influence by becoming the prerogative of ceremony and royalty, thus remaining outside the mass production—well into the Victorian period—of boxes in silver, papier mâché and wood.

Boxes

a) Marriage box of silver; Friesland, Netherlands, c. 1660; ht. 2¾″ (6.98 cm.).

Small coffrets for jewels are among the earliest boxes as accessories to personal costume, occurring frequently in 14th century inventories. Both the coffered shape and the association of such boxes with marriage persisted for several centuries. In this characteristically Frisian version, a hexagonal box was filled with ducats and presented by a young man to his intended bride. Engraved around the sides and on the cover are allegorical figures allusive to marriage which is further symbolized on the top of this and other examples by clasped hands.

b) Silver box; The Hague, Netherlands, 1666; dia. 2½″ (6.4 cm.).

Made with a detachable cover, this is probably one of several ointment or patch boxes from a toilet service. The bold repoussé decoration is characteristic of Dutch silver work at this period, but it is unusual to find so complete a representational composition on such a small scale. It is a measure of the skill of the unknown silversmith that the effect is at once vigorous without being untidy. In each hand the child holds a tulip, the flower that, since the peak of the tulip craze in 1637, had become a favourite motif of silversmiths on the Continent and in England (see p. 253a).

c) Box, of silver engraved with armorial design, initials I.L. and P.S. and 1674; Germany, 1674; dia. 1 11/16″ (4.28 cm.).

At the end of a visit to the King of Arakan in 1630, the Portuguese friar, Sebastião Manrique, obtained permission to build a Catholic church in that country (now Burmese). The King presented Manrique with a gold betel box which he promptly decided would serve nicely as a pyx on the altar of his promised church. So, to attribute an exclusive function to a box is to ignore the unpredictable needs or tastes of its owner. The decoration of this box—armorial, with initials and date—is obviously commemorative; but the occasion, and the use to which it was actually put, can only be conjecture.

d) Box, of steel, partly gilded, with foliate design; France, late 17th century; wdth. 2⅞″ (7.3 cm.).

When handled with the attention and skill usually reserved for precious metals, copper, brass and steel could be fashioned into beautifully made boxes which intrigued early collectors. Cardinal Mazarin owned several gilded copper boxes, some decorated with coral arabesques. The styles of base metal boxes generally followed those of gold and silver, but an occasional independence of design is evident, as in this steel example. Although conventional, its polygon form and shallowness, the boldly designed decoration of pierced sunflowers and scrolling leaves, applied on the cover and base, gives the box an unusual sculptural quality.

a) Tobacco box, silver; maker: Edward Cornock (ent. 1707, mentioned 1731), London, England, 1718; lgth. 6" (15.2 cm.).

The flat plain surfaces of English silver tobacco and snuff-boxes provided scope for engraved decoration, at its height from c. 1685–c. 1715. Armorials were common, the arms being en-framed in elaborately scrolled mantlings. A standard of highly finished decoration, combining representational figures with formal baroque motifs, was set by Simon Gribelin (1661–1733), a Huguenot refugee from Blois. The influence of Gribelin's *Book of Severall Ornaments* (1682) is evident here in the vigorous scroll- and strapwork. But departing from Gribelin's balanced, rather stately manner, the engraver has included a simple and refreshing genre figure of a pipe smoker.

b) Tobacco box, brass, engraved with a portrait of John Law, and inscribed HEER JOHAN LAWR & WIND IST BEG WIND IST END; *Netherlands, 1720–25; lgth. 6⅛" (15.6 cm.).*

Dutch tobacco boxes were long enough (average 6") to house a *carotte* of tobacco com-fortably, and are fitted with hinged lids. While some were well made in silver, by far the majority were of brass or copper (or a combination of the two) and were often made and decorated in a rather slap-dash manner. The covers and bases are engraved with biblical, genre or historical subjects. As these base metal boxes are never marked or signed, only those with specific topical decoration are readily datable. This example is contemporary with John Law's bubble schemes of 1718–20.

Boxes

EARLY 18TH CENTURY

---

c) Snuff-box, enamel; Germany, c. 1730; lgth. 2¾" (6.9 cm.).

The decoration of snuff-boxes was particularly subject to political overtones. Obliquely, in the form of a gold presentation box set with a portrait of the ruler; topically, in boxes painted with current political heroes, battle scenes and maps; commemoratively, in boxes like this decorated with allegories of past events: here, William III's invasion of Ireland in 1689 (on the cover).

The box is later, exemplifying the technique of applied gilding practised in Berlin and Dresden. The seriousness of the main subjects is charmingly offset by the painted miniature: the same hand can be assumed from the idiosyncratic drawing of the birds.

d) Snuff-boxes, hard-paste porcelain; decorator: Christian Friedrich Herold (1700–1779); Germany (Meissen), c. 1735; lgth. of larger 2¾" (6.9 cm.).

The production of small boxes at Meissen was encouraged under the directorship of Count Bruhl whose own collection of gold boxes was well known. In shape and decoration the earliest Meissen boxes, generally unmounted, reflect the mixed influence of Japanese lacquer and *kakiemon* porcelain painting. After c. 1730 they assumed the conventional forms dictated by metalwork proto-types, but their decoration was quite independent. To his miniature scenes of Chinoiseries and Oriental harbours, Herold (see p. 173*d*) brought the same care and refinement as he did to the decoration of larger table-wares. In this small-scale perfection Meissen boxes parallel those of Parisian gold.

Box of porcelain, painted enamel colours; St-Cloud, France, c. 1735.

Boxes

a) Snuff-box of tortoiseshell, piqué in silver and mother-of-pearl; France, c. 1740; dia. 2⅞″ (7.30 cm.).

The decoration of snuff-boxes often assumed a topical character; scenes alluding to popular interest or events were often, as on this example, copied from prints. The subject of the cover scene is the fireworks display on the Seine on the night of August 29th 1739, one of the festivities accompanying the marriage of Louise-Elisabeth with Philip of Spain. Shown are the Temple of Hymen on the Pont Neuf and, in mid-river, the music pavilion. The composition was probably repeated on many boxes, which would have been made as popular souvenirs of the occasion.

b) Snuff-box of gold, made by Pierre Croissant; (w. 1721-1747) Paris, France; 1741-2; base lgth. 3″ (7.6 cm.).

The primary visual distinction of Parisian gold boxes of the 1740s and 1750s is the continuity of their design. Of simple oval, oblong or circular form, with straight or only slightly curved walls, each box was conceived either as a single unit or as six faces of which each presented an unbroken decorative subject. To this period belong the continuous geometric patterns of which this is an example; the *quatre-couleur* architectural, pastoral and hunting scene boxes; boxes with bouquets set against sunburst grounds, and those with genre and flower subjects enamelled *en plein* on engraved diapered panels.

c) Snuff-box of tortoiseshell piqué in gold; probably France, 1740-50; dia. 2⅞″ (7.2 cm.).

The abstract design and technical virtuosity of this example are in sharp contrast to the simple pictorial stripwork of northern baroque piqué boxes. Decoration in this manner was popular in Italy, and Neapolitan craftsmen have been credited with very similar piqué work; certainly, the flamboyant design is uncharacteristic of French work. The form of the box itself, however, was well known in Paris as either a *tabatière en oignon* or sometimes as a *boîte à ballon*. Examples in tortoiseshell were sold by Lazare Duvaux in 1749; German rock crystal and Meissen porcelain versions were also made.

d) Snuff-box of heliotrope, gold, emerald and diamonds; Germany; 1745-50; lgth. 3⅜″ (7.9 cm.).

Diamond-studded hardstone boxes were especially favoured by Frederick the Great. The so-called Potsdam boxes, of which some were designed by J. W. G. Kruger (active 1755-68), were simply hollowed out, smooth-surfaced chunks of stone smothered in diamond landscapes or bouquets. A more subtle use of hardstones is seen in the boxes of heliotrope, chalcedony and bloodstone boldly carved with a mixture of baroque and rococo motifs. Their cartouche and shaped oblong forms derive from Paris boxes of c. 1735-45 but, allowing for time lag, may date as late as c. 1755. The gold rims, plain or enamelled, are almost always set with a jewelled thumb-piece. No marked examples of this type of box appear to be known.

a) Snuff-box, gold with diamonds and en plein enamelling; by Daniel Baudesson (w. c. 1730-80), Berlin, Germany, c. 1745-55; lgth. 3⅜″ (8.57 cm.).

The influence of French gold boxes spread north to Stockholm and east as far as St. Petersburg. In this illustration, the use of diamonds to outline scrollwork and architectural elements and the *en plein* enamelling, have been borrowed from a Paris style of the 1740s. The interplay of the two—usually kept separate by Parisian goldsmiths—and the richly jewelled thumb-piece indicate its German origin. Although unmarked, the rim of this box is inscribed with the name of Daniel Baudesson; the inside of the lid holds a miniature portrait on ivory of Frederick the Great, for whom Baudesson is known to have worked.

b) Box, of soft-paste porcelain, in the form of a sheep; Mennecy, France, mid-18th century; lgth. 2½″ (6.4 cm.).

The French porcelain factories of Saint-Cloud, Chantilly and Mennecy (see pp. 182b-183c) produced a wide range of small figural boxes whose influence extended to the Chelsea porcelain 'toys' (see p. 189d) and, to a lesser extent, German hardstone boxes. Because of the rigorous marking system, many of these boxes can be dated by their mounts, the majority of which fall into the period 1735-55. But, since the three factories were roughly contemporaneous, and since interfactory copying was normal practice, the mounts alone cannot be used to isolate a given model; this little sheep is of a type familiar to all the factories.

c) Snuff-box, gold with gouache miniatures; maker: possibly Pierre François Delafons (w. 1732-87), the miniatures by Louis Nicolas van Blarenberghe (1734-1812), Paris, France, marked for 1750/1; lgth. 3⅛″ (7.9 cm.).

The *tabatière à cage* was fully exploited (and probably invented) by the *marchand mercier* who found it—from *c.* 1740—an ideally flexible medium, easily and inexpensively renewed from time to time with new-fashioned panels replacing the old. The frame of this box is dated 1750-1, but the views of the Château of Chanteloup—the country seat of the duc de Choiseul—are dated 1767, and almost certainly replaced plaques of a quite different sort, perhaps carved mother-of-pearl, more usual around 1750. Gouache miniatures do not occur with any frequency until after *c.* 1760.

d) Snuff-box of enamelled gold, with inset porcelain plaques; Jean François Breton (w. 1737-c. 1791), Paris, France, 1752-53; lgth. 3¼″ (8.25 cm.).

One of the services offered by the Parisian *marchand mercier* was the repair and modernization of out-of-fashion pieces. That the present cartouches of Meissen porcelain in this box are replacements is apparent from close examination of their slightly damaged frames. The plaques themselves were probably cut down from a rectangular Meissen box about ten years after Breton's box was completed; the *marchand mercier* Lazare Duvaux, in particular, is known to have acquired porcelain plaques for use in gold boxes. The original panels were perhaps agate or another hardstone, stylistically more in keeping with the colourfully enamelled gold.

Box in soft-paste porcelain, painted enamel colours, silver mounts; Mennecy, France, c. 1750.

a) Tobacco box of brass and copper; Johann Heinrich Giese; Iserlohn, Westphalia, Germany, c. 1758; lgth. 6½" (16.5 cm.).

Iserlohn was the German centre for manufacturing brass tobacco boxes in the mid-18th century. Of elongated form with hinged lids like their Dutch counterparts (see p. 63b), they were more highly finished, their covers being decorated with stamped raised scenes of compositional intricacy and skill. Favourite subjects were Prussian victories of the Seven Years' War, a theme also found on contemporary German porcelain and enamel boxes. This scene commemorates Ferdinand of Brunswick's success in pushing the French back over the Rhine (1758). Most of these commemorative boxes are signed; J. H. Giese and I. H. Hamer are the two names most often encountered.

b) Snuff-box of enamelled gold, with panels of Japanese lacquer; Jean Ducrollay (w. 1734–60/61), Paris, France, 1753–54; lgth. 3⅜" (8.57 cm.).

The guild of the *marchands merciers* was not a craft guild, and its members were not permitted to work the materials they handled; they were dealers, retailing jewellery and furnishings with something of the purpose and flexibility of the modern interior decorator. One of their exclusive privileges was the trade in Oriental lacquer; the day books of Lazare Duvaux contain numerous references to lacquer boxes. In addition to selling complete pieces, Duvaux also cut up larger (or damaged) ones into conveniently small panels. Ducrollay purchased such plaques from Duvaux on several occasions for incorporation in his *tabatières à cage.*

Boxes

MID 18TH CENTURY

c) Snuff-box, vernis martin with silver-gilt; Paris, France, c. 1760; lgth. 4" (10.2 cm.).

Unlike japanning and papier mâché, in which coats of shellac and opaque (usually black) paint were laid on a metal, wood or paper body, *vernis martin* involved the application of several dozen layers of a clear varnish derived from gum copal to which colour or gold powder could be added. The prevailing ground colour was a lustrous honey tone on which were painted genre and landscape subjects in a manner evocative of the *en plein* enamelling on gold boxes. Popular from c. 1745–c. 1765, *vernis martin* boxes are generally larger than gold ones and are commonly rimmed in silver gilt.

d) Box for scent bottles, in heliotrope, gold, diamonds and rubies; England, 1760–70; lgth. 2⁷⁄₁₆" (6.19 cm.).

A miniature—presumably pocket—version of the *nécessaire* this box, despite its small size, is filled with six crystal scent bottles. Although a few German and French boxes of this type are known, the style of the cagework, and the *nécessaire* itself are both characteristic of English goldsmiths' work of c. 1750–70. No marked examples are known and there are occasionally such stylistic similarities between English and German versions as to make an informed attribution difficult: the simple flower swag and C-scroll combination present here is, however, repeatedly echoed in larger variants set with English watches.

a) Snuff-box of enamelled copper mounted in gilt metal, painted with birds; Staffordshire, England, 1760-70; lgth. 3¼″ (8.25 cm.).

At least two of these birds, painted in the reserves, appeared in the many pattern books published in London by Robert Sayer. *The Ladies Amusement* (1759-60) was a potpourri of original and plagiarized illustrations by Robert Hancock, Pillement, Francis Barlow, and other anonymous artists. The original engraving of the kingfisher in the left end panel is attributed to Hancock, but it appears in Sayer's work over the name of Charles Fenn. Borrowing and adaptation were the stock-in-trade of box decorators whose skills in this line are as evident in French gold boxes as in English enamel ones.

b) Snuff-box of quartz and assorted hardstones, mounted in gold with country scenes; probably Dresden, Germany, 1760-70; lgth. 2⅞″ (7.3 cm.).

Tradition more than evidence indicates a Dresden origin for quartz boxes with relief decoration, genre scenes, flowers or insects carved from coloured stones and cemented into prepared hollows in the surface of the box. Based on a piece signed by a member of the Hoffman family of Dresden, it is likely that boxes such as this—*tabatières à cage* in which the subtly coloured relief ornament seems to float on the pale translucent quartz—are all Dresden work. Jewel-studded variants, often formed of a single opaque stone of pronounced colour, are more in the Berlin style preferred by Frederick the Great.

Box of enamel on copper; Staffordshire, England, c. 1750–1800.

---

c) Patch box, silver; U.S.A., 2nd half 18th century; lgth. 1⅜″ (3.5 cm.).

Box-making in America was largely confined to New York state, New England and Philadelphia, and certain stylistic mannerisms can be traced to the Dutch or English origins of those settlements. Although insignificant in quantity, American boxes are of interest for their fresh interpretation of European styles. This unmarked example fits in a tradition of vigorously designed boxes of provincial character of which marked variants are known from both New York State and New England. A common feature is the border of sketchy, stylized leaf tips also known on Dutch base metal tobacco boxes.

d) Box of painted enamel, in the form of a bird; Staffordshire, England, c. 1770; ht. 4″ (10.2 cm.).

Boxes in the form of birds can be traced to Egyptian cosmetic boxes of the XVIII Dynasty, modelled as trussed ducks. A more direct influence on the Staffordshire enamellers, however, were probably the bird sculptures of Meissen porcelain (c. 1740) later imitated at the Chelsea, Bow and Derby factories (see p. 194*d*). Although generally referred to today as *bonbonnières*, these bird boxes were certainly designed for varied use; 24 'Double Doves Snuff Boxis' are cited in the Chelsea bills between 1770 and 1773.

Boxes

Gold snuff-box set with various stones; Dresden, Germany, late 18th century.

a) Snuff-box, gold and enamel; maker: D. M. C.; Switzerland, c. 1780; lgth. 2½″ (6.4 cm.).

Almost nothing is known of the Swiss box-makers of the 18th century whose work generally followed current Paris styles. Among those recorded only by their initials are the goldsmiths 'F.S.', 'L F.T.', 'F.M.' and 'D. M. C.' The last is represented in several collections by well-designed and executed boxes in the neo-classical style of the 1770s. The majority of his pieces were in *quatre-couleur* gold; here, a two-colour gold frame is contrasted with panels of foil-flecked translucent green enamel. Characteristically the box bears, in addition to the maker's mark, other marks that appear to be officially unrecorded.

b) Snuff-box of wood; Scotland, c. 1800–25; lgth. 2½″ (6.4 cm.).

Wooden boxes tend to fall into two categories: those of good design and workmanship inspired by metalwork prototypes and the mass market ones, like those of post-Revolutionary France, with impressed decoration of current political and social interest, or fantasy boxes modelled as shoes (see p. 69d), books, animals, hats, etc. This example, although recalling the shallow reeding of English silver boxes, is unusual for the vigour and independence of its design. It is typical of the well-made Scottish boxes of the early 19th century which are also noted for their beautifully-fitted integral hinges, as clearly shown in this photograph.

c) Snuff-box, gold and enamel; Switzerland, c. 1810; lgth. 3 7/16″ (8.7 cm.).

From the 17th century the enamellers of Geneva depended for their livelihood on the international watch trade. In the 19th century their work extended to snuff- and music-boxes, often incorporating watches and automata—frequently for export. Subjects for decoration included exotic harbour scenes, trophies of music or flowers, and allegorical and pastoral scenes characterized by a staginess of composition and a rendering in bright opaque colours. Borders of boldly designed geometric patterns were not uncommon. Few artists have been identified; signed work by Jean-Louis Richter (1766–1841) places him among the most accomplished enamel painters.

d) Vinaigrette, gold, with pierced and hinged inner lid, Italian mosaic cover; maker's mark N.F.D., Paris, France, c. 1810; lgth. 1¼″ (3.17 cm.).

Although in the English goldsmiths' repertoire from c. 1760 as part of a *châtelaine*, the vinaigrette reached its peak of inventiveness and popularity in the 19th century when Birmingham silversmiths made them as animals' heads, flowers, books, hearts and other whimsical forms. The vinaigrette was less common in France. This elegant vinaigrette has all the stylistic authority of larger Parisian gold boxes. In England the pierced inner lid was either hinged or completely removable.

The miniature of the spaniel is probably Roman; there was a thriving export of such mosaic panels to England and France c. 1800–30 for silver or gold box lids.

a) Snuff-box, gold and diamonds; maker: probably John Northam (entered 1793), London, England, c. 1825–30; lgth. 3½″ (8.8 cm.).

The two most prominent gold box-makers in England from c. 1800 through the reign of George IV were A. J. Strachan and 'I. N.', thought to be John Northam. Both goldsmiths specialized in elaborate presentation boxes. Although this box frame was made in 1825–26 the diamond monogram was added after William IV's accession in 1830; the cast decoration, too, was probably applied at that time. This assembly-line method on the part of an individual craftsman is also seen in gold jewellery of the period; it was clearly an efficient way for a goldsmith to keep abreast of his orders.

b) Snuff-box, silver; Nathaniel Mills (w. 1826–50), Birmingham, England, 1843; lgth. 3⅛″ (7.93 cm.).

Long the centre of England's toy-making industry, Birmingham became the centre for 19th century box-makers. From the Regency into the early decades of Victoria's reign, Birmingham silversmiths, of whom Nathaniel Mills was among the most prolific, produced a steady supply of snuff-boxes and vinaigrettes. The prevailing fashion throughout this period incorporated cast views of English castles or churches, and elaborate engine-turned patterns. In this unusual example, Mills adapted to silver a shape and style of ornament more usually found in the bright-enamelled gold Swiss boxes of the period, many of them made for the Eastern market.

Staffordshire box with tiny scent bottles.

c) Imperial presentation box of gold, enamel, pearls and diamonds; maker CB, for the firm of K. Hahn; St. Petersburg, Russia, 1896–1903; lgth. 3⅞″ (9.84 cm.).

The shimmering effect of depth, achieved by covering an engine-turned ground with a layer of translucent enamel, is enhanced here by an airy lattice of gold strips, studded with diamonds, that rests lightly on the surface of the cover. In the centre is the monogram in Cyrillic of Nicholas II (1868–1918). The unusual outline of the box is an attenuated version of the cushion shape often seen in mid-19th century Austrian boxes.

The firm of Karl Karlovitch Hahn, although not well known today, was competitive with Fabergé's in St. Petersburg at the turn of the century.

d) Snuff-box of wood, in the form of a boot, with metal trim; England, c. 1875–1900; lgth. 2¾″ (6.9 cm.).

Snuff-boxes in the form of shoes attained widespread popularity after c. 1750, made of French porcelain, English and Dutch pottery and Staffordshire enamel. Perhaps this predilection for ceramic variations was due to a familiarity with Near Eastern pottery exemplars. In the 19th century shoe boxes were generally made in wood. The model, that of a simple high-heeled slipper, remained essentially unchanged until the Victorian era when it was altered to reflect specific boot styles. Comparable to examples dated in the 1880s, this box is fitted with a hinged lid rather than the more usual sliding one.

Bottles and Boxes Glossary

Bottles

BLACK BOTTLE: Very dark green or brown bottle in use in 18th century. Originally produced probably by chance because of the nature of the raw materials used, it became highly prized as the ideal bottle to protect wines from the light. Glass from the recently excavated Gawber glass-house (near Barnsley, Yorks.) seems particularly 'black'.

BURST-OFF PENNY GREEN WORK: Name for the method of finishing off the tops of bottles by merely knocking them off the glass at the end of the blowing iron without any 'fire finishing'.

CODD'S PATENT BOTTLES: The ball-stoppered mineral bottles of the style invented by Hiram Codd and made by Dan Rylands, Barnsley, Rylands & Codd, Barnsley, and John Kilner, Wakefield—all in Yorkshire, England (Codd himself was from Camberwell, London). Many other similarly-sealed bottles were also patented in the 1870s and '80s.

FINISH: The top of a bottle neck, so called as it was the last operation in making a bottle.

FLINT: Clear, more or less colourless glass. In the period of the Excise regulations (1745-1845) flint glass-houses made lead glass and other high quality ware and also had to make bottles and vials of less than 6 oz. capacity. Bottle houses made the larger bottles.

GREEN: The greenness of much bottle glass comes from iron oxide in the sand used. Today, decolourizers are used and strict control is kept over raw materials.

KICK-UP or PUSH-UP: The raised base of a bottle. Originally to give a stable base when the pontil was broken off and the body of the bottle was basically spherical.

PARISON: The first stage blank in blowing a bottle; modern bottles are first formed in a parison mould and then transferred to a blowing or finishing mould.

PUNT MARK: From *pontil*, the solid rod that was used to hold the base of the bottle when it was being reheated and finished. Often known as the punty iron—hence, the mark on the base of the bottle became known as the punt mark and this is the term used for the manufacturer's trade mark, usually found on the base of bottles from the second half of the 19th century. Ricketts was probably the first modern glass manufacturer to mark his bottles.

SEALS: Were applied to wine bottles frequently as indicators of ownership in the 18th century; however, the general practice of having one's own bottles died out in the 19th century, except for Colleges and Inns of Court, once the import of wine in bottle was again permitted.

WEATHERING: On bottles is the result of a reaction between chemicals in the glass and those in the soil at the exact spot where they are unearthed. Apparently similar pieces of glass found in adjacent positions could have much weathering and none at all.

Boxes

BASSE TAILLE ENAMELLING: Translucent enamel laid over a sunken ground so as to be level with the surface; used on Parisian gold boxes from c. 1755.

BOITE A PORTRAIT: A gold, often jewel-studded, box set with a portrait miniature; used throughout the 18th century to distinguish snuff-boxes with portraits and those without (*tabatière*).

CAGEWORK: All-over floral and/or figural decoration in open-work gold encasing a hardstone box; a technique common in England and Germany c. 1750-1770.

COUNTER BOXES: Small cylindrical pierced silver boxes, about 1" (2.54 cm.) diameter, designed to hold 20 or more counters; chiefly English, c. 1625-1650.

ENGINE TURNING: A geometric pattern engraved on a surface by means of a rose engine lathe; French term is *guilloché*. In evidence on Parisian gold boxes from c. 1750 and also common in the decoration of English and French boxes of tortoiseshell, horn and ivory.

EN PLEIN ENAMELLING: Painting in opaque enamel colours on the surface of a box; a technique popular in Paris c. 1745-55 and used occasionally in Germany and England.

FANTASY BOXES: An informal name for sculptural boxes.

FERMIER GENERAL: The French tax farmer responsible for the payment of duty on gold and silver; each farmer, who served an average 7-year term, employed a charge mark (*poinçon de charge*) and a discharge mark (*poinçon de décharge*): the former registered an unfinished piece at the Mint, obliging the goldsmith to return it upon completion, pay the required tax, and have it discharged for sale.

FREEDOM BOX: A hinged box, usually gold, of snuff-box size containing a scroll proffering the freedom of a city on the recipient, and generally engraved with the arms of the city; chiefly English 17th and 18th centuries; some American examples are known.

INTEGRAL HINGE: A hinge formed of metal cylinders soldered alternately on the back edge of a box and its cover at such an angle as to be flush with the vertical wall, and held in place by a transverse pin.

LANCASHIRE BOXES: Brass boxes with hinged covers, fastened by a combination lock, with two or more decorative dials; Prescot, Lancs., c. 1800-50.

MAUCHLINE BOXES: Hinged wooden boxes painted either with scenes in black or with tartans; originally from Laurencekirk, later made in many Ayrshire towns, including Mauchline; early 19th century.

MOCHA STONE: Moss agate.

Glossary (contd.)

MOSAIC PAINTING: Representational subjects (landscapes were a favourite) executed in mosaic on small plaques to be set into box-lids. Italian, early 19th century.

MULL: The traditional Scottish snuff-box; formed of a ram's horn and fitted with a hinged silver lid.

NIELLO: An alloy of sulphur, lead, copper and silver, fused, powdered, and pressed into lines engraved on silver, producing black-line decoration; standard decoration for Russian boxes c. 1770-1870, and sometimes at Birmingham and Paris, c. 1825-1850.

PAPIER MACHE: A substance composed of layers of thick paper pressed into shape over a wood core. A popular material for German and English snuff-boxes c. 1780-1850 which were lacquered in black and painted.

PIQUE: Pieces of silver embedded in tortoiseshell, horn or ivory that has been softened by heat and that, when cool, hardens and holds the metal. In *piqué point* the patterns are in pinpoints of silver; strips of the metal are used in *piqué posé*; widely used in England and the Continent c. 1690-1750.

PRESENTATION BOX: A variant of the freedom box, common in England, c. 1780-1820; silver or gold, of snuff-box size, presented for some service or to commemorate an event; decorated and inscribed accordingly.

'PRESTIGE' MARKS: Certain pseudo-French marks (the most common being the Paris charge mark of the harrow, 1756-1762) struck on late 18th and early 19th century Swiss gold boxes of unquestioned authenticity; presumed to reflect genuine admiration for the French gold boxes rather than an attempt to deceive.

QUATRECOULEUR: Varicoloured gold, used generically to designate any number of tints, although red, blue, green and white were the usual ones. Red gold was an alloy of gold and copper; the addition of arsenic or steel filings produced blue; green and white gold were both differing alloys of silver and gold; used extensively on Parisian boxes, rarely elsewhere.

RELIC BOXES: Snuff-boxes composed in part—whether actually or traditionally—of material from some popular relic, e.g. Nelson's ship, *Victory*, etc.

SINGING BIRD BOXES: Gold snuff boxes of Genevan origin with a small bird that flutters and sings when wound up, c. 1790-1830.

STOBWASSER BOXES: Papier mâché boxes made at the Brunswick manufactory of Georg Siegmund Stobwasser (d. 1776); surviving examples are almost entirely 19th century.

TABATIERE A CAGE: A metal box frame fitted with panels of a different material, as lacquer, porcelain, miniatures, etc.

VERNIS MARTIN: A varnish derived from gum copal applied in numerous layers on a core of pressed paper, and enriched by painted decoration; so called from its development by Guillaume Martin who obtained a patent for the process in Paris in 1730.

Repairs and Maintenance

Having been for the most part objects in active use, boxes can be expected to show signs of wear and damage that do not require attention. By now, old gold boxes will have lost some of their enamelled borders, the rims and corners of papier mâché and enamel boxes will be chipped, and inlaid fragments of mother-of-pearl or silver or ivory will be missing. In addition to the effects of normal wear, however, there is the damage caused by internal stress resulting from the combination of materials in a given box.

Particularly vulnerable are tortoiseshell and horn boxes, either piqué or overlaid with gold stripes, on which the metal tends to spring loose. A relatively constant, not too dry, humidity (about 45-50 relative to a temperature of 65°-70°F.) can minimize this effect, and is desirable as well for boxes of wood, *vernis martin* and ivory.

Perhaps the sturdiest boxes are those made entirely of silver, but care should be taken, in cleaning, to avoid rubbing which will efface monograms and other lightly engraved ornament. Silver and base metal boxes can safely be cleaned with a non-abrasive polish and a soft cloth or brush: a preliminary washing in soapy water will loosen some surface dirt and lessen the need for rubbing. As the metal of small silver and brass boxes is often very thin and brittle, additional care should be taken while cleaning not to break it. Apart from the routine cleaning of simple all-metal boxes, however, the collector is advised to leave treatment and repair to a professional.

Bottles and Boxes
Fakes and Forgeries

Bottles

Although there does not appear to be any serious faking of old bottles, a number are made in an antique style for decorative purposes. The colour and proportions tend to be wrong so that the cardinal rule is to look at as many of the originals as possible.

Imitations of old wine bottles are made as proprietary lines and can usually be identified by mould marks at the sides or a more 'modern' base than would be consistent with the original shape. Bottles made for Oxbridge colleges and Inns of Court continued to be 'sealed' until the early part of this century.

Pharmaceutical bottles can sometimes be found in an old chemist shop but appear irregularly at antique sales or shops. The fact that some appear cloudy inside has nothing to do with age but merely reflects on the type and condition of the contents. Recessed hand-painted labels were done until well into this century—the old ones have pontil marks. Look out for mould marks and manufacturers' identification marks and remember that blue containers are still made today.

Boxes

French gold boxes have been the most extensively altered and forged. 'Alteration' means the forger's practice of cutting up genuine boxes—either because of unsightly or irreparable damage, or because the maker's prestige makes it worthwhile—and creating 'new' boxes. Failing an obvious disparity in design elements or techniques inconsistent with the period or style, or faults such as truncated borders or badly fitted bases, such pastiches are often revealed by their marks. Since there was much contemporary repair and alteration, genuine boxes may have two sets of marks, differing both as to maker and date. Their location and the amount of difference is important. The law required each separate metal piece to be marked at the onset of manufacture so there should normally be three sets of three marks (the maker's, charge and warden's marks) inside a gold box (inside the bottom, inside the cover and one vertical wall) and the discharge mark struck on the bezel of the completed piece. An impossible conflict between these sets should be fair warning. By far the majority of these pastiches involve boxes like the *tabatières à cage* whose marked gold linings could be easily detached and used again.

There are also outright wholly modern fakes with forged marks, usually betrayed by discrepancies in the marks or in their location. Other forgers so stretched and distorted their marks that they seemed plausible, merely unidentifiable. The technical level is often very high; their principal weakness is an incompatibility of stylistic features, either in relation to each other or to the purported date of the box, and/or the style and palette of the enamelling.

Further Reading

Bottles

CRELLIN, J. K., and SCOTT, J. R. *Glass and British Pharmacy 1600-1900. A Survey and Guide to the Wellcome Collection of British Glass.* London, 1972.

DAVIS, D. C. *English Bottles and Decanters 1650-1900.* London, 1972.

FOSTER, K. *Scent Bottles.* London, 1966.

MCKEARIN, H. *Bottles, Flasks and Dr Dyott.* New York, 1970.

MEIGH, E. *The Story of the Glass Bottle,* 1972.

MOODY, B. *Packaging in Glass.* London, 1963.

MOSS, H. M. *Chinese Snuff Bottles.* London, 1971.

MUNSEY, C. *The Illustrated Guide to Collecting Bottles.* New York, 1970.

RUGGLES-BRISE, S. *Sealed Bottles.* London, 1949.

TOULOUSE, J. H. *Bottle Makers and their Marks.* Camden, N.J., 1971.

Fruit Jars—A Collector's Manual. Camden, N.J., 1969.

Boxes

BEDFORD, J. *All Kinds of Small Boxes.* New York, 1964.

BERRY-HILL, H. and S. *Antique Gold Boxes.* London, New York and Toronto, 1960.

BRAMSEN, B. *Nordiske Snusdaser.* Copenhagen, 1965.

DELIEB, E. *Silver Boxes.* New York, 1968.

FREDERIKS, J. W. *Dutch Silver,* vols II and III. The Hague, 1958, 1960.

HONEY, W. B. *Dresden China.* London 1934.

HUGHES, G. B. *English Snuff-boxes.* London, 1971.

HUGHES, T. and B. *English Painted enamels.* London and New York, 1951.

LE CORBEILLER, CLARE. *European and American Snuff-boxes 1730-1830.* London, 1966.

NOCQ, H. and C. D. *Tabatières, boîtes et étuis . . . du Musée du Louvre.* Paris, 1930.

PINTO, E. H. *Wooden Bygones of Smoking and Snuff-taking.* London, 1961.

Further Reading (contd.)

RACKHAM, B. *Catalogue of the Schreiber Collection*, Vol. III. London, 1924.

SNOWMAN A. K. *Eighteenth Century Gold Boxes of Europe*. London, 1966.

SNOWMAN, A. K. *The Art of Carl Fabergé*. London, 1953.

UKHANOVA, I. N. *Russkie laki v sobranii Ermitazha*. Leningrad, 1964.

WATSON, F. J. B., and DAUTERMAN, C. C. *The Wrightsman Collection*, vol. III. New York, 1970.

Museum Collections

Great Britain

BIRMINGHAM: The City Museum and Art Gallery.
BRISTOL: Harvey'sWine Museum.
CAMBRIDGE: The Fitzwilliam Museum.
LANCASHIRE: The Liverpool City Museum.
LONDON: The British Museum, Goldsmith's Hall; The Victoria and Albert Museum; The Wallace Collection.
NORFOLK: The Castle Museum, Norwich.
SOMERSET: The Holbourne of Menstrie Museum of Art, Bath.

U.S.A.

MASSACHUSETTS: The Museum of Fine Arts, Boston.
NEW YORK: The Brooklyn Museum, The Metropolitan Museum of Art, New York City; The Corning Museum of Glass.
OHIO: The Toledo Museum of Art.
WASHINGTON, D.C.: The Smithsonian Institution.

Index

Carpets and Rugs

The Oriental carpet has been an object of veneration in the West for many centuries. Like other expressions of art emanating from the East, the painstaking obsession with detail so exquisitely carried out at no matter what cost in time—and effort—awes the Western world into humble acknowledgement of this peculiar genius of the Eastern craftsman.

It is not only in the mechanics of production that the Oriental weaver excels, but also in the art of design as applied to this particular field. Indeed, in Persia there have been Shahs in the past who have devoted their very considerable gifts to creating designs for carpets, and many exquisite patterns have been created by these Royal patrons of the arts.

Fine carpets have been made by hand in the West too, as is witnessed by the old Axminsters of England, the products of the Killybegs factory in Donegal—which still, by the way, produces hand-knotted carpets to order—and the famous Savonnerie carpets of France, which firm still produces State carpets at a fabulous cost. But none of these carpets has a fineness of knot that will in any way compare with the products of the East, where large carpets are made with two hundred, three hundred or more knots to the square inch, each individually tied by hand.

Just imagine a man from the West even contemplating making a carpet the size of the Ardebil, which measures 34′ 6″ (10.5 m.) by 17′ 6″ (5.3 m.), and has approximately three hundred and twenty knots in every square inch of its area. No, the Occidental mind is not attuned to this way of thought; we are too impatient for results. Nothing is more humbling than to stand before one of these gigantic masterpieces and realize that it has been painstakingly constructed knot by individual knot. There is not only the warp and weft of a carpet there, but also the very warp and weft of a man's life: truly something to treasure.

Opposite:
Old Lavah Kirman; Persia.

Carpets and Rugs
The Craft

Weaving Techniques

Generally speaking, the technique of producing a hand-knotted Oriental rug is the same no matter which country the rug is produced in. There were basically only two types of loom—upright and horizontal. The upright looms are used by town and village dwellers who either attend at a factory as in Tabriz, or work in their own homes as in Isfahan and many other towns, and they can be used for producing either rugs or carpets of almost any size, the width of the loom being the only limiting factor.

The horizontal loom, on the other hand, is only used by nomads, and is a very primitive affair that can easily be packed up and carried about, and just as easily re-erected when new grazing grounds are reached and a short stay is made until such time as there is need to move to fresh pastures.

By the very nature of things these horizontal looms automatically limit the size of the weavings produced, and most of the output of these nomadic weavers is in rugs, with an occasional larger piece.

Reduced to its simplest terms, the warp threads are stretched on the loom as the framework upon which the rug is constructed. First a small end-web is woven as a basis for the first rows of knots which are then tied, each knot encircling two threads of warp. After one or two rows of knots are tied, according to the district custom, one, two, or more weft threads are then passed through the warps, and the whole is then beaten down tightly with heavy metal combs. More rows of knots are tied, followed by the insertion of weft threads and the beating down, and this cycle is repeated until the rug is complete, when another few rows of end-web are woven to finish off the rug.

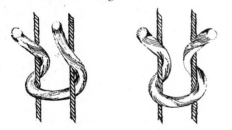

Persian or Senneh knot.   *Turkish or Ghiordes knot.*

The knots used are either of Persian or Turkish origin, and are referred to as either a Persian or Senneh knot or a Turkish or Ghiordes knot. The Turkish knot is used throughout all the Turkish weaving areas, and also throughout the Caucasus, and in areas of Persia where there are Turkish enclaves left by the tides of invasion by the Turki tribes from Turkestan many centuries ago. The Persian knot is employed by many areas in Persia (strangely enough not in Senneh, the district from which the knot takes its alternative name!), China, Turkestan, and some districts of India.

There are variations in tying techniques: the knots may be very evenly tied, one side or the other may be pulled more firmly, or the general lay of the knot may be in a left-handed or right-handed direction. No matter which technique is used the basic difference still exists: in the Turkish knot the two ends come together between the warp threads, giving a two warps, two tufts, two warps alternation (..//..//..//), whereas with the Persian knot the result gives alternate warps and tufts (./././././). It is the opinion of experts that finer designs can be executed with the Persian than are possible with the Turkish knot.

The finish at the sides of a rug also varies considerably, from single overcast in one colour, striped in two colours or more, and short sections single overcast in plain but differing colours along the length of the rug. Sides can also be finished in one, two or even three-cord selvedges.

Warps can be of cotton, wool, goat-hair, linen or silk, and weft threads vary tremendously, being of differing colours in particular areas, different fibres like the warp threads, different thicknesses, from very fine to very coarse, and they are inserted through the warp threads in a number of different ways, each of which is usually characteristic of a particular category.

Each and all of these differences are used in determining the category of a rug, and it is the sum of these characteristics which is the determining factor in difficult cases. A knowledge of these typical points can only be obtained by careful study, and it takes a very long time to acquire. Books can be a useful aid, but it is imperative that they be allied to practical handling of actual examples, for, apart from making clear the points made by a writer, there is also literally the feel or 'handle' of a rug which also helps in deciding its category.

Oriental Carpets and Rugs
Introduction

For centuries it had always been assumed by writers on Oriental rugs that piled or knotted rugs, as distinct from woven rugs such as kelims, Soumaks, etc., had not been made farther back than about a thousand years.

These conclusions had not been arrived at in any arbitrary fashion, but were drawn from a careful study of the works of such ancient writers as Strabo, Plutarch, Herodotus and Pliny, as well as many others. It was clear from these writers that all the early sumptuary carpets were woven and not knotted. Indeed, such a world-famous carpet as 'The Spring of Chosroes' which was 106′ (41.5 m.) square, was woven of silk in a garden design so that King Chosroes could use it at such times as the weather made it impossible for him to enjoy the amenities of his outdoor garden.

This carpet truly represented the height of luxury for, according to Dr. Karabacek of Vienna, it consisted of silk, gold and silver, and precious stones. His description continued, 'On it was represented a beautiful pleasure ground with brooks and interlacing paths, with trees and flowers of springtime. On the wide borders surrounding it were represented flower beds in which precious stones coloured blue, red, yellow, white and green denoted the beauty of the flowers. Gold imitated the yellow-coloured soil and defined the borders of the brooks, where the waters were represented by crystals. Gravel paths were indicated by stones of the size of pearls. The trunks of trees were of gold and silver, the leaves and flowers of silk, the fruits of many-coloured stones.'

Prior to World War II, the earliest known knotted carpets were of the thirteenth century, the evidence in part derived from Marco Polo's reports and descriptions of knotted carpets: he saw them during his travels (1270s) in Eastern lands. There are still a number of carpets in existence dating from the fourteenth century, which can be seen in various museums.

This accepted theory concerning the time at which knotted carpets were first made received a rude shock in 1949 when S. I. Rudenko, a Russian archaeologist, investigated the last of five Scythian burial mounds at Pazyryk, in the Gorny Altai region of Southern Siberia, not far from the borders of Outer Mongolia.

In common with other burial mounds, its covering cairn of small stones sheltered a timber-lined pit containing in the southern half a small burial chamber made of dressed logs. The strange thing is that, owing to the work of grave robbers soon after the burial, water had seeped in, and frozen. Although the subsoil of this region is not subject to perennial freezing, the ice in the tomb appears to have been permanent—a fortunate phenomenon. On melting the ice by means of hot water, the excavators discovered embalmed corpses, clothing, textiles, saddles and bridles, objects of leather and wood, and a rug, almost all of which had been perfectly preserved in the ice.

The rug measured 6′ 6″ by 6′ (2 by 1.9 m.), and was very finely knotted with approximately three hundred and fifty knots to the square inch—the same fineness of knotting as the famous Ardebil Carpet in the Victoria and Albert Museum, London. This knotting, and the sophisticated design, argued that carpet knotting was an art that had already been practised for a very considerable number of years to have reached such a standard. What was even more important, however, was the fact that the other contents of the tomb enabled its discoverers to place the date of the burial at around 500 B.C., some 2,400 years ago.

Traditional patterns are strongly entrenched in Oriental weaving, scarcely changing from century to century. Rugs from the thirteenth to the sixteenth centuries are almost all in museums; the collector will soon find that occasionally a late sixteenth or seventeenth century example comes on to the market, but the largest number of fine carpets available are of eighteenth and even nineteenth century date and even these are getting scarcer year by year.

a) Ghiordes prayer-rug; Turkish, early 17th century; lgth. 6' 1" (185.4 cm.), wdth. 3' 8" (111.7 cm.).

One of the most prolific weaving areas of Asia Minor was the town of Ghiordes, the source of this prayer rug, with cream-coloured field and main border.

The double pilasters supporting the niche are typical of the period, and in the centre of the *mihrab*, or arch, is a reproduction of the hanging lamp that depends from the *mihrab* in the mosque. Borders are of highly specialized flower and leaf forms. The reds and dark and light blues, which are the main colourings, are rather faded.

b) Oushak; Turkish, late 16th century; lgth. 11' 4" (345.4 cm.), wdth. 8' 9" (266.7 cm.).

This is a typical medallion Oushak with a rounded pole medallion. Warp and weft, as in all these early Oushaks, are both of wool, the weft being dyed red. Medallion and corners are on a dark blue ground in contrast with the red of the field. It will be seen that the corners do not exactly complement the medallion, in the style of Persian weavings. The use of a pale golden yellow to highlight the outlines of so many of the figures, is very characteristic.

c) Ghiordes 'Saph', or family prayer rug; Turkish, late 17th or early 18th century; lgth. 9' 4" (284.5 cm.), width. 5' 5" (165.1 cm.).

This mat shows many of the characteristics typical of the Ghiordes weavers. Note the shape of the *mihrabs*, the well-ornamented spandrels, and

the typical squaring-up of the border design. The passion for quandrangular treatment of design extended to the panels above the prayer arches, with its serrated leaf, paired off with two stylized flower forms.

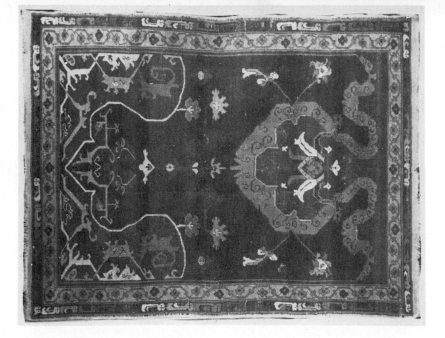

a) Oushak prayer rug; Turkish, 17th century; lgth. 5' 2" (157.5 cm.), wdth. 3' 11" (119.4 cm.).

This is a very unusual piece. It has an almost impressive simplicity of design, with a clean-cut vine and flower main border stripe on a pale yellow ground, in contrast to the deep indigo of the field and the red of the spandrels. The stylized cloudband occupying much of the field is quite a common motif in Oushaks, but is usually much more subordinate to the overall design. The touches of white provide a startling note of contrast.

b) Mudjur rug; Turkish, late 17th or early 18th century; lgth. 4' 10" (147.3 cm.), wdth. 3' 10" (116.8 cm.).

The area of Mudjur in Central Asia Minor is responsible for some of the most colourful rugs in the Turkish group. The stepped arch of the *mihrab* is usually delineated in multiple rows of different colours, ending in a vandyke, and the left and right-pointing *ubrechts*, or water jugs, in the spandrels are typical. Equally characteristic are the reciprocal vandykes in the panel above the field. The particular glory of the Mudjur, however, is in the main border stripe which consists of a series of squared-off motifs, each in a different colour. Some twelve or more colours are used, including a very unusual mauve.

c) Ladik prayer rug; Turkish, early 18th century; lgth. 5' 6" (167.6 cm.), wdth. 3' 9" (114.3 cm.).

One of the rarer types of Turkish rugs which always brings joy to the heart of a collector is the Ladik, very rarely in any other form than a prayer rug. This is one of the more usual designs, with a triple arch at the top of the field, and vandykes and downward-growing lilies in the panel below the field. The border is very typical, with its alternating rosettes and lilies, each succeeding lily pointing in the opposite direction. Colours in these rugs are always pleasing, with red and light and dark blue predominating, and lesser amounts of green, brown, ivory, and a rich characteristic canary yellow.

a) *Bergamo rug; Turkish, late 18th century; lgth. 3′ 8″ (111.8 cm.), wdth. 3′ 5″ (104.1 cm.).*

Bergamo rugs differ from other Asia Minor pieces in having a longer pile, and a very-nearly square format. They have a very wide range of designs carried out in coarse but sturdy weave, on warps of wool, or occasionally of goat hair. The surprisingly fine woolen weft is dyed red. Prayer rugs were made, but are not very common. There is nearly always a red end-web at the foot of the rug. The design of this late 18th century piece is fairly typical, and the adventitious arrangement of some of the fill-in motifs, coupled with the long pile, show that the rug was of nomad origin.

b) *Kulah prayer rug; Turkish, 18th century; lgth. 4′ 3″ (129.5 cm.), wdth. 3′ 6″ (106.7 cm.).*

This Kulah prayer rug has the typical low-pitched arch. The Tree of Life in the field is very elaborate, and is set on a red ground, while the border carries alternate rosettes and formalized flowers on a white ground. The knotting of this piece is finer than most of this type, and the weave is altogether firmer. The narrowing border at the top and bottom of the rug is normal practice. That this was intended to be a fine rug is evidenced by the addition of a silk fringe at top and bottom, which is carried part way along the sides.

c) *Konieh rug; Turkish, late 17th century; lgth. 5′ 0″ (524 cm.), wdth. 4′ 0″ (121.9 cm.).*

Konieh has always produced interesting rugs, particularly *namazlyks*, in which the prayer arches vary over a wide degree of form. Most of these rugs have an exceptionally wide border that is not too crammed with ornament, resulting in an air of spaciousness that is lacking in many other rugs. The plain red field is set off by the busy, dark blue spandrels filled with stylized floral forms. The wide border has a light tan background, against which the rosettes and rather primitive flower shapes stand out clearly. The weave is typically coarse and loose. Warp is of wool, as is the medium-thick, red-dyed weft.

a) Transylvanian rug; Turkey, 17th century; lgth. 6' 10" (208 cm), wdth. 5' 3" (160 cm.).

These rugs were made in Asia Minor, but the vast majority of those now in existence were discovered in the churches of the province of Transylvania, in Romania, where they had been presented by merchants journeying on the perilous roads between their own towns and the trading centres of Asia Minor, as a thanks-offering for their safe return. The Germans refer to these rugs as *Siebenbergen* (seven towns) from the seven walled towns of Transylvania.

Most Transylvanian rugs date from the 17th century, but there are some from the latter half of the 16th century, and at the other end of the time scale, production continued into the 19th century.

The main colours were red, light and dark blue, brown, black and a great deal of tan or fawny yellow; this colour scheme gives them a very distinctive appearance.

The weavers were very superstitious, making numerous odd changes of colour and design in their endeavours to avoid being stricken with the Evil Eye. Note the difference in the designs in the lozenge shapes in the top border compared with the sides, and also with the lower border. There are several other variations easily discovered by making a careful scrutiny of the illustration.

---

b) Early Kuba or Couba rug; Caucasian, lgth. 11' 7" (353 cm.), wdth. 7' (213 cm.).

Here is a classic rendering of a Kuba, or Couba design (Shirvan), which is obviously of Persian origin and stems back to the time when this area was part of the Persian empire. The border, too, is more Persian than Caucasian. The main colours of blue, red, sable brown and yellow of the design impart a richness to the whole against a ground of deep indigo in the field and red in the border. The treatment of the flowers is far more natural than in any other Caucasian type. The knotting is finer, too, and the weave in general is tighter, giving a firmer handle to the rug. There is some *abrash* visible in the photograph, particularly on the right-hand border.

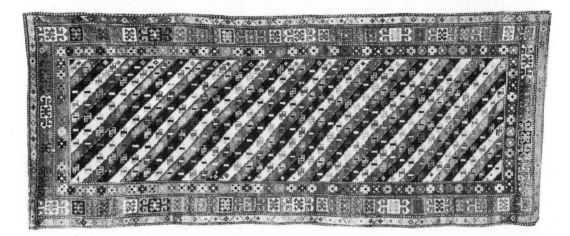

a) Gendje (Gengha or Yendje) rug; Caucasian; 19th century; lgth. 9' 5" (287 cm.), wdth. 3' 8" (112 cm).

These rugs are of a coarse construction and a fairly loose weave, with a reddish wool weft that can have two, three or more shots between every two rows of knots, and is therefore very obvious on the back of the rug.

Patterns can vary quite a lot, but this diagonally striped field is quite popular with the weavers of this area, though the designs carried by the stripes are more usually of highly stylized flowers rather than these geometric forms.

The dark blue, red and white of the stripes are the main colours, but light blue, green, yellow and brown have also been used.

---

b) Shemakha (or Soumak) rug; Caucasian, 19th century; lgth. 5' 4" (162 cm.), wdth. 3' 0" (91.2 cm.).

This is a rug with a knotted pile which is made in the district which turns out the Soumak pileless carpets. These rugs are not very frequently met with, and often are not recognized for what they are.

The stepping of the medallions is a technique probably used in Soumaks to avoid long 'breaks' in the fabric, and the use of an ornamented octagon in the centre of each medallion is also closely allied to the Soumak. The saw-tooth inner edge of the border is noticeably uneven on the long sides, while being perfectly matched across the two ends.

The main colours are deep red, a dark rich blue, green, yellow, brown and ivory. The warp and weft are both woollen.

a) Chichi rug; Caucasian, early 19th century; lgth. 4′ 10″ (147 cm.), wdth. 3′ 9″ (114 cm.).

One of the lesser-known products of the Caucasus is the Chichi or Tchetchen, shown here. Everything about this rug is characteristic of Chichi weavings; the border stripe of rosettes separated by diagonal 'ribbons', the profusion of border stripes with every symbol carefully delineated, and the field covered with horizontal rows of stylized leaves alternating with rows of geometric medallions on a red ground. There are two border stripes of carnations, flowers which very often appear in both Caucasian and Turkish rugs. The main colours used are blue, red and ivory with a little green and brown.

b) Shirvan rug; Caucasian, 19th century; lgth. 4′ 4″ (132.1 cm.), wdth. 2′ 10″ (86.4 cm.).

This Shirvan rug of the 19th century has a number of the characteristics of the type. Generally speaking borders are usually common to more than one category of rug in the Caucasus, but this leaf and wine-glass border appears more often in Shirvans than in any others, and the multiple medallions in the field are also typical. The *abrash* or colour shading in the dark blue field is very apparent in this piece, but many lovers of oriental rugs prefer to have some *abrash* as they think it adds to the hand-made character. Like all Caucasian pieces the knot used is Turkish.

c) Cabistan prayer-rug; Caucasian, mid 18th century; lgth. 4′ 11″ (149.9 cm.), wdth. 3′ 9″ (114.3 cm.).

A truly fascinating piece is this Cabistan prayer-rug, with the whole of the field and the spandrels covered with the *boteh* design; this has called for a great deal of ingenuity in covering the *boteh* with differing designs. Cabistans are a sub-group of Daghestans with which there are some differences. The knots of Cabistans are more tilted as against the perfectly straight knots of Daghestans when seen from the back, and the weft may be of wool or cotton as against the invariable wool weft of the Daghestan.

a) *Daghestan prayer-rug; Caucasian, early 19th century; lgth. 5′ 6″ (167.6 cm.), wdth. 3′ 7″ (109.2 cm.).*

Unlike Persian and Turkish prayer-rugs the *namazlyks* of the Caucasus only have these hard angular arches at the head. The diapered pattern of the field on a white background, with its hard, clean-cut brilliant look caused by the short clipped pile, is very typical of this genus. Note the space below the arch which is to take the sacred relic, etc., to be touched by the man's forehead when making his obeisances, and the indication in the spandrels as to where the hands should go, and the quaint animal forms. Alignment of knots is very even on the back. Main colours are blue, red, and ivory with green and yellow.

b) *Traditional Soumak rug; Caucasian, lgth. 7′ 7″ (231.1 cm.), wdth. 5′ 5″ (165.1 cm.).*

An excellent example of a flat woven Soumak rug from the Caucasus, where the weft forms the face of the rug. The large diamond-shaped medallions with octagonal centrepieces and crosses incised into the diagonal sides are very characteristic of the type, as are the reciprocal latch-hooks of the outer border. The large ornamented octagons with their attendant triangular T-pieces which fill in the gaps left by the medallions are also typical. The border, which often occurs in Soumaks, can only be a highly stylized running vine and flower. Unlike most kelims the loose ends of warp threads are left hanging on the back, so that the pieces are not really reversible.

c) *Dragon carpet; Caucasian, late 16th century; lgth. 7′ 2″ (184.4 cm.), wdth. 5′ 1″ (154.9 cm.).*

A superb example of a late 16th century 'Dragon' carpet from the Caucasus which has very strong Persian influences, the large palmettes in particular recalling the very old Ispahan carpets. The dark blue field is broken up with broad red bands carrying floral and other forms connected by a stem, and there are various mythical creatures dispersed over the field, including two elongated spotted dragons rampant about a third of the way up from the bottom on either side. The borders, too, with their leaves and rosettes, look distinctly Persian. The main colours are dark blue, red and tan, with some brown, ivory, rusty-black and a pale blue with a greenish tinge.

Opposite:
Rare Transylvanian prayer rug; Turkey, early 17th century.

Turkish Kulah prayer rug, early 18th century.

Turkish Ghiordes prayer rug, late 18th century.

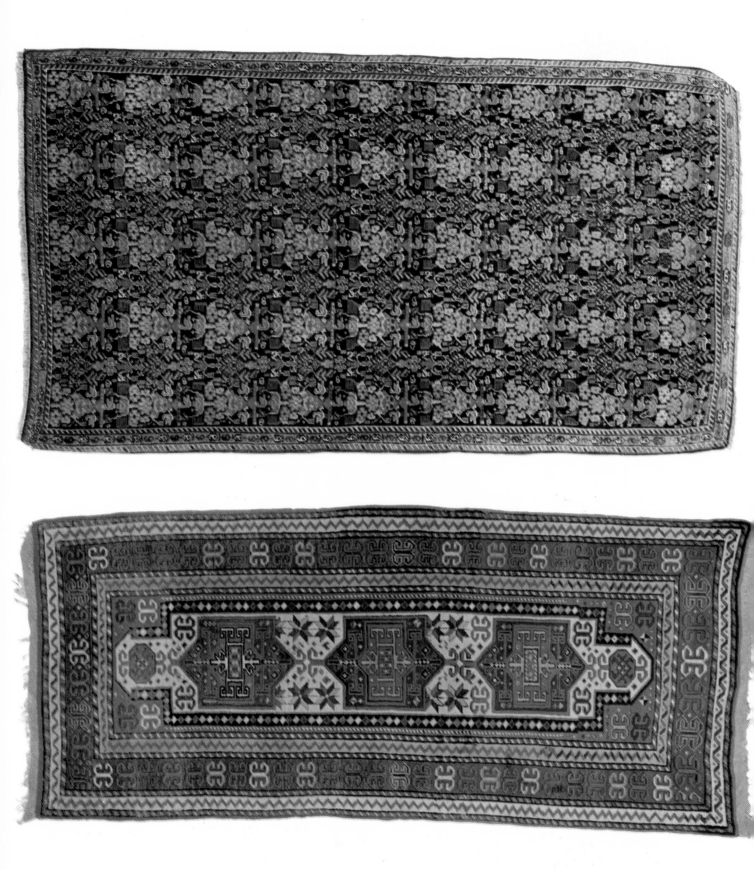

Top: *Malayer rug; Persia, early 19th century.*
Bottom: *Fine Kazak rug; Turkey, second half of 19th century.*

a) Kazak rug; Caucasian, 19th century; lgth. 7′ 9″ (236.2 cm.), wdth. 5′ 1″ (154.9 cm.).

Like most Kazak rugs this one has a strong forthright design in bold uncompromising bottle green, bright red, yellow and white, with some brown and a little blue. Kazak weavers use a great deal of green in their rugs whereas all other Caucasian weavers use green very sparingly, and the pile of their rugs is longer than any other Caucasian rugs with the possible exception of the Tcherkess. There is no set pattern that may be regarded as Kazak; the only rule seems to be a liking for large bold patterns and bright colours. Warps are of wool, as are the rather coarse weft threads, which are usually dyed red or brown. There is a marked *abrash* all over this rug.

---

b) Derbend rug; Caucasian, late 19th century: lgth. 6′ 6″ (198.1 cm.), wdth. 4′ 7″ (139.7 cm.).

A fine Derbend of the latter part of the 19th century, this rug has an ivory ground to the field with the pattern carried out in navy blue, rusty-black, dark brown, light blue and a glaucous blue. Warp and weft are both of natural brown wool. The border is slightly unusual in that it consists of three main border stripes of equal width, the outer Georgian stripe being rather more ornamental than is usual, and the inner stripe showing an interesting variation of the serrated leaf and wine-glass motif (see p. 81*b*).

c) Tabriz carpet; Persian, late 19th century; lgth. 13′ 4″ (406.4 cm.), wdth. 9′ 5″ (287.0 cm.).

Tabriz, in the north-west of Persia, is the home of this carpet. There is no design which is truly Tabrizi for the weavers here have always produced a multiplicity of designs of their own and have also reproduced the designs of other areas. This design is the well-known Shah Abbas, named after the famous and most enlightened Persian ruler who ruled from 1587 to 1629, who was a great patron of the arts. Tabriz rugs are always well woven, and are knotted with the Turkish knot. Fineness of knotting can vary from about 120 to 400 to the square inch, and the pile is clipped short, giving it a rather harsh feel. Warp and weft are made of cotton.

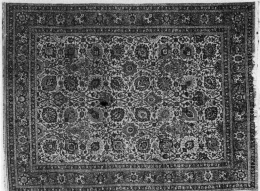

Carpets and Rugs

Oriental
PERSIAN

a) *Silk Tabriz rug; Persian, 19th century; lgth. 5 10" (177.8 cm.), wdth. 3' 11" (119.4 cm.).*

Like most Persian silk rugs, those of this type are eagerly sought after, and are always a good investment. The ground colour of the field is oyster coloured on the surface, but this has faded from a pale blue which can be seen at the foot of the tufts. Doubtless owing to the pile being of silk, the reds of the medallions and borders are more of a madder red than the brick red of the woollen rugs. The Turkish knot is used, but having silk warps and wefts the knots are very much finer than in woollen rugs of this area.

b) *Kirman carpet; Persian, early 19th century; lgth. 6' 6" (198.1 cm.), wdth. 4' 4" (132.1 cm.).*

The town of Kirman in south-east Persia has been noted throughout the world for centuries for the quality of its carpets. This rug was woven at the beginning of the last century, for the date is woven in the centre cartouche at the bottom of the rug— 1225 in the Moslem chronology, which is equal to 1810 by our system. The rose reds and rose pinks of Kirman weaves are very distinctive, as is the use of quite a lot of cream, and three shades of blue. Like all Kirman weavings, the drawing is impeccable.

c) *Ispahan prayer-rug; Persian, 17th century; lgth. 5' 5" (165.1 cm.), wdth. 3' 5" (104.1 cm.).*

An exceptionally fine piece is this 17th century Ispahan prayer rug with its deep blue field and lacy *mihrab*. The field is covered with a vine tracery behind which appears a miniature version of the Shah Abbas design (cf. p. 83c) so dear to the weavers of this district at this period. The red spandrels also carry a complementary tracery in light colours with a shadowy cloud-band in deepest blue. The inner and outer guard stripes are rich green, and the red cartouches stand out vividly against the white of the main border stripe, and themselves provide a fine foil for the elegant Arabic script of the quotations. The knotting is extremely fine.

a) Souj Bulak, Persian, early 19th century; lgth. 15' 1" (459.7 cm.), wdth. 6' 11" (210.8 cm.).

Like most Kurdish weaves, this *kelleyi* from Souj Bulak is a sturdy product with woollen warps and medium-thickness woollen wefts, the whole being beaten down very firmly. Close examination of the field shows ornaments that are distinctly Persian in style—palmettes that are similar to those of Ispahans, several varieties of rosettes, and here and there a typical Herati leaf. The arrangement, however, is Kurdish, as are the rich colourings of dark blue as the ground of the field and a glowing red for the border which carries the same disjunct assortment of floral forms in red, blue, green, brown, yellow and ivory.

---

b) Bidjar rug; Persian, mid 19th century; lgth. 7' 3" (221 cm.), wdth. 4' 9" (144.8 cm.).

The very naturalistic roses, both in drawing and in colour, of this Bidjar, should not lead one to think that it is in any way delicate, for there is not another type of Persian rug that is so solid and sturdy. Indeed, Bidjars must always be rolled as they cannot be folded. The reason is twofold; first is the weavers' habit of pulling one side of the Turkish knot so tightly that one of the two warp threads encircled by the knot is doubled up behind the other, thus giving a double thickness to the backing fabric. Allied to this is the fact that woollen warps and wefts are unusually stout. The ground colour of the field is a lovely light blue, with the design picked out in crimson, pink, ivory, green, yellow, and brown.

c) Senneh rug; Persian, late 18th century; lgth. 6' 4" (193 cm.), wdth. 4' 5" (134.6 cm.).

Although in the Kurdish group of weaves, the rugs of Senneh are the lightest and daintiest of all Persian rugs. The pile is clipped exceedingly short, and this, together with the fine knotting, gives a rug that is at once extremely flexible yet having a firm handle.

The back of the rug is very distinctive, the way the knots are tied giving it a rough feel unlike any other rug. The field can be diapered with a small repetitive pattern such as this, or could consist of small rows of *boteh*, or sharply angled medallions and corners covered with the Herati pattern. The border is the characteristic 'Turtle' pattern, lit up by the use of bright yellow in addition to green, white, red and blue. Warps are very fine cotton or silk; if the latter, the warp fringes are striped in different colours. A fineness of 400 and 500 knots to the square inch is frequently encountered, and the knot is Turkish.

a) *Fereghan rug, Persian, late 18th century; lgth.*
6′ 6″ (198.1 cm.), wdth 4′ 5″ (134.6 cm.).

A rare and delicate design that comes from the
Fereghan weavers is this Musta Hafiz pattern, an
asymmetrical design carried out in yellow, blue,
green, ivory and red picked out in black against
a background of light glowing red. The whole rug
is alight with colour. The border has the normal
'Turtle' motif, emblem of constancy, alternating
with finely drawn rosettes and palmettes. The
knotting of this rug is much finer than is usual with
Fereghans, counting some 250 Persian knots to the
square inch.

---

b) *Fereghan rug, Persian, late 18th century; lgth. 6′ 1″*
(185.4 cm.), wdth. 4′ 0″ (121.9 cm.).

Rugs from the Fereghan district more normally
have a pole medallion as the centrepiece of the
arrangement, in contradistinction to the carpets
which almost invariably have all-over repetitive
patterns. As in this rug, the medallion is mostly
set on a plain field of elongated diamond shape,
the edges of which are stepped, with small tri-
foliate shapes projecting into the field from the
stepping. The large corners of the field are always
closely covered with a diapered pattern, often the
Herati, but in this case stylized flowers.

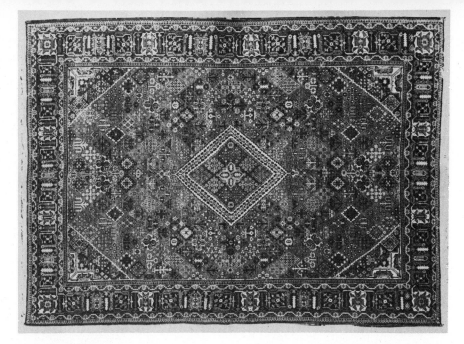

a) Joshaghan carpet; Persian, early 19th century; lgth. 10' 2" (309.9 cm.), wdth. 7' 0" (213.4 cm.).

Joshaghan was an area which was at one time noted for the excellence of its products. Here is an antique carpet from that area which shows the trellis arrangement of the pattern which is characteristic of so many Joshaghan carpets, each panel being embellished with a floral motif. The colours are rich, being deep blue and red, enriched with yellow, green, brown and ivory. The knot used is Turkish and the quality is medium, some large pieces being fairly coarse in texture. Warp is of cotton, with a ribbed appearance on the back, and the weft is of wool of a reddish brown colour, though it could be natural.

b) Wool Heriz of traditional design, Persian; lgth. 16' 9" (510.5 cm.), wdth. 12' (365.8 cm.).

Carpets made in Heriz have always been noted for being some of the hardest wearing of all Persian types. The carpets themselves are usually rather square in format, and the designs are hard and angular. Knotting is coarse to medium, with the Turkish knot, and warp and weft are both of cotton, rather stouter than in most other Persian rugs. The pattern is characteristic, with a dark blue medallion on a field of brick red, the corners and centre of the medallion in ivory. In spite of its geometric appearance the design is based on floral concepts; the border even has a recognizable variation of the 'Turtle' motif. There is nearly always a little black used in Heriz designs, a colour that never appears in Ghorevans which are similar in design. Other colours used include light, dark and medium blue, green and a brownish-red.

c) Silk Heriz rug; Persian, mid-19th century; lgth. 5' 0" (152.4 cm.), wdth. 4' 1" (124.5 cm.).

Heriz is also noted for its silk rugs, and it seems incredible that the same area that produces the rugged, uncompromising four-square Heriz wool carpet should produce the light, airy concepts that make up the silk rugs. This is a really elegant prayer-rug with a red field showing considerable *abrash* and carrying a quite naturalistic tree, and spandrels with well-drawn flowering plants. The dark blue panels above and below the field bear foliate forms and the curvilinear pattern in the main border contains many dainty little flowers. The knotting of these silk rugs is very fine.

a) Khorassan carpet; Persian, early 19th century; lgth. 5' 10" (177.8 cm.), wdth. 4' 2" (127 cm.).

The Khorassan province of Persia is in the far north-east and harbours the sacred city of Meshed. Certain types of older carpets are not assigned to any specific origin such as Meshed or Birjand, but are termed Khorassan after the province. Usually this category has the field covered in very large *boteh* motifs, but in this case the field has a most unusual repetitive motif undoubtedly of floral origin. Closely examined, it reveals that each rosette is the centre of an oval design, each oval interlocking and forming part of the four neighbouring ovals. The border is a classic example of a leaf and flower motif arranged as a running vine. The ground colour is ivory with the design in rose red and blue with touches of yellow and green.

b) Bokhara carpet; Central Asian, early 19th century; lgth. 10' 2" (309.9 cm.), wdth. 6' 7" (200.7 cm.).

This old Bokhara carpet has the typical rounded *gul* of octagonal form of the Tekke tribes, and the characteristic more angular octagons in the main border stripe. The warp threads are of undyed goat hair and the weft is of undyed wool of a brown colour. The *guls* are quartered by dark blue lines running both vertically and horizontally along and across the field, the opposing quarters being of matching designs, one pair being on red and ivory and the other on dark blue and red tones, the *guls* being outlined in dark blue. The field is a rich tone of red, and the whole carpet is knotted in a soft silky wool that gives the appearance and feel of velvet. The woven end-webs of red and blue are often found on older pieces.

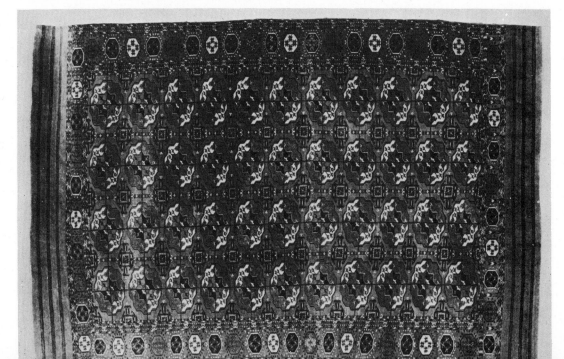

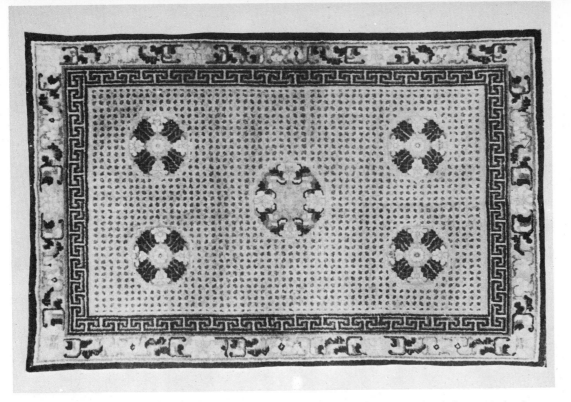

a) Chinese rug; late 17th century; lgth. 7′ 10″ (238.8 cm.), wdth. 4′ 10″ (147.8 cm.).

This antique Chinese rug was woven about the end of the reign of the Emperor Kien Lung, in the latter part of the 18th century. The inner T-border stripe is a design of great antiquity, but the shading which can be observed here did not occur before the middle of the century. The main border stripe, too, is also characteristic of this period of production. The pattern in the field, apart from the adornment of the five medallions, is known as the 'Grain of Rice' pattern, and appears in quite a number of rugs of this period. The field is a faded tangerine colour with the other colours used being ivory, yellow and dark blue. The structure of the rug is loose.

---

b) Chinese rug; late 18th century; lgth. 7′ 10″ (238.8 cm.), wdth. 5′ 6″ (167.6 cm.).

A late 18th century Chinese rug in which the field is occupied by several representations of the mythical lion-dog, with the cloud bands of eternity, and flying butterflies symbolizing happiness. The ground colour is a rich deep blue, with the other main colours being tan, persimmon and ivory. The inner border stripe with the large dot was not in use before the middle of the century. Like all Chinese rugs the knot used is Persian, and the texture of the piece is on the loose side. The warps and wefts are both of cotton, the weft threads being rather coarse.

European Carpets and Rugs
Introduction

The French industry, like the English, was formed with the idea of copying the Turkish and other Eastern carpets which were being brought into Europe, and in 1608, one Pierre Dupont was granted a licence to use a workshop under the Bouvre Gallery in Paris. Here, he made hand-knotted carpets 'in the style of the Levant and of Turkey'.

He took a partner in 1627, a former pupil of his named Simon Lourdet, who set up in business in buildings which had been acquired by the Crown near the Colline de Chaillot, and which had formerly been a soap factory or *savonnerie;* thus the carpets acquired the name by which they have been known ever since.

In that same year the Council of State enacted a decree that gave the ateliers a constitution of their own, which, among other things, prohibited the entry into France of carpets from the East. Both the masters were declared noblemen, and each was granted a large annuity, together with free lodging and certain privileges, in return for which they had to teach an agreed number of children from the workhouse.

Like any other manufacturing concern, the Savonnerie works had their ups and downs, and at the end of the seventeenth century, the works actually closed down for a few years.

At the beginning of the eighteenth century, taste and fashion changed a good deal; a restrained, more elegant line affected all the aspects of French life—dress, architecture, art and of course, carpets.

French taste was, by now, considered the most civilized in the world, and was copied everywhere in Western Europe, and in many other countries as well. Their carpets were no longer 'in the Oriental style', and the designs were entirely French. Belin de Fontenay and Pierre J. Perrot were two among the many painters who created Savonnerie carpet designs.

Nonetheless, by the late 1700s, the factory was again in difficulties. Increasing costs, the havoc caused by the Revolution, and the competition from the Aubusson works all helped to cause financial problems. But with the Napoleonic era, there was a revival in production as the new Empire re-built, re-furnished, and re-carpeted. The works were moved again in 1826 to the buildings which housed the Gobelins factory, and the two were amalgamated by Royal decree.

The Aubusson tapestry industry had existed since 1665. Their technique was based on the work of the Soumak carpet-makers of the Caucasian mountains; the surface was smooth, with the cut threads hanging down on the reverse, or wrong side. After c. 1750, they started making carpets as well, using the same method. Their work was never considered as fine as that of Savonnerie and Gobelins, but it was

intended for a much wider market, and these carpets have a style and freshness of their own, often more appealing than the elaborate, highly decorated Court designs.

British carpets really owe their start to the cupidity of Cardinal Wolsey; having been the recipient of a gift of seven fine Damascene carpets as a bribe from Venetian traders who hoped to have a prohibitive tariff removed, he promptly demanded one hundred more! In the end, he only received sixty-one, but the display at his Hampton Court Palace encouraged other nobles to acquire fine carpets for their own homes.

This was in 1520; by 1539, weavers were brought from the East to make a large carpet for the Earl of Ormond. From then on, many upright looms were installed all over the country, and the craft grew in both quantity and quality of output. After Wolsey's death, an inventory included 'eleven carpets of Englyshe making'.

Most early English work was knotted on warps of hemp or flax, and usually being made to order, often had coats of arms or similar devices incorporated into the design, together with the date—a fortunate circumstance for the collector. The English weavers soon stopped making slavish copies of Oriental originals, and designed carpets in their own idiom. Many had local maps, and illustrations from the herbals.

Later, the main English works were re-established at Paddington, Fulham, Moorfields, Exeter and Axminster; most started production during the eighteenth century.

The Axminster works first started manufacture in 1755. The owner, Thomas Whitty, got his idea for a horizontal loom from the factory of a Mr Parisot, who had not long before introduced the art from France, and had established a factory at Fulham. Many fine carpets came from this factory during the following years.

In 1834, Blackmore, who had earlier started a hand-knotting factory in Kilmarnock, took over the Axminster factory and transferred it to the town of Wilton, near Salisbury, where he installed looms capable of producing carpets thirty-three and even forty feet wide. Over the next one hundred and twenty years, many beautiful carpets were made but owing to economic problems, the Wilton factory regretfully sold its last hand looms in 1958.

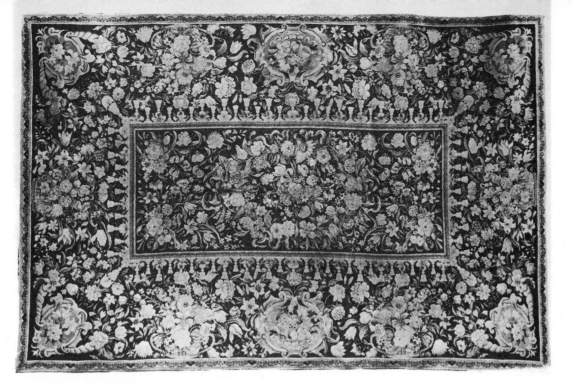

a) *Savonnerie carpet, France; made during the second half of the 17th century, lgth. 14' 3" (434 cm.), wdth. 9' 3" (281 cm.).*

The earlier Savonnerie products ranged from carpets to chair covers and included tapestries and other fabrics. However, in 1662, the Manufacture Royale des Gobelins was organized under the patronage of Colbert, Minister to Louis XIV; Gobelins took over all the tapestry and fabric work and left the Savonnerie factory to concentrate on carpets.

Strict control of design from the painters of the Royal Academy ensured that the carpets showed less Eastern influence, and French floral patterns became pre-eminent.

There is a great similarity between the figuratively and literally 'carpets of flowers' so popular during this period, usually on a dark background, and the marquetry on dark-stained wood which typifies furniture of the same era.

b) *Savonnerie carpet, of the early Louis XV period; France; c. 1720–40; lgth. 11' 4" (345 cm.), wdth. 9' 4" (284 cm.).*

The new designs at the beginning of the 18th century were lighter and more delicate versions of the flower patterns for which Savonnerie was famous. Many different flowers were interspersed with various decorations, such as the Royal arms; in this case, the blue central medallion encloses four gold *fleurs-de-lis*. The photograph shows quite clearly that three corners have been re-woven —not unusual with a carpet of this age.

a) *Savonnerie carpet of the Louis XVI period; France, late 18th century; lgth. 14' 10" (452 cm.), wdth. 13' 6" (411 cm.).*

The classical world began to influence French design towards the middle of the 18th century, although the flowers and scrolls remained part of the overall pattern. Many carpets had classical scenes as part of the design, and even predominantly floral examples, such as this lovely oval, often had a border of laurel leaves, tied with crossed ribbons. Another popular pattern of this era was the Greek key design. Marie Antoinette encouraged the use of classical motifs, and the excavations of Roman ruins were an additional impetus. Shepherds and shepherdesses sported in Arcadian landscapes in paintings, on porcelain, tapestries, and of course, on carpets. Colours became lighter and fresher, and although the Revolution might have apparently been the ruination of such a Royal, luxury industry, in fact it had a salutary effect. The elaborate designs were so expensive to make that buyers had become scarce and prices too high; with the change to the *Directoire* that swept away panniers and powdered wigs, the basic simplicity of classical line came to the fore.

b) *Detail of Savonnerie carpet, France; late 18th, early 19th century; lgth. 16' 6" (503 cm.), wdth. 12' 9" (389 cm.).*

This is an interesting transitional stage between the floral curves of the earlier period, and the more geometrical designs which began to develop. The garlands are still there, but in more restrained curves and disciplined to fit within the geometrically precise borders.

With the Napoleonic era, the Savonnerie works were again reprieved; there had been a huge amount of damage and destruction during the Revolution, and the new government set about restoring the national inheritance. The Savonnerie works were re-named the *Manufacture Nationale des Tapis et Meubles façon de Perse dits Savonnerie*, and an enormous output of new designs poured out incorporating all the new motifs we associate with the Napoleonic era; the *N*, the bees, the Imperial crown, etc. The classical influence was still very strong; indeed, they were part and parcel of the French Empire style. In addition, the Egyptian campaigns of Napoleon brought more exotic shapes and motifs into the vocabulary of designers and artists throughout the country.

a) Small Aubusson rug, France; made in the first half of the 19th century; lgth. 6′ 6″ (198 cm.), wdth. 5′ 6″ (168 cm.).

In 1665, Louis XIV's Minister, Colbert, organized the Aubusson factories into a *Manufacture de Tapisseries*; from then on, their products were signed MRDA—Manufacture Royale d'Aubusson. But carpet production did not really get under way until the end of the 18th century. Less expensive than the Savonnerie carpets, Aubussons were usually lighter and less formal in design, made largely for the middle classes rather than the aristocracy.

b) Aubusson carpet; France, mid-19th century; lgth. 11′ 7″ (353 cm.), wdth. 9′ 7″ (292 cm.).

During the 19th century, Aubusson carpets continued to rival those made at the Savonnerie factory. During the first half of the century, in particular, many very fine carpets were made, as beautiful in design and colouring as any produced elsewhere in France. Their only serious disadvantage was durability; the flat weave did not wear as well as the pile of Savonnerie carpets, and many magnificent examples have undoubtedly perished. Many patterns, such as in this illustration, have a three-dimensional effect, and apparently sometimes were actually used on the ceiling instead of carved and painted stucco decoration.

Carpets and Rugs
European
ENGLISH

a) Tapestry map; England; c. 1580: ht. 6' 2" (188 cm.), wdth. 4' (122 cm.).

In addition to the knotted carpets made in England, there were also carpets made using the tapestry technique, and many made on an embroidery frame. This particular map is a tapestry, but it illustrates the kind of design that was very popular in England, typical of a very local and personal approach. It was made by the Sheldon family, who lived in the district, and shows part of Gloucestershire, Somerset, Wiltshire, and Monmouthshire.

The river is the Severn (the top of the picture is east, right-hand side to the south). Kingswood Park, in the centre, was the home of Mr Hopkins, a witness to Shakespeare's signature.

b) Detail of a carpet in a neo-classical design; England, c. 1780.

For the next three centuries, knotted English carpets followed either the Oriental or the fashionable French patterns. It was not until the advent of Robert Adam, and his total approach to the ideal home, that English carpets once more reflected an original style which was itself copied and admired in other countries. At Osterley Park, for example, Adam designed the facade, the interior, architectural work, the furniture, the ceilings, fabrics and the carpets.

---

c) Carpet made in the 'Redcar' pattern; by William Morris; England, late 19th century; lgth. 11' (335 cm.), wdth. 8' 2" (249 cm.).

After the lightness of the neo-classical era, the Victorian patterns merged into an overall heavy, florid effect common to both England and France. The Arts and Crafts Movement, spearheaded by William Morris, was intended to improve the artistic taste and understanding of the Victorian family, and he designed furniture, carpets, tapestries, etc. It was the last attempt to revive hand-made craftsmanship before machine weaving took over the English carpet industry completely. This particular pattern has a strong resemblance to the entwined floral Persian designs and an equally strong connection with the sinuous Art Nouveau line which was to follow.

Carpets and Rugs Glossary

ABRASH: Shading of a solid colour caused by different batches of dyeing.

BAFF: Knot.

BOTEH: The cone or pear design on which the so-called Paisley and Kashmir shawl designs are based.

DJUFT: Pair.

DJUFTI KNOT: A fraudulent knot which encircles four warp threads instead of the normal two.

DOZAR: A rug measuring about 6′ 6″ × 4′ 3″ (198 × 130 cm.).

FARSIBAFF: Persian knot—see p. 76.

FIELD: In prayer rugs the central panel with the arch at the top; in ordinary rugs and carpets it is the area inside the borders.

GHALI, KHALI or QALI: Carpet.

GIREH or PUNZEH: A measurement of length equal to one-sixteenth of a *zar*, approximately 2¾″ (6.9 cm.).

GUL: A quartered polygon that is a characteristic feature of Turkoman rugs.

GOL-I-HINNAI: A representation of the henna flower, usually a straight stem with side branches, each bearing a stylized flower at the tip.

HERATI: The basic design of an all-over repetitive pattern that appears on Persian carpets from many areas. The basis of the design is a rosette enclosed within a quadrant flanked by serrated lanceolate leaves.

JUVAL or CHOVAL: A large single bag used by nomads for storage purposes, approximately 41″ to 44″ (104 to 112 cm.) in width.

KELLEYEH or KELLEGHI: A long narrow carpet of which the length is usually from two to three times the width, ranging from about 10′ × 5′ to 20′ × 7′ (305 × 152 cm. to 610 × 213 cm.).

KENAREH: A long narrow strip or runner, approximately 2′ 6″ to 3′ 6″ (76 to 107 cm.) in width by from 8′ to 20′ (244 to 610 cm.) long.

KELIM: A flat woven pileless carpet or rug: also the end-web on some rugs between the knotted portion and the fringe.

KHALI: See 'ghali'.

KHARAK: A rug measuring about 5′ 6″ × 2′ 3″ (168 × 69 cm.).

KHATCHLI: A Turkoman rug in which the field has been quartered by a design in the form of a cross.

MIHRAB: The niche or arch at the top of the field of a prayer rug.

MINA KHANI: An all-over pattern of rosettes joined by straight or curved stems.

MOSUL: A rug measuring about 6′ 6″ × 3′ 3″ (198 × 99 cm.).

NAMAZLYK or NAMAZI: a prayer rug.

PUNZEH: See 'gireh'.

PUSHTI: A small rug about 3′ × 2′ (91 × 61 cm.).

QALI: See ghali'.

SAPH: A family prayer rug or carpet with several praying panels in the one piece.

SEDJADEH: Sofa rug.

SHOT: A passage of the shuttle across the web.

SPANDRELS: The portions of the panel on either side of the 'mihrab' in a prayer rug.

TORBA: A small single woven bag used by nomads for transporting goods.

TURKBAFF: Turkish knot—see p. 76.

UBRECHT or UBRIK: Water jug.

WARP: The foundation threads that run lengthways from the top to the bottom of a rug.

WEFT: The foundation threads that run across a rug from side to side.

YASTIK: A very small rug measuring about 17″ × 33″ (43 × 84 cm.).

ZAR: A measure of length that is approximately 41″ to 44″ (104 to 112 cm.).

ZARONIM: A rug measuring about 5′ 0″ × 3′ 6″ (152 × 107 cm.).

ZAROQUART or ZARCHEREK: A rug measuring about 4′ 6″ × 2′ 3″ (137 × 69 cm.).

Top row:
Left: The Mina Khani pattern.
Centre: Detail from a Shah Abbasi design which shows a spiral arabesque.
Right: Detail of a Bid

Majnum design showing weeping willow and flowers.
Bottom row:
Left: The 'Gol-i-Hinnai' design.
Right: Detail of Herati pattern.

Carpets and Rugs
Repairs and Maintenance

Like any other textile product, a carpet needs care, most of which can and should be based on common sense. It is obvious that the older the carpet, the greater care should be exercised in handling it, for great age can cause a carpet to become frail.

The greatest enemies of carpets are grit and moths. Grit with its sharp edges can cause a great deal of damage, especially if it is allowed to get down to the roots of the tufts where it exercises a cutting or abrasive action every time that portion of the carpet is trodden upon. Vacuum cleaners will not harm carpets in good condition, nor will a good sweeping from a broom, but one should never resort to hanging a carpet over a clothes line and beating it with a stick.

Oriental carpets should never be cleaned with proprietary cleaners and detergents because these are apt to remove the essential oils from the wool and allow it to become harsh and brittle with consequent loss of durability. Nor should an Oriental carpet be sent to any ordinary cleaning firm for the same reasons. They should always be sent to firms which specialize in their cleaning for they understand the product.

Repairs, too, are a very specialized business, and should only be entrusted to a firm of repute. Any rug that is damaged should be sent for repair at the earliest possible moment so as to minimize the spread of the damage, and also to restore the value of the piece.

Fakes and Forgeries

Insofar as Oriental carpets are concerned there are very few fakes as the cost of production—remembering that pieces are all hand-knotted—would be out of all proportion to the return.

What does happen, however, is that occasionally an existing carpet or rug is 'aged' by various means, usually by burning off the pile and then vigorously brushing it. Sometimes the faker will also discolour the back of the rug by burning it over to match the front.

Here it is of value to know something of the designs which are relevant to both the period and the area to which the rug is alleged to belong. If either of these suggest that

something is wrong, and there is a suspicion that the rug may have been burned off, or aged by burning or singeing, then place a handkerchief over a portion of the suspected area and breathe heavily outwards through the handkerchief and the pile. Whip the handkerchief away quickly and smell the pile: a distinct smell of charred wool will be apparent if the rug has been 'doctored'.

Sometimes woven portions may have been painted over to disguise the fact that part of the pile has been worn down to the backing but this is usually easily detected by the eye, and may be confirmed by rubbing with a damp cloth, when some colour will be transferred to the cloth.

Further Reading

General

BERNHEIMER, O. *Alte Teppiche des 16.-18. Jahrhunderts.* Munich, 1959.

HAACK, H. *Echte Teppiche.* Munich, 1956.

NASSERI, G. S. *Vierzig Jahre Suchen und Sammeln.* Wiesbaden, 1970.

SCHLOSSER, I. *European and Oriental Rugs and Carpets.* London, 1963.

KENDRICK, A. F., and TATTERSALL, C. E. C. *Hand-woven Carpets, Oriental and European.* London, 1922.

Oriental

BIDDER, H. *Carpets From Eastern Turkestan.* London, 1964.

BODE, W. VON, and KUHNEL, E. *Antique Rugs from the Near East.* London, 1970.

CAMPANA, M. *Oriental Carpets.* London, 1969.

DILLEY, A. U. *Oriental Rugs and Carpets.* New York, 1931.

EDWARDS, A. C. *The Persian Carpet.* London, 1953.

ERDMANN, K. *Oriental Carpets: an Account of their History.* London, 1960.

Seven Hundred Years of Oriental Carpets. London, 1970.

FOCSA, M. *Scoarte Romanesti.* Bucharest, 1970.

GANS-RUEDIN, E. *Orientalische Meisterteppiche.* Bern, 1966.

GROTE-HASENBALG, W. *Der Orientteppich, seine Geschichte und Kultur.* Berlin, 1922.

Teppiche aus dem Orient. Leipzig, 1936.

HAWLEY, W. A. *Oriental Rugs, Antique and Modern.* New York and London, 1913.

HILDEBRAND, H. *Der persische Teppich und seine Heimat.* Zurich, 1951.

HOPF, A. *Oriental Carpets and Rugs.* London, 1962.

LARSON, L. *Rugs and Carpets of the Orient.* London, 1966.

LETTENMAIR, J. G. *Das grosse Orientteppich Buch.* Munich, 1972.

LORENTZ, H. A. *A View of Chinese Rugs from the Seventeenth to the Twentieth Century.* London, 1973.

MACEY, R. E. G. *Oriental Prayer Rugs.* Leigh-on-Sea, 1961.

MCMULLAN, J. V. *Islamic Carpets.* New York, 1965.

ORENDI. *Das Gesamtwissen über antike und neue Teppiche des Orients.* Vienna, 1930.

POPE, A. U. *A Survey of Persian Arts.* New York, 1939 and 1970.

REED, S. *Oriental Rugs and Carpets.* London, 1967.

SARRE, F., and TRENKWALD, U. *Altorientalische Teppiche.* Leipzig, 1926 and 1928. (Eng. trans. also published.)

SCHMUTZLER, E. *Altorientalische Teppiche in Siebenbürgen.* Leipzig, 1932.

SCHURMANN, U. *Caucasian Rugs.* Brunswick, 1964.

Central Asian Rugs. Frankfurt, 1969.

UHLEMANN, H. *Geographie des Orientteppichs.* Leipzig, 1930.

VEGH J. DE, and LAYER, C. *Tapis turcs provenant des églises et collections de Transylvanie.* Paris,

European

CAMPANA, M. *European Carpets.* London, 1969.

JACOBS, B. *Axminster Carpets (hand-made) 1755-1957.* Leigh-on-Sea, 1970.

The Story of British Carpets. London, 1968 and 1972.

JARRY, M. *The Carpets of the Manufactory de la Savonnerie.* Leigh-on-Sea, 1966.

MAYORCAS, M. J. *English Needlework Carpets 16th-19th Centuries.* Leigh-on-Sea, 1963.

TATTERSALL, C. E. C., and REED, S. *A History of British Carpets.* Leigh-on-Sea, 1966.

Carpets and Rugs
Museum Collections

Great Britain

LONDON: The Victoria and Albert Museum.

U.S.A.

MASSACHUSETTS: The Fogg Art Museum, Harvard University, Cambridge; The Museum of Fine Arts, Boston.
NEW YORK: The Metropolitan Museum of Art, New York.
PENNSYLVANIA: The Museum of Art, Philadelphia.
WASHINGTON D.C.: The Textile Museum.

Egypt

CAIRO: The Museum of Islamic Art.

Turkey

ISTANBUL: Türk ve Islam Eserleri Müzesi.

Index

Opposite:
Bidjar medallion rug with delicate floral border; Persia, early 19th century.

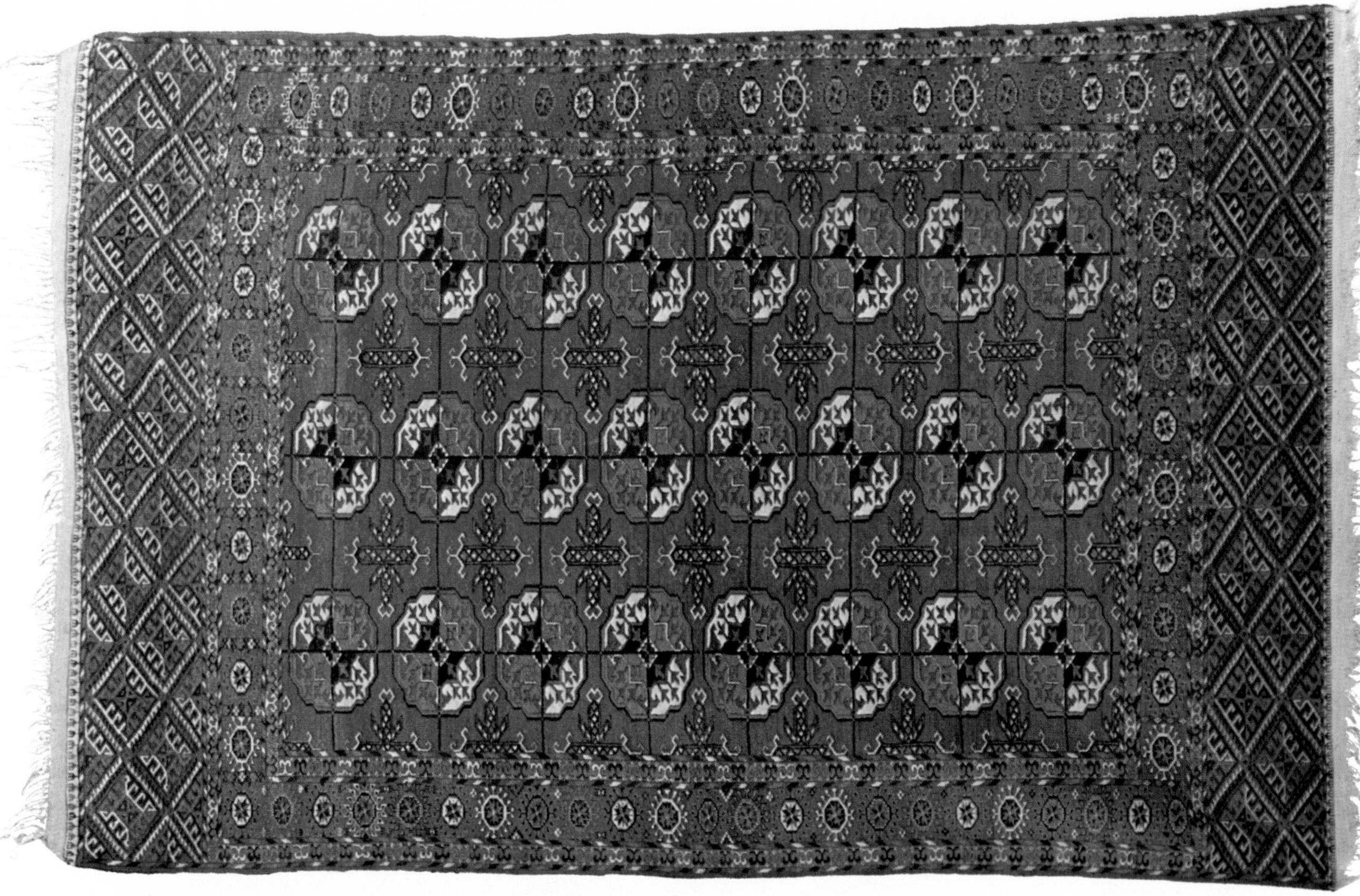

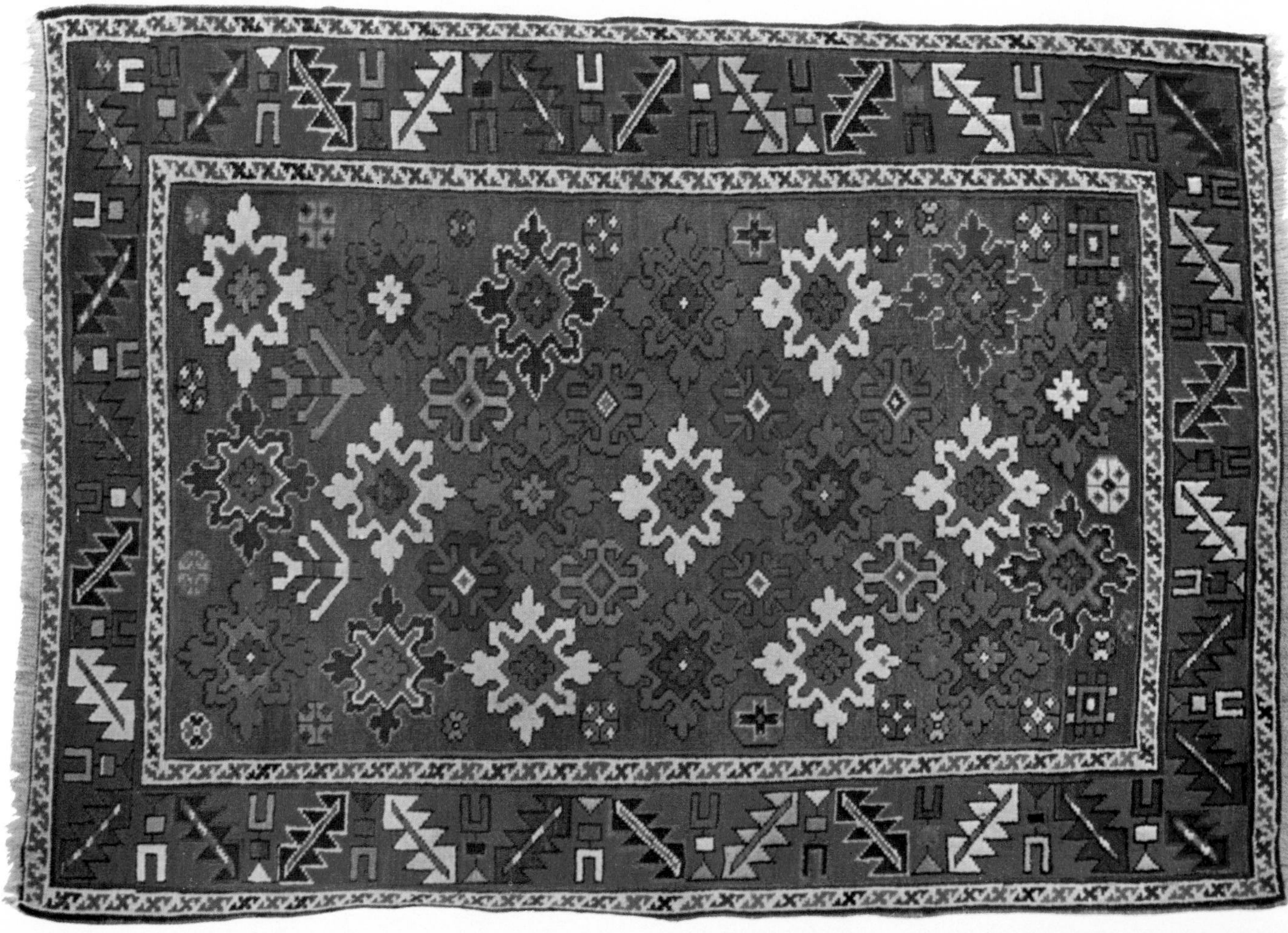

Top left: Central Asian Tekke Bokhara rug, mid–19th century.

Left: Caucasian Kouba Shirvan rug, second half of the 19th century.

Above: Two of a set of four Savonnerie carpets woven in France, mid–19th century.

Ceramics

Today the love of all types of antiques is probably greater than at any time in history. Those fortunate ones who were able to participate in the Grand Tour during the eighteenth century were very few, and usually very wealthy. At the present time easy, comparatively cheap, travel has brought the art treasures of the world within the range of the majority of those interested in such subjects. This familiarity with beautiful art objects has inspired today's collectors, and there is little doubt that of all the decorative arts, those in the field of pottery and porcelain are the most popular, normally requiring less experience to identify, and collectable according to one's purse.

The material of earthenware, and later porcelain, has always been used to serve a dual purpose; first, the essential needs of cooking and serving food and drink, secondly to give visual pleasure. The great houses of Europe would have looked very stark without their treasures; the palaces of Italy had their colourful tin-glazed earthenwares (maiolica), the courts of France their Vincennes and Sèvres porcelain, and the great houses of the Adam period were brought to life by the neo-classical creations of such potters as Josiah Wedgwood.

One of the most successful ways of learning about ceramics is to acquire an example of almost every type. Expensive? By no means—individual pieces can be so badly damaged that they are worth very little, but the material is right, the various styles of decoration similarly so, and in this way you will be able to train your eye to readily recognize genuine examples. In addition, you will discover which of the many kinds of ceramics appeal to you, and why.

With this basic knowledge and appreciation, a collection should be both interesting to acquire and infinitely satisfying to own.

Opposite:
Dish; porcelain decorated in underglaze blue; China, 15th century.
Jar and cover; tin-glazed earthenware decorated in high-temperature blue; Delft, Holland, early 18th century.
Coffee-pot and cover; porcelain painted in underglaze blue; Meissen, Germany, c. 1740.
Sweetmeat dish in underglaze blue; Bow, England, c. 1750-55.

Ceramics
The Craft

Man has been using clay to fashion both figures and useful wares for many thousands of years. At first simple objects made of hand-moulded clay were baked in the sun, but in order to change a soft clay vessel to a composition that will not again revert to a plastic nature wherein contact with water, it is necessary to bake it at a temperature varying between 450-700°C. Such temperatures were not successfully reached until about 4000 B.C., when the Near Eastern potters first learnt how to build vertical kilns. At this period the technique of glazing was still unknown, but a thin layer of refined clay applied to the surface of the wares burnished both before, and sometimes after firing, helped to make the ware less porous and thus capable of containing liquids. Alkaline glazes (a form of coloured glass) had been used for decoration at a very early date in Egypt, but a complete coating of lead-glaze to seal at least the inside surfaces of jugs and pots, etc. was not used until about the seventeenth century B.C.

The earliest clay wares were formed without any mechanical aids. Authorities differ as to the date of the introduction of the potters' wheel, but Near Eastern pottery of about 3500 B.C. gives clear evidence, in both form and surface patterns, that a fast-turning wheel was almost certainly established. Later Egyptian wall-paintings, showing potters at work, also depict a wheel in use (c. 1900 B.C.).

There are certain clay bodies richer in natural fluxes than those used for earthenware. When fired to a temperature of about 1250°C., these clays vitrify, and so become completely impervious to liquids; this material is called stoneware. Chinese potters first produced fine stonewares during the Han dynasty.

Probably towards the end of the fourteenth century A.D. the technique of salt-glazing was first introduced in the Rhineland (see p. 130). The soda in common salt, which was thrown into the kiln at the peak firing temperature, volatilized and combined with the silica and alumina in the clay, to produce a tight-fitting colourless glaze which usually had a fine 'orange-peel' texture. These salt-glazed stonewares were sometimes decorated by adding a clay slip before firing, rich in iron-oxide, creating various tones ranging from orange to rich browns, after firing. Wares of this material were produced in England by John Dwight at his Fulham factory from 1672. Up until recently ginger-beer bottles were still being manufactured from this material.

During the eighteenth century Staffordshire potters improved the coarser stoneware of the earlier centuries by adding white ball-clay and calcined flints, thus producing a refined body. Later, this body was fired at a lower temperature to make the popular lead-glazed earthenware, perfected by Josiah Wedgwood as 'Queensware' (c. 1765).

Mesopotamian potters (c. 800-900 A.D.) learnt how to coat their comparatively low-fired (about 900°C.) earthenwares with an opaque white glaze by adding tin-oxide (ashes of tin) to their normally transparent lead-glazes. The glazed but unfired pots were decorated in a more colourful range of high-temperature colours (blue from cobalt, green from copper, purple from manganese and yellow from antimony) and fired with the glaze at about 900-1000°C. This technique later spread to the West, resulting in the Hispano-Moresque wares, Italian maiolica, French and German faience and the Delftware of Holland. Similar tin-glazed earthenwares were produced at various centres in England.

During the T'ang dynasty (A.D. 618–906) the Chinese potter first learnt how to produce a hard-paste porcelain from two forms of granite in varying stages of decomposition; china-clay (kaolin) and china-stone (petuntse), materials which when fired to a temperature of about 1350°C. fused together to form a translucent white body. The glaze, which fitted tightly and rarely 'crazed', was produced from china-stone, fluxed with lime and potash, and fired with the body. By the 1300s Chinese potters were using cobalt to produce many wares with underglaze-blue decoration; such pieces could be fired to completion in a single operation.

The full range of enamel colours made from coloured glass was not used in China until c. 1450. These colours were fused on to the surface of the already-fired glaze, by re-firing at the comparatively low temperature of about 800°C. A separate low-temperature kiln was always used for these enamels.

Various attempts were made to imitate the hard-paste porcelains of China in artificial or soft-paste porcelains in both Italy and France during the sixteenth and seventeenth centuries. The secret was, however, retained by the Chinese until the early eighteenth century, when an even whiter hard-paste porcelain was produced in Saxony at the Meissen factory of Augustus the Strong, Elector of Saxony and King of Poland. Soft-paste porcelain from white-firing clays and other materials, such as bone-ash, and powdered glass, was also produced in England from about 1745, but it was 1768 before William Cookworthy established his factory at Plymouth, in south-west England, to produce a true hard porcelain.

Chinese Ceramics
Introduction

In China, ceramics have always been highly esteemed; quality was preferred to quantity, perfection of form and glaze to ostentation. China's ceramic tradition developed over a period spanning more than four thousand years.

As early as 3000 B.C., neolithic wares were painted with splendid geometrical designs, and by the Shang Dynasty white glazed ware with impressed designs reflected contemporary bronze shapes. The fusing of feldspar in the body and glaze to produce stoneware was discovered around 1100 B.C. Thereafter, the development of high-fired wares followed an intermittent course; green-glazed stoneware of the third/fourth centuries A.D., was more far advanced technically, but true porcelain was not discovered until the beginning of the T'ang dynasty.

The T'ang period produced a wide range of funerary wares, perhaps the most colourful ever made in China. The predominating combination was chestnut, green and yellow. By the tenth century in the kingdom of Wu Yüeh, splendid celadons which were greatly to influence Sung ceramics had been perfected.

The Sung dynasty was the classical age of China. The earlier wares, particularly the white wares, continued the T'ang tradition, but by the reign of Emperor Hui Tsung (1100–1125), the Sung potters had developed their own distinct style, the 'growing form of Sung'. Both incised and impressed decoration reached a high degree of perfection: flowing lines depict plants, birds and other natural motifs favoured by the scholar artists. Splendid monochrome glazes were introduced; the most famous was the lavender-blue glaze of Ju, made for Hui Tsung's Court. At their best, however, the opalescent blue Chün wares, often flushed with red, are equally lovely. From the north came the brown-black wares of Honan and celadons of Yao-chou and Lin-ju; Hopei made particularly beautiful cream-glazed Ting wares with superb floral decoration. Only Tz'u-chou wares retained the colourful T'ang tradition throughout the Sung and Yüan dynasties; these were later to inspire Ming polychrome porcelains.

In 1127, the Court fled before the advancing Tartars, and the southern Sung dynasty was established at Hangchou, where Imperial kilns were set up. Southern celadons were made at Lung-ch'üan and neighbouring kilns, and the Chien and Kian kilns are famous for *temmoku*, so admired by the Japanese—the term refers to the browny-black wares of China. Old traditions, however, lingered on and the Ch'ing-Pai wares continued the elegant Ting forms. Ch'ing-Pai subsequently developed into Shu-fu and thence evolved into early blue and white porcelain during the Yüan dynasty, a period of intense ceramic development.

The Ming dynasty is famous for its underglaze blue and white porcelain developed at the kilns of Ching-tê-chên, which remained the ceramic centre of Chinese porcelain manufacture for five hundred years. Exquisite Imperial pieces were made there as well as more massive export wares.

During the fifteenth century the development of overglaze enamels inspired many new polychrome wares; the products of Chêng-hua, Chêng-tê, Chia-ching and Wan-li are famous. They were made in a variety of colour combinations on a white ground, such as *san ts'ai* (three colour), *tou ts'ai* (contrasting colours), *wu ts'ai* (five colours), as well as a red and green family. Some of the most spectacular are the *fa hua* wares—simple, strong designs using rich colours of turquoise, deep blue, purple and yellow-brown. Fine Ming monochromes were also made, such as Imperial yellow, in successive reigns.

With the Ch'ing dynasty, two new techniques were perfected; *famille rose*, introduced c. 1721, was a gold-based pink enamel borrowed from Europe. The second was the development, c. 1729, of high-fired glazes and the subsequent introduction of new monochromes with European names (peach bloom, *sang-de-boeuf*, etc.). Although the main development centered on the Court and Ching-tê-chên, interesting provincial pieces include the cream white figures of Tê-hua in Fukien, the red and green wares of Swatow, and the brown I Hsing stonewares.

During the late Ming and the Ch'ing dynasty Europeans imported large quantities of porcelain, particularly blue and white. This was known as 'Kraak' porcelain, because it was carried in Carracks of the East India companies. Later the term 'Nanking' was used. Polychrome wares, ranging from punch-bowls to *famille rose* dinner services and commemoratives dishes etc., were much in demand, and many European families ordered armorial services depicting their coat of arms.

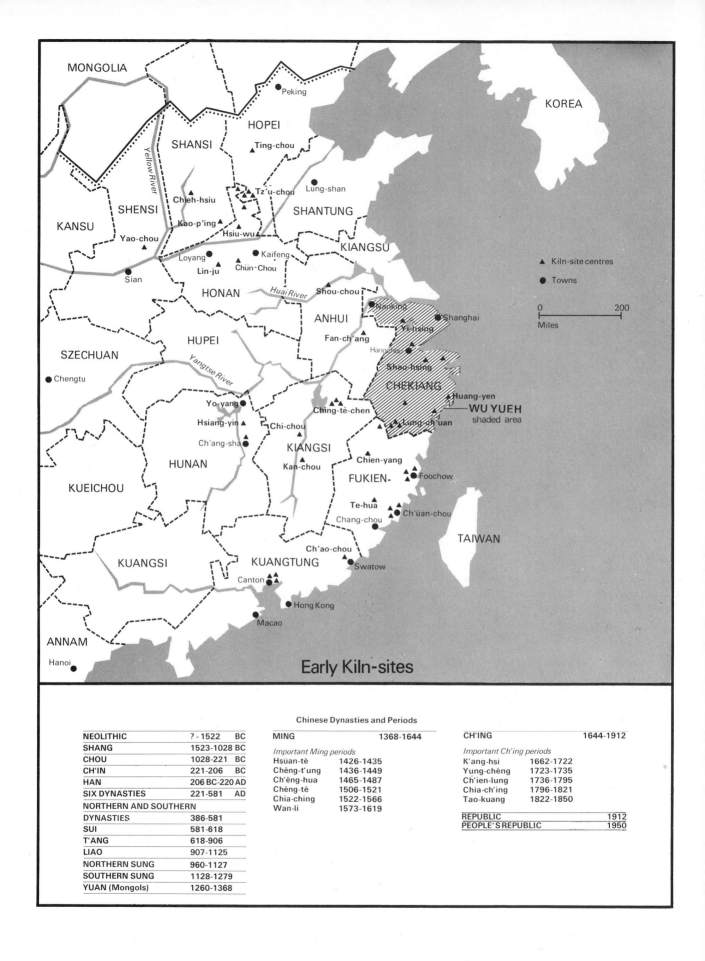

MONGOLIA

KOREA

HOPEI

• Peking

SHANSI

SHENSI

▲ Ting-chou

Tz'u-chou

• Lung-shan

SHANTUNG

KANSU

Chieh-hsiu ▲

Yao-chou ▲

Kao-p'ing ▲

Hsiu-wu ▲

KIANGSU

Loyang •

• Kaifeng

• Sian

Lin-ju ▲

Chün-Chou ▲

HONAN

Huai River

Shou-chou •

Kiln-site centres ▲

Towns •

0   200
Miles

ANHUI

Nanking ▲

HUPEI

Fan-ch'ang ▲

• Shanghai

Yi-hsing ▲

Hangchow •

SZECHUAN

Yangtse River

Shao-hsing ▲

• Chengtu

CHEKIANG

Huang-yen ▲

WU YUEH
shaded area

Yo-yang •

Hsiang-yin ▲

Chi-chou ▲

Ching-tê-chen ▲▲▲

Lung-ch'uan ▲

Ch'ang-sha •

KIANGSI

Chien-yang ▲▲

• Foochow ▲▲

HUNAN

Kan-chou ▲

KUEICHOU

FUKIEN

Te-hua ▲

Ch'üan-chou ▲

Chang-chou •

TAIWAN

KUANGSI

KUANGTUNG

Ch'ao-chou •

Swatow •

Canton • ▲▲

• Hong Kong

• Macao

ANNAM

• Hanoi

Early Kiln-sites

Chinese Dynasties and Periods

NEOLITHIC	? - 1522	BC
SHANG	1523-1028	BC
CHOU	1028-221	BC
CH'IN	221-206	BC
HAN	206 BC-220 AD	
SIX DYNASTIES	221-581	AD
NORTHERN AND SOUTHERN		
DYNASTIES	386-581	
SUI	581-618	
T'ANG	618-906	
LIAO	907-1125	
NORTHERN SUNG	960-1127	
SOUTHERN SUNG	1128-1279	
YUAN (Mongols)	1260-1368	

MING	1368-1644

Important Ming periods

Hsüan-tê	1426-1435
Chêng-t'ung	1436-1449
Ch'êng-hua	1465-1487
Chêng-tê	1506-1521
Chia-ching	1522-1566
Wan-li	1573-1619

CH'ING	1644-1912

Important Ch'ing periods

K'ang-hsi	1662-1722
Yung-chêng	1723-1735
Ch'ien-lung	1736-1795
Chia-ch'ing	1796-1821
Tao-kuang	1822-1850

REPUBLIC	1912
PEOPLE'S REPUBLIC	1950

Ceramics

Chinese

NEOLITHIC

CHANG

CHOU

HAN

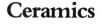

a) Neolithic urn with painted decoration from Pan-Shan, Kansu Province; ht. 15½" (39.5 cm.)

Pre-historic pottery (about 2500-3000 BC) has been found in many parts of north and central China, particularly in Kansu, Shensi, Shansi, and Honan. Those from central China are of red clay covered with burnished white slip with the upper part of the body decorated in black geometrical designs. The pots from the grave fields of Pan-Shan are richly painted, their necks either high and cylindrical, or short and flaring. The handles seem disproportionately small. This buff earthenware urn has a globular body, two loop handles, and a cylindrical neck with spreading lip. It is painted in black and maroon with spiral scrolls and chequered roundels.

b) White earthenware jar of Shang dynasty (1523-1028 BC); ht. 13 1/16" (33.2 cm.).

In addition to grey and red wares, Shang dynasty potters produced a white ware of such fine texture that it has been mistaken for porcelain. These wares have a pinkish tinge and are often quite hard and heavy. Although the kaolin content is high, the body lacks the vitreosity of true porcelain and is brittle and fragile. The vessels are beautifully made; many, like this jar, reflect contemporary bronze shapes.

Here, the decoration comprises a narrow band of dissolved dragons round the shoulder, with alternating plain and decorated chevrons on the body and three pierced animal heads—one near the base; two on the shoulder.

---

c) Covered glazed vase of bronze form with impressed decoration from the Chin tsun tombs at Loyang, Honan. Late Chou dynasty, c. 800-700 BC; ht. 7¾" (19.4 cm.)

By the third century BC finely potted, high-fired vessels of red clay were being made; some are covered with a thin greenish or greyish glaze, which is generally perished. The slight glaze on some earlier wares is thought to be accidentally caused by wood ash falling on the pottery during firing. Late Chou wares have characteristic bronze forms and this typical example is glazed with olive green. There are two pierced animal heads on the shoulder with a band of impressed design above and below. The lid has three bosses, a similar impressed design around the edge, and in the centre.

d) Basin of bronze form; Yüeh ware of Shao-hsing type (probably Han dynasty); dia. 9¾" (24.4 cm.).

Stoneware and porcelain with an olive-green glaze was made in various parts of China; one kiln site known to produce this type was at Chiu-yen in the Shao-hsing district, the modern Yüeh-chou in Chekiang. It has been identified as the Yüeh ware referred to in Chinese literature, and was made between the first and sixth centuries AD.

This basin of bronze form has three animal mask feet; on the sides are four *tao tieh* masks in relief, and a wave pattern is incised inside the bowl. There are spur marks on the base.

Ceramics

Chinese

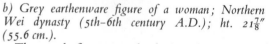

a) Lead-glazed hill jar and cover; Han dynasty, late 1st century BC or 1st century AD; ht. 9½″ (24.1 cm.).

The lead-glazed wares of the Han dynasty have been found throughout North China. The low-fired soft lead yellow glaze often appears tawny-brown over the red body, and a splendid silvery iridescence due to the degradation of the glaze through burial is characteristic.

This 'hill jar' is typical. Made of red earthenware, it stands on three feet in the shape of bears, and is decorated in moulded relief under a yellowish-brown lead glaze. A frieze around the side shows a hunting scene with mounted and foot archers, and tiger masks with pendant rings. The cover is in the form of mountains with animals, birds and a mounted archer on the slopes.

b) Grey earthenware figure of a woman; Northern Wei dynasty (5th-6th century A.D.); ht. 21⅞″ (55.6 cm.).

The tomb figures made during the Northern Wei dynasty are amongst the finest produced in China. Towards the end of the Han dynasty, the type of tomb figures changed, warriors and priests becoming more numerous.

This grey earthenware figure, slender and tall, is typical of the Wei dynasty. The woman has a serene expression and she wears a low-cut dress with long sleeves, belted at the waist. Her clothing is indicated by incised lines.

c) Covered jar with blue lead glaze, T'ang dynasty (8th century); ht. 16⅕″ (41.2 cm.).

The beauty of the T'ang glazes is very evident on the vases, jars, bowls and dishes made as funerary wares. Similar wares were made for everyday use, some reflecting the style of Sassanian metal ware, their stamped designs filled in with glazes of different colours. However, the potters usually let the colours run and mix with each other: examples of dappled amber, green and white glazes are common; blue was more rarely used.

Single colour glazes were also used effectively, running unevenly and finishing in an irregular line short of the base. If the glaze was applied in several layers, an uneven effect was produced and this earthenware ovoid jar with domed cover is a splendid example of this technique. It is covered with an applied deep blue glaze which stops just short of the base.

d) Pottery dancers, T'ang dynasty; ht. 7⅞″ (20.1 cm.) and 8⅛″ (20.6 cm.).

During the T'ang dynasty, pottery figures continued to be made for burial, including earth spirits, attendants, tomb guardians, musicians, dancers and animals—particularly horses and camels—reflecting aspects of everyday life. Generally the T'ang figures are made of a whitish or pinkish pottery although some are dark grey.

The unglazed figures were often painted in red, green, blue and black over a white slip and sometimes gilded; they must have been brilliant originally, but burial has sobered their appearance. These graceful dancers, their hair dressed in a high whorl, have long sleeves and scarves over their shoulders. The unglazed white pottery shows traces of red and black pigment.

a) Saddled horse of T'ang dynasty; ht. 27" (68.6 cm.), lgth. 27".

The T'ang glazed figures, since they have suffered less by burial than the unglazed, display vividly the brilliant colours used by the potters. The glazes—dappled amber, green and white with the occasional addition of blue, in combination—give a splendid effect.

T'ang camels and horses are well known but other tomb animals include ducks, geese, pigs and oxen. This splendid standing horse has a cream glaze with amber striped mane, textured green-glazed saddle-cloth and amber saddle; the dark-brown harness has elaborate amber studs and moulded green trappings; the hooves are amber, the tail bound in green.

b) Bowl covered with an olive-green glaze—Yüeh ware, probably 10th century; dia. $5\frac{11}{16}$" (14.5 cm.).

Wares similar to those from Shao-hsing have been found some twenty miles away at Shang-lin-hu, dating from around the end of the T'ang dynasty. These wares, which continued into the Five Dynasties (907-960), are generally incised or carved and covered with an olive-green or olive-brown glaze. Many have close affinities with Northern celadon.

This bowl is carved on the outside with a petal design; inside are incised two confronting phoenixes with a petal border round the rim. It is covered with an olive-green glaze.

---

c) White porcelain vase of Northern Sung dynasty (960-1127); ht. $14\frac{3}{8}$" (36.6 cm.).

Ting ware was made at kilns in Hopei during the Northern Sung dynasty, reaching perfection towards the turn of the 11th century. It has a white, often opaque body which may show a reddish-orange glow to transmitted light, where thin; its creamy white glaze congeals into thick, brownish globes, known as 'tear-drops', on the underside of bowls and dishes, and towards the base of vases.

This prunus vase (*mei p'ing*) with its swelling shoulder tapering to the foot is a fine example. Often called the 'rain drop vase', its form and decoration, an incised design of peonies and foliage, with bands of petals around the base and shoulder, reflects the love of nature of the Sung scholar artists.

d) Northern celadon (Northern Sung dynasty—960-1127) probably from Yao-chou, late 11th century; dia. 7" (17.8 cm.).

The term Northern celadon covers a number of closely related stonewares made at various kilns, many unlocated, in North China during the Northern Sung dynasty and even earlier. They have a distinctive olive-green glaze and closely resemble Ting in form and decoration which may be incised, carved or moulded. Like Ting, they were at their best in the late 11th century. Recently two kiln sites have been excavated at Lin-ju in Honan, and Yao-chou in Shensi.

This Northern celadon box, with olive-green glaze, is decorated with a carved design of peony scrolls enclosed by foliage scrolls and petals, a typical Sung design.

a) Stoneware globular jar, Northern Sung dynasty (11th–12th century); ht. 3¾″ (9.5 cm.).

Chün wares take their name from Chün-Chou, the modern Yü Hsien in Honan, but there is evidence that they were also made elsewhere in North China. At their best, they rival Ju wares but vary considerably in quality, although even the rougher types are attractive. They were made from the Sung dynasty through the Yüan to Ming.

Tradition has it that the numbered bulb bowls were made specially for the Palace. The body is generally dark grey but burns to a warm buff where free of glaze. The colour of the glaze (often opalescent) varies from rich blue to bluish grey, sometimes suffused with crimson, a technique that the potters skilfully controlled. This fine jar has a thick turquoise glaze with large purple patches.

b) Stoneware ewer, Northern Sung dynasty (11th century); ht. 8″ (20.4 cm.).

The term Tz'u-chou embraces a group of wares made in North China from the 10th century to the present day. A rugged stoneware, they contrast sharply with the refined white Ting wares. Some are decorated with black, brown or white glazes, others are painted in red and green enamels whilst some have reserved or *sgraffiato* designs.

They are of interest for their beauty and freedom of decoration, and as illustrations of the underglaze and overglaze painting techniques so brilliantly developed during the Ming dynasty. It is not easy to date Tz'ü-chou wares but this grey stoneware ewer with *sgraffiato* peony scrolls, carved through a white slip, is a splendid 11th century Sung example.

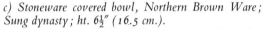

c) Stoneware covered bowl, Northern Brown Ware; Sung dynasty; ht. 6½″ (16.5 cm.).

Those brown and black Sung wares made in the north, often called Honan wares, were undoubtedly made elsewhere and some are closely related to the Tz'u-chou wares. Their beauty lies in the lustrous brown-black glaze often painted with rust brown.

Other northern types have a brownish-black glaze with oil-spot markings. Some tall bottles and jars have sharp-edged vertical ribs of white slip applied to the body which show through the glaze. A white glaze is applied to the lips of some bowls and occasionally to the inside of a vessel. This covered bowl with straight sides is painted rust-brown on a lustrous black glaze.

d) Stoneware bowl stand, Northern Sung dynasty (early 12th century); dia. 6⅜″ (16.3 cm.).

Although Ju ware has been identified from literary evidence, the kiln site has not yet been found. Ju was made specially for the Northern Sung Court during a few years at the beginning of the 12th century, just before the Court fled to the south in 1127 AD. It is thus extremely rare and only about 30 pieces are known in the west.

All are of high quality and this bowl-stand is no exception. The five-lobed saucer rim is carved above and below in a design of overlapping petals on a circular spreading foot, and it is covered with a beautiful crackled greyish-blue glaze.

a) Stoneware tea bowl, Southern Sung dynasty (1129–1279); dia. 4⅞″ (12.4 cm.).

This tea bowl comes from Kian fu, the ancient Chi-chou (south of Ching-tê Chen, the great pottery centre in Kiangsi). Surviving Kian wares consist largely of conical or splayed bowls, and are frequently damaged. The interior of this bowl is decorated with two butterflies and two phoenixes around a central rosette and has a dark brown glaze.

Sometimes leaf patterns were made by pressing actual leaves into the glaze; other Kian bowls have on the outside white slip streaks or spots incorporated in the glaze; a streaky effect inside the bowl was obtained by spraying slip into the still molten glaze.

b) Carved Ch'ing-p'ai porcelain bowl with pale blue glaze; Sung dynasty; dia. 7¹¹⁄₁₆″ (19.5 cm.).

Ch'ing-p'ai embraces a group of similar wares with a pale-blue glaze ranging from bluish-green to near white. The whitish-yellow body, often flecked with brown iron specks, is very translucent. Made at Ching-tê-chên and at kilns in Fukien and in the vicinity of South China ports, they were exported in large quantities throughout the Middle and Far East. Decoration was incised, carved and moulded, perfected towards the end of the Sung dynasty. Fine quality Ch'ing-p'ai continued well into the Yüan dynasty.

This fine hexagonal Sung bowl with foliate rim, is carved inside with an althea flower; the glaze is translucent pale blue.

---

c) left: Celadon porcelain vase, Southern Sung dynasty; ht. 10″ (25.4 cm.).

This mallet-shaped porcelain vase, of Imperial quality, has a long tubular neck slightly everted at the mouth and is covered with a bluish opaque greyish-green celadon glaze with a faint crackle.

d) centre: Porcelain dish with relief design, Yüan dynasty; dia. 16⅞″ (43.1 cm.).

The Lung Ch'uan porcelain dish with wide flat base, moulded sides and flat rim has a biscuit design in relief, burnt brown, of a dragon surrounded by clouds chasing a flaming pearl, and around the rim seventeen prunus blossoms. Around the well is a carved water design.

e) right: Porcelain dish with incised design, Ming dynasty (15th century); dia. 18″ (45.7 cm.).

The large porcelain dish is decorated inside with an incised peony encircled by radiating petals. It is covered with a green glaze except for an unglazed ring on the base, the central area inscribed in Persian, 'Husain Khan melk' (the property of Husain Khan).

The southern celadons include these from the Lung Ch'uan kilns in south Chekiang. These three pieces illustrate the wide range of Lung Ch'uan celadons from the Sung dynasty to the 15th century.

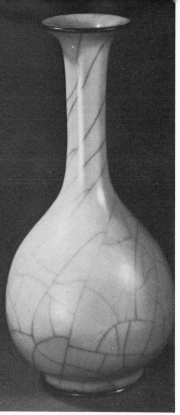

a) *Stoneware vase of Southern Sung dynasty (early 12th century); ht. 7⅛″ (18.2 cm.).*

With the Southern Sung Imperial Court established at Hangchou, there were set up in the neighbourhood potteries making wares for Court use, first at *Hsiu-nei-ssu* ('Phoenix Hill') kiln, and subsequently at *Chiao-t'an* ('Suburban Altar') kiln.

These kilns made 'Kuan' (official) ware, the main characteristics of which are a very thin, dark, hard body covered with several layers of glaze, in such a manner that the body is frequently thinner than the glaze. In colour, this celadon glaze varies from a deep bluish-green to lavender and ash-grey, and often has an irregular crackle.

The stoneware vase illustrated here, with its pear-shaped body, slender neck and spreading lip, is covered with a greyish blue crackled glaze, and has a metal-bound mouth and foot-rim. A splendid example of Kuan ware, it reflects the taste of a cultured and sophisticated Court.

Ceramics

Chinese

SOUTHERN SUNG
YÜAN

b) *Shu fu bowl with rounded sides and everted lip, moulded and incised decoration; Yüan dynasty, 14th century; dia. 8″ (20.3 cm.).*

Shu fu developed during the Yüan dynasty from the Sung white wares, in particular *Ch'ing-p'ai*. The term *Shu fu* is derived from the two characters denoting official ware, which frequently appear on this type, although other characters are also used. The decoration, whether moulded or incised, is often barely visible beneath the thick unctuous blue glaze. The inside of this typical bowl has moulded decoration of flying geese with the character *fu* (happiness), and *lu* (emoluments), in slip beneath the bluish semi-opaque glaze. The outside is incised with scrolls at the rim, and five lotus panels at the base.

c) *Temple vase painted in underglaze blue; Yüan dynasty (1260–1368); ht: 25″ (63.6 cm.).*

Early Chinese blue and white porcelain was developed during the Yüan dynasty; though there is a tradition that it was made during the Sung dynasty, supporting evidence is lacking. Blue and white attributed to the early 14th century is generally similar in form to the Yüan celadons such as covered jars, bottles, vases and stem-cups. The freely drawn decoration consists chiefly of flowers, sprays of leaves and scrolls in blue-black with an occasional hint of grey-brown. The potting has little of the Sung quality

A notable exception, however, are the David temple vases, the only fully documented 14th century blue and white pieces known, and proof that complete mastery of the medium had been reached. This vase, one of a pair, is decorated in brilliant underglaze blue; around the body is a dragon among waves and clouds, on the foot are bands of waves, a peony scroll and panels with emblems. There is a lotus scroll on the narrow shoulder and above this, a design of plantain leaves, including on one side the date equivalent to 1351 AD. Around the mouth is a chrysanthemum scroll. This vase shows the wave pattern in its early form.

d) *Early blue and white porcelain stem-cup; horizontally grooved stem with spreading foot, rounded bowl and everted rim, Yüan dynasty (1300–1350); ht. 3⅞″ (9.8 cm.)*

The sturdy *shu fu* wares with their characteristic slip and moulded decoration displaced during the Yüan dynasty the delicate *Ch'ing-p'ai* wares, and from the *shu fu* the early 'blue and white' porcelain was developed. Many of the earliest pieces still retain raised slip or moulded decoration. This stem-cup is painted on the outside with a blue three-clawed dragon. The bowl has a flaming pearl inside, a classic scroll encircling the rim. A transparent, blue-tinged *shu fu* glaze covers two four-clawed dragons moulded in low relief. This stem-cup provides a link between *shu fu* wares of Yüan and early blue and white.

a) Rare ewer painted in copper red; late 14th century, ht. 12¾" (32.3 cm.).

Red designs using copper as the colouring agent were also made at this time. Copper red was, however, difficult to obtain and the potters seldom achieved good results.

This rare, fine ewer is one of an interesting and very scarce group of underglaze copper red wares (sometimes with underglaze blue). Pear-shaped, its long spout is connected to the neck by a strap. Two ogival panels enclose a stylised floral scroll, surrounded by sprays of flowering plants. Petals and a fret border ring at the foot, scrolls and fern fronds border the neck, with scrolls on both the handle and foot.

b) Prunus vase (mei p'ing) of blue and white porcelain, painted with parrots and flowering branches; Ming c. 1400–1450, ht. 13" (33.0 cm.).

Between 1351 AD and the Hsuan tê period (1426–1435), there were considerable changes in blue and white design and technique. The early 15th century wares, large vases, bowls etc. are always unmarked. The pigment was applied in broad strokes over the simplest outlines; later, carefully drawn outlines were filled in with a uniform wash. In these early pieces, the thick application caused depressions in the surface, known as 'heaped and piled'.

This prunus vase (*mei p'ing*) is particularly fine and quite distinct in form and decoration with parrots on flowering branches above a peony scroll and a diaper pattern on the shoulder.

c) Stem-cup with red glaze; Ming, early 15th century; ht. 4⁵⁄₁₁" (10.7 cm.).

Although monochromes in the Sung tradition—particularly celadons—continued to be made for a time in the Ming dynasty, by the 15th century they had been generally replaced by the fine quality blue and white porcelain made at Ching-tê-chen in Kiangsi. However, Ming monochromes produced include bowls and dishes in yellow (an Imperial colour), of the finest quality, and others covered with turquoise, cobalt blue and green glazes.

The red wares obtained by using copper are remarkable by any standards, and this stem-cup is no exception. It has a widely flared mouth-rim and a hollow stem spreading slightly at the foot. It is covered with a brilliant copper-red glaze unevenly streaked and paling to white at the rim. The glaze inside the stem is white.

d) Palace bowl, painted in blue; Ch'eng hua period (1465–1487); dia. 5¹¹⁄₁₆" (14.5 cm.).

The reign of Ch'eng-hua marks the second great 15th century ceramic period. One group of these wares follows closely the traditional 15th century subjects and styles, another introduces a style completely new and consisting mainly of the famous palace bowls, their characteristics including delicate floral scrolls and thinner, smoother glaze.

Although the drawing is less vigorous and certain than the earlier wares, it has much charm. The flowers and foliage are lightly stylised and difficult to identify: frequently a flower appears with an unrelated leaf. The bowl illustrated has a slightly flared rim and is painted inside and out in underglaze blue with a lily scroll and, in the centre, a floral scroll.

119

Ceramics

Chinese
MING

a) Jar with polychrome decoration; Ming dynasty, Ch'êng-hua period (1465–1487); dia. 5⅛" (13.0 cm.).

The *tou ts'ai* wares which are decorated in underglaze blue delicately combined with overglaze enamel colours, red, green, yellow and pale aubergine, are perhaps the most famous innovation of the Ming potters. Briefly *tou ts'ai* means not so much contrasted colours as appropriateness of decoration. This style was introduced in the Ch'êng-hua period (1465–1487) but subsequently lapsed until the end of the 16th century when a few pieces were made, and was then later revived in the 18th century when Ch'êng-hua pieces were reproduced. Most *tou ts'ai* pieces, although small, are of fine quality and the chicken cups are particularly famous.

This beautiful potiche, with its short straight neck and wide mouth decorated in *tou ts'ai* style, with rocks, growing plants and butterflies, outlined in underglaze blue and with overglaze washes of green, yellow, aubergine and red enamels, is an outstanding example. (In the Fogg Museum of Art is a Yung-chêng period (1723–1735) copy.)

b) Rectangular box painted in blue; Ming dynasty, Chêng-tê period (1506–1521); ht. 7½" (19.1 cm.).

During the reign of Chêng-tê, state affairs were mainly controlled by the Mohammedan eunuchs. In addition to the Imperial wares, nearly all dishes, bowls and ewers are decorated with dragons and lotus scrolls, there is an interesting group of blue and white known as 'Mohammedan wares' bearing formal scrolls enclosing medallions with Arabic or Persian inscriptions. These pieces were probably made in the Imperial factory, since they bear the mark of the Emperor in good calligraphy, and include brush rests, boxes and articles for the writing table as well as various types of vases.

This covered box is decorated with floral scrolls enclosing circular medallions with Arabic inscriptions. That on the cover reads 'the reins are no use to a blind man' and that on the base 'a fool finds no contentment'.

c) Leys jar with polychrome decoration; Ming, Chêng-tê period (1506–1521); dia. 5¾" (14.7 cm.).

San ts'ai means three colours and has been applied to the green, yellow and aubergine decorated wares of the Ming dynasty. The term is also applied to the three colours, green, yellow and white, of T'ang pottery. There are, however, fundamental differences in technique: the glaze of T'ang wares was applied direct to the unfired body; for Ming wares, these colours were applied to the biscuit porcelain body which thus required a second firing.

Although probably not introduced before the mid-15th century, the method increased in popularity from the Chêng-tê period. This leys jar, with bulbous body and widely spreading neck decorated in green and yellow enamels on the biscuit with an incised design of dragons, clouds, pearls and lotus panels, is early 16th century.

d) Bowl with enamel colours in biscuit; Ming, 16th century; dia. 7" (17.8 cm.).

The Ming *fa hua* wares are perhaps the most spectacular of the polychromes. Their main characteristic is the use of threads of slip or clay in the style of cloisonné to confine the different colours used in decoration, often in combination with incised designs. Although the *fa hua* wares are earlier than *san ts'ai*, they are closely related. Their range of colours, however, differs from that of the *san ts'ai* group but green, aubergine and yellow are used, the dominant background colour being either deep cobalt blue or a brilliant turquoise. This stoneware bowl shows clearly the use of the 'cloisonné' technique. Decorated with lotus sprays in aubergine and white against a turquoise background, it is truly 'dazzling to the eye'.

a) Bowl painted in blue; Ming dynasty (2nd half, 16th century); dia. $5\frac{11}{16}''$ (14.5 cm.).

Very large quantities of porcelain were made during the reigns of Chia-ching, Lung Ch'ing and Wan-li—over one hundred thousand pieces each year with a thousand of one design. The deteriorating quality of the Imperial porcelain was largely offset, however, by the emergence of new styles with great artistic merits, based mainly on landscape paintings.

This bowl, inscribed 'made for the President of the six Boards', is an example of the non-Imperial ware, as fine as any Imperial piece. The bowl, with its rim mounted in metal, is decorated on the outside with a landscape of mountains and clouds; inside is a central panel depicting a river scene.

b) Wine jar with polychrome decoration; Ming dynasty, Chia-ching period (1522-1566); ht. 17'' (43.2 cm.), dia. 17'' (43.2 cm.)

The term *Wu-ts'ai* (five colours) is defined nowadays as decoration used in washes, with overglaze enamels and with the outlines of the decoration drawn in overglaze red or sepia or black. Although the *wu ts'ai* palette first appeared in the Chia-ching period, it became even more popular during that of Lung-ch'ing and continued into the Ching dynasty.

This covered fish jar with its wide mouth, short straight neck and wide shoulders is a fine example of *wu ts'ai* style decoration. Round the body are fish swimming among lotus and other water plants and there is a band of *ju-i* motif on the shoulder and of petals around the base.

---

c) Octagonal jar with polychrome decoration; Ming dynasty, mid 16th century; ht. 15'' (38.1 cm.)

The 'red and green' family were exported in quantity to Japan where the gilded types were popular and to the Near East. They reached Europe in the 16th century: several survive in Elizabethan silver mounts. Although few pieces bear a Chêng-tê (1506-1521) reign mark, many carry that of Chia-ching (1522-1566)—testimony to their increase in popularity.

This octagonal jar is decorated in red, green and yellow enamels with designs in gilt of the Eight Buddhist Emblems and lotus scrolls; it has red and green borders in a rectangular frame of red diaper patterns with sections of chrysanthemums in the corners. On the shoulders are *ju-i* shaped panels enclosed in lozenge diaper and inscribed in gold, which may be translated 'Happiness like the Eastern Sea, longevity like the Southern Mountains'.

d) Vase decorated in blue and white; Ming dynasty, Chia-ching period (1522-1566); ht. $17\frac{1}{2}''$ (44.5 cm.).

Blue and white of the reign of Chia-ching is noted for its fine dark purplish blue, called 'Mohammedan blue'. Chia-ching was a Taoist and consequently the subjects chosen then for decoration show this strong influence. Thus the eight immortals and other Taoist figures are often depicted, whilst the emblems of immortality: the pine tree, deer and crane are used in various combinations.

A favourite device is a peach tree, its trunk twisted into the character *shou* (the symbol for long life). This double gourd vase shows a peach tree so twisted whilst the lower gourd is decorated with cranes.

a) Box painted in blue; Ming dynasty, Wan-li period (1573–1619); dia. 4⅛″ (10.4 cm.).

Imperial porcelain of the Wan-li period followed closely the style of Chia-ching and the reign saw a steady and rapidly increasing deterioration in the quality of blue and white. Not only were supplies of high-grade clay more difficult to obtain but, unfortunately, the attitude of the Court restricted porcelain designs. Mass production of vast quantities of porcelain during this and the preceding reigns inevitably led to artistic decline. Many wares were produced for export to Tibet, and carry Tibetan inscriptions.

There was also an unfortunate tendency to twist the branches of trees into Chinese characters. This circular box and cover is decorated with a dragon and a phoenix among fungus scrolls, whilst on the cover there are four medallions with the characters *feng shen yu t'aio*, 'may the winds be favourable and the rain seasonable'.

b) Swatow dish, decorated in red, green and turquoise enamels; late 16th–17th century Ming; dia. 14¼″ (36.2 cm.)

The red and green Swatow wares stem from the red and green painting of Sung and Yüan, which, with a change in style, continued into the Ming dynasty, resembling the later Ming red and green wares. Exported to south-east Asia, India and Japan, they were made for everyday use, and decorated with diapers and panels of red outlined in green. Plants, (especially chrysanthemums) animals, birds, dragons and phoenixes, were painted in a free style. Dark turquoise, blue and lavender glazes were also used, and in addition to landscapes the decoration often has a maritime flavour depicting ships, fish, etc.

c) Peach-bloom vase, K'ang-hsi period (1662–1722); ht. 8¼″ (21.1 cm.).

An innovation of the Ch'ing dynasty was the production of high fired monochromes in a variety of colours, showing little sign of Ming influence. New ranges of colour were introduced, one of the most unusual being the 'peach blooms', ranging from a reddish pink to various shades of brown and green, often intermingled, including celadons and moss-greens with scarcely a hint of red.

This example has an oviform body with moulded petal pattern around the ower part, and long expanding neck. It is covered with a light pinkish glaze with darker mottling. The six character reign-mark of K'ang-hsi is inscribed on the base in underglaze blue.

d) Famille jaune vase, K'ang-hsi period (1662–1722); ht. 20¼″ (51.6 cm.).

Although no new techniques in decoration were developed in *San ts'ai* style, the existing techniques were extended during the Ch'ing dynasty, and applied to the decoration of large vases, particularly with black or yellow grounds. These are known as *famille noire*, and *famille jaune*.

The soft quality of this decoration on the biscuit is well shown by this rectangualr vase with tall neck expanding towards the mouth, dragon handles, painted flowers of the four seasons in *famille verte* enamels on the biscuit, and yellow ground (*famille jaune*).

a) Brush-pot of I-Hsing ware; late 17th or early 18th century; ht. 4⅕" (10.7 cm.).

Unless their products were celebrated for quality, it was seldom economic for the numerous potteries throughout China to market them beyond their immediate neighbourhood. I-Hsing in Kiangsu Province is famous for its red-pottery unglazed teapots, akin to stoneware, made during the Ming and Ch'ing dynasties. These small teapots were exported in large numbers with tea, at the end of the 17th century, and influenced the design of early English silver teapots.

In addition, I-Hsing wares include brush-rests and brush-pots for the scholar's study. This brush-pot of unglazed brown stoneware is in the form of a hollowed tree trunk with branches and prunus blossom in relief. The potter's mark *Yang lu Ch'ien* is incised on the base.

b) Famille verte dish of K'ang-hsi period (early 18th century); dia. 9⅞" (25.1 cm.).

Early in the Ch'ing dynasty, the underglaze blue, characteristic of Ming, was replaced by a violet-blue enamel which was generally opaque and unsuitable for the large splashes of colour so effective in Ming wares. Blue, therefore, became subservient to the brilliant transparent green enamels of the splendid and decorative wares termed *famille verte*.

However, a particular group of *famille verte* is decorated mainly in red and green with no blue. An example is this plate inscribed within a gold brocade border *wan shou wu chiang*, 'a myriad longevities without end'; these were made to commemorate the birthday of the K'ang-hsi Emperor in 1713. The centre is decorated with a river scene of ducks, plants and rocks.

---

c). Famille rose, ruby back dish of Yung-chêng period (1723–1735); dia. 8" (20.3 cm.).

An important development during the Ch'ing dynasty was the introduction of a pink enamel deriving its colouring from gold, a technique discovered in Europe during the mid-17th century. This new style, called by the Chinese *Yang ts'ai* (foreign colours), is known as *famille rose*. Early examples appeared in China about 1721, but the technique only reached perfection during the Yung-chêng period.

This 'ruby back' dish is a fine example; made of egg-shell porcelain, it has rounded sides and is decorated in *famille rose* enamels with a singing bird on a branch of flowering magnolia, the outside covered with a ruby-pink enamel.

d) Blanc de Chine figure of Kuan Yin, 18th century; ht. 15" (38.4 cm.)

It is not known when *blanc de chine* porcelain was first made at Te-hua in the province of Fukien. Although many of the finest pieces have been dated to the 17th century, the kilns may have existed there even earlier. It resembles opaque glass and is generally a cream colour although there are many fine gradations in shade. Its beauty lies generally in form and colour, decoration being limited to relief ornament and incised designs. Dating is not easy and colour an unreliable guide.

Since it gives an extremely sharp moulding, *blanc de chine* is very suitable for making figures. Here Kuan Yin, the Goddess of Mercy, is seated on a rock with her hands clasping her raised right knee: her eyes are half closed in meditation. She is wearing a long voluminous robe and a shawl over her shoulders whilst by her side is a bundle of three scrolls. The impressed potter's mark is that of *I Mo-tzu*.

a) Celadon vase; Yung-Chêng period (1723–1735); ht. 10¼" (26.2 cm.).

During the Ch'ing dynasty (particularly in the reigns of Yung-Chêng and Ch'ien Lung), the traditional Chinese reverence for the past led to some very fine copies of the classical Sung and Ming wares. T'ang Ying, the gifted Director of the Imperial factory, compiled a list of fifty-eight types of decoration used in Impérial porcelain between 1729 and 1732, about half imitating older designs.

This vase with its tapered cylindrical body, horizontally ribbed sides, sloping shoulders and short neck is covered with a semi-opaque bluish-grey celadon glaze after the style of Sung *Kuan* yao. Under the glaze on the base is the six character mark of Yung-Chêng.

b) Famille rose armorial plate; Yung-chêng period (c. 1730); dia. 9⅞" (25.1 cm.).

During the Ch'ing dynasty, the porcelain exported in large quantities greatly influenced the development of European pottery and porcelain. Some export ware was made to special order, many pieces being decorated with armorial bearings. Although not always of high quality, these pieces have great historical interest for they often indicate very closely their date of manufacture, particularly where they commemorate a marriage.

This plate painted in *famille rose* enamels shows the arms of Lee quartering those of Astley. The crest is a squirrel cracking a nut and an oak branch 'fructed all proper'. The border contains views of London and Canton.

Ceramics

Chinese
CH'ING

c) Apple-green vase of early 18th century; ht. 9.4" (23.9 cm.)

Monochrome glazes fired at a medium or low temperature were a feature of Ch'ing dynasty porcelain and include a variety of colours such as green, aubergine and yellow. 'Apple green' was obtained by superimposing a translucent green enamel on a greyish-white crackled felspathic glaze. An example is this vase in bronze form with a flattened pear-shaped body and two tubular handles covered with a green enamel over a greyish-white crackled glaze. The base, which is unglazed, is dressed with a brown wash.

d) Porcelain vase Ku Yüeh Hsuan; Ch'ien Lung (1736–1795); ht. 3½" (9.6 cm.).

The term Ku Yüeh Hsuan is applied to a small group of Imperial porcelains of the finest quality. Translated as 'Ancient Moon Terrace', its meaning is not clear despite many attempts to determine it.

The first pieces are rare and invariably inscribed with a poem in black enamel accompanied by red seals, and varying from piece to piece. This small vase is decorated with orchids and wild roses and a poem with the seals *chia li* (beautiful), *ssŭ shih* (four seasons) and *ch'ang ch'un* (enduring spring). The poem has been translated:

It is their purpose to hold fragrance,
And in due season to display their
many colours

e) Bowl decorated in enamel colours; Tao Kuang (1821–1850); dia. 6" (15.2 cm.)

During the reign of Tao Kuang (1821–1850), porcelain deteriorated both in body and glaze whilst the mixed enamels of the *famille verte* and *famille rose* then in vogue were apt to be overpowered by the iron red. Nevertheless there are some fine imitations of K'ang-hsi underglaze blue and *wu-ts'ai* enamels. This bowl decorated in enamel colours was made for a granddaughter of Tao Kuang who married a Mongolian Prince of the Tumed banner. It was made at the Imperial factories.

Opposite:
Porcelain bottle decorated in enamel colours in Ku-yüeh style; Chien-lung period; China, 1736–95.

Korean Ceramics Introduction

Korea was originally divided into three small states: Koguryō in the north, Paekche to the south, Silla in the south-east. Few, if any, wares appear to be earlier than the Silla dynasty (founded 57 B.C.) and there is scant evidence of ceramic remains from either Koguryō or Paekche. By the mid-seventh century A.D., Silla had absorbed both her neighbours.

The majority of early Korean wares are tomb wares, but undoubtedly domestic wares were not dissimilar. Early Silla ceramics include ash-grey stonewares, some resembling Han bronzes, and a distinctive range of covered vases, stem-cups and covered circular boxes. The later Silla unglazed wares recall those of T'ang China, with their impressed and incised decoration of rosettes, circles, trefoils, chevrons, etc. Glazed wares, similar to Chinese proto-porcelain, with olive-brown glazes and the same sort of decoration, were also made.

During the Koryo dynasty, excellent ceramics were produced, including some of the finest celadons ever made and, in particular, some notable inlaid wares. The former reflect the Chinese influence of Yüeh, the Northern celadons, with their incised and impressed decoration, and the Southern celadons of Lung-ch'üan and nearby kilns. White wares resembling Sung Ting, but Korean in form and feeling, were also made. Inlaid decorated Koryo wares are purely Korean in shape and style and are quite distinctive; those in reverse inlay are particularly splendid. Painted wares were made towards the end of the Koryo dynasty and although influenced by the Chinese wares from Tz'u-chou, they have their own characteristics. Some black, brown and cream-glazed stonewares found in Korea are Chinese; nevertheless similar pieces were undoubtedly made in Korea from the tenth century onwards.

During the Yi dynasty the Koryo style continued for a time but eventually was replaced by the Punchŏng group of wares. An important characteristic of these often very fine wares is the use of a white slip, either as a base for painting in iron-brown in the Tz'u-chou style, or for *sgraffiato* type decoration. Other Yi wares include fine white porcelain, especially in the early 18th century, as well as blue and white.

Although the Korean ceramics often reflect Chinese influence and inspiration, they remain nevertheless distinctly individual in form and feeling.

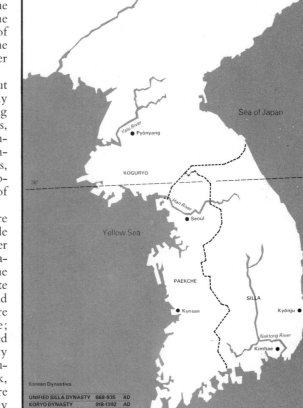

Opposite:
Bowl with incised decoration; Korea, 12th century.
Wine cup and stand with incised decoration; Korea, 12th–13th century.

127

a) Koryō celadon wine pot and cover with incised, carved, and moulded lotus design; 13th century; ht. 7" (17.8 cm.).

Some of the most beautiful glazed pottery ever produced was made during the Koryō period. The celadons are particularly famous and rival the Chinese Sung wares in form and glaze. Chinese influence is strong, stemming first from the Yüeh wares and subsequently from both the northern celadon and southern Lungch'nan wares. These Koryō celadons reached perfection from about the mid-12th century to the end of the 13th century over a period of some 160 years. This splendid wine pot and cover is typically Korean in feeling although Chinese influence is apparent.

Ceramics

Korean
KORYŌ

b) Inlaid Koryō mae-pyŏng; late 12th century; ht. 15½" (39.4 cm.).

During the Koryō period, both black wares and white wares as well as celadons were made and all show strong Chinese influence. Typically Korean, however, are the inlaid celadon wares which are perhaps the outstanding achievement of the Koryō potters. This form of decoration is known as *sanggam* and was first introduced early in the 12th century. Freely-drawn designs of ducks and cranes, peony and chrysanthemum sprays, and willows replaced the traditional Buddhist lotus. This celadon vase (*mae-pyŏng*) with its inlaid decoration of cranes under willows illustrated the wonderful freedom of design often attained.

c) Reverse inlaid Koryō covered wine pot; 12th century; ht. 10⅞" (27.6 cm.).

Some celadons were decorated in an elaborate reverse method whereby the background is inlaid in white, or more rarely in black, whilst the design is in celadon. This is most effective particularly where the whole vessel is so treated. Such vessels however, are scarce and more frequently this technique is confined to narrow strips of decoration around the edge, often in the form of a border of overlapping lotus petals. This rare and beautiful celadon wine pot and cover has an overall floral design in reverse inlay.

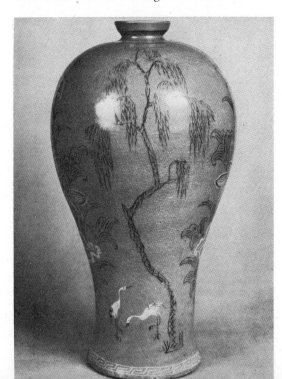

a) Punch'ŏng deep bowl and cover decorated with flower heads inlaid with brushed slip; 15th century; dia. 7 3/16" (18.3 cm.).

The early Yi vessels owe much both in form and glaze, to the Koryō wares. Although incised and painted decoration replaced inlay, it was not immediately abandoned. The term *punch'ŏng*, indicating a green or bluish celadon type glaze, embraces a large group of stonewares made with a greyish clay somewhat coarser than that in Koryō celadons. The types are generally distinguished by Japanese terms. *Mishima*, or *koyame-de* (almanac ware) is decorated with a stamped ground of white mesh or hatching known as 'rope curtain' pattern, like this covered bowl which has 'Sŏngju Changhŭng-go' (Sŏngju Warehouse) inlaid on the cover.

b) Punch'ŏng ware decorated in sgraffiato style; 15th to 16th century; dia. 5 1/2" (13.9 cm.).

Another type of Yi *punch'ŏng* ware is decorated in underglaze iron oxide whilst others are decorated in reverse in a *sgraffiato* technique similar to the Chinese Tz'u-chou wares. Some of the coarser of these wares were made at Chollomando whilst others of finer quality come from Kyeryong-san, where the kilns at Hakhong-ri in South Chungcheong province also produced both black and white pottery. This dish is decorated in *sgraffiato* style, the floral decoration being cut through a coating of slip. It is from the Kyeryong-san kiln site.

c) Yi dynasty blue and white covered box, said to depict Han River scene near Seoul; 18th–19th century; ht. 3 3/4" (9.5 cm.), dia. 5" (12.7 cm.).

During the Yi dynasty, blue and white porcelain was made at the Punwon potteries in the Kwanju district south-east of Seoul. Although production started in the mid-15th century, many of the finest pieces were made in the early 18th century. The output included large jars for use at important ceremonies as well as wine jars and smaller objects such as brush-holders and water droppers, particularly the latter which were made in great variety in an infinity of charming shapes. On the lid, a design in underglaze blue depicts a crane flying amidst clouds.

d) White Yi porcelain covered bowl moulded in bamboo style; 18th century; ht. 5 1/2" (13.9 cm.), dia. 6 1/4" (15.9 cm.).

The Yi period white porcelain, although often as elegant as the Koryō white wares, is nevertheless distinctive in style. Some have square-cut or faceted sides whilst others rely for effect on their flowing curves. All have simple forms and purity of glaze. The form of the larger pots is frequently splendid whilst many smaller objects for the scholar's table, such as water-pots, have great quality and are often made in the form of animals, fruit etc. This white porcelain bowl and cover has in the centre of both bowl and cover a small flower in underglaze blue.

Continental Pottery
Introduction

The Arab invasion of Spain in the eighth century—the time-honoured starting-point for a history of European pottery—is almost too convenient; it is as if the magnificent lustre-wares had sprung unheralded from virgin soil. It is true that these wares gave the impetus to an extraordinary flowering, tending to overshadow the more commonplace development that went before, although pottery had been made continuously in Europe from the calcolithic age. Behind the splendours of Hispano-Moresque and the different tin-glaze techniques, hangs a permanent backcloth of peasant and even sophisticated pottery, varying in style and material with the indigenous qualities of soil and population. The art of pottery is like a kaleidoscope; beginning with the simplest craft and raw materials, adding here a new element, there a different technique, its reflections change with all the accumulated skills and grow even more complex, brilliant and repetitive, showing a thousand facets which tempt the mind and eye to explore the history and art of the European potter.

To the first porous pots more or less efficiently fired, or even sun-dried, simple lead glazes were added to make them watertight. Later, slip was applied and patterns scratched through to reveal the white or coloured body beneath. This technique, called *sgraffiato,* is popular even today; many cooking pots sold in continental markets are still made of soft, low-fired earthenware, only partially glazed. Such pots are universal—their origin, in the absence of decoration can only be devined by shape and colour, combined with an instinct for the habits of a community.

Whilst the Middle East artists, far ahead of the West, discovered and improved the glazes and colours that later came to Europe in the wake of Islam, thirteenth century Rhine potters had, like the Chinese artisans centuries before, discovered stoneware. Stoneware is impervious to liquids, but the Rhinelanders soon discovered that it could be improved by throwing salt into the blazing kiln. The effect is that of a flux, causing the surface of the vessel to melt into a glassy film with a texture like pitted orange-peel. This produces the brown and light grey wares still used today where a plain, non-porous material is required. It is a strange coincidence that in Europe the Germans invented that hard, tough material—of all European pottery the closest in the quality of its body to the translucent Oriental porcelain, that became the ultimate model—until Böttger, another German, discovered the secret of making hard-paste porcelain at Meissen in 1709.

Lead glazes suffered from one great disadvantage—the colours ran—a difficulty overcome in the Near East by working in relief, and by two different reserve techniques called *cuerda seca* and *cuenca* used by the Moors in Spain. Italian lustre-wares are the direct offspring of the Moorish metallic lustre colours developed in Mesopotamia, and brought to Egypt in the tenth century. Early pieces were in well-tried potters' shapes: pitchers, ewers, dishes and pharmaceutical jars, crudely and sparsely decorated in colours limited to manganese purple, copper green and later a thick dark blue. These are evident in the Tuscan school centred on Florence; the Faenza school followed Tuscany, the blue still dominant until the palette was enlarged in the early sixteenth century by yellows, orange, brown and different greens, allowing the artists freedom to develop their painting skills and produce the *istoriato* style associated with Urbino. In the late fifteenth and early sixteenth centuries Europe, especially Italy, was in the full flower of the Renaissance, an age of passionate enthusiasm for experiment, resulting in almost unlimited advances in style and design. The status of the painted tin-glaze wares rose above the purely utilitarian to one of prestige and ornamentation, giving free rein to the imaginative skill of the painter.

Eventually, the Courts of Europe were vying with one another for the decorative skills of the migrant workmen, and tin-glaze wares for every use remained in constant demand until the arrival of large quantities of Oriental hard-paste porcelain in the sixteenth century. The activities of the East India Companies initially acted as a fresh stimulus and tin-glazed wares seemed to offer a perfect substitution for the too-expensive porcelain. This perfection rang a death knell, and the true fire died; copying became stereotyped and only in exceptional cases did the new over-glaze enamelling produce original work, and not simply an imitation of a different medium. In the eighteenth century the Dutch, like the late Renaissance Italians, displayed their skill as draughtsmen and painters, and designed with almost unimaginable virtuosity on the space and material available. Then the mind turns away with relief to the freer brushwork of earlier days, when shape governed decoration and was not subservient to it.

a) Storage jar in earthenware, Grotte de Maurous, La Vacquerie (Herault), France, c. 3000 BC; ht. 19¾″ (50 cm.).

During the winter of 1933-34, two hunters retrieving a ferret from the fissured rock, found the cave of La Vacquerie. Archaeologists later confirmed that the cave had been untouched since prehistoric times. Eight large jars were intact, some half-buried in the floor. Made without a wheel, i.e. coiled, they are crudely potted in a low-fired, very impure clay. Each probably collected water reserved from the dripping roof, linking La Vacquerie with other cistern caves. Two jars held a carbonized deposit, perhaps charcoal stores. These utilitarian jars show a surprising urge towards decoration, considering the rigours of existence in the 2nd millennium BC.

b) Tubular-spouted pot of stoneware, dull red decoration; Pingsdorf, Germany, 900-1050 AD (found in London); ht. 7¼″ (18.4 cm.).

From the late Frankish period a considerable pottery industry inherited from the Romans flourished in the Rhineland, especially at Trier. After exhausting fuel and clay deposits, the centres moved further down the Rhine, establishing a growing trade across the North Sea to England.

This typical, globular pitcher has a foot-ring added by hand, and a characteristic comma-like pattern painted on the shoulder. Other linear designs included bands of sloping lines and cross-hatching. The yellowish body is fired to vitrification, and may be classed as stoneware. Pingsdorf ware has been accurately dated by studies of local stratified river layers.

---

c) Dish, tin-glazed earthenware painted in green, manganese and purple; Paterna, Spain, c. 1375-1425; dia. 9½″ (24 cm.).

The Hispano-Moresque style was developed by Moorish potters after the Catholic reconquest of Spain. Paterna and Manises were the most important centres; the earliest Paterna ware may date from the 14th century. The palette, of copper and manganese on a white ground, is similar to that of Orvieto. The vigorously executed designs—birds, animals, foliage, etc.—have a strong Islamic flavour. Heavy outlines on this dish may perhaps derive from contours used by the tile-makers to separate coloured lead glazes (see *d*, right); painting on unfired tin-glaze was a difficult technique, and this is a very early example.

d) Set of four glazed tiles, earthenware, with blue, green and yellow glazes; Hispano-Moresque, Spain, 15th-16th century.

These tiles exemplify the Islamic tradition in Spain, developed in North Africa as early as the 11th century. The earlier method of keeping brilliantly-coloured glazes apart and unimpaired by running was mosaic work. This laborious process was simplified by the Islamic potters, who painted lines of manganese pigment, combined with a greasy substance that disappeared in the firing, between the enamels. The enamels remained heaped up along the dividing lines, and traditionally this technique has been known as *cuerda seca* (dry cord). However, Arthur Lane (*Guide to Tiles*) questioned whether the term originally referred to this method.

Early Dutch tile, which followed the Hispano-Moresque tradition (see p. 141).

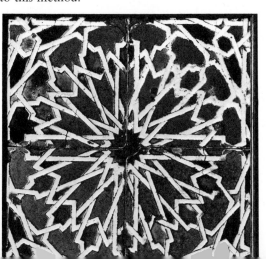

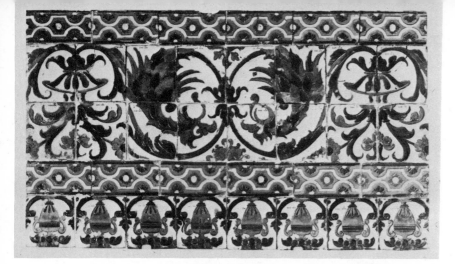

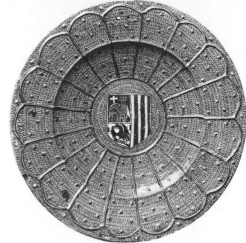

a) *Panel of tiles, earthenware, glazed in the cuenca technique in ochre, blue, green and cream; Southern Spain, 16th century.*

There was so great a demand for tiles in Europe that it was clearly worthwhile to replace the method of individual hand-cutting. At first, moulded stamps impressed hollow channels into the clay, which were subsequently filled with the greasy manganese mixture. Finally, potters found that a raised-outline pattern, pressed into the soft clay, kept the glazes apart without grease. This *cuenca* technique developed naturally from *cuerda seca*.

Elaborate foliate, Gothic and heraldic designs superseded the first patterns, and were themselves gradually re-absorbed and reshaped into old mosaic designs. *Cuenca* was revived in the 19th century, without ever recovering its former excellence.

b) *Dish of tin-glazed earthenware painted in copper lustre; Hispano-Moresque, Manises, Spain, late 15th century; dia. 20″ (51 cm.).*

The Caliph of Damascus invaded Spain in 711; northern Christians resisted successfully, and the whole peninsula was eventually reconquered. The Islamic invasion lasted until 1492.

Moorish potters, fleeing from Malaga, settled at Manises. Their original green, purple and blue palette was later enriched with lustres, well-known in Islam but only perfected in Spain after c. 1400. Exported lustreware greatly influenced Italian pottery, although its popularity declined during the 16th century. The red or buff body was tin-glazed, fired, and sometimes painted with a blue design. Silver or copper lustre was added, and fired in a special low-temperature kiln. Modern lustreware is very coppery and slick, far removed from early styles.

Ceramics

Continental Pottery

SPANISH

c) *Drug jar, or albarello, tin-glazed earthenware painted in blue and lustre; Manises, Spain, 1450–1475; ht. 15½″ (39.3 cm.), dia. 9½″ (24.1 cm.).*

The shape of this magnificent apothecary's jar derives from the Middle East, and was used for dry drug and powder jars in every European pharmacy. The device indicates the hospital or religious order for which it was made.

Sometimes Spanish wares had illiterate Arabic script and other Islamic motifs and these gradually merged with equally-misunderstood Gothic lettering and Christian symbols. Everyday decoration was rather sterotyped; this vine and bryony-leaf was very popular. Large pieces for the nobility, however, were embellished with heraldic devices and coats of arms. The *albarello* shape was very common in Spain.

d) *Vase of tin-glazed earthenware, decorated in pale blue, and inscribed* Silva Coronel; *Talavera, Spain, 17th century; ht. 16″ (40.5 cm.).*

Talavera's early green and white 15th century wares were similar to those of Toledo, but its later pottery is more famous: pharmacy jars made for wealthy patrons, unsophisticated polychrome wares in blue and a muddy orange, outlined in blackish-purple, and, on more everyday pieces, even cruder paintings of birds, deer and hare in a very dark blue. Talavera flourished throughout the 17th century producing all kinds of useful wares, painted principally with buildings, animals and hunting scenes often in yellow, orange and green. This vase is encircled with groups of horsemen and men holding guns and pikes in a landscape.

a) Wall-fountain of tin-glazed earthenware in poly-chrome; Alcora, Spain, c. 1750; ht. 21" (53.3 cm.).

The Duke of Aranda founded Alcora in 1726. He summoned Joseph Olérys from Moustiers, entrusting him with its organization. Frenchmen were employed at first, but after a year the Spaniards took over. The large, high-quality output sold throughout Spain, with several tax concessions.

This wall-fountain *en fleur de solanée* (potato-flower pattern) is typical of the designs Olérys brought from France. At Alcora, he learned to fire high-temperature colours of orange, purplish-black and green, all much stronger than the slightly pallid Moustiers palette.

These grotesque masks would have seemed out of date at Louis XV's rococo court!

b) Bowl of earthenware with sgraffiato decoration, green and brown glazes. Italy, 15th century; dia. 5⅛" (13 cm.).

Sgraffiato was common throughout Europe on simple pottery and later, on more ceremonial pieces. Clear, yellowish lead glazes, sometimes discoloured with iron impurities, were used throughout the Middle Ages. For variety, potters dipped an unglazed vessel in slip (pipe-clay and water) incising the decoration through this coating, like scratching (*sgraffiato*) the icing to reveal the cake. It was then covered in clear, or occasionally tinted, glaze and fired. The *sgraffiato* itself could be coloured (blue, green, purple, yellow, brown); however, the lead glaze often ran, and the resulting mottled effect, though often attractive to us, was far from intentional!

---

c) Polychrome dish, tin-glazed earthenware, inscribed E non se po mangiare sensa fatiga; Faenza, Italy, late 15th century; dia. 16¼" (41.3 cm.).

Faenza dominated maiolica from the late Gothic period until after the beginning of the High Renaissance, although the history of Italian maiolica is one of style rather than place, since workmen and fashions moved from centre to centre. Early manganese purple, copper green and dark blue pigments were joined, about 1480, by antimony-yellow, orange, pale turquoise, and sparingly, red.

This colouring, plus the vigorous brushwork of the leaf and trefoil border, are typical of the Faenza period, although the actual tones of the palette suggest a Florentine attribution.

The angel riding an owl (presumably Wisdom) piously cautions 'The lazy man will starve'.

d) Drug-jar, tin-glazed earthenware, painted with cobalt blue, manganese and purple; Italy, probably Florence; c. 1450, ht. 12½" (31.8 cm.).

This drug-pot belongs to the 'oak-leaf jars' from early 15th century Tuscany. Decorations were heraldic designs or devices, like this ladder of the hospital of Santa Maria della Scala, Siena, enclosed in manganese and blue and surrounded by 'oak-leaves'. The dark *impasto* blue can be felt under your fingers. Here the blue was a wash with purple outlines; towards the mid-16th century they perfected an ultramarine capable of linear treatment. The oak-leaf pattern is found on jugs, vases and pharmacy jars; all have a dignified strength and integrity notably lacking from some later, more decorative, maiolica.

Ceramics

Continental Pottery
ITALIAN

a) *Polychrome dish, tin-glazed relief-moulded earthenware with blue and yellow lustre; Deruta (near Perugia), Italy, c. 1500–1525; dia. 13⅞″ (35.5 cm.).*

Deruta had been producing pottery since the end of the 15th century. Although influenced by Faenza, Deruta has an individual style. The early potters imitated frescoes familiar to them through the painters of Umbria. The highly-developed Italian fresco technique may account for the apparent ease with which maiolica painters handled the difficult tin-glaze; both media allow no alterations to the decoration. The first silver lustre wares at Deruta were pale; this example is typical of the later style, a rich yellow combining with blue. The vigorous high-quality relief includes grotesques, fruit and foliate scrolls.

b) *Vase, white-enamelled earthenware, Andrea Della Robbia; Florence, Italy, c. 1500; ht. 16″ (40.7 cm.).*

The work of the Della Robbia family is very sculptural in quality, the immense size of the plaques and lunettes almost excluding them from a history of pottery. The rather late example shown, by Andrea Della Robbia (1435–1525), is typical of its period, using high-relief masks, swags and moulded handles akin to ornamental bronze-casting. It is an example of clay used by a master modeller, contrasting with the maiolica of Castel Durante and Urbino, where the clay becomes a frame for the painter's brush. Most Della Robbia work is thickly glazed in white, or a characteristic blue.

---

c) *Maiolica dish, painted in polychrome with a Papal Procession; mark: P; Caffaggiolo, Italy, c. 1516; dia. 19½″ (49.5 cm.).*

The Caffaggiolo pottery (c. 1506–1600) was founded and controlled by the Medici family. Maiolica had reached such technical perfection that large quantities were made purely for decoration. Fattorini, an outstanding painter, was brought from Montelupo; his family managed the factory until it closed. Caffaggiolo boasted several very gifted, anonymous painters; one of them perpetrated this lively commentary on current events in Florence, commemorating Pope Leo X's visit in 1516.

Mounted foot guards in green and brown stripes, with musicians and bearers, follow a mauve elephant (clearly an unreliable form of transport). The Pope is silhouetted against a dark blue landscape.

d) *Maiolica dish, polychrome; Castel Durante, Italy, c. 1520; dia. 11¾″ (30 cm.).*

This dish, Actaeon turning into a stag while pursuing Diana in a typical early Renaissance landscape, was probably painted by Nicola Pellipario (b. 1480), who worked at Castel Durante and Urbino. Pellipario is recognized as a great master of *istoriato*, first developed at Faenza. His compositions, inspired by classical mythology, were interpreted with skill, delicacy and originality. Style apart, one must admire the virtuosity which produced such masterly painting on the unfired and difficult tin-glaze. *Istoriato* was very popular in the 19th century; such imitations never achieve the original brilliant drawing or colour, and are fairly easy to detect.

Mark on c.

a) Two-handled vase, or drug-jar, tin-glazed earthen-ware, decorated with blue, green, ruby and gold lustre; Gubbio, Italy, c. 1510; ht. 9¼" (23.5 cm.).

The workshop at Gubbio run by Maestro Giorgio Andreoli (d. 1553), was famous for its lustres. Indeed, wares were sent from Deruta especially to have the ruby lustre added. This vase (it probably originally had a cover) is a good example of the moulded designs invented by Andreoli to show off his coloured lustres. Such gadrooned, embossed pieces with fluted neck and finely scrolled handles were more decorative than practical, as lustre-pigments wore badly. In the late 19th century, reproductions of Gubbio and Deruta lustres were made in Florence by Ulysse Cantagalli, usually bearing his blue cockerel mark.

b) Wine-cooler, tin-glazed earthenware with poly-chrome decoration; probably Urbino, Italy, c. 1550; ht. 10" (25.5 cm.), dia. 16" by 12¼" (42 cm. by 31 cm.).

The vivid colours and brilliant blue interior of this wine-cooler indicate the period after 1550; it is typical of the monumental pieces imitating bronze or metal examples. One panel holds the portrait of a young nobleman; the other his arms— a black eagle displayed on a rock below three castles. The background of cupids, satyrs and *groteschi* is familiar from Raphael's work.

By this time the earlier designs of Florence, Castel Durante and Faenza had become outmoded. The Renaissance revival of classical antiquity did produce beautiful, restrained compositions, but sometimes led to a misplaced fantasy and virtuosity that approached the degenerate.

---

c) Dish, tin-glazed earthenware, polychrome painting of Bacchus and autumn fruits; Venice, Italy, c. 1550; dia. 17¾" (45 cm.).

Faenza workmen strengthened the previously unimportant Venetian potteries and by 1550 pro-duction was greatly enlarged. This dish is an interesting hybrid, perhaps from Domenigo da Venezia's workshop. The realistic detail and superb drawing reveal the hand of a master-painter. Venice, the greatest Eastern trading port in Europe, was well-acquainted with Chinese porcelain and Near Eastern pottery such as Isnik; their maiolica reflects this in a blue-stained ground-colour, touched with opaque white or yellow. The slight relief effect on this plate is half-way between the earlier Faenza-Urbino tradition and the richly-sculptured vessels made later in the century.

d) Dish, tin-glazed earthenware, painted in purple on turquoise ground; marked with crowned shield of Savoy in purple; Savona, perhaps Turin, Italy, late 17th century; dia. 12" (30.5 cm.).

Late 17th-century Italy produced a crop of some-what insipid blue and white maiolica, after Oriental porcelain had overwhelmed the European world. No work of the known Turin potters apparently survived; some in the Savona style, marked with the crowned shield of Savoy, may be by Giovanni Giacomo Bianchi at the Pavio factory.

Savona (the general term for the work of Ligurian potters) produced some clumsily potted, over-decorated pieces, in the old late Renaissance style. The Spanish-influenced animal and foliage designs are much more attractive, with a linear delicacy seldom found in the later Ligurian wares.

Mark on d.

Ceramics

Continental Pottery

ITALIAN

GERMAN

a) Plate, tin-glazed earthenware, painted in pale yellow, beige and greenish-brown tones; Castelli, Italy, c. 1750; dia. 7" (17.8 cm.).

Carlo Antonio Grue, a well-known maiolica painter, established the first documented Neapolitan factory late in the 17th century, developing the style now called *Castelli* which his four sons continued. The Gentili family also painted landscapes and mythological subjects in the Grue style. Perhaps Grue's fourth son, Liborio (1701–1776) who worked in miniature, painted this typical scene in rather sombre pale yellow, beige, and greenish-brown tones, although without red. Surprisingly the *istoriato* style still continued well into the 18th century.

b) Jug, stoneware, the so-called Hafnerware, decorated with coloured glazes, probably the work of Paul Preuning; Nuremberg, Germany, c. 1550; ht. 21" (53.3 cm.).

Hafnerware has acquired a traditional meaning in English, over and above its actual translation; *Hafner* simply means potter. Nevertheless, in English, Hafnerware is associated with the *stove-tile* potters of Germany and Austria, who made the great wood-burning stoves of those cold forest regions. Their early green-glazed tiles gave way to colours and then to opaque tin enamels. Hafnerwares also include Silesian pieces with tin-enamels separated by incision (*cuerda seca*), and stonewares, chiefly made by the Preuning brothers. Inspired perhaps by the stove-tilers, they decorated large vessels with Gothic and Renaissance subjects in brilliant reliefs.

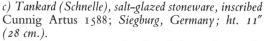

c) Tankard (Schnelle), salt-glazed stoneware, inscribed Cunnig Artus 1588; Siegburg, Germany; ht. 11" (28 cm.).

German stoneware developed from the mediaeval pottery industry. Salt-glazing was discovered about 1450–1500, and the potteries clustered in the Rhineland, using the almost unlimited fuel and rich clay deposits.

Siegburg, a distinguished centre from the 14th century until the Swedes sacked the town in 1632, used a fine white clay. The slender *Schnellen*, made after 1550 and influenced by Cologne, were decorated with excellent relief patterns. This example has moulded figures and shields, and a dated inscription. The contemporary pewter mount, with its fine knop and hinge, complete the elegant lines of this distinguished piece.

d) Rhenish bottle of salt-glazed stoneware, Bellarmine, with masks and medallions in relief, signed W E (William Emens) and dated 1607; Frechen, Rhineland, Germany; ht. 12½" (31.6 cm.).

These heavy bottles are traditionally named after Cardinal Roberto Bellarmino (1542–1621); 'Old Greybeard', another nickname, is nearer the German *Bartmannkrug*, and there seems no genuine link with the Cardinal. Bellarmine is probably an old English corruption of *Bartmannkrug*. Ornamental reliefs were made from moulded plaques fixed onto the vessels and occur much earlier than the first salt-glaze (c. 1450). The rich, treacly colour and vigorous modelling remained unimpaired by the enormous quantity probably made. Heraldic devices came rather later, as witness the date and signature of this magnificent bottle.

Bellarmines were also made in England during the 17th century.

a) Tankard of salt-glazed stoneware with enamel colours, contemporary pewter mount, with a later monogram, JS; Kreussen, near Bayreuth, Germany, 1660; ht. 8½″ (21.5 cm.).

Kreussen is famous for glass-enamelling. The enamelling technique was commonly used by decorators working at home (*Hausmaler*) and not confined strictly to Guilds. *Hausmaler* worked independently of the factories, except for acquiring, often illicitly, the basic pottery and glass wares. Here the deep brown salt-glaze forms a background for enamels laid thickly over moulded patterns. Corded blue and white bands, striped ribbons and unfired gilded dots are typical Kreussen decorations. The unworn gilding, the important-looking portrait (perhaps the Great Elector) and the garlanded fleur-de-lis borders, suggest ceremonial rather than everyday use. Dated pieces begin around 1622.

b) Owl jug, tin-glazed earthenware, initialled LS below the cover, for Lorenz Speckner; early 17th century; ht. 10¼″ (26 cm.).

Lorenz Speckner made this, one of his famous early faience pieces, at Kreussen, when the Vest factory was still producing stoves decorated only with coloured glazes. The jug, glazed with white tin-enamel, has blue-painted moulded feathers; others have coats of arms and cold gilding. This first German faience—as opposed to Italianate maiolica—was apparently Speckner's speciality. Their nickname—*Eulenkruge*—has linguistic origins; in Hesse, potters were *Euler* or *Auler* from Middle High German, *Ule*, a pot. *Eulenkruge* means, literally, potters' jugs. *Eule* also means owl, hence 'owl jugs': in this case it happens to be a pigeon!

Mark on b.

---

c) Bouillon pot, tin-glazed earthenware decorated in blue with splashes of orange, inscribed and dated 1631; Hamburg, Germany; ht. 6⅞″ (17.5 cm.).

Unknown potters in Hamburg, a leading member of the Hanseatic League, produced German tin-glazed wares from the early 1600s to 1680. Rare dated pieces range from 1628 to 1656, mostly painted in a strong blue, combined with yellow, green and orange-red. The yellowish body shows patchily through the thinly-applied, often crackled, glaze. The powerful, scrolled handles of this unusual bowl reflect a mediaeval and indigenous feeling and the vigorously-painted motifs have travelled far from the delicate late Ming designs so popular at this period. The interior has a strainer to separate the bouillon from the vegetables.

d) Dish, tin-glazed earthenware, painted in blue; Frankfurt, Germany, mid-17th century; dia. 13⅛″ (33.5 cm.).

Frankfurt (founded 1666) produced some of the finest European imitations of Chinese porcelain. Blue is dominant, occasionally with manganese and yellow; a brilliant glaze without the Dutch *kwaart* covers a harder body than the Dutch type, and there is no Delft orange-peel effect. It is unlikely that the excellent painting was done by local men; significantly, many Dutch potters worked at Hanau and Frankfurt. There is a remarkable similarity between this free painting, typical of Frankfurt, and the decoration of *De Grieksche A* (p. 140d). Frankfurt made all kinds of vessels: double gourds, large fluted and plain-rimmed plates with a deep centre well, flower cases, tiles, pharmacy jars, etc.

Ceramics

Continental Pottery
GERMAN

a) Salt in the form of a monkey, stoneware; Westerwald, near Bonn, Germany, c. 1700, perhaps earlier; ht. 6" (15.3 cm.).

The Westerwald mountains supplied abundant fuel for the kilns of a great pottery industry, probably continuous there since Roman times. Westerwald apparently produced nothing very outstanding till the late 17th century, when a vigorous sense of modelling inspired the use of masks and rosettes in relief and a curious knife-cut technique, normally separating the colours but here suggesting fur.

The monkey might conceivably be by Dwight of Fulham, but the base looks typically German and these characteristic figures, lion-salts, or pierced inkstands with birds were the main Westerwald products of the 18th century.

b) Enghalskrug (narrow-necked jug), tin-glazed earthenware, unpainted, with pewter mount; Ansbach, South Germany, mid-18th century; ht. 9½" (24 cm.).

Ansbach (founded 1708 by Matthias Bauer and Johann Kaspar Ripp) was an early, very successful faience pottery; important names include G. Kohnlein and G. C. Popp, subsequently owner-manager until 1807. Cheap creamware continued production until 1839.

Snail-twisted, pointed handles and the evenly-fluted belly are Ansbach variations on a basic shape; pinkish tinges indicate the body under the creamy-white glaze. Ansbach's fame included copying green and blue K'ang-hsi enamels and Imari wares with unfired gold; other colours were yellowish-green, iron-red, black, yellow and purple. True enamels were never used at Ansbach.

Mark on b.

---

c) Tankard, tin-glazed earthenware, painted in Schwarzlot and signed MS, perhaps Mathias Schmid, with contemporary pewter mount; Germany, probably Nuremberg, Hausmalerei, c. 1720; ht. 5½" (14 cm.), dia. 3¾" (9.5 cm.).

Nuremberg and Augsburg were important centres for *Hausmalerei*—work produced by outside decorators. Contemporary factories used only high-temperature colours, especially blue and white, whereas *Hausmaler* were mostly glass or enamel painters, guild members, trained in the muffle-kiln palette, including fired-gold and silver.

Schwarzlot was an early delicate grey and black style, sometimes with gold; later baroque decoration enclosed landscapes and Biblical scenes (cf. p. 453a). Elaborate pieces for noble patrons had gold or silver mounts.

Important *Hausmaler* included Johann Schaper (using *Schwarzlot*), Abraham Helmhack (who enhanced enamel colours with *kwaart*) and the two Preisslers.

d) Jug, part of a tea-set, earthenware, brown manganese glaze with silver Chinoiseries, the lid attached with a silver chain; Bayreuth, Germany, c. 1730-40; ht. 5⅞" (15 cm.).

Early pieces from the Bayreuth factory (1714-1800) are very rare, especially before the Margrave (Georg Wilhelm) took over (1724). Johann Georg Knoller leased Bayreuth from 1728-1744, producing the best wares. Earthenware and faience used the same clay, one with brown manganese glaze, the other tin-oxide. The brown, much in demand, was described by contemporary writers as red porcelain, although it was soft earthenware. Decorators are well known from occasional signatures. Some famous artists working at Bayreuth included Johann Andreas Fiechthorn (gold and silver), Adam Friedrich von Löwenfinck (Chinoiseries and enamel colours), Joseph Phillip Dannhöfer and Johann Friedrich Metsch.

Mark on c.

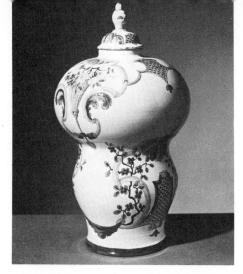

a) Vase and cover, tin-glazed earthenware, painted in blue, green, crimson and yellow enamel; Fulda, Germany, c. 1745; ht. 10¼″ (26 cm.).

The Fulda factory was short-lived (1740–1758) but its late beginning and employment of the best artists (the two Löwenfincks, the Hess and Ripp brothers, and J. P. Dannhöfer) account for the quality of its enamelling and gilding. Best known are its Chinese imitations, and freer Chinoiserie style associated with Löwenfinck. Blue painting outlined in manganese, baroque scrollwork inspired by the Rouen *ferroneries*, and domestic wares in quantity were also produced.

This cumbersome 'Chinese' double gourd, with incongruously small cover, shows the lengths to which ambitious potters could go; however, the skilful decoration reaches the standard expected of Fulda.

b) Butter-boat, tin-glazed earthenware, painted in enamels; mark: a wheel and 2 in grey enamel; by Zeschinger; Höchst, Germany, 1750–53; ht. 3¼″ (8.3 cm.).

Höchst, unusually successful from the start, was founded by two Frankfurt merchants and Adam Friedrich von Löwenfinck, a supreme enamel-decorator trained at Meissen and employed at Bayreuth, Fulda, Ansbach and possibly Chantilly. This well-preserved butter-boat in brilliant red and other colours, shows the close imitation of porcelain practised at Höchst with the precise shape and applied flowers appropriate to a hard-paste body. Faience was gradually replaced by porcelain, ceasing production by 1757.

Wares included tureens in the shape of birds, animals or vegetables, decorated in enamels over a brilliant milky white glaze.

F.v.L.

Mark of the Fulda factory.

---

c) Helmet-shaped ewer, tin-glazed earthenware, painted in enamel colours; Stockelsdorff, Germany, about 1775; ht. 7¾″ (19.5 cm.).

This rather late faience establishment started c. 1771. Its wares are of surprisingly high quality, undoubtedly because of Johann Buchwald and Abraham Leihamer, who came in 1772. Buchwald remained director till after 1785.

Stoves were the most important but all kinds of decorative domestic ware was made: wall-fountains, trays and table tops, typical of Baltic faience factories. This helmet-shaped ewer, vigorous in form and colouring, has greenish-yellow and black scrolling, and the Strasbourg-type flowers are deep purple and blue, giving the piece a life and brilliance frequently lacking on such late wares.

d) Pierced dish, cream-coloured glazed earthenware; Hubertusburg, Germany, probably after 1798; dia. 9¼″ (23.5 cm.).

This Saxon faience factory never really succeeded. Count von Lindenau, directing it himself after 1774, could hardly compete with Meissen porcelain! By then even long-established potteries found that faience itself was losing popularity. The Elector of Saxony took control, appointing Count Marcolini director; he produced only cream-coloured earthenware; the factory was sold and then finally closed in 1848.

This typical example, imitating Leeds cream-ware, has a yellowish-white glaze and a Leeds pierced border. This plate was probably part of a service, with the arms of Poland, Lithuania and Saxony.

Ceramics

Continental Pottery

NETHERLANDS

a) Drug or pharmacy jar, tin-glazed earthenware with leaf decoration; Northern Netherlands, 1600–1625; ht. 7½" (18.5 cm.).

Pottery in the Netherlands dated from the 10th century; there had always been contact with the great Rhineland centres. This jar was made by refugees settling in the North after the revolt against Spain, and Antwerp's defeat in 1585. It carries the faded memory of the great Hispano-Moresque pottery and the promise of future development by men of independent spirit. Netherlands maiolica cannot be attributed to individuals or even towns; most potters simply repeated their traditional work, but the Northern influx of experienced tin-glaze workmen was the stimulus leading to the widespread dominance of later Dutch earthenware.

b) Plate, tin-glazed earthenware, polychrome; Northern Netherlands, first part of the 17th century; dia. 9½" (24 cm.).

Border decoration can help in dating early pieces such as this, with the heavy potting and crude painting typical of Netherlands maiolica. However, the early rims were plain, or hatched with simple motifs; these foreign and more sophisticated designs round the central figure indicate the appearance of a new model, the Chinese Wan-Li porcelain imported after 1602 by the Dutch East India Company.

Oriental porcelain remained the model throughout the next two centuries. The impact of these fashionable and expensive pieces caused a revolution in European pottery before which Netherlands maiolica quickly gave way.

---

c) Bottle with Chinese decoration, tin-glazed earthenware; Delft, Netherlands, c. 1670; ht. 10⅜" (26.5 cm.).

After an explosion in 1654, the town of Delft was rebuilt and many breweries became potteries, without changing their name. They soon outstripped other faience producers, till Delft became a generic term for blue and white tin-glazed earthenware. The potters were Guildsmen of St. Luke, but the factories were usually run by wealthy merchants. Guild rules prevented craftsmen from being directors or managers; this was occasionally circumvented, e.g. the Eenhoorn family of The Greek A, and Johannes Knotter, '*meester- porceleyn-backer*', managed *De Porcelyne Fles*. This bottle is typical of the high quality Delft Wan-Li imitations.

d) Baluster-shaped vase, tin-glazed earthenware decorated in blue, cover probably missing; mark: SVE 22; Delft, Netherlands, De Grieksche A c. 1674; ht. 12½" (32 cm.).

The mark serves merely as confirmation in attributing this vase to Samuel van Eenhoorn, manager of his family's *De Grieksche A* from 1674–1678, when his father gave him the factory as a wedding present.

The close-grained body with orange-peel glaze is brilliantly painted in soft blues and violets, with figures delicately outlined with *trek* (blue or dark blue-black) following the curved surface with all the freedom of a Chinese original. The carefully drawn details—i.e. clothing, faces, delightful T'ang pony—are all typical of Samuel's work. He used *trek* more discreetly than his imitators who produced heavier outlines.

Mark on d.

a) Two candlesticks, tin-glazed earthenware with blue Chinese decoration; mark: D with a shaft and the number 24 for De Dissel; Delft, Netherlands, late 17th century.

De Dissel (The Thistle) factory is relatively well documented; from 1640-1666 the Cruyck family left no identified marks; for 1666-1694, usually the thistle, a 'D' and a date; 1694-1697, Cornelius van der Kloot, painter, occasionally added 'CK'.

The declining business was bought (1694) by Adriaen Kocks, owner of *De Grieksche A* who transferred everything there after 1701, but presumably continued to use the *De Dissel* patterns and mark. Designs such as these candlesticks with butterflies and flowering plants continued to be made into the 18th century.

b) Dish, tin-glazed earthenware, painted in blue; Delft, Netherlands, c. 1675-1700; dia. 13¼″ (33.5 cm.).

Similar dishes made both in England and the Netherlands were sometimes confused, as the English ware was decorated at Lambeth by Dutchmen. One distinguishing Dutch mark is the *kwaart*—a coating of clear lead glaze over the tin-enamel, imparting a brilliant sheen to the final product. The Italian equivalent on maiolica was *coperta*.

The decorating in very dark blue gives a slightly pompous effect with its heavily-painted flowers and fruit border, presumably oranges. Both the Dutch and English seemed to agree about the stolid, hideous Queen Mary, although allowing Stadholder William III (1689-1702) a somewhat sly look.

---

c) Circular dish, tin-glazed earthenware with Chinese decoration, painted in blue and white; Delft, Netherlands, second half of the 17th century; dia. 10¼″ (26 cm.).

This dish belongs to the very popular type which imitated the blue-and-white Wan-li (see p. 121) style (1573-1620). Chinese porcelain was imported in huge quantities during the late 17th century and Dutch tin-glaze suffered by comparison with the harder Chinese body, and more brilliant decoration. These plates are difficult to distinguish immediately from the almost violet colour of the Chinese originals.

d) Gourd-shaped bottle, tin-glazed earthenware, painted in blue with Chinese decoration, mark; GK for Gerrit Kam; Delft, Netherlands, made either at De Paeuw, 1701-1705 or at De 3 Vergulde Astonnekens 1680-1705; ht. 19¼″ (49 cm.).

The history of these Delft potteries is unbelievably complicated. In 1622 *De Paeuw* was sold, half to G. L. Cruyck, half to Willem Cleffius and Wouter van Eenhoorn. Wouter soon sold out to Willem's son, Lambert. The Cleffius family also owned *De Metalen Pot*.

Gerrit Kam and Wouter van Eenhoorn had owned *De 3 Vergulde Astonnekens* since 1668. On Wouter's death Gerrit presented that pottery to his son, and bought *De Paeuw*. Hence the difficulty in attribution. The style of this bottle, however, is typical of Gerrit's work, especially its shape and up-to-the-minute imitation of K'ang-hsi porcelain.

Tiles are one of the most popular forms of Delftware.

Ceramics

Continental Pottery
NETHERLANDS

Mark for the Young Moor's Head factory.

a) Two polygonal dishes, from reistafel sets, polychrome with gold Chinese decoration, mark: R I H S; Het Jonge Moriaenshooft, Delft, Netherlands, 1680-1692; 10⅜″ by 13⅜″ (26.5 by 33.5 cm.).

The Young Moor's Head factory is renowned for the work of the Hoppesteyns; Jacob, owner 1664-1671, his wife, manager after his death, followed by their son, Rochus (d. 1692). So many different themes were used—Chinese imitations, mythological and biblical stories, Italianate landscapes—that presumably several good artists were employed there. The blue or polychrome vine-tendril border, similar to late Ming or early Ch'ing cloud scrolls may have been invented by Rochus. However, he did commission outside decorators, including workers at The Hague using polychrome high-fired colours, so there is some doubt about the origin of these dishes.

b) Tea-pot, red stoneware, mark: fox on an oval medallion surrounded by an inscription, Ary de Milde; Delft, Netherlands, late 17th/early 18th century; ht. 3¾″ (8.7 cm.), lgth. 4⅘″ (11.8 cm.).

Cleffius and Lambert van Eenhoorn imitated the red I-hsing tea-pots in earthenware; Ary de Milde finally achieved something nearer the hard, water-tight Chinese body.

De Milde's red stoneware was an important model for the Elers brothers in England, and for Böttger, whose red stoneware only succeeded after a de Milde pupil came to Meissen. This tea-pot has polychrome ornament set with garnets, often imitated by Böttger, sometimes, it is claimed, down to the mark.

De Milde's official mark (reg. 1680) is rare; usually his name accompanies a fox running to the left.

c) Inkstand, tin-glazed earthenware, painted in enamel colours, mark: PAK De Grieksche A; Delft, Netherlands, c. 1720; ht. 4¾″ (12.3 cm.), lgth. 7⅞″ (20 cm.).

Japanese Imari porcelain first arrived in Europe about 1700. The decoration is underglaze blue combined with an overglaze pattern of gold and red requiring a second firing in a muffle-kiln. Soon the straightforward imitations gave way to Delft versions decorated in gold combined with bright blue, red and green.

This piece was signed by Pieter Adriaenson Kocks, director of The Greek A (1701-1722) which employed several good decorators. Only a few Delft factories used muffle-kilns but the introduction of enamel enabled the industry to compete with the Oriental and later European porcelain.

d) Hexagonal oil-cruet and cover, tin-glazed earthenware with olive-green ground, mark: LVD; Het Jonge Moriaenshooft (1692-1730), Delft, Netherlands; ht. 6⅛″ (15.5 cm.).

This rare jug can be dated and attributed with almost complete certainty; Lieven van Dalen bought The Young Moor's Head from Rochus Hoppesteyn's widow and his work has a very limited range. No polychrome or blue wares can be attributed to him.

The grounds, always dark brown or olive-green, had a meticulously painted Chinese and Japanese-inspired linear design with birds, insects and flowering branches. His borders are simple hatching or arches, with slight scrolling on handles and spouts. Although this shape appears Middle Eastern, it is probably a copy of a Chinese ewer, itself of Persian derivation.

Opposite:
Reeded vase in tin-glazed earthenware painted in enamel colours; Delft, Holland, late 17th century. Tin-glazed ware is often fragile; early pieces are rare and even damaged pieces such as this are sought after.

a) Dish, tin-glazed earthenware painted in colours with a subject depicting Paris and Venus in a landscape; Lyons, France, 1550–1600; dia. 9¼″ (23.5 cm.).

Until the late 16th century, tin-glazed earthenware in France remained closely related to Italian maiolica, made in the southern province by Frenchmen imitating Italians, or, as is probable here, by Italian potters living and working in Lyons. At Lyons, tradition tended towards classical or biblical scenes, often adapted from woodcuts, and followed the rather unsatisfactory *istoriato* (see p. 134*d*) style usually associated with Urbino. Sometimes the painting wandered right over the edge of the dish and even this design, apart from the determined little cupid and brilliant colours, is rather crude and stereotyped.

b) Plate, decorated with masks in relief and painted with coloured glazes; by Bernard Palissy; France, c. 1550; dia. 9″ (23 cm.).

Bernard Palissy (1510–1590) was a glass painter who traditionally turned potter after seeing work from Saint Porchaire. A Huguenot under court patronage, he was nevertheless persecuted, dying in prison, (see p. 163*d*).

Clear sharp designs were enhanced by brilliant, mingled glazes; white was achieved without tin oxide, by allowing the low-fired white clay body to show through a translucent lead-glaze.

This rare plate is much more attractive than his large elaborate dishes, overburdened with snakes, foliage, rocks and marine creatures, and so often faked.

c) Drug-jar, tin-glazed earthenware, painted in colours; Nîmes, France, 16th century; ht. 9½″ (24 cm.).

Early French faience was made at Rouen, Lyons and Nevers in the north and centre, at Nîmes and Montpellier in the south; however, wet drug-jars made in southern France have a small ring between the spout and body. The reserved-leaf decoration is a traditional Faenza pattern, *a quartieri*. Many pieces formerly ascribed to Nîmes are now attributed to Montpellier, which, in the late 16th and early 17th century, supplied two hospitals. The potter families of Montpellier—Estève, Ducoin, the Faviers, Olliviers and Boissiers—did a great deal of original work decorated in a free style with masks, fruit and flowers.

d) Baluster vase, tin-glazed earthenware, white on blue, the so-called 'Bleu Nevers' decoration; Nevers, France, mid-17th century; ht. 13¾″ (34.9 cm.).

During the Italian Renaissance a deep blue-pigmented lead-glaze was used at Faenza, Venice, and later Nevers. Several factories (Rouen, St. Omer, Delft, Bristol) tried to emulate the opaque brilliance of Nevers blue, made from 1630 till about 1700.

Some vases were directly inspired by China, others were influenced by Isnik and Islamic interpretations of Chinese originals. A bold opaque white tulip and carnation design, sometimes overpainted in yellow, is called '*bleu persan*'. However, the shape of this vase and the scene within a medallion of cloud-scrolls are typically Chinese.

Opposite:
Dish in tin-glazed earthenware with copper lustre; Hispano-Moresque; Spain, c. 1520.

a) Dish, tin-glazed earthenware painted in colours with the so-called 'inlaid yellow' decoration; Rouen, France, 1725–1750; dia. 22" (56 cm.).

This decoration, difficult and expensive to produce, was confined to Rouen. The blue and white *lambrequins* (also more accurately called *broderies*, or lacework), invented at the Normandy factory, were copied occasionally in France and the Netherlands, but the central yellow rosette appears nowhere else. Not, of course, truly 'inlaid', but a complicated design of mosaic, arabesques and fine scrolls in black or purple, closely resembling the elaborate goldsmiths' work on watch-cases. The yellow ground is embellished with figures—putti, musicians or huntsmen—reserved in white. Very rare pieces are painted in yellow monochrome; only one or two examples are known.

b) Plate, tin-glazed earthenware, polychrome decoration; Rouen, France, 1720–1740; dia. 10" (25.5 cm.).

This style is usually attributed to Giullibaud, who married the widow of Levavasseur, a pottery owner. Rouen still used high-temperature colours of magnificent quality. The dominant *style rayonnant* was giving way, rather belatedly, before Oriental and rococo influence. The Rouen craftsmen expressed their symmetrical feeling with motifs regularly spaced within the green-and-red mosaic border, and central, rather stereotyped, flowers. This distinctive style is still used in modern French versions. Early pieces have a rather heavy body, and a greenish-blue, often very crackled glaze, caused by impurities in the clay and by the pewter added to the glaze.

c) Wine-cistern in the form of a Child Bacchus, tin-glazed earthenware painted in blue; France, perhaps Rouen, mid-18th century; ht. 21¼" (54 cm.).

After initially copying Nevers and Delft, Rouen became the leading and most influential factory in France. Sinceny had over forty Rouen potters by 1740. Lille also employed Rouen workers, making almost slavish copies in extremely light faience with a rather yellowish ground, distinguishable from Rouen.

This cheerful little Bacchus is one of three known to the writer, each with a different attribution—one Lille, one, doubtfully, Sinceny and one Rouen. Apparently from the same mould, one still has its cover. The decoration on this piece is presumably unfinished; the jug is unpainted and the vine-leaf design summary in comparison with the others.

d) Covered ewer, tin-glazed earthenware painted in colours, mark: S in underglaze blue; Sinceny, France, mid-18th century; ht. 11¼" (28.5 cm.).

The small factory at Sinceny was at first entirely run by potters from the parent factory at Rouen. It began (1734) with the already outmoded monochrome blue—later developing a personal quality while still following Rouen designs, and excelling particularly in Chinese figures in landscapes, more freely-painted waterplants, and flowers such as this familiar carnation pattern. After 1760, before the introduction of enamels, Sinceny became more independent, devising the Yellow Rose pattern and naturalistic tulip bouquets. Sinceny suffered acutely from other small potteries luring away its employees, so care should be exercised in making attributions.

a) Plate, tin-glazed earthenware, opaque white and manganese on a blue-tinted ground; Saint-Amand-Les-Eaux, France, mid-18th century; dia. 8¾″ (22.3 cm.).

In 1775 two factories were reported at Saint Amand, reputedly 'as good as Rouen'. However, the factory run by descendants of Barthélémy Dorez, of Lille, is less well known than the Fauquez faiencerie, 1718–1802.

Fauquez decoration was a rather prim Chinoiserie, as in this example, and, of course, imitations of Rouen rococo. But their most interesting work is a delicate opaque-white on a pearly, bluish-grey ground called *bianco-sopra-bianco* (white on white, of Italian origin) usually with blue or violet flowers. It bears a deceptive similarity to some tin-glaze produced at Bristol, England.

b) Plate, tin-glazed earthenware painted in high-temperature colours, the figure-subject a greenish-blue monochrome; Joseph Fauchier II; Marseilles, France, mid-18th century; dia. 11⅛″ (28.4 cm.).

The work of the Fauchier family is outstanding; several large models thickly glazed in white are signed and dated by Joseph Fauchier I, manager of St. Lazare, 1711–1724, until he founded the Pentagon at Marseilles. After his death (1751) it passed to his nephew, Joseph Fauchier II, flourishing until the 19th century.

The Fauchiers preferred *grand feu* colours and skilfully adapted them to changing tastes, although they must also have used enamels. They invented the thick, popular yellow glaze, but their delicate naturalistic flowers show up better against white. This 'Watteau' scene has a rococo border of scrolling flowers and leaves.

---

c) Plate, sugar-bowl, jug and spoon; tin-glazed earthenware painted in enamel colours; Sceaux, France, 1750–1800.

The absolute monopoly of the Sèvres Royal porcelain factory accounts in a devious way for the fine quality of Sceaux faience. Jacques Chapelle, prevented from competing with Sèvres, determined to make the best possible imitations. His very fine, close-grained lead-glazed body was advertised as *faience japonnée*.

Many of the best artists come from Sèvres, Mennecy, Strasbourg and possibly Marseilles, consequently the decoration was varied and of the highest quality: birds, flowers, landscapes, illustrations to Aesop's fables, vegetable and bird tureens as well as small figures in the manner of Niderviller. The factory made popular faience throughout the 19th century.

d) Ewer and cover, tin-glazed earthenware painted in enamel colours; Marseilles, France, 1750–1760; ht. 9½″ (24 cm.).

Marseilles had great influence on the development of French enamels on tin-glaze. Widow Perrin was one famous producer whose mark is often faked. However, modern copies rarely match the brilliant painting of the originals.

This ewer is probably by Honoré Savy who taught Perrin apprentices enamel-painting, and muffle-kiln firing. Traditionally, he specialized in this predominantly black and green painting, using his own green enamel.

However, fruit, flowers and marine subjects on rococo shapes, a fine white glaze and the famous yellow ground are all general characteristics of Marseilles, and one cannot be too dogmatic about attributions.

Ceramics

Continental Pottery
FRENCH

a) *Oval dish, tin-glazed earthenware decorated with grotesque figures, after Jacques Callot, mark: OL; Moustiers, France, c. 1750; 16⅝" by 12½" (42.2 cm by 31.7 cm.).*

Joseph Olérys of Marseilles (1697–1749), trained by Clérissy at Moustiers, became manager at Alcora in 1726 (cf. p. 133a). There he learned to manage new underglaze colours which revolutionized production at the Olérys-Laugier factory, founded in 1738. It continued until 1793.

Olérys' *grotesques* were imitated everywhere in southern France—fanciful, feathered savages with bow or sword, attenuated hybrid birds, palm trees on little hills and perhaps a ruin or two. The best have curving rims with growing flowers and foliage; colours are orange, yellow and green; monochromes are also found. The rare blue *camaïeu* is normally attributed to Spain.

Mark of the Olérys-Langier factory.

b) *Wall-fountain and basin, tin-glazed earthenware painted in blue; Strasbourg, France, 1735; fountain ht. 19⅛" (48.5 cm.), basin ht. 5¼" (13 cm.), dia. 17¼" (44 cm.).*

Strasbourg is so famous for its vivid polychrome that one overlooks the earlier period (until c. 1744) when first Charles François Hannong, but principally his son Paul, worked in blue and white. This magnificent piece has relief masks, swags, garlands and lambrequin borders still dominating the rococo influence of foliate scrolls, beautifully-carved shell motifs and asymmetrical leaves on the mount. Although clearly derived from Rouen, the designs are freer and less monotonous. Later Paul abandoned this style altogether, favouring the polychrome wares of the *grand feu*, and then the full palette of enamels fired in the muffle-kiln (*petit feu*).

c) *Boar, tin-glazed earthenware painted in naturalistic colours; Strasbourg, France, c. 1755; lgth. 8⅞" (22.5 cm.).*

Strasbourg flourished with every plastic technique, *grand* and *petit feu* colours and many fine artists. Until porcelain manufacture moved to Frankenthal, evading the French Royal monopoly, the Lanz brothers sculpted the larger pieces, and probably most of the figures at Strasbourg, which specialized in huntsmen, animals and monumental bird-shaped tureens.

The boar exhibits the technical mastery achieved by the 1750s: brilliant modelling, perfect firing control even to the fragile unsupported legs, realistic enamels—greenish-black hide, manganese-pink snout, and grassy-green base. Altogether a *tour de force* from the classic period of Paul Hannong's administration at Strasbourg.

d) *Stove of tin-glazed earthenware, painted in monochrome red; Strasbourg, France, c. 1760.*

This splendid stove was made in Strasbourg, so renowned for exceptional virtuosity that it was imitated all over Europe. Monumental in size and very rococo, it retains a certain baroque feeling with pediment, urn and swag. Medallions of female busts represent the four seasons, other scenes are after Boucher and Lancret. This pale, purplish-red colour was invented by Andreas Cassius of Leyden with nitric acid, red pigment and gold. It was very difficult to control and probably expensive, so that such a large stove would have been a matter of prestige as well as warmth.

Mark on c.

a) Plaque decorated with a stag-hunt in a landscape, tin-glazed earthenware painted in blue and white; Röstrand, Sweden, c. 1726-50; 18" by 13½" (46 by 35 cm.).

The factory at Rörstrand started in 1726 and produced mainly blue and white wares until Anders Fahlstrom, the first native director, developed the range of colour and Swedish-designed decoration. This table top, typical both in shape and painting, is an excellent example of the whole genre. Rörstrand generally followed faience styles—Marseilles, Strasbourg, and *bianco-sopra-bianco* from St-Amand-les-Eaux or Bristol; the English influence (creamware and transfer-printing) was growing by the mid-seventies. After 1796 'Wedgwood' creamware was almost the only product. The factory finally returned to Swedish design and fine modern pottery.

b) Candlestick, tin-glazed earthenware in the form of a seated Chinaman, polychrome enamels, painted by Johann Otto Franzén; Marieberg, Sweden, c. 1758-1766; ht. 14" (36 cm.).

Johann Ehrenreich, a German, established Marieberg (1758) on Kungsholmen Island, Stockholm. Many early pieces were unpainted, the modelling and applied decoration being effective alone. Colours included a bright, rather violet-toned blue, crimson, purple, black and a strong green (far superior to the enamels then used at Rörstrand) with very little gilding.

This splendid Chinaman recalls the elaborate Chinese figures made in contemporary German porcelain.

After Ehrenreich's backers dismissed him in 1766 for financial reasons, Pierre Berthevin brought a French influence from Mennecy. Transfer-printing and English style creamware were introduced before Marieberg was finally sold to Rörstrand in 1782.

Rorfl 2769 / 5 / H 5

Mark on a.

---

c) Oval dish, tin-glazed earthenware, marked: OB, painted in blue; Østerbro, Denmark, c. 1765; 12⅜" by 18" (31.5 by 46 cm.).

The short-lived Østerbro factory (1763-1769) was started by Peter Hofnagel from Herrebøe, Norway. He was accused of luring workmen from existing factories and infringing the rights of Gierloff at Store Kongensgade in Copenhagen. Gierloff had all Hofnagel's stock and equipment seized pending the lawsuit in 1769, after which Østerbro had to close.

Hofnagel advertised a purple-painted tureen, and rococo candlesticks, which are consequently attributed to him. The mediocre faience was painted normally only in blue or manganese, sometimes lightly gilded. Marks are the only distinction between Østerbro and Store Kongensgade.

d) Ice-pail, tin-glazed earthenware painted in enamel colours; Kastrup, Denmark, c. 1760; ht. 8¼" (21 cm.).

Jacob Fortling, the Danish court architect, received a privilege in 1755 to make stoneware on Amager Island. First Joseph Adam Hannong from Strasbourg, and then a colour chemist supervised the enterprise, which obviously has a wider range of production. Fortling died in 1761; the business ended up after 1772 making industrial stoneware and, as usual, English-style creamware.

Kastrup faience is largely influenced by Strasbourg. Enamel-painted sprigs of yellow tulips and a crimson rose are said to be characteristic. The Watteau-scene was probably copied from a print of a south European landscape.

English Pottery Introduction

Pottery was made in Britain from time immemorial but little of it concerns the collector of antiques. Sturdy and useful at first, gradually it assumed elegance of form and refinement of ornament. Mediaeval pottery points the way. All the techniques available to the seventeenth century slip-potter were known then: trailing, appliqué, incising, impressing, modelling, the lot. Pottery as a collectable was beginning.

Two glazes emerge in the Middle Ages to be fully developed later—lead-glazes stained with copper oxides (the primitive forerunner of Wedgwood's green glaze) and a black glaze produced from iron.

The impetus to improvement came from increased domestic amenity and improved communication. The first resulted in more care in local manufacture, the second in new kinds of pottery: stoneware salt-glazed which came from the Rhineland, and polychrome pottery like that made at Faenza and Antwerp, introduced by refugees from persecution and economic depression.

Makers of tin-enamelled pottery established themselves first at Norwich and soon after in London at Aldgate. Before long, they moved to South Bank at Southwark and Lambeth. A new industry was born. From Lambeth, potters went to Bristol and from thence to Liverpool. Soon tin-enamelled pottery was being made in Scotland and Ireland also. At first the styles were Renaissance and Italianate; Chinese-Dutch styles came afterwards.

But tin-enamelled pottery, gay as it was, chipped far too easily. More durable pottery took its place and to all intents and purposes, the industry was dead by 1780.

Salt-glazed stoneware, as far as tableware is concerned, suffered the same fate. After sporadic attempts to produce it, John Dwight of Fulham devised a formula, and patented it. The secret soon leaked out. Staffordshire and Nottingham potters were quick off the mark. Nottingham stuck to brown and excelled in it. Staffordshire sought after something finer, more like porcelain, and by dint of constant experimentation and innovation, succeeded in making a white stoneware of superlative quality.

Tea-pots and figures, puzzle-jugs and jelly moulds were made in it. Potters cast it in elaborate moulds, made imitation agate-stone cats and rabbits, scratched floral ornament in the clay, rubbed cobalt into the incisions and enamelled it in bright colours. But salt-glaze was rough on the furniture and cutlery. Soon this too disappeared from the table, underground, to find a use in sewage pipes and chemical stoneware.

Native pottery had not stood still either. In Staffordshire slip decoration was taken to a high level of technical excellence. Regional styles began to emerge in Kent, Sussex, Devonshire, Somerset, North Wales and Yorkshire. Elers developed the Staffordshire red clay into a fine 'red porcelain' and made expensive little tea-pots in it. Staffordshire potters flattered Elers by imitation. Soon fine tableware made in Staffordshire began to appear on the market.

To make these finer wares, white plastic clay was imported from Dorset and Devon. Flint was introduced into the earthenware body to make it stronger and whiter; the potters' wheel was improved and the lathe introduced. Plaster-of-Paris moulds enabled the potter to make all kinds of unusual shapes; improved glazing and firing techniques enabled him to manufacture better pottery with less loss.

The scene was set for a great advance when Josiah Wedgwood appeared. He gathered up the strands of development made by Astbury, Whieldon, Booth, Daniel and his own forebears, and after incessant experimentation, transformed the local product into the beautiful cream-coloured earthenware, which he called—after Royal patronage—Queensware.

He took Elers' 'red porcelain' and from it made Rosso Antico, the native Black Egyptian he changed into Basaltes, a new porcellanous stoneware he called Jasper; and in these bodies he made functional vegetable dishes and tea-pots, and ornamental vases in the antique style.

Cream-colour, jasper and basaltes were to be seen everywhere; but man, and more particularly woman, hankers for novelty. A new kind of pottery was soon wanted, as good as cream-colour, as white as porcelain and more durable than either. Stone china—ironstone china—was the answer. Pictures were wanted on pottery. Blue underglaze transfer-prints met the demand with scenes from contemporary history, religion, drama and topography.

Figures made gay many a cottage mantelpiece. Wesley might rub shoulders with Palmer the poisoner, or Wellington with Van Amburgh the lion tamer. Garden seats and umbrella stands were made in maiolica; shrimp measures and beer jugs in tobacco-spit ware.

By the middle of the nineteenth century, vast quantities of pottery were being manufactured; good, bad, and indifferent—mostly indifferent. Revival set in after the Great Exhibition. The bid for greater simplicity resulted in better shapes and finer glazes.

a) Jug, light buff coloured earthenware, baluster shape with pronounced roll at lip and bold loop handle, under a lead glaze; found at Oxford, c. 1325–1350; ht. 13½" (34.3 cm.).

The tall baluster shape is characteristic of many early mediaeval jugs made in England and France, although later examples tend to be less elegant and much more robust and sturdy in appearance. Developed almost as a decorative feature are the irregular ridges or wheel marks of the thrower. Such articles were made in many parts of England with regional variations but, as they are generally associated with archaeological excavations, few turn up in the antique trade.

b) Oval dish, tin-enamelled earthenware; made at Lambeth, c. 1633–1697; lgth. 19¾" (50.2 cm.).

This dish is moulded in relief with circular and oblong wells separated by masks and bunches of fruit on the rim, and a reclining naked woman and five children in a formal setting in the centre. It is painted in the traditional four colour palette of the makers of maiolica, faience and delft. Such dishes, adapted from Bernard Palissy's model *La Fécondité* (cf. 153*d*), are known from dated examples to have been made in England from 1633–1697. The earlier ones are generally in polychrome, the later ones in blue and white. Some bear the arms of the City Companies of London.

---

c) Monteith (glass cooler), tin-enamelled earthenware, decorated with Chinese figures in a landscape; Lambeth, c. 1680–90; dia. 2" (5.1 cm.).

In opaque white enamel upon a royal blue ground, this montieth is in the *bleu persan* style of Nevers *faience* (cf. p. 145*d*). Potters at Nevers in France introduced this type of decoration about 1650 and later scholars mistakenly thought it was of Persian origin, hence the term *bleu persan*. It was imitated at Delft in Holland, and at Bristol and Lambeth in England from about 1680. Late Ming floral and figure subjects are frequent on the attractive jars, jugs, wine coolers, plates and mugs decorated in this manner.

d) Vase and cover, tin-enamelled earthenware, baluster form, painted in blue on unfired raw glaze; Liverpool, c. 1735–40; ht. 17½" (44.5 cm.).

The vase is decorated with peonies and rocks and the helmet-shaped cover with a peony and a butterfly. The pleated-petalled peony, a common Chinese decoration emblematic of summer and having sexual overtones, occurs frequently upon porcelain and tin-enamelled earthenware made in emulation of the Chinese. Such tin-enamelled earthenware made in Britain at Lambeth, Bristol and Liverpool is frequently called delft after the town in Holland which became famous as a centre for its manufacture.

Ceramics

English Pottery
TIN-ENAMELWARE

RED AND BROWN
EARTHENWARE

a) Tea-pot, tin-enamelled earthenware, oviform in shape with an inset flat lid and rounded knob; Lambeth, c. 1740; ht. 4" (10.2 cm.).

The high elliptical loop handle on this example terminates in a scroll and is balanced by a straight spout. It was painted in cobalt upon the raw glaze with sprays of flowers and insects, and round the shoulder of the pot and the edge of the lid there is a border of Chinese cloud-scroll ornament. This is an excellent example of the direct and dexterous brushwork of the Lambeth delft potters.

b) Bough or flowerpot, tin-enamelled earthenware, hollow rectangular brick, decorated with flowers on raw unfired glaze; Bristol, c. 1740; lgth. 5¾" (14.6 cm.).

Characteristic of Bristol 'bricks' is the large central rectangular hole in the top flanked by smaller circular ones, and the shaping of the feet from the fronts and sides of the vessel. Similar bricks were made at all the English delftware potteries, Lambeth, Bristol and Liverpool. It is believed they were used to display flowers or leaves, or as pen and ink stands.

---

c) Tyg or posset pot, red earthenware, multi-handled and covered with a shiny iron-black glaze; Staffordshire, c. 1660; ht. 5¼" (13.3 cm.).

Black-glazed pottery was made from late in the 15th century until the beginning of the 18th century at many places in England, but particularly in Yorkshire in the 16th and 17th centuries, and in Staffordshire. Because many early examples have been found on monastic sites it was called 'Cistercian' ware, but obviously most of the pottery within the class was made for domestic purposes.

The glaze of this piece is brownish, less lustrous and flecked with dark streaks due to over-firing in the kiln.

d) Tyg, brown earthenware, cylindrical with four double loop handles, inscribed J L, T ᴾ E and 1636, by John Livermore (d. 1658); Wrotham, Kent; ht. 6" (15.2 cm.).

Livermore's initials occur on Wrotham pottery from 1612 until 1649. Wrotham wares are distinctive in style; early shapes and decorations are simple, later ones are often rather fussy and over-ornamented with excessive use of dots and 'stitches' of slip. Handles are often grooved and filled with a twisted cord of brown and white. The term 'tyg' is of obscure origin but is generally applied to a multi-handled beaker.

This tyg is decorated with pads and rosettes of white clay under a clear lead glaze.

a) left: Earthenware dish with close trellis border on the rim, interrupted by a panel with the name thomas toFT; *Shelton, Staffordshire, c. 1660; dia. 16¾″ 42.5 cm.).*

In the centre of this dish is a lady holding a fleur-de-lis and a rose, flanked by sprays of leaves and triple vessica shapes. It is coated on the upper surface with white slip and decorated with trails of dark brown and white slip.

b) centre: Dutch oven, red earthenware; Staffordshire, c. 1690; wdth. 9½″ (24.1 cm.), ht. 8½″ (21.6 cm.),

The vigorous and spirited use of the slip-trailer has here resulted in a particularly fine piece. It is decorated with two tulips in a double-handled vase framed on each side by a running band of S-curves, and at the top by a chevron and dot border under a clear lead glaze. A number of basic motifs were used by the Staffordshire potter to build up decorative patterns, among them the triangle, chevron, wave, vessica, S-curve and dots.

c) right: Cup, buff coloured earthenware, inscribed with initials and date I B 1700 in brown slip jewelled with white dots; Staffordshire, 1700; ht. 3¼″ (8.3 cm.).

Thistle-shaped with a bold loop handle, the lower part of this cup is decorated with alternate stripes of open and fine marbling.

Cups in slip-decorated pottery are comparatively rare; this example provides a masterly combination of trailed, jewelled and combed decoration.

---

d) Holdall in the form of a cradle, red earthenware, inscribed Made by Ralph Shaw October the 31 Cobridg: gate *on the sides and* MT 1740; *North Staffordshire; lgth. 10¾″ (27.3 cm.).*

Cradles were made in North Staffordshire and elsewhere from the second half of the 17th century until early Victorian times. Having the same fertility significance as the delftware *La Fécondité* dishes (see p. 151b) they were frequently given as presents to newly married couples. Some cradles were made in cream-coloured earthenware at the end of the 18th century and beginning of the 19th century, occasionally with the figure of a child in them.

This holdall is decorated in trailed white slip.

e) Earthenware dish, red clay; Staffordshire, c. 1750; dia. 14¾″ (37.5 cm.).

Here the red clay is covered with an orange-red slip and decorated with white slip freely trailed over the surface. On the rim is a border of interlaced Gothic arches with elliptical shapes and dots underneath; in the centre a Chinese figure holding a parasol stands beside a house and tree on the banks of a river, while two birds fly overhead. Such Chinoiserie subjects are rare on Staffordshire slip-decorated pottery—usually it is decorated with patriotic, religious or topical emblems.

a) Harvest jug, brown earthenware, bulbous form with a cylindrical neck, by Edward Reed; Bideford, North Devon, 1741; ht. 14½" (36.8 cm.).

The handle of this jug is a bold loop ending in a coil; the jug itself is covered with an engobe of white slip through which the decoration was drawn with a pointed stick and the background scraped away. Under the lip are the Royal Arms and Supporters with the initials 'G.R.' and the date. At the front is a woman holding a flowering plant; the shoulder is surrounded by a long inscription including the words 'made by me Edward Reed'.

Note the skilful use of the *sgraffiato* technique (see p. 133b), and the typical coiled handle terminal.

b) Tea-pot, dark brown earthenware, possibly made by John Astbury of Shelton, Staffordshire, c. 1735–40; ht. 4½" (11.4 cm.).

This globular tea-pot has white crabstock handles and spout, and is decorated with applied leaf-shaped pads of white pipeclay, grapes, stems and tendrils growing from the handle. The applied leaves and stems are cracked and fissured because of unequal shrinkage during the drying and firing process.

Many shards of tea-wares in brown clay edged with white have been found on the site of Astbury's factory. Similar wares were made by Samuel Bell at the Pomona factory, Newcastle-under-Lyme, Staffordshire, from 1725-1745.

---

c) Tea-pot, solid agate earthenware, unmarked but probably by Thomas Whieldon; Fenton, Staffordshire, c. 1750; ht. 6" (15.2 cm.).

This example is in the form of a pecten shell with a bird spout, fish handle and lion knob. The pecten shell motif was used extensively for the shape of jugs and tea-pots and as a form of ornament in mid-18th century.

The agate clay is formed from wedging together fine slices of white, blue-stained and brown clay. When agate ware was abandoned for table wares, Wedgwood used solid agate for vases. He also used granite, pebble and marbled glazes frequently for application on cream-coloured bodies.

d) Lovers seated within an alcove, surmounted by a bird, earthenware, probably by Thomas Whieldon; Staffordshire, c. 1755; ht. 5¾" (14.6 cm.).

This alcove group has a clear lead glaze stained green and purple with copper and manganese oxides. Each part was formed by hand and luted together with slip in the same manner as the celebrated 'Pew Groups'.

Such groups represent the witty manipulative skills of the Staffordshire potter at their best, but it is doubtful if the type originated in Staffordshire. Similarly-fashioned alcove groups were made in tin-enamelled earthenware at Delft in Holland c. 1745–50.

Staffordshire 'Pew Group'.

a) Two-handled loving cup, brown salt-glazed stoneware; Nottingham, c. 1725; ht. 9″ (22.9 cm.).

Decorated with a narrow band of engine-turned ornament, this cup has an incised floral decoration on one side and an inscription 'Edward Taylor and Elizabeth His Wife March the 25th Anno Domini 1725', on the other. The incisions were made with the point of a nail or stick in the unfired clay.

Nottingham was an important centre of stoneware manufacture from c. 1690-1800; the lustrous nut-brown colour and extremely fine potting are characteristic of its wares. Similar brown stonewares were made in Derbyshire and at Fulham, London.

b) Cup, white salt-glazed stoneware; Staffordshire, c. 1735-40; ht. 2¾″ (7 cm.).

This cup is decorated with three applied sprays of prunus blossom and the bold flat-sided handle is embellished with scrolls and applied floral ornament. This type of sprig-moulded ornament was derived from Chinese Fukien porcelain and also occurs on Chelsea, early Derby and Bow porcelain. It is now known that North Staffordshire potters worked at the Bow and Chelsea factories, which may account for similarities in style.

---

c) Rabbit, salt-glazed stoneware; Staffordshire, c. 1745; ht. 2½″ (6.4 cm.).

The body and mound are moulded in brown and white clay, the head and applied flowers in white clay with touches of brown slip for the eyes. Cats, birds and other creatures were similarly made in cobalt-stained clay and white clay, sometimes with additional splashes of blue (see p. 192b).

Country potworks in Staffordshire, the West Country and Sussex produced cruder imagery in lead-glazed red and yellow agate ware from the 17th century on.

d) Jug, white salt-glazed stoneware; Staffordshire, c. 1750; ht. 5½″ (14 cm.).

The jug is decorated with a freely incised floral spray spreading on both sides, and a narrow rouletted border stained with cobalt. Such decorations are classified as 'Scratch Blue', although in the 18th century the technique was called 'flowering' and was done by women and girls, who decorated the ware with flowers 'traced with the point of an iron nail' in the unfired clay. Dated pieces have been recorded from 1724 until 1776, when salt-glazed stoneware was fast going out of favour. The clean line and careful shaping of the lip as well as the bold calligraphy of the drawing should be noted.

155

Ceramics

English Pottery
SALT-GLAZED WARE

a) Tea-pot, salt-glazed stoneware, of globular form by Aaron Wedgwood and William Littler; Brownhills, Tunstall, Staffordshire, c. 1750; ht. 5½" (14 cm.).

The tea-pot is on three masked feet, has a crab-stock handle and spout, and an acorn knob on the lid. Tea-pots of this shape were described in contemporary invoices as 'cut feet teapots'. The fine blue colouring is due to a coating of cobalt stained slip applied to the ware in the 'green' state before the salt-glaze firing.

William Littler (see p. 194d) appears to have abandoned manufacture of stoneware about 1750 in order to concentrate upon the production of porcelain at Longton Hall.

b) Figure group, white salt-glazed earthenware, thought to be modelled by Aaron Wood; Staffordshire, c. 1755; ht. 5¼" (13.3 cm.).

In this group the lovers embrace upon a mound of earth against the stump of a tree. Except for the eyes, which are picked out with dark brown slip, the group is uncoloured.

This is a characteristic example of the 'image toys' made in salt-glazed and lead-glazed earthenware by Staffordshire potters such as Thomas Whieldon, Aaron and Thomas Wedgwood between 1735 and 1760. The treatment of the heads should be compared with the masks at the back of some of the celebrated 'Pew' groups.

WEDGWOOD POTTERY

c) Vase and cover, blue and white jasper, with the mark WEDGWOOD impressed, by Josiah Wedgwood; Etruria, 1790; 13½" (34.3 cm.).

This is decorated with white relief figures representing Hercules in the garden of the Hesperides. The white handles rising above the blue ovoid shape effectively balance the vase-like knob.

Jasper is a fine white porcellanous stoneware capable of being stained throughout its substance with metallic oxides. Wedgwood produced many colours including sage green, lilac, yellow and various blues. Jasper was introduced in 1774 after Wedgwood had made thousands of trials, and became extremely popular for decorative pottery ranging from bell-pulls and beads to insets for fireplaces and furniture. Other potters made jasper, among them Turner, Adams and Neale.

d) Jug, black basaltes, mark: WEDGWOOD in small upper case letters impressed; Josiah Wedgwood, Etruria, c. 1785; ht. 7½" (19.1 cm.).

This jug has a bold loop handle terminating in a mask and a finely shaped lip, the cover surmounted by a spherical knob. Basaltes is a refinement of the traditional Staffordshire Egyptian Black into an extremely dense black stoneware with a smooth silky surface, capable of taking slight patina with time. Wedgwood used it for vases, library busts, plaques and medallions, and said of it 'the Black is Sterling and will last forever'. It is still made today. Note the beauty of line and quality of finish.

a) Sucrier and cover white stoneware, mark: Turner impressed; John & William Turner, Lane End, Staffordshire, c. 1790–1795; ht. 5¼″ (13.3 cm.), sq. base 2⅝″ (6.7 cm.).

The body is moulded in relief, with projecting handles, the cover floriated, pierced and surmounted by a lion. The background to the relief medallion is painted with dark brown enamel. Turner's white stoneware is a hard, dense vitrified body, opaque but essentially porcellanous in character. It was first made by John Turner the elder (1738–1787) about 1780 and was continued in production for about twenty-five years. Shapes are generally hard and severe in line and in the neo-classic taste.

b) Tea-pot, white stoneware, moulded in relief with a sliding lid and flower knob and bright blue enamel panels; unmarked, probably made by David Dunderdale, Castleford, Yorkshire; c. 1795–1800; ht. 5¾″ (14.6 cm.).

Although unmarked examples are rare, the Castleford type tea-pot is easily recognized by the shape and fit of the lid, and the parapet or collar of the pot. Some examples have painted polychrome landscape panels instead of figural reliefs. Other manufacturers made relief decorated white stoneware tea-pots, among them Heath & Son of Burslem, Benjamin Plant of Longton, Clulow & Co., Fenton and Sowter & Co., Mexborough, Yorkshire.

TURNER

Mark on a.

---

c) Plate, cream-coloured earthenware, mark: 38 in brown, Josiah Wedgwood, 1773–74; dia. 9¾″ (24.8 cm.).

This is part of the service made by Josiah Wedgwood in 1773–74 for the Chesmen Palace of the Empress Catherine of Russia. The service consisted of 952 pieces, each painted with a different view of English scenery. The rim of this plate is painted with a wreath of oak leaves and in the centre in purple-brown, is a view of Fowey Castle, Cornwall. Wedgwood's costs in producing this service, including artists' fees for drawings, prints and factory costs amounted to £2,600: he was paid £2,700 for it.

d) Plate, cream-coloured earthenware, decorated in enamel colours in the Delft style with an image of Our Lady of Kevelaar; mark: $\frac{Turner}{2}$ impressed, John Turner, Lane End, Staffordshire, c. 1780; dia. 9¾″ (24.8 cm.).

John Turner and his sons exported considerable quantities of earthenware 'in the white' for decoration in Holland. The subjects most commonly found on Delft decorated Turner ware are the 'Virgin and Child' which is frequently inscribed 'Onse Live Vrouw Tot Kevelaar', and was painted on wares sold as souvenirs to pilgrims to the shrine of Kevelaar, and the 'Prodigal Son'. Dutch enamelling also occurs on earthenware made by Heath and the Leeds Pottery.

TURNER
2

Mark on d.

English Pottery
CREAM WARE

a) Tureen, cover and ladle, mark: Neale & Co. *in large letters impressed under the tureen, the lid inscribed 12 by James Neale & Co., Hanley, c. 1785; ht. 6″ (15.2 cm.).*

This cream-coloured earthenware tureen is decorated with .strawberry leaf and has a beaded border in green and two shades of brown. The perfecting of cream-coloured earthenware was Wedgwood's greatest achievement but he was not alone in this field. The fine earthenwares made by his rivals and competitors such as Baddeley, Whitehead and Bacchus, often pass unrecognized because they are rarely marked. James Neale was one of his most important and successful rivals and produced utility pottery of great elegance and beauty.

NEALE & CO
Mark on a.

b) Candlestick, cream-coloured earthenware; unmarked, Staffordshire, c. 1780–85; ht. 10¾″ (27.3 cm.).

This candlestick is moulded in relief with masks, swags and acanthus leaves; the handles are flattened scrolls, and the base is beaded and gadrooned. Although unmarked, it has been identified as the work of James and Charles Whitehead of Hanley from plate 107 of their extremely rare *Designs of Sundry Articles of Earthenware,* 1798. The business, started by Christopher Charles Whitehead, lasted from c. 1775–1815. Jasper, Egyptian Black, and printed and enamelled earthenware were made; they commanded a sufficient overseas trade to warrant issuing a finely printed catalogue in four languages. Many Whitehead cream-coloured wares were pierced in the Leeds style.

c) Food-warmer, cream-coloured earthenware, comprising covered jug, stand and godet; Leeds, c. 1790; ht. 10″ (25.4 cm.).

The hollow stand is decorated on each side with a human mask and star-shaped piercings: the aperture is surrounded with scrolls and foliage and around the base is a band of gadrooning. There are two entwined strap handles terminating in flowers and leaves. The jug which nests into the rim of the stand has a small loop handle; its cover is shaped to fit over the spout. Similar articles were made for tea.

d) Jug, earthenware, Staffordshire (attributed to Adams factory, Tunstall), 1814; ht. 7″ (17.8 cm.).

This is decorated with an anvil and flowers and foliage in enamel colours in the 'Peasant' style. Under the lip a floriated heart encloses the initials and date 'J W 1814'. Similar wares were made by many Staffordshire potters, including Spode, Davenport, Rogers and Allerton to name but a few. Jugs, mugs, bottles and flasks are the vessels most commonly decorated in this style. Many of them were made as love tokens, or as wedding, anniversary or seasonal gifts.

a) Roman Charity, earthenware figure, painted with coloured lead glazes; Ralph Wood, Burslem, c. 1770; ht. 8" (20.3 cm.).

The inscription near the figure of the man is 'Roman Charity' and impressed inside at the back is mould number '92'. The Wood family comprising Aaron, three generations named Ralph, and Enoch, were all gifted block-cutters, modellers and manufacturers of pottery figures. They gave an impetus to this popular and lucrative branch of the pottery industry in Staffordshire. John Voyez, modeller, was associated with Ralph Wood, and the special understanding of the relation of coloured glazes to the tooling of the original models was probably due to him.

b) Madonna and child, earthenware figure group in coloured enamels on simulated marble base; unmarked, but made by Wood & Caldwell, Burslem, c. 1800; ht. 14" (35.6 cm.).

Wood and Caldwell made this figure from a terracotta *bozetta* by Lucas Fayd'herbe (a pupil and friend of Rubens) which is now in the British Museum, London. Enoch Wood was in partnership with James Caldwell from c. 1792 until 1818. He was himself a capable modeller and produced many figures, often of large size, including a famous portrait bust of John Wesley, modelled from life. Other of his models were based upon the Antique.

c) Lion and unicorn, mark: Walton within a scroll at the back; John Walton, Navigation Rd., Burslem, probably 1820; hts. 6¼" and 6" (15.9 cm. and 15.2 cm.).

These earthenware chimney ornaments are decorated in bright enamel colours. They were probably made for the coronation of King George IV as part of a garniture including as centrepieces the Royal Arms. The parts of these figures were made in separate moulds and assembled, luted together with slip, dried and fired. Painted with brilliant colours they commanded a ready sale in the trade. Some of Walton's moulds passed into the hands of Kents of Burslem and have been extensively used for re-issues.

d) Portrait figure of John Wesley (1703-1791), earthenware; unmarked, probably made by Sampson Smith of Longton, c. 1860; ht. 11" (27.9 cm.).

Wesley is shown in gown and cassock standing within a Gothic niche, the details of which are sparingly picked out in flesh-colour, blue, black and gold. The 'body' is of poor quality earthenware and the glaze is crazed. Such figures were made by pressing bats of clay into three-part moulds. A large number of them were produced over a considerable period of time. Almost identical and extremely rare is the figure of Dr Henry Cooke (1788-1863), the Irish Presbyterian opposed to the disestablishment of the Irish Episcopal Church.

Ceramics

English Pottery
STONE CHINA

a) *Sucrier, cover and plate, stone china, mark on plate:* Turner's-Patent N 6 *in red; John & William Turner, Staffordshire, c. 1800–1803; ht. 5¾″ (14.6 cm.), dia. 6¼″ (15.9 cm.).*

These are decorated in 'oven' blue, red and gold in the Chinese style. Turners' patent No. 2367 was taken out 19 January 1800 for 'a real Porcelain, wholly different from any previously made' which was produced from ground Tabberner's Mine Rock and an equal proportion of Cornish stone. It is grey in colour and not unlike Mason's Patent Ironstone China which succeeded it. Decorations are usually in the Chinese style (see below) although important painted specimens are known.

b) *Centrepiece to a breakfast or supper service, stone china, marks:* M. Mason *impressed and the pattern no. 6 in red; Miles Mason, c. 1806; ht. 7⅛″ (18.1 cm.).*

This centrepiece is transfer-printed in underglaze blue with the popular Broseley willow pattern, and enamelled over in colours. Miles Mason (1752–1822) was originally a chinaman in London (1784–1802) and a manufacturer of porcelain, earthenware and stone china. His stone china, first produced c. 1806, was a strong, durable earthenware which is often translucent. It was the forerunner of the Ironstone China patented by Charles James Mason in 1813, and the so-called granite china of later 19th century manufacture.

M. MASON

Mark on b.

---

c) *Plate, stone china, mark: blue seal enclosing the word* Spode *and* Stone China *beneath, pattern no. 2061 in red; Josiah Spode, c. 1814; dia. 7¼″ (18.4 cm.).*

Josiah Spode began to make stone china about 1813 soon after C. J. Mason (son of Miles Mason) had taken out his patent for Ironstone China. It is a fine, grey porcellanous body, always well potted and frequently translucent. The 'cabbage' pattern, which was based upon a Chinese decoration, proved extremely popular and is still in production. It was introduced c. 1814. This plate is transfer-printed in underglaze blue, enamelled overglaze and gilded, with the 'cabbage' or 'tobacco-leaf' pattern.

d) *Tureen stand, earthenware, transfer-printed in underglaze blue and enamelled, mark:* Mason's Cambrian Argil *impressed; G. M. & C. J. Mason, Fenton, Staffordshire, c. 1820–25; lgth. 14⅜″ (36.5 cm.).*

In 1819 important mineral deposits were opened up by Thomas Ryan at Middletown Hill, North Wales, just over the border from Shrewsbury. Wedgwood experimented with 'Cambria Rock' for a stone china body in 1819, and when the business of Harley & Seckerson of Lane End was sold in 1825, Cambrian Clay was included in the stock. Mason's are the only potters who included the word 'Cambria' as part of their mark.

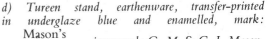

Opposite:
Top: Slipware dish made by Ralph Toft, and slip-decorated earthenware posset pot; England, 1677 and 1696.
Bottom: Earthenware tureen, cover and stand, probably made by Thomas Whieldon; England, c. 1755.

160

a) Plate, ironstone china, mark: Mason's *over a crown and drapery label enclosing the words* Patent Ironstone China *in purple-brown; C. J. Mason, Fenton, Staffordshire, c. 1830–35; dia.* $10\frac{3}{8}''$ *(26.4 cm.).*

The decoration, transfer-printed with a bold 'tobacco-leaf' design in brown and filled in with a dark blue and enamel colours, gilded, was copied from export Chinese porcelain. Mason's Ironstone China varies considerably in colour, weight and quality. For his auction sales which started in 1818, if not earlier, ware was decorated extremely crudely, but other wares were highly finished like this plate.

b) Earthenware plate, circular with eight indentations, mark: W. Mason *in blue under the rim; William Mason, Fenton, Staffordshire, c. 1811–22; dia.* $10''$ *(25.4 cm.).*

William Mason was the elder son of Miles Mason and made earthenware at Fenton, first in partnership with his father and then from 1811 until 1822 on his own account at Sampson Bagnall's works, Fenton. Two patterns only have been identified, namely, 'Broseley Willow' and 'Gothic Ruins'; marked examples are extremely rare. This plate has a flat rimless base: transfer-printed in underglaze blue, with a scroll and flower border enclosing four landscape vignettes and a picture of a gothic ruin in the centre.

Andrew Stevenson of Cobridge made a similar pattern to the 'Gothic Ruins' printed in dark blue and marked *A. Stevenson Staffordshire Warranted.*

Mark on a.

---

c) Plate, earthenware, mark: blue scroll inscribed Water Works Philadelphia, *enclosing initials* R.S.W; *Stevenson & Williams, Lower Manufactory, Cobridge, c. 1825–30; dia.* $10''$ *(25.4 cm.).*

Ralph Stevenson worked the Cobridge factory c. 1802–1835 when he became bankrupt. He manufactured earthenware and ironstone china. His younger brother, Andrew, also made blue-printed American views at another factory in Cobridge. This plate is transfer-printed in underglaze blue, with a wide oak leaf and acorn border framing a landscape including trees, wagon and classical building. The oak leaf border has been used in modern times.

d) Oval dish, earthenware, marks; Minton *impressed with MC conjoined—the date mark for 1871; lgth.* $19\frac{1}{4}''$ *(48.9 cm.).*

This dish is moulded in relief with a figure of Ceres in the centre, and masks, cherubs' heads and cornucopias alternating with oval depressions on the rim and decorated with coloured glazes. The decoration is in the style of Bernard Palissy (see p. 145*b*). Majolica, the name given to coloured glazed pottery in Victorian times, was introduced by Leon Arnoux (1816–1902) at Mintons, Stoke-on-Trent, c. 1851, for ornamental pottery (see p. 204*a*). Subsequently it was used for architectural ceramics, flowerpots, garden seats, umbrella stands and domestic pottery. Many other factories produced majolica including Wedgwoods.

MINTON
Minton mark on d.

Opposite:
Top: Salt-glazed stoneware coffee-pot, tea-pot and vase in 'Littler Blue' made by William Littler, England, c. 1745–50.
Bottom: Bull-baiting figure group in enamelled earthenware, made by Obadiah Sherratt of Hot Lane; England, c. 1825.

Ceramics

English Pottery
MOCHA WARE

STUDIO POTTERY

a) Mug, earthenware, mark: One Quart *impressed underneath a rosette painted in red; Staffordshire, c. 1880; ht. 6" (15.2 cm.).*

This mug is decorated with bands of coloured slip into which dendritic effects have been introduced by an infusion of ceramic pigment and tobacco. The earliest known piece of Mocha or tobacco-spit ware, in Christchurch Museum, Ipswich, is inscribed *M. Clark 1799*. Such wares were made throughout the 19th century by many factories including C. T. Malıng, Newcastle-on-Tyne, the Leeds Pottery (recorded as 'Moscha' ware) and Spode, Stoke-on-Trent. William Evans (1846) says the fern-like effects were produced by a 'saturated infusion of tobacco in stale urine and tobacco'. Early pieces are much more thinly potted than later ones.

b) Jug, buff stoneware, marks: Doulton 1878 Lambeth *in a circle,* 508 *and* W *impressed, with* H B B *in monogram incised; Doultons, Lambeth, 1878; ht. 9½" (24.1 cm.).*

Incised salt-glazed stoneware was first shown by Doultons at the Paris Exhibition in 1867 and Hannah Barlow was the best known artist who used the technique. Vigorous spirited drawing, skilful suggestions of modelling and effective placing characterize all her work which deservedly became popular. This brown and blue jug is incised with a drawing of donkeys in a landscape by Hannah Barlow.

---

c) Vase, earthenware, with snake handles, painted in enamel colours with fête galante *subjects, signed* E. Lessore; *marks:* WEDGWOOD, WUS *and* S *impressed; Wedgwoods, Etruria, Staffordshire, 1864; ht. 10" (25.4 cm.).*

Emile Lessore (d. 1876) came to England from Sèvres in 1858 and after a brief period at Mintons (see p. 204a) moved to Wedgwoods where he remained until 1863. After returning to France, he continued to decorate Wedgwood pottery until he died. His signature occurs also, but much less frequently, on marked Davenport porcelain. His touch is free and sketchy, reminiscent of Watteau who inspired him.

d) Vase and cover, earthenware, mark: W DE MORGAN & Cº SAND'S END POTTERY, *by William de Morgan in partnership with Halsey Ricardo; Fulham, London, c. 1888-90; ht. 13½" (34.3 cm.).*

This is painted in lustre with a series of wide bands of conventional bird, fish and animal motifs. The mark and phoenix wings are impressed within a circle.

As a potter, William de Morgan concentrated his attention first upon reproducing the styles and techniques of Syria and Persia, and subsequently upon producing lustre-decorated pottery by firing metallic salts in a reducing atmosphere similar to that of the Hispano-Moresque potters (cf. p. 132b), the ruby Gubbio lustres (cf. p. 135a) and the more brassy lustres of Deruta.

A mark of William de Morgan (see d).

American Pottery Introduction

Among tradesmen listed in 1610 to be sent from London to the struggling English colony in Jamestown, Virginia, were four 'potters of earth'. Whether or not these particular potters ever arrived, there is archaeological evidence that pottery was certainly being made in Virginia by the second quarter of the seventeenth century, and probably earlier. Similarly, in Massachusetts three potters were at work in 1635, and in New York no later than 1655.

These early colonial potters were trained in European traditions handed down from the Middle Ages. What they made in the New World reflected both those traditions and the impact upon them of a frontier environment, unfamiliar materials, and changing needs. In succeeding generations during the colonial period, hundreds of potters developed a thriving industry, many were American born, and apprenticed to their pioneer elders. Regional ceramic styles soon became apparent.

Few examples survive to define early Anglo-colonial American pottery; especially for wares made in Massachusetts; yet there are sufficient archaeological evidences and scattered whole pieces to indicate the red earthenware of New England which reflected its Puritan origins in natural lead glaze colours, skilfully controlled thin body, and minimal decoration combined with elegant proportions.

Except for an abortive attempt to make delftware in 1688, the first innovation in American ceramics was the introduction of salt-glazed stoneware. The credit for this appears to belong to Anthony Duché, a Rhenish-born potter of Philadelphia, who applied in 1730 for a monopoly to make stoneware in Pennsylvania, noting that he had first produced it several years previously. William Crolius, who emigrated to New York City from Neuwied, near Coblenz, Germany, in 1724, was listed as a potter in 1729. He probably made stoneware by then; certainly he and his descendants continued to make only stoneware until 1870. Both Crolius and Duché worked in the Rhenish tradition that influenced most American stoneware for 150 years. An exception was introduced independently in Virginia by William Rogers. Rogers was described by Governor Gooch in his reports to the Board of Trade (in which he disguised the extent of local manufactures) as the 'poor potter of Yorktown', although he was a large scale producer, and by no means poor. Sometime after 1725, Rogers began to make an excellent brown salt-glazed stoneware, barely distinguishable from contemporary English prototypes.

In 1741, Isaac Parker of Boston sent for James Duché, Anthony's son, to teach him the system of making stoneware. Duché discovered that stoneware clay would have to be imported from Perth Amboy. This expense proved too great and the pottery reverted to earthenware production.

In 1794, Jonathan Fenton moved to Boston from New Haven. Attempting to make stoneware, he also found that he had to import the clay from Perth Amboy, and Fenton's pottery closed in 1796. His stoneware reflected the Germanic influence that spread from New York to New Haven, and no doubt touched Fenton during his apprenticeship.

Elsewhere, the materials were more widely available, and stoneware production increased rapidly after the Revolution, becoming the traditional potters' mainstay across the entire country until the late nineteenth century. Many large urban stoneware potteries filled a growing need for domestic and chemical wares, and for water and sewer pipe. Decoration on household stoneware developed into a characteristically American form of ebullient folk art by the 1830s. Bold blue floral and pictorial subjects took the place of earlier, more tightly executed incised designs.

Radical changes began to take place by 1828; a Scot, David Henderson, the first of a large influx of British potters, introduced Staffordshire-type factory techniques. Henderson began to make moulded stoneware at his Jersey City pottery, expanding soon into Rockingham and moulded yellow wares. His example was followed by the industrially-organized potteries of East Liverpool, Ohio; Bennington, Vermont; Baltimore, Maryland, and innumerable lesser centres from coast to coast.

The Arts and Crafts Movement, stimulated by the ideas of Morris and Ruskin in England, spearheaded a reaction against the factory-made wares. During the 1880-90s, this resulted in the growth of studios and *fabriques* for making art pottery. Rookwood, Grueby, the Robertsons' Chelsea Keramic Art Pottery and Dedham Pottery, and the Low Art Tile Company were among the most influential.

Meanwhile, the use of traditional earthenware gradually declined, as domestic and imported cheap stoneware and cheap mass-produced earthenwares replaced the mellow, lead-glazed redwares.

An early example of Massachusetts pottery.

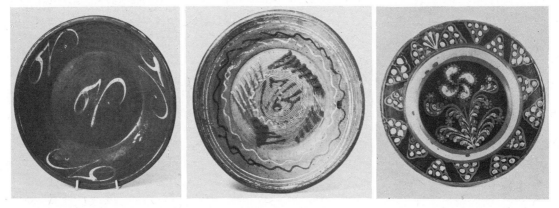

a) Slip-decorated earthenware dish; eastern Massachusetts, second half of 18th century, dia. 9″ (22.8 cm.).

Although the potters of Pennsylvania, New York, and south-western Connecticut made plates and dishes by rolling out sheets of clay like dough, then 'draping' them over moulds, the potters of Massachusetts, Rhode Island, and New Hampshire 'threw' their dishes in a pan shape on the wheel. A whole class of such dishes, possibly originating in the large cluster of colonial potteries in Charlestown, across the Charles River from Boston, is notable for the calligraphic slip decoration that chastely ornaments them.

b) Earthenware pan, Dedham, Massachusetts; 1764; dia. 11⅜″ (28.8 cm.).

Over a century of pottery making in Essex County, Massachusetts, led to a concentration of potters there, and a regional style that was diffused throughout eastern and northern New England. In 1764, the young Joseph Wilson moved from Essex County to Dedham, south of Boston, where competition was less severe. This pan, attributed to Wilson, was reportedly his children's baptismal

bowl. The style of banded decoration, utilizing both black and white slips, reveals the extended influence of German potters in Philadelphia. After Wilson moved to Providence, Rhode Island in 1767, he advertised ware 'glazed in the Same Way as Practiced in Philadelphia.'

c) Slip-decorated earthenware plate; made in Moravian community of Wachovia at Salem, North Carolina, 1774–1829; dia. 11⅞″ (30.1 cm.).

Gottfried Aust was trained in Herrnhut, the original Moravian community in Germany. He built a pottery in 1755 at Bethabara, and later another at Salem. His apprentice, Rudolf Christ, succeeded him, and this plate, decorated with white and red slip over brown slip on a red body, was made by Aust or Christ. William Ellis, a Staffordshire potter stranded by the failure of Bartlam's Queensware Pottery in Charleston, Carolina, taught Christ to make Queensware (see p. 110) a rare product in America. Simultaneously conservative and innovative, the Wachovia potteries represent a significant long chapter in American ceramic history, lasting over 150 years.

d) Sgraffiato-decorated earthenware plate, Johannes Neesz, Montgomery County, Pennsylvania, c. 1810, dia. 12½″ (31.7 cm.).

The great German enclave in the counties west and north-west of Philadelphia formed a homogeneous folk culture with continental traditions of slip-decoration and clay ornament. Although utilitarian wares were often as unadorned as those from New England (if more robust in form), the outstanding pieces are elaborate presentation wares using the *sgraffiato* techniques.

e) Slip-decorated earthenware churn; Morgantown, West Virginia, c. 1820; ht. 9⅝″ (24.4 cm.).

By 1785 a potter, Jacob Faulk, had settled in Morgantown. John W. Thompson, his apprentice and by 1814 owner of the shop, produced fine lead-glazed red earthenware with handsome glaze colours. Reflecting Faulk's German influence, his early wares are boldly slip-decorated with tulips and other devices. This churn's semi-transparent greenish-yellow glaze was called 'china glaze' by Thompson.

a) *Salt-glazed stoneware pot; New York, by David Morgan; late 18th century; ht. 10″ (25.4 cm.).*

The rich supply of high-grade stoneware clay in the Amboy, New Jersey clay-banks stimulated the development of stoneware manufacture in New York City, Staten Island, and north-eastern New Jersey during the 18th century. The first Rhenish-trained stoneware potters, such as William Crolius or John Remney used Germanic decorative techniques, incising designs in the wet clay and filling the spaces between with blue cobalt. This exemplifies the shape and decorative style of New York and New Jersey stoneware during the post-revolutionary period, including the treatment of shoulders and neck.

b) *Salt-glazed stoneware cooler, by Franklin Wight; Ashfield, Massachusetts, 1850–54; ht. 11¾″ (29.8 cm.).*

By the mid-19th century there were many rural stoneware potteries. One was in Ashfield, in the Berkshire hills, where this four-gallon water cooler was made by Franklin Wight, a journey-man in the employ of Hastings & Belding, the pottery's proprietors in the early 1850s. It has the conventional blue cobalt floral decoration of the period, but also bears in relief a moulded full-length portrait of George Washington, sprigged on to the front surface. The enduring patriotic symbolism of George Washington is shown repeatedly in pottery and other forms of folk art dating from before the Civil War.

c) *Salt-glazed stoneware butter crock, by John Bell; Waynesboro, Pennsylvania; c. 1840; ht. 6½″ (16.5 cm.).*

This grey crock with brilliant blue cobalt decoration represents mid-19th century stoneware of south-central Pennsylvania, Western Maryland, and the Shenandoah Valley of Virginia. This strongly Germanic pottery was influenced by the Bell family of whom Peter Bell of Hagerstown, Maryland, was the first. In nearby Waynesboro, Peter's son, John, produced a variety of earthen and stonewares.

d) *Ash-glazed stoneware molasses jug; probably Randolph County, North Carolina; late 19th century; ht. 17″ (43.1 cm.).*

The greater isolation of the rural south encouraged deep-rooted folk traditions. Small potteries in remote villages supplied local needs skilfully, using robust and massive shapes. Fired in primitive wood-burning, 'ground-hog' kilns, ash glazes (usually wood-ash, clay and water) ranged from lustrous greenish-black, to beady, broken-textured dark green, startlingly reminiscent of Oriental ash-glazed wares.

e) *Ash-glazed stoneware effigy jug; probably Aiken, South Carolina, c. 1860; ht. 5″ (12.7 cm.).*

The considerable role of black potters in the south is not fully documented, although there were many slave potters, and blacks freed because of their skill. Most of their work was anonymous, made for a local market. A remarkable series of grotesque face jugs, however, used by black field hands to carry water to their work, are among the few examples which indicate a surviving relationship to African sculptural art.

Ceramics

American Pottery
STONEWARE

ROCKINGHAM

FAIENCE

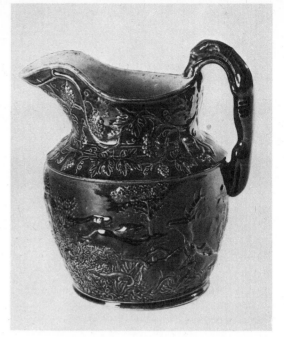

a) Stoneware jug with satirical embellishment, by Cornwall Kirkpatrick; Anna, Illinois, 1876; ht. 9⅞″ (25.0 cm.).

Pottery dedicated to political objectives was not uncommon in 19th century America, where potters sometimes incised their support of candidates into their wares. Probably no other potter, however, has matched the Hieronymus-Bosch-like fantasies of Cornwall Kirkpatrick whose convoluted imagination and sculptural skills produced a unique series of tortured, snake-entwined jugs, pigs with maps incised in them, fantastic chimney pots, and surrealistic urns.

b) Rockingham pitcher; American Pottery Manufacturing Co., Jersey City, New Jersey, 1833–1845; ht. 10″ (25.4 cm.).

The industrial revolution came to American ceramic manufacture with David Henderson (see p. 165). Beginning with moulded stoneware, he expanded into moulded yellow and Rockingham wares in 1830, and later into white ware, both hand-painted and transfer-printed. In 1833, his firm became the American Pottery Manufacturing Company; Daniel Greatbach, the principal designer, probably designed this pitcher.

c) left: Faience vase, painted by A. R. Valentien; Rookwood Pottery, Cincinnati, Ohio; c. 1885; ht. 5½″ (13.3 cm.).
d) centre: Vase, by Crueby Faience Co., Boston, Mass; c. 1900; ht. 6¾″ (17.1 cm.).

The art potteries, many only making tiles, flourished c. 1880–1900. Devoted to fine, 'artistic' ceramics, they re-directed American ideas away from the decadent, commercially-produced wares. The Arts and Crafts Movement was especially influential, and Japanese ceramics, exhibited at the Philadelphia Centennial Exposition were an additional inspiration. Maria Longworth began the Rookwood Pottery in 1880. Rookwood Faience had rich, lustrous glazes and skilful decoration.

e) right: Earthenware poodle with brown Rockingham glaze; Lyman Fenton & Co., Bennington, Vermont, c. 1852; ht. 9¼″ (23.4 cm.).

In 1793 Captain John Norton established an earthenware pottery in Bennington, Vermont, which later made stoneware. His son Julius was joined by Christopher Webber Fenton. Fenton was impressed by Henderson's ideas, left Nortons in 1847, and built a new factory. He brought in several Staffordshire potters, including Daniel Greatbach, and patented (1849) a superior flint-enamel glaze, distinguishable from the brown Rockingham by green, blue and orange tones, either singly or in combination. Although one of the most elaborate 19th century potteries, Fentons closed in 1858.

Continental Porcelain
Introduction

The first attempts to reproduce Chinese porcelain in Europe were made in Italy during the sixteenth century. In 1575 the Grand Duke Francesco I de 'Medici sponsored experiments which resulted in the production of a very limited quantity of glassy soft-paste porcelain, decorated in underglaze-blue with the occasional addition of purple outlines derived from manganese. This production virtually ceased when the Duke died (1587). Only about sixty surviving examples of this ware are known; most are marked in a fashion seemingly in imitation of the Chinese. These bear either an underglaze-blue sketch of the dome of the Florence Cathedral, or the six-ball armorial device of the Medici family.

There is no record of any further successful European experiments until 1673 (this was probably due to the ready supply of all the Far Eastern porcelain required by European customers). In that year, Louis Poterat of Rouen was granted a special licence to produce porcelain, in addition to the faience he was already making. Poterat's output of soft-paste porcelain must have been very limited and it is very difficult to attribute any example with certainty.

The beautiful soft-paste porcelains made at Saint Cloud by the family of faience-producer Pierre Chicaneau are well documented. Other early French factories manufacturing good quality soft-paste porcelain were situated at Chantilly and Mennecy. The most important Chantilly wares produced from c. 1725 were enamelled in the well-known Japanese style referred to as *Kakiemon*. In order to help their creamy-coloured soft-paste porcelain more closely resemble hard-paste porcelain made at Arita in Japan, the glaze was opacified with tin-oxide, a process normally reserved for earthenware. This same technique was sometimes used at the Italian factory at Doccia, near Florence.

In 1710 the Royal Saxon Porcelain Manufacture was set up in the Albrechtsburg fortress of Meissen, about twelve miles from Dresden. This first factory to produce true hard-paste in Europe was to set the porcelain fashions for all the other factories established up until about 1760. The wares and figures first produced at Meissen were fashioned in the Baroque style of the period. It was not until the Seven Years War (1756-63) when the troops of Frederick the Great of Prussia occupied the Meissen factory that their position as the foremost porcelain manufactory in Europe was successfully challenged by the more recently established factory at Sèvres in France.

The first experiments were carried out at Meissen by the physicist Count von Tschirnhaus, aided by a very capable young alchemist, J. F. Böttger. Their research first resulted in a very fine red stoneware somewhat similar to the earlier Yi-hsing wares of China but of a much finer grain, and so hard that it could be cut, engraved and polished in the same manner as precious stones. This was made at Meissen until at least 1730.

Around 1709, a hard white porcelain was produced from china-clay and alabaster; it was nearer 1718-20 before the preferable material of china-stone was located and used. This resulted in a porcelain even whiter and slightly higher fired than the Chinese was. Outstanding names associated with Meissen are J. G. Herold (or Höroldt) and J. J. Kaendler. Herold, previously at the Vienna porcelain factory of Du Paquier, joined Meissen in 1720; very soon after his arrival Meissen porcelain was being decorated in a wide range of beautiful enamel colours used in a variety of new and exciting styles. These included fantastic scenes associated with Chinese life. The new fashion of Chinoiserie was sometimes inspired by earlier and contemporary engravings. Stylized and Oriental flowers, naturalistic botanical specimens and charming little harbour scenes were also based upon engravings.

J. J. Kaendler, the most famous modeller of porcelain figures, was engaged at Meissen from 1731-75. Together with his assistants, he designed nearly all the early lively porcelain figures, ornate table-decorations and services that were in such demand at the time. From c.1750 the secret of the manufacture of hard-paste porcelain became widely known, often through the renegade Meissen workmen, resulting in the establishment of many factories throughout Germany and Italy.

The Vincennes factory of France was established as early as 1738, but it was probably nearer 1745 before a good soft-paste porcelain was successfully produced in quantity, in the new rococo fashions. They moved to a new building at Sèvres in 1756, but despite the outstanding quality of their work, the factory was almost certainly only saved from closure by the timely intervention of King Louis XV, who purchased the concern thus enabling it to continue operations as a Royal subsidized factory.

Hard-paste porcelain was not produced at Sèvres until c. 1772, and gradually more pleasing, but costly, soft-paste was replaced by the so-called hard 'Royal Porcelain'. In 1793 the factory was taken over by the French Republic.

Together these two major factories dictated the fashions for all European porcelain made throughout the eighteenth century.

Ceramics

Continental Porcelain

ITALIAN:

MEDICI
VENICE
DOCCIA

Mark on a.

a) Flask of Medici soft-paste porcelain painted in underglaze-blue; mark: dome of Florence Cathedral and F between two dots in blue; Florence, Italy, c. 1580; ht. 6⅞" (17.4 cm.).

The earliest attempts to imitate the hard-paste porcelain of China appear to have been made in Florence. The chances of the average collector finding a piece of this rare Medici porcelain are very slight: there are only about sixty specimens known to exist and most are accounted for. The material consisted of about 80% white-firing clay and 20% 'frit' (the ingredients of glass), the latter used as a substitute for china-stone. The manufacture was the private venture of the Grand Duke Francesco I de Medici and lasted from 1575 until his death in 1587.

b) Tea-pot of hard-paste porcelain, moulded in relief and decorated with enamel colours; Venice (Vezzi's factory), Italy, c. 1725; ht. 4¾" (12.1 cm.).

One of the earliest European productions of hard-paste porcelain was that of Francesco Vezzi, who was making both useful wares and a small number of figures from about 1720-27. Their palette included the entire range of enamel colours, preferences being shown for an iron-red, rose-pink, purple, emerald green and an opaque yellowish green.

Vezzi's porcelain was very similar to that of Meissen, which is not surprising: his clays came from the same source, and he was aided to a certain extent by the renegade Hunger, who had previously worked at both the Saxon factory and Vienna.

---

c) Figure of a harlequin in glazed hard-paste porcelain, probably Vezzi's factory; Venice, Italy, c. 1720-27; ht. 5¾" (14.6 cm.).

Meissen was already acknowledged as the fashion-setter for European porcelain, and in consequence very few original forms or styles of decoration can be attributed to Vezzi. This white porcelain harlequin, inspired by the popularity of the *Commedia dell'Arte* (Italian Comedy), has a lot in common with the early Meissen figures modelled by ivory carvers.

Similar figures were also painted in bright enamel colours on Vezzi's thickly potted octagonal tea-pots. The majority of Vezzi's table-wares were marked with 'VENEZIA', 'Venᵃ', or 'Va' in either gold, underglaze-blue or red-enamel.

d) Tea-pot of hybrid hard-paste porcelain, decorated in underglaze-blue transfer-prints and stencils; Doccia, Italy, mid-18th century; ht. 6⅜" (16.2 cm.).

Early experiments were started with Italian clay at Doccia, near Florence, by Carlo Ginori in 1735. Their material was a hybrid hard-paste porcelain (*masso bastardo*) which had a distinctly grey appearance. This tea-pot is typical of the 1740s, when their wares were of a robust baroque style, with snake-like spouts, heavy handles and high-domed lids. The blue on the lid was applied by stencilling, whilst the design of the 'performing dog' is an exceptionally early form of transfer-printing.

Ceramics

Continental Porcelain

ITALIAN:

DOCCIA
CAPODIMONTE
BUEN RETIRO (SPAIN)
VENICE

a) Cup and saucer of hybrid hard-paste porcelain, decorated with enamel colours; Doccia (near Florence), Italy, c. 1760; dia. of saucer 5" (12.7 cm.).

Wares with relief decoration of mythological, religious and hunting subjects have for many years been wrongly confused with the soft-paste porcelain of Capodimonte. The style was created at Doccia in the factory's early years, and can frequently be traced to Italian bronze plaquettes of the 16th century, which were later copied in lead. Decoration employed the full range of strong enamel colours, with flesh tones applied in a stippled manner.

The majority of wares seen with this style of decoration were, despite the Neapolitan mark of a crowned 'N', made in Germany since the middle of the last century.

b) Figure in soft-paste porcelain, painted in enamel colours and gilt; mark: a fleur-de-lis impressed; Capodimonte (northern suburb—Naples), Italy, c. 1750; ht. 6⅝" (16.8 cm.).

One of the most beautiful of all soft-paste porcelains was that made at Capodimonte. The enamel colours are usually of soft pastel tones with a slight, tasteful use of gilding. The factory was founded in 1743 by Charles of Bourbon, and continued until 1759, when Charles succeeded to the throne of Spain and the porcelain concern was re-established at the Buen Retiro palace in Madrid. Apart from many well-described, useful and decorative wares mentioned in the Neapolitan State Archives, mention is also made of the large variety of figures of this type, modelled by Giuseppe Gricci.

Mark on b.

---

c) Sugar-bowl of soft-paste porcelain decorated in soft enamel colours and gilt; mark: a fleur-de-lis in blue; Buen Retiro, Madrid, Spain, c. 1785; ht. 4" (10.2 cm.).

When Charles of Bourbon moved his Neapolitan factory to Madrid, he transferred staff members and their families, equipment, and four-and-three-quarter tons of the fine Italian clays. The Spanish clays were very inferior and produced a creamy body which compared very unfavourably with the beautiful white paste of Capodimonte. Figures were also made at Buen Retiro, but were of a very poor quality decorated in harsh and opaque colours and appropriately likened by Arthur Lane in *Italian Porcelain* to those of late 18th century Staffordshire. The same fleur-de-lis mark in blue, gold or impressed, was used at both factories.

d) Coffee-pot in hard-paste porcelain, decorated in enamel colours and gilt; mark: anchor in red enamel; Venice, Italy (Cozzi's factory), c. 1770; ht. 8⅜" (21.3 cm.).

Geminiano Cozzi started to produce a hard grey porcelain at Venice in 1764. In 1765, he was granted a twenty year privilege and financial support from the Venetian Board of Trade and the Senate. The Italians never really captured the true feeling of rococo, and Cozzi's wares were usually heavily potted and ill-balanced: this rather ugly inserted leaf-moulded spout with matching handle is very typical. Cozzi's table-wares were usually marked with an anchor painted in red enamel; gold was sometimes used on outstanding pieces. His limited range of figures are difficult to separate from those of Le Nove.

Mark on d.

Ceramics

Continental Porcelain

ITALIAN:

NAPLES
LE NOVE

GERMAN:

MEISSEN

Mark on a.

a) *Plate in soft-paste porcelain, painted in enamel colours and gilt; mark:* F.R.F. *monogram (Fabbrica Reale Ferdinandea) under a crown in red enamel; Naples, Italy, c. 1780; dia. 9¼″ (23.5 cm.).*

Although excavations had been taking place at Herculaneum in secrecy since 1738, the finds were not made public until the 1757 publication of *Le pitture antiche d'Ercolano*. The classical figure on this plate was illustrated in the fourth volume of this series, published in 1765. The original source was a fresco-painting found at Herculaneum. The four surrounding heads were taken from classical gems. The Royal Porcelain Factory of Naples was revived in 1771 by King Ferdinand IV. The factory was taken over by a French firm, Jean Poulard Prad & Company, in 1807, and closed in about 1830.

b) *Jardinière and stand in hard-paste porcelain painted in enamel colours and gilt; mark:* Nove *above an eight-pointed star in gold; Le Nove, Italy, second half 18th century; ht. 8¼″ (20.9 cm.).*

Pasquale Antonibon was already the owner of a prosperous tin-glazed earthenware factory at Le Nove, near Bassano, prior to starting the manufacture of a hard-paste porcelain in 1762. From 1781-1802 the factory was under the direction of Francesco Parolin, during whose time the fan-shaped *jardinière* seems to have been most popular. This form was originally introduced at the Vincennes factory of France in about 1750.

From 1802-25 the factory was under the directorship of Giovanni Baroni, whose porcelain and cream-coloured earthenware was mostly fashioned in the new Empire style.

---

c) *Tea-pot in Böttger brown stoneware with wheel-engraved decoration; Meissen, Saxony, Germany, c. 1715; ht. 3⅞″ (9.84 cm.).*

Since the mid-17th century, the Chinese had been exporting high-fired brown stoneware tea-pots: tea had become a popular European beverage. These wares were imitated in Holland and England, but the finest of the type were produced at Meissen, near Dresden, from about 1708—one year before Johann Friedrich Böttger finally succeeded in producing a white hard-paste porcelain.

This stoneware was so highly fired, and of such fine-grained material, that it was made to appear glazed if merely polished on a glass-engraver's wheel. Production of this material continued at Meissen until about 1730.

d) *Tea-pot in hard-paste porcelain with relief decoration picked out in enamel colours, enamel decoration probably added between 1730-35 in Augsburg, by Bartholomaus Seuter; Meissen, Saxony, Germany, c. 1720-25; ht. 4¾″ (12.1 cm.).*

The Royal Saxon Porcelain Manufacture was established in 1710 at the Albrechtsburg fortress of Meissen, about twelve miles outside the city of Dresden, where the Court of Augustus II, Elector of Saxony, was situated.

The early white porcelain of Böttger was produced from china-clay, together with a calcareous flux in the form of alabaster; this was an alternative to china-stone, which was not used until nearer 1720. These early undecorated wares were often acquired by outside decorators (*Hausmaler*) who embellished them with the full range of enamel colours and gilt decoration.

a) Tankard in hard-paste porcelain, painted in enamel colours and gilt with silver-gilt mounts; Meissen, Saxony, Germany, c. 1724; ht. 6⅝" (16.8 cm.).

Following the death of Böttger in 1719, the Meissen porcelain works was completely re-organized. Prior to this time their enamel decoration was very inferior to that of Chinese porcelain.

In 1720 Samuel Stölzel, a renegade Meissen kilnmaster, returned from Vienna bringing with him the talented decorator Johann Gregor Herold, who had a sound knowledge of the production and technique of applying brilliant enamel colours to hard-paste porcelain. His earliest decoration consisted of Chinoiserie (see p. 140*b*), a style which included theatrical-like figures of Chinese characters, but entirely unrelated to the decoration on the original Oriental wares.

b) Vase and cover in hard-paste porcelain decorated with enamel colours, probably by Johann Ehrenfried Stadler; mark: A.R. monogram in underglaze-blue; Meissen, Saxony, Germany, 1727-30; ht. 15½" (39.4 cm.).

This very fine vase is one of the few genuine pieces made to the order of *Augustus Rex*, Elector of Saxony, King of Poland (d. 1733). Wares of this type, with the 'A.R.' monogram, were intended for his personal use or as a gift to a Court favourite or the head of a foreign state. The early flower-painting (*Indianische Blumen*) and Chinoiserie is in the style of J. E. Stadler, the palette including the early pink lustre (*Perlmutter*), sometimes seen on Böttger porcelain. The 'A.R.' mark was later imitated on many inferior wares made in Germany between 1850-1900.

The rare A.R. monogram

---

c) Tea-pot in hard-paste porcelain painted in underglaze-blue and enamel colours; mark: crossed swords in blue; Meissen, Saxony, Germany, 1730-35; ht. 3¼" (8.25 cm.).

One of the most popular forms of decoration on Japanese porcelain from the late 17th century is known as *Kakiemon*, the 'nickname' of the Arita potter considered to have introduced this attractive style. Wares were later decorated in this same fashion in many of the major European porcelain factories. The Meissen decorators were able to copy direct from the Japanese porcelain already in the extensive collection of Far Eastern wares acquired by Augustus. The crossed swords factory mark, adopted in 1723, was often painted in blue enamel instead of the more usual underglaze-blues on wares decorated in this manner.

d) Chocolate-pot and cover in hard-paste porcelain painted in enamel colours and gilt; mark: crossed swords in underglaze-blue, and '50' in gilt; Meissen, Saxony, Germany, c. 1730; ht. 7½" (19.1 cm.).

Between 1725 and 1730, the fine enamel colours including black and deep reddish-brown, introduced by Herold, were being used for the painting of harbour scenes, which in many instances were inspired by Augsburg engravings of Italian port scenes by Melchior Kysell, after the paintings of J. W. Baur. The earliest of these scenes were in many instances the work of C. F. Herold, a kinsman of Johann Gregor Herold. The heavy ornate baroque-like frames (*Laub und Bandelwerk*), usually indicated an earlier date than the simple gilt surrounds.

Japanese Kakiemon bowl (see c, p. 182d, p. 191c).

173

a) Figure of a beggarman in hard-paste glazed porcelain, modelled by J. G. Kirchner (b. 1706); Meissen, Saxony, Germany, c. 1730; ht. 6¼″ (15.9 cm.).

The few early Meissen figures in brown stoneware, or white porcelain, were most probably modelled by Court ivory-carvers. The first full-time modeller to be employed at the factory appears to have been J. G. Kirchner, whose brother was a Court sculptor. Kirchner was dismissed within the year for being 'frivolous and disorderly' but was re-engaged between 1730-33.

This small and attractive figure is in complete contrast to many of the large animals and figures Kirchner modelled for the furnishing of the Japanese Palace which Augustus had purchased in 1717 to house his vast collection of porcelain.

b) Figure of a harlequin in hard-paste porcelain decorated in enamel colours, modelled by J. J. Kaendler; Meissen, Saxony, Germany, c. 1738; ht. 6½″ (16.5 cm.).

The modeller responsible for the finest Meissen figures of the baroque period was J. J. Kaendler (1706-1775). Kaendler started his career at the factory in 1731, and soon became the firm favourite of Count Heinrich von Bruhl (appointed Director of the porcelain factory following the death of Augustus II in 1733); Kaendler was first engaged on the production of large table-services, such as the famous 'Swan Service', which comprised over 2200 items. The Italian Comedy figures were modelled after the engravings used to illustrate Riccoboni's *Histoire du théâtre italien* and were invariably painted in strong red, yellow and black.

---

c) Jug and cover in hard-paste porcelain and in enamel colours; mark: crossed swords in underglaze-blue; Meissen, Saxony, Germany, 1745-50; ht. 5⅜″ (13.7 cm.).

Because almost all the Chinese porcelain brought into Europe from the 17th century came via the vessels of the East India Companies, there was a misunderstanding as to the original source: even the early sale catalogues of the English Chelsea porcelain factory referred to decoration as 'India plants'. The stylized Chinese-type flowers painted on early Meissen were similarly attributed to India. These fine cut flowers (*Schnittblumen*), painted in natural colours, became fashionable about 1740 and were usually based on earlier botanical engravings. The name of J. G. Klinger, a Meissen decorator, is usually associated with this manner of decoration.

d) Figure of cook boiling eggs, hard-paste porcelain painted in enamel colours and gilt; mark: crossed swords in underglaze-blue, modelled by J. J. Kaendler and J. P. Reinicke; Meissen, Saxony, Germany, c. 1753-63; ht. 6½″ (16.5 cm.).

By the middle of the 18th century, porcelain figures were still popular throughout Europe as decorations for the dining-table. Horace Walpole writing in an essay in 1753 stated that even in England '. . . jellies, biscuits, sugar-plumbs, and creams, have long given way to harlequins, gondoliers, Turks, Chinese and shepherdesses of Saxon china. But these, unconnected, and only seeming to wander among groves of curled paper . . .' Many of these figures took the form of peasants, tradesmen or craftsmen, painted in the softer tones of yellow and mauve.

Mark on c.

a) Bacchic Revel, symbolic of Autumn in hard-paste porcelain painted in enamel colours and gilt, mark: crossed swords in underglaze-blue and Z202 impressed; modelled by J. J. Kaendler; Meissen, Saxony, Germany, c. 1754; ht. 11″ (27.9 cm.).

This group well illustrates the new fashion for extreme rococo which became so popular from about 1755. Whilst this wave-like form of modelling was often extremely pleasing on table-wares, it was less successful when used as a base for figures, and often gave the impression of castaways huddled on an island, sometimes in danger of falling off. This cleverly modelled group consists of three separate sections which when accurately assembled appear as a single group. The softer enamel colours are now being accompanied by the more generous use of gilding.

b) Figure of a Japanese actor (?) in hard-paste porcelain; Du Paquier's factory, Vienna, Austria, c. 1720; ht. 16½″ (40.6 cm.).

Claudius Innocentius Du Paquier had been experimenting for several years before finally producing hard-paste porcelain with the assistance of two renegade Meissen workmen, Hunger and Stolzel. The factory remained under Du Paquier's direction until 1744, when the undertaking was purchased by the Empress Maria Theresa. The early Vienna table-wares were extremely baroque in style, the decoration consisting of scrollwork, shell-like palmettes and intricate lattice-like gilding. The rare figure illustrated is one of a pair of white figures which has only recently been attributed with certainty to the Du Paquier period of the Vienna factory.

c) Figure of a man loading a pistol, hard-paste porcelain painted in enamel colours; Vienna, Austria, c. 1755; ht. 6½″ (16.5 cm.).

There were very few original figures made at Vienna during the State period (1744–84), the majority being modelled after those produced at Meissen. One of their principal modellers was J. J. Niedermayer, who was in charge of that department from 1747 until his death in 1784. His versions of the Meissen figures were usually 'prettier' and rather doll-like compared with the originals. From 1744, the factory-mark of Vienna consisted of a two-bar shield which was used until the factory closed in 1866. Minor German and Austrian factories have used versions of this mark to the present day.

d) Pastoral group in hard-paste porcelain painted in enamel colours; mark: a six-spoked wheel in underglaze-blue, and 41/N50 incised; Höchst, Germany, c. 1770; ht. 6⅜″ (16.2 cm.).

It was not until the middle of the 18th century that any further porcelain factories were established in Germany. The earliest of these was at Höchst-on-Main, where J. Benckgraff and J. J. Ringler in 1750 produced what was at first a rather coarse hard-paste porcelain. The factory was patronized by the Elector Emmerich Joseph, and his successor Friedrich Karl.

Pastoral groups of this type were produced by Laurentius Russinger, the Höchst *Modellmeister*, from about 1760, and invariably have the same grassy bases. The painting of the figures included very pink flesh tones and gaily-coloured costumes, pale blue dominating.

Höchst wheel mark (see d).

175

Ceramics

Continental Porcelain

GERMAN:

HÖCHST
FÜRSTENBERG

a) Cup and saucer in hard-paste porcelain painted in enamel colours and gilt; mark: a wheel in blue; Höchst, Germany, c. 1780–85; dia. (of saucer) 5⅜″ (13.7 cm.).

This form of cup, with a saucer which has a deep well to receive its base, is termed a *trembleuse*, a shape probably first introduced at the French factory of Saint-Cloud. The style of decoration is very similar to that seen on later Sèvres, the subject being that of Leda and the Swan. The painters favoured a rich purple or lilac with profuse gilding.

The Höchst factory had a very short period of prosperity, from about 1765–75, after which it rapidly declined and finally ceased in 1798.

b) Figure of Ragonda in hard-paste porcelain painted in enamel colours and gilt; mark: I/F incised, modelled by Simon Feilner; Fürstenberg, Germany, c. 1754; ht. 7¾″ (19.7 cm.).

Although Duke Carl I of Brunswick founded the factory at Fürstenberg in 1747, no porcelain was produced until 1753, when the arcanist Johann Benckgraff was engaged.

Simon Feilner, the modeller who had previously also worked at Höchst, moved together with Benckgraff, and continued to model some very attractive figures of the various Italian Comedy characters. The early simple form of base, as used here, is seen to be ideal for these animated figures, which were painted in the same strong enamel colours as used at Meissen.

c) Group in hard-paste porcelain painted in enamel colours and gilt, mark: CB incised; Fürstenberg, Germany, c. 1760; ht. 6¼″ (15.9 cm.).

This amusing figure of a lady endeavouring to catch a flea is typical of the satirical subjects favoured by A. C. Luplau during the period he was a modeller at the Fürstenberg factory.

J. C. Rombrich, another modeller employed at the factory, is generally associated with the very competent figures of monkeys playing various musical instruments, based of course on the famous Meissen *Affenkapelle*, or 'Monkey Band'. The modeller Desoches produced some very good biscuit porcelain in the manner of Sèvres, including a bust of Friedrich Augustus, Duke of Brunswick.

d) Tea-pot in hard-paste porcelain painted in enamel colours and gilt, mark: F in blue; Fürstenberg, Germany, c. 1765–70; ht. 4″ (10.2 cm.).

The early useful wares made at Fürstenberg were often designed with high-relief rococo scrollwork, a style which according to some authorities was deliberately designed to help hide the many imperfections in their paste. By 1760, their material was so improved that plain surfaces offering plenty of scope to the enamel painters were more customary.

The factory passed into private ownership in 1859, and continues to this day. Their mark has always been a cursive 'F' in underglaze-blue, the only exception being the impressed mark of a running horse which was used on their biscuit porcelain busts made in neo-classical style.

Mark on d.

a) *Coffee-pot and cover in hard-paste porcelain painted in enamel colours and gilt, mark: G in gold; Gotzkowski's factory, Berlin, Germany, 1761-3; ht. 8¼" (20.9 cm.).*

The early Berlin factory of W. K. Wegely was only in production from 1751-57. The founder had been granted many monetary privileges by King Frederick, but his plans to rival the wares of Meissen were thwarted by the outbreak of the Seven Years War (1756-63).

The later factory of J. E. Gotzkowski was begun in 1761, but ran at a loss until taken over by Frederick the Great of Prussia in 1763. The King is said to have favoured the *Mosaik*, or scale-pattern, as seen on this coffee-pot, where the scaling is in varying shades of green.

b) *Group of Mars and History in undecorated glazed hard-paste porcelain, modelled by W. C. Meyer; Berlin, Germany, c. 1767; ht. 18½" (46.9 cm.).*

The large models created by Friedrich and Wilhelm Meyer may well be criticized by lovers of earlier porcelain figures as being too large. They followed very much the neo-classical style, which at the time was becoming increasingly popular and in consequence may often be likened to early Roman marble sculpture. W. C. Meyer's work can often be identified by the very elongated limbs and unusually small heads. The large groups produced later by J. G. Muller are usually less pleasing than the group illustrated, due to their exaggerated poses.

c) *Figure of Columbine in hard-paste porcelain painted in enamel colours and gilt; mark: shield of Bavaria, impressed, modelled by Franz Anton Bustelli; Nymphenburg, Germany, 1755-60; ht. 7¾" (19.7 cm.).*

Whilst J. J. Kaendler must be acknowledged as the finest modeller of porcelain figures during the baroque period, the master modeller during the succeeding rococo period was undoubtedly Franz Anton Bustelli of the Nymphenburg factory. Experiments concerned with the manufacture of porcelain commenced at this Bavarian factory as early as 1747, but it was about 1753 before a high quality hard-paste porcelain was produced. Bustelli arrived to take charge of the modelling one year later and produced a wide range of figures, including gallants, lovers, Chinoiserie groups, centrepieces, hawkers, and his well-known figures from the Italian Comedy.

d) *Dish in hard-paste porcelain painted in enamel colours and gilt; mark: the shield of Bavaria, impressed; Nymphenburg, Germany, c. 1760; dia. 11¾" (29.8 cm.).*

This very beautiful plate, painted in natural flower colours, is from the service made for the Electoral Court in Munich. The service was probably made at nearby Neudeck, prior to the move in 1761 to new buildings adjacent to the Palace of Nymphenburg. The life of the Elector and his courtiers appears to have consisted solely of entertainment: The Italian Comedy, opera, tournaments, shooting, hunting, firework displays and boating, all accompanied of course by lavish banquets, necessitating large services of finely decorated porcelain.

Nymphenburg mark: shield of Bavaria (see c).

Ceramics

Continental Porcelain

GERMAN:

NYMPHENBERG
FRANKENTHAL

a) Plate from a 14-piece fish service painted in enamel colours and gilt, marks: the shield of Nymphenburg and Nymphenburg *impressed and in blue; Nymphenburg, Germany, c. 1901-6; dia. 9½″ (24.1 cm.).*

This attractive fish service is known through the factory records to be associated with the sculptor and painter Louis Levallois, who was employed from 1901-6. A sketch for the sauce-boat of the same service is signed by Levallois and dated 1903. The decoration, in varying tones of green, purple and brown, was most probably the work of Professor Gradl, who was employed as a free-lance painter between 1904-6. The Nymphenburg factory was run by the State until 1862; since then production has continued under a private company.

Frankenthal factory mark (see b).

b) Cup and saucer in hard-paste porcelain painted in enamel colours and gilt, mark: C.T monogram under a crown in underglaze-blue; Frankenthal, Germany, c. 1775; dia. (saucer) 4¼″ (10.8 cm.).

Paul Hannong succeeded in making a hard-paste porcelain at Strasbourg prior to 1755, but due to the various privileges granted by King Louis XV to the Sèvres factory, he was prevented from continuing his manufacture and forced to move to Frankenthal where he found a new patron, the Elector of the Palatinate. Carl Theodor permitted him to establish a factory in some old army barracks, where by the end of 1755, a high quality porcelain was being produced in quantity. Decoration included some pleasing fabric-like patterns, striped gilt grounds and trellis patterns, favouring crimson and green.

c) Group of a man and a servant-girl in hard-paste porcelain decorated in enamel colours and gilt, mark: C.T monogram under a crown in underglaze-blue; Frankenthal, Germany, c. 1770-75; ht. 6″ (15.2 cm.).

This amusing group is credited to the modeller Karl Gottlieb Lück, who came to Frankenthal with his brother Johann Friedrich in 1758. They had both previously been working at Meissen as pupils of J. J. Kaendler. K. G. Lück's work can usually be identified by the rather fussy and highly coloured compositions, invariably mounted on high grassy mounds, with rococo scrollwork edges picked out in gilding.

During the last quarter of the 18th century, groups, figures and busts in the neo-classical style were produced by Adam Bauer and J. P. Melchior.

d) Tea-pot in hard-paste porcelain painted in underglaze-blue; marks: C.T monogram under an electoral crown, and AB in blue; Frankenthal, Germany, c. 1750-1800; ht. 4¼″ (10.8 cm.).

It is rather surprising to learn that the Frankenthal porcelain factory produced such comparatively humble wares as this tea-pot, which in the absence of a mark would more probably have been attributed to one of the many late 18th century Thuringian factories.

This so-called *Zwiebelmuster*, or 'onion pattern', was initially introduced at Meissen in about 1740. It became very popular and wares decorated in this fashion have been produced throughout Europe up to the present day, especially in Scandinavia.

Opposite:
A group in underglaze blue porcelain modelled by Anton Grassli; Vienna, Austria, c. 1780-90.

Ceramics

Continental Porcelain

GERMAN:

LUDWIGSBURG

SWISS

DUTCH

a) Miniature group in hard-paste porcelain painted in enamel colours; mark: interlaced C's in underglaze-blue; Ludwigsburg, Germany, 1765-1770; ht. 3⅛" (7.94 cm.).

This miniature group of a tailor's shop is one of a series referred to as the 'Venetian Fairs'. This title is said to have been suggested as a theme for a Court Festival by the Duke himself, after he had visited Venice in 1767. They are attributed to J. J. Louis, who was chief modeller at Ludwigsburg from 1762 until his death in 1772. Other subjects in this same series include inns, booksellers, men playing dice, etc.

The most common Ludwigsburg factory-mark is two back-to-back interlaced C's, under a ducal coronet.

b) Figure of Ceres in hard-paste porcelain, painted in enamel colours; Ludwigsburg, Germany, c. 1770; ht. 9⅜" (23.8 cm.).

In 1758 J. J. Ringler, the nomadic arcanist, helped establish a hard-paste porcelain factory at Ludwigsburg for the Duke Carl Eugen of Württemberg. The factory flourished until the Duke died in 1793, after which it declined and finally closed in 1824. At the peak of their prosperity in 1766, 154 workers were employed, and although heavily subsidized by the Duke, the staff were at times forced to receive a portion of their wages in faulty wares, which they in turn had to sell.

Models of this type are probably the work of J. C. W. Bayer, who was employed as a modeller from 1759-67.

Mark on d.

---

c) Figure of a man being attacked by a dog, hard-paste porcelain painted in enamel colours; Zurich, Switzerland, c. 1775; ht. 5¼" (13.3 cm.).

Unlike the majority of other 18th century continental porcelain factories, the proprietors of the Zurich factory had no wealthy patrons. The factory was established in 1763 and for a short period only, they produced a creamy-white soapstone porcelain, similar to that made at Worcester in England. Soon, however, they managed to produce a hard-paste porcelain. J. V. Sonnenschien, who had previously worked at Ludwigsburg, is credited with the modelling of the majority of the simple but pleasing figures of peasants, soldiers, musicians and other humble characters, all made about 1775.

d) Saucer in hard-paste porcelain painted in enamel colours; mark: crossed swords with three dots in underglaze-blue; Weesp, Holland, c. 1762-71; dia. 6" (15.2 cm.).

Count van Gronsveldt-Diepenbroil succeeded in producing a hard-paste porcelain at Weesp, by 1762. He was aided by Nicolaus Paul, the arcanist who had previously worked at Wegely's factory in Berlin. Their wares can be briefly summed up as being of a fine white porcelain—comparable with that of Meissen—with high quality but usually dull painting of loudly-coloured flowers, exotic birds or landscapes. In 1771 the factory was purchased by Johannes de Mol, and transferred to Oude Loosdrecht.

Opposite:
Back: Plate, hard-paste porcelain from the Swan Service made for Count Brühl; Meissen, Germany, 1736-38.
Left: Vase, soft-paste porcelain; Capodimonte, Italy, c. 1750.
Right: Figure of a Russian peasant; St. Petersburg, Russia, c. 1817.
Front: Flower-pot, soft-paste porcelain, possibly painted by Ledoux; Sèvres, France, 1757.

Ceramics

a) Dish in hard-paste porcelain painted in enamel colours; Oude Loosdrecht, Holland, c. 1771–1784; lgth. 7½" (19.1 cm.).

Following the transfer of the Weesp factory to Oude Loosdrecht, the first wares produced had much in common with those of the earlier factory. These German fashions were shortly abandoned in favour of the more popular *Louis Seize* styles of France (the transitional style between rococo and neo-classical). Their pleasing landscape painting can often be identified by the deep rich colours of brown, black or purple monochromes.

The factory mark of 'M.O.L.' could be intended for either the name of the proprietor (Johannes de Mol), or *Manufactuur Oude Loosdrecht*.

b) Spice-box and cover in soft porcelain painted in underglaze-blue; Saint-Cloud, France, first half 18th century; wdth. 6" (15.2 cm.).

There is little known about early French soft-paste porcelain. Louis Poterat of Rouen was granted a patent in 1673 for the manufacture of both faience and porcelain, but he appears to have been concerned primarily with the production of earthenware. About this time, records indicate that Claude and François Reverend were similarly engaged but their porcelain, if any, remains unidentified.

This spice-box was produced rather later at the Saint-Cloud factory, initially established by Pierre Chicaneau (d. 1678). The wares were thickly potted and often decorated in the same *lambrequin* style so often seen on the faience of Rouen.

c) Pastille-burner in the form of a hare in soft-paste porcelain painted in enamel colours of pale green and yellow, very sparsely applied; Saint-Cloud, France, c. 1750; ht. 10½" (26.7 cm.).

In his book *French Faience*, Arthur Lane stresses how essential the sweet-smelling potpourri was to make life in the French Courts more tolerable. This is a particularly pleasing example of the beautiful soft-paste porcelain of Saint-Cloud, mounted on an equally fine gilt bronze ormolu base.

Marks were not consistently used at the Saint-Cloud factory, but among those recorded, the most common included an early underglaze-blue 'sunface' and 'St. C' over 'T', either incised or in blue. The latter mark indicates a date post-1772, when the factory was under the direction of Henry Trou II.

d) Bowl in soft-paste porcelain, painted in enamel colours in the Kakiemon style; mark: a hunting-horn in red enamel; Chantilly, France, c. 1735; wdth. 6¼" (15.9 cm.).

The porcelain factory of Chantilly was first established in 1725 under the patronage of Louis-Henri de Bourbon, Prince de Condé, and continued under various directors and owners until 1800. The majority of porcelain made there up to the middle of the 18th century was decorated in the *Kakiemon* style of the popular Japanese Arita porcelain (see p. 173c) which often depicted events in Japanese mythology.

The glaze on this example has been made white and opaque to make this soft-paste porcelain look more like the hard-paste of Japan.

Mark on d.

182

a) Tureen, cover and stand in soft-paste porcelain painted in underglaze-blue, mark: a hunting-horn and A in blue enamel; Chantilly, France, c. 1750; lgth. of stand 9" (22.9 cm.).

From about the middle of the 18th century, the practice of 'dressing up' Chantilly porcelain to resemble the hard-paste porcelain of Japan was abandoned. A translucent lead-glaze was used, which showed the creamy soft-paste porcelain to greater advantage and the majority of their wares were decorated with underglaze-blue. The most popular of the blue designs used were *à l'épi* (ear of corn) and *à la brindille* (sprig or twig), styles of decoration that were imitated on the English porcelain made at Caughley in Shropshire in about 1780-85.

b) Ink-stand in the form of a River God, glazed white porcelain, soft-paste, marks: DV incised and in blue; Mennecy, France, 1750-75; lgth. 8½" (21.6 cm.).

The soft-paste porcelain made at Mennecy (Dept. of Seine-et-Oise) from 1748 is probably the most beautiful ever produced. The factory was started in 1734 in the rue de Charonne, Paris, then moved to Mennecy, where production continued until 1733, when a further move to Bourg-la-Reine took place. The factory continued here until 1806, but the majority of the later output almost certainly consisted of cream-coloured earthenware, or *faience fine*.

---

c) Custard-cup and cover in soft-paste porcelain painted in enamel colours, mark: DV incised; Mennecy, France, c. 1755-60; ht. 3½" (8.89 cm.).

The table-wares produced at Mennecy were as beautiful in their simplicity as their figures: this reeded custard-cup is typical. The palette invariably includes rose-pink, bright blue and a brownish-green, colours which tend to melt into the brilliant, wet-looking glaze. This flower decoration is very similar to the *Deutsche Blumen* of Meissen. It was probably due to the generous monopolies enjoyed by the Vincennes and Sèvres factories that the deep purple enamel was used as an edging, in place of the more customary gilding.

d) Cup and saucer in soft-paste porcelain painted in underglaze-blue and gilt; mark: crossed L's enclosing A; Vincennes, France, 1753; dia. of saucer 6" (15.2 cm.).

From about 1740, attempts were made to produce porcelain in the old royal château of Vincennes by Gilles and Robert Dubois, who were financed by Orry de Fulvy. It was 1745 before success was finally achieved, with the aid of Louis François Gravant who had worked at Chantilly, and a beautiful soft-paste porcelain was produced by the company formed under the name of Charles Adam. The early ground colour on this cup and saucer is a dark blue, applied under the glaze and referred to in the factory records as *bleu lapis*.

Mark on d.

Ceramics

Continental Porcelain

a) Ewer and basin of soft-paste porcelain painted in enamel colours and gilt; marks: K within interlaced L's (date-mark for 1763) and interlaced S's, mark of the painter Catrice, who decorated at Sèvres from 1757-75; Sèvres, France, date-mark for 1763; ht. of ewer 6⅝" (16.8 cm.).

Among the most sought-after of Sèvres ground colours is the yellow (*jaune jonquille*), which was first introduced by Jean Hellot, the factory chemist, in 1753. This example is particularly pleasing: the children are painted in a rich royal blue enamel, with the exception of the naturally painted flesh tones. This ewer and basin might well be that referred to in the contemporary sale catalogue as '*1 pot à l'eau, enfans camayeux*' which was made for the Duc d'Orléans in 1764.

b) Part of a cabaret-service in soft-paste porcelain painted in enamel colours on bleu céleste ground; mark: crossed L's enclosing L, and N in blue; Sèvres, France, 1764; lgth. of tray 13½" (34.3 cm.).

Cabaret-services, or *déjeuners*, as they were at times also called, were particularly popular in France during the third quarter of the 18th century. These 'tea-for-two' sets of matching porcelain were sometimes fitted into ornate boxes, intended for use whilst travelling. The *bleu céleste*, a turquoise blue, was used from about 1752, and was probably suggested by the early Chinese wares. The 'N' mark is that of the decorator F. J. Aloncle, who specialized in bird-painting between 1758-81.

c) Plate in hard-paste porcelain decorated in enamel colours and gilt, the E II for Ekatarina II (Catherine II), marks: double I cypher with AA enclosed, and painter's and gilder's marks; Sèvres, France, date-mark for 1778; dia. 10¼" (26.0 cm.).

This plate is from one of the largest and most lavish services ever produced at the Sèvres factory. The service was ordered by the ambassador of the Empress Catherine II of Russia in 1777 and eventually delivered in June, 1779. In all, it comprised a total of 744 pieces, and the cost was so great that negotiations took place until 1792 before the bill was eventually paid—just in time to prevent the factory going into bankruptcy.

The main ground colour is in turquoise-blue; the attractive border reserves in imitation of classical gems are in sepia on a reddish-brown ground.

d) Chocolate cup and saucer in hard-paste porcelain decorated with coloured enamels and gilt; Sèvres, France, c. 1785; dia. of saucer 5⅜" (13.7 cm.).

The ingredients essential for the production of true porcelain, china-clay and china-stone (kaolin and petuntse), were discovered near Limoges in 1768. By 1772 Sèvres was producing both soft and hard-paste porcelain, the latter being known as *Porcelaine Royale*.

'Jewelled Porcelain' was introduced as early as 1773, but did not become popular until later. The effect was achieved by fusing enamels over gilt or silver foil, giving the radiance of precious stones. Wares of this type were produced in quantity during the 19th century by other French factories.

a) Vase in hard-paste biscuit porcelain with white classical figures applied on a blue ground; mark: AB for Alexandre Brachard jeune; Sèvres, France, 1813; ht. 16″ (40.6 cm.).

Wedgwood's blue-and-white jasper-ware vases, made in the neo-classical styles of the late 18th century, were copied by several contemporary English potters in similar material. This vase is a surprisingly late reproduction of similar vases, but in a hard-paste porcelain. The work is that of Alexandre Brachard *jeune*, who was active at Sèvres as a *sculpteur-répareur*, from 1784-92, 1795-9, and 1802-27. Other continental porcelain factories made cameo plaques in the same style as those produced by Josiah Wedgwood at his factory of Etruria.

b) Figure of a dancer playing pipes, hard-paste biscuit porcelain, mark: S and 1904 within impressed triangle; Sèvres, France, dated 1904; ht. 16½″ (41.9 cm.).

This figure is one of a set made as table decorations at the Sèvres porcelain factory between 1903-5. The original models appear to have been first produced in gilt bronze by Agathon Léonard in about 1900. They were made by Siot-Decauville for the Paris Exhibition of 1900. The white hard-paste figures represent the popular American dancer of the day, Loïe Fuller (1862-1928), who danced to the music of Chopin, Schubert and Debussy at the *Folies-Bergère* (see p. 488c).

---

c) Clock case of hard-paste porcelain with gilt bronze ormolu mounts, mark: Manufacture de Mr. le Duc d'Angoulême à Paris, in gilt; factory of Dihl and Guérard, rue de Bondy, Paris, France, c. 1785-90; lgth. 20½″ (52.1 cm.).

This very large and ornate clock was produced at the Paris factory of Dihl and Guérard, who were patronized by the Duc d'Angoulême. The biscuit figures flanking the clock represent Bacchus and Cupid. The enamel dial is signed by *Cardinaux à Paris*.

The well-known cornflower spray, used as a form of decoration at so many English and French factories, was probably first introduced at this factory, and is referred to as the 'Angoulême sprig'.

d) Bowl in hard-paste porcelain painted in enamel colours; mark: an imitation of a Chinese seal in red enamel; France, late 19th century; dia. 9⅞″ (25.1 cm.).

This bowl has been painted in imitation of Chinese *famille rose* export porcelain like that being exported by the East India Companies a century before. The porcelain is a hard-paste like the original but the glaze has been tinted with cobalt to give the Far Eastern look. Wares thus decorated are very common and usually attributed to the Paris firm of Samson which started in 1845 and is still in operation.

Samson lists the various marks they admit to having used on their reproductions and this simulated Chinese character does not appear, so may well be by another contemporary 'reproducer'.

Ceramics

Continental Porcelain

FRENCH:

PARIS

BELGIAN

b) Plate in hard-paste porcelain painted in enamel colours and gilt; mark: crossed torches in underglaze-blue; La Courtille, rue de la Fontaine-au-Roi, Paris, France, 1773–93; dia. 9½" (24.1 cm.).

Mark on b.

a) Cup and saucer in hard-paste porcelain painted in blue and gilt, marks: L.S.X in monogram form, stencilled in red, and M incised; Clignacourt, near Paris, France, 1775–91; dia. of saucer 5" (12.7 cm.).

The hard-paste porcelain factory at Clignacourt was started in 1767 by Pierre Deruelle. Their early mark was a stylized windmill in underglaze-blue, but from 1775–91, whilst under the patronage of Louis-Stanislas-Xavier, Comte de Provence, the brother of King Louis XVI, the early mark was abandoned in favour of the L.S.X monogram. Their table-wares were of a fine quality, with decoration signed at times by George Lamprecht, who was formerly at Sèvres.

The factory of La Courtille was established in Paris by J. B. Locre in 1772, and the concern sold in 1787 to Laurentius Russinger, the German modeller, who was later joined by François Pouyat, a potter from Limoges. The factory finally closed in 1840. Their table-wares were of a high quality and usually marked with either crossed flaming torches or crossed arrows, which had obviously been chosen to look like the more famous crossed swords of the Meissen factory. This plate is painted in the full range of enamel colours, the main subject being in black.

c) Ice-pail (sceau) in soft-paste porcelain painted in enamel colours and gilt; Tournai, Belgium, c. 1790; ht. 4" (10.2 cm.).

The soft-paste porcelain factory of Tournai was first established by François Joseph Peterinck in 1751, after having a monopoly granted by the Empress Maria Theresa.

This ice-pail is decorated with bird paintings taken from the drawings of Buffon made for his *Natural History*, first published in 1787. The style seemingly proved very popular and wares of this type are by no means uncommon. The naturalistically coloured birds are painted in reserves on a band of royal-blue enamel—the *fleur-de-roi* of Sèvres, their names written on the reverse.

d) Group in soft-paste white porcelain with glaze, Tournai, Belgium, c. 1760; ht. 5⅝" (14.3 cm.).

Even the more experienced porcelain collector may be confused between the white porcelain groups and figures produced at Tournai and those made at Derby. This is undoubtedly due to the fact that F. J. Peterinck is known to have engaged workmen who had previously been employed at the English factory. Groups of the type illustrated were seldom marked and were probably modelled by Nicolas Lecreux; other modellers known to have worked at Tournai included N. J. Gauron, who had previously been at Mennecy, and Joseph Willems who for a time was engaged at Sprimont's Chelsea factory in London.

Tournai factory marks (see c).

English Porcelain Introduction

When discussing the development of porcelain manufacture in England, it is essential to remember that unlike the large factories of the Continent, the English concerns were purely commercial ventures of their various proprietors. They were not in any way subsidized by the State or wealthy patrons and if they were unable to show a profit they were forced to close. The only English porcelain factory that was established in the eighteenth century and is still in production today is that of the Worcester Royal Porcelain Company.

To the best of present-day knowledge the first factory to produce porcelain in England was that established by Nicholas Sprimont and Charles Gouyn in about 1745 at Chelsea, a district of south-west London. The majority of the wares produced throughout the independent years of this factory (1745-70) were fashioned after those first popularized by Meissen. By about 1758 the quality of Sprimont's soft-paste porcelain had deteriorated and their wares were mostly in the rococo fashions of the French factory of Sèvres. It was during the so-called Chelsea-Derby period (1770-84) that so many good quality table-wares in the neo-classical style were produced.

Although the proprietors of the Bow factory in east London took out a patent concerning the materials necessary to the manufacture of porcelain as early as 1744, it was almost certainly nearer 1747 before wares were being produced in commercial quantities. The wares of Bow were less costly than those of Chelsea and usually more practical. At the peak of their production, three hundred workers were employed. Bow was the first factory which to our knowledge used calcined bone as an ingredient, resulting in a much tougher ware than the glassy paste of Chelsea. The Bow factory was known as 'New Canton', the factory was said to have been laid out as a Chinese establishment, and a large proportion of their table-wares were decorated with underglaze-blue in the Chinese export porcelain fashion. There is a great similarity between the wares produced at Bow and those of the later factory started at Lowestoft in East Anglia in 1757, and the new collector might well be forgiven for confusing the blue and white wares of these two factories. Work continued at the Bow factory until 1776 but the Lowestoft concern survived until about 1799.

Prior to establishing a factory at Derby in 1756, William Duesbury was engaged as an independent decorator; his account books for 1752 tell us of his adding either unfired or enamel colours to Bow, Derby and Staffordshire wares. Duesbury was one of the first English porcelain manufacturers to produce 'biscuit' figures in the fashion of Vincennes and Sèvres, but his rather chalky, open-grained soft-paste porcelain was not a suitable material to leave without the protection of a glaze, and was inclined to stain very easily and soon become dirty. The factory continued into the nineteenth century and from about 1812-48 is referred to as 'Bloor Derby' after Robert Bloor, who took over the factory from Michael Kean, who was the sole proprietor after the death of William Duesbury in about 1796.

A new form of English soft-paste porcelain was first introduced by Benjamin Lund and William Miller at Bristol in 1748. Their material contained soapstone (steatite) quarried under licence in the area of the Lizard, near Helston in south Cornwall. Their factory was very short-lived for in 1752 it was purchased by a group of Worcester business men, who in the previous year had formed a porcelain company known as the 'Worcester Tonquin Manufacture', the principal partners being Dr. Wall and William Davis. The table-wares produced at the Worcester concern up until 1776 when Dr. Wall died were of outstanding quality in material, form and style of decoration, but from 1776-93 in the years now referred to as the 'Davis & Flight' period, their wares were often of a very poor quality, decorated mainly in underglaze-blue with designs transferred from engraved copper-plates. These pieces were very inferior to those of the rival concern established by Thomas Turner at Caughley in Shropshire in about 1772.

It was not until 1768 that hard-paste porcelain was produced in England by William Cookworthy, a Plymouth chemist. There seems little doubt that Cookworthy had located the necessary china-clay and china-stone on the property of Lord Camelford, near Truro, at a much earlier date. It is unfortunate he delayed his manufacture for so long as by 1770 Chinese blue and white porcelain could be purchased in England at very low prices.

It was in about 1794 that Josiah Spode II introduced the material of bone-china, a body consisting approximately of 50 per cent of calcined animal bone, 25 per cent china-clay and 25 per cent china-stone. This material was in turn produced by nearly all the major English china factories of the nineteenth century and remains one of the most admired ceramic bodies throughout the entire world to this day.

Ceramics

English Porcelain
CHELSEA

Mark on a.

Mark on b.

a) Jug, soft-paste porcelain, painted in enamel colours; mark: incised triangle; Chelsea, 1745-49; ht. 4¾″ (12.1 cm.).

To the best of our knowledge the first English porcelain factory was established at Chelsea, London, in 1745, by a Huguenot silversmith, Nicholas Sprimont. The early period porcelain consisted of a fine soft-paste, which apparently was difficult to model and fire.

Many of Sprimont's early shapes were similar to those he had formerly created from silver. Jugs, such as this, were shaped by pouring slip (watered-down clay) into hollow plaster-of-Paris moulds. The mark often used up until about 1749 was a small incised triangle, and so collectors refer to these early years of Chelsea as the 'triangle-period'

b) Figure of Scapin, soft-paste porcelain, painted in enamel colours; mark: raised anchor on oval applied medallion, picked out in red; Chelsea, c. 1749-52; ht. 4¾″ (12.1 cm.).

Up until about 1755 the porcelain fashions of Europe were dictated by the famous Meissen factory in Saxony. Sir Everard Fawkener, secretary to the Duke of Cumberland, was a patron of the Chelsea factory and arranged for their modellers and decorators to have access to the Meissen collection of Sir Charles Hanbury Williams, British Ambassador at the Court of Dresden. This figure, a character from the Italian Comedy, is modelled after a Meissen original.

---

c) Plate, soft-paste porcelain, painted in purple enamel; mark: anchor in red enamel; Chelsea, c. 1755; dia. 9¼″ (23.5 cm.).

Very little is known as to the names of the early Chelsea painters, but Jeffrey Hamet O'Neale, who later worked in Worcester, is thought to be responsible for these Meissen-like scenes, described in the Chelsea sale catalogues as 'purple landskips'. In common with Meissen, the Chelsea decorators often painted insects or small flowers to help hide any minor blemishes in the paste or glaze.

From about 1752-58 the Chelsea factory mark was a small anchor painted in red enamel, hence the 'red-anchor period'.

d) Tureen and cover, soft-paste porcelain, painted in enamel colours; mark: anchor in red enamel; Chelsea, c. 1755; lgth. 14½″ (36.8 cm.).

It was at Meissen that porcelain was first fashioned in the form of animals and vegetables. Banqueting tables in the German courts were often set with complete services of matching porcelain designed to a common theme, such as the famous 'Swan Service' (p. 174b) with porcelain swans 'swimming' on 'lakes' of mirror.

This very fine tureen was purchased by Lady Charlotte Schreiber, a great 19th century collector, in Rotterdam in 1876, where the dealer asked '£5 for it and took £4'. Similar tureens were made in the form of a hen with chicks, and a boar's head.

Mark on c.

a) Plate, soft-paste porcelain, painted in enamel colours; mark: anchor in red enamel; Chelsea, c. 1755, dia. 9¼″ (23.5 cm.).

Very few wares made at the Chelsea porcelain factory were entirely original. In earlier years they tended to imitate Meissen, and after c. 1755 their wares were modelled and decorated after those from the French factory of Sèvres.

This plate is one of an original botanical series, some of which have been traced to the engravings of George D. Ehret, a German botanical painter who settled in Chelsea in 1737. The old term of 'Sir Hans Sloane' plates is a misnomer. Sir Hans was in fact a patron of the Apothecaries' Physic Garden in Chelsea.

b) Figure of a hawker, soft-paste porcelain, painted in enamel colours and gilt; mark: anchor in gold; Chelsea, 1760–65; ht. 5¾″ (14.6 cm.).

From about 1758 the porcelain made at Chelsea included the added ingredient of calcined animal bone, which made a tougher, but rather more porous material. This was combined with a new glaze that tended to develop minute cracks over the surface (crazing). The result was a ware inclined to stain rather badly. At this same time the fashion for bases with rococo scrollwork modelling, which had just begun, ruined the lively animation so apparent on the early figures.

From about 1758–70 the Chelsea mark took the form of a gold anchor, a device often seen on recent hard-paste fakes.

Mark on a.

Mark on b.

---

c) 'The Chesterfield Vase', soft-paste porcelain, painted in enamel colours and gilt; mark: anchor in gilt; Chelsea, c. 1765; ht. 23½″ (59.7 cm.).

This very heavily decorated large vase was once the property of the Earl of Chesterfield who purchased it at Christie's in 1770. One of a pair, it is typical of the later Chelsea wares fashioned in the style of Sèvres.

The ground colour of 'mazarine-blue' is in imitation of the *bleu lapis* used on Sèvres porcelain from about 1749. The enamel painting is probably the work of J. Donaldson, from a print by R. Gaillard after the François Boucher painting of *Le Panier Misterieux*. Similar painting signed by Donaldson is known on Worcester porcelain of about 1770.

d) Two scent-bottles and stoppers, soft-paste porcelain, painted in enamel colours; Chelsea, ('Girl-in-a-Swing' factory), c. 1752–54; ht. 4″ (10.2 cm.).

In the early part of the 1960s it was proved beyond doubt that from 1749–54 there were two Chelsea porcelain factories in operation. Named after a key figure, the second concern is referred to as the 'Girl-in-a-Swing' factory. Among the wares made at this second factory were many 'toys', or miniatures, including scent-bottles, which can now be readily identified by their rather poor style of modelling and distinctive coloured enamels, which include a deep yellow, a strong crimson, and a dark chocolate brown, usually used to colour hair.

Ceramics

English Porcelain

a) Pair of Sphinxes, soft-paste porcelain, heads thought to be of actress Peg Woffington (d. 1760) adapted from the painting of Arthur Pond, engraved by James McArdell; Bow c. 1750; lgth. 4½″ (11.4 cm.).

Although a patent was applied for as early as 1744, it was more likely nearer 1747 before a soft-paste porcelain containing calcined animal bone (bone-ash), was made in commercial quantities at the factory of Thomas Frye and Edward Heylyn. The factory is referred to as Bow, but was in fact sited on the Essex side of the River Lea. The proprietors called their factory 'New Canton' and large numbers of their early wares were made in the style of Chinese export porcelain (see p. 123b).

b) Figure of a lion, soft-paste porcelain, glazed; Bow, c. 1750-55; lgth. 11½″ (29.2 cm.).

In common with most other porcelain factories the early proprietors of Bow were constantly endeavouring to improve upon their material. The glaze in particular, which often differed in hue, tends to make quick recognition difficult. Bow porcelain was usually heavy, for unlike Chelsea, they made their figures, and some table-wares and vases, by pressing thin slabs of clay into the walls of the moulds by hand (press-moulding).

This lion is modelled after the early classical marble statue at the bottom of the steps of the *Loggia dei Lanzi*, in Florence.

---

c) Sauce-boat, soft-paste porcelain painted in underglaze-blue; mark: a script G in blue; Bow, c. 1752; lgth. 7½″ (19.1 cm.).

The early Bow table-wares were very thickly potted and often followed slightly earlier silver shapes. Their underglaze-blue decoration was a strong royal blue and to preserve the clarity of the design, the glaze appears to have been slightly underfired, often resulting in a mass of minute bubbles. This feature is not so apparent on the later blue-and-white.

The 'peony and fence' is one of the more popular designs that was often used at Bow, in this instance by a painter who marked his work with a script 'G'.

d) Figure of a shepherdess, soft-paste porcelain, painted in enamel colours; Bow, c. 1755; ht. 5¾″ (14.6 cm.).

The early Bow figures appear to have been the work of a single modeller, and in consequence their faces show a family likeness throughout. This is particularly noticeable with their groups of the Nine Muses, most of which were sold 'in the white'. The enamel decoration, sometimes seen on figures thought to have been made prior to about 1753, was most probably added by outside decorators. The work-books of William Duesbury, working in London (1751-53), mention the decoration of 'Bogh' figures.

This shepherdess of slightly later date shows a distinct improvement in modelling, and factory-applied colours, but has no factory mark.

Mark on c.

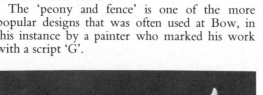

Detail showing heart-shaped terminal of handle (see a).

a) Mug, soft-paste porcelain, with enamel colours over a printed outline; Bow, c. 1760; ht. $3\frac{3}{4}''$ (9.5 cm.).

Bow was among the earliest English factories to decorate their wares with prints taken from engraved copper-plates. In addition to a few early wares with fully engraved prints, some taken from the plates of the famous engraver Robert Hancock, they also used simpler designs, usually of Chinoiserie style, which merely provided an outline. This enabled unskilled hands, or even child labour, to fill in the pattern with coloured enamels. A feature often seen on mugs of the shape illustrated, and other Bow handles, is a small heart-shaped terminal at the lower point of attachment to the body.

b) Sweetmeat centrepiece, soft-paste porcelain, painted in enamel colours; Bow, c. 1760; wdth. 6'' (15.2 cm.).

Sweetmeat dishes, in the form of scallop-shells on a mound of smaller shells, were produced at several English porcelain factories, and were in some cases the work of a single 'repairer' (assembler), who often impressed his work with 'T' or 'T°'. These initials have been found on some dishes such as the one illustrated, and other wares or figures attributed to Bow, Worcester or Plymouth. This mysterious 'Mr Tebo' (or Thibaud), of whom little is known, eventually worked for Josiah Wedgwood. The Bow examples usually include a strong translucent emerald green enamel in the palette.

'Mr Tebo's' marks (see b).

c) Butter-dish, soft-paste porcelain, painted in enamel colours in Japanese Kakiemon style; Bow, c. 1760; dia. $4\frac{1}{2}''$ (11.4 cm.).

Prior to the establishment of the Meissen factory in 1710, the only true porcelain available throughout the entire world was that made in the Far East, primarily in China. From about 1658 hard-paste porcelain was also made at Arita in Japan. One particular form of Japanese decoration became very popular in Europe and was imitated at many factories, it was known as 'Kakiemon', the nickname of the potter considered responsible for its introduction. The Kakiemon design on this dish is called the Quail, or Partridge, pattern.

d) Figure symbolic of Fire, from a set of the Elements, soft-paste porcelain, painted in enamel colours; Bow, c. 1760-65; ht. $9\frac{5}{8}''$ (24.2 cm.).

The form of the bases is a good clue to approximate dating of figures considered to be genuine. From about 1755 Bow, in common with other English porcelain factories, began to perch their figures, or groups, on high four-footed pedestals, modelled in rococo fashion. From about 1763 many Bow examples were marked with a small anchor alongside a dagger, painted in red enamel.

Bow figures of this type have been reproduced in hard-paste porcelain. These can usually be easily identified by their crisp modelling, 'tight-fitting' glaze, and bright colouring.

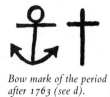

Bow mark of the period after 1763 (see d).

191

Ceramics

English Porcelain
DERBY

a) Figure of a boar, soft-paste porcelain; Derby, c. 1750; ht. 5″ (12.7 cm.).

Although the Derby Porcelain Manufactory was not established until 1756, there is a class of wares attributed to Derby dating from c. 1750. These rather primitive but pleasing figures are thought to be the work of André Planché, a foreign potter who learnt of the manufacture of soft-paste porcelain on the Continent.

This figure is modelled after the antique marble boar now in the Uffizi Gallery at Florence. This model and other known Derby examples have been copied in England during recent years, but reproductions can usually be easily detected by their very poor colours, which include tones of grey-black and salmon pink.

b) Figure of a gallant, soft-paste porcelain, painted in enamel colours; Derby, c. 1757–8; ht. 10⅞″ (27.6 cm.).

The Derby factory of Duesbury and Heath was first established in 1756. The concern was advertized as 'the second Dresden' and during their early years many of their productions, particularly figures, were modelled after those of the Meissen factory. In order to give the impression of hard-paste the glaze was usually tinted with cobalt, resulting in an all too obvious pale blue glaze, which tended to obscure any fine modelling.

Recent research has proved that an almost identical model was also produced at the Liverpool factory of Samuel Gilbody.

---

c) Mug, soft-paste porcelain, painted in enamel colours; Derby, 1756–60; ht. 5¾″ (14.6 cm.).

To rely solely upon factory-marks as a means of attribution can be very misleading. It is necessary to learn to recognize not only the main difference between hard and soft-paste porcelain, but also the various types of soft-paste. In addition various styles of decoration and characteristics of certain painters and their range of colours, must also be considered. In *Old English Porcelain* the late W. B. Honey wrote of many such guides, and compares the 'dishevelled' Derby birds, as seen on this mug, with the exotic birds of Chelsea and Worcester.

d) Base of a Derby figure showing typical 'patch-marks' and incised model number; Derby, c. 1760.

Up until about fifty years ago there was a great deal of confusion over Derby figures, made from about 1760, and those made during the 'gold-anchor' period of the Chelsea factory. It was then observed that figures, and some table-wares of this type, which lacked the gold-anchor mark, invariably had three or more small round dark blemishes on the base, and were in fact of Derby manufacture. These 'patch-marks' were the result of supporting the wares on pads of clay during the glaze firing. The incised numbers refer to the model and factory price-list.

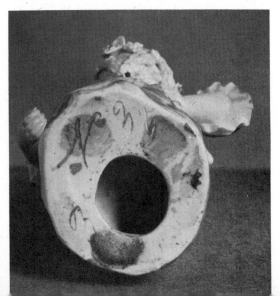

a) Dish, soft-paste porcelain, painted in enamel colours and gilt; Chelsea-Derby, c. 1775; lgth. 12¾″ (32.4 cm.).

In 1770 the Chelsea factory was purchased by William Duesbury of Derby (see p. 190d), who continued to run both undertakings until 1784, when Chelsea was finally closed. It was during this 'Chelsea-Derby' period that some of the most pleasing, and practical, table-wares were produced.

Porcelain was not an ideal material for reproducing earthenwares of early Antique form to cater for the popular neo-classical taste of the period. But swags, garlands, vases and heads from the Antique, which were all so tastefully applied at Derby and Chelsea at this period, were ideal for the purpose.

b) Jug, soft-paste porcelain, painted in enamel colours and gilt; mark: D under a crown in purple; Derby, c. 1782; ht. 7½″ (19.1 cm.).

This fine jug with the pouring lip in the form of the head of Lord Rodney, was made to celebrate his victory over the French Admiral De Grasse in the West Indies. The flower-painting is similar to that seen on some Sèvres porcelain and is attributed to the factory painter Edward Withers. A further Derby feature is the royal blue enamel border, referred to as 'Smith's blue', after a workman credited with introducing the colours.

The painting is in marked contrast to the naturalistic style of their contemporary painter, William Billingslev.

Mark on d.

c) Figure of a dwarf, soft-paste porcelain, painted in colours and gilt; Derby, 1770–84; ht. 6⅝″ (16.8 cm.).

Dwarfs of this type were originally modelled at the Meissen factory after the engravings of Jacques Callot, published in 1622. This particular model has been reproduced by the modellers of the Chelsea factory, who also 'invented' a matching female figure.

The first Derby dwarfs were made during the 'Chelsea-Derby' period (1770–84) and were described in their price list under No. 227 as a 'Pair of Grotesque Punches'. An interesting variation on some of the Derby models is advertising matter written on the large hats, said to be after an actual character known as 'The Mansion House Dwarf'

d) Soup-tureen and stand, soft-paste porcelain, painted in enamel colours and gilt; mark: crown, crossed batons and D in blue; Derby, late 18th century; lgth. 18″ (45.7 cm.).

William Duesbury died in 1786. He was succeeded by his son, William Jr., who took Michael Kean, an Irish miniature-painter, into partnership. After Duesbury died in 1797, Kean continued to run the factory until its purchase in about 1811 by Robert Bloor. Production finally ceased in 1848.

During the late 18th century the Derby tradition of fine flower painting continued with such painters as John Brewer and William ('Quaker') Pegg. The latter's painting ranks amongst the finest to be seen on English porcelain. Pegg worked at Derby from 1795–1800 and 1813–20; the blue factory-mark suggests his earlier period.

Japanese Imari vase, the style of decoration an important influence on English porcelain.

193

Ceramics

English Porcelain
LOWESTOFT
PINXTON
LONGTON HALL

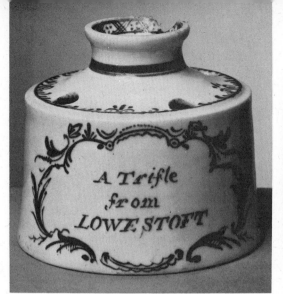

These straight spouts are typical of Chinese pots (compare b).

a) Inkwell, soft-paste porcelain, painted in underglaze-blue; Lowestoft (Suffolk), c. 1785; ht. 2½" (6.4 cm.).

Lowestoft might well be considered the 'peasant' porcelain factory of England. They produced modestly decorated and inexpensive items, catering primarily for the local market. Many wares were painted with inscriptions giving the name and the date of the owner, or recipient of a gift. Some, such as this inkwell, were intended as souvenirs for the visitor or holidaymaker to Lowestoft, at that time a fashionable seaside resort.

The porcelain of the Lowestoft factory was similar to that made at Bow; it contained a similar high percentage of calcined bone and consequently was very liable to staining if chipped or cracked.

b) Teapot, soft-paste porcelain, painted in enamel colours; Lowestoft (Suffolk), c. 1780–85; ht. 6" (15.2 cm.).

For many years the term 'Chinese-Lowestoft' was wrongly used to refer to Chinese porcelain of the type made for export to Europe. It is now generally appreciated that there is no connection between the Far Eastern ware and the soft-paste porcelain made at the small East Anglian fishing village of Lowestoft which was in production from 1757 to about 1799. Only after 1770 were some of the Lowestoft wares decorated in enamel colours, in addition to the underglaze-blue which had been used from the start. Special note should be taken of the curving spout on the pot illustrated; this differs from the straight Chinese version.

---

c) Coffee-can, soft-paste porcelain, painted in colours and gilt; mark: bow and arrow in red enamel; Pinxton (Derbyshire), 1796–1812; ht. 2½" (6.4 cm.).

William Billingsley started his career as a decorator at Duesbury's Derby factory. For many years he experimented with the materials of soft-paste porcelain, but lacked the necessary capital to start his own factory. In 1796 he persuaded John Coke to invest in a new concern at Pinxton, in Derbyshire. Billingsley was only associated with the factory from 1796–99, during which period he produced some attractive table-wares, very much in the style of those made at Derby. Due to high costs and no profits, Billingsley left Pinxton in 1799. These little sprigs of flowers on a white ground are typical of Pinxton.

d) Figure of a pheasant, glazed soft-paste porcelain; Longton Hall (Staffordshire); c. 1750; lgth. 7¾" (19.7 cm.).

For many years Staffordshire potters had concentrated on either earthen or stonewares made and fired with local materials. They therefore found it difficult at first to adapt their skill to the more refined material of soft-paste porcelain, produced for the first time in Staffordshire at Longton Hall between 1749–60.

This porcelain had much in common with that used at the short-lived Chelsea 'Girl-in-a-Swing' factory (1749–54) (see p. 189d). It was probably the well-known potter, William Littler, who took the knowledge of porcelain from London to Longton Hall.

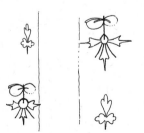

Typical Pinxton sprigs (see c).

a) Potpourri, soft-paste porcelain, decorated with relief flowers, enamel colours and gilding; Longton Hall (Staffordshire), c. 1755; ht. 16½″ (41.9 cm.).

These extremely ornate potpourri remained popular in England for almost one hundred years. Longton Hall produced a large variety of wares and figures of varying quality and was one of the earliest factories to reproduce figures after bronzes. Their mugs and jugs can often be distinguished by extremely ugly and impractical handles, and were often decorated with transfers by the Liverpool printing firm of Sadler and Green.

It is now known that when the factory closed in 1760, William Littler went to West Pans in Scotland, where by 1764 he was working as a 'China Maker'.

b) Sauce-boat, soapstone porcelain, painted in enamel colours; mark: BRISTOLL moulded in relief on base; Bristol (decoration added at Worcester), 1748-52; lgth. 7½″ (19.1 cm.).

The early Bristol porcelain factory was established by Benjamin Lund and William Miller in 1748. Soapstone was probably an ingredient in the porcelain made at one of the London factories, of which we know so little, but it was at Bristol that the advantages of this new body were fully recognized—a resistance to cracking if immersed in hot water, and a glaze that rarely 'crazed'.

The moulded 'BRISTOLL' on the base of this sauce-boat has been overpainted with a green-enamel leaf, suggesting that the decoration was added after the factory had been taken over by Worcester in 1752.

Ceramics

English Porcelain

LONGTON HALL
BRISTOL
WORCESTER

---

c) Jug, soapstone porcelain, decorated with black enamel prints; Worcester, dated 1757; ht. 5½″ (14.0 cm.).

During the Seven Years War, Frederick the Great, King of Prussia, was an extremely popular figure in England. His portrait and loyal inscriptions were often used to decorate earthenware or porcelain. The engraver responsible for the majority of the prints seen on Worcester porcelain at this period was Robert Hancock, who left London for Worcester around 1756. His work was invariably after earlier or contemporary engravings; in this instance the original painting was by Antoine Pesne, and the first line-engraving by Richard Houston. Under the trophy of arms and inscribed flags is the Hancock's signature 'R H Worcester'.

d) Vase and cover, soapstone porcelain, painted in underglaze-blue; workman's mark: a TF monogram in blue; Worcester, c. 1760; ht. 8″ (20.3 cm.).

Dr. Wall was one of the most important of the original fourteen partners who established the early Worcester factory in 1751. Wares made up to the time of his death in 1776 are referred to as of the 'Wall-period'. During this period Worcester produced their finest pieces, the majority of which were decorated in the typical grey-blue underglaze colour. This subject of the owl being 'mobbed' by birds was sometimes painted in the full enamel palette. The knob in the form of a flower was often used at Worcester, but also copied at other factories, including Caughley.

Bristoll

Mark on b.

R.H. Worcester

Mark on c.

a) Jug, soapstone porcelain, moulded with overlapping cabbage-leaves and decorated in enamel colours with a scene and coat of arms; Worcester, c. 1760; ht. 10½" (26.7 cm.).

Some of the finest enamel painting ever produced at Worcester decorates these large jugs moulded in the form of cabbage-leaves. This shape remained popular for many years and was also produced at both Caughley and Coalport.

The flower painting is in the naturalistic style seen on mid-18th century Meissen. The landscape is in the manner and palette of a Worcester painter named James Rogers, whose signature 'J. Rogers Pinxit 1757' is on a mug in the British Museum. This attribution is best used to suggest a style, rather than the work of the actual painter (cf. p. 199c).

Mark on b.

b) Vase and cover, soapstone porcelain, painted in colours and gilding on an underglaze-blue scaled ground; Worcester, c. 1770; ht. 6¾" (17.1 cm.).

In about 1768 the Worcester factory began to produce more highly decorated wares, somewhat in the style made at Chelsea during their late years as an independent concern. Today, Worcester porcelain, decorated with a blue ground and painted in a fish-scale pattern, is very much in demand—new collectors should beware of the many recent French hard-paste porcelain reproductions made to resemble these pieces. Both the old and the new are often marked with a blue 'fretted square' factory mark.

---

c) Two vases, porcelain, painted in enamel colours and gilt; marks: Flight, Barr & Barr and London address in red and F.B.B. under a crown, impressed; Worcester, c. 1830; ht. 10" (25.4 cm.).

The Worcester porcelain factory was owned by Joseph & John Flight from 1783-93 (John died in 1791); in 1793 Martin Barr became a partner (Flight & Barr period, 1793-1807). Barr's son joined the firm in 1807, and wares were marked with the names, or initials, of 'Barr, Flight & Barr' (1807-13). The last years of the factory was the 'Flight, Barr & Barr' period, 1813-40, when the concern was taken over by Robert Chamberlain.

d) Vase, porcelain painted in enamel colours and gilt, the decoration attributed to John Barker; mark: Chamberlains Worcester in red script; Worcester (Chamberlain's factory), c. 1815; ht. 9¼" (23.5 cm.).

It was probably nearer 1790 before Robert Chamberlain and his son Humphrey started to produce their own porcelain, rather than only decorate that of other factories. Their 19th century wares were generally decorated in the lavish and expensive styles of the period, and were especially popular in London. They opened showrooms, first in Bond Street and later Piccadilly.

The form of this vase is still earlier neo-classic, such as Josiah Wedgwood produced in his stonewares. The decoration of beautifully painted feathers was probably by John Barker.

Flight, Barr & Barr mark (see c).

Opposite:
English porcelain, left to right: top, dwarf, Chelsea; Polyhymnia, Bow; both soft-paste, c. 1750; bottom: figure; squirrel; both Derby soft-paste, c. 1765; boys and goat; hard-paste, Plymouth, c. 1768-70.

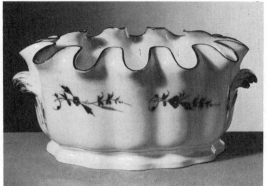

a) Dessert-dish, soapstone porcelain, printed in underglaze-blue with 'The Travellers' pattern; mark: Salopian *impressed; Caughley (Shropshire), 1775–80; dia. 6⅜″ (16.2 cm.).*

Thomas Turner (b. 1749) was apprenticed at the Worcester Porcelain Manufactory, where he acquired sufficient knowledge of the manufacture to enable him to start up his own concern in about 1772 at Caughley (pronounced Calf-ley) in Shropshire.

Turner was joined in 1775 by Robert Hancock, the engraver, who was responsible for several of the printed designs used at Caughley, which so closely resemble those of Worcester. This particular design was probably taken from an 18th century French engraving and is attributed to Hancock.

b) Monteith (or Verrière), soapstone porcelain, painted in underglaze-blue; mark: S *in underglaze-blue for Salopian; Caughley (Shropshire), c. 1785; lgth. 12″ (30.5 cm.).*

Thomas Turner was obviously very keen on the form and decoration of the contemporary French porcelain being made at Chantilly and Tournai. Known to have visited France during the 1780s, it is said he persuaded some French potters to return with him to England and work at Caughley.

This monteith, fashioned after silver, was used for cooling wine glasses in ice. The underglaze-blue decoration is referred to as the 'Chantilly sprig', other similar patterns include the 'Carnation', 'French sprigs' and 'Salopian sprigs' (see p. 183a).

Mark on b.

c) Jug, soapstone porcelain, decorated in enamel colours and gilt; enamel decoration added at Chamberlain's Worcester workshop; Caughley (Shropshire), 1785–90; ht. 8½″ (21.6 cm.).

Soon after Thomas Flight purchased the Worcester factory in 1783, Robert Chamberlain left the concern and started his own porcelain decorating business. During the late 1780s Turner sold large quantities of his Caughley wares to Chamberlain in the glazed, but undecorated state. Many of the finely-decorated Caughley pieces, such as this jug, are considered to be Chamberlain's work. There is still a little confusion over those Caughley wares decorated in a less sophisticated manner, as some enamel and gilt decoration was also added at the factory.

d) Tea-pot, hard-paste porcelain, painted in enamel colours; made at Caughley during the management of John Rose of Coalport, c. 1800; ht. 6¾″ (17.1 cm.).

In 1799 Caughley was taken over by John Rose of the Coalport concern. Rose continued to run both factories until 1814, when his entire production was concentrated at Coalport.

Excavations during the 1960s on the old Caughley site indicated that a hard-paste porcelain, of a type previously attributed to the New Hall factory, was also made at Caughley from about 1796. These Caughley/Coalport hard-paste porcelains are discussed in David Holgate's book on New Hall, which stresses that identical patterns were often used at both factories, the main differences being the moulded handle, spout, lid and knob shapes.

Opposite:
One of a pair of pot-pourri vases and covers in porcelain; Chelsea, England, c. 1765.

Ceramics

English Porcelain
LIVERPOOL
PLYMOUTH
BRISTOL

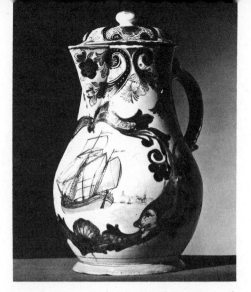

a) Mug, soft-paste porcelain, painted in enamel colours; Liverpool (Samuel Gilbody's factory), c. 1760; ht. 5⅜" (13.7 cm.).

During recent years research and on-site excavations have enabled collectors to allocate certain wares, previously only classed as 'Liverpool', to specific potteries.

There were at least eight major potteries in Liverpool during the second half of the 18th century. This mug is attributed to Samuel Gilbody's Shaw's Brow pottery, where porcelain was made from about 1754-61. Many other wares made by Gilbody were decorated with enamel printing signed by Sadler, with whom Gilbody is known to have been well acquainted. Another early and important factory was that of Richard Chaffer (d. 1765) and Philip Christian, who continued the factory until 1775.

b) Jug and cover, porcelain, painted in enamel colours and underglaze-blue; Liverpool (William Ball's factory), dated 1765; ht. 11¾" (29.8 cm.).

From the beginning of the 18th century many Liverpool potters specialized in tin-glazed earthenware. The decoration on this jug, which is inscribed 'THE UNION', 'REIN VOS 1764', continues the early Delft-ware tradition of painting items to order for the captains of visiting ships. Customarily the merchant owners of new vessels presented their captains with similarly-inscribed bowls at the start of a maiden voyage.

Very little is known about the potter William Ball, who was making porcelain in Liverpool from about 1755-69. His underglaze-blue decoration was extremely bright and is often referred to as a 'sticky-blue'.

---

c) Selection of wares of hard-paste porcelain, the cup and mug being decorated in underglaze-blue; Plymouth, 1768-70; ht. (of mug) 4¾" (12.1 cm.).

For collecting purposes the wares made at Plymouth and Bristol between 1768-81 are considered together. The factory of William Cookworthy, and twelve other shareholders, only remained at Plymouth for two years, before moving to Bristol.

Cookworthy was obviously interested in hard-paste porcelain at a much earlier date; unfortunately, by the time he started his production, the material was no longer a novelty, and the genuine Chinese article could be purchased very cheaply.

Due to the high temperature their underglaze-blue was applied rather sparingly, but usually still fired to a blackish-grey, as was the case with some early Chinese wares.

d) Vase and cover, hard-paste porcelain decorated in a Sèvres style with enamel colours and gilt; Bristol, c. 1775; ht. 15½" (39.4 cm.).

Cookworthy had located essential supplies of china-clay and china-stone, on the property of Lord Camelford, near Truro, Cornwall. In 1768 he took out a patent for the sole right to use these in porcelain manufacture. In 1774, when Cookworthy retired, the patent was transferred to one of the original partners, Richard Champion. He was granted an extension of the patent for a further fourteen years, but only in relation to translucent porcelain, other potters being allowed to use them in their stonewares and earthenwares.

Painting of the type seen on this vase is usually attributed to a French painter, a Monsieur Soqui.

a) Pair of figures, hard-paste porcelain, painted in enamel colours; Bristol, c. 1775; ht. 7¼" (18.4 cm.).

Almost all the limited range of figures that can be safely attributed to the Plymouth period were apparently produced from moulds first used at the earlier Staffordshire factory at Longton Hall, and most probably sold at Salisbury in 1760, when about 90,000 pieces of their porcelain were also put up for sale.

These later Bristol figures with the rocky mound bases are considered to be from the models made for Champion by Pierre Stephan, who at the time was working at Derby, where he modelled similar coarse figures for that factory.

b) Tea-pot and stand, hard-paste porcelain, painted in enamel colours; Bristol, c. 1775; ht. 6½" (16.5 cm.).

From the time that Richard Champion took control of the factory he seems to have concentrated on tea and coffee-services, and other table-wares and vases. He rather rashly claimed that his wares had the hardness of Dresden (Meissen) and the elegance of Sèvres. His claim was hardly justified, and the later Bristol flower-painting was particularly dull.

This tea-pot shows two typical Bristol features, the 'ear-shaped' handle and the inverted pear-shaped body. Matching tea-pot stands, to protect the elegant tea-tables, appear to have been supplied with the majority of Champion's later tea and coffee-pots.

c) Tea-pot, hard-paste porcelain, decorated in under-glaze-blue and gilt; mark: Ralph Clowes New Hall, fecit incised; New Hall (Staffordshire), c. 1787-90; ht. 6" (15.2 cm.).

By the end of the 18th century many competent potters were producing wares in Staffordshire, which makes attribution to a particular factory very difficult at times. This is the case with many pieces made in the style of the New Hall China manufactory. The New Hall factory was formed by a group of six Staffordshire potters, who purchased from Richard Champion the remaining years of his patent for the production of hard-paste porcelain. The body of the New Hall porcelain was almost identical to Bristol, but the glaze was much softer, and had a 'wet' appearance.

d) Coffee-pot and cover, bone-china, painted in red and blue; mark: New Hall printed in reddish-brown within a double circle; New Hall (Staffordshire), c. 1814-25; ht. 8¾" (22.2 cm.).

The New Hall factory continued producing hard-paste porcelain until c. 1814 when, with many other English factories, they turned to the more popular bone-china, as introduced by Josiah Spode II (c. 1794).

Their earlier hard-paste wares, made from 1781, were only very inconsistently marked with pattern numbers, but from the time they produced bone-china they often added also the printed factory-mark of 'New Hall'. These bone-china wares were often decorated in bright colours with jasper patterns, gold or silver (platinum) prints (patented by Peter Warburton 1810) and the conventional black-enamel prints often of a mother and child.

New Hall mark (see d).

201

Ceramics

English Porcelain
SWANSEA
NANTGARW
COALPORT

SWANSEA

Mark on a.

NANT-GARW C.W

Mark on b.

a) Plate, soft-paste porcelain, painted in colours and gilt; mark: Swansea and the name of the bird (hoopoe) in red enamel; probably painted by Matthew Colclough; Swansea (Wales), 1814–17; dia. 8¼″ (21.0 cm.).

After the move to Swansea, the early paste of Billingsley, which had a translucency likened to 'sodden snow', was modified for economic reasons. The result was a paste with a 'duck-egg' green translucency.

Painting of the simple type, as illustrated, is acceptable as factory work. However, a large proportion of the Welsh porcelain was enamelled and gilded in London to the orders of such retailers as Mortlocks of Oxford Street, with rather garish results.

b) Plate, soft-paste porcelain, with enamel and gilt decoration almost certainly added in London; mark: NANTGARW C.W. impressed (Nantgarw China Works); Nantgarw (Wales), c. 1815; dia. 10″ (25.4 cm.).

In 1813 William Billingsley, his two daughters, and Samuel Walker, his son-in-law, started to manufacture a fine, but wasteful and costly, soft-paste porcelain at Nantgarw, north of Cardiff. Billingsley, partly financed by a local surveyor, W. W. Young, was soon in financial trouble. This necessitated his accepting the invitation of L. W. Dillwyn, of the nearby Swansea Pottery, to move his porcelain production to the older factory. He worked there from 1814–17, when he returned to Nantgarw.

A good indication of Billingsley's fine soft-paste is that the moulded decoration on plate rims etc. often shows as slight indentations on the reverse.

c) Plate, porcelain, painted in enamel colours and gilt; Coalport (Shropshire), 1820–30; dia. 9¼″ (23.5 cm.).

By the early 1820s John Rose had purchased both the moulds and stock in trade of both the Swansea and Nantgarw factories. This has resulted in a great deal of confusion among collectors, who are often disappointed to learn that their wares are of the later factory, despite their having the identical forms as the earlier Welsh porcelains.

The moulded design of the rim of this plate can be seen on both Swansea and Nantgarw porcelain, but the style of decoration is of the later period and the body is of a bone-china, rather than the fine soft-pastes of the originators.

d) Plate from a service made by command of Queen Victoria for presentation by her to Nicholas I, Czar of Russia, exhibited in the Great Exhibition of 1851; mark of the retailer A.B. & R.P. Daniell of London; Coalport, c. 1850; dia. 10″ (25.4 cm.)

From about 1845 Coalport wares were mainly in the styles of 18th century Sèvres. Their coloured grounds of pink (*rose*) and dark-blue (*bleu-de-roi*) were good, but no later porcelains ever equalled the beauty of the original French soft-paste porcelain, although at times some Coalport wares with faked marks were sold as the genuine article.

The factories of both Minton and Copeland, who also produced similar wares, did at least use their own factory marks.

a) Cup and saucer, bone-china, decorated with pale underglaze-blue print; mark: imitation Chinese seal in blue; Lane Delph (Staffordshire), Miles Mason's factory, early 19th century; dia. (saucer) 5¾″ (14.6 cm.).

Some of the finest Staffordshire pottery of about 1800 was the work of Miles Mason (b. 1752). Although involved in the china and glass trade, and various partnerships with other potters for quite a long period, Mason did not become an independent potter until about 1800.

Mason produced a variety of materials including earthenware, porcelain of a New Hall type, bone-china and stone-china. This cup is one of four popular Mason shapes, the distinctive feature being the curved-back thumb-rest at the top of the handle.

b) Pair of flower-pots, bone-china, painted in enamel colours and gilt; mark: WEDGWOOD printed in red; Etruria (Staffordshire), Wedgwood's factory, 1812-22; ht. 2½″ (6.4 cm.).

Josiah Wedgwood died in 1795. He had been an independent master-potter since 1759, producing many kinds of earthenwares and stonewares. Although he was known to have been interested in the production of porcelain, he apparently did not make any in a commercial quantity. Probably the loss of overseas business, due to the Napoleonic Wars, prompted Josiah Wedgwood II to start producing bone-china in 1812.

These wares were finely potted and tastefully decorated and always marked with the name 'WEDGWOOD' in either red or blue. Bone-china production came to a halt in 1822 and was not revived until 1878.

Ceramics

English Porcelain

MILES MASON

WEDGWOOD

MINTON

---

c) Coffee-can and saucer, bone-china, painted in enamel colours and gilt; Stoke (Staffordshire), Minton's factory, c. 1820; dia. (saucer) 5½″ (14.0 cm.).

Prior to becoming a master-potter on his own account, Thomas Minton (1765-1836) was apprenticed to Thomas Turner at the Caughley factory, where he learnt the art of engraving copper-plates for transfer-printing. He later worked as an engraver in London for Josiah Spode, William Adam and Josiah Wedgwood, prior to starting his own factory at Stoke in 1796.

Minton's wares were always of a superior quality, but his earlier pieces were usually unmarked. This coffee-can shows a typical Minton shaped handle, with a distinct ring as opposed to an oval.

d) Tea-warmer, bone-china, painted in enamel colours and gilt; Stoke (Staffordshire), Minton's factory, c. 1820; ht. 8⅞″ (22.5 cm.).

The tea-warmer was almost certainly derived from the earlier continental *veilleuse*, a vessel made most likely as a food-warmer for the sick-room; a small bowl for soup, or gruel, warmed by an oil-lamp (*godet*).

The tea-pot form is also a continental shape, produced at various Paris factories in hard-paste porcelain. This particular example has been traced by the early pattern-books to Minton's factory. These same pattern-books have revealed that Minton produced many unmarked tea-wares decorated in styles made popular at Worcester and the Welsh factories of Nantgarw and Swansea.

Mark on a.

Detail of Minton ring handle (see c).

Ceramics

English Porcelain
MINTON
COPELAND & GARRETT
ROCKINGHAM
BELLEEK

a) Plate, bone-china, painted in enamel colours and gilt; same form and decoration as on a dessert-service presented by Queen Victoria to the Emperor of Austria, and shown at Great Exhibition of 1851; Stoke (Staffordshire), Minton's factory, c. 1850; dia. 9½″ (24.1 cm.).

Thomas Minton died in 1836 and was succeeded by his son Herbert, who took John Boyle into partnership. The initials 'M. & B.' sometimes seen on transfer-printed wares relate to 'Minton & Boyle' (1836–41).

Herbert Minton (d. 1858) continued to produce high quality wares decorated by the finest hands available, in some instances ceramic artists and potters who had worked in continental factories. These included Leon Arnoux, Christian Henk, Emile Lessore and Louis H. Jahn, who ended his career as curator of the Hanley Museum, Staffordshire.

b) Figure of 'Narcissus' moulded in 'Parian' porcelain; modelled by John Gibson R.A.; Stoke (Staffordshire), Copeland & Garrett's factory, 1846; ht. 11¾″ (29.8 cm.).

The term 'Parian' was introduced in the early 1840s to describe a new type of porcelain, intended to simulate the famous statuary marble from the Greek island of Paros. Credit was given in 1842 to the firm of Copeland & Garrett (1833–47), for the introduction of this ideal material, but some doubt still remains as to the actual inventor.

'Narcissus' was the first work commissioned by the Art-Union of London in 1846. They purchased from Copeland & Garrett scaled-down Parian-ware copies of Gibson's original sculpture to give as consolation prizes in their annual lottery, held to raise funds for the arts.

Mark on c.

Mark on d.

c) Cup and saucer, bone-china, painted in enamel colours and gilt; mark (on saucer only): griffin and Rockingham Works Brameld Manufacturer to the King, printed in mauve; Swinton (Yorkshire), 1830–37; dia. (saucer) 5¾″ (14.6 cm.).

Fine quality bone-china was only made at the Rockingham Works at Swinton from 1826–42. The factory was on the estate of their patron, the Earl Fitzwilliam, the factory name being that of his kinsman, the Marquis of Rockingham.

For many years, wares have been wrongly attributed to this factory merely because they were decorated in a revived rococo style. Pattern numbers on Rockingham do not appear to go beyond about number 1,560. Handles of tea-ware are a good aid to identification. Rockingham appears to have used a distinctive variety of eight shapes.

d) Cup and saucer, hard-paste porcelain, decorated with lustrous glaze and enamel colours; mark: Irish wolf-hound and harp, printed in black over a ribbon, inscribed BELLEEK; Belleek (County Fermanagh, Ireland), c. 1875; dia. (saucer) 5¼″ (13.3 cm.).

Despite the fact that Belleek porcelain was not produced in commercial quantities until about 1863, the wares made prior to about 1890 are eagerly sought by present-day collectors. The outstanding feature of this manufacture is the 'mother-of-pearl' lustrous effect seen on the glaze.

Collectors are cautioned against buying any so-called early wares, which are marked with the country of origin (i.e. Ireland, England etc.). Not until 1891 did the McKinley Tariff Act of America compel all American imports to be marked with the name of the country where made.

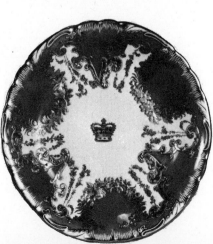

American Porcelain Introduction

The history of American porcelain was brief before 1825, although it began even in advance of the history of porcelain in England. In 1739, Andrew Duché, a son of Anthony Duché, the first stoneware potter in Philadelphia, attempted to make porcelain in Savannah, Georgia. Although he resisted showing the results of his experiments, he did allow William Stephens, Secretary of the Georgia Colony, to look at a bisque-fired tea cup, which Stephens reported 'was as transparent as any ordinary strong china cups commonly are'. It is probable that Duché actually made porcelain experimentally; if so, he was the first American to do so, followed by Bonnin and Morris in Philadelphia, c. 1770-72.

Much later, Dr. Henry Mead made porcelain in Jersey City and possibly in New York City. The first sizeable American production of porcelain was by the Jersey City Porcelain and Earthenware Company, founded in 1825. It made porcelain for only three years and anticipated by a few months the most famous of nineteenth century American porcelain works, that of William Ellis Tucker in Philadelphia.

Tucker, having begun as a decorator of porcelain from his father's import shop, turned to experimenting with kaolin and feldspar to make porcelain. From a small kiln behind the store he moved to a larger one which he built after leasing the old Philadelphia waterworks for a pottery in 1826. The following year he went into production, taking John Hulme as a partner in 1828. Judge Alexander Hemphill succeeded Hulme in 1831, enabling Tucker to build a new factory. Tucker died in 1832, leaving the business to Hemphill, who ran it until finally closing down in 1838.

There were a few short-lived porcelain works during the mid-century, the best known having been Lyman and Fenton's factory in Bennington, Vermont. Its elaborately varied production included the first Parian ware made in the United States and also porcelain table and toilet wares. The factory closed in 1858. Two years earlier a group associated with it established the Southern Porcelain Company in Aiken, South Carolina. Parian and porcelain were also made there during the few years it existed.

Charles Cartlidge made porcelain at Greenpoint, Long Island, between 1849 and 1856 and William Bloor produced Parian ware there from 1859 to 1862. The Union Porcelain Works, also of Greenpoint, made hard-paste porcelain, including ceramic sculpture, after 1862. A third porcelain works at Greenpoint was the Faience Manufacturing Company, directed by Edward Lycett. Belleek ware was made by Ott and Brewer and other firms in Trenton, New Jersey, and by Knowles, Taylor and Knowles in East Liverpool, Ohio. The latter made a fine porcelain called Lotus ware between 1890 and 1898. Virtually all the late nineteenth century factories were run by potters trained in Staffordshire. In general most of their products are notable for embodying the more appalling qualities of late Victorian art, although the often intricately and elegantly designed Lotus ware was sometimes able to rise above this criticism. For the most part, porcelain was seldom a success in America, either aesthetically or economically. Only in strictly utilitarian wares, such as the contemporary Coors laboratory porcelain, has the American commercial porcelain potter been wholly successful.

Lamp with tea-pot by Tucker and Hemphill of Philadelphia, c. 1836.

Ceramics

American Porcelain

18TH CENTURY
BONNIN AND MORRIS

19TH CENTURY
BENNINGTON

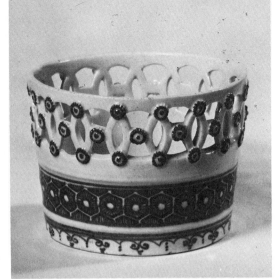

a) Soft-paste porcelain open-work dish, painted in underglaze blue; mark P, Bonnin and Morris, Philadelphia; 1770–1772; ht. 2½″ (6.35 cm.).

Until recently there has been no agreement that the supposed first American porcelain factory operated by Gousse Bonnin and George Anthony Morris in Philadelphia actually made porcelain. Neither has opinion been unanimous that a key piece, a broken fruit basket in the Philadelphia Museum attributed to Bonnin and Morris in 1841 by its original owner's son, was porcelain, having been described by Barber in 1893 as 'cream-coloured earthenware', and later successively by Spargo, Ramsay, and Clement as 'white earthenware'. It remained for Graham Hood to apply historical scholarship, archaeological method, and scientific analysis to prove beyond question in 1972 that bone-ash, soft-paste porcelain was the factory's sole product and to identify positively twelve surviving examples.

b) Soft-paste porcelain sweetmeat stand, painted in underglaze blue, unmarked; Bonnin and Morris, Philadelphia, 1770–1772; ht. 5½″ (13.9 cm.).

Bonnin and Morris porcelain's resemblance to Bow, Lowestoft and other English 18th century porcelains is belied by occasional pooling, 'dragging', pitting, and bubbling of the glaze and by uneven body thickness.

There are also distinctive traits in the underglaze blue pseudo-Chinese decorations. This is usually painted, although, as in English counterparts, it is sometimes transfer-printed. The rather turgid body is not easily translucent. The surviving whole pieces comprise the following forms: fruit basket, large sauceboat, small fluted sauceboat, openwork dish, shell pickle tray, sweetmeat stand. Wasters from the kiln site and documentation add evidence of punch bowls, dinner and tea services. A reversed 'S' mark, found on a fruit basket and a shard, probably signifies Southwark, the factory's neighbourhood, while the more frequent 'P' stands for Philadelphia.

c) Parian ware from Bennington, Vermont; c. 1850–58; ht. of tall vase 8 13/16″ (22.3 cm.).

The Victorian predilection for making something of a cheap material to imitate something else made of an expensive material is exemplified by Parian ware. Formed either by pressing wet clay against the interiors of moulds, or by casting with liquid slip, Parian ware emerged from kiln as biscuit porcelain, resembling the marble for which it was named. At Bennington, Christopher Webber Fenton (see p. 168e) always attuned to his own times, was the first to produce this popular English innovation in America, in the late 1840s.

a) Blue and white pitcher; Grape pattern; ht. 16⅛″ (40.9 cm.).

Bennington's success with its Parian ware led to experimentation with colour. Fenton, avoiding the cheap, painted surface colour used by some of his competitors, brushed blue slip on the parts of the mould where colour was desired. This adhered to the white slip poured into the mould in the casting process and fused with it when fired. Thus the blue colour is integral with the body.

b) Blue and white Parian ware pitcher and vase; Bennington, Vermont; c. 1850–58; ht. 7½″ (19.0 cm.).

Bennington's blue and white Parian vases and trinket boxes were usually the epitome of Victorian fussiness. Frequently, they fairly crawled with applied flowers and tendrils that have now and then been permitted to survive by the grace of some miraculous intervention. In several examples an indigenous American source is revealed in symbolic motifs, such as the American eagle.

---

c) Pitcher, white Parian ware, Corn-husk pattern, c. 1860; ht. 10⅛″ (25.7 cm.).

These later Parian wares reflect the increasing grossness of ceramic design after 1850. This Corn-husk pitcher is typical; one can scarcely imagine a more infelicitous shape or a more obtrusive confusion of three-dimensional decoration. Yet such was the taste of the period and the romantic inappropriateness of its furnishings that a person of ordinary means could imagine that on his very own table, for such a lowly purpose as pouring his breakfast milk, there sat a piece of marble sculpture in the latest fashion. As an American, he could also point with pride to the ears of corn so faithfully represented.

d) Vase, hard-paste porcelain; Union Porcelain Works, Greenpoint, Long Island, New York; c. 1870; ht. 8½″ (21.5 cm.).

The Union Porcelain Works was established about 1857 by William Boch as a manufactory of soft-paste porcelain knobs and hardware. When Boch failed it was taken over by Thomas C. Smith, who by 1888 converted the works into a hard-paste porcelain factory, which made a variety of decorative wares, including this turtle and pitcher-plant vase.

American Porcelain

GREENWOOD
OTT & BREWER
WILLETTS
KNOWLES

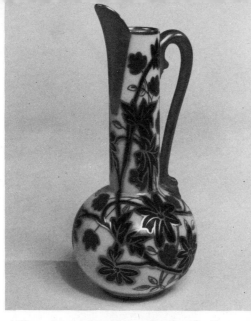

a) Ewer decorated in blue, red and gold; Greenwood Pottery Company, Trenton, New Jersey; c. 1876; ht. 6" (15.2 cm.).

The Greenwood Pottery Company was one of several American firms founded by Staffordshire potters whose aim was to make commercial white wares, porcelain hardware trimmings, telegraph insulators, etc. in America. Established in 1861 by Stephens, Tams, & Company, this firm, like several of its competitors, extended into porcelain table and decorative wares. Barber mentions their 'ornamental designs, richly decorated in the Royal Worcester style'. This piece was exhibited in Greenwood's display at the Centennial Exhibition in Philadelphia in 1876.

b) Belleek porcelain tea-pot; made by Ott & Brewer, Trenton, New Jersey; c. 1882–1892; ht. 3¾" (9.52 cm.).

A refinement of the cast Parian ware was the fragile egg-shell porcelain known as Belleek ware. The Belleek works in Ireland, which developed the ware, was founded in 1863 (see p. 204d). Many English potters were employed there, among them members of the Bromley family. In 1882, Ott & Brewer in Trenton decided to imitate Belleek ware. They imported William Bromley and his two sons from Belleek to manage their factory. From then on Ott & Brewer were producing high-quality Belleek-type porcelain, much of it designed under the growing influence of Japanese porcelain.

c) Belleek porcelain cup and saucer; made by Willetts Manufacturing Company; Trenton, New Jersey; after 1879; ht. of cup, 2⅛" (5.39 cm.).

Ott & Brewer's success with Belleek ware was emulated by another Trenton firm, Willetts Manufacturing Company. After luring William Bromley Sr. away from Ott & Brewer to manage their firm, Willetts produced Belleek ware of similar style and quality. There were other efforts to make Belleek ware, notably by the Delaware Pottery in Trenton. This was managed by Thomas Connelly, who had also trained in the Irish Belleek factory.

d) Vase in 'Lotus Ware', made by Knowles Taylor, & Knowles, Company; East Liverpool, Ohio; c. 1892; ht. 7½" (19.0 cm.).

East Liverpool in Ohio vied with the Trenton, New Jersey factories as a principal centre for the factory production of commercial yellow, white and granite wares, as well as of decorative porcelains. Of the latter, probably the most successful is the 'Lotus Ware' of Knowles, Taylor, and Knowles. Lotus Ware was a thin bone porcelain with an appealing texture and with frequently interesting reticulated and applied decoration. It was featured at the Columbian Exposition in Chicago in 1893.

One of a pair of vases by Tucker and Hemphill, c. 1835 (see Introduction to American Porcelain, p. 205).

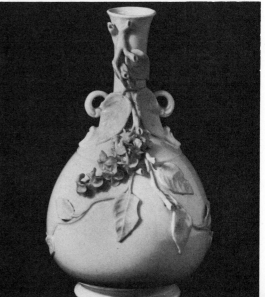

Ceramics Glossary

ALKALINE GLAZE: A glaze composed of soda or potash and sand, used on a clay body which also includes the same elements.

ARABESQUES: Foliate and scrollwork surface ornament perhaps imitating and derived from the Islamic script.

ARCANUM: Literally a secret, but especially the secret formula for making porcelain.

BISCUIT: A ceramic body, fired once and lacking glaze.

BLEU PERSAN: White enamel decoration on a stained blue ground (at Nevers).

BERRETTINO: Dark or light blue glaze obtained by staining the tin-enamel with cobalt. Characteristic of 16th-century Faenza.

BODY: 1) The combination of prepared materials from which ceramics are made (see also 'paste'); 2) The body of a piece, as opposed to lids, handles, spouts, etc.

CHINA-CLAY: A white refractory clay formed over a long period from decomposed granite.

CHINA-STONE: A fusible stone which, when fired at about 1350° together with china-clay, forms the hard, white and translucent material of hard-paste porcelain.

CHINOISERIE: Generic term for Chinese ornamental motifs, particularly for those executed by European craftsmen with rather distant knowledge of Oriental art.

COPERTA: See 'kwaart'.

CRAZING: A fault in the glaze resulting in minute surface cracks; the larger so-called crackle sometimes seen on Chinese wares was deliberately caused to simulate antiquity.

DEUTSCHE BLUMEN: Naturalistic flower-painting as introduced at Meissen about 1740 (literally 'German flowers').

ENAMEL: A form of coloured glass used for decoration of ceramics by fusing to the glaze at about 800°C.

FAIENCE PARLANTE: 19th century French faience decorated with sayings, records of family events and so on.

FAMILLE ROSE: A style of Chinese porcelain decoration used from the early 18th century which includes the pinks and crimsons derived from chloride of gold.

FAMILLE JAUNE: A style of Chinese porcelain decoration dominated by a yellow enamel, often as a ground colour.

FAMILLE NOIRE: A style of Chinese porcelain decoration which uses black as a ground colour.

FAMILLE VERTE: A style of Chinese porcelain decoration where various tones of green enamel dominate.

FELDSPATHIC GLAZE: A glaze rich in feldspar (alumino-silicates).

FERRONNERIES: Intricate linear design said to be derived from wrought iron work. Adapted from engravings by Bos and Floris, designers of Antwerp in mid-16th century.

FLINT-POSLIN: Swedish name for English creamware.

FRIT: A powdered form of the ingredients of glass used in soft-paste porcelain as an alternative to china-stone.

GADROONING: A pattern of large loops, joined at the base forming a petal design, adapted by potters from metal shapes.

GALENA: A lead sulphide used for early lead glazes.

GILDING: The application of various forms of gold to the surface of wares. Early gilding consisted of ground gold-leaf or gold powder with honey as a medium. This was applied in liquid form and then fired on to the glazed ware. From the late 18th century the honey was replaced by an amalgam of mercury and then similarly fired. After firing the gilding was burnished.

GLOST-KILN: Kiln used to fuse the glaze to ceramic ware.

GROTESCHI: ('Grotesques') half-figures, masks, foliate designs and arabesque derived ultimately from Roman wall-paintings.

HARD-PASTE PORCELAIN: The type of porcelain first introduced by the Chinese potter; made from china-clay and china-stone.

IMARI: Japanese decoration of red and gold enamels over an initial pattern of underglaze blue and white.

IMPASTO: Colour applied thickly, standing proud of the surface.

INDIANISCHE BLUMEN: Literally 'Indian flowers'; floral decoration copied from East India porcelain, mainly chrysanthemums and foliage, cf. *Deutsche Blumen*.

INTAGLIO: Incised or sunken decoration.

ISTORIATO: Literally narrative-painting; in fact usually mythological, biblical or historical subjects covering the whole surface of a piece.

KAAPSCHE SCHOTELS: Literally plates from the Cape; so-called because the Dutch ships carrying the cargo came round by way of the Cape of Good Hope.

KAKIEMON: A 17th-century Japanese potter's family who specialized in an asymmetrical style of enamel decoration holding a subtle balance between areas of white and those decorated with fine drawing.

KAOLIN: The Chinese term for china-clay, meaning 'high hill'.

KWAART: Final coating of lead glaze composed of oxide of lead, sand, potash and salt.

LACQUER COLOURS: (Cold colours) decoration in unfired lacquer colours on Böttger's glazed red stoneware and some early animal figures to avoid a second firing, before the prefection of enamelling.

LAMBREQUINS: Pendant design of rosettes and fine lacework patterns invented at Rouen and much copied elsewhere.

LEATHER-HARD: Term referring to the condition of the clay after shaping, but before firing.

LUSTRE DECORATION: Metallic colours fused to the surface of wares in a reduction kiln; copper resulting in copper-

Ceramics
Glossary (contd.)

coloured tones, silver firing to a brassy yellow, chloride of gold looking like copper when applied to a dark brown body, and turning pink on a white clay body. Platinum was used to give the effect of silver; this does not oxidize to black like true silver.

LUTING: The use of liquid clay or slip either to assemble various parts of a moulded figure or to apply separately-moulded decoration to the surface of a vessel.

MOULDING: The shaping of clay with the use of prepared moulds. The clay is used in a plastic state and hand-pressed into the hollow moulds.

MUFFLE-KILN: The low-firing kiln or *petit feu* (about 800°C.) used for applying enamel colours to ceramics.

OXIDIZING-KILN: A kiln into which air is freely admitted. This kiln-atmosphere produces different colours on the wares or decoration.

PARIAN WARE: A white ceramic body introduced about 1849, used primarily for the scaled-down reproduction of life-size sculpture. Also used for decorative and table-wares, when it is usually glazed.

PASTE: The body (*q.v.*) of a piece and especially porcelain.

PATE-SUR-PATE: Technique invented at Sèvres for painting and low-relief appliqué modelling using a white porcelain paste. Copied by Solon at Minton after 1870.

PETUNTSE: A French word expressing phonetically the Chinese *pai-tun-tzu* (meaning 'little white bricks'), i.e. the china-stone after it has been prepared for the potter.

PLATEELBAKKER: (Dutch) a potter. Used very freely and only to be distinguished from *Meesterplateelbakker*, who was the factory owner.

PURPLE OF CASSIUS: Crimson colour discovered by Andreas Cassius of Leyden. Made by dissolving gold in nitric acid and sal ammoniac.

REISTAFEL: Literally 'rice-table'. Actually sets of dishes to hold the different meats served with rice for a traditional Indonesian meal adopted by the Dutch.

REDUCTION KILN: A kiln where a smoky atmosphere is deliberately produced to achieve certain effects and colours on the wares being fired.

ST. LUKE, GUILD OF: Saint Luke was the patron saint of artists. A Dutch guild.

SCHWARZLOT: Black and grey decoration on German porcelain and faience.

SLIP-CASTING: Formation of clay wares or figures by pouring slip into hollow plaster-of-Paris moulds; the plaster absorbs the water and so builds up a layer of clay on the inside wall of the mould. When a sufficient thickness of clay has accrued, the surplus slip is emptied out and, after a short period, the remaining cast can be removed from the mould.

SLIP: Clay watered down to a creamy consistency.

SOFT-PASTE PORCELAIN: Artificial porcelain made from various white-firing clays and the ingredients of glass—bone-ash, steatite, etc.

SPRIGGING: The application of separately-moulded decoration to the surface of wares, as on salt-glazed stonewares or 'Astbury' type pottery.

STEINGUT: Creamware.

STEINZEUG: Stoneware.

TEGGELBAKKER: Dutch tile-maker.

THROWING: The process of forming a hollow circular form from clay by hand, by means of a fast-turning wheel.

TIN-GLAZE: Lead glaze opacified by the addition of tin-oxide. The first European tin-glazed wares were made in Spain, where Hispano-Moresque pottery was decorated in lustre colours. The Italians, who imported it via Majorca, called it 'maiolica', and soon copied the technique. At first the term 'maiolica' was applied only to lustreware, but gradually it has become the generic term for Italian tin-glazed pottery. Faenza was an important centre; its craftsmen travelled to Northern Europe, and 'faience' indicates tin-glazed ware made principally in France and Germany. The Dutch developed their own individual style, and their influence spread to England, where 'Delftware' was made in a few factories. To add to the confusion, English potters in the nineteenth century adopted the name 'majolica' for relief-decorated pottery covered in coloured glazes. Today, 'majolica' is used in America as a synonym for 'maiolica'.

TRANSFER-PRINTING: The transfer of a design engraved into a copper-plate or woodblock, by means of a thin paper or slab of gelatine, onto the surface of the body or glaze of a ceramic ware. High temperature colours are applied before glazing, low temperature colours (i.e. enamels) are fused over the fired glaze. This process was also used on enamels on a copper base.

TROMPE L'OEIL: Literally 'deception of the eye'. Hence pieces designed to simulate something different by means of modelling and/or decoration.

UNDERGLAZE BLUE: Decoration in cobalt-blue pigment on the once-fired porcelain body before the final glaze and enamels (if any) were applied.

WASTERS: Wares which are defective as they come from the kiln. Usually sought as evidence of manufacture on the sites of old potteries.

ZWIEBELMUSTER: The Meissen onion pattern, actually originally an imitation of the Chinese peach.

Repairs and Maintenance

Repairs of ceramics can be so well executed today that they are at times dangerous: they will often escape detection by all but the very experienced. It is now possible to attend classes where the art of ceramic restoration is taught, but for those who need to seek the services of professional repairers, the only advice is to be sure to get an estimate of the cost first, as a repair can sometimes cost far more than the value of the damaged article.

Too many restorers today tend to carry the treatment far beyond the damage, and a simple hair-line crack is often more acceptable to the serious collector than paint sprayed over a large area, causing the extent of the fault to remain in doubt. Until recently, many of the paints and varnishes used were very apt to discolour after a short period, but with modern developments in chemistry and the introduction of acrylic resins there is less likelihood of this happening if the work is undertaken by a skilled repairer.

Care should be taken with all good ceramics, both old and new, to avoid washing in very hot water or subjecting them to any extreme forms of heat, as this is likely to cause the glaze to 'craze' (crackle) and thus permit staining of the body. Hard-paste porcelain is less vulnerable to this hazard.

Finally, if plates must for convenience be stacked, the uppermost side of one plate should be protected from the foot-rim of that above by at least a sheet of plain paper, preferably a felt pad; this prevents possible abrasion and the marring of the decoration.

Fakes and Forgeries

The most common deception encountered by ceramics collectors concerns the marks. During the nineteenth and early twentieth centuries many genuine reproductions were made of popular wares. These pieces often bore a genuine maker's marks. Today such examples are offered as originals, the late, but honest mark having been removed and replaced with a fake, much earlier mark.

Marks which have been either incised or impressed into the clay before firing can be accepted, to the extent that they must have been applied at the time of making. This is also true of some marks in underglaze-blue, or the later underglaze colours of green and pink, which became possible in the early years of the nineteenth century. But one should be highly suspicious of underglaze-blue marks covered with just a small patch of glaze, on an otherwise unglazed base; the Meissen crossed-swords mark is the most frequently used.

The most dangerous marks are those in the lower fired enamel colours, or gold. A very common trick is to grind away the late mark, and substitute an enamel or gilt early mark. This practice is easily revealed, since it makes a small saucer-shaped indentation, free of glaze, on what should be a smooth surface. A further bad sign is a small, gilded nonsensical device or flower, usually found with a popular mark, such as a gold anchor, a two-bar armorial shield, crossed 'L's or swords in blue. This gilded device, easily removed with an abrasive, such as wire-wool (steel wool), usually reveals a later enamel or underglaze mark such as those of the various Limoges, Thuringian or Bohemian factories, which often included the country of origin, i.e. 'Made in Limoges France'. This invariably indicates a post-1891 date, when the American McKinley Tariff Act came into operation, necessitating all imports to be marked with the name of the manufacturing country. The absence of such a mark does not, of course, necessarily imply a pre-1891 date; generally, only the larger manufacturers exporting to the U.S.A. adopted trade-marks to comply with the regulations.

Modern Far Eastern hard-paste porcelain is often marked 'Made in China' or 'Made in Japan'; unfortunately not all Oriental manufacturers are so honest. The *nien hao*, or reign-mark of a Chinese Emperor, has been used fairly consistently since the 1300s, but it became the practice in China at a very early date to use older marks, not necessarily to mislead, but often as a form of veneration for certain 'vintage porcelain' reigns, including Hsüan Te (1426-35), Ch'eng Hua (1465-87), Chia Ching (1522-66) and Wan Li (1573-1619). This same excuse cannot be made for much later blue and white wares which bear the four-character reign-mark of the Emperor K'ang Hsi (1662-1722) instead of the more correct six-characters; these are deliberate fakes, and date from the nineteenth century onwards.

Among the earliest classes of European earthenware which attracted the attention of the faker were French wares made by Bernard Palissy or his followers, c. 1560, and into the seventeenth century (see p. 145*b*). These dishes and figures were imitated by the French potters Charles Avisseau and Georges Pull and the Portuguese firm of Mafra & Son. Since these nineteenth century reproductions were often made from moulds taken from original examples, they are invariably smaller; this is due to the shrinkage of the clay by about one-seventh during the initial 'biscuit' firing.

Italian maiolica was also extensively copied during the nineteenth century. The most common mark seen on wares

Ceramics
Fakes and Forgeries (contd.)

decorated in the more popular styles such as the Urbino grotesques is the broadly painted sketch of a cockerel, the admitted mark of Ulysse Cantagalli of Florence (d. 1901). Many late tin-glazed wares can be dated by the use of a pink colour derived from chrome, and not available prior to the nineteenth century.

The firm of Samson of Paris was established in 1845. Originally concerned only with making replacements or matching wares to enlarge existing services, they prospered so that before long their notepaper bore the inscription advertising 'Reproductions of Ancient Works emanating from the Museums and from private collections'. Various marks are also shown as being Samson versions of the

originals used on reproductions of 'Japanese & Chinese', 'Persian and Hispano-Moresque', 'Limousin enamels' (Limoges enamels), 'Sèvres and terra-cotta', 'Meissen', 'French, Italian, Spanish, English porcelain', and 'European enamels'. When imitating English soft-paste porcelain, Samson fortunately used hard-paste, making these fakes more easily detected than his other wares, especially when the admitted Samson marks have been removed by less honest vendors.

Intriguingly, at a large sale in London, Samson fakes of large Chelsea groups of the 'gold anchor' period were sold, as reproductions of course, and made very high prices. The new fashion of collecting fakes is now with us.

Further Reading

General

CHARLESTON, R. J. (ed.) *World Ceramics*. London and New York, 1968.

CUSHION, J. P. *Pottery and Porcelain*. London, 1972.

CUSHION, J. P., and HONEY, W. B. *Handbook of Pottery and Porcelain Marks*, 3rd ed. London, 1965.

HAGGAR, R. G. *Pottery Through the Ages*. London (new ed.) 1966; New York, 1959.

HANNOVER, E. *Pottery and Porcelain*, 3 vols. ed. and tr. Bernard Rackham, London and New York, 1925.

HONEY, W. B. *The Art of the Potter*. London, 1946; Boston, n.d.

JACQUEMART, A. *History of the Ceramic Art* (tr. Mrs. B. Palliser). London, 1873; 2nd ed. 1877.

LANE, A. *A Guide to the Collection of Tiles*, 2nd ed. London, 1960

SAVAGE, G. *Porcelain Through the Ages*. London. 1954; rev. ed., Baltimore, Md., 1963.
Pottery Through the Ages. London, 1958; New York, 1963.

Oriental

ASHTON, L., and GRAY, B., *Chinese Art*. London, 1945; New York, 1953.

AYERS, J. *The Seligman Collection of Oriental Art*, vol. 2. London, 1964.

DONNELLY, P. *Blanc de Chine*. London and New York, 1969.

GARNER, SIR H. *Oriental Blue and White*. London, 1964; New York, 1971.

GOMPERTZ, G. ST. G. M. *Chinese Celadon Wares*. London, 1958.
Early Chinese Pottery and Porcelain. London, 1953.
Korean Celadon. London, 1963.

Korean Pottery and Porcelain of the Yi Period. London and New York, 1968.

GRAY, B. *Early Chinese Pottery and Porcelain*. London, 1953.

GRIFFING, R. P. JR. *The Art of the Korean Potter, Silla, Konyo, Yi*. New York, 1967.

HONEY, W. B. *Ceramic Art of China and Other Countries of the Far East*. London, 1944.
Korean Pottery. London, 1947.

JENYNS, S. *Ming Pottery and Porcelain*. London and New York, 1953.
Later Chinese Porcelain. London, 1951.

KIM, DR. C., and GOMPERTZ, G. ST. G. M. *The Ceramic Art of Korea*. London, 1961.

KOYAMA, F., and FIGGESS, J. *Two Thousand Years of Oriental Ceramics*. New York, 1960; Tokyo, 1961.

TRUBNER, H. *The Far Eastern Collection (Royal Ontario Museum)*. Toronto, 1968.

WILLETTS, W. *Foundation of Chinese Art*, vols. 1 and 2. London, 1958 and later editions.

Continental

CHARLESTON, R. J. *Three Centuries of Swedish Pottery*. London, 1959.

CUSHION, J. P. *Continental China Collecting for Amateurs*. London, 1970; Alhambra, 1971.
Pocket Book of French and Italian Ceramic Marks. London, 1965.
Pocket Book of German Ceramic Marks. London, 1961.

DE JONGE, C. H. *Delft Ceramics* (tr. Marie-Christine Hellin) London, 1972.
Dutch Tiles. London, 1972.

Further Reading (contd.)

DUCRET, S. *German Porcelain and Faience*. London, 1962.

FROTHINGHAM, A. W. *Lustreware of Spain*. New York, 1951.

GIACOMOTTI, J. *French Faience* (tr. Diana Imber). Freibourg, 1963.

HAGGAR, R. G. *The Concise Encyclopaedia of Continental Pottery and Porcelain*. London, 1960, repr. 1968; New York, 1968.

HONEY, W. B. *Dresden China*. London, 1954.
French Porcelain of the Eighteenth Century, 2nd ed. London, 1972.
European Pottery and Porcelain, 2 vols. London, 1949-52.

IMBER, D. *Collecting Delft*. London, 1968.

LANE, A. *Italian Porcelain*. London, 1954.
French Faience. London, 1948.

RACKHAM, B. *Italian Maiolica*. London, 1952.

SAVAGE, G. *Eighteenth Century German Porcelain*. London, 1947.
French Porcelain of the Eighteenth Century. London, 1960.

English

BELL, R. C. *Tyneside Pottery*. 1971.

BEMROSE, G. *Nineteenth Century English Pottery and Porcelain*. London, 1952.

CHARLESTON, R. J. *English Porcelain, 1745-1850*. London, 1965.

COOPER, R. G. *English Slipware Dishes 1650-1850*. London and Levittown, N.Y., 1968.

CUSHION, J. P. *Pocket Book of English Ceramic Marks*. London, 1965.
English China Collecting for Amateurs. London, 1967.

EYLES, D. *Royal Doulton*, London, 1965.

GARNER, F. H., and ARCHER, M. *English Delftware*, 2nd ed., 1972.

GODDEN, G. A. *Lowestoft Porcelain*. London, 1969.
Mason's Patent Ironstone China, London, 1971.
Caughley & Worcester Porcelains, 1775-1800. London, 1969.

HAGGAR, R. G. *English Country Pottery*, 1950.
The Masons of Lane Delph. 1952.
Staffordshire Chimney Ornaments. London, 1955.

HONEY, W. B. *Wedgwood Ware*. London, 1948.
Old English Porcelain. London and New York, 1948.
English Pottery and Porcelain (rev. ed. by R. Charleston). London, 1962.

LOCKETT, T. A. *Davenport Pottery and Porcelain*. 1972.

MANKOWITZ, W., and HAGGAR, R. G. *The Concise Encyclopaedia of English Pottery and Porcelain*. London, 1957.

MOUNTFORD, A. *Staffordshire Salt-glazed Stoneware*. 1971.

WAKEFIELD, H. *Victorian Pottery*. London, 1962.

WATNEY, B. *English Blue and White Porcelain of the Eighteenth Century*. London, 1963.

WHITER, L. *Spode*. London and New York, 1970.

American

BARBER, E. A. *The Pottery and Porcelain of the United States*, 2nd ed. (enlarged). New York and London, 1902.
Tulip Ware of the Pennsylvania-German Potters. Philadelphia, 1903; 2nd ed. 1926; repr. New York, 1970.

BARRET, R. C. *Bennington Pottery and Porcelain: A Guide to Identification*. New York, 1958.

BIVENS, J. JR. *The Moravian Potters in North Carolina*. Chapel Hill, 1972.

HENSKE, L. *American Art Pottery*. Camden and New York, 1970.

HOOD, G. *Bonnin and Morris of Philadelphia, the First American Porcelain Factory, 1770-1772*. Chapel Hill, 1972.
The Pottery and Porcelain Collector's Handbook. New York, 1971.

RAMSAY, J. *American Potters and Pottery*. Boston, 1939; 2nd ed., New York, 1947.

SPARGO, J. *Early American Pottery and China*. New York, 1926; repr., 1948.

WATKINS, L. W. *Early New England Potters and their Wares*. Cambridge, Mass., 1950; repr. Hamden, Conn., 1969.

WEBSTER, D. B. *Decorated Stoneware Pottery of North America*. Rutland, Vt., 1971.

Ceramics
Museum Collections

Great Britain

BIRMINGHAM: City Museum and Art Gallery.
CAMBRIDGESHIRE: The Fitzwilliam Museum, Cambridge.
GLOUCESTERSHIRE: The Corinium Museum, Cirencester.
LANCASHIRE: The Liverpool City Museum.
LINCOLNSHIRE: The Usher Art, Gallery, Lincoln.
LONDON: The British Museum, The Geffrye Museum, The Guildhall Museum, Victoria and Albert Museum, The Wallace Collection, The Wellington Museum.
SOMERSET: The Holburne of Menstrie Museum of Art, Bath.
SUSSEX: The Brighton Art Gallery.
YORKSHIRE: Temple Newsam House, Halton, Leeds.

U.S.A.

CALIFORNIA: The Fine Arts Society of San Diego.
KANSAS: The University of Kansas Museum of Art, Lawrence.
LOUISIANA: The Isaac Delgado Museum of Art, New Orleans.
MASSACHUSETTS: The Museum of Fine Arts, Boston.
MINNESOTA: The Walker Art Center, Minneapolis.
NEW YORK: The Cooper-Hewitt Museum of Design, The Frick Collection, The Hispanic Society of America Museum, The Metropolitan Museum of Art.
OHIO: The Cincinnati Art Museum.
VERMONT: The Bennington Museum.
WASHINGTON, D.C.: The Smithsonian Institution.

Index

Left to right: Lead-glazed red earthenware gallon jug with manganese decoration, William Pecker Pottery, Merrimacport, Massachusetts, U.S.A., 1784–1820. Red earthenware jar, Thompson Pottery, Morgantown, West Virginia, U.S.A. Lead-glazed red earthenware spice bottle inscribed D. Thompson, Thompson Pottery. Salt-glazed stoneware three-gallon butter crock with blue cobalt decoration, Barnabas Edmonds Pottery, Charlestown, Massachusetts, U.S.A., c. 1845. Stoneware quart pitcher, stamped WISTATRS, Stonnington Point, Connecticut, U.S.A., 1811–23.

Overleaf:
A 'Schippertje' clock for use on vessels plying the inland waterways of Holland. The rapid movement of the pendulum overcomes the rolling of the vessel.

Clocks, Watches and Barometers

The mechanical clock made its appearance about 1300; the earliest examples were for ecclesiastical use. The material was wrought iron and the parts were large but by the 15th century, smaller clocks were made for domestic use—still of iron but with the metal worked cold (see p. 528). During the fifteenth century, the spring was applied as motive power in place of the weight and the clock became portable. As techniques advanced, these portable clocks became small enough to be carried on the person and so the watch came into being. About 1560, brass began to replace iron: the movements were now more finely finished and themselves objects of beauty; previously, all decoration had been applied to the outer cases.

The greatest revolution in the history of timekeeping was the application of the pendulum by Huygens in 1657 (see p. 226b), which was followed by the balance spring (hairspring) for watches in the 1670s. For the first time real accuracy was possible, and further technological improvements resulted in clocks and watches of exquisite workmanship and fine performance.

Production in specialized workshops had begun by the end of the seventeenth century, replacing the independent craftsman, but it was the nineteenth that saw real factory production taking over from the hand worker and by the twentieth, this transformation was complete.

Because clocks have been produced in factories does not mean they are devoid of interest. Many of the examples here are factory products: their appeal depends on what one's collection is attempting to illustrate rather than on the characteristics of the piece itself.

Barometers show less variety. They were first made in the mid-seventeenth century when timekeepers were first developed as precision instruments and can be broadly divided into two groups: those for scientific and those for domestic use. We are here only concerned with the second group, which tended to follow contemporary furniture styles to suit a room's decor. The shape of a barometer is controlled by scientific requirements and mercury instruments must be at least 33″ (83.8 cm.) long, but the invention of the aneroid about 1850 (see p. 260) made much smaller instruments possible.

Clocks, Watches and Barometers
The Craft

The beginning of clockmaking is connected with the monastic life, although it does not necessarily follow that monks themselves were the original craftsmen. The legend of Peter Lightfoot (see Glossary) in the West of England has now been exploded in favour of groups of workmen who had come over from the Continent to ply their craft.

The workers in iron had their heyday in the Middle Ages: iron production was primitive and wasteful but with the lack of good quality steel to make accurate cutting tools, the rough shaping of pieces by forging was the obvious way to create objects in metal. Files were needed to finish parts, but filing would naturally be kept to a minimum. Many people believe that the small chamber clock preceded the large clocks, but in view of the fact that larger pieces are more accurate in proportion than smaller ones, and that the metal for smaller clocks would be worked cold it seems more likely that the larger, forged iron clocks came first.

The smaller work belongs to the realm of the locksmith, and beginning with the Gothic chamber clock, production then advanced to making clocks driven by springs. The making of a spring is a tedious process and could only have come about with developments in steel production and more accurate tools. The latter would also have been necessary to produce the small clocks which were the forerunners of the watch.

Developments in the production of brass led to its use in clocks and watches about 1560. It is easy to work with and suitable for plates and wheels, but pinions need to be of hardened steel to resist wear. A brass wheel working against a steel pinion is the best arrangement for clock and watch movements, but in time even the steel pinion wears because particles of dirt get embedded in the softer brass and act as an abrasive. Steel can be hardened by heating and rapidly quenching but brass can only be hardened by work hardening, i.e. hammering, rolling or being drawn into wire.

The chief difficulty in horological production is the cutting of wheels. They must be concentric, all teeth must be as near alike as possible and of the proper profile to give the minimum of friction when in use. The wheel cutting engine with a division plate containing the numbers of holes to represent the numbers of teeth mostly in use is believed to date from about 1670, but in view of the exquisite work produced at earlier dates, some sort of apparatus must have been available previously. Brass for wheels must be carefully hammered to produce uniform hardness.

Turning has always been an important part of horological production: a bow giving a to and fro motion of the work was used up to the end of the nineteenth century and in fact has never died out. Turning by continuous rotary motion was probably in use in horology by the early eighteenth century although other trades were quicker to employ it. The developments in general engineering tools begun in the early nineteenth century led to special lathes for clockmakers and watchmakers being used by mid-century, and with the extension of factory production in the second half of the century, the tools were multiplied both in number and variety. Not only tools themselves, but those required to produce them were extensively developed.

Production in factories probably began about the late seventeenth century, but such establishments were small and would not now qualify for the name. Factory production as we know it really began in Connecticut about 1807, when Eli Terry undertook to make 4,000 wooden-wheeled clocks using water-powered machine tools. His undertaking was extensively copied, and with the increased production of rolled brass, wooden-wheeled movements had disappeared from production by about 1850. France began producing high quality factory-made clocks in the early nineteenth century and maintained production for well over a hundred years. The Black Forest of Germany produced large numbers of cheap clocks made principally of wood under a system of outworkers, but began to change to organized factories about 1870 in direct imitation of America. The earliest German factory clocks were cheap like the Americans', but by the end of the century, high class movements of a quality equal to the French were being turned out. Britain stuck mostly to handwork and the horological industry virtually died as a result of competition from abroad. It was revived after 1945.

The making of barometers involves the techniques of the glass-blower and the cabinet-maker. The glass-blower draws out a long thin tube of uniform section and then fills it with mercury, making sure that no air bubbles are trapped (see p. 260).

Clocks
Introduction

The collector of antique clocks has a wealth of material from which to choose his collection, and it is a matter of personal taste coupled with the amount he is prepared to spend that determines the kind of clock he wishes to collect.

An attempt has been made here to illustrate as many types as possible but no book, however large, could hope to illustrate every kind. Clocks from the Continent have usually remained there and are thus less common in Britain and the U.S.A. However, Holland and the Black Forest in particular both engaged in the export trade, while France was one of the countries to pioneer factory production, also exporting many clocks during the middle and late nineteenth century.

The styles characteristic of nations such as Germany (apart from the Black Forest), Austria, and Italy have mostly remained in these countries, but as people in Europe have generally been unable to hoard possessions, the casualty rate has been much higher than in Britain and consequently the clocks are much more difficult to find.

Examples from before 1650 from any country are extremely rare and very expensive, most of them being in museums, but they do appear in sales from time to time. Clocks by late seventeenth century London makers such as Tompion, Quare and Knibb are among the most desirable pieces to own, but have been particularly sensitive to demand, with prices continually establishing new records.

Even clocks of this period by lesser-known makers are expensive, but as works of art they rank high in the history of English clockmaking. The eighteenth century brought in the arch dial and figured walnut together with mahogany and lacquered cases, while the movement also changed in that the contrast in size between the wheels in the lower and upper parts of the train became less apparent. Plates fastened with latches gave way to those fastened with pine and in many cases five pillars gave way to four.

The history of French clocks is also the history of French furniture (q.v.). The maker of the case was considered as important as the maker of the movement, and French movements were usually very conventional. In England, styles of clock cases changed as furniture styles changed, with the remarkable exception of the bracket clock which retained its ebony case until quite late in the eighteenth century. During the Regency period, however, this type of clock also underwent severe modifications to bring it into line with furniture styles.

There was a brief period at the beginning of the nineteenth century when English makers favoured French styles of case, but later in the century the French product swamped the British market for dining room and drawing-room clocks while America and Germany catered for the other rooms in the house. At the end of the century, the English clock was all but eliminated.

America followed English models in Colonial days and immediately after the Revolution, but soon began to develop styles of her own. The chief difficulty was the shortage of raw material and many cases were made of lesser quality wood and veneered with mahogany. Birmingham factories supplied movements and dials for long case clocks, but once Eli Terry had established the principle of mass production, the making of long case clocks died away and the Connecticut product dominated the home market. Cheaper clocks had wooden movements; the better ones were of brass, but once Jerome had brought out his brass OG clocks in 1839 the making of wooden wheeled clocks faded out. The American product became more sophisticated as the century wore on but rarely reached the standard of European work.

The early German factory products were based on American types but were very rough indeed. By 1900, however, such firms as Winterhalder and Hoffmeier were producing clocks of as high a quality as the English or French and were even including fusees and quarter chimes.

Once the pendulum was established as a regulator, the other countries of Europe seemed to follow the lead of England or France. In particular, Scandinavia adopted the long case clock which in a different form was also made in North Germany. Holland made long case clocks in the eighteenth century generally similar to British ones but usually more elaborate; at the end of the century she began to base her clocks on French models. Austria and Sweden also did this and even England was not immune to French influence. This borrowing of ideas by clockmakers from various lands is probably the most fascinating aspect of the subject.

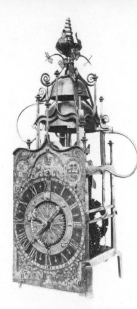

a) Gothic wall clock and movement, iron, by Erhard Liechti; Switzerland, 1583; ht. 20″ (50.8 cm.).

For generations, the Liechti family of Winterthur were celebrated clockmakers, and, unlike many of their contemporaries, initialled their work.

This example has highly decorated finials and bell canopy. It strikes hours, quarters, and shows the phases of the moon; the dial was repainted in 1748 and a minute hand added, which is interesting but spoils the clock's original condition. The quarter hour dial has been superimposed on the main one, with the figures inside the hour figures; this is a feature of many southern European clocks. Here, the long hand indicates minutes, and the short one, hours.

The right-hand photograph shows the decoration of the balance and the verge; the latter has been filed and not turned. The lowest arbor on the middle (quarter) train carries the count wheel, and the frame of the movement bears a little decoration in punch marks, the maker's initials and the date. The dial is carried by two hooks formed on the ends of a horizontal bar riveted to the front uprights of the movement. The side pieces of the little turret for housing the bell and balance are held in position by lugs, skilfully inserted into the upright corner pieces.

---

b) Late Gothic wall clock, iron; Switzerland, 1533; ht. 16½″ (41.9 cm.).

This is a fine specimen of the Gothic wall clock. The teeth are well cut and the iron in the frame appears to have suffered very little over the years. The finials and decoration of the bell canopy show very skilful work. Beside the moon dial is a tiny window to show the moon's age.

Not uncommon is the wheel balance with rim formed into a pattern. The alarm is set by inserting an ornate pin in a hole in the central disc of the dial, which is of sheet iron painted. The decoration on the bell canopy is also painted.

c) Gothic clock in iron, with coat of arms of church in Thurgau, by Andreas Liechti; Switzerland, 1612; ht. 18½″ (46.9 cm.).

This example by Andreas, Erhard Liechti's son, resembles closely his father's clocks. It has the usual alarm movement and moonphase and although fitted with quarter striking, the plain form of the balance is employed. The finials are simpler, with plain ball-shaped ends turned slightly outwards. The most noticeable difference between this clock and the elder Liechti's is the solid decorative lugs on the frame uprights.

The rear bar of the going train is cranked to save space, so the fly for the quarter train has to be made smaller and given four vanes. Unfortunately the alarm work is missing.

a) Wall clock in beech, painted, with wooden move-ment; probably from Davos, Switzerland, 1669; ht. 11" (27.9 cm.).

The small dial below the main one indicates quarter hours, its hand the equivalent of the modern minute hand. The pediment is character-istic of clocks of this region. The alarm disc in the centre rotates with the hour hand and is set by inserting a pin in one of the holes; it can sound at an hour or half hour.

The wheels behind the dial are not visible but in the next compartment is the going train with

scapewheel consisting of a disc with iron pins pro-truding from its face which act on the vertical verge. In the compartment above is the wheel balance reinforced with an iron band. Cords sup-port the weights, needing a light counterpoise to prevent slipping.

The striking train, in the second compartment, is released and locked by the arm on the right of the lower horizontal arbor. There is no 'warning'; the striking train begins to run when the arm has reached a certain height.

---

b) Wooden clock with painted decoration; Switzerland, 17th century; ht. 11" (27.9 cm.).

Southern Europe, round the Alps, has long been noted for clocks, and this example has a wooden movement as did many from that region. Its features include a quarter-hour dial, an alarm set by inserting a pin into one of twelve holes on a disc which revolves with the hour hand, a dial for indicating the day of the month and a ball to show the phases of the moon. The clock is controlled by a wheel balance and is, of course, weight driven.

c) Wall clock in softwood by Isaac Brandt; La Chaux de Fonds, Switzerland, 1716; ht. 13" (33.0 cm.).

This simple single-handed timepiece shows the country style of Swiss clocks becoming more sophisticated by the early 18th century. The orna-ment on top even suggests the decoration of factory made clocks of the late 19th century. The primitive painting of the earlier clocks has been abandoned for a style of decoration that relies on simple mouldings and the wood grain. The narrow chapter ring and well-executed brass hand give a very clear indication of the time. The weight is still of the primitive design found on earlier clocks.

Clocks

Swiss
EARLY 18TH CENTURY

Typical Swiss hood design of the period.

a) *Louis XIV style clock in walnut with bronze mounts, movement signed Adam Droz; La Chaux de Fonds, Switzerland, c. 1720; ht. 36″ (91.4 cm.).*

This Swiss clock is based on French models of the Louis XIV period but is simpler, with an all-over white dial which may be later, as one-piece dials were difficult to make at this period, and the fashion for minute figures nearly as large as those for the hours began in the mid-18th century: The hands are of brass. The movement is provided with quarter striking and repeating work. The pendulum is concealed by the elaborate decoration placed in front of the glass.

b) *Louis XIV style clock in painted softwood by P. Jaquet Droz; La Chaux de Fonds, Switzerland, c. 1740; ht. 31″ (78.7 cm.).*

The plainness of this clock when compared to its French model is remarkable, and the pewter dial is more of a South German design than French. The wooden case is painted green and the feet are of gilded bronze, while a certain amount of gilding is also applied to the woodwork. The movement has a verge escapement, pull repeat and alarm. The plain pendulum will be noted. The hands are well finished with plenty of contrast between them, and the quarter hour marks retained, although the minute figures are very prominent.

c) *Long-case clock in softwood painted black, by P. Jaquet Droz, La Chaux de Fonds, Switzerland, c. 1750; ht. 82″ (208 cm.).*

The hood of this clock has been based on the design illustrated on the left, a common one in Switzerland, but in order to obtain extra precision the going side is weight driven with a compensated pendulum, and maintaining power is provided to keep the clock going when being wound. Hour and half hour striking is also fitted but it is spring driven, and rather out of place in a precision clock. The pendulum beats seconds, and the centre seconds hand against the white dial makes for legibility. There is a certain affinity with the early Vienna Regulators (*q.v.*).

d) *Bracket clock in softwood painted in red and black, by Terrot and Thuillier; Geneva, Switzerland, c. 1750; ht. 16″ (40.6 cm.).*

The dial with brass centre and pewter chapter ring with quarter and half hour marks suggests the earlier part of the century while the shape of the clock with its carrying handle above suggests an English rather than a French model. A pull repeat arrangement is fitted with a double hammer alarm, but no provision is made for striking. The hands are of brass while a pierced brass screen covers the glass in front of the pendulum. No gilding has been applied to the woodwork of this example.

a) Wooden-wheeled clock in beech; Davos, Switzerland, 1760; ht. 12½" (31.8 cm.).

This clock illustrates how slowly new fashions penetrated some parts of Europe. Still controlled by a balance without a spring, it has a separate quarter-dial, and would seem to have been made a century earlier. In spite of being so primitive, it chimes the quarters and tells the day of the week, the month and the phases of the moon. The distinctive pediment of the type has been modified to incorporate birds in its design.

The movement would normally be boxed in by brightly painted side doors. The three trains of wheels and some of those which operate the subsidiary dials are visible here. The wheel balance comes in the space below the bells and the scape-wheel with its iron pins can be seen just below it.

Decorative turning has been applied to as many parts as possible, including hammer arbors, wheel arbors etc. Note the sturdy construction of the frame which had to be made from properly seasoned wood to prevent warping. Iron is used minimally—mostly in the form of wire.

b) Bracket clock in gilded wood, by P. Jaquet Droz; La Chaux de Fonds, Switzerland, c. 1760; ht. 18" (45.7 cm.).

The shape of this clock is based on English models although the dial, hands and detail decoration are different from the prototype. The movement is provided with fusees and strikes hours and quarters. A special escapement is provided and also alarm work. All four sides of the case are glazed allowing the movement to be visible. The dial and Strike/Silent dial in enamel are typical continental features as are the two redundant finials beside the carrying handle. The complete gilding of the case is unusual, and was probably done to a special order.

c) Baroque wooden-wheeled clock in beech by Emanuel Brugger; Teufen (Appenzell), Switzerland, 1767; ht. 34" (86.4 cm.).

This clock, although possessing wooden wheels, is much more sophisticated than the Davos type. It has a minute hand and a short 'cow tail' pendulum swinging before the dial, along with striking and alarm work. The painting is very elaborate, featuring a blue ground, white pillars and marbling effect on the moulding below the dial, with corner paintings representing the four seasons. In the arch over the dial is the figure of Time with a skull and an hour-glass. The painting on the bracket below symbolizes death.

Clocks

Swiss

On the dial, a plain, steel indicator shows the day of the month.

Italian
17TH CENTURY

a) Louis XV style clock in palissander with gilt bronze ornaments, by Jaquet Droz; La Chaux de Fonds, Switzerland, 1770; ht. 41" (104 cm.).

This example retains a number of French features but the polished wood surfaces are exceptional. Unsymmetrical features in the ornament occur here and there but the rococo style is outmoded at this period, with designs progressing towards the symmetry of the latter part of the century. Note the long hour figures and prominent minute figures in conjunction with the very elaborate brass hands. The key at the side is for locking the door covering the dial and pendulum. As on many such clocks, the latter is obscured by a metal decoration in front of the glass door.

b) 'Directoire' style clock with mahogany veneer and bronze mountings, signed D. P. Bourquin; Villeret, Switzerland, c. 1800; ht. 40" (102 cm.).

The end of the 18th century brought modifications to the design of the clock case with veneer and inlay replacing painted wood and gilding, the latter being limited to the bronze mounts. The minute numbers on the dial have become less prominent and curves in the case are replaced with straight lines. This clock illustrates the same type of development that was occurring in Britain during the Regency period. The shaped door has now been replaced by the solid circular brass bezel with a separate door giving access to the pendulum.

---

c) Table clock in gilded brass by Camerini; Italy, 1656; ht. 5" (12.7 cm.).

Huygens (see p. 226b) made his experimental model of a pendulum clock on Christmas Day, 1656, and did not get his patent till 1657. This clock by Camerini of Turin, dated 1656, bears a short pendulum and as there is no indication of conversion from balance control, it may well have been an independent application of the pendulum. It has going and striking trains and may once have had an alarm. The pendulum rod bears a thread through much of its length, which may suggest that a lot of trial and error occurred before the clock could be persuaded to keep time.

d) Lantern clocks, brass; left: Italy, mid-17th century, ht. 6" (15.2 cm.); right: Italy, 1694, ht. 5" (12.7 cm.).

Until the 19th century, the Italian timekeeping system counted 24 hours to a day, beginning at sunset. Early clocks used in Italian monasteries also featured a rotating dial in conjunction with a fixed pointer. *Left* illustrates the rotating dial principle. Its alarm is set by a concentric hand and it has a wheel balance.

The 24 hour system made striking a problem, so clocks were devised to treat the 24 hours as four groups of six hours each, as in *right*. In the days of one-handed dials, this gave a clearer indication of the time, and economized on the power required for striking.

224

a) Night clock, ebony case with brass claw feet, by Petrus Thomas Campanus; Rome, Italy, c. 1680; ht. 24" (60.9 cm.).

About the middle of the 17th century, night clocks were first made, containing a lighted lamp: its rays shone through openings cut in the shape of numbers. The glowing numeral represented the hour, and took one hour to travel round a semi-circle, its position denoting the quarters. When one hour figure had passed by, it was replaced by the next. This example is in the form of an 'altar clock'. When repeating work was invented during the 1680s, the night clock went out of fashion so that it was comparatively short-lived, although the idea was later revived in different forms.

b) Clock with rotating hour dial, brass, by Bartolomeo Antonio Bertolla; Italy, mid-18th century; ht. 9" (22.9 cm.).

Clocks with a single hand showing only quarter hours were produced in Europe for timing sermons. This example extends the idea: it includes a rotating dial which indicates the hours as well, and it shows the minutes by means of the quarter-hour hand. The clock is weight driven. The inscription on the dial means 'I made this clock at the age of 80 years'. The maker is unlisted, but the general appearance of the clock suggests country work.

c) Bracket clock in ebony case, by Joseph Dominici; Italy, late 18th century; ht. 13" (33.0 cm.).

The English bracket clock provided a model here, though the main differences are the bottom drawer for the key and the slender wooden supporting pieces at the corners of the case. The dial plate is of embossed brass with no separate spandrels, but the silver chapter ring and little slot to show if the clock is going suggest the prototype. The figures taper towards the centre, a feature sometimes found on Dutch clocks, and the hands are less distinctive than on a contemporary English clock. Quarter hour and half hour marks are used.

Clocks

French

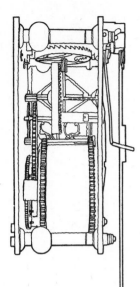

The movement of b, virtually a table clock turned on its side.

a) Table clock in gilt brass; France, c. 1560; ht. 6″ (15.2 cm.).

The tower type of table clock was popular in France; this illustration shows the usual arrangement of the movement in two storeys. Note the long tapered fusee with its arbor extended below the bottom of the clock to form the winding square, and the going barrel fitted on the striking side. Often a small door was placed on the side of the case so that the fusee could be inspected to see if winding was necessary. The movement is solidly made and its pillars meticulously decorated.

b) Clock, ebony case with brass ornaments by Thuret, based on Dutch model; France, c. 1670; ht. 10″ (25.4 cm.).

The world's earliest pendulum clocks were made by Salomon Coster of The Hague working under a patent obtained by the Dutch scientist, Christiaan Huygens. They were the model for similar clocks produced by French makers during Huygens' time in Paris (1665–81): this is a typical example by Isaac Thuret.

The chapter ring, backed by red velvet, has every minute numbered; the cartouche below gives access to the pendulum, allowing the clock to be started easily. The case front and the pediment above are much more elaborate than on the original Dutch clocks, marking the beginning of distinctive French styles.

c) right: Mantel clock, oak veneered with ebony and boulle by André Charles Boulle; France, late 17th century; ht. 26″ (66.0 cm.).

Boulle, who worked in the Louvre from 1673, became famous for the furniture decoration he devised: designs cut with a fine saw through sheets of tortoiseshell and brass, and the pieces combined for decorative surfaces (see p. 375*b*).

This example shows this type of work as well as early French use of decorative bronze figures (Love triumphing over Time). The dial is also interesting: every minute is numbered; each hour figure is on a separate piece of enamel. Later, enamel dials were made in one piece. The movement is probably by a member of the Martinot family.

d) Clock on pedestal, boulle: green, red, yellow and blue tortoiseshell, ormolu by Rabby; Paris, France, early 18th century; ht. 113½″ (288 cm.).

As the French spring-driven clock began to get larger, it became customary to provide a pedestal for it. Sometimes a long pendulum would swing inside the pedestal so that the clock virtually became a long case clock, although the idea of a clock standing on a separate pedestal was maintained.

This example has a short pendulum. There are separate enamel plaques for the numbers on the dial and each minute is numbered. Surmounting the whole is a putto with a helmet and a shield bearing the arms of France.

a) *Clock in gilded bronze, movement by J. A. Lepaute, working 1748–74, the dial marked* Horloger du Roy; *France, c. 1760; ht. 15″ (38.1 cm.).*

Louis XV's reign covered the rococo period: this clock dates from the end of that time, when symmetry in design was returning. Notice the minute numerals which are nearly as large as those of the hours, and the asymmetrical placing of the winding holes (the latter a legacy from the rococo period). The small panel in the base was developed as the century wore on, becoming a dominant feature in the design. The figures depict Venus cutting the wings of Cupid and are in the manner of Falconet (1716–91).

b) *Regulator clock, oak veneered with purplewood, tulipwood and kingwood, bronze mounts, case believed to be by N. Petit (1752–91); France, c. 1760; ht. 84″ (213 cm.).*

As fashionable at the time, these minute and hour numerals are nearly the same size; two additional concentric hands indicate the day of the year, and seconds. Note the enamel dial: by this time, they were being made in one piece. The weight, suspended on an endless rope, hangs behind a gridiron pendulum.

The straight-lined case, decorated with bronze ornaments and a large figure group, contrasts with contemporary typical French mantel clocks.

---

c) *Two clocks in Sèvres porcelain; left: movement by Dubois (1757–89), gilding by Chavaux, 1780; ht. 9″ (22.9 cm.); right: movement by Cranier (working 1781–93), case painted by Tandart (1754–1803), c. 1785; ht. 9″ (22.9 cm.); all working Paris, France.*

Left: The neatness of French clocks just before the Revolution is evident here. The tiny dial has Arabic hour figures; the minute figures, although only a third smaller, are not obtrusive, and are also upright to match the position of the hour figures. The piercing of the hands is delicate as is the work on the garland of flowers and fruit surrounding the dial.

Right: The plain outline shows how greatly French designs had changed from those of the previous reign. What is lost in decorative outline is made up in colourful painting and porcelain with a lot of blue in the bands surrounding the case and dial. The hour hand, with its bold fleur-de-lis motif, contrasts well with the minute hand.

d) *Clock in gilded bronze and porcelain by Robin (1742–1809); France, c. 1780; ht. 18″ (45.7 cm.).*

With the reign of Louis XVI, French clocks became more delicate and more symmetrical in design. Robin worked for both Louis XV and Louis XVI and it is believed that this clock may have belonged to Marie Antoinette.

The dial is small in comparison with the clock as a whole and very neat. An unusual feature of the movement is that it has to be wound from the back, implying that the clock was intended for a centrally-placed table rather than a mantelpiece. Cupids, which predominate here, are a favourite motif on French clocks.

French
MID–LATE 18TH CENTURY

Delicate ormolu work on a Louis XVI clock, c. 1780.

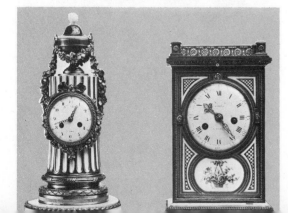

Clocks

French

Pressed brass decoration on a Comtoise clock, (see d, right).

a) Clock by Ferdinand Berthoud (1727–1807); Paris, France, late 18th century; ht. 18″ (45.7 cm.).

Berthoud's careful workmanship and attention to detail greatly improved the accuracy of timepieces; he also published many essays on their making.

This example is plain but still an object of beauty and a precision instrument. The pendulum is compensated for temperature changes with the 'gridiron' system: the differential expansion of brass and steel rods overcomes the tendency of the whole pendulum to become longer in heat and shorter in the cold. This type was a model for many 19th century French clocks, which usually have the pendulum compensated by the expansion of mercury in glass jars.

b) Capucine in brass; France, c. 1800; ht. 5″ (12.7 cm.).

The Capucine came into fashion about 1800—a small portable clock for desk or bedside use. Most examples are fitted with repeat and alarm; they usually have very clear white enamel dials and plain brass cases. The name is supposed to be derived from 'Capucine Nun', presumably for the clock's austerity, decoration being kept to a minimum.

The first pendulum clocks made in France based on Dutch models were called '*Religieuses*' because of their plainness, retaining the name even when they became more decorative than their prototypes.

c) left and centre: The 'pendule d'officier' (produced for officers in the Napoleonic campaigns), bronze, by 'Leroy & Fils'; Paris, France, early 19th century; ht. 7″ (17.8 cm.), wdth. 4½″ (11.4 cm.); overall ht. 9″ (22.9 cm.).

Such clocks had an alarm and sometimes repetition work. The cases were of metal, incised and gilded, and the enamel dials had Arabic figures. Note the carrying handle and the bezel's decoration. The straight hand is for setting the alarm.

The scapewheel and pallets at the top of the movement actuate the alarm hammer; the right-hand cord shuts off the alarm; the left-hand cord actuates the repeat, and the two small hammers (left) are for the hours and quarters. On the right, the pierced bridge covers the balance and spring; the regulator dial below has a square for a key.

d) Comtoise movement with enamel dial, pressed brass surround, iron case; France, c. 1830; ht. 14″ (35.6 cm.).

The Comtoise movement was supplied as a self-contained unit, ready for use if supported by a wall bracket, as in this example. The pendulum is plainer than on many others, but a little decoration is supplied by the flower painting on the dial. The weights are plain castings, hanging directly from the lines. The chief decoration is supplied by the pressed brass surround to the dial and the pierced brass hands. The pierced ornament over the dial is rather unusual: pressed brass decoration was more common.

a) *Group of three carriage clocks with brass cases and enamel dials; Paris, France, c. 1830; ht. 4" (10.2 cm.).*

The more typical centre clock contrasts with the other two which have cases of oval section. They differ further in having circular enamel dials with metal ground. The carrying handles of all three are more elaborate than usual, and all cases have a knob in the top to set off the repeating mechanism. Note the different style of hands and the numbering of the five minute intervals on the clock on the left. These clocks exemplify the high finish of the type.

b) *Comtoise clock; long case in oak; France, c. 1840; ht. 84" (213 cm.).*

Comtoise movements were sent to many parts of France and cases were constructed locally to receive them. The glazing of the hood revealed the decorated dial surround, and the decorated pendulums, which swung near the front of the movement, were also visible. The large diameter bob usually required the case to be widened where it swung, a feature also found in the older French long case clocks of the Louis XIV and XV period. However, the Comtoise was generally found in a simple country-made case like this one.

c) *French mantel clock in gilded wood; Paris, France, c. 1860; ht. 8" (20.3 cm.).*

The 19th century French factories began to produce circular movements with striking work which were all similar in appearance but of very high quality. During the Second Empire, say 1850-70, an attempt was made to revive styles of former periods and this example suggests that of Louis XVI, while bearing the typical 19th century movement. Clocks of this type were usually covered with a glass shade and were the pride of Victorian drawing-rooms. The cases could be of wood or cast metal, were always gilded, and sometimes incorporated decorative china panels.

d) *Crystal regulator in polished brass; Paris, France, c. 1900; ht. 11" (27.9 cm.).*

This is a commercially produced clock that is a direct descendant of *a*, p. 228. It has a dead beat escapement with agate pallets, and the pendulum has two jars of mercury to compensate for temperature changes. The movement is basically a typical French factory product, but a precision clock is spoiled if fitted with striking work. The compensated pendulums are usually only fitted to these movements when they are visible, as in this example. Hidden pendulums are usually of the conventional type.

French
19TH CENTURY

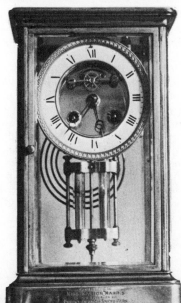

229

Clocks

a) Table clock in gilded brass, by Nicholas Vallin, London, England, c. 1600; dia. 2½" (6.35 cm.).

About 1600, there were scarcely any English clockmakers and the London trade consisted of men from the Continent, such as N. Vallin whose table clock illustrates the type of work they produced. The case is comparatively plain but the dial contains various astronomical indications as well as telling the time. It shows the position of the sun and moon in the zodiac, age and phase of the moon, difference between solar and lunar time and high water in London. An important feature of the clock is the beautifully clear engraving of the figures.

b) Lantern clock in brass, by William Bowyer; London, England, c. 1630; ht. 12" (30.5 cm.).

The first design considered English in origin is that of the 'lantern' clock, which appeared early in the 17th century. It was virtually the continental Gothic wall clock made slightly broader and constructed almost entirely in brass instead of iron. The bell became a dominating feature of the design, and all the early clocks had wheel balances; there is no known example with a foliot. This example has been fitted for a single weight on an endless rope though originally there were two separate weights, one on each side of the clock.

c) right: Lantern clock in brass, by Jo Snow; England, 1630; ht. 10" (25.4 cm.).

This is an example of a provincial lantern clock. It has a single hand with a tail to facilitate setting it to time and a wheel balance placed behind the frets. The chapter ring is narrow and the engraving rather coarse. Note the handle of the door near the figure IX. The hole above the figure XI is for the pivot of the alarm release, but the alarm disc is missing. This clock may be of West Country origin, as members of the Snow family are recorded at Salisbury and Lavington about this time.

d) Long case clock in 'architectural' style case, oak with ebony finish, by A. Fromanteel (introduced pendulum to England, 1658); England, 1660-70; ht. 72" (182.8 cm.).

This must be one of the first long case clocks made in England. It has a short pendulum, reaching only to the bottom of the dial, and the conventional verge escapement with a horizontal scapewheel. The winding holes are covered by shutters, and the clock cannot be wound until a cord is pulled to release them, providing power to keep the clock going during winding. The dial is very plain with a narrow chapter ring for legibility; the hands are characteristic of the period. The small square aperture over the figure VI shows the day of the month. It is smaller than the usual long case clock.

a) Bracket clock, ebony on oak, by Thos. Wise; England, c. 1690; ht. 11″ (27.9 cm.).

The bracket clock is shown here in one of its simplest forms, being a timepiece fitted with repeating mechanism that functioned when a cord was pulled. The winding hole is placed unsymmetrically as is often found on these clocks. The dial is very legible, and has the single cherub's head spandrels popular at the period. Note the elaborate basket top and carrying handle, together with the metal finials which contrast with the plainness of the case. The dial has prominent half hour and quarter hour marks but unobtrusive numbering of the five minute intervals.

b) Hood and dial of long case clock, marquetry on oak, by Richard Baker (member Clockmakers' Company, 1685); London, England, 1700; dia. 11″ (27.9 cm.).

This close-up of the hood and dial shows that the veneer round the glass has been applied in small pieces. There is no door in the hood which has to be slid upward to expose the winding holes. The dial is legible and the two hands are not surrounded by the usual rings. Note the name of the maker written along the bottom edge of the dial below the chapter ring and the antique form of the figure 1 in the date aperture, also the cleanly finished cherub's head spandrels.

c) Long case clock, oak with walnut veneer, Francis Stamper; London, England, after 1682; ht. 78″ (198 cm.).

The invention of the anchor escapement with seconds pendulum led to larger long case clocks around 1680, and the architectural design with ebony finish was replaced by more decorative styles. This example relies on the grain of the walnut veneer for decorative effect. The twisted columns beside the hood are a development from the architectural style, but the engraving round the centre of the dial is a feature taken from older clocks. Notice the very elaborate hands and spandrels. Clocks at this period usually had a convex moulding below the hood, but this anticipates later fashions with a concave one.

d) Long case clock, marquetry on oak decoration, Robert Clements; London, England, c. 1695; ht. 84″ (213 cm.).

This case shows just how complicated the marquetry designs could be at this period. Every surface is highly decorated: the moulding round the hood, the dial surround, the convex moulding below the hood and panels on the trunk door and base, with panels of veneer on the sides for good measure. The spandrels are very complicated and the half hour marks prominent with hands more decorated than usual; even the date aperture is surrounded by engraving. The straight pillars imply a date near the end of the century.

Clocks

English

Detail of d; the pendulum hook is used when moving the clock.

a) Lantern clock in brass, by John Drury; London, England, c. 1700; ht. 11″ (27.9 cm.).

Here, the lantern clock is entering its third stage of development. It still has only a single hand, but its most important feature is the anchor escapement and the long pendulum introduced about 1670–80; the striking is of the rack type which appeared about the same time. The dolphins on the frets were a favourite design on lantern clocks. This illustration shows how the movement is constructed of top and bottom plates with removable bars to carry the wheel arbors and shows the iron spur which keeps it away from the wall when hanging so that the pendulum can swing.

b) Hooded lantern clock in oak with brass dial, by Edwin Adams; England, c. 1730; ht. 16″ (40.6 cm.).

The lantern clock is shown here in its last phase as a wall clock. The dial is now square and the movement covered with a hood; the next stage of development will be to put the movement into a long case standing on the floor. This clock's movement has its wheels between plates instead of a 'birdcage' frame, but no striking work is fitted. The lantern clock held on as an alarm clock longer than as a striking clock, and examples are known dating from the painted dial period at the end of the 18th century.

c) Long case clock in oak decorated with lacquer, movement by John Ellicott; London, England, c. 1750; ht. 87″ (221 cm.).

Although the minute hand was a well-established feature by 1750, the quarter hour marks remain on the inner side of the chapter ring. The painted face with moving eyes is rather discordant and may be a later addition; it is flanked by dolphin spandrels. In the corner of the dial are spandrels of an elaborate pattern. When lacquering was fashionable, cases were made in England and sent to China to be decorated. The ground colour might be black, green, scarlet or yellow, and while the colours in most remaining clocks are muted by age, they must originally have been extremely bright.

d) Bracket clock, veneer on oak, decorated with heavy bronze castings, by John Ellicott; London, England, c. 1740–50; ht. 12″ (30.5 cm.).

The English bracket clock was usually quite restrained in design, but occasionally a custom-made item would break the bounds of convention. Such a piece is this by one of London's most celebrated makers. The decoration suggests French work, but there is symmetry in the design unlike the French rococo style (see p. 368). The wood grain contributes to the decoration, a feature then common on long case clocks but not on bracket clocks which retained the conventional ebony. Even the shape of the dial and its decoration is unusual. The hands and chapter ring are more restrained, the former contrasting effectively with the matted background.

a) Long case clock in oak, by E. Billington; Harbrough, England, c. 1750; ht. 78" (198 cm.).

The country-made long case clock with a single hand was a well-known type during the 18th century. The similarity of the movements suggests that there may have been centres for producing them and that the name of the local clockmaker was engraved later. The English 30 hour movement is very solid and will virtually last forever, although if a rope is used to support the weight it is usually preferable to convert the clock to chain drive. This clock is a typical example with large spandrels, silver chapter ring and matted dial centre with a small date aperture.

b) Mural clock in oak, by Thomas Mudge; London, England, c. 1760; lgth. 62" (157 cm.).

Thomas Mudge went into partnership with William Dutton in 1755, but their products did not at first bear both names. 1760 is a likely date for this example, a mural clock sometimes included in the 'Act of Parliament' category, and anticipating the developments in the type. The lacquered case is an 18th century feature, like the elaborate hands, but such a clock could well have been made nearly a century later. The dial is intended to be legible at a distance, but the very ornate hands make this difficult.

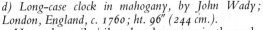

Dial of Wiltshire long case clock, c. 1785. A bird is often found on country-made clocks.

---

c) Bracket clock, ebony on oak, signed by Hall; London, England, c. 1760; ht. 13" (33.0 cm.).

Here is a typical example of the English bracket clock just after the middle of the 18th century. The case is surmounted by a top known as an inverted bell (i.e. upper part concave, lower part convex). The spandrels are more elaborate than previously and the maker's name is on a small plate applied to the dial. The quarter hour marks are still shown, together with spots to make the half hours more prominent; the dummy pendulum (see p. 240c) is used to show if the clock is going. It strikes and can be made to repeat hours and quarters.

d) Long-case clock in mahogany, by John Wady; London, England, c. 1760; ht. 96" (244 cm.).

Here, the strike/silent hand appears in the arch, flanked with the usual dolphin spandrels. The dial corner spandrels have become nondescript while the minute figures have increased in size. The quarter hour circle is retained but the maker's name now appears on a small plate fastened to the dial. Beside the dial are fluted columns finished with brass caps and bases produced in Birmingham, the motif repeated in the trunk. In the latter 18th century, the long case clock lost favour in London, but remained popular in the provinces. Those still made in the capital were probably intended for provincial use.

Dial of clock, with English 'maker'. An identical dial exists with an American name.

a) Long case clock in mahogany, by Benson; Whitehaven, England, c. 1780; ht. 96″ (244 cm.).

Particularly in the North of England the long case clock held its own during the 18th century and began to develop in a style somewhat different from that produced in London. Cases were wider and by the early 19th century had become very wide indeed (Yorkshire style). There tended to be more decoration on the cases and dials than in the Regency period, as exemplified here.

Note the decorated centre of the dial which makes the hands indistinct, the date ring inside the chapter ring, and a third concentric hand as date indicator. The subsidiary dial in the arch contains various astronomical indications.

b) Long case clock in mahogany, by Adam Gordon; Dunkeld, Scotland, c. 1780; ht. 84″ (213 cm.).

This example is by a Scottish maker. The dolphin designs so often found at this period decorate the arch, but the spandrels in the corners of the dial are of the single cherub's head type found on much earlier clocks. Such combinations often appear on a clock which originates far from the capital. The fluted pillars and scrolls over the hood persisted into the early 19th century, but were then usually accompanied by a painted iron dial. The hands match. Cases of later clocks would not have had such good quality veneer.

c) Bracket clock of oak with ebony finish; by Thomas Chantler; London, England, late 18th century; ht. 16″ (40.6 cm.).

From 1750, modifications to the bracket clock began which would change it beyond recognition by the early 19th century, and this clock shows the early modifications. Though it retains the old style case with ebony finish and carrying handle, the dial is now enamel and has figures for the days of the month indicated by a separate concentric hand instead of a date aperture. The matching hands were used after the white dial was introduced. This dial's decorated brass background is a poor substitute for spandrels, and the way is being prepared for the painted iron dial.

d) Mural clock in oak, decorated in lacquer on black background, known as 'Act of Parliament' clock, by Humphrey Sellon; London, England, late 18th century; ht. 60″ (152 cm.).

In 1797, an Act of Parliament imposed a tax on all clocks and watches, and the legend has it that people disposed of their timepieces and relied on large mural clocks specially made then and hung in taverns. As the Act was repealed the next year, it is improbable that every remaining clock of this type was made in 1797–8. In fact, such mural timepieces were well-known in the 18th century and were made until about 1860 although later examples had dials smaller in proportion to the trunk and glazed. Here the motif is a picture of Bacchus, suggesting use as a tavern clock.

French-style English carriage, or travelling clock, c. 1820–25.

a) 'Balloon' clock in oak, by Perigal and Browne; London, England, c. 1783; ht. 15" (38.1 cm.).

The makers of this so-called 'balloon' clock were in partnership from 1782 to 1799 in Coventry Street. The first balloon ascent was made in 1783 and about this time the Prince of Wales was becoming a leader of fashion, hence his crest of three feathers incorporated in the design. The style was copied throughout the 19th century, often with an inferior movement, but the high winding holes on this example indicate the use of fusees. The hour hand appears to be a replacement; the original would have been more slender, matching the minute hand.

b) Bracket clock in ebonized fruitwood with brass inlay, by Tupling; London, England, c. 1820; ht. 16" (40.6 cm.).

This example illustrates the development of the bracket clock in accordance with Regency furnishing styles (see p. 358a). The dial is now painted white and is circular with a solid brass bezel to hold the glass. The case is much plainer, relying on the brass inlay for decoration. The turned feet replace the former pattern made to fit the corners of the case. This clock is fitted for repeat and has a strike/silent lever over the figure XII. The boss for the carrying handle is unusual with its shell design instead of the usual lion's head.

c) Skeleton clock with striking, brass; England, c. 1840; ht. 14" (35.6 cm.).

The type is most common as a simple timepiece striking one blow at the hour, but this example incorporates hour striking on a gong, reserving the single blow for the half hours. The side supports are somewhat plainer than the usual frame of skeleton clocks but this is compensated for in the elaborately pierced dial which is extremely difficult to read. It features a typical English striking movement controlled by a rack and snail mechanism; the fusees and barrels are connected by chains instead of gut lines. The bell above for sounding the half hours is an unconventional shape for such a clock.

d) Bracket clock, mahogany, with three trains, musical, by French maker; Royal Exchange, London, England, c. 1840; ht. 15" (38.1 cm.).

During the Regency period, the bracket clock became very austere, but at the beginning of Victoria's reign the process reversed itself. The gilded bronze ornaments and complicated spandrels of this clock are more ornate than those of the previous century, and the figuring of the mahogany also adds to the decoration. As well as playing tunes the clock chimes 'ting tang' quarters. The hands are typical of the 19th century but seem plain for a clock of this type. The hour hand could be larger for more contrast.

A return to ornamentation in the early Victorian period.

235

a) left: Regulator in mahogany, by Lowenstark & Sons; London, England, c. 1860; ht. 78" (198 cm.).

The regulator clock was a precision timepiece used for astronomical observations or as a standard for regulating the other timepieces in a clockmaker's shop. The movement had to be simple and sturdy and was therefore not complicated by striking mechanism. Three separate hands obviated the necessity for motion work and thereby reduced friction, a feature which also made the dial easier to read. A dead beat escapement was fitted and the pendulum compensated for changes in temperature. The gravitational effect of the weight on the pendulum bob was minimized by the weight cord being led to one side.

b) Striking dial with inlaid mahogany case by M. Rhodes; Bradford, England, c. 1830; ht. 23" (58.4 cm.).

The 12" dial clock became popular at the end of the 18th century, and the design was later modified to have a longer pendulum and striking work. Here, the evolution of the design about 1830 is shown and this style was to be imitated by American and German factories later in the century. The movement is of the traditional English type with fusees and an anchor escapement. The bell can be placed either above or behind the movement. The case is of solid mahogany veneered with the same wood, and the brass inlay is typical of late Regency work.

German
16TH–17TH CENTURY

c) Augsburg table clock of gilded brass; Augsburg, Germany, mid-16th century; ht. 6" (15.2 cm.).

Augsburg became famous for these clocks in the 16th and 17th centuries. Many had dials giving astronomical indications; many also featured automata. The distinguishing mark of the city is a pineapple, often stamped in the plates of the movement The cases were richly decorated and gilded. Originally having a balance, many have been converted to pendulum control, the pendulum often swinging in front of the dial.

This example possesses an alarm, a date dial, an aperture for showing the phases of the moon and a small dial showing the quarter hours (commoner on clocks of the early 17th century).

d) Octagonal table clock in gilded brass inscribed Davidt Weber, Aug. *(presumably Augsburg); Germany, c. 1690; dia. 4" (10.2 cm.).*

Much plainer than the average Augsburg piece, this example is not a striker, but is fitted with an alarm. The solidly made hand can be set only by a key on the square. There are no quarter hour marks: perhaps the clock was only for night use. Note the winding squares (right-hand photograph) marked 'G' (*Gehwerk*, going mechanism) and 'W' (*Wecker*, alarm).

The back-plate of the movement is shown on the right. The balance cock is fastened by a screw, but its neck filed very narrow—a link with the earlier part of the century. There is no balance spring, regulation being achieved by altering the tension of the mainspring.

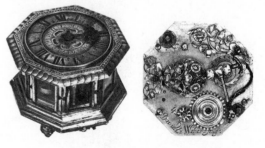

a) Metal cased Stockuhr in gilded brass, by Leopold Hoyss; Bamberg, Germany, c. 1760; ht. 10" (25.4 cm.).

The German *Telleruhr* or 'dish clock' was originally a wall clock, its shape resembling a dish. Subsequent developments modified its shape, leaving a circular metal dial with an irregular gilded metal surround and making it a standing clock.

This example has three trains but no glass to protect the dial. The prominent half hour marks are repeated on the linear track of the chapter ring where quarter hours are usually shown. Above XII, the day of the month is shown; the opening below houses the indicator to show whether the clock is going.

b) Neuchâtel style clock in ebony with gilt decoration, by Hoyss; Germany, 1770; ht. 20" (50.8 cm.).

Here, Hoyss has taken the Swiss 'Neuchâtel' style as his model. The ebony case remains but the metal decoration is more restrained. The clock still has three trains, and the day of the month shows just below figure XII. The small dial below VI is for strike/silent. In contrast to the *Stockuhr's* handle, a key secures the door of this case. The statuette is more elaborate than the usual decoration on Neuchâtel clocks. The hands contrast nicely.

c) and d) Bamberg clocks in ebony with gilded brass, designed by Leopold Hoyss (1713–1797), and c) signed by him; Bamberg, Germany, c. 1770; ht. of both 20" (50.8 cm.).

Hoyss is best known for the *Bamberger Stockuhr*, a type based on the English bracket clock but with many modifications. The ebony case is retained as is the basket top, but the separate gilded brass castings applied to the cases are new. Unlike English clocks, these do not stand on a firm base but are raised on curved wooden legs with gilded brass feet. Urns, symbolic of death, feature as ornaments for the top. The door hinges are also prominent and decorative.

The greatest differences are in the dials. Both of these have the little slot to indicate the pendulum, but the design is different. *d* has the curved minute band so often seen on Dutch clocks; both have foliage decorating the centre of the dial but *c* is a casting and *d* engraved. Both have very prominent half hour marks. The dial plate of *c* shows a certain French influence with the high chapter ring and pendulum visible below it.

Both clocks chime the quarters in addition to striking the hour. *d* has subsidiary dials marked in German 'repeat/not repeat' and 'strike/not strike'; much richer than *c*, it was no doubt made for a very special customer.

Clocks

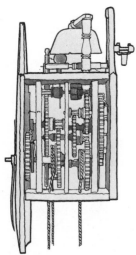

Black Forest movement (c. 1800) with weights supported by cords instead of chains.

a) Black Forest clock with mahogany rim, convex glass in brass bezel, designed for British market; Germany, early 19th century; dia. 12" (30.5 cm.).

The Black Forest clock industry was deeply involved in export by the early 19th century. Most export clocks had painted dials, but this type was based on the 'English dial' clocks made at the time, though the latter did not have the exposed weights and long pendulum.

Such clocks were usually time and strike¯only with the striking mechanism at the rear, but this example possesses alarm work at the side of the movement, operated by a weight carried on a cord (cf. the chains of the going and striking weights).

b) A cheaper than standard Black Forest product, painted dial, wood motion work; Germany, c. 1830; ht. 12½" (31.6 cm.), wdth. 8½" (21.6 cm.).

The industry was always concerned with producing clocks as cheaply as possible. Here, the main arbor which carries the sprocket actuated by the chain rotates once per hour, and carries the cannon pinion which bears the minute hand; thus, fewer teeth have to be cut, but the clock only runs for 12 to 15 hours. The driving weight for the going train is on the 3 o'clock side in contrast to the usual 30-hour clock. The dial is slightly smaller than usual. Notice the minute hand secured by a pin instead of the usual nut.

c) Black Forest 8-day wall clock, painted dial; Germany, c. 1840; ht. 16" (40.6 cm.), wdth. 12" (30.5 cm.).

The usual running period of a Black Forest wall clock was 30 hours but a limited number were made to run for 8 days. The weights were suspended from gut lines wound on barrels as on an English long case clock, but the barrels and the frame were of wood. The size of the dial was about the same as that of a normal 30-hour clock, and they are easily recognizable by the presence of the winding holes. These clocks were intended to be hung up, but they are often met with in English long cases which have been divorced from their original movements.

d) Black Forest striking clock in imitation ebony with brass inlay, alabaster pillars; Germany, c. 1860; ht. 14" (35.6 cm.).

Under the spur of American competition, Black Forest makers tried to produce something more refined than the old pull wind wall clocks. This clock has the traditional wooden framed movement with brass wheels, but possesses fusees.

The pillar and pediment design was a well known feature of Black Forest work at this period, and often the pillars were made of porcelain. The inlaid brass forms a pleasing contrast to the shiny black finish. As with many experimental clocks, a window is provided so that the owner can see at a glance whether the pendulum is still swinging.

a) German OG clock in pine with walnut veneer, by I.B. Sayer; Saig, Germany, c. 1860; ht. 30″ (76.2 cm.), wdth. 17″ (43.2 cm.).

The American OG clock (p. 245a) captured the British market in the 1850s and even began to penetrate Europe, threatening the Black Forest cottage industry. When German factory production began in the 1860s, they imitated the American clocks. This OG is incomplete: the painted glass tablet in the door is missing, but the movement is much more solid than that of the American model, even the dial is of much heavier sheet metal, and the case finished with greater care. German factories soon designed new case styles, and production of OG clocks did not last long, hence German examples are rarer than the American.

b) Cuckoo clock in softwood, walnut veneered; Germany, c. 1865; ht. 9″ (22.9 cm.).

The cuckoo clock has only been in its present form for about 100 years. It began in the style of the ordinary Black Forest wall clock and later developed into the style shown here before appearing in the cases decorated with carved leaves that we now know.

This clock is driven by brass cased weights and has a brass pendulum. The movement is of the traditional Black Forest style with a beechwood frame and brass wheels, but the enamel dial and glazed door represent a step forward from the old Black Forest wall clock to a more sophisticated design.

Black Forest 'picture frame' c. 1850–60. The eyes move with the pendulum.

c) Alarm clock in softwood, veneered; Germany, c. 1870; ht. 8″ (20.3 cm.).

Black Forest makers were trying to imitate American designs and the cottage style clock shown here is provided with a spring driven movement although the plates are still made of beechwood. The dial is of sheet zinc and the glass has a gilded rim; in the lower part of the case the glass is decorated, all features of the American clocks.

This type was not long on the market but soon replaced by similar clocks with brass movements, and later still by clocks with movements of even better quality than the American ones.

d) Small striking 'drop dial', pine case, mahogany veneered, brass inlay, vendor's name on dial; Germany, c. 1875; ht. 17″ (43.2 cm.), dial dia. 13″ (33.0 cm.).

This is an example of the early penetration of the British market by German models in the early days of German factory production. The frame of the movement is of wood with brass bushes to take the pivots as in the old Black Forest wall clocks, but the springs are in barrels and the hands are of steel instead of brass, although much thicker than contemporary British hands. The general design of the clock resembles the English drop dials of 1830–40, especially in having brass inlay.

239

Clocks

German
LATE 19TH CENTURY

Interior view of 240a, showing paper pasted in the back.

a) Teutonia alarm clock, pine case; Germany, 1875–80; ht. 11½″ (29.2 cm.), wdth. 7″ (17.8 cm.).

Here is another factory copy of an American model. They can often be distinguished by the wood of the case which is stained and polished rather than veneered, and instead of the door fitting inside the top and sides of the case, the whole of the front forms the door, which may be veneered or not. Rules for distinguishing between German and American clocks are very flexible and there are many exceptions.

The Teutonia Clock Manufactory of St. Georgen was well known as an exporter to Britain. This is one of their earlier efforts.

b) Kitchen timepiece, pine case; Germany, late 19th century; ht. 14½″ (36.8 cm.), wdth. 8½″ (21.6 cm.).

This clock is typical of German factory productions of the period. There is much pressed brass ornament, the dial centre, the pendulum bob, and plaques on the case. Notice the pendulum is slightly offset to one side. The two turned decorations at the base of the door are popular on German clocks at this period. There is no maker's name or trademark which indicates one of the smaller producers, for the larger firms used a paper stuck on the back of the case in imitation of the American factories, or else embossed their trademark on the movement.

German–Austrian
REGULATORS

c) 'Regulator' clock in mahogany veneer on softwood; Germany, late 19th century; overall ht. 42″ (107 cm.).

This type was developed from the weight-driven 'Vienna Regulator'. Some movements approach French work in quality, having solid plates and pinions and a high finish; others have open plates and lantern pinions like American factory products. They are known as regulators because they feature the 'gridiron' pendulum. Unfortunately most of the pendulums met with are dummies. This is so if all the rods are held by one fastening; for the compensation to work they must have separate fastening pieces. Some were highly decorated with carving and turning while others were plainer.

d) Laterndluhr in mahogany; Austria, c. 1820; ht. 56″ (142 cm.).

The style of Vienna regulator with enlarged hood and base is called *Laterndluhr* (lantern clock); its movement is sometimes larger than on the normal clock.

This is a fine specimen with a beautifully made case. There are no hinges, access to the mechanism being provided by sliding panels. The weight is oval and well to one side, while the movement has circular plates unlike usual examples. It runs for a month on one winding. Note the delicacy of the hands and the quiet dignity of the dial.

a) Group of Vienna regulators in mahogany; Austria, 1810–30; hts. from 30″ to 60″ (76.2 cm. to 153 cm.).

The Vienna regulator developed in the early 19th century from the long case clock. The cases of earlier examples were in three distinct parts—hood, trunk and base—but later cases tended to be straight. The movements were hand-made except for the cutting of the teeth of the wheels.

This is a group of early examples; the one on the right, however, has no separate base. The two outside clocks (extreme left and right) go for a year and are provided with two weights hanging from one pulley. The centre clock shows the date and the day of the week.

b) Vienna regulator in mahogany by Leopold Hörrer; Austria, c. 1850; ht. 54″ (137 cm.).

Here, the Vienna regulator is developing towards its best-known style: a long slender case with decoration at the top and bottom. The one-piece dial and slender hands are features of the earlier clocks. The curved door follows the top of the dial. The carving is based on small units of design and is very unobtrusive; the backboard of the case is inlaid. The weight is large because the clock is designed to run for a month. The screw for steadying the clock on the wall is visible bottom left.

---

c) Vienna regulator in mahogany by V. Häusler; Austria, c. 1850; ht. 42″ (107 cm.).

The plain lines suggest a typical Vienna regulator of the so-called 'Biedermeier' period (c. 1815–1830), but V. Häusler is known to have been in business from 1842–82.

The only decoration is on the dial rim and the base. Note the prominent steadying screws at the bottom of the case; these are smaller in later clocks.

d) Vienna regulator in mahogany by Franz Weitzendorfer; Austria, c. 1855; ht. 42″ (107 cm.).

Weitzendorfer worked 1853–58 but the clock could well be considered late 19th century in style. The dial is in two sections, but retains the earlier cast decorated rim and slender hands. The sides of the case have lost their sharp edges and incorporate pillars with a hint of capitals and bases top and bottom. The top pediment and the bottom edge of the door are curved, the base developing the bulbous lines of later clocks.

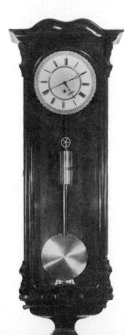

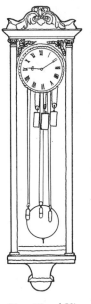

Transitional Vienna Regulator, c. 1840. The flat top relieved by a carved pediment.

Clocks

Dutch, Danish, Maltese

Miniature Japanese work of the 19th century, only 6¼″ high.

a) 'Stoelklok' in oak painted; Holland, c. 1780; ht. 26″ (66.0 cm.).

In the Netherlands, the Gothic wall clock developed into the *stoelklok*, with a brass movement and a verge escapement connected to the pendulum through a long wire over the top of the movement. The bracket was decorated in bright colours and the frets round the dial and above the canopy were also painted and gilded. The back of the bracket usually carried decorations in the form of mermaids as shown here or in pieces of wood shaped like the handles of a vase. The type was made throughout Holland but is particularly associated with the province of Friesland.

b) 'Staartklok' in mahogany; Holland, c. 1850; ht. 4″ (10.2 cm.).

About the beginning of the 19th century, the *staartklok* developed in the Netherlands, replacing the *stoelklok*. This is a typical example. While the movements were similar (except that the *staartklok* had an anchor escapement and long pendulum), the rest of the clock underwent a complete change: the pendulum is contained in a long box at the rear, and can only be seen through the window covered by the plaque with the vase design. The painted iron dial is reminiscent of long case clocks and has the typical Dutch scalloped minute track. The small weights in front are for the alarm.

c) Bornholm clock in painted softwood; Denmark, 1848; ht. 84″ (213 cm.).

The Baltic island of Bornholm is noted for long case clocks based on the English model. The movements are similar to those of English eight-day clocks, but the cases have additional decoration in the form of carving and painting, and some clocks are finished in light colours which contrast greatly with the English prototype. The hood of the clock may be square, as here, or round as in many long case clocks made in Scotland. The Swedish 'Farmhouse' clock has an affinity with the type.

d) Later Maltese clock, deal case, painted and gilt; Malta, c. 1840-50; ht. 30″ (76.2 cm.), wdth. 21″ (53.3 cm.).

This type owes something to the Italian altar clock; there is an affinity with contemporary American clocks, although any connection at that time is tenuous. The earliest had a single hand; later ones also had a minute hand. The going period was usually short, winding needed every 12 hours. Maltese clocks usually have a slot in the dial through which the pendulum bob can be seen to indicate whether the clock is going. The highly-coloured cases are decorated in gold leaf. This dial is built up from separate boards; note the typical 'ear pieces' at the top of each side, and the carved pediment.

a) 'Case on case' clock, mahogany veneer; U.S.A., c. 1800; ht. 36″ (91.4 cm.).

Among the earliest of native American designs produced after the Revolution was the 'case on case' clock. The movement was a scaled down version of that of the English long case clock but the design of the case itself suggested an English bracket clock on a small cabinet, and tried to disguise the clock's being weight driven. Note the painted dial with 'tumbling' hour figures and the inlay of the hood and trunk. A bell gives one blow at the hour and the weight is suspended from a pulley hung on a gut line exactly as on an English long case clock.

b) Long case clock in pine, mahogany veneer, with typical Birmingham movement and dial but bearing the name Mitchell and Mott, New York (27 Pearl Street, c. 1790–1809); U.S.A., c. 1805, ht. 87″ (221 cm.).

The clock trade has relied for years on specialist workshops that produced rough movements for finishing by the nominal maker, or even finished movements for which the vendor took credit. In the early 19th century the centre for long case movements was Birmingham, which supplied dealers not only throughout England but also in the U.S.A.

Although generally English in design, this has more decoration than a contemporary English clock. The various panels of veneer, the inlay and the slender feet would be rare on English clocks. The painted roses in the upper part of the hood may be later additions.

c) Banjo clock in mahogany veneer, brass side ornaments, acorn finial, marked S. Willard's Patent; U.S.A., c. 1810; ht. 30″ (76.2 cm.).

Simon Willard of Roxbury, Mass. patented a timepiece in 1802. The idea was to produce an elegant clock without using springs, which were difficult to obtain then. It was driven by a heavy tapered weight with limited fall, the loss of distance compensated by the use of a small barrel and a large main wheel. The barrel arbor was at figure 2 instead of 6 to allow for another inch or two of drop. The pendulum was just behind the dial. Note the 'tumbling' hour figures, plain hands and delicately painted glass tablets. Their appeal to collectors has resulted in numerous fakes.

d) Dial of wooden hang up clock in pine, from Merriman and Dunbar; Bristol, Connecticut, U.S.A., c. 1815; ht. 16″ (40.6 cm.).

The dials of the American hang up clocks were based on the English painted iron dials which were being imported at the time. The clocks were wound by pulling cords attached to the barrels which raised the weights, and therefore winding holes were unnecessary. The weights were tin cans filled with stones by the purchaser of the clock. The hands were of pewter and could not withstand manual setting, hence if the clock needed correcting it had to be done by moving the dial wheels with the fingers. The corner and arch paintings were in bright colours, embellished by gilding.

American
EARLY 19TH CENTURY

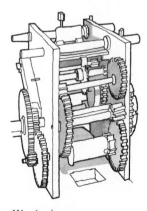

Wooden hang up movement in cherry, laurel and oak, c. 1807.

243

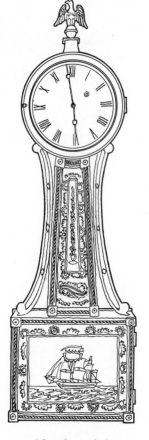

a) Pillar and scroll shelf clock with mahogany veneer, by Chauncey Ives using Eli Terry movement; Bristol, Connecticut, U.S.A., c. 1825; ht. 25" (63.5 cm.).

Terry received a conventional training as a clockmaker, but turned to mass production of wooden movements, producing 4,000 hang up type clocks in 1807-1809. He later sold his factory and established a new one, where he worked on the idea of a weight-driven shelf clock—a cheaper version of Willard's patent timepiece (p. 243c).

This clock illustrates the well-known features of the type although the wooden finials are unconventional. The hands are of the same length and are distinguished by their design. The painted tablet is executed by hand and a piece of ivory surrounds the keyhole.

He produced several types of movement which were fitted into pillar and scroll cases, and the design shown here on the right is that of 1823. His movements were made by other manufacturers, some by arrangement and others without any acknowledgment. The movement exhibits two features introduced by Terry the escapement and the count wheel are on the front plate and the motion work for providing the 1:12 movement of the hands is between the plates.

b) Patent looking-glass clock in mahogany veneered on pine (Joseph Ives' patent); Connecticut, U.S.A., c. 1820; ht. 60" (152 cm.).

Ives obtained a U.S. government patent for applying a looking-glass to the front of a clock case and made many, this particular example having a movement with iron plates and his 'roller pinions', intended to reduce friction. The movement ran for 8 days and, like many American clocks, had the cords for the weights carried over pulleys at the top of the case for increased distance through which to fall. These clocks have very small dials banished to the top of the case, allowing the maximum size of looking-glass. The type is also associated with the state of New Hampshire.

c) Empire shelf clock in mahogany veneered on pine, by J. C. Brown; Bristol, Connecticut, U.S.A., c. 1840-50; ht. 36" (91.4 cm.).

The painting on this Empire style clock portrays the residence of its maker, a subject often used on his clocks but as he purchased the house in 1847, this clock is probably a very late example of the style. The dial still has the conventional corner ornaments, but the figures are becoming longer and the aperture is smaller. The case shape was developed later, being given much broader pillars which were gilded; the style in its new form lasted about 1850-80. The wood grain provides a pleasing decoration. The carving on the pillars is more restrained than on earlier examples.

A later banjo clock, (cf. 243c) with more elaborate decoration.

a) left: OG clock with veneered case and brass movement by Chauncey Jerome; Bristol, Connecticut, U.S.A., 1839–45; ht. 26" (66.0 cm.), wdth. 15½" (39.4 cm.).
centre: Clock paper, less elaborate than later examples with ornate type, often illustrating the clock factory; here an extra piece explains how to set the alarm.
right: Here the closed door reveals the painted tablet; the building may represent the Independence Hall at Philadelphia.

The U.S. financial crisis in 1837 affected all manufacturing including that of wooden movement clocks, which was virtually dead by the middle 1840s. Chauncey Jerome knew that rolled brass was being produced in Connecticut and decided to make a cheap clock with a brass movement. Housed in an OG case, the clock (designed by his brother Noble) was patented in June 1839.

In 1842 the first of these clocks were exported to Britain, and later to all parts of the world. Produced by the thousand up to 1914, it is the most common American clock.

This example is from Jerome's Bristol Conn. factory and can be dated between 1839 and 1845, when the factory burnt down. It is fitted with alarm in addition to striking, though many movements in these clocks have holes drilled for the alarm mechanism even if it is not actually fitted. The cases were pine veneered with mahogany or other wood. The crudely painted flowers in the corner of the dial are seen only on earlier examples. Later dials are plain or ornamented with a monochrome transfer. The lower part of the glass door is covered by a scene painted in reverse, i.e. highlights done first, then background.

---

b) Wagon spring clock, mahogany veneer, by Birge and Fuller with Ives' movement; Bristol, Connecticut, U.S.A., c. 1844; ht. 22" (55.9 cm.).

The 'wagon spring', invented by Joseph Ives, was one of the solutions offered to overcome the difficulty in producing steel springs. A number of steel strips are fixed to the bottom of the case forming a leaf spring similar to that used on wagons. The clock is provided with a virtually weight driven type of movement and winding the cords

on the barrels puts the wagon spring in tension, providing the power to drive the clock. A serious disadvantage is the modifying gear consisting of chains and drums which convert the short powerful pull of the spring into a longer weaker one to drive the clock. The movement is based on the well-known OG design, but modified by the addition of an extra arbor on each train to give an 8-day period of running.

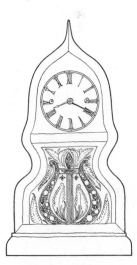

The 'Acorn' shape (c. 1850) had sides of laminated wood; difficult to make, it is now rare.

245

Clocks

American
MID-19TH CENTURY

a) OOG clock in pine with mahogany veneer, by Chauncey Jerome; Bristol, Connecticut, U.S.A., c. 1850; ht. 26" (66.0 cm.), wdth. 15½" (39.4 cm.).

The standard OG type soon captured the American market and even penetrated the rest of the world as an export commodity; most factories produced the double OG or OOG along with it. In addition to the main moulding containing the ogive, the motif was repeated in the surrounding moulding and the door, which were respectively convex and concave. OOG clocks were a little more expensive than the plain types, but their production cost must have been only fractionally more.

b) 'Drop dial' design clock in pine inlaid with mother of pearl; U.S.A., c. 1850; ht. 22" (55.9 cm.).

The British 'drop dial' of the Regency period provides the model for this clock, but the decoration suggests a date in the 1850s. The movement is a typical American 8-day weight driven movement adapted for spring drive, and the hands are mass-produced stampings. A gong replaces the bell for striking, and the sheet iron dial of the English clock is here replaced by one of sheet zinc. Such clocks formed part of the increasing flood of American exports to Britain from 1850 onwards.

c) OG Gothic clock, mahogany veneer on pine, by Brewster and Ingrahams; Bristol, Connecticut, U.S.A., c. 1850; ht. 13" (33.0 cm.).

This design of case was produced by Ingraham and housed the Brewster type of movement with a reinforcing channel stamped into the plates. The springs were brass, one way of overcoming the difficulty of manufacturing them in steel. Brass springs are satisfactory when new, but become weaker with constant use. The tablet is of etched glass and there is a small ivory surround to the keyhole. This, together with the free-standing pillars suggests the pillar and scroll design, but the shape of the door embodying the square tablet and circular wooden dial surround is like that of the 'Beehive' or 'Round Gothic' style.

d) Marine or locomotive clock in softwood, by Ingraham; U.S.A., 1870; dia. 6" (15.2 cm.).

Mass production of watches in the U.S.A. did not become well established until the 1870s. Transport undertakings needed timekeepers for use on ships and locomotives and as pendulum clocks were unsuitable for the purpose, a balance-controlled movement was evolved and housed in a simple wooden case. This example is by Ingraham, who produced several similar models up to the early eighties. The hands are of a design often met with on American clocks, the spade ends having a circular hole punched in them. The dial is of paper with a metal backing.

A 'Beehive' or 'Round Gothic' mantel clock, c. 1840.

a) 'Blinking eyes' clock in iron, painted; New York, U.S.A., c. 1875; ht. 12″ (30.5 cm.).

This type of clock was made in a variety of designs of which 'Topsy' and 'Sambo' are the best known. The movement is a cheap lever type, but as it runs it moves the eyes of the figure. The idea was intended as a novelty rather than a serious essay in timekeeping, and the general effect depends on the colouring. No makers' names appear, but such clocks were featured in the catalogue of the Waterbury (Connecticut) Clock Co.

b) Gothic design timepiece in pine with mahogany veneer, Ansonia Clock Co.; New York, U.S.A., c. 1880; ht. 12″ (30.5 cm.), wdth. 6½″ (16.5 cm.).

The Sharp Gothic design was popular with all American manufacturers from its introduction by Ingraham in the 1840s until the end of the 19th century. Its usual form was as a striking or alarm clock, but this example is a timepiece. The finials are decorated and the design on the door is partly transparent, allowing the swing of the pendulum to be seen; the design is also carried to the upper part of the glass leaving just a circular opening so the dial is visible. The pendulum itself bears an ornate design.

The name 'cottage' was applied to a flat-topped rectangular case.

c) 'Drop' dial inlaid with white metal lacquered to look like brass; U.S.A., c. 1880; ht. 27″ (68.6 cm.).
d) Drop dial of walnut veneer on pine, by Jerome & Co. (Newhaven Clock Co.); Newhaven, Connecticut, U.S.A., c. 1875; ht. 27″ (68.6 cm.).
e) Drop dial of walnut veneer on pine, by E. N. Welch; U.S.A., c. 1880; ht. 27″ (68.6 cm.).

This type was made in imitation of the English clocks of the late Regency period, but is of a much inferior quality. The movement of *c* is a typical American factory product with open plated and exposed springs. The striking is on a wire gong. An attempt has been made to reproduce an old English pattern of hands, but the bezel is pressed brass, not a solid casting as on English clocks.

d and *e* illustrate how similar were the products of American factories about a century ago. Both clocks strike on a bell which is unusual for an American clock of this period, wire gongs being preferred. The hands are almost identical. The dials of the prototypes were usually convex and made of sheet iron, but on these clocks they are flat and of sheet zinc. The low position of the winding holes indicates that the clocks have no fusees. The bottom sections of the cases are redundant, but on the English prototype would have served to house a much longer pendulum. The fret, which allows the pendulum bob to be seen, would have been omitted on the English clock.

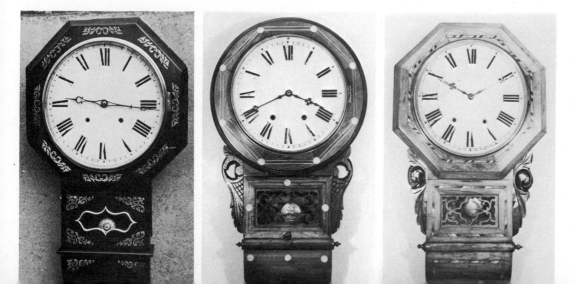

Clocks

American

a) Kitchen clock with 8-day movement, in oak, stained and polished; U.S.A., c. 1880; ht. 23″ (58.4 cm.).

The American Sharp Gothic design remained popular for many years but in face of German competition, factories devised variations. This model is entitled 'Clyde'; it was usual for each variation to have such a name. Cases were often decorated with designs embossed by a mould while the wood was hot and damp. The dial is divided by a brass ring; the pendulum is not only decorative but shows how alterations in the height of the bob affect timekeeping: a device among many 19th century U.S.A. clock patents.

b) 'Venetian' strike and alarm clock in rosewood; U.S.A., c. 1880; ht. 18″ (45.7 cm.).

Although Elias Ingraham had invented the Sharp Gothic case, the firm gave up using it about 1865. Other factories continued its use to the end of the century, but Ingraham was anxious to put new models on the market. The 'Venetian' style shown here was patented in 1861 and produced in various modifications up to 1902. This particular clock has an alarm in addition to striking, and this cost 50 cents extra. Innovations are the brass rim round the dial and round the dial aperture. The design of the movement was used for many years with only slight modifications.

c) Calendar clock in oak; St. Louis, Missouri, U.S.A., c. 1880; ht. 42″ (107 cm.).

Calendar clocks were fashionable in the U.S.A. from after the Civil War, and several firms went into business making them. The movements were supplied by well-known manufacturers. This model, known as 'Fashion' was supplied by the Southern Calendar Clock Co., and the clocks were sold by teams of salesmen who would canvass a whole town at a time and then pass on to the next. A pamphlet was supplied with the clock purporting to be a guide to its maintenance and repair, but consisting largely of advertising material. These pamphlets are now very rare.

d) Mantel clock, 'Doric', in softwood; Bristol, Connecticut, U.S.A., c. 1880; ht. 16″ (40.6 cm.).

The patent for this type of case was granted to Ingraham in 1861, and the design manufactured up to 1902 along with the 'Venetian'. The 'Doric' was the cheaper of the two models costing about three-quarters of the price of the 'Venetian'. The circular rim surrounding the pendulum aperture should be covered by painted glass, and this together with the bezel and the intermediate turned buttons forms the door. The catch securing it is visible on the left side just above the centre. The dial and hands are similar to the lever timepiece of p. 246d.

a) Mural clock, maple veneer on pine, probably by E. Ingraham & Co., but unmarked; U.S.A., late 19th century; ht. 34″ (86.4 cm.).

American factories began to feel German competition in Europe in the 1880s and 1890s and produced new styles in retaliation. In accordance with popular taste, more turning was incorporated in the cases which were also decorated with inlay. Dummy compensation pendulums were a selling point too; in this example the pendulum suggests a jar of mercury and a looking-glass behind it lightens a somewhat sombre effect. This type of clock was made by several American factories.

b) Kitchen clock with calendar in redwood; U.S.A., c. 1900; ht. 22½″ (57.2 cm.).

This type was fashionable about the turn of the century, with the cases produced by compressing wood in a mould under hot and moist conditions (cf. p. 248a). The movement is an 8-day one, and the design on the glass allows the elaborately decorated pendulum bob to be seen. The hands are derived from French models and the day of the month is shown by the long hand pointing to the figures on the outer edge of the dial. Attached to the case are a thermometer and a weather-glass. The gong is of a deeper tone than mid-19th century American clocks.

Clock, c. 1900, with a 'real Bonn porcelain' case.

---

c) 'Crystal regulator' in white metal gilded; made by Ansonia Clock Co.; New York, U.S.A., c. 1900; ht. 12″ (30.5 cm.).

French makers during the 19th century produced pendulum clocks having an affinity with the carriage clock: precision clocks with two tubes of mercury to form the pendulum bob. The Ansonia Company produced their own version, but the movement was of inferior quality. The visible escapement was retained, and the circular plates for containing the parts, but the pendulum had only dummy compensation. Like other American imitations of French clocks, they are easily detectable: the winding holes are in the chapter ring instead of in the sunk portion of the dial. The cases are more highly decorated than the French ones, and so many different designs were produced it was possible to issue a whole catalogue of the one type.

The rear view shows the unusual support for the gong and the way that the wheels project beyond the area of the plates. Unlike most Ansonia products, rack striking is fitted but is on the back of the movement instead of behind the dial. Regulation is by a square above the figure XII which alters the effective length of the pendulum suspension spring.

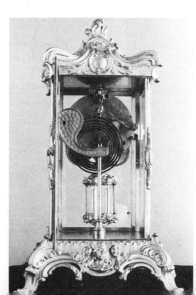

Watches
Introduction

Watches have tended to show less variation in their basic design than clocks, the chief differences being in the outer decoration. While the verge escapement continued in use, most European watches were very similar, the main difference being that English watches possessed a cock to support the balance, while continental makers used a bridge for this purpose.

English watches had their top plates covered with pierced work in the early days of the balance spring but later they became much plainer, even the pierced cocks being replaced by solid ones decorated with engraving in the early nineteenth century. The continental makers usually restricted the decoration to the balance bridge.

Sizes of watches were fairly consistent during the period late seventeenth to early nineteenth centuries, the general tendency being towards a thinner watch, but with the verge escapement there is a limit to what can be done, and only improved escapements made this possible. This tendency was reversed by the French 'onion' watches of the late seventeenth and early eighteenth centuries, but French watches eventually settled down to more moderate sizes.

Enamelled cases were developed in the early seventeenth century and continued to be made until the nineteenth. Many people have collected watches for their enamelled cases alone, caring little about the movements inside them, and such pieces are still extremely popular. Indeed, it is fortunate that this has occurred, as many interesting movements have been preserved which, had they been housed in silver or gold cases, might have been scrapped for the sake of the precious metal. Many watches have been ruined for the sake of the balance cocks which have been used to make items of jewellery such as bangles or brooches, but even if an old watch is not in working order it should be preserved: even the functional parts of the mechanism have a beauty of their own.

Metal watch cases were at first the main items to be decorated and, of course, base metal ones have more frequently survived. The earliest cases protected the dials, as glasses did not come in until the seventeenth century, and some of the dial covers were perforated to allow the hand to be seen without opening the case. The minute hand was uncommon until after 1675. By this time, the watch had acquired something like its present-day appearance: circular with a pendant above the XII and designed for carrying in the pocket. The case was a pair case, i.e. the watch case proper contained the movement and glass but had an exposed winding hole at the back which was protected from dust by means of another hinged case without glass which snapped over the first one. And more than one outer case has sometimes been fitted. Outer cases were not always metal but might be tortoiseshell, shagreen (prepared skin), leather etc. Precious metal cases were often replaced in the eighteenth century by pinchbeck cases, composed of a copper-zinc alloy named after its inventor and claimed to be indistinguishable from gold.

The pair case was less popular on the Continent as many watches were made there which wound through the dial, rendering the outer case unnecessary. British makers after about 1830 began to abandon the outer case and add a hinged door to the back of the watch. Continental makers copied this and provided an inner door which contained keyholes for winding and hand setting, dial winding being abandoned, but British watches still had their hands set from the dial side as long as the full plate movement was used.

Jewels, which resist wear better than brass, are inserted in watch plates to form hard bearing surfaces for the pivots. The principle was invented by a Swiss, Facio, who applied for a patent in 1704. The craft of jewelling was long an English monopoly because the drilling and polishing of the jewels was formerly a difficult operation.

The nineteenth century brought in the factory-made watch which is usually extremely plain, and many were made on the Lepine principle whereby every wheel had its own removable cock. England did not take kindly to the factory system and the industry all but died. The Swiss captured the British market, to be challenged after 1860 by the Americans.

The American watches rapidly established a reputation for accuracy and were all built from interchangeable parts, greatly facilitating repair. English watches at the time were constructed in the rough (*ébauches*) and finished off by the vendor's workmen, each watch being an individual job and only the basic parts such as the wheels and barrel being interchangeable.

The final development of the watch during the nineteenth century was the provision of keyless work, which really only became popular after the abandonment of the fusees.

a) Watch, silver with gilt dial, inscribed Barnes in Dorcest *(Dorchester); England, 1600; 2" by 1½" (5.03 by 5.81 cm.).*

London is often assumed to have been the only place where watches were made in England in the early 17th century, but this example disproves that. The movement shares the hinge with the dial cover; previously, such movements were loose and could be tipped out into the hand. There are four lugs to locate the movement in its correct position in the case. The square aperture below VI may have originally held a date indicator. The little finial at the bottom of the case precludes its being carried in the pocket: it would have been worn on a chain round the neck. The single hand is stoutly made to allow the time to be corrected by the fingers, and it bears a long tail to distribute the load when this is being done. The narrow chapter ring is typical of the period.

b) Watch by the London maker, Edmund Bull, greatly resembling that by Barnes, Dorcest; England, c. 1600; 2" by 1½" (5.08 by 3.81 cm.).

This suggests a common origin, even at this early date. Later on, watches and clocks were produced in specialist workshops and only finished by the man whose name they bore, but no very early date for this practice has ever been established. The Bull watch lacks the finial but the general design closely corresponds to the previous example.

---

c) Watch, fanciful shape with rock crystal case, by Edward East (c. 1610–1693); London, England, c. 1635; lgth. 1¾" (4.45 cm.).

East was the most celebrated of the early English makers, and master of the Clockmakers' Company in 1645 and 1652. His career covers a period of great development in watchmaking, beginning about 1632 when they were still worn mainly for decoration, and ending after the balance spring and the minute hand were well established, with watches worn in the pocket, not round the neck.

This is an early example with splendid finish: even the ends of the pillars and the stud or 'pottance' bear a little design. It is not surprising that East became watchmaker to Charles I.

d) Watch, open to show movement, enamel decorated case (prob. French made), movement by East; London, England, c. 1640; dia. 1⅝" (4.13 cm.).

Although early, this is a step nearer the modern watch in appearance. The movement is circular, the cock is held by a screw, the pillars are of the Egyptian style favoured later in the 17th century and the support for the mainspring set-up is finer, having a worm gear with indicator disc instead of a simple ratchet. The old type of train is retained, containing one arbor fewer than watches made after the introduction of the balance spring.

Watches

English

a) *left: Movement of clock-watch in brass, by Thomas Chamberlain of Chelmsford; England, c. 1630-40; dia. 2″ (5.08 cm.).*
right: Dial side of case of the clock-watch showing delicate pierced work.

This family evinced high class work outside London at a comparatively early date, as with this fine specimen predating the introduction of the balance spring (hairspring). The balance cock is pinned on as is the count wheel. The latter has notches at increasing intervals to control the number of blows struck. The bell is inside the pierced case. The pillars are nicely turned and the border of the top plate decorated by engraving. The setting up mechanism for the going mainspring is missing; the striking mainspring has a decorated guard.

The cover serves the protective function of a glass, and can be opened by releasing the catch at the bottom. The design represents the Angel preventing Abraham from sacrificing Isaac; the head of the ram is shown at the left. The pendant is also decorated: the watch would be worn round the neck.

---

b) *Watch in brass by Simon Hackett (member Clockmakers' Company, 1632, and Master 1646, d. 1664); London, England, c. 1660; dia. 1½″ (3.81 cm.).*

This watch has certain modern features: the circular movement, the hinge shape (cf. Barnes and Bull watches) and though the balance cock is of the old type, fastened by a pin, the setting up of the spring is more sophisticated, having a worm gear with an indicator disc to show how far the worm has been moved. The edge of the plate bears a little engraving.

The alarm is fitted with stopwork (a pinion gearing with a segment of a toothed wheel) to prevent the spring being overwound. The pierced case contains the bell with the movement inside it.

c) *Watch by East; London, England, c. 1660; dia. 1¾″ (4.45 cm.).*

This watch shows further signs of the modern period. The hand, although single, is more delicately made and is set by a key. The watch is circular and has a glass over the dial, while below figure VI is a tiny catch for holding the movement in the case. The chapter ring is slender, suggesting the earlier part of the century, but is very legible.

'Pendulum watch' by Markwick, London, c. 1700.

a) left: Traveller's alarm watch in brass, by Daniel Quare; London, England, 17th century; dia. 2¼″ (5.72 cm.).
right: The Quare watch opened, showing the elaborate decoration of the movement; dia. 1¾″ (4.45 cm.).

Increases in travel and the use of coaches made alarm watches invaluable. This example has a pierced case for the bell to sound: the alarm is set by rotating the numbered disc in the centre of the dial. The bezel is split in the middle of the hinge above the figure XII to allow the glass to be snapped in, and the little catch at the figure VI fastens the movement in the case. The dial is calibrated for quarter and half hours only.

The alarm spring has no fusee and is guarded by a decorated and pierced piece of metal. Even the foot of the balance cock is pierced. The pillars are of the 'tulip' pattern fashionable in the late 17th century, after the so-called 'tulip mania' of the middle of the century. Note the extreme thickness of the watch and the somewhat small pendant and ring.

Watch with pierced case, by Daniel Quare, London, c. 1700.

---

b) Novelty watch, silver inner case, piqué outer case (silver and tortoiseshell with decorative pins), by Joseph Windmills (admitted to the Clockmakers' Company in 1671, Master in 1702); London, England, c. 1690; dia. 2″ (5.08 cm.).

The late 17th century produced a number of novelty watches. This example has the usual long minute hand, but the hours have been calibrated from VI to VI round a semi-circular opening in the upper half of the dial and are shown by a disc which rotates once in 24 hours bearing on one half a sun for the hours of the day and the other, a moon for the hours of the night. The aperture over the 30 minute mark is for the day of the month.

c) left: Watch in brass by George Etherington (Master of the Clockmakers' Company 1709); London, England, early 18th century; dia. 1⅝″ (4.13 cm.).
d) right: Watch in brass by J. Paulet; London, England, 1703; dia. 1¾″ (4.45 cm.).

Once the minute hand gained popularity, it was fashionable for the figures denoting every five minutes to be nearly as large as the hour figures. The practice began in the late 17th century and lasted well into the 18th. These two watches illustrate this feature. Note the very short hour hands and the inner track denoting half hours. The dials at this time were still metal, the plain white enamel ones coming much later. Many watches of this period had their dials replaced later by enamel ones. The pendants should be noted.

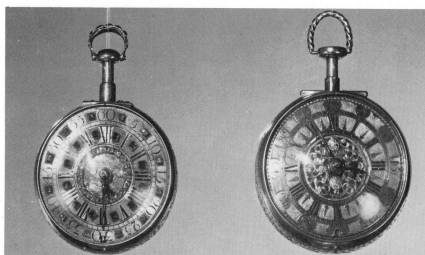

Watches

English

18TH–19TH CENTURY

a) *left: Brass repeating watch by Mudge & Dutton, made for Thomas Raikes (later Governor of the Bank of England, and for many years in his family); London, England, 1783; dia. 1⅜″ (3.49 cm.).*
right: The rear of the case, bearing the owner's initials; dia. 1⅞″ (4.76 cm.).

The repeating watch was designed to denote time in the dark by striking on bells or gongs when a slide was pushed or the pendant pressed in. This particular watch repeats the time to the nearest 'half quarter' i.e. 7½ minutes.

The foot of the balance cock is solid, the only pierced work appears in the table of the cock itself. It has the old form of disc regulator, operated by a key placed on the square in its centre. Despite extra mechanism for repetition, the type is seldom larger than ordinary watches.

It has a 'pair' or double case, but the front of the outer case is open and the glass in a bezel fitted to the inner case. Usually a paper was put in the outer case after a watch had been repaired and often several are found, mainly as advertisements for the repairer although some are in needlework (spoiling the title of 'paper') and were probably presents from the sweetheart or wife of the owner. These 'papers' also provided a soft bed for the watch.

---

b) *Movement by Barraud with cylinder escapement (usually associated with 19th century Swiss watches, though invented by George Graham of London); originally in 18 ct gold case; London, England, 1815; dia. 1⅝″ (4.13 cm.).*

The layout is similar to the usual verge watch, with the scapewheel parallel instead of at right angles to the plates, so that the cylinder escapement was sometimes called 'horizontal'. It was not widely used until the 19th century, allowing watches to be made thinner. Earlier English watches retained the fusee and the chain abandoned by 19th century Swiss makers in favour of the barrel with toothed periphery ('going barrel'), which made the movement smaller.

The encased cylinder is of sapphire to resist wear. The plainness of the movement is remarkable as watches of this period usually had some—if little—decoration.

c) *Movement of watch, plain, with only cock engraved, large jewel bearings, by Adam Burdess; Coventry, England, typical of late 19th century; dia. 1½″ (3.81 cm.).*

The lever escapement was usual for English watches a century ago, the layout of the movement still based on the earlier verge watches. The balance is compensated for temperature changes and fitted with screws in its rim for exact adjustment.

This movement possesses one unusual feature: the keyless work patented by Adam Burdess in 1869. The lever at the bottom left is worked to and fro to wind the watch though the hands are set by turning the milled disc below the lever, which is not the best of arrangements. The barrel containing the mainspring can be seen below the plate marked 'Coventry'.

Details of three watches c. 1760 illustrating variations in regulation indicators.

a) Gold watch with tourbillon, by Fordsmand; London, England, c. 1900; dia. 2" (5.08 cm.).

A watch tends to change its rate if its position is altered and the French maker, Breguet, devised the tourbillon to overcome this. The balance and escapement are mounted in a cage which revolves about once per minute, thereby tending to cancel the position errors. In the Karrusel, a later variation of the idea, the rate of rotation was much slower.

This watch is a late example of British craftsmanship. It has a tourbillon, compensated balance, overcoil balance spring, and is jewelled. The 'Maltese Cross' stopwork, limiting the winding of the spring, is more typical of Swiss work.

b) Early pocket chronometer with silver case by the firm of Barraud of Cornhill; London, England, c. 1797; dia. 2" (5.08 cm.).

For extra legibility there are two subsidiary dials for hours and seconds leaving only the minutes on the main dial. The seconds dial has each fourth division numbered, a feature which was not perpetuated. This chronometer was worn for over a year in 1962/63 and performed very well although it dates from 1797. The escapement is of the Arnold type which differs from the Earnshaw (*c* below). The bow (hanging loop) and the case hinge are characteristic of the period as is the legibility of the dial.

---

c) left: Pocket chronometer, brass dial and movement inscribed invenit et fecit; *by Thomas Earnshaw (1749-1829); London, England, early 19th century; dia. 2" (5.08 cm.).*
right: Movement of the Earnshaw pocket chronometer.

Accurate results obtained from marine chronometers inspired the making of pocket watches with the same escapement and compensated balances. Their timekeeping was extremely accurate but they were easily stopped. Indeed, it would seem illogical to wear such a delicate mechanism on the person when a marine chronometer, of much more robust construction, is contained in a stout box and mounted in gymbals to prevent disturbance or damage. Earnshaw is virtually responsible for the

marine chronometer of today.

The movement is plain except for some engraving on the balance cock. It contrasts with the usual verge watch movement of the period; note the absence of a regulator; a chronometer was too delicate to be adjusted by its owner and was returned to the maker if its performance was unsatisfactory.

The balance has trapezium-shaped weights which are moved inwards or outwards by temperature changes acting on the bimetallic rim of the balance and cancelling the effect of the same change in temperature on the balance as a whole. Note the wire restraining one weight from flying off.

Chronometers

English
19TH CENTURY

a) *Pocket chronometer movement, silver case, hall-marked 1825, by Earnshaw; London, England, 1825; dia. 2" (5.08 cm.).*

This is another example by Earnshaw, made near the end of his career (d. 1829). There are no wires for restraining the weights on the rim of the balance. Only the balance cock bears decoration and that is in the form of engraving. Pierced work was much less popular at this period, and when seen is usually on verge watches that were more traditional in design than those with the new precision escapements.

b) *Marine chronometer, with brass and mahogany case, by Jas McCabe; London, England, mid-19th century; dia. 4" (10.7 cm.).*

This typical marine chronometer is mounted in gymbals in a stout mahogany box with brass corners to protect it at sea.

The first maker named James McCabe died in 1811 and his business was carried on under the same name by his descendants till 1883, making it difficult to date any given piece.

The seconds dial is large and clear. Beside the figure XII is an indicator to show if the chronometer needs winding. It is imperative that a chronometer should not stop at sea. The key is kept in the top right hand corner of the case.

Watches

German

c) *Watch movement of iron with gilt metal case; Germany, c. 1550; dia. 2" (5.08 cm.).*

The earliest watch movements were iron and somewhat roughly finished; then, decoration was applied only to the cases.

In Germany, the varying power of the spring was usually modified by a brake ('Stackfreed') which is shown here. The arbor for the spring has a pinion which meshes with a wheel carrying a special cam. Some of this wheel's edge is uncut to limit the turns of the pinion and thereby the winding of the spring. The roller is pressed against the edge of the cam by its spring, resisting it when fully wound, aiding it when nearly run down.

d) *Carriage watch in brass; German, c. 1700; dia. 3" (7.62 cm.).*

This example is decorated with repoussé (i.e. a design beaten out from the back of the metal), and fitted with an alarm set by turning the centre disc until the desired hour comes opposite the tail of the hour hand. Four holes in the disc will take a steel point to assist in this operation. Between 55 and 60 is a slot with a peg marked 'S' and 'N' (*schlagen, nicht schlagen*—'strike' and 'silent'). Quarter hours are not marked on the inner ring of the dial but diamond marks in the minute track indicate 'half quarters'.

a) Cruciform watch in silver, embossed and gilt, brass movement; France, c. 1630; dia. 2½″ (6.35 cm.).

The earliest watches were probably drum-shaped; later, cases were made in the form of stars, animals, books and other objects, such as the cross shown here. Note the substantial hinge and the lugs to locate the movement in the case. The dial has a narrow chapter ring and a tasteful hour hand. Its centre design consists of four cherubs representing the four winds; the rest of the dial is decorated with religious motifs. The watch has an outer leather case.

b) Watch in brass by Pierre Duhamel; Paris, France (and Geneva), early 17th century; dia. 1⅝″ (4.13 cm.).

This watch has no balance spring, regulation being effected by increasing or decreasing the tension of the mainspring using the worm at the top of the movement. The case is enamelled, but the movement plainer than those later in the century and the cock for holding the balance has pierced feet longer than on later movements.

c) Watch in brass (anon.); France, last half 17th century; dia. 1½″ (3.81 cm.).

The case is enamelled inside and out, and the movement decorated with pierced work; the pillars are of the 'tulip' type fashionable at the time. The balance is held by a bridge, not a cock.

d) Thick watch, called 'oignon' (onion), with silver gilt rim; by De Lisle; Paris, France, late 17th century; dia. 2¼″ (5.72 cm.).

This is a late example with two hands—many have only one. Most of these watches are time-pieces, but this one repeats hours and quarters; the case is pierced so the bell can be heard clearly. The one-piece enamel dial has a hump at each hour figure and a hole at 4 o'clock to allow winding through the dial (common in continental watches). The 'glass' is rock crystal and very high—no less than 11 mm.—making the whole watch 38 mm. thick.

Watches

French

Swiss

a) left: Breguet lever watch in gold; France, c. 1830; dia. 2″ (5.08 cm.).

The work of Breguet is characterized by plainness and neatness and this lever watch is a good example. The narrow chapter ring and the matted background to the dial make for good legibility, and the hands are plain and form a good contrast. This pattern of hand is often known as a 'Breguet' hand.

The style *Breguet et Fils* (below the seconds dial) was adopted in 1816 and therefore this watch can be dated after that year. The thinness of the case should be noted.

right: Movement of the Breguet lever watch.

At this period, English makers were producing thick movements with fusees and a certain amount of decoration on them: this one is devoid of anything that is not absolutely functional.

The balance is compensated for temperature changes and the balance spring is of the 'Breguet' type, whereby the outer coil is bent to a smaller diameter and fastened at a point higher than the rest of the spring. The spring then expands and contracts on both sides and relieves the balance pivots of side pressure. Note the shape of the securing screws at the edge of the movement.

---

b) left: Enamel dial of watch by Nicolet Monnier (unlisted); Switzerland, early 19th century; dia. 2″ (5.08 cm.).

Among the features typical of the period are the Arabic figures, the 'Breguet' hands, and the holes for winding through the dial. Note also the minute divisions with triangular marks for the quarter hours and special marks showing the other 5-minute intervals.

right: Movement of the Monnier watch; dia. 1¾″ (4.45 cm.).

Even complicated examples of continental movements were comparatively plain by the early 19th century. This is a clock watch, i.e. it strikes the hours in regular progression and is also a repeater. The striking can be set to give hours only, or hours and quarters *grande sonnerie*, where the number of blows for the preceding hour is sounded at every quarter, before the blows denoting the quarter. The striking can also be silenced. The escapement of this watch is the little-used 'virgule', which includes a piece shaped like the tail of a comma.

The balanced bridge is supported by a screw at each side and the stopwork consists of a finger which engages with a wheel having only part of its edge cut into teeth (used to prevent overwinding). The dial for regulation has a square to take a key which moves the indicator between 'A' and 'R'—*avance & retard* ('fast' and 'slow').

*a) Watch movement by Larpent and Jurgensen;
Copenhagen, Denmark, early 19th century; dia. 1½″
(3.81 cm.).*

The firm was founded in Roskilde in 1780,
continuing into the 19th century. This movement
by them is interesting for being a full plate watch
without a fusee; also it is wound through the dial.

The extreme plainness of the movement contrasts with watches made in other countries at the
period, as its purpose is purely functional. The
thick plates give good bearing surfaces to the pivots
and are fastened to the pillars by screws instead of
being pinned.

*b) Watch movement by Larpent and Jurgensen; early
19th century; dia. 1½″ (3.81 cm.).*

This example is more typical of French or Swiss
work. A fusee is provided and the bridge supporting the balance is decorated with pierced work;
winding is done through the dial.

The top plate of the movement is thick but
unlike the preceding example, it is pinned on; its
thickness makes jewelled bearings less essential.
The engraving of the name is very distinctive as is
the catch at the bottom for securing the movement
in the case. There is no separate bar for supporting
the barrel.

---

c) left: Silver watch marked Copenhagen, *by Jules
Jurgensen; Denmark, c. 1860; dia. 2″ (5.08 cm.).
right: Movement of the same watch.*

Urban Jurgensen (1776–1830) was the most
famous of the watchmaking family. His son Jules
founded a factory at Le Locle, producing high
quality watches: this example is very pleasing
having no unnecessary ornament and a clear
dignified dial. Note the large seconds dial for extra
legibility, and the slide near the figure III for

operating the repeating mechanism.

It has a chronometer escapement with a pivoted
detent, but is classed as a watch because of its
repeating work (top left hand corner of movement). The balance spring is of the Breguet overcoil
type and again unlike a chronometer, there is a
regulator bearing the words 'Fast' and 'Slow' in
English; also this movement is built up of separate
bars whereas a marine chronometer has the full
plate type with the balance above.

Barometers
Introduction

The barometer originated in 1643 when the Italian scientist Torricelli, a pupil of Galileo, took a glass tube of about 36″ (91.4 cm.) long and filled it with mercury. By placing his finger over the open end and inserting the tube into a container of mercury he found that on removing his finger the tube remained full to a height of about 28″ (71.1 cm.) above the surface in the container. The space between the top of the mercury and the end of the tube was a vacuum, later called the Torricellian vacuum. This space tends to fill with mercury vapour, but the effect on the reading of the instrument is negligible.

The outer surface of the tube which is immersed in the container or cistern always carries a very thin layer of air with it; this air may eventually creep into the tube as a result of the up and down movement of the mercury and penetrate the Torricellian vacuum, causing the instrument to give a false reading. Over a long period, the readings become less and less accurate, and many amateur scientists have compiled records over the years which thus lose value the later they are made.

When the mercury in the tube falls, the surface in the cistern rises and vice versa: consequently the true reading of the barometer will not be shown. This can be allowed for by making the divisions on the scales fractionally smaller or by making the scale movable. The main scale is often furnished with a Vernier scale to give a more accurate reading. The diagonal barometer was intended to serve this purpose, but the Vernier scale can overcome the problem quite exactly enough for domestic use.

Another variation of the original idea was the wheel barometer (siphon barometer) where the tube was bent to a J shape, one arm being very short and having a small weight floating on the mercury. The weight was attached to a cord which ran over a pulley and terminated in a counterbalance weight at the other side. Any difference in the level of mercury caused the weight to rise or fall and thereby move a hand over a dial by means of the cord and pulley. This magnified the movement of the mercury level but could stick, hence the practice of tapping the barometer before taking a reading. The difference in level of a wheel barometer gives a less accurate reading, for a drop of one inch (2.54 cm.) in the height of the mercury column as measured by a cistern barometer actually involves a drop of half an inch (1.27 cm.) in the long tube and a rise of half an inch in the short one. This is sometimes compensated for by having a large bulb on the top of the long tube which enlarges the surface of the mercury so that practically all the variation in height takes place in the short limb.

The aneroid barometer, invented about 1850, can be made as small as a pocket watch. Many made for domestic use have a frame shaped like that of the wheel barometer, as the stem is a convenient place to mount a thermometer. The principle of the aneroid is to record the expansion and contraction of a metal box which has been exhausted of air, and magnify the movements by a series of levers which operate a pointer on a dial. Once again, the instrument should be tapped before reading.

A barometer with a dial usually has an indicator to be set each time it is read, and so gives the day to day variation. Occasionally, barometers without dials will have a sliding pointer to indicate daily readings or a special manual dial is provided.

The barometer's main use in the home has been as a weather predictor, but the words, 'Rain, Change, Fair' etc. are somewhat misleading. In order to predict the weather, other factors such as temperature and direction and strength of the wind have to be taken into account. It is also more important to note whether the mercury is rising or falling than its exact height. The Fitzroy barometer (p. 263*d*) was designed to state simply the basic rules for predicting weather, and the paper included the famous words 'Long Foretold, Long Last; Short Notice, Soon Past'.

Before the days of radio and television, the barometer was a much more important instrument in the home than it is today when weather forecasts are regularly broadcast. It took its place with the clocks that indicated the phases of the moon, high water at a certain port or the day of the month, and many of the early clockmakers also made barometers. The instruments' cases often resembled clock cases.

*a) Lacquered barometer, oak; England, c. 1700; ht. 36"
(91 cm.).*

The case of this barometer is a pleasant piece of
turning, and the shape well calculated to protect
the glass tube inside. It is a little early for the lacquer
finish which may have been applied later. The dial
contains two pointers for indicating two daily
variations and the wording is 'Rising Fair or
Frost/Dry Serene, Variable, Falling Rain Snow or
Wind/Rainy Stormy'. There is no thermometer.

The three finials suggest the hood decorations
of a contemporary long case clock, and the frame
of the dial bears a little carving.

*b) Wheel barometer, walnut veneer on oak, by John
Hallifax of Barnsley; England, early 18th century;
ht. 52" (132 cm.).*

Hallifax (1695-1750) was a clockmaker; this
barometer is inscribed with his name and marked
'*Invenit et Fecit*' (invented and made). The case indicates that it was perhaps made to match a clock.

The brass dial has the early 18th century spandrels; the maker's name plaque and the hand are
both typical of clock work of the period. The dial
half way down the trunk is for recording the daily
variations, the inches being divided into ten parts,
and there is also a circle of thirty numbers to record
the day of the month.

*c) Wheel barometer, walnut veneer on pine, by John
Hallifax of Barnsley, England, c. 1826-50; ht. 40"
(102 cm.).*

This bears the same inscription as Hallifax's
earlier example.

The two dials have the same graduation, an
inner ring with the numbers 1-30 and an outer
ring with only 28-31. The present reading of the
barometer is given by the upper dial and this is set
by hand on the lower one. The following day this
will provide a record to compare any variation in
height.

*d) Siphon barometer, lacquer on oak, by Isaac Robilou;
London, England, 1719; ht. 38" (97 cm.).*

A barometer decorated with lacquer is very
unusual, especially when it dates from early in the
period when this finish was popular. Latin was
fashionable at the time: note the inscription; the
dial has English also. The thermometer has a very
long tube, but is calibrated only up to temperatures
usual in Britain, the highest called 'Excessive Hot
Weather', the lowest 'Excessive Cold'. Zero is at
the zone marked 'Temperate Weather' and lower
temperatures are shown by an increase in the
number of degrees of cold: this instrument was
made before the Fahrenheit scale was devised.

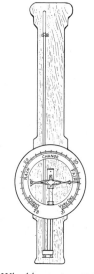

*Wheel barometer, 1924.
Type attributed to Robert
Hooke, 1664.*

261

Barometers

English

a) Diagonal barometer, mahogany; England, 1753; ht. 40″ (102 cm.).

The diagonal barometer cannot be truly symmetrical but an attempt has been made here to produce an instrument that would blend with the decor of a room. The thermometer and barometer tubes balance each other, and the intervening space is filled with a table giving all kinds of information such as the Dominical letter, date of Easter, sovereigns of England, etc.

Various adjustable indicators are provided to show high water at London Bridge, day of the week, day of the month, zodiac signs, fixed feasts, etc.—information reminiscent of that supplied by the elaborate astronomical clocks of mediaeval cathedrals.

b) Carved mahogany barometer with enamel plaques; England, late 18th century; ht. 40″ (102 cm.).

The dial's wording is fuller than usual: 'Settled, Fair or Frost, Changeable, Dry, Doubtful, Wet, Settled, Rain Snow or Wind'; an ornate hand records the day to day variation. The lettering and figures suggest that of early painted iron clock dials.

The very thick tube of this barometer—exposed for most of its length—makes it more vulnerable. The shape of the case is similar to that of a long case clock, though the carving style suggests a later period. There is no thermometer. Unfortunately, this instrument is not signed, though its likely origin is the North of England.

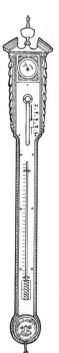

Carved mahogany barometer by H. Pyefinch, London; late 18th century.

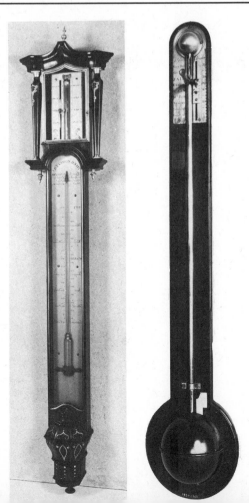

c) Barometer and thermometer in mahogany inlaid with brass, by G. Adams at Tycho Brahe's Head in Fleet Street; London, England, 1760; ht. 36″ (91 cm.).

This very neat instrument anticipates later fashions. It has very legible scales, including a Vernier for measuring the exact height of the mercury in the barometer tube. The dials for the barometer and thermometer reading have a glass for extra protection, and the two flanking pillars protect the door from being accidentally opened. The wording of the dial is simple, in keeping with the general design of the instrument: 'Fair/Frost, Variable, Rain/Snow'. The thermometer dial indicates 32° as 'Just Freezing'.

d) Fixed cistern barometer, mahogany, by J. Sisson; London, England, c. 1800; ht. 38″ (97 cm.).

Here is a barometer intended more for scientific use. The case is plain and functional and there is a small brass tube with a lens for reading the mercury level very accurately. This is coupled to the Vernier scale and moves with it.

Note the spherical container for the cistern and the brass cover for the top of the tube. The dial is silvered. Although the wording is similar to that on a modern barometer, the last two items read 'Fair if a Rise, Foul if a Fall'.

a) Diagonal barometer, mahogany, by one of the clock-making Finney family; Liverpool, England, early 19th century; ht. 34″ (86 cm.).

If the top of a barometer tube is bent over at an angle slightly inclined to the horizontal just above the 27″ (68.6 cm.) level, a rise of 1″ (2.54 cm.) in the mercury will be spread over several inches of the tube and a more exact reading can be obtained. The diagonal barometer was useful for scientific readings, but its lack of symmetry made it unpopular for domestic use.

This example shows 28″ (71.1 cm.) as 'Stormy' and 31″ (78.7 cm.) as 'Drought', both exaggerations. Diagonal barometers were more popular in the early 18th century: later, such exactness could be obtained by using a Vernier scale.

b) Cistern barometer, mahogany, by J. Ayscough; London, England, c. 1800; ht. 40″ (102 cm.).

The elaborate carving on this barometer would suggest the period after the Great Exhibition, but the lettering and figures on the scales and the carving of the sun over the cistern point to an earlier date. The thermometer is calibrated up to the boiling point of water, which seems unnecessary, and temperatures such as 'Spirits Boil', 'Fever Heat', and 'Water Freezing' are quoted on the scale.

The maker's name appears at the top of both barometer and thermometer scales. The Vernier is adjusted with a knob at the right side of the case.

Barometers

English

c) Marine barometer, mahogany; England, 1820; ht. 36″ (91 cm.).

A marine barometer must be protected from the movement of the ship which might cause damage; it would also give a false reading if not truly vertical. Usually, the tube is encased in a wooden box which is left closed except when a reading is taken. This example has the thermometer on the inside of the door which gives access to the scale.

It can be hung from the top ring, its own weight keeping it vertical, but in very strong seas would have to be fastened down; the holes half way down are for supporting it by means of gymbals.

d) Fitzroy barometer, oak; England, 1860; ht. 45″ (114 cm.).

Robert Fitzroy (1805-65) who retired from active service in the Royal Navy in 1850 was appointed Meteorological Officer to the Board of Trade in 1854. He is remembered for the cheap and serviceable barometer he designed which not only registered the height of the mercury, but gave simple notes on the type of weather to be expected from other factors taken into account at the same time: two movable pointers showed the height of the mercury at 10 a.m. yesterday and at 10 a.m. today. The instrument included a storm gauge and a thermometer graduated up to 120° F.

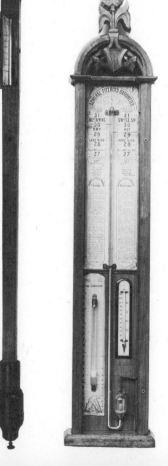

Barometers
French

a) Wheel barometer, ormolu with Sèvres plaques, by Passemant au Louvre; Paris, France, early 18th century; ht. 40″ (102 cm.).

The carved fruit and coloured plaques may suggest an article made for decoration, but the large legible dial confirms the instrument's purpose. The dial is calibrated in French inches, 27 to 29, divided into *douzièmes* (12ths). The indicator is very functional and the hand for recording the daily variation is correctly subordinated to it. This barometer's shape is original, tending to minimize its height.

b) Wheel barometer in boulle and ormolu; France, early 18th century; ht. 40″ (102 cm.).

Here, an attempt has been made to vary the traditional style of the wheel barometer with a dial of unconventional shape. It is decorated with small coloured sprigs and flowers. The instrument is apparently intended as an article of furniture, for there are no figures to give the height of the mercury despite the very long thermometer tube, only three plaques to indicate weather and a small dial showing possible wind direction. The S-shaped indicator hand for the daily variation is redundant in this instance.

c) Cistern barometer in tulip and kingwood with gilt brass mounts, by Lange de Bourbon; France, mid-18th century; ht. 40″ (102 cm.).

This instrument is very plain by contemporary French standards—probably a reaction after the rococo period. The maker's name appears on the enamel plate which has a little foliage decoration and divisions that are not numbered. Note the graceful bronze mounts, particularly that covering the cistern, and the way the graining of the veneer follows the outline of the cistern and the plate, providing a decorative background. There is no provision for recording daily variations.

d) Wheel barometer in casuarina wood and bronze, chased and gilt; France, mid-18th century; ht. 36″ (91 cm.).

This example is in the shape that became so well known in the 19th century, but differs in having the bronze mounts applied in accordance with the French principle of a century earlier, that all furniture in a room including clocks and barometers, should match.

The thermometer tube is extremely long and is graduated beyond the range of temperature normally needed in Europe; perhaps it was intended for use in a tropical climate, or done for purely artistic reasons. The dial is graduated in French inches. The adjustable S-shaped pointer does not obscure the reading of the index.

Opposite:
OG weight-driven clock by E. N. Welch of Forestville, Connecticut; U.S.A., c. 1870.

Clocks, Watches and Barometers Glossary

Clocks and Watches

ANCHOR: The escapement used in pendulum clocks from c. 1675 onwards, taking its name from the shape of the pallets.

ARBOR: A horological term for axle.

BALANCE: A bar or wheel which oscillates and allows the escapement to function, at the same time controlling the speed. The pendulum is the clock's modern counterpart of this. The earliest clocks had bar or wheel balances.

BALANCE WHEEL: The scapewheel of a verge watch. Not to be confused with 'balance'.

BARREL: A drum containing a spring or, in a long case clock, the drum on which the gut lines are wound. On a chiming clock the drum on which the pins for lifting the hammers are mounted.

BEZEL: Metal frame around the glass of a clock or watch.

BOB: The weight on the end of the pendulum; its actual weight has no significance in timekeeping, only its distance from the point of suspension.

BRACKET CLOCK: An English spring driven clock, mid-17th to 19th centuries. As these clocks are not usually stood on a bracket the name is inappropriate though it has now become common usage.

BRIDGE: Metal support with two feet—used in watch movements, especially by European makers, to support the balance.

CHAPTER RING: The circular band on the dial which contains the figures.

COCK: In a clock this is (a) the bracket which supports the pendulum or (b) a support with only one foot. In a watch, it is the bracket which protects and covers the balance.

COUNT WHEEL: A wheel with notches in its edge at increasing intervals that controls the number of blows struck.

DETENT: Catch by which striking is regulated.

ESCAPEMENT: A device which allows the last wheel in the going train to escape one tooth at a time. It is controlled by the balance or pendulum to which it gives impulse to keep it going. The escapements mostly in use in antique clocks are the anchor and verge which cause a recoil as each tooth is caught. The Graham escapement is dead beat i.e. no recoil. In watches the lever, cylinder and duplex escapements are all dead beat.

FLY: The last piece in the striking train, this revolving vane controls the rate of striking.

FOLIOT: A bar balance used in the earliest clocks in connection with the verge escapement. At the end are a number of small grooves giving alternative positions for the small weights which are used for regulation.

FUSEE: A piece of metal shaped like a truncated cone with the base extended, round which a spiral groove is cut to take a gut line or chain. It is used to equalize the power of the mainspring in connection with the barrel.

GOING BARREL: A barrel with teeth round its edge to mesh directly with the train in cases where no fusee is fitted.

LEVER ESCAPEMENT: Invented c. 1758 by Thomas Mudge, its importance being that the balance was left free for the majority of its swing, allowing it to fulfil its role as controller.

LIFTING PIECE: A lever which controls the release or locking of the striking.

LIGHTFOOT, PETER: It was long believed that the clocks of Wells Cathedral, Wimborne Minster, Ottery St. Mary Church and Exeter Cathedral were made by a monk of this name.

MOTION WORK: The gearing behind the dial which causes the hour hand to rotate once in 12 hours and the minute hand once every hour.

OG and OOG: A name applied to certain German and American clock cases because the front moulding is shaped in an ogee curve.

PALLETS: The steel surfaces which interrupt the passage of the scapewheel teeth, giving impulse to the balance or pendulum. Sometimes the term is applied to the anchor-shaped piece of which the two pallets form a part.

PENDULUM: The suspended body in a clock which regulates and controls the movement of the works; it consists of a rod and 'bob' (q.v.).

Compensation—in a pendulum allows for the effects of changes in temperature on its operation by various means, one of which is:

The Gridiron—a pendulum composed of alternate brass and steel rods: the differing rates of expansion compensate for any change in the length of the pendulum as a whole, which would affect the timekeeping.

PINION: In theory, a wheel with fewer than 20 teeth. The name is sometimes applied to the pinion and the arbor that bears it. The teeth of a pinion are called 'leaves'. In the train of a clock or watch each wheel except the scapewheel drives a pinion. In the motion work the reverse is the case.

PIVOT: The end of an arbor made to smaller diameter to run in a hole in the frame, forming a bearing surface. Pivots should bear a high polish to minimize friction.

RACK AND SNAIL: Invented by Edward Barlow, 1676, this is a method of controlling the number of blows struck so that it always corresponds to the position of the hour hand and can be used for repeating. The snail is a cam that travels with the hour hand and allows the rack to

Clocks, Watches and Barometers Glossary (contd.)

fall a certain distance, corresponding to the hour shown. When the clock strikes, one tooth of the rack is gathered up for every blow struck.

SCAPEWHEEL: The last wheel of the going train of a watch or clock that operates the escapement.

SPANDREL: A corner ornament of a clock dial.

TABLE CLOCK: A spring driven clock of the 15th-17th centuries usually in a metal case. Sometimes the dial is placed horizontally on top.

Barometers

ANEROID BAROMETER: One where the pressure of air is measured by its action on the elastic lid of a box exhausted of air, as opposed to:

CISTERN BAROMETER: Where a straight tube filled with mercury, and closed at the top, is inverted with its end in a small container of mercury; the mean height of the mercury is the indicator of the air pressure.

SIPHON BAROMETER: Has a curved tube, J-shaped, with the mercury in the shorter limb exposed to the air.

TIMEPIECE: A clock that does not strike.

TRAIN: A set of wheels and pinions gearing with each other to motivate 'going', 'striking', etc.

VERGE: A long spindle provided with 2 pallets that are alternately moved by the scapewheel in the verge escapement. In America the term is also used to denote the anchor.

VERNIER SCALE: A short movable scale which enables minute measurements to be taken; it was invented in 1631 by Paul Vernier.

WHEEL BAROMETER: An adaptation of the siphon barometer where the mercury in the shorter limb has a float placed upon it with a cord attached which passes over a pulley; as the float rises or falls, it moves the indicating hand of the circular dial.

Repairs and Maintenance

Clocks, watches and barometers are delicate instruments which cannot function properly if neglected. It must be stressed that they should never be taken apart or repaired except by a properly skilled person, for ignorance can cause very expensive damage or ruin a piece forever. Skilled work nowadays is not cheap, and there is a shortage of craftsmen to carry it out, so the temptation to employ unskilled labour is all the greater.

Maintenance is essential for all kinds of machinery and while people will regularly have their cars serviced, they begrudge this expense for a clock or a watch. This is false economy. If timekeepers are properly maintained, they will last virtually forever.

However good the quality of oil used, it will eventually dry up, leaving a residue that will grind away pivots, and therefore watches should be cleaned every two years or so with a slightly longer interval for clocks. After cleaning, it will usually be necessary to adjust the regulation again. Gut lines can become dry and fray, and they should be kept moist with a little neat's foot oil. Oil should not be applied to the movements. Let the repair man do this. Only special clock or watch oil should be used, and this should be applied to pivots and pallets only. The teeth of the wheels are designed to run dry. The old trick of keeping a rag soaked in paraffin in the bottom of the case achieves absolutely nothing.

Uncontrolled central heating can cause problems with furniture of all kinds, clocks and barometers included: a dry atmosphere may cause wood to crack, and precautions with the cases of clocks and barometers should be the same as for other antique furniture. Always watch for any signs of woodworm and take action as soon as fresh holes or dust are discovered. The insides of clock cases should always be kept clean and the outsides of clock and barometer cases protected with a good wax polish. Use modern polishes only on modern furniture! As with movements, repairs to the cases of antique clocks and barometers should be left to an expert.

Fakes and Forgeries

Inevitably there are many clocks and watches in circulation which are not what they seem to be. From the mid-seventeenth century, English work was the most highly esteemed and consequently many pieces were produced on the Continent with the signatures of English makers of repute. A particular favourite was Daniel Quare, and many pieces of obvious continental origin bear his name. Breguet of Paris was also a great target for the forger. Many forged watches were made in Switzerland and Holland; for instance, a watch with a scalloped minute hand bearing the name of an English maker immediately makes one suspect a Dutch origin.

Of course, the important thing to remember is that any early forgery was produced with contemporary tools and materials, using contemporary methods, and such a piece is therefore interesting in itself. A specialized collection of forgeries could be made, ranging from the mid-seventeenth to the late nineteenth century.

It is present day work in faking and forging that gives the most concern. Forged watches are less popular than clocks because there is less skilled labour available to make them and clocks are easier to produce. A very clever fake is most difficult to detect because the faker will have paid special attention to the workmanship and material as well as the design. The colour of the brass, the profiles of the teeth, the finish of the steelwork and the engraving will all have received attention. After the clock has been made, signs of wear in a 'life' of, say, two hundred years have to be produced and special techniques are available for this purpose.

An easier form of deception is to take a genuine old clock by a lesser-known maker and re-engrave the name of a famous maker on it. The forger is assisted in this by the fact that the number of engravers and dial makers was limited and they were patronized by both the well-known and lesser-known clockmakers.

The only safeguard against fakes and forgeries is intensive study: the more one sees of top quality pieces that can be authenticated, the easier it is to detect something that is not right.

Further Reading

Clocks and Watches

BAILLIE, G. H. *Watchmakers and Clockmakers of the World*, London, 1963.

BASSERMANN-JORDAN, E. VON. Fully revised by H. von Bertele. *The Book of Old Clocks and Watches*. London and New York, 1964.

BEESON, C. F. C. *Clockmaking in Oxfordshire 1400–1850*. Oxford, 1967.

BELLCHAMBERS, J. K. *Devonshire Clockmakers*. London 1962. *Somerset Clockmakers*. London, 1968.

BRADBURY, F. *British and Irish Silver Assay Office Marks*. Sheffield.

BRITTEN, F. J. *Old Clocks and Watches and their Makers*, sixth edition, London and New York, 1933.
Old Clocks and Watches and their Makers, seventh edition, extensively revised by G. H. Baillie and others. London and New York, 1956.

BRUTON, E. *The Long Case Clock*. London 1964; New York, 1968.
Clocks and Watches, 1400–1900. London and New York, 1967.
Clocks and Watches. London, 1968.

CAMERER CUSS, T. P. *The Country Life Book of Watches*. London, 1967.

CLUTTON, C., and DANIELS, G. *Watches*. London and Centerville, Mass., 1965.

DANIELS, G. *English and American Watches*. New York, 1967.

DINSDALE, REV. N. V. *The Old Clockmakers of Yorkshire*. Clapham, Lancs., 1946.

DREPPERD, C. W. *American Clocks and Clockmakers*. New York, 1947.

DROST, W. E. *Clocks and Watches of New Jersey*. Elizabeth, New Jersey, 1966.

DRUMMOND ROBERTSON, J. *The Evolution of Clockwork*. Wakefield, 1972.

EDEY, W. *French Clocks*. New York, 1967; London, 1968.

EDWARDES, E. L. *The Grandfather Clock*, Altrincham, 1971.
Weight Driven Chamber Clocks of the Middle Ages and the Renaissance. Altrincham, 1965.

FENNELL, G. *A List of Irish Watch and Clock Makers*. Dublin, 1963.

GORDON, G. F. C. *Clockmaking Past and Present*. Kingston Hill, Surrey, 1948.

JAGGER, C. *Paul Philip Barraud*. London, 1968.

JOY, E. T. *The Country Life Book of Clocks*. London, 1967.

LEE, R. A. *The Knibb Family, Clockmakers*. Byfleet, 1964.

LLOYD, A. H. *The Collector's Dictionary of Clocks*. London, 1964, Cranbury N.J., 1966.
Old Clocks. London, 1970.

Clocks, Watches and Barometers
Further Reading (contd.)

LOOMES, B. *Yorkshire Clockmakers*. Clapham, Lancs., 1972.

MILES BROWN, H. *Cornish Clocks and Clockmakers*. Newton Abbot, 1970.

PALMER, B. *The Book of American Clocks*. New York, 1967. *A Treasury of American Clocks*. New York, 1968.

PEATE, I. C. *Clock and Watch Makers in Wales*. Cardiff, 1960.

REES, A. *Ree's Clocks, Watches and Chronometers (1819-20) a selection from the Cyclopaedia*. Newton Abbot and Rutland Vt, 1970.

ROBERTS, K. *The Contribution of Joseph Ives to Connecticut Clock Technology*. Bristol, Conn., 1970.

ROYER-COLLARD, F. B. *Skeleton Clocks*. London 1970.

SYMONDS, R. W. *Thomas Tompion—His Life and Work*. Feltham, Middx.

TYLER, E. J. *European Clocks*. London, 1968; New York, 1969.
The Craft of the Clockmaker. London, 1973.

WARD, F. A. B. *Time Measurement*. London, 1966.

Barometers

BELL, G. H., and E. F. *Old English Barometers*. Winchester, 1952.

GOODISON, N. *English Barometers 1680-1860*. New York, 1968; London, 1969.

MIDDLETON, W. E. K. *The History of the Barometer*. Baltimore, 1964.

Museum Collections

Great Britain

CAMBRIDGESHIRE: Fitzwilliam Museum, Cambridge.

ESSEX: Colchester Museum.

HAMPSHIRE: Willis Museum, Basingstoke.

LANCASHIRE: City of Liverpool Museum.

LEICESTERSHIRE: Newarke Houses Museum, Leicester.

LINCOLNSHIRE: Usher Collection, Lincoln.

LONDON: British Museum; Guildhall; London Museum; National Maritime Museum, Greenwich; Science Museum; Victoria and Albert Museum; Wallace Collection.

NORFOLK: Bridewell Museum, Norwich.

OXFORD: Ashmolean Museum; Museum of the History of Science.

SUFFOLK: Gershom Parkington Collection, Bury St. Edmunds.

SUSSEX: Hove Museum.

YORKSHIRE: Tolson Museum, Huddersfield.

SCOTLAND: Royal Scottish Museum, Edinburgh.

WALES: St. Fagans Welsh Folk Museum.

U.S.A.

CALIFORNIA: California Academy of Science, San Francisco.

CONNECTICUT: American Clock and Watch Museum, Bristol; Clockshop, Mystic Seaport.

HAWAII: Bernice P. Bishop Museum, Honolulu.

ILLINOIS: Hunter Collection, Springfield; Time Museum, Rockford (formerly Denver, Colorado).

MICHIGAN: Henry Ford Museum, Dearborn.

NEW YORK: Metropolitan Museum of Art, New York City.

PENNSYLVANIA: Franklin Institute Museum, Philadelphia; NAWCC Museum, Columbia.

TEXAS: Old Clock Museum, Pharr.

WASHINGTON D.C.: Smithsonian Institution.

Index

a   b   c   d

Embroidery and Needlework

Embroidery is the decoration of material, and, unlike tapestry with which it is often confused, has no existence without a basic fabric. It is a craft which has flourished for several thousand years, and the Book of Exodus in the Old Testament refers in detail to the work of seamsters and embroiderers. It is not too much to suggest that the craft stems from the time when animal skins were first sewn together with the stitches forming a pattern.

It is infinite in variety, ranging from stitchery so fine that it has to be held up to the light to be seen, to work in vivid colours in thick rug wool on hessian. It has been and is practised by men and women, rich and poor, professional and amateur with the minimum of equipment. In fact, it is probably this immense versatility which has prevented embroidery from being collected and enjoyed except by the percipient few. There is just too much variety. The range includes ecclesiastical vestments and church furnishings, dress and accessories, domestic articles, coverings for furniture, stage decorations and curtains, enormous wall coverings for office foyers and purely decorative hangings and panels for the house. An incomplete list, but already formidable in extent.

As embroidery is not seen in isolation, but is usually part of another craft such as furniture or dress, it follows that it changes and develops according to the current fashion. Thus, it varies in both style and technique according to the period and the country it comes from.

Embroidery is sometimes an art as well as a craft, and the combination of designer/craftsman in one person often produces superb results; but in general it is a craft which has been practised by generations of ordinary men and women, and in some part it is the history of the lives they led.

Opposite:
Very fine man's embroidered night-cap; England, 18th century.

Embroidery and Needlework
The Craft

In embroidery, the most important technical aspect is to understand the different stitches and their use.

It is not easy to distinguish between the main types of bead work but they are as follows:-

1. Beads either alone or combined with cross stitch, in either case each bead is sewn separately onto canvas.
2. Beads strung onto thread and secured to the material, which need not be canvas. In this case the beads will not be in parallel lines, and may well overlap.
3. Bead knitting. Difficult to tell from No. 1, as here the beads are strung onto fine cotton and then each bead is knitted in pattern and so the same effect is obtained as in No. 1.
4. Beaded knitting. Here odd beads are knitted on during the course of the knitting, and so they are above rather than in, the knitting.

Pearls and paillettes of glass and metal are also sewn onto fabrics to give a rich, enamelled effect.

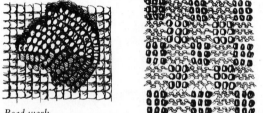

Bead work.

Cross stitch, gros point, and tent stitch are the stitches most commonly used in the Berlin work and other canvas work of the nineteenth century. They can only be worked on an even weave material. Cross stitch is self-explanatory; tent stitch, or petit point, is the same stitch as gros point but worked either on a finer canvas or over one thread instead of two; while gros point is one half of the cross of cross stitch. Tent stitch is used for filling in large spaces which need frequent colour changes—it is very flexible, especially useful where a naturalistic effect is needed.

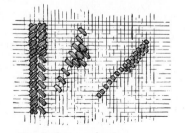

Detail of canvas showing cross stitch, gros point, petit point (or tent stitch).

Dresden work.

Dresden work was a type of embroidery in vogue in the 18th century consisting of various pulled stitches with some outline stitches worked in white thread on very fine muslin or linen. It was used instead of expensive lace for ruffles, tuckers, aprons, kerchiefs and other light accessories.

Plush stitch is worked on a fine canvas in tent stitch with as thick a thread as is practicable. Each row is worked over a gauge and then the loops are cut. The work may be done over one size of gauge, or the gauge can vary, giving variety of height to the stitch.

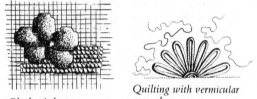

Plush stitch.   *Quilting with vermicular ground.*

Basically, quilting is the joining of two or more layers of material by stitching through them all to make one piece. There are, however, several different types of quilting and the one in the drawing is typically eighteenth century. Here the main design consists of two rows of back stitching with a soft cord run through the back. The ground is backstitched in a 'wormy' or vermicular pattern which contrasts with the raised main design.

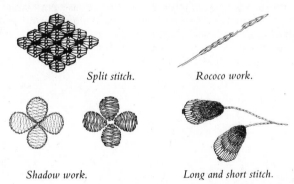

Split stitch.   *Rococo work.*

Shadow work.   *Long and short stitch.*

The rococo stitch is difficult to use with shaded colours, and the effect is always formal, but it was popular in the seventeenth and nineteenth centuries.

In contrast, the split stitch is used where very fine graduations of light and shade are needed, and is nearly always used in working a face or hands. The thread is always a fine untwisted silk, which the needle splits in every stitch.

English Embroidery and Needlework Introduction

The earliest known English embroidery is the stole and maniple of St. Cuthbert in Durham Cathedral. These are believed to be tenth century, which is comparatively late compared to work in Egypt and China, but the technique and quality of their design proves that by then the craft had reached a high level of skill.

From the manuscripts and monumental brasses it can be seen that the clothes of mediaeval men and women were decorated with embroidery, but clothes become worn out with the result that all the embroidery which is left from before the late sixteenth century is ecclesiastical, but as this was the great period of Opus Anglicanum perhaps the lack of secular work does not matter too much.

From about 1250 to 1350 English ecclesiastical embroidery was known as Opus Anglicanum—'English work'—with no need to specify what kind of work or trade it was, as in embroidery England led the world. This superb needlework used for enriching the furniture and vestments of the Church was exported all over Europe and specimens can be seen in Spain and Italy as well as in England. The Syon Cope, probably one of the best examples of Opus Anglicanum, is in the Victoria and Albert Museum in London, and shows clearly the high level of skill in both drawing and technique as well as the tremendous sweep of imagination. From this high point ecclesiastical work gradually declined over the next two centuries, but another peak was reached at the end of the sixteenth century—this time in secular work.

Portraits of both men and women in the time of Elizabeth I show dresses and chemises, undersleeves and shirts, all exquisitely embroidered, sometimes in silks and metal threads but more often in blackwork; and at the same time household furnishings such as cushions and hangings were being worked in diapered or scrolling patterns with insects, animals, flowers and leaves. These designs were, in general, taken from pattern books, herbals, bestiaries and all kinds of illustrated books, and this has always been the practice in England. The man or woman who is both designer and craftsman is rare, and generally adapts some one else's design.

The seventeenth century was notable for crewel work, quilting, and raised, or as it was later called, stump work; but while the first two carried on into the eighteenth century in different forms, raised work had a fairly brief life of about fifty years. It still showed the flowers and animals so loved by the English, but the designs became more pictorial and the work was characterized by padding, either with cotton wool or small pieces of wool underneath the silk, thus making some parts raised. Raised work was used for articles such as jewel caskets, mirror frames, and, very unsuitably, cushions. Crewel work was a bold heavy embroidery much used for curtains and bed hangings; it continued into the eighteenth century, becoming lighter and more delicate as did furniture.

There are few samplers extant earlier than the seventeenth century, but from about 1700 to the present day they are far from rare and make a fascinating study. Originally a reference sheet of patterns to be kept for later use, they later became a method of teaching children to sew; and while map samplers and darning samplers are generally charming the stereotyped alphabets and pious verses of the nineteenth century can become very monotonous.

The use of muslin for dress and accessories gave much scope for fine embroidery and Nancy Woodforde in her diary gives a clear description of the way in which ladies used to exchange patterns and discuss needlework when they met. In the eighteenth century the embroidery for ruffles, aprons, and kerchiefs was generally Dresden work, but later this was combined with tambouring. From there it was a short step to the sewed muslins and Ayrshire work of the early nineteenth century followed by Broderie Anglaise which, although it can be coarse and uninspiring, occasionally shows real beauty.

The nineteenth century, however, is best known for its canvas and bead work, and more especially for Berlin woolwork. Middle class ladies of this date had more time at their disposal than ever before, and found that canvas work in cross stitch or gros point which was not too difficult and only entailed following a chart with each stitch clearly shown, exactly suited them. Nothing was too slight or too unlikely to be embroidered in this way, from Father's braces and carpet slippers, and Mother's reticule, to the drawing room chair seats and fender stools, with an affecting copy of Rubens' 'Descent from the Cross' over all.

The main impression left after seeing a representative collection, is that English embroidery has a charm and liveliness often allied to excellent technique which cannot be excelled anywhere.

Embroidery and Needlework

English

17TH–18TH CENTURY

a) Panel of plant slips with animals and insects, worked with silk and metal threads on satin; early 17th century; 18½" by 11½" (46.9 by 29.2 cm.).

In the late 16th and early 17th centuries great interest was taken in all forms of natural history; this is reflected in contemporary embroideries. This panel shows a number of slips interspersed with homely animals and various insects, all intended to be cut out later and applied to other embroideries. The technique used for the plants is interesting in that the shapes are completely filled in with tent stitch and then the petals and leaves outlined with wire and filled in with buttonhole stitch. These then curl back realistically. In contrast, the insects are worked flat, mostly in long and short stitch.

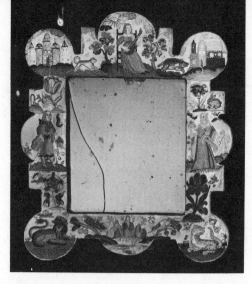

b) Mirror with frame in stump work; c. 1640; 22" by 18" (55.9 by 45.7 cm.).

Raised work, or as it came to be called much later, stump work, was a type of embroidery much in vogue in the 17th century. It consists of animals and people, together with houses, plants and insects, all in glorious juxtaposition and with absolutely no idea of scale. Parts of the embroidery are flat, while other parts such as the friendly-looking lion and the spotted leopard shown here are padded to give a three-dimensional effect. Stump work is often seen on jewel caskets, mirrors and cushions, as well as pictures.

c) left: Miniature of Charles I worked in split stitch and padded satin stitch, with silk and some metal threads couched; inscription: DEUS MEUS EST RUPIS MEA PSAL[M]IS; 2¾" by 3½" (6.99 by 8.89 cm.).

This is one of an unknown number, all based on portraits, but varying slightly in quality. It was long thought that they were worked after the King's execution, as a memorial, but it seems more likely that they were made c. 1700 for the Stuart supporters.

d) centre: Chair with back and seat worked in gros point with wool on canvas; c. 1680; seat 28" by 25" (71.1 by 63.5 cm.), back 24" by 28" (61 by 71.1 cm.).

Hard-wearing wool and canvas was a favourite combination for chair and stool seats; its popularity has never really waned. The subjects chosen were often pictorial and when gros point was the stitch used, the result looked like tapestry. Unfortunately such work was then called 'tapestry work', a mistake continued today. This back, which may be a little later in date, was perhaps taken from another chair.

e) right: Detail of bed cover in corded quilting with background quilted in back stitch; early 18th century; 22" by 41" (55.9 by 104 cm.).

Quilting has a long history, and has never gone out of favour. The necessity for warmth was made into a virtue by the exquisite stitchery and charming designs used. Quilting can also be used together with embroidery or patchwork. This cover has the design in corded quilting, while the background has a vermicular pattern.

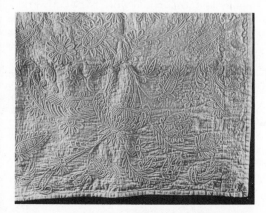

a) *Apron worked with silk and gilt threads on stiff cream silk; c. 1750; wdth. at bottom 40″ (102 cm.), dpth. 19″ (48.3 cm.).*

The decorative apron was an integral part of dress in the 18th century; many have survived. Muslin ones are generally long. This one is quite short and heavily embroidered. Smooth metal thread, couched in pattern, gives a wonderful sheen to the flowers; the awns are worked in purl. Though carefully designed to fill the available space, the work was probably by an amateur; it is very gay and attractive.

b) *Pillow cover worked with silks on fine over heavier linen (unfinished detail); 18th century; 34″ by 16″. (86.4 by 40.6 cm.).*

Because of its unfinished state this would interest a collector primarily for its embroidery techniques. In a drawer since it was laid aside, the colours are fresh as the day they were worked, disproving the myth that 18th century colourings were subdued. The ground is quilted in back stitch, with sprays and birds worked in silk, a favourite 18th century combination. The ink outline has several blots, which may be why the work was never finished.

Embroidery and Needlework

English
18TH CENTURY

c) *left: Kerchief of white muslin worked in a variety of pulled and surface stitches (detail); mid to late 18th century; 33″ square (83.8 cm.).*

Whitework in various forms was a feature of both the 18th and 19th centuries; Dresden work was amongst the most decorative. This was exquisitely fine pulled work combined with surface stitches, much used in place of the more expensive bone lace for ruffles and all kinds of light dress accessories. This kerchief or small shawl has two deep corners.

d) *centre: Panel worked with coloured wools on linen twill; c. 1750; 17½″ by 15½″ (44.5 by 39.4 cm.).*

This illustration shows yet another example of the English love of naturalistic flowers in embroidery. The designs of the crewel work hangings on twilled linen of the 17th century owed much to Eastern influences; here, a hundred years later, are the same crewel wools and the same twill, but the

design is taken straight from the garden of the embroideress, and the result is more akin to a Dutch flower painting. The stitches used are very simple, mostly straight stitch and long and short stitch, but the beauty lies in the varied and brilliant colours and in the feeling of luxuriant growth.

e) *right: Panel worked in cross stitch on scrim; 1798 24½″ by 15″ (62.2 by 38.1 cm.).*

The piece illustrated is a fascinating enigma, apparently part of something, worked with dull green and navy blue thread on scrim in cross stitch by a number of people. It tantalizes the imagination. The most plausible explanation is that it is a 'friendship' piece on the lines of the friendship quilts common in America, and that a number of friends worked their initials and the date (1798) into an irregular pattern as a present for one of their number. Without all the initials it could be a sampler, but this seems unlikely. Very collectable!

Embroidery and Needlework

English

EARLY 19TH CENTURY

a) Picture worked in single thread black silk on a painted silk ground; 1805; 10" by 6½" (25.4 by 16.5 cm.).

An unexpected type of needlework of the late 18th and early 19th century was the working of pictures in hair or in fine black silk with a painted ground. Often these were copies of prints but, according to a note on the back of the one illustrated, it was worked by Ann Roper, aged 13½, to the design of John Cross of Norwich, her drawing-master, who also painted in the ground. The scene is of the Ruins of Athens with the Temple of Minerva in the distance—probably true, but it is hard to believe that such meticulous work could be done by a child of 13.

b) Panel worked in ribbon, silk and chenille on painted silk ground; c. 1815–20; 18" by 16" (45.7 by 40.6 cm.).

At the beginning of the 19th century pictures with a painted silk ground and embroidered subject were popular. As always these could be of superb workmanship or extremely naive. This illustration belongs definitely to the latter category. The trees are beautifully worked in many shades of green and blue chenille with the trunks in ribbon, but the embroideress has found the figures rather beyond her capacity. However it is difficult to resist the lamb which is licking the Virgin's foot or the other lamb wanting to play with the child.

c) left: Cap for a baby, of white muslin, decorated with Ayrshire embroidery; c. 1830.

Ayrshire work is a type of whitework or 'sewed Muslin', identifiable by the fine and varied point fillings in the design, and done mainly in Scotland from c. 1820–c. 1870. It was used on dresses (1820s) and on such accessories as pelerines, chemisettes, caps, cuffs, etc. (1830s and 1840s), but it is usually found on babies' clothes. Look for lightness of design and variety of point-filling stitches.

d) centre: Sampler worked with blue cotton in cross stitch on scrim; 1832; 6¼" square (15.9 cm.).

The range of samplers is very wide indeed—so wide that the collector would do well to concentrate on one aspect. This is one of the 'school' group, interesting to the social historian, as frequently the school has vanished. Such samplers are a link with the past. Other groups include those showing houses, ships, or those dated within a certain period.

e) right: Hand screen worked with wool and silk in cross stitch, bound with chenille, lined and fringed in silk; c. 1840; dia. 7" (17.8 cm.).

Until this century, no lady allowed sun or fire near to her complexion; both were considered equally disastrous! A variety of indoor screens evolved; such as this. The turned-ivory handle could be held gracefully between the lady and the fire, while talking or listening. The even white canvas is sufficiently decorative not to require filling. The design of tropical birds with European flowers, very common at this period, would be worked directly from a chart.

a) *left: Panel worked with Berlin wool in cross stitch, with a band of bead work either side (detail); c. 1860; 13½" by 40" (34.3 by 102 cm.).*

Bead and wool embroidery was popular around 1850–1890, and used, not always happily, as cushion covers, chair seats, purses—in fact, as anything which ingenuity could suggest. The design was worked in cross stitch or gros point on to double canvas, then each bead was sewn on separately. Sometimes, as here, the beads were a fraction too big for the size of canvas. The puckered result is probably why this panel was unused.

b) *centre: Pin-cushion in blue furnishing silk embroidered with opaque, clear and gold beads, and blister pearls; c. 1870–80; 8" by 6½" (20.3 by 16.5 cm.).*

From the 18th century, some pin-cushions were more decorative than useful. The early ones were often of white satin with the design in pins, given as christening gifts. Later, they were embroidered in all types of beads, leaving little or no space for

pins. This tightly-stuffed example has the usual looped bead fringe, and the design shows two motifs which have appeared before; the bouquet of flowers with barley (p. 277a), and the bunch of grapes (p. 276d).

c) *right: Bookmarker in rococo stitch (detail); mid-19th century; 2" by 9" (5.08 by 22.9 cm.).*

Embroidered bookmarkers fall into the same endearing category as embroidered braces, smoking caps and all the other trivia of the Victorian age. They are essentially small embroideries with no pretensions to professionalism, unashamedly amateur but none the less charming for that. This bookmarker is worked in rococo stitch which is generally associated with the work of the 17th century and was frequently used in stump work pictures. The use of the stitch was then revived in the 19th century, often for small embroideries such as this. The tassel in the form of a hand is of mother of pearl.

d) *Needlework picture in Berlin wools; 1875; 24" by 15" (61 by 38.1 cm.).*

Needlework pictures such as this are in a class by themselves. This type of needlework did not follow any style, nor did it lead anywhere, it just happened. These straightforward pictures of ships appeared in the middle of the 19th century and in nearly every case, if not in all, were the work of sailors. The ships they portrayed may not have been seen with the eye of an artist, but they certainly were with the eye of an expert, for the hull, sails and rigging are always immaculate. This ship was depicted by Samuel Peter Harvey, Master Mariner, 1825–1900.

e) *Panel on canvas with birds in cut chenille work and flowers in silk; late 19th century; 12" by 10" (30.5 by 25.4 cm.).*

A photograph cannot do justice to the effect of these humming birds worked in plush stitch with chenille. As the stitch is made over gauges of varying sizes the birds stand out from the canvas from a mere ⅛" (3 mm.) to a full ½" (13 mm.) while the flowers and insects in shiny silk are worked flat, providing a telling contrast. This three-dimensional type of embroidery, very different from the raised work of the 17th century, was a favourite of the 19th century and is found on firescreens, cushions, and other articles of this kind. Compare this panel with p. 277b and note the continuing tradition of birds and insects with flowers.

Embroidery and Needlework

English

MID–LATE 19TH CENTURY

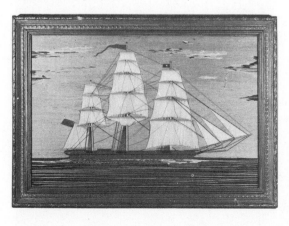

Continental Embroidery and Needlework Introduction

Archaeologists have found interesting specimens of embroidery in various parts of Europe and ancient writers have documented various types. Embroidery was valued highly in the non-Christian and, more especially, in the early Christian world. Eastern embroidery penetrated into Europe during the early Middle Ages, its influence on design and workmanship continuing through the centuries.

Embroidery became the handmaid of the Christian Church. It also served monarchs in brilliant pageantry and ordinary people in their everyday life. Byzantine ideas were absorbed as were designs, such as the pairing of animals and birds around a central arrangement of the Persian Tree of Life, which featured in the teachings of Zoroaster. Hagiology played its part and military saints were much admired. The illiterate learnt from pictorial scenes. Heraldry was especially important during the Crusades and the ancient symbolism of design and colour was used on embroidered coats of arms, flags, pennons and scarves. The many complications of heraldic patterns led to a marked development in stitchery. Mediaeval embroideries often reached a very high standard. Even so, continental embroiderers emulated and envied *Opus Anglicanum*, which enjoyed the highest repute.

Christianity experienced many vicissitudes in Europe between the twelfth and late fifteenth centuries but monasteries and Royal Courts preserved throughout the vestiges of culture. Embroidery was not confined to women; men also prided themselves on their craftsmanship. Embroideries were created on rich fabrics for the Church. Particularly magnificent were ecclesiastical vestments such as copes, chasubles, dalmatics, orphreys and mitres, and furnishings for churches such as hangings, altar frontals, lectern covers and funeral palls.

The guilds of the flourishing cities and towns also commissioned robes and furnishings of elaborate embroidery, Emperors and monarchs encouraged its use in their Courts, and many of these Royal examples have become treasured national possessions. Moriscoes, the Medici family, and other exalted patrons, ensured the preservation and also the evolution of the craft.

The influence of the Renaissance spread from Italy throughout Europe. The embroiderer's needle came to vie with the painter's brush in artistry, colour, technique and finesse. Skilled and eminent artists created designs, and sometimes painted small areas of fabric, e.g. with a face. Post-Renaissance time brought in a more peaceful era and higher living standards. Embroidery became a lavish adjunct of costume and of house furnishings; the paintings of the Flemish school, the engravings of Abraham Bosse and the work of Murillo in Spain give ample evidence of this.

Western Europe, as a whole, practised freely-worked embroidery, based on the threads of the material and worked in linear patterns; design and colour schemes were traditional in the various countries, and are at their best in European national costume.

Due to direct and flourishing trade with the East, there was a new and very strong Oriental influence in mid-seventeenth and eighteenth century Europe. The embroiderer used a rich cornucopia of fabrics with bizarre designs—Chinese and Indian landscapes, pagodas, costumes, trees, birds and flowers. The furniture and lacquer work of the East had a direct influence on colour in needlework. Silks, cottons and wools were dyed to meet the prevailing taste—there were blacks, browns, subdued shades of green, and blue and some yellows.

The Industrial Revolution brought multifarious inventions and innovations which militated against originality and the true spirit of craftsmanship. Yet once machine-made goods were established, a reaction arose among people of discriminating taste, in favour of hand-made work. There was a revival of traditional skills and an interest in exploring possible areas where mechanization had no place; in short, embroidery was impregnated with new life when it ceased to compete with the machine. During the nineteenth century, Berlin wool work, first practised in Germany, found enthusiastic advocates throughout Europe.

In twentieth century Europe there has been less leisure time available for the amateur practitioner of needlework. Many embroiderers have experienced the pleasure of co-operative work, especially in the creation of large-scale pieces for cathedrals and civic buildings. International trends and developments have been encouraged by women's organizations, schools of needlework, and governmental interest.

A variety of embroidery is constantly being evolved, based on new techniques, new designs and on the use of traditional and man-made fabrics.

a) The Martyrdom of St. Thomas, detail from orphrey; Flanders, mediaeval.

Some of the most magnificent embroideries created in the Middle Ages were made in Flanders. Pride of place was given to ecclesiastical robes. Designs on vestments are attributed to famous artists, such as the brothers Van Eyck. Figures are shown under the customary architectural arch. The *nué* work used came to be known as Burgundian technique. It was so fine that the stitchery appears as woven silk. Red shades prevail. There are many shades of blue, set off with greens, mauve, and brown; appliqué of shot silk heightens the effect.

b) Panel of embroidered orphrey; Florence, Italy, mediaeval; lgth. 32″ (81.3 cm.), wdth 21″ (53.3 cm.).

During the Middle Ages Florence developed as a commercial centre. Under powerful patrons, particularly Lorenzo de Medici (1448–92), the arts advanced. This embroidered orphrey has a linen base. Stitchery is in silk and gold thread and appliqué work. Split satin stitch is used for the faces. Features are outlined in fine black silk pulled tightly to the back of the work to suggest fine brush work. The background is filled in with satin, chain and Hungarian stitches. The figures are set in the usual architectural framework.

Orphrey is fabric richly embroidered in gold; also, a band of such embroidery, especially on ecclesiastical garments.

c) Embroidered bag; French, late 14th or early 15th century; 6½″ (16.5 cm.) by 5½″ (14.0 cm.).

The Italian influence on France in the later Middle Ages was strong; embroidery was used lavishly on secular costume. Bags were used instead of pockets. Made of heavy material, they were covered with embroidered scrolls of gold thread, and small rings of gold and silver were introduced.

Closely woven linen is used for this bag, with red silk a prominent part of the design, which is based on geometrical forms. Gold thread is also introduced, and the outstanding effect is made by the Royal arms of the House of Burgundy (the form fleur-de-lis).

d) Embroidered panel; France, 17th century; lgth. 38″ (96.5 cm.) wdth. 16½″ (41.9 cm.).

The reign of Louis XIV, the Sun King, marks an epoch in the history of art. The Grand Monarch was himself a lavish patron of embroidery and Mme de Maintenon established a college of embroidery at St Cyr. The design in this panel is grouped around conventional flower vases. There are caryatid figures in gold embroidery. Buds and flowers and fruits including pomegranates and grapes are worked in satin stitch in coloured silk and wools.

a) Fragment of church embroidery; Spain, 16th century; lgth. 36" (91.4 cm.), wdth. 42" (107 cm.).

An example of Renaissance work which flourished in most European countries. Black and white work was inspired by the outline embroidery of the Moors, and also by the invention of printing. All-over patterns characterized these pieces. Climbing stems and tendrils linked and supported garlands of flowers and fruit. Black silk is used on white linen and metallic thread is introduced. Careful stitching is seen: prominent are stem and back stitch, couching and French knots.

b) Panel in fine stitchery; Saxony, Germany; 16th century; 15" (38.1 cm.) by 12" (30.5 cm.).

This work shows the influence of Italian linen embroidery which flourished in the 16th century. Solid stitching is used on open-textured fabric. The ground fabric resembles fine gauze; threads are drawn out to give the desired light effect. A design of flower motifs and scrolls is worked in a close linen thread. The stitches are even, forming diaper patterns, with bold outline stitches. Much of the work seems to imitate needlepoint lace.

Embroidery and Needlework

Continental

16TH–18TH CENTURY

c) Panel of linen embroidery; Poland, 17th century; lgth. 22" (55.9 cm.), wdth. 18½" (47 cm.).

This panel is typical of the linen embroideries of central and northern Europe. Designs are based on and indeed controlled by the right angles formed by the warp and weft of the irregularly woven linen. Traditional designs are arranged in lines interspersed with plain panels; stars, rosettes, wheels and stylized flowers are worked in bright reds, and browns, and black. Some of the designs were inspired by objects in the daily life of the peasants. A decorative panel such as this was often an heirloom, and served as a ceremonial cloth or as a sampler, to preserve traditional patterns.

d) Embroidered panel showing figure, tree, and flower motifs; Finland, 18th century; lgth. 10½" (26.7 cm.), wdth. 8" (20.3 cm.).

Though much of the embroidery of Finland was devoted to ecclesiastical, Royal and civic functions, it also served prominently in the homes of the ordinary people. Designers introduced into their work motifs depicting plants and flowers, animals, birds, and familiar figures. Carved woodwork, so prominent in northern Europe, provided inspiration. The embroidery shown here has in it a suggestion of patterned weaving, at which the Finns were highly skilled. The tree was a prominent feature in Scandinavian mythology as the symbol of life and often appeared as a central motif in Adam and Eve scenes.

Opposite:
Top: Sampler of darning stitches worked with silk and cotton on fine linen scrim; England, 1795.
Bottom: Waistcoat in purple velvet embroidered with narrow ribbon and filoselle silk; England, c. 1840.

a) Embroidery on fine linen; Greece, 18th century; lgth. 28″ (71.1 cm.), wdth. 26″ (66 cm.).

There is distinct freedom and lightness and grace in the embroideries of eastern and central Europe. They express art for the people by the people. The work is vital and spontaneous. Shown here is an embroidery worked in coloured threads on handwoven linen, in linear patterns. Freely-worked embroidery is seen in animal and plant forms. Colours are all bright-red, yellow, blue, green, orange and purple. Predominant is a rich red, a firm favourite and familiarly called 'rotten cherry'.

b) Skirt with wool embroidery; Holland, 1725–50.

Holland, a sea-faring country, experienced the full impact of trade with the Far East. Rich fabrics were imported. Individuals, and established embroidery workshops, in Amsterdam and other Dutch centres, copied the elaborate fabrics or embroidered the somewhat florid designs on plain grounds. The use here of wide, coloured embroidery on a plain dress is highly effective. Coloured, worsted yarn and some polychrome silk were used. Bold motifs are set off with garlands of green leaves and coloured branches.

Satin stitch, outline stitch, herring-bone stitch and French knots were used.

---

c) Oval fringed cloth with all-over design; Norway, late 19th century; wdth. 48″ (122 cm.).

Much Norwegian embroidery is in white work. Here it is incorporated into a colourful pictorial design showing the generic affinity between embroidery and folk culture. A well-known Norwegian folk tale is depicted. Huntsmen, horses, dogs, dwellings and landscape are shown in remarkable perspective. The snow-covered hills and trees stand out in contrast to the rich colourings of the costume. The surface of the cloth is covered in with embroidery stitches, satin stitch predominating; outline stitch and French knots are also used.

d) Detail of previous folk-tale embroidery; Norway, late 19th century.

A dramatic moment in the tale is embroidered on a fringed cloth. Shadings of green, grey, red, brown and black are thrown into relief by embroidery depicting a snow landscape. The detail we have illustrated is a dramatic moment with the hunter advancing on the bear, spear at the ready.

Opposite:
Top: Large 'star of Bethlehem' quilt comprising hundreds of diamond patches in printed calicoes; U.S.A. Bottom: Bride's quilt showing evidence of having been made by several people; Baltimore, Maryland, U.S.A., c. 1845.

a) Child's sampler; Spain, 1844; lgth. 12" (30.5 cm.); wdth. 14¾" (37.5 cm.).

This inscribed and dated sampler is Spanish work. It is an example of a sampler worked for its original purpose—to illustrate patterns and colourings; ornamental work is secondary. Cross stitch is used on coarse linen.

Most Spanish and Mexican specimens are worked in bright coloured silks and some drawn work is characteristic.

Venetian pattern books of the 16th century established designs in Europe: lettering, conventional flowers, bird and animal forms are shown here, and the 19th century craze for depicting buildings is evident. Plants—botanical and indefinable—form borders.

b) Detail of embroidered apron; Italy, 19th century.

On medium meshed linen, continuous scroll patterns with leaves and flowers are worked in polychrome silks. Satin, long and short, and stem stitch are used.

An Italian girl began to embroider her trousseau at an early age; an apron was a usual article for initiation into the craft.

Typical of the Abruzzi is this article showing excellence of work and appropriateness of traditional design despite the simplicity of materials as usual with the embroideries of Italy, it is preeminently an expression of Italian peasant craft.

Embroidery and Needlework

Continental
LATE 19TH–20TH CENTURY

---

c) Child's tunic; Russia, late 19th century; lgth. 38" (96.5 cm.).

Skilled embroidery was made in Russia, especially in the workshops set up in centres such as Kiev. The fusion of two cultures and their needlework traditions was felt in Russia. Designs based on the threads of the material such as were practised in northern Russia were embroidered in conjunction with those designed in the East. Here a border design has been produced to meet the exigencies of the tunic. Satin, outline and filling-in stitches have been worked effectively in colours of orange, browns and yellow.

d) Panel showing leaf and fruit design; Vienna, Austria, 1900/25; lgth. 36" (91.4 cm.); wdth. 19" (48.3 cm.).

German and Austrian interest in wool embroidery dates from the late Middle Ages. This interest was maintained, and mainly devoted to furnishings. Fabrics thus embroidered resembled tapestry. Designs were often pictorial or of plants and flowers. They were stylized or realistic and were given in remarkable detail. Coarse canvas forms the background of this panel. Worsted thread made from sheep's wool and with very little twist is used for couch work which is held in place with small stitches of the same wool.

American Embroidery and Needlework Introduction

Although a universal craft, needlework developed over the centuries with strong national characteristics—and perhaps this is most evident in America. From a European background and with a common vocabulary of stitch forms, colonial women developed trends which reflected their cultural origins but became expressions of their new way of life.

To the early settlers, needlework was entirely practical. Conditions dictated extreme economy in the use of cloth so that mending and patching was the primary challenge. The New England climate demanded warmth, hence the early importance of quilting. The scarcity of cloth gave impetus to the art of patchwork which became such an important branch of American needlework.

After the first tenuous settlements in Virginia and New England had become established, women could turn to more than the bare necessities of life. Through needlework they expressed a love of colour and beauty that even the harsh years of adversity had not stamped out. Formal art did not exist, nor the richness and beauty of stained glass windows, nor the trappings of Church and State; these had been part of the old way of life that they had left behind. Perhaps these memories account for the popularity of crewel embroidery and the silk and wool pictures produced in some profusion in parts of New England at the end of the seventeenth century. Still with its roots in Europe, it was usually the work of women with some degree of education, and the needlework of this period is strangely sophisticated, compared to much of the folk art that followed many generations later. Some of the subjects portrayed in these early pictures were far from everyday life, expressing the nostalgia still felt for the old country.

By the early eighteenth century, schools were established in Boston for teaching intricate techniques of needlework which, according to a broadside of 1716, were an essential part of the education of young ladies aspiring after culture and refinement. Shops in Boston, at any rate, were surprisingly well stocked with materials and patterns. At first these designs were either imported or diligently copied from London, but soon local artists took over, producing patterns with a strong American flavour.

Crewel embroidery, especially, developed along particularly individual lines, largely a result of the expense and scarcity of imported wools, and the consequent use of homespun wool and early dyes which were difficult and limited. From this economical use of wool grew the much lighter American style; fewer stitches were used, and designs were traced in outline, rather than heavily filled in. The designs, originally English, were soon adapted to include representations of the local flora and fauna that women found around them.

During the nineteenth century it was the enormous development of quilting with ever-increasingly elaborate patch and appliqué work that distinguished American needlework. The rich harvest of this American tradition is still enjoyed today in the many beautiful quilts preserved in museums and countless private homes.

On the frontier as well as in the rapidly growing towns, all women made quilts and the names of their designs reflected the experiences of their lives—'Corn and Beans', 'Indian Hatchet', 'Bear's Paw', 'Rocky Road to California' were just a few of these. Their deep religious feeling showed in names such as 'Crown of Thorns', 'Star of Bethlehem', and 'Golgotha'. The legendary 'quilting bee' was often the most important feature of a social life drastically restricted by distance. The number and quality of quilts that resulted from these gatherings were not only a status symbol but an essential part of every girl's equipment for marriage.

No review of American needlework would be complete without reference to the work of the American Indians. Long before the first European settlers arrived, Indian women from tribes all over the continent were expressing their love of beauty in embroidery, using beads and dyed porcupine quills; this quill work was unique to North America. Although it varied from tribe to tribe, the standard of artistry was uniformly fine. Both quill and bead embroidery on the skins of a wide variety of animals goes back to pre-historic times. Before the introduction of glass beads this embroidery was done with seeds, shells, animal teeth and claws, horn and bone, and various mineral substances such as copper, quartz, turquoise and silver.

In older cultures art and painting reflected the contemporary scene but long before painting had gained a foothold, the life of New England was being recorded in needlework pictures and samplers. Even by the nineteenth century it was as much in the patchwork and appliqué quilts, as in other forms of folk art, that life was spontaneously and graphically recorded. For this reason and for its technical excellence, American needlework has a special significance.

Embroidery and Needlework

American
INDIAN

a) *Indian porcupine quill embroidered sheath; 18th century; lgth. 5¾″ (14.6 cm.), wdth. 3″ (7.6 cm.).*

This sheath, which was found to contain a document, is a particularly fine example of quill embroidery on birch-bark. It shows how quills were laid on the surface and secured with a fine thread as well as the rare technique seen in the small star-shaped flowers where minute sections of very fine quills were inserted end-on giving the impression of French knots. The floral design, unusual in such an early example, as well as its function as a container for letters or papers indicates that it was influenced by the white man and probably made for sale or presentation to him; nonetheless, porcupine quill embroidery existed in a comparatively sophisticated form long before the first European settlements—used mainly by the Plains Indians and the Great Lakes and eastern woodland tribes for decorating garments and accessories. Design differed from one area to another, inspired largely by tribal religion. The first quill work was done only on prepared hides, perforated with sharply pointed stones. A thin strip of animal sinew was moistened, the end twisted and dried into a sharp point. This 'needle' was used to pull the sinew in small back stitches through the perforations, holding the quills in place. A similar technique was later used for birch-bark quill work.

b) *Black broadcloth hood, possibly for a cradle; Iroquois, or eastern woodlands tribe; lgth. (including fringe) 24″ (60.9 cm.).*

A hood for a cradle made of black broadcloth comes from the eastern woodlands region and shows the European influence in the floral design. The effective use of white beads to accent certain parts of the design was a feature of the Iroquois and other eastern woodland tribes, as was the inward double curve motif seen here. The 'overlay' stitch was essential for designs such as this—every bead being separately secured. Bead fringes became a popular substitute for the cut hide so beloved of all Indians.

c) *Buckskin jacket with porcupine quill embroidery, made for Chief Two Leggings; dated 1890; lgth. 14″ (35.5 cm.), wdth. 22″ (55.8 cm.).*

Made of buckskin, this jacket was part of a suit that belonged to Chief Two Leggings of the Crow Indians when he was a boy. The quills have been dyed red, green and yellow and the rather stylized design is nonetheless an advance on most earlier patterns that were purely abstract. It can be seen how the stems were worked with a couched stitch and the quills, laid so closely together and with such a regular outline, stamp it as a work of fine craftsmanship. No matter what region quill work comes from, the quills were always dyed with vegetable substances.

a) Indian saddle-cloth and moccasin of bead work on skin; Mississippi river area.

This saddle-cloth and moccasin are typical examples of a technique that was widely used by the tribes who inhabited regions around the Mississippi River. It clearly shows the 'lazy' stitch which consisted of threading a given number of beads on a strand which was then secured only at either end. By counting the beads on the string according to the colours a pattern could be worked out in proper sequence but the pattern was necessarily restricted to the abstract. When sewn in close rows and firmly secured this type of work can give the appearance of weaving. The predominating colour on these two examples is a vivid turquoise blue with the pattern in dark blue, white and a small touch of pink which shows an artistic restraint in the use of colour characteristic of some tribes.

b) Seat of walnut Queen Anne chair, dated 1740–50; lgth. 21" (53.3 cm.), dpth. 18" (45.7 cm.).

Flame stitch was a very popular canvas stitch used for working the particular zigzag pattern known also as Florentine work. The simplest form consists of straight stitches worked over from horizontal threads of canvas, each stitch rising or falling two threads above or below the last. It was much used for seats, pocket books and other small items and being specially suited for abstract design, it was less demanding for a busy housewife than sophisticated needlepoint embroidery. It was also useful for using up precious fragments of wool. This seat is worked in beautifully muted shades, typical of the early vegetable dyes.

c) Sampler made by Hannah Taylor; Newport, Rhode Island, dated August 18, 1774; lgth. 19" (48.3 cm.), wdth. 14½" (36.8 cm.).

In the days when fine needlework was considered an essential accomplishment for girls of refinement and education there was a proliferation of samplers in which they demonstrated their skill and knowledge of stitch forms. This one, made by Hannah Taylor in 1774 when only eleven years old, is as much picture as sampler because not content with letters and numbers in rows, she has indulged her artistic sense in a wealth of imagery which has given this needlework its great charm and exuberance.

Embroidery and Needlework

American
19TH CENTURY

a) Mourning picture, dated 1803; ht. 26¾″ (67.9 cm.), wdth. 32⅞″ (83.1 cm.), framed.

This is a typical example of the mourning pictures that were such a favourite outlet for emotional expression. They were produced in large numbers by educated young ladies, embroidery stitches being combined with painting and, as in this case, they were usually executed in silk thread on white satin. The tomb itself was always represented complete with inscription—here it was to Daniel Goodman who died at the age of 18. Traditionally, pious symbols of death were included such as the cyprus trees and weeping willows while members of the family were depicted in appropriate attitudes of grief.

b) Needlework picture, with painted water and sky; a woman standing by a river, or coast; embroidered with the name of Mrs Nancy Monroe; 19th century; ht. 15″ (38.1 cm.), wdth. 18″ (45.7 cm.).

This delightful example of 19th century folk art combines needlework and painting and has all the characteristics of an untutored but vigorous artistic expression. Using the simplest of embroidery stitches and with little regard for scale it is, nonetheless, a good attempt at recording an actual scene. Whether Mrs Nancy Y. Monroe is the subject or the artist is a matter for conjecture.

c) Show towel, embroidered in red and black, Pennsylvania; probably 19th century; lgth. 59¼″ (150.5 cm.), wdth. 20″ (50.8 cm.).

Executed in very fine cross stitch in red and black on fine linen, this towel is typical of Pennsylvania German decoration used extensively on all domestic articles. With its roots in central Europe this type of design has retained a remarkable consistency over generations. This is what is known as a 'show towel' used to cover up the towels actually in use and which might have borne traces of hands being dried before they were quite clean—extreme evidence of the rule of the *Hausfrau* and a tribute to the loving pride taken in beautifying her home.

d) Detail from bedcover of homespun linen, crewel embroidered in all-over Tree of Life design; late 18th century.

·Typically American, this 'Tree of Life' motif, in slightly different renderings, has been repeated at widely spaced intervals. The embroidery has all the characteristic economy of American work both in the variety of stitches as well as in the area actually covered. Although very faded now with age, the wools show the subtle and muted shades obtained from vegetable dyes, an art which was learned to quite a considerable extent from the Indians.

Crewel work was mainly devoted to bed furnishings, but it found its way onto petticoats, chair seats, and a variety of small items—aprons, purses, etc.

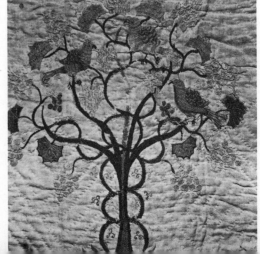

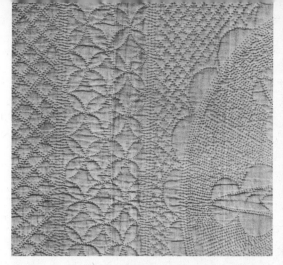

a) Detail of bed coverlet in deep red cotton twill, with central medallion in fine straight-line quilting; probably from the eastern U.S.

Plain quilted coverlets usually pre-dated patchwork. This example shows the traditional single and double diamond pattern, with a band of what was known as 'wine glass' in England and 'tea cup' in America. The co-ordinated design indicates the high degree of artistic skill used in planning these quilts.

In colonial Virginia quilting provided warmth and protection from Indian arrows. Later, it became fashionable for petticoats and doublets; the top layer ranged from homespun to rich silk, the padding was sheep's wool, later largely replaced by cotton. Nonetheless, the continued popularity of quilting has been in coverlets; indeed, coverlet and quilt have become synonymous.

b) Detail of bedcover in white candlewick embroidery on white homespun, dated 1818.

This embroidery on homespun linen, white on white, is literally done with a large needle and the wick used in candle-making, a supply of which all prudent families kept in hand. The bulk of the embroidery is padded or couched with only an occasional use of French knots. Candlewicking more frequently involved looping the wick over a small piece of wood and then cutting the loops to give a foretaste of the candlewick bedspreads we know today.

In this instance the couched stitch has retained a wonderful sharpness of outline and is particularly well suited for the bold design of flowers and foliage.

---

c) Detail of bedcover of trapunto embroidery; by Mrs Nexon, 1821.

Another example of a white quilt, this one shows the use of 'trapunto' or 'stuffed' work—a technique whereby the whole area was not padded but only certain parts of the design were picked out for stuffing with cotton to give the effect of bas-relief. This quilt was made by Mrs Mary Waldron Nexon when she accompanied her husband, a Lieutenant-Colonel in the U.S. Army, while he toured the frontier forts in Indian territory. She has included a number of military subjects—a flag and liberty cap, drum, cannonballs, stars and spread eagle in flight—all of which are accentuated by being stuffed while every inch of the area between is closely covered with very fine quilting.

d) Detail of rug in looped wool embroidery; dated 1833.

This is an example of a rare type of needlework very little of which is still in existence in America. Using a technique similar to candlewicking, these coverlets were worked with wool on coarse homespun, and the surface was so covered with embroidery that the foundation was completely hidden. Work such as this is frequently classified as being 'hooked' but a close examination of the back shows that they were worked with a needle looped over a small piece of wood. The pile could be cut or left in loops as in this case.

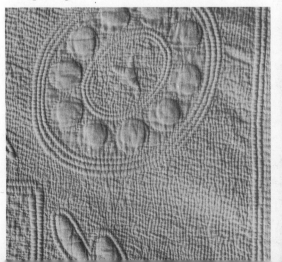

Embroidery and Needlework

American
18TH–19TH CENTURY

a) Detail of coverlet in appliqué work, motifs divided by bands of red calico; late 18th century.

This appliquéd 'top' is of an exceptional standard of craftsmanship. Its fine condition is accounted for by the fact that it is only the top layer and was never quilted or even lined—it was customary to keep a store of 'tops' against the day when a daughter married; then they were brought out for quilting. A good supply of quilts was an essential part of every girl's dowry.

This coverlet is typical of what is known as the Revolution period when flower sprays and other motifs were cut from French *toile* and appliquéd onto plain material.

b) Detail of coverlet in blue and white appliqué work.

'The Little School House', in this case in deep blue and white, was a favourite design and shows the effective use of a simple appliquéd motif. The technique of stitching a shape onto a backing was the logical extension of joining pieces together, which, as the pieces were of simple geometric images inspired the use of appliqué and to increase the effect of realism, materials—usually imported calicoes—were specially bought by the yard.

c) Detail of coverlet in patchwork quilting of hexagon design; very early 19th century.

This pattern is known as 'Mosaic' or 'Grandmother's Flower Garden'. The system of organizing patches of geometrical shape into a clearly defined design was the first stage in the evolution of patchwork from the realm of pure necessity into that of artistic expression. Originally coverlets were created by the random joining together of fragments of material, often from worn garments, and their merit lay in the fact that something was being made from nothing; but by the end of the 18th century when cloth was more readily available, coverlets became the most important, often the only, outlet for women's need to create something of colour and beauty for their homes.

d) Detail of patchwork quilt, combining patchwork and quilting techniques; 1824.

This quilt shows a combination of exceptionally elaborate quilting with simple patchwork in the form of a double eight-point star in a deep pink printed calico. The wealth of quilting patterns includes stars, rosettes, lilies, large flower medallions with tulips and roses, fans at the corners and along the margin of the centre panel interspersed with blocks of diamonds. The universally popular running feather pattern is used for the border elaborated with sprays of flowers. The stitching is of an outstandingly fine and even quality throughout.

a) Hawaiian appliqué quilt; lgth. 82" (208 cm.), wdth. 78" (198 cm.).

To bring the story of quilt-making right up to date, this modern Hawaiian quilt shows another technique in appliqué. Here the whole design is planned and cut out from one single piece of material in a manner similar to that used in paper cut-outs. In this case it is in plain bright red cotton and the whole piece is then laid on the white background, the edges turned in and then sewn down. Finally the whole area is quilted with the quilting following the intricate shape of the applied red design. In all Hawaiian quilts the design is symbolic: in this case it represents Queen Kapiolani's fans and *Kahilis*—a type of canopy used in Royal processions.

b) Coverlet in crewel work; made by Abbiah Thomas; Massachusetts, 1730–40.

Abbiah Thomas, using the subtle colours of home-dyed crewels and all the usual stitches, embroidered this beautiful coverlet in Duxbury Massachusetts between 1730–40. It is worked on a hand woven twill and she has incorporated into the design the birds and stylized flowers that were so popular—the birds are a strange mixture, some obviously of native origin while others were evidently inspired by the Oriental designs that were known in 18th century New England.

A similar combination of motifs is shown in the flowers while the meandering nature of the border is typical of American embroidery, demonstrating how much economy in the use of stitch forms produced the overall delicacy of design that distinguished it from its English source.

c) 'Deerfield' blue-and-white head curtain; Massachusetts, c. 1895; lgth. 77" (196 cm.), wdth. 62" (157 cm.).

In Deerfield Massachusetts in the 1890s, there was a deliberate revival of the 18th century embroidery and under the guidance of Margaret C. Whiting and Ellen Miller, the Deerfield Society of Blue and White Needlework was founded and remained active from 1896 to 1926. Although linen threads were used in place of the perishable crewels, the colonial patterns and stitches were used, and so was indigo dye to produce three shades of blue.

Every piece of embroidery produced by the Blue and White Society, if considered of a sufficiently high standard, carried somewhere the 'trademark' of a spinning wheel with a *D* in the centre.

The design here is the characteristic open meandering pattern using Stem, Romanian, lattice and longarmed cross stitches, typical in every way of the 18th century.

Embroidery and Needlework Glossary

AYRSHIRE WORK: A form of white work known as sewed muslin. It consists of surface stitches, such as satin stitch, combined with quite large areas where the material is cut away. These holes are then filled with a variety of point lace fillings (*q.v.*). In vogue during the first half of the 19th century and much used for christening gowns and bonnets.

BERLIN WOOL: A soft, untwisted fairly thick wool in many bright colours, which has the merit of covering canvas very well. It was used in the 19th century in conjunction with coloured charts, and both originated in Germany.

BLACK WORK: A 16th and early 17th century type of embroidery which has had a slight revival in the 20th century. Usually only black thread was used. Different surface stitches formed the outlines of the scrolling stems, flowers and leaves, with the fillings of double running stitch in a wide variety of diaper patterns.

CHENILLE: A thread which is almost a cord. It is generally of silk, though sometimes of silk and wool, or even wool alone, and is furry, like a caterpillar (*chenille*).

COUCHING: Threads (usually metallic) laid along the outlines of a pattern, and secured by small stitches.

DRAWN WORK: Prescribed threads of the warp or weft were removed, with decorative stitches then worked on the remaining threads.

FILOSELLE: A fine, lightly twisted spun silk. Any number of threads up to six, usually two or three, can be used together.

HARDANGER: A technique associated with Norway; geometrical patterns on drawn threads.

OPUS ANGLICANUM: The name given to ecclesiastical embroidery in England between about 1250 and 1350. It combined great inventiveness with technique which has never been surpassed. Worked only in silks and metal threads.

ORPHREY: A band of gold embroidery, usually ecclesiastical.

PURL: Gold or silver-covered wire twisted in a tight spiral leaving a hollow through which the needle passes. The metal can be cut to any length required and is then sewn like beads.

SAMPLER: These were originally samples, examples of patterns, stitches, colours, etc. Later they acquired artistic value in themselves, and were often done by young girls as practice lessons.

SLIPS: The name given to a plant form, much used in embroidery in the 16th and 17th centuries. It may have fruit and flowers shown together, as well as leaves, but it always has a small piece of broken-off stem at the bottom.

STUMP WORK: Properly called raised work, this is a pictorial type of embroidery made up of isolated motifs. There may be a centre piece of an Old Testament scene, such as David and Bathsheba, or the Judgment of Solomon, and this could be surrounded by slips and animals, especially the lion, leopard and stag, birds and insects. In vogue during the 17th century.

TAMBOUR WORK: A quick method of working chain stitch. The material is stretched over a round frame (tambour), and a very fine steel hook is used. Working with the right hand and hook above, and the left hand and thread below, the hook is pushed through the muslin, and brings up the thread, forming a line of chain stitches. Very popular method of decorating the muslin dresses of the early 19th century.

THREAD DYES: Natural dyes were used until the 19th century; after c. 1848, synthetic dyes came into general use.

TWILL: Material which is woven so that the line of weave appears diagonally rather than vertically and horizontally. In linen or linen and cotton, much used for the ground of crewel work in the 17th and 18th centuries.

Repairs and Maintenance

In collecting embroideries two things have to be borne in mind. The first is the state of the piece and the second is the practicability of displaying it.

Unless very old and very valuable, a piece in a poor state of repair is not a wise buy. Embroideries are not easy to repair and there are few professional conservationists. Threads can be stitched down if they have come loose; white work can be washed and will generally come up like new, as will a large number of eighteenth century quilts, but there is little that can be done to an eighteenth-century silk picture worked on satin if the satin has split, and samplers from the nineteenth century which have moth holes are very difficult to mend. They must all be accepted with their blemishes and the collector must decide between these and the charm of the work.

In so far as maintenance is concerned, the problems of display must also be considered. As a general rule those pieces which are already framed and glazed are the easiest to show, but they should never be in sunlight, or indeed any strong light, which rots silk and fades colours. Small pieces such as coifs, night caps and handbags can be shown in the round in a cabinet, provided the light is not too strong and the cabinet dust-proof, but larger pieces such as waistcoats, dresses and aprons should be kept in boxes or drawers with wads of acid-free tissue paper to stop the material from splitting down the folds. They must be taken out frequently and examined for deterioration and should be put back into different folds. That should be no problem, as obviously the appreciative collector will wish to look at them and show them as often as possible.

The range of embroideries is very large. This being the case, it is probably wisest and more rewarding to collect in groups—either choosing one type of article embroidered in as many different styles as possible, or else specializing in one kind of work and finding as many articles as possible which are worked in it. Into the first category might come framed pictures or panels of differing dates, samplers, aprons, waistcoats, caps, handbags and reticules, hand-screens and firescreens, and pieces of furniture with embroidered covers. Into the second would come white work, canvas work, black work, bead work, work with metal threads, quilting and crewel work; all these groups can be subdivided.

Fakes and Forgeries

Luckily, the prices paid for pieces of needlework have never been high enough for the art to attract forgers. Added to which no one has yet found a way to overcome the fact that the main constituent of every piece of embroidery is—time. Machine embroideries have been made since the nineteenth century and in Japan you can buy silk embroideries by the yard, but in these cases the machine work is quite obvious. So no collector is likely to have to worry about fakes and forgeries.

What he will have to worry about, however, are copies. Embroidery is a domestic art and these copies were made with no thought of deceiving, but were, and still are, made to fill a need. If someone owns an eighteenth century chair with a seat worked in canvas work which has, with much use, become completely worn out, what is more natural than that the owner should work a new seat copying the old one as nearly as possible? It is easy to buy tapestry or crewel wool of the same type and colour as the old, and a well loved pattern can be copied stitch by stitch, but it must be emphasized that these are not fakes—they are copies.

Embroidery is a craft about which the majority of dealers as well as collectors know very little, and often a dealer will tell a prospective buyer that a piece is, for example, seventeenth century black work, when it is, in fact, twentieth century; but this is generally ignorance and not the wish to defraud, and the piece in question could be neither fake, forgery, nor copy, but a genuine piece worked by a modern embroideress trying her hand at a type of embroidery practised by her forebears.

What is needed is for the collector to develop a keen eye helped by looking at good pieces in musuems and collections as often as possible, so that he can learn to distinguish between embroidery made by hand and that made by machine, and also between genuine tapestry which is woven and the canvas work which simulates tapestry which is embroidered.

Embroidery and Needlework
Further Reading

BETTERTON, S. *American Textiles and Needlework.* Bath, 1972.

BOISSERT, H. T. *Peasant Art of Europe and Asia.* London, 1959; New York, 1969.

CAVE, O. *English Folk Embroidery.* London, 1965; New York, 1966.

COLBY, A. *Quilting.* New York and London, 1972.
Samplers Yesterday and Today. London, 1964; New York, 1965.

DIGBY, G. F. W. *Elizabethan Embroidery.* London, 1963.

EDWARDS, J. *Bead Embroidery.* London, 1966.

FEL, E. *Hungarian Peasant Embroidery.* London, 1961.

FINLEY, R. E. *Old Patchwork Quilts and the Women Who Made Them.* Philadelphia, 1929; London, 1971.

FISHER, E. *Swedish Embroidery.* London, 1953.

HALL, C. H., and KRETSINGER, R. G. *The Romance of the Patchwork Quilt in America.* New York, 1935.

HARBESON, G. B. *American Needlework. The History of Decorative Stitchery from the Late Sixteenth Century to the Twentieth Century.*

HUGHES, T. *English Domestic Needlework.* London, 1961.

JOHNSON, P. *Greek Island Embroidery.* London, 1961.

JONES, M. E. *The Romance of Lace.* London, 1950.
A History of Western Embroidery. London, 1969.

JOURDAIN, M. A. *The History of English Secular Embroidery.* London, 1910.

KENDRICK, A. F. *English Decorative Fabrics of the 16th–18th Centuries.* Benfleet, Essex, 1934.
English Needlework. London, 1933; rev. ed. by Wardle, P., London, 1967.

KING, B. *Creative Canvas Embroidery.* New York, 1967.

KINMOND, J. *Anchor Book of European Embroidery.* Branford Newton Center, Mass., 1966.

LEVEY, S. M. *Discovering Embroidery of the 19th Century.* Tring, Herts, 1971.

MORRIS, B. *Victorian Embroidery.* London, 1962.

SCHUETTE, M., and MILLER, C. S. *Pictorial History of Embroidery.* New York, 1964.

SNOOK, B. *English Historical Embroidery.* London, 1960.

SWAIN, M. *Historical Needlework.* London and New York, 1970.
The Flowerers, the origin and history of Ayrshire needlework. Edinburgh, 1955.

WILLIAMS, E. S. *Bargello Embroidery: Florentine Canvas Work.* New York and London, 1968.

Museum Collections

Great Britain

CAMBRIDGESHIRE: The Fitzwilliam Museum, Cambridge.
LONDON: The London Museum; The Victoria and Albert Museum.
NORFOLK: Strangers' Hall Museum, Norwich.
SOMERSET: The Museum of Costume, Bath.
SCOTLAND: The Royal Scottish Museum, Edinburgh.

U.S.A.

DELAWARE: The Henry Francis Dupont Winterthur Museum.
MASSACHUSETTS: Historic Deerfield; The Museum of Fine Arts, Boston.
NEW YORK: The Metropolitan Museum of Art, New York City; Sleepy Hollow Restorations, Tarrytown.

Index

Furniture

An introduction to the subject of furniture in an encyclopaedia of antiques calls for a definition of 'furniture'.

The 'wardrobe' of a monarch originally included the beds, tables, cupboards, stools, chests and so forth, which we would now call 'furniture'; these and other items in their turn included the velvets, damasks and other 'rich stuffs' with which they were padded or decorated, together with the tapestries or carpets which clothed the walls. All these things moved with the court from palace to palace. Now it is usual to divide the contents of the wardrobe, in its old sense, into 'furniture', and 'furnishings', or 'soft furnishings', as department stores describe them.

Nevertheless, antique upholstered chairs, sofas, couches, beds, etc., are regarded as furniture, although their modern equivalents might find their way to the 'soft furnishings' department; and this usage holds irrespective of the amount of 'show-wood' or visible framing which the piece displays.

Furniture, therefore, is chiefly of wood, but it is also necessary to encroach on the subject of metalwork which not only plays a structural part in many objects, but is extensively used for handles, drawer-pulls, inlays, mounts and other adornments. Papier mâché is also included as so much domestic furniture was once made of this material, which may be regarded as a distant cousin of the modern moulded plastics.

Of all the wide variety of antiques collected—and the term covers the spectrum from pre-Christian artefacts to wireless sets of the 1930s—furniture probably gives the most pleasure, as it can still perform its original function. Few would risk drinking wine from a rare seventeenth century glass or pouring tea from a valuable eighteenth century porcelain pot, but the owner of a fine eighteenth century chair may happily sit in it as he contemplates the harmonious proportions and mellow colour of the even older bureau at which he should be working.

Opposite:
The dining room of an English country house, 18th century.

Furniture
The Craft

The craft of the furniture maker has so many branches that only the bare structure can be described. It is a business with a long history, and the fluted columns of a Graeco-Roman temple or the hood of an eighteenth century long case clock are both derived from the bundles of papyrus with which the ancient Egyptians built their huts at the dawn of civilization.

Most early northern European furniture was made of oak, while in the south fruitwood was popular. The structure of pre-Renaissance furniture is often needlessly massive; planks were smoothed with the adze and joints were very simple, the most complex being the mortice and tenon, and were locked together by wooden wedges or pegs known as 'tre nails'. Carved decoration was sometimes picked out in colours, and the simplest staining and bees-wax polishing processes were used.

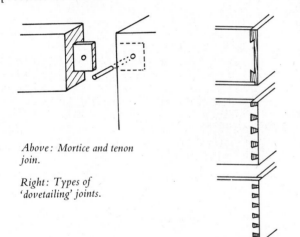

Above: Mortice and tenon join.

Right: Types of 'dovetailing' joints.

As life became more settled and prosperous the heavy carpentry was enhanced by new joinery techniques, and the 'joint' (i.e. joined) stools, benches and cupboards reflect the growing nicety of the joiners' craft. Simple inlays of vari-coloured woods, or pieces of dyed horn and bone, augmented or replaced carved decoration and elegantly-wrought iron hinges and lock-plates became decorative as well as functional. In Italy particularly, the wood-carving so popular in northern Europe was largely replaced by early forms of carved and painted gesso work on chests, tables, etc.

Slowly the craft of the cabinet-maker began to emerge as a refined extension of the joinery business. New methods of jointing, such as dovetailing, and the use of glue in place of wedges, made lighter forms of construction possible.

Experiments with spirit based stains and polishes began and the despised Victorian 'French polishing' really has an honourable ancestry. Improved tools made it possible to produce new forms of convex, concave or ogival mouldings and the plane or 'shave' made the production of smooth planks easier and less wasteful. These techniques saved timber and also made the production of lighter, more elegant, styles possible. The forms of classical architecture—pediments, friezes, architraves etc.—were increasingly applied to domestic furniture.

The development of tools and finer saws also made it possible to cut panels thin enough to use as veneer. Though veneering can be a kind of sham, clothing a cheap wood with a more costly one, the original object was to make full use of the decorative 'figure' of woods such as walnut, laburnum or olive which did not yield large enough planks for economical use as carcass material.

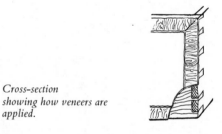

Cross-section showing how veneers are applied.

By slicing the tree trunks into rounds, and 'quartering' the thin slices, most attractive mirror-images and patterns of the striations, or figure, could be used on panels, drawer fronts etc. These were often cross-banded, i.e. with a margin of narrow veneers cut across the grain. Similarly, matched patterns could be taken from longitudinal slices. Early veneers are very thick, sometimes nearly $\frac{1}{8}''$ (0.3 cm.), but later they were thin enough, $\frac{1}{32}''$ (0.07 cm.) or less, to be adapted to sharp curves. Early in the nineteenth century paper-thin machine-cut veneers, 'peeled' by multiple knives in a lathe, began to degrade the art of veneering whilst greatly reducing the cost.

The development of veneer-cutting methods, developed first in the Netherlands, c. 1660, made possible a new form of inlaying known as marquetry (naturalistic forms) or parquetry (geometric forms).

Opposite:
Writing-cabinet in deal veneered with walnut inlaid with various woods and bone; attributed to Anton Herman; Mainz, Germany, 1738.

Furniture
The Craft (contd.)

Marquetry: an example of a design.

Parquetry: an example of a design.

The simplest form of marquetry involves taking two sheets of veneer, one light and one dark, and glueing them together with thin paper between them: a design is cut with a fine fret saw, and then the veneers are soaked to dissolve the glue and separate the sheets. The dark wood cut from one veneer can then be used to fill the space in the light wood, and vice versa. By using a great number of sheets of vari-coloured woods, natural or stained, elaborately variegated designs can be built up into a 'master' sheet with which the article of furniture is faced. The process was expensive as it required great skill, and used material wastefully. A type of marquetry using thin sheets of metal (brass or pewter) and tortoiseshell was evolved by André-Charles Boulle (see p. 375*b*) in the time of Louis XIV, but was not much made in England.

'Japanned' decoration, imitating oriental lacquer painting, developed at the same time as marquetry; it never quite equalled the real thing for brilliance and durability, but it was far cheaper and never went wholly out of fashion. By the 1730s walnut began to be scarce (see p. 323*c*) and mahogany from the Indies made its appearance. The first imported mahogany was rather dull in figure, and so hard that it was used in the solid, because the veneer cutting techniques of the time could not cope with its toughness.

Later, as more sophisticated techniques were available, veneers could be cut from more decoratively figured or 'feather' mahogany, from Honduras. The best quality pieces were of Honduras veneers mounted on Cuban mahogany carcasses. Other woods (satinwood, harewood or stained sycamore, ebony, holly, boxwood, tulipwood, etc.) were used, particularly for inlays; ivory, tortoiseshell, and especially in France, plaques of porcelain and gilt-bronze mounts, were employed to create elaborate decorative effects.

Carved and gilded furniture was made, often on a softwood carcass, complete mouldings and decorative detail being made of gesso or composition instead of wood. It was cheaper and also necessary in order to produce the very light and intricate decoration characteristic, for example, of Robert Adam's designs for wall sconces or mirror frames (see p. 350*b*).

'Ormolu', i.e. chased and mercurial-gilt brass or bronze handles and ornaments, were most elaborate in France, but plain brass drawer pulls and lock escutcheons were used in England, originally gilded or preserved from tarnishing with 'gold lacquer', which gives almost as good an effect at much less cost. More elaborate ormolu *was* produced in England, notably from Boulton & Watt's famous Soho Foundry at Birmingham, although some authorities have said otherwise.

Machine processes for sawing, planing, carving, etc. developed from c. 1790 onwards, and steam engines were used to drive the machines. Rosewood, amboyna and other decorative woods became fashionable with elegant gold-lacquered brass inlays. The nineteenth century saw many new modes, like Thomas Hope's Egyptian style, and the new processes reduced costs, but the basic eighteenth century qualities of restraint, harmony and sound proportions were still paramount.

These good qualities began to disappear just as the machine age really got into its stride, and new advantages were dissipated by bad design. Early Victorian furniture is often delicate and charming, but in general furniture grew increasingly ponderous, ill-proportioned and smothered with incongruous applied decoration and paper-thin machine-cut veneers with die-stamped 'hollow-ware' brass handles and mounts. Towards the end of the century, simpler ideas, often using painted and stained finishes, began to emerge. With the Arts and Crafts movement in England, and the *Art Nouveau* in France, a gradual return took place to fine woods, well planned proportions, and respect for the craft of cabinet-making.

Opposite:
Cabinet on stand; Antwerp, Belgium, mid–17th century.

Continental Furniture
Introduction

Furniture belongs to domestic architecture but is less permanent. To gain a clear picture of what was actually made and used in the seventeenth and eighteenth centuries—a very necessary exercise in view of the amount of alteration, not to mention downright faking, which has taken place since—we need to look at furniture not in isolation, but in its proper setting. Sometimes it is possible to find a house which has escaped any major alteration during the past centuries, such as Skokloster Castle near Stockholm or Castle Amerongen near Utrecht. But more often, we must turn to museums: not only for the rooms they preserve from demolished houses, but for prints, pictures and—what is unexpected to English readers because there are few equivalents outside the Continent—dolls' houses. In Germany and the Netherlands these are no toys but contemporary, accurate and expensive family records which reproduced in perfect miniature the complete contents, as well as the room arrangement of well-to-do houses, mainly of the late seventeenth and early eighteenth centuries. Such a house, made for Petronella Oortman (now in the Rijksmuseum, Amsterdam) is initialled 'B.O.'. Presumably it dates from her marriage with Johannes Brandt in 1686. It has a hall and a reception room with doors and furniture of rosewood; there are even wall paintings of arcadian landscapes. It is not dissimilar to some of the rooms in Ham House (Richmond, England); on the same floor is the main bedroom, with rosewood panelling. The bed is in an alcove and flanked on either side by a cupboard and a wardrobe. The house contains a number of other rooms and holds a miniature collector's cabinet. The entire house is mounted in a cabinet on a stand, and was doubtless itself a collector's piece. Collecting was a major pastime of the seventeenth and eighteenth centuries and collectors' cabinets were made in numerous styles and woods.

Dolls' houses of this quality are rare, of course, but fortunately the cult of domesticity which they represent and for which the Dutch especially were famous, has left its mark in numerous prints and pictures. Prints are particularly helpful for an understanding of the period in question; paintings of interiors tend to concentrate on gentle, domestic scenes with innumerable linen-presses and the great cupboards of northern Europe. But it is the prints which show how company was received: Marot's designs for great beds in reception rooms, for example, or the elaborate protocol of chairs and stools according to rank which can be seen in the engraving of the dinner for the King of Denmark and Sweden at Frederiksborg Castle in 1658. Less well known than the Dutch interiors of the Golden Century are those of the next century, which nonetheless are perhaps even more informative. Those by Cornelis Troost (1697-1750), well represented in the Royal Museum at The Hague, are particularly evocative. Troost's work is reminiscent of his English contemporary, Hogarth, but it lacks Hogarth's satirical bite. One of Troost's engravings shows a scene of the 1730s or 1740s although the group of people are sitting on tall-back chairs which appear to date from about 1700. The tables are of the tilt-top tripod style; their light comes from chandeliers and candles in reflecting sconces; and they are warmed not only by a great log fire below the architectural chimney-piece but also by a huge corner stove. This last is a characteristic continental touch (see p. 148d), like the use of carpets on tables in the Netherlands, or the universal Delft-tiled tea tables in Scandinavia. But for all the conviviality of his company, Troost's interiors are still essentially architectural and have relatively little furniture. Towards the end of the century the opposite was the case: elaborate chimney-pieces, door and window surrounds and ceilings were all but eliminated and more and more attention was given to furnishings. Certainly there were more objects in rooms, particularly during and after the Empire period. For a record of the arrival, first of informality and then of over-furnishing, we must turn to the water colours of the late eighteenth and early nineteenth centuries. These affectionate and even sentimental reminders of middle and upper-middle class comfort and security are most readily available in Professor Mario Praz's indispensable history of furnishing (see bibliography). Written descriptions of furniture in letters, novels or elsewhere are relatively sparse, uninformative and open to a certain amount of confusion: hence the overriding importance of visual evidence which allows us a generous glimpse into the life of a vanished period.

a) Coffer or cassone with carving in high relief; made of chestnut; Italy, c. 1560; ht. 30" (76.2 cm.); lgth. 71½" (182 cm.); detail, below left.

The basic shape of this coffer is that of a sarcophagus, but its form is complicated by the carving: putti at the angles, and in the centre where they support a cartouche with heraldic arms; this cartouche, and its two fellows to either side are surmounted by heads of putti and acanthus leaves; and framed in strapwork. The flanking cartouches are further carved with putti in chariots drawn respectively by dogs and bulls. These, and much else in this design suggest an antique Roman inspiration, e.g. the lion-paw feet, the carving on the lid—palmettes, leaves, masks—and the sarcophagus form itself: on the other hand, the strapwork and the putti are throughly Renaissance in character.

b) Folding chair of x-form, made in carved oak; Italy, c. 1515; ht. 41" (104 cm.); wdth. when open, 27½" (69.8 cm.).

These folding chairs have a long history. There was a folding x-form in Tutankhamen's tomb (18th dynasty of Egypt) and many were depicted in Greek and Roman paintings, often with the lion's paw feet that obviously have remained popular. They were made throughout the Middle Ages and by the 16th century in Italy, had acquired a back-rest. In the great palaces of the Renaissance, movable furniture was comparatively simple, and a chair very similar to this one stands beside a rectangularly plain but elegant table in the private study of Francesco I de' Medici in Florence.

c) Mirror of engraved glass and frame; Venice, Italy, early 18th century; ht. 40" (106 cm.); wdth. 28½" (72.3 cm.).

The carved and gilt frame provides the maximum contrast with the Precht frame (see p. 317a). 18th century work was often of mediocre or poor quality, and this example is not only perfunctorily executed but also shows little style or skill. The delicacy of the engraving on the glass is quite another matter: it is as elegantly stylish as the frame is inelegantly lumpish.

Furniture

Continental

ITALIAN

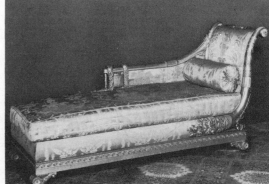

a) Pier-table of gilded pine with marble top; north Italy, mid-18th century; ht. 36½" (92.7 cm.); lgth. 65" (165 cm.).

Carved and gilt pine frame, surmounted by a slab of brown and *verde antico* marble. The design is a riot of writhing forms among which dolphin-heads, eagles and putti can be distinguished amid a confused mass of flowers, leaves, stems, etc. The legs are midway between a cabriole and a hocked-leg. The total effect is very far from the subtlety of French rococo: this is a jungle.

b) Day-bed with initials 'CM'; from a large suite of gilt and white painted Empire furniture; Italy, c. 1810; ht. 38" (96.5 cm.), lgth. 66" (168 cm.).

The suite was probably collected by William Noel-Hill, later the third Lord Berwick during his term (1824–1833), as Minister to the court of the Two Sicilies in Naples, and is now at Attingham Park, Shropshire. There is a family tradition, without documentary proof but going back to the 1840s, that the suite previously belonged to Caroline Murat, Queen of Naples. This day-bed, or sofa, belongs to the well-known French style forever associated with Madame Recamier. The scrolls of that parent type, however, are mini-mized here; the strongly rectangular base is severe and only the scroll at the head, which ends in a kind of cornucopia, suggests the opulence of the Recamier model.

c) Chair from the same suite; ht. 38" (96.5 cm.), dpth. 23" (58.4 cm.).

Essentially a late 18th century type in overall shape, but the dolphin arm-supports, and the stout back legs and uprights, among other details, point to the early 19th century. There is an un-resolved conflict in style between the outward-curving back legs (cf. the scimitar legs in contemporary English furniture, p. 357b) and the tapering, cylindrical, fluted front legs which look back to the late 18th century. Like much 18th century Italian furniture, the quality of workman-ship is not very high.

d) Chair from the same suite; ht. 41" (104 cm.), wdth. 26" (66 cm.).

By contrast with the preceding chair, this one is entirely early 19th century in conception. In the first place, it is much heavier; in the second, its design is strongly archaeological. The total effect is throne-like. Again, the carving is not distin-guished: acanthus and anthemion on the legs, Vitruvian scroll on the seat-rail, lion mask, scroll, etc., on the arms, garlands and floral sprays on the back.

a) left: Vargueno in two sections; Spain; 17th century; ht. 55″ (140 cm.); right: Detail.

A distinctively Spanish type, the *vargueno* was a precursor of the cabinet with many small drawers in its interior. It was first developed in the early 16th century, evidently from Moorish origins—as the decoration of this one, brilliantly gilt and coloured, indicates. Its purpose was to store documents, and to act as a writing desk, hence the fall-front usually found on these pieces. The term *vargueno* is actually a 19th century one: the original term *escritorio* is proof of its function in relation to the writing and storing of documents. The *vargueno* evidently inspired the 17th century cabinets, being first copied in various German cities and thence generally.

b) Dark rosewood games table, inlaid with ivory and silver mounts; Lisbon, Portugal, mid–18th century; dia. $37\frac{1}{2}″$ (95.3 cm.).

The rococo design has close affinities with English and French work. The slender cabriole legs and scrolled feet, the circular drum top with drawers, the *rocaille* carving on the apron, are essentially international. The specifically Portuguese character derives from the double serpentine 'break' placed centrally between the legs and linked to the curved receptacles (for money or counters) on the table-top, also from the almost Moorish design of the ivory inlay.

c) Arm-chair from a set in the Yellow Room of the Royal Palace, Madrid, Spain; late 18th century; ht. 34″ (86.4 cm.).

This chair belongs to the transitional style between neo-classicism and the more archaeological 'purist' approach which took Greek and Roman furniture as models (cf. p. 316c). The figures on the top rail of the back and on the seat rail are derived from Greek vase painting. However, this chair also shows interesting Spanish variants on the more scholarly forms found especially in France and England, e.g. the unconventional form of Greek fret on the back and seat; the 'ears' attached to the back which perhaps belong to a baroque past; the octagonal shaping of the legs and the flanged arm rails; the interlaced central section of the back.

Furniture

Continental
DUTCH

a) Cabinet on stand; probably Antwerp, South Netherlands; c. 1600–50; ht. 65¼″ (166 cm.).

The stand consists of four carved blackamoors; the drawers of the cabinet are decorated with painted scenes from Old Testament history. The Bible was a favourite source for Dutch decorators (cf. p. 310c). The importance of such cabinets, with others made in Paris, is difficult to appreciate today. They were used for the keeping of papers, jewels, etc., but above all for the housing of collections of objects of *virtue*, so dear to 17th century scholars and collectors. On the whole they belong to upper-class surroundings, as opposed to the middle-class houses from which examples like the following probably came.

b) Cupboard or press; North Netherlands, c. 1689; ht. 89½″ (227 cm.).

This type of cupboard, of almost monumental size, was found throughout northern Europe in the 17th century. In middle-class houses they were among the most important prestige-pieces. Numerous examples survive in Germany, the Low Countries, and Scandinavia. They are certainly large but not ponderous, if allowance is made for the ample scale of their original surroundings and the relatively few other pieces of furniture. A characteristic feature is the boldness of the mouldings of the doors, cornice, etc. and a good point about the design is the restriction of the rich carving to well-defined areas.

---

c) Doll's house interior, detail of sitting room; Holland, mid to late 17th century; ht. 18½″ (47 cm.), wdth. 26¾″ (68 cm.).

These models are important in furthering our knowledge of prosperous middle-class interiors in the late 17th and early 18th centuries. This example shows some features not usually found in contemporary *English* interiors: the parquetry floor, the ceiling, the twisted columns of the chimney-piece, its frill and, of course, the Dutch costumes of the dolls. However, close English counterparts did exist for the set of chairs with straight backs and turned legs and stretchers, a table with similar turning, a china cabinet on stand—also with twisted legs, and a chest on stand, its doors decorated with a striking star inlay.

d) Table and candlestand, marquetry; ascribed to Jan van Mekeren, Netherlands, c. 1685.

Sets of this kind (the other candlestand is not shown), sometimes including a mirror, were often supplied in the late 17th century, according to the evidence of inventories, but they rarely survive as sets. The stand had an octagonal top, supported by a turned baluster, which itself rests on a tapering member of square section, which is supported by three scroll feet. The table rests on four tapered legs of square section with cube and bun feet, joined by a flat stretcher.

a) Table with top of delicately engraved brass on a tortoiseshell ground; by Michel Verbiest, Antwerp, 1689; lgth. 58¾″ (149 cm.); left: The top.

The table-top informs us in an inscription that it was designed in Antwerp by Pieter Loose and made by Michel Verbiest in 1689. Its Antwerp origin is significant, for that city was a major centre for marquetry in brace, tortoiseshell, and mother-of-pearl. (cf. colour-plate). Such marquetry was applied, above all, to cabinets, but also to other furniture including tables. The design of flowers and leaves, figures, birds and monkeys probably owes something to contemporary Italian design, as it certainly does to French. The frame's lively carving is also influenced by France, notably in the diagonal stretchers and claw-feet. But the profusion of flower and fruit swags, reminiscent of 'Gibbons' carvings or still-life paintings, is thoroughly Dutch.

---

b) Cabinet on stand, marquetry; by Ph. van Santwijk; The Hague, Holland, c. 1700; ht. 80½″ (204 cm.), dpth. 24½″ (62 cm.); left: A detail of the door.

This type of marquetry (usually on cabinets but also on tables etc.) was a speciality of Amsterdam and The Hague, just as Paris was the centre for ebony cabinets and Antwerp for those of tortoiseshell and inlaid with semi-precious stones, etc. (cf. p. 308a). In this example the marquetry is technically superb, but the design is more than a little confusing because, in a typically Dutch manner, it 'overflows' from the panels into the borders and indeed everywhere, without any plain surface as relief. The tapering square legs are characteristically Dutch (cf. p. 308d).

Furniture

Continental
DUTCH

a) One of a pair of chairs, Netherlands, c. 1700; ht. 47¾" (121 cm.).

Chairs of this type were widely made throughout northern Europe, especially in England and the Netherlands, but also in Germany and Scandinavia. Typical features include the caned seat and back, the turned back uprights, the generous use of carved scrolls in legs, stretchers, back and cresting. An opulent effect is achieved with the minimum of outlay.

b) Chair, walnut; North Netherlands, c. 1700-50; ht. 44" (118 cm.).

Tall back, caned, framed by elegantly curving uprights and double scrolled crest culminating in a boldly carved shell, below which is a delicate interlaced scroll 'pendant'. The shell is repeated, again surmounting scrolls, at the base of the back. All four legs are fully cabriole (indicating a date well into the 18th century) with club feet and a shell carved on the knee. Note the manner in which the seat rail 'breaks' at the angle.

c) Interior of a room; Hindeloopen, south-west Friesland, Holland; early 18th century.

The small seaside town of Hindeloopen was famous for its painted furniture. It was quite different from most contemporary European painted or japanned furniture. Hindeloopen folk art which represents—unlike the other furniture in this section—peasant life, was derived from the voyages of her skippers. They loaded their ships in Amsterdam and sailed thence mainly to Scandinavia, where they came in contact with the many-coloured folk art of the north. Some examples of the cheerful, and charming, rooms and furniture have been preserved, e.g. the National Museum, Copenhagen, has a room from Zealand of about 1800 with settles, cradle, and long case clock—all in green and vermilion; the Fries Museum has a small room with wainscotted bed dated 1763 and painted biblical scenes, and a large room (illustrated) with carved oak bed wainscot and four-door cupboard, blue tiles with biblical scenes and painted 18th century furniture including a bed-stool of 1720 with painting of the Prodigal Son, and a charming three-legged table.

a) Secretary, walnut; North Netherlands; c. 1750; ht. 89¾" (228 cm.).

Walnut secretary-cabinets were characteristic pieces of furniture in both England and Holland in the early 18th century. From originals which were virtually common to both countries, they began to diverge in design about 1700; in Holland they continued to be made long after they had gone out of fashion in England. This example contains a panel of mirror-glass in its door which, owing to the cost of glass, indicates high quality. The scrolly carved ornaments belong to north European style. Note the half-round moulding which frames the mirror: its ogee shaped top is typical of the early 18th century. Note also the way in which the drawers are shaped in the serpentine sections separated by a flat central section. An English maker would have kept the drawers flat.

b) Secretary-cabinet, walnut; North Netherlands; c. 1753; ht. 102½" (260 cm.).

This should be compared with the previous example. Its main interest is that it bears the date 1753. Since this piece is still in the mainstream of walnut furniture design, i.e. of about 1700 and subsequent years, it provides ample proof of the conservatism of Dutch makers. Note also that it still retains mirror-doors, long after these had been abandoned by English cabinet-makers. The scrolly tops of the mirror-frames, and the metal mounts, are thoroughly rococo. Note the architectural cornice and canted pilasters, the crest engraved·on the upper glass panel, and the monogram in the centre of the fall-front.

---

c) Marquetry commode; Netherlands, c. 1760; lgth. 65½" (166 cm.); left: A detail of the front panel.

This is an excellent example of the international influence of French furniture design at this date. Very similar commodes were then being made in Germany and England as well as in the Netherlands. This one is thoroughly 'French': the marble top, the serpentine ends, the superb marquetry, the rococo mounts in ormolu. The latticework and quatrefoil flowers are found on much French and Franco-German furniture of this date. The floral marquetry of the central panel is of the kind favoured by English marqueteurs. Note particularly the assured way in which a complex design is firmly controlled by stringing lines.

b) Clothes press with marquetry of walnut and other woods; Lubeck, North Germany; early 18th century; ht. 72" (183 cm.).

Furniture

Continental

GERMAN

a) Table, partly gilt, with marble top; Dresden, Germany, c. 1720; ht. 30½" (77.5 cm.).

The similarity between some German and some English and French furniture has often been noticed: in this case the table bears a marked resemblance to James Moore's parcel-gilt or gilt gesso furniture, made about the same time in London. Indeed, it would be easy to mistake this for his work. The special feature of this type of furniture is its deployment of a variety of masks e.g. 'Indian'—with reference to the then current cult of the Americas; in this case all the masks are of satyrs. This table was made for the Elector's Residence.

Not only is this piece clearly German, it is specifically North German, from Lubeck. The cupboards and presses of the northern cities possessed certain local characteristics, particularly the pediment shape; at Danzig the cresting took the form of a broken pediment, at Hamburg a straight cornice, and at Lubeck it was arched. Another feature to note is the triple pilaster on the doors. It is easy to condemn the apparent 'heaviness' of such furniture, but it must be stressed that pieces such as this were intended for relatively sparsely furnished houses, where they were the dominant items which carried much prestige.

c) Gilded upholstered arm-chair; Berlin, Germany; c. 1725; ht. 153½" (390 cm.).

The chair has gilt arms, legs, and scrolled stretchers surmounted by an urn; there is rich acanthus carving on the arms. The legs, of square section, have pronounced 'knees'. The general appearance has much in common with English and French gilt furniture at the turn of the century. It should also be compared with the splendid silver furniture (for which the gilt wood furniture was a substitute) which Louis XIV commissioned, and which was imitated in England. One of the finest surviving silver sets (which also has Frenchified scrolls, stretchers, and urn finial) was made in Augsburg for the court of Hanover, c. 1720.

d) Walnut cabinet on pear wood stand; Germany; c. 1720-30; ht. 69" (175 cm.).

The marquetry is of box, apple, ebony, and ivory. The design represents an interesting transition between baroque and rococo: the cabinet, though lighter in feeling, derives from the great baroque presses (cf. *b*, above); it closely resembles contemporary English cabinets in such details as the architectural pilaster. But the inlay shows signs of rococo influence (the contrasting black and white central pendant motif is characteristically German), and the cabriole stand, with serpentine stretchers and scrolled apron, is distinctly rococo. Note the fine detail, especially the subtle cross-banding which, together with delicate stringing, defines the panels of the drawers and cupboard.

a) Secretary veneered in walnut, with gilt carving; Dresden, Germany, c. 1725; ht. 59¾″ (152 cm.).

This secretary is in two stages: the lower section has three drawers, the upper section is enclosed by two doors with inset mirror-panels. The whole design is architectural, and culminates in a bold cornice with 'Indian' busts and vases. National characteristics are always easier to assert than to explain, but this piece shows several undoubtedly 'German' features: (a) the lower pilasters and feet, which originate in 16th and early 17th century architectural design and must be regarded as archaic at this date; (b) the curly frame of the mirror panels; (c) the concave shape of the cornice which—with many variations—is often found in early 18th century German architecture. It appeared also in English baroque design but was later to be condemned by classicists like Sir William Chambers as 'incorrect'.

b) Single chair in walnut; Hamburg, Germany; c. 1720–30; ht. 41″ (104 cm.).

A superlative example of the art of the chair-maker, who was at this time usually working separately from the cabinet-makers. It greatly resembles contemporary English chairs, especially in the cabriole front legs. However, the splat, back uprights, and seat are composed of scrolled, undulating members; this gives a restless effect, entirely attuned to German rococo architecture but contrasting with the general repose of English Palladian design. It is of very high quality in its workmanship and can certainly compare well with its English counterparts, notably in the fine veneers used, and in the low-relief carving on the back, knees, and central apron.

c) Bureau of walnut and palisander; inlaid; by Abraham Roentgen; Neuwied, Germany, c. 1765; ht. to the fall-front surface 29⅜″ (74.5 cm.).

The inlay includes ebony, mother-of-pearl, and silver. One major feature is obvious; the exceptional elaboration of the marquetry, which is superbly executed. Its very splendour is its undoing, however, for its exuberance makes the design confused. The throne-room shown on the fall-flap is that of the Elector of Trier, Johann Philipp von Walderdorff, whose desk it was. There are a good many concealed features including a footstool which drops from the knee-recess, and platforms which swing out from the sides to hold books. Such complex interiors were a speciality of Roentgen.

Furniture

Continental

GERMAN
AUSTRIAN

b) Bonheur-du-jour, mahogany veneer inlaid with silver wire stringing and Wedgwood medallions; Vienna, Austria, c. 1780–90; ht. 27½" (69.8 cm.).

a) Commode of walnut, carved in light relief; from the Rhineland; c. 1775–80; ht. 29¼" (74.3 cm.).

A piece such as this may be regarded as provincial. However, its carving (of musical instruments, festoons of bay or olive leaves and berries, ribbons, leaves, rosettes, etc.), if not of really high quality, is far from countrified. The border of stopped fluting, the fluted cylindrical legs, the paterae, etc., all announce the penetration of the neo-classical style in the Rhineland. Note how the overall design (the beading 'frame', the festoon of leaves and berries, and the oval border round the musical instruments), flows across the two drawers and the division between them.

The high quality of much Viennese furniture was encouraged and maintained by the guild of furniture-makers. Stylistically, it is interesting to see the combination of French and English influences: the Greek fret on the gallery and feet, and the roundels, stiles, etc. on the drawers are not English and this type of furniture was originally French, but the light simplicity and elegance are strongly characteristic of some Sheraton designs, enhanced by the blue and white Wedgwood inlays. These were not restricted to English furniture, of course—Wedgwood exported them for this purpose—but they certainly add an English flavour.

c) Commode, probably made by David Roentgen; Neuwied (The Rhineland) Germany, c. 1785–95; ht. 34½" (87.6 cm.), lgth. 53" (135 cm.).

David Roentgen worked for his father from 1768 and took over the business in 1772. He became one of the most celebrated of all German 18th century cabinet-makers. Introduced at the French Court in 1779, he became a *maître-ébéniste* of the Paris guild in 1780 (see p. 381b). He built up a series of depots in important European centres, including St. Petersburg, as outlets for his products. These were distinguished by their superb marquetry which, besides the conventional 18th century motifs, often included musical instruments such as here, at each side of the commode. His other speciality was complicated built-in mechanisms similar to the spring-operated devices on late 18th century English and French pieces and early 19th century American pieces. Note the superb figure-drawing in the front panels, and the masterly perspective of the centre Italian comedy scene.

a) Baroque commode with marquetry decoration; by Paul Bech; Denmark, 18th century; ht. 51½″ (131 cm.).

The Danish baroque commode form is a compromise between that of a chest on stand (here consisting of four hairy-paw legs) and of a chest of drawers. The upper section of four drawers is of pronounced German style in its series of concave and convex curves with a pair of sharp breaks in the plane towards each end. The marquetry decoration of flowers and leaves belongs to the naturalistic Dutch tradition, but its free-flowing character contrasts with the stiffer 17th century style of inlay, and emphasizes that this piece belongs to the 18th century.

b) Chest of drawers, veneered in walnut with gilt decoration; made by Linnart Larsen, Denmark; early 18th century; ht. 35¼″ (89.5 cm.).

This excellent chest also shows obvious German traits in the block-front elevation, and provides an interesting comparison with contemporary English work. Cross-banded veneers, drawer-edges which overlap the body, and bracket feet are common to both, but the baroque breaks are very rare in England, although they occur in American design. These give a strong vertical emphasis which balances the horizontal drawers, whereas English makers habitually imparted a vertical lift by reducing or grading the proportions of the drawers. The key-escutcheons and the handles are fully in the Franco-German rococo tradition.

c) Cabinet of walnut, inlaid and partly gilt, made by C. F. Lehmann; Copenhagen, Denmark; completed 1737; ht. 153½″ (390 cm.).

In style and proportion, this cabinet contrasts in every way with p. 316a. If this extraordinary piece were not documented it would not be unreasonable to think of it as a hoax; its tortured style seems to embrace the wildest Teutonic rococo of the 18th century, English 19th century rococo revival and Great Exhibition excess, and something of Art Nouveau. It is a far cry from the controlled indiscipline and organized asymmetry of French rococo: it is as though we (or the maker) were looking through a distorting mirror.

d) Secretary-cabinet veneered in walnut, partly gilt; made by Bengtsson, Denmark; mid-18th century, ht. 32⅞″ (83.3 cm.).

This piece, superlative in its figured veneers and finely-judged proportions, is similar to *b* (above) but has scroll-feet instead of bracket-feet, a writing-desk with fall-front, and an upper cupboard surmounted by a cornice and fretted gallery. The corners are canted, i.e. sloped diagonally, and even the diagonals are cross-banded. In addition to the breaks in the lower stage, the breaks in the cornice and the console-brackets beneath give a decided baroque architectural character. This is lightened by the rococo handles and escutcheons, and the finely-carved festoons of flowers.

Furniture

Continental
DANISH

a) Bureau with display cabinet, palisander veneer; made by Albrechtsen, Denmark; mid-18th century; ht. 60" (152 cm.).

The general lines of this piece are strongly reminiscent of contemporary English cabinets: it is in two stages, the upper one consisting of shelves enclosed by glass doors; the lower comprising a bureau with fall-front and drawers. There is also a Germanic character, imparted by the wavy cornice (cf. p. 312*b*) and by the inlay of contrasting veneers within lozenge-shaped borders, which extends below the drawers to the base (itself, like the diminutive bracket-feet, un-English) and to the sides. The metal mounts are fully rococo. Note the drawer in the base.

---

b) Dressing-table of mahogany, signed and dated by J. Pengel; Copenhagen, Denmark, 1793; ht. 32⅞" (83.3 cm.).

J. Pengel was a master-joiner of Copenhagen; inlay on the top of his table is by David Roentgen (cf. p. 313*c*). The simple elegance of this piece, and its material (mahogany) is very similar to English work of the 1780s and 1790s: such items, usually fitted with rising mirrors and various trays and boxes for soap, brushes, shaving gear, etc. in the top, and with either a cupboard door or a tambour front (as here) were widely made, and undoubtedly exemplify the use of English pattern-books which are known to have been widely disseminated in Scandinavia. There are some un-English points: the Greek fret in the top; the metal swag across the lower drawer; and the five 'cones' (from classical architecture) at the top of the legs.

c) Mahogany-veneered chair in Greek style, designed by N. A. Abildgard, Denmark; end of the 18th century; ht. 35½" (90 cm.), wdth. 21" (53 cm.).

This simple but stylish chair reflects the impact of contemporary archaeological work and above all the influence of the Greek Revival. It closely parallels chairs by Thomas Hope and others in England a century later. It is made of veneered mahogany with painted anthemion; the back rail is a frieze with classical figures, based on Greek vase painting. The colours are black, brown, yellow and white: the colours of Greek vases. Abildgard was a painter and architect who has been called the founder of an independent Danish tradition in furniture. A substantial group of his work is in Frederiksborg Castle, near Copenhagen.

a) Mirror with etched decoration and carved frame, from the workshop of Burchard Precht; Stockholm, Sweden, c. 1700; ht. 86″ (218 cm.), wdth. 42¼″ (107 cm.).

Precht was of German origin but settled in Sweden in the 1670s. He specialized in the production of high-quality carving on gilt mirrors, tables, candelabra etc. Precht often drew on late 17th century French designs, often Jean Bérain's. Here, the exquisite delicacy of the design can be regarded as French if not typically Bérain's. The finely-drawn scrolls and the refinement of the seated figures are distinctly Gallic, as are the baskets of flowers. But the smaller details are equally fine: the cartouche and crown, the mask, the eagle-headed scrolls at the sides, and the palmettes on the border.

---

b) Commode made by Johan Niclas Eckstein, Stockholm, Sweden; mid-18th century; ht. 34¾″ (88 cm.), lgth. 47¾″ (121 cm.).

The overall design of this piece with bombé front and sides, is in the French tradition, but the gilt channels between the drawers are typically Scandinavian. The ormolu mounts are of fine quality; the handles and keyplates are in the French style with controlled asymmetry. Note how the drawers are 'framed' (thus accentuating the curves) by ormolu beading. The quality of the design is enhanced by the delicate contrast between the drawers—with finely-figured veneers and inlaid lines forming lozenges or 'diamonds', cross-banded—and the controlled floral marquetry in the central panels, also artfully asymmetrical.

c) Guard's bed, made in the form of a commode, by G. Haupt; Stockholm, Sweden. 1769; ht. 40½″ (103 cm.).

Georg Haupt trained for several years in Paris—it is thought under the great Riesener—(see p. 381c) and spent a year in London before returning to Stockholm in 1769. This example is especially French—e.g. the lattice inlay and the festoon round the central medallion. The side panels with their semi-circular insets combine to produce a shape characteristic of Haupt. Another favourite motif was the Vitruvian scroll (or wave) on the central frieze. Charmingly wayward sprays of flowers trail from the scrolls—a naturalistic addition which would not have been tolerated when Vitruvian scrolls were much in vogue in the early 18th century.

Furniture

Continental
SWEDISH

a) *Guard's bed, disguised as a commode; made by G. Haupt, Stockholm, Sweden; ht. 47¼" (120 cm.).*

The general appearance is similar to the previous example, but here the Vitruvian scrolls are even more pronounced and the leaves which grow from them are less delicate than the flowers in 317c. Note the G (for Gustavus III) in the side panels, and the central urn (fully neo-classical with its flutings, rams' heads, etc., set off by fringed draperies). The urn motif was used also by English makers, but usually based on French engravings which were one of the most important sources for cabinet-makers everywhere. The exceptionally elegant stringing in light woods which confines the panels in both examples should be noted. A particularly interesting feature about both pieces—which correspond closely to Haupt's chests and commodes—is that they are in fact press-beds (i.e. beds folding into a chest) for the use of guards in the Royal Palaces of Stockholm and Drottningholm. Such convenient dual-purpose furniture was not uncommon, to judge from the numbers recorded in inventories, but has not often survived.

b) *Neo-classical commode by Johan Christian Linning; Stockholm, Sweden, late 18th century.*

Linning was one of the leading cabinet-makers of his day. The influence of the numerous French craftsmen who were brought to Stockholm to decorate and furnish the Royal Palace after 1732 was seen not only in the dominant place occupied by French rococo in upper-class houses but also in working methods such as the signing and dating of furniture which adds much interest. Makers who followed this practice included Linning and his distinguished contemporary Lars Nordin; the equally-famous Georg Haupt and his pupils Petter Kyhlberg and Gustav Adolf Ditzingen; Gottlieb Iwersson; Anders Hellman, Erik Öhrmark; Johan Lindgren; Melchior Lundberg; and Carl Tollström, all of Stockholm. This commode, a magnificent one in neo-classical style, is inlaid with a floral motif of which Linning was especially fond. The quality of the inlay and of the delicately-strung panel which 'frames' it, is superlative.

Opposite:
Fine small Sheraton satinwood secrétaire bookcase with painted and decorated pediment; England, c. 1790.

English Furniture Introduction

The value of antique furniture has increased so much that the aesthetic pleasure it gives might seem in danger of being overlooked. However, the most hard-headed investor will find that his acquisitions are much more than mere hedges against inflation. The pleasure of a wider understanding of history, and the appreciation of craftsmanship, add greatly to the satisfaction of having made a wise investment.

Classification by reigning monarchs is convenient, but misleading as obviously the accession of a new sovereign does not automatically usher in a new style; their names are only a rough guide. Jacobean covers the last years of Queen Elizabeth I and the reigns of James I and Charles I. Carolean indicates Charles II and James II (abdicated 1688), but the growing popularity towards the end of the century of walnut veneers, marquetry, high-backed chairs and barley-sugar-twist legs makes it convenient to distinguish these later pieces as 'William and Mary', There is no clear distinction between 'Queen Anne' (1703-14) and 'George I' as walnut still reigned supreme, but the cabriole leg and other graceful curves softened outlines; however the accession of George II (1737) coincides with the widespread introduction of mahogany and new forms which the new timber demanded. Georgian refers generally to George III, but he reigned so long (1760-1820) that the sub-divisions of 'Chippendale', 'Adam', 'Sheraton', and 'Hepplewhite' are useful. The Prince of Wales became Regent for his blind, deranged father in 1811, but often the blanket label of Regency is put on the period circa 1795-1820. His own reign as George IV (1820-1830) is variously described as 'late Regency' or 'late Georgian'. The furniture made during his brother William IV's brief reign (1830-1837) merges into 'early Victorian'. The many changes during Victoria's reign justify the divisions into 'early', 'mid' and 'late' Victorian.

English furniture, even of the highest quality, is very seldom stamped with the maker's name; consequently, it is very important to understand that 'Sheraton', 'Hepplewhite' and 'Adam' refer to furniture styles based upon published drawings and designs, not the work of individual craftsmen. However, Thomas Chippendale both designed and produced furniture, although pieces actually made by the firm of Chippendale and Haig rarely come on the market.

Although the work of such scholars as Ralph Edwardes has put things into better perspective, showing us that cabinet makers such as Vile & Cobb or George Seddon did better 'Chippendale' work than Chippendale, there is still too much importance attached to these few names. An ill-proportioned long-case clock will be called 'Chippendale' merely because of some blind-fret carvings and a swan-neck pediment, whilst an inlaid shell motif will label an item 'Sheraton', even though it bears no relation to his published designs.

The modern collector must break away from too-rigid definitions and rules. Dogmatic pronouncements that dovetails of such-and-such angles were never seen before such-and-such a date, and similar assertions, are to be mistrusted; there are such wide variations in dating features that the only fixed rule is that there is no fixed rule. This applies to broad generalisations of style as much as to constructional details: Chippendale's firm made furniture designed by Robert Adam, and country cabinet makers were still turning out admirable ribband-back Chippendale chairs about sixty years after the publication of Chippendale's book.

Trade with Western Europe and elsewhere naturally brought foreign influences to bear, but the isolation of an island, coupled with native idiosyncrasies, put a distinctive English gloss on foreign modes soon after they had been introduced.

The Renaissance took root later in Britain than in western Europe. Its seventeenth century impact upon domestic architecture, decoration and furniture coincided with an upsurge of English technical inventiveness. These two influences persisted for nearly two centuries. The principal result was greater mastery of jointing, veneering, polishing and inlaying coupled with better understanding of the rules of proportion. This gave full play to developing new styles whilst keeping the purely decorative aspect of furniture in second place. Generally speaking, even the most exuberant fancies—however apparently incongruous—were kept in check; designers knew that a chair was primarily for sitting on, and a clock for showing the time of the day or as Sheraton put it, '. . . the case is always proportioned from the figure and size of the dial plate. . . .'

After 1830, elegant furniture continued to be made, but in general the lines grew coarser, the shapes bulkier and the outlines blurred by heavy machine-made mouldings and incongruous applied decoration. But the essential feeling for good design and fine workmanship of most surviving *pre*-Victorian furniture (for the badly made, shoddy items are less likely to have lasted), accounts for its increasing value.

Opposite:
Bed, part of suite of painted green and white furniture supplied by Chippendale for David Garrick's villa at Hampton; England, 1775.

Furniture

a) Oak draw-table and bench; first half 16th century; table, ht. 34½" (87.6 cm.), lgth. 62" (157 cm.); bench, ht. 23" (58.4 cm.).

This extending oak table and bench, a matched set, are attributed to the first half of the 16th century. The end supports of the table retain traces of the Gothic arch form and the stretcher below the bench-seat matches the structure of the table. The bench ends also show strong Gothic influence. The length of the table-top can be extended to nearly 10 feet (305 cm.) by pulling out the draw-leaves—a method of extending-table construction which is still widely used. The dowels holding the joints together can just be discerned at the upper parts of the legs.

b) Carved oak linen-fold chest; 16th century; ht. 21" (53.3 cm.), lgth. 51½" (131 cm.).

This chest is attributed to the late 16th century, but one should be wary of carved chests: it was a sensible economy for 18th century country joiners to use pieces of old carved wainscot or wall-panelling; so the typical 15th- or 16th-century linen-fold decoration does not necessarily confirm the date of the piece. Also, Victorian and later dealers made up chests and other pieces using genuine carved timbers—pew-ends for example.

However the massive framing and hinges of this chest support its claims to Tudor origin. The lock fitted above the old key-plate is new.

c) Ark in jointed oak; 16th century; ht. 44" (111 cm.), dpth. 31" (78.7 cm.).

The useful box, here seen as an early 16th century panelled oak 'ark', is one of the basic items of domestic furniture. It is the ancestor of the 'chest-with-a-drawer' and 'chest-of-drawers', and could serve as table or seat as well as for storage. The simple jointing with tenons and tre-nails survived into the 19th century on such workaday pieces as stable-corn-bins or butchers' blocks. Traces of shallow incised decoration on the left-hand front panel suggest that the other two panels may be replacements.

d) Hutch, oak; late 16th century; ht. 23" (58.4 cm.), dpth. 17½" (44.4 cm.).

Before the term 'hutch' became associated with rabbit-keeping, it signified a ventilated cupboard (in the modern sense) for food, particularly bread. It was usually secured to a wall and, as the photograph shows, furnished with a stout lock. Even so functional an object was given a little decoration, such as the thumb-moulding of the one shown here together with its shapely wrought iron handle. A close look shows that no two of the spindles are precisely alike—they would have been turned in a primitive pole lathe with nothing but the turner's hand and eye as a guide.

a) Draw-leaf table, cedar; late 16th century; lgth. 78" (198 cm.) extending to 142" (361 cm.), ht. 32" (81.3 cm.).

This imposing cedar draw-leaf table exemplifies the rather half-hearted flirtation with Renaissance forms found on late-Elizabethan furniture. The arcaded decoration on the frieze below the table-top is still based on a Gothic motif and the quadre-foils carved above the bases of the baluster legs are of Gothic inspiration, but Corinthian capitals are incongruously squeezed between the balusters and the frieze. The toe-recesses in the stretchers are uncommon.

b) Documents cabinet on original stand, oak; early 17th century; ht. 35" (88.9 cm.).

Special-purpose furniture was made at all periods. This oak cabinet-on-stand was almost certainly made to special order for storing documents. As it belongs to no specific type one might call it a Jacobean filing-cabinet. The rising top lifts to disclose a compartment suitable for large plans or charters, whilst the lockable doors enclose five shallow drawers, one of which is 'secret' or concealed. Gothic influences linger in the shape of the wrought iron hinges and the projecting buttress mouldings of the upper part.

c) Cup-board, mahogany; early 17th century; ht. 49½" (125 cm.).

The 'cup-board' in its original form was a one- or two-tier table designed to stand against a wall to store and display silver and gold cups, goblets, salts and other valuables. Enclosed compartments on one or other tier led to the development of the closed cupboard in the modern sense. Court-cupboard (i.e. French 'court') is a lower or short-ened version; 'buffet' is of a fairly recent origin. In addition to being magnificently carved, this example is rare for being made of mahogany, which did not come into general use until about 1740.

Almost all surviving early furniture is oak, a hard heavy wood that, although difficult to work, is exceedingly durable. During the Elizabethan era, walnut came into fashion because of its more beautiful figure, and its fine texture more suitable for carving. However, as native supplies dimin-ished, much had to be imported from Europe, and a particularly bad winter in 1709 killed off a large proportion of the usable trees. The first imports of mahogany arrived from Jamaica during the 17th century but large quantities were not imported until the 1730s.

a) Jacobean buffet, oak; c. 1620; wdth. 48″ (122 cm.).

This small buffet shows the intermediate stage between the original cup-board (see previous example) and the type we know. With its incongruity of decorative styles, the piece also shows that early 17th century designers lost their way as badly as the Victorians. The old simplicity was abandoned: rich clients wanted plenty of decoration, but the new Renaissance ideas were not fully understood in England until the architectural work of Inigo Jones, Christopher Wren and others began to influence furniture.

Behind the over-blown pillar (right) a panel of intarsia inlay foreshadows the marquetry of 60 or 70 years later.

b) Buffet, oak; 17th century; wdth. 39½″ (100 cm.).

Here is another form of the 17th century buffet which illustrates the development from the open two- or three-tier cup-board into both the sideboard type of dresser, and the fully enclosed 'press', as our ancestors called a cupboard enclosed by doors. Only the central panel of this buffet opens; not a very convenient arrangement. The bulbous pilasters of the previous example have given way to shapely baluster legs below and pendent knops above. The chequered effect, given by the alternate rectangular projections and flattened sections is interesting and ingenious.

c) Elm chest with carved inscription Elezabeth Lovell 1649; *17th century; ht. 20″ (55.8 cm.), lgth. 30″ (76.2 cm.), dpth. 17″ (43.1 cm.).*

'Marriage chest', 'dower chest', 'linen chest', 'coffer' are but a few of the names given to the simple storage-box/side-table/bench without which no home was complete. Many were completely plain and many plain ones were 'improved' by Victorian carvers, or were assembled from odds and ends of carved panelling from various sources. The 17th century carver of this chest has made a mistake in the spelling of 'Elezabeth'; such mistakes were not uncommonly made by semi-literate craftsmen. This example is of elm instead of the more usual oak.

There are two varieties of elm used in furniture making, the English variety, and the Wych or Scotch elm. In both, the colour is brown in tone, hard and flexible in texture. Wych elm was preferred for the famous English long-bows, and also for cabinet making, because of its finer grain. A great deal of country furniture was made in elm, and Windsor chairs often have elm seats. The finest figure from the elm wood is cut from the burrs which mar the tree trunk. These burrs were cut into round slices, like oysters (see p. 326c), and were often used during the early 18th century as veneers on fine furniture.

a) Carved oak dresser; 1659; ht. 51″ (129 cm.), wdth. 41″ (104 cm.), dpth. 21″ (53.3 cm.).

The inscriptions 'WATCH AND PRAY', 'LIVE WELL AND DIE WELL', and 'REPENT THE LORD IS AT HAND' suggest a dual purpose for this standing chest or dresser, which might well have served as a Bible lectern during family prayers. The more familiar 'Bible box' served a similar purpose, and all such sloping-topped chests or boxes were forerunners of the fall-front bureau.

The initials 'W.S.' are doubtless those of the original owner, and the improbable bird in the centre panel appears to surmount a baby in swaddling-clothes—possibly representing the infant Jesus.

There are carvings of rather primitive female figures on either side, standing on flowers, whose heads are enclosed in a circle. The same flower motif divides the three panels. Because of the date, this dresser does fall into the Cromwellian era.

---

b) 'Day-bed', walnut; 17th century; lgth. 67″ (170 cm.).

This 17th century forerunner of the familiar couch is of carved walnut. It could be used as a bench for three or four people, or as a lounging chair on which one person could recline with his feet up. Its length meant that it could also be used as an extra bed. The boldly carved stretchers and back rest are more massive than they seem to be and are thick enough for the carving to be deeply undercut. The cane seat doubtless originally supported a thick full-length squab or cushions probably covered with damask or silk. (See p. 327a for details of early cane work.)

The difference in style between the earlier pieces and this day-bed is immediately obvious. Fairly simple, straightforward shapes have given way to elaborate, three-dimensional scrolled carving, and the paw feet are a departure from the simple bun, or square. As cabinet-making became more highly developed, the production of even lighter and more elegant versions of fashionable styles became possible—compare this with the arm-chair in p. 328c.

Furniture

English

MID–17TH CENTURY

a) Table on triangular frame with 3 turned legs connected by turned stretchers, walnut; 17th century (Charles II); ht. 27¾" (70.4 cm.), top (closed) 21" (53.3 cm.), top (open) 26" (66 cm.).

The envelope table of the 19th century traces its ancestry from this rare form of 17th century triangular table which opens to form a hexagon. When opened, the flaps are supported on lopers, or slides, similar to those found on fall-front bureaux. The view of the closed table shows the head of one of these lopers above a flush-fitting drawer. As the 21" triangle only becomes a 26" hexagon the arrangement is perhaps more ingenious than useful, which doubtless accounts for the extreme rarity of such tables.

b) Chair in turned walnut; mid–17th century; ht. 42" (107 cm.), wdth. 20½" (52.1 cm.).

The bobbin-turning of this chair is a simplified form of the barley-sugar twist (see p. 327a). Bobbin-turned chair frames and table stretchers, etc. remained popular, particularly in country districts, from the 16th to the 19th century. Oak, elm or beech are the most usual woods and the fact that this specimen is of walnut probably—but not necessarily—suggests 17th-century construction. Regional variations existed, but there was considerable overlapping. This example came from Shropshire, and similar bobbin-turning is also associated with Lancashire, Yorkshire, and the Welsh borders.

c) Charles II cabinet enclosing drawers, on original stand; olive wood; ht. 59" (150 cm.), wdth. 40" (102 cm.).

The whorled effect on the drawer and door fronts of this Charles II cabinet is known as oyster veneering. The 'oysters' are slices cut from the junction of branch and trunk. 'Oysters' were often cut from walnut but in this example they are of olive wood, which was fashionable at the time. The high quality of this piece is reflected in the way the expensive oyster veneering is carried round the sides of the cabinet. The stand is original and pleasantly simple.

The olive wood used in Stuart times was imported from southern Europe. It is hard and close-grained with a green tone, and was usually used as a veneer, in 'oysters' as in this piece, or in marquetry.

There are typical features of inlaid cabinets during the late 17th century which are clearly exhibited in the example above; the rounded frieze at the top is a drawer, as can be seen by the drawer pulls, another pair of which indicate the two drawers in the frame of the stand. The stand itself has a projecting top moulding, turned legs, and flat, slightly shaped stretchers. (See also p. 329c.)

a) Refectory table, oak, c. 1640; ht. 30" (76.2 cm.), lgth. 102½" (260 cm.), and set of 6 identical chairs, and 2 similar arm-chairs, walnut; c. 1670.

The long, narrow refectory table is of a type made, with variations, for several centuries. It derived from the 'board' with trestles or supports which could easily be stored and moved. In place of the slightly tapered baluster legs, seen here, the earlier Elizabethan refectory tables were often disfigured by over-large, carved, bulbous legs.

The six walnut upright chairs, with typical barley-sugar twist components, date from around 1670. The two carver, or elbow chairs, though similar, are not *en suite* with the rest.

Cane-back chairs came to England with the restoration of Charles II to the throne (1660). The East India Company shipped the necessary canes to England from the Malay peninsula.

This early cane was woven in fairly large mesh; as the technique developed the cane was more closely woven. Walnut and cane chairs were made in many variations; sometimes the walnut was replaced by beech, for economy. Gradually the cane back panel was replaced by carving and the cane seat by upholstery.

---

b) Chest of drawers, oak; c. 1650-70; ht. 31¾" (80.6 cm.), wdth. 31¼" (79.4 cm.).

The simple chest of drawers was a 'must' for every well-furnished house by the second half of the 17th century, when this example was made. The wainscot or panelled structure with external framing soon passed out of fashion in London, but continued elsewhere for another hundred years. It will be seen that the four long drawers are disguised (apart from the central keyholes) as eight short ones. Inevitably, the original handles have been replaced by Victorian knobs, these in turn removed, the holes filled (traces are still visible) and brass handles appropriate to an 18th century chest fitted.

c) Bookcase, oak; c. 1670; ht. 96" (244 cm.), wdth. 57" (145 cm.), dpth. 21" (53.3 cm.).

Although made in about 1670, this imposing bookcase has features which are more characteristic of 18th-century practice. These include the concave frieze below the cornice, the brass escutcheon plates, and the partly concealed hinges, the plates of which are inside the structure. The rivet heads on the edges of the upper doors show that the hinges, though inconspicuous, are massive enough to support the weight of the large doors. Although this is described as a bookcase, glazed cabinets were coming into use then for the display of porcelain and other valuables.

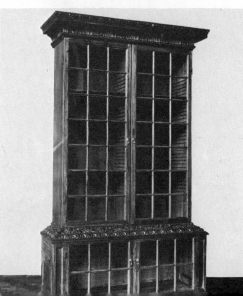

a) Sleeping chair in gilt wood (one of a pair); c. 1675; ht. 55″ (139 cm.), wdth. 29″ (73.6 cm.), dpth. 34½″ (87.6 cm.).

Dual purpose furniture is far from new, as this rare 17th century bed-chair testifies. A hinged rest at the upper edge of the back-rest supports it in the horizontal position. The crest-rail, or stretcher, between the front legs is adorned with a carved mask, and the legs themselves stand on recumbent horses. The carved wood frame is gilded and the fringed red damask upholstery is said to be original.

Furniture

English
LATE 17TH CENTURY

b) Mirror-frame, walnut marquetry; c. 1690; ht. 45″ (114 cm.), wdth. 29″ (73.7 cm.).

The peonies, tulips, scrolling foliage and exotic birds in reserves, or small panels, are characteristic of early English marquetry. The art has been developed sufficiently here to apply the veneers to the sharply radiused frame of the looking-glass. The shaped panel of marquetry and its fretted cresting are all too often missing from mirror-frames of this sort. The wide, shallow bevelling of the edges of the glass suggest that it is probably original, but it is unwise to be dogmatic about the age of silvered glass.

c) Arm-chair, walnut; c. 1675; ht. 54½″ (138 cm.), wdth. 28½″ (72.3 cm.), dpth. 22½″ (57.1 cm.).

Grinling Gibbons (1648-1721) raised the craft of wood-carving to the status of art, as this fine walnut chair, by an unknown maker of the Gibbons 'school', testifies. Note particularly the open scrollwork of the legs repeated in the supports of the armrests. The crest-rail is typical of the period; similar cresting topped the otherwise plain hoods of contemporary long case clocks. Much of the finest work of the period was executed in lime wood which is easy to work, but being soft, is also appetizing to the furniture beetle, or woodworm.

Gibbons was born in Rotterdam; he had settled near London by 1671, when his talent was discovered by John Evelyn, who brought the talented young woodcarver to the attention of architects and patrons. Only one known piece of furniture is attributed to him, although he undoubtedly carved frames, chimney pieces, etc. Gibbons was the leading member of a considerable group of woodcarvers, and was held in esteem as a designer and artist as well as a craftsman-carver. His 'school' is noted for festoons of fruit, flowers and foliage, often in lime wood, pear wood and walnut.

a) Cabinet, painted with flowers in natural colours on dark blue ground; c. 1680.

Lacquered English furniture falls into three main categories: either it was sent to the Far East to be decorated and returned, a long and expensive process, (cf. p. 232c) or made from genuine imported Chinese screens, cut up for the purpose; or 'japanned', in imitation of the real thing. The latter, commonest, solution led also to occasional production of painted furniture which did not attempt the Chinoiserie style—like this little cabinet on a stand, a rare and early example of the genre. The vase-shaped baluster legs, bun feet, and convex frieze of the stand suggest the date.

b) Single gate-leg table in walnut; c. 1690; ht. 28¼″ (71.8 cm.), lgth. 32¾″ (83.1 cm.).

Our forbears were as much concerned with space-saving as we are, and even in large houses it was the custom to keep the centres of the rooms clear of furniture which was not in use. Folding tables were produced very early, this example dating from about 1690.

The slender elegance of the baluster-turned legs should be noted in contrast to those of the earlier refectory table (p. 327a). The scrolled hoof feet are characteristic of the period 1690–1710 and were followed by the claw-and-ball form.

c) Cabinet on stand, walnut with marquetry; late 17th century; ht. 64″ (162 cm.), wdth. 46″ (116 cm.).

This cabinet is opulent without being ostentatious. Contemporary cabinets decorated with japanning were often supported by carved and gilded, or silvered, stands which tend to be over-decorated. Similarly, French furniture, of great technical excellence, began to be too curvaceous (see p. 378b & c) and somewhat overloaded with applied decoration, for modern taste. However, the finest work was characterized by the nice balance of decorative effect and fitness for purpose. The blend of oyster veneers in walnut and multi-coloured marquetry inlays enhances the simple lines of this splendid cabinet.

Cabinets on stands were intended to hold important papers, valuables, etc. Some examples had elaborate floral or 'seaweed' marquetry, and inlays of precious metal.

The simplest form of marquetry involves taking two sheets of veneer, one light and one dark, and glueing them together with thin paper between them: a design is cut with a fine fret saw, and then the veneers are soaked to dissolve the glue and separate the sheets. The dark wood cut from one veneer can then be used to fill the space in the light wood, and vice versa. By using a great number of sheets of vari-coloured woods, natural or stained, elaborately variegated designs can be built up into a 'master' sheet with which the article of furniture is faced.

a) Table top, floral marquetry of various woods on pine; late 17th century; lgth. 37″ (94 cm.), wdth. 25″ (63.5 cm.).

This· is an illustration of the art of marquetry in about 1700. The carcass is of pine instead of the oak used earlier, not for cheapness but because it had been found that the constant movement of oak, with changes of humidity, tended to crack and lift veneers. Ebony, box, holly, hornbeam, and harewood (stained sycamore) are amongst the woods used to construct the elaborate flowers and foliage. By one of those now obvious 'mistakes' sometimes found in early work, the central oval design of flower sprays is upside down in relation to the two birds outside the oval border.

b) Dressing-table glass or toilet mirror, walnut frame; c. 1700; ht. 32½″ (82.6 cm.), wdth. 18″ (45.7 cm.).

This form of looking-glass, adjustable for angle between uprights rising from a plateau, came into favour toward the end of the 17th century. The base took either the form shown here, with one or more small drawers, or was made as a miniature bureau (see p. 356a). This example has a mirror plate with shallow bevelling set in a prettily-shaped frame with a 'slip', or inset border, of gilded gesso between the wood frame and the glass. Gesso is a form of finely-ground Plaster of Paris or gypsum, mixed with pulverized chalk, and often used for mirror frames.

c) Small William and Mary bureau in walnut; c. 1700; ht. 39¼″ (99.5 cm.), wdth. 27½″ (70 cm.).

This choice, small bureau illustrates the technique of using veneers for their decorative effect. The matched left- and right-hand patterns of figured wood on the fall front are enclosed by a narrow herring-bone border (narrow strips of cross-banding arranged so that the lines of grain suggest a 'V' or herring-bone form); a wider band of veneer cut across the grain surrounds the herring-bone. The ledge on the fall front allows the slope to be used as a book rest. The inverted vase shape of the legs is reflected in the brass drawer-pulls.

a) Upholstered settee; early 18th century; wdth. of seat 61″ (155 cm.).

Our forebears looked upon lounging or sprawling on sofas or chairs as most unbecoming and their furniture was designed accordingly. This settee reflects this abhorrence, yet it is, in fact, more comfortable than many a modern piece. The height and depth of the seat and the angle of the back-rest are well proportioned to the human frame. The covering is of contemporary Soho tapestry, and the wide seat would take three in comfort, or four at a pinch. The Soho tapestry works were famous for their upholstery coverings during the first half of the 18th century.

b) Gate-leg table, oak; early 18th century; lgth. 56″ (142 cm.).

The classic gate-leg table was made in many sizes and shapes: this example opens to an oval nearly 84″ (312 cm.) across its greatest dimension, which is about the practicable limit. The larger it is, the more difficulty in making a folding table rigid; also, the wide, thick oak planks were apt to warp unless secured to very heavy cross-bracing. Later, large, rectangular gate-leg tables were often made of solid mahogany—less prone to warping; these are known as 'cottage diners' although it is hard to imagine an 18th century cottager rich enough to dine off mahogany.

c) Dining chairs, burr-walnut; wdth. 21½″ (54.6 cm.), dpth. 17″ (43.2 cm.), ht. 38″ (96.5 cm.).

The high-backed, cane-panelled dining room chairs of the 17th century (p. 327a) fell out of fashion, and walnut chairs of less exaggerated height were popular during the reigns of Queen Anne and George I. Apart from the broad vase-shaped splats of the back rests, the most striking features of the new style were the cabriole legs and the absence of stretchers. Very accurate jointing and curvature is needed to get the required rigidity without stretchers. 'Cabriole' signifies a goat's leap; the shape is supposed to be derived from a goat's fore-leg.

a) Lobby chest of cross-banded walnut veneers; c. 1710; ht. 32½″ (82.6 cm.), wdth. 31¾″ (80.6 cm.).

These small pieces were called lobby chests in the 18th century and they were used in lobbies, or small rooms, which also had to serve as occasional bedrooms. The fold-over top lined with baize is a desirable feature which allows the chest to serve also as a dressing- or writing-table. As a simpler alternative many chests have a pull-out slide for writing upon, often mis-called a 'brushing slide'. This arose from the erroneous supposition that clothes were laid across it while being brushed; the slide is not sufficiently rigid for such a purpose.

These chests are an obvious development from the earlier, simple oak pieces (see p. 327b). At first, half round mouldings divided the drawers, as can be seen in that example. Later pieces often had cock-beaded decoration around the drawer fronts. In this piece the beautifully matched veneers have been cross-banded on the drawer fronts.

The use of the term 'bachelor's chest' for this type, with fold-over top, is indefensible.

b) Queen Anne or George I bureau-cabinet, walnut; ht. 91″ (231 cm.), wdth. 38″ (96.5 cm.), dpth. 24″ (60.9 cm.).

This bureau-cabinet is such as to set the collector's mouth watering. It is not over large, and is of the highest quality in every detail, from the matched patterns of the figure of the veneers to the intricacy of many concealed compartments and drawers. For example, the pilasters flanking the inner doors of both bureau and cabinet form the fronts of narrow, deep drawers for documents. At the base of the cabinet are two pull-out slides for supporting candlesticks.

Bureaux with cabinets or book-cases above, developed in the 18th century. Early examples are either walnut or japanned. This practical combination of a chest of drawers, desk and cabinet continued to be made in walnut for some 50 years; later examples were in mahogany. After 1750 the compartmented cabinet was gradually replaced by glazed doors, which enclosed shelves for books, or for the display of china.

a) Queen Anne dressing- (or writing-) table, walnut; c. 1710; ht. 28½" (72.4 cm.), lgth. 30½" (77.5 cm.).

The drawers in tables of this sort were placed in such a way that the user could sit close to the table surface. Mostly used as dressing-tables, many have suffered damage to the top, which has then been faced with tooled leather to hide the blemishes, though this was not common practice originally. The herring-bone cross-banding around the drawer fronts is matched by a similar border, inset 2" (5 cm.) from the edge, around the top.

b) Lowboy, fruitwood; c. 1700–1730; lgth. 30¾" (78.1 cm.).

Pieces of furniture like this were made at the time as writing-tables, dressing-tables or, without the finished table surface, as stands for cabinets or chests of drawers. The American name of lowboy is an appropriate general term as they could be put to so many uses. Most were veneered with walnut, but this one is of fruitwood, most probably apple, which has an agreeable pale colour that takes polish well. It is a rather soft wood and after two centuries, drawer runners show signs of wear, as seen in the lop-sidedness of the right-hand drawer.

c) Chest-upon-chest, matched walnut veneers; c. 1710–1720; ht. 70½" (179 cm.), wdth. 41¼" (105 cm.).

From the 16th century onwards, the chest or coffer—one of the oldest items of domestic furniture—sometimes had one or more shallow drawers fitted below the base. This developed into the familiar chest of drawers during the 17th century. A chest of drawers on a stand, similar to that of contemporary cabinets, is a tall- or high-boy, names often given to the type of chest-upon-chest or double chest, shown here. Because it was above eye level, the top surface of the upper chest was not veneered; a veneered or ornamented top surface would suggest a 'marriage', or alteration.

Double chests came into use at the beginning of the 18th century, and generally followed the styles for walnut furniture of the period. They were made throughout the century, and examples from the second half of the century are usually in mahogany. The problem of reaching the top drawers led to the general replacement of tallboys by wardrobes. Those versions made in the 19th century were usually considerably reduced in height.

a) Rush-bottomed, ladder-back chairs, elm; c. 1720; ht. 39″ (99.0 cm.).

This type of chair was popular amongst country craftsmen throughout the 18th century and the style was re-introduced by William Morris in the second half of the 19th century. Beech was the usual material but elm examples, such as these, were made in quantity. Yew, oak and mahogany are seen less often. The chair shown on the left is slightly different, and more clumsily proportioned than the matching pair beside it. A probable date is c. 1720 but country styles changed so slowly it is unwise to be dogmatic.

Furniture

English

EARLY 18TH CENTURY

b) Gilded table, pine coated with gesso; c. 1714; ht. 34½″ (87.6 cm.).

Continental influences were strongly shown in some types of English furniture and this gilded table would have been quite at home in a French nobleman's *hôtel*, an Italian *palazzo* or the *residenz* of a Bavarian prince. It is probably the work of James Moore (*c.* 1670–1726), and bears the crest and cipher of Richard Temple, Baron Cobham. As was usual with 18th century gilded furniture, the material is pine coated with fine gesso, which provided a good basis for gold leaf but does not always take kindly to central heating. Moore is known for gilt gesso work, and also made some pieces designed by William Kent (see *d* below).

c) Reading chair, carved mahogany, upholstered in leather; c. 1720; ht. 33″ (83.8 cm.), wdth. 31″ (78.7 cm.), dpth. 30″ (76.2 cm.).

Special reading and writing chairs were made from the early 1700s until Queen Victoria's reign. This early example is said to have belonged to John Gay. The user straddles the seat and rests his forearms on the 'arms', using the adjustable 'table' to support a book or for writing. The arm-rests conceal hinged trays for pens, pen-knife, ink- and pounce-bottles; a drawer for paper is fitted into the seat. The feet conceal small castors with leather trundles. Because one is shown in a famous picture of a cock-fight, the misnomer 'cock-fighting chairs' has been given to these ingenious devices.

d) Chest of carved oak with gilt gesso; c. 1720; ht. 31″ (78.7 cm.), wdth. 57″ (144 cm.), dpth. 26½″ (67.3 cm.).

The humble oak coffer of farmhouse or cottage had its carved and gilded counterpart. The sarcophagus form and the boldly carved masks of this example suggest the influence of William Kent (1686–1748) or Batty Langley (1696–1751). Although chests such as this were used for storage, their primary purpose was as display or side-tables in large state rooms or entrance halls.

Kent was primarily an architect and painter, but after returning from Italy (1719) he created designs for houses, furniture, decorations, etc. His work, highly decorated, is on the large scale suitable for the mansions of his aristocratic patrons.

a) Knee-hole desk, matched walnut veneers; c. 1720-40; lgth. 30" (76.2 cm.).

The classic knee-hole desk, seen here, with its shallow cupboard at the back of the knee-hole recess grew up into the pedestal desk, or library table, designed to be seen from both sides and with no cupboard between the pedestals. The original form was usually small, like this one, and they are much sought after. The walnut veneers of this example are beautifully matched. In addition to the seven visible drawers, an eighth is concealed by the apron above the knee-hole.

The later pedestal desks were often much larger, and highly decorated. William Kent designed elaborate examples with carved and gilt ornamentation, and later ones by Chippendale were made in Chinese Gothic and neo-classic versions.

b) Bureau, oak, with label; London, c. 1750; ht. 41" (104 cm.), wdth. 36" (91.4 cm.), dpth. 32" (81.3 cm.).

Oak furniture of this period is generally described as 'country made' and, indeed, most provincial pieces were oak. However, a great deal was still made in London and occasionally an original label survives as proof. Notice the spelling of 'Buro'; 'Wisk' and 'Ombre' tables were for whist and the old game of *ombré*. Dutch and India tea-tables probably refer to inlaid, and japanned or lacquer-painted decoration, respectively; but best of all, the price is shown: if the dealers could sell this handsome piece for two guineas—and profitably—one wonders how much was paid to the poor devil who made it.

Furniture

English

EARLY 18TH CENTURY

a) Pier-table, gilt wood and gesso, composition top, jasper veneered; c. 1725; ht. 32″ (81.3 cm.), lgth. 56″ (142 cm.).

The fashion for gilded furniture with marble tops is usually regarded as French, but English cabinet-makers produced much fine work in this genre, usually stamping robust English overtones on the original styles. This is a fine example; the use of human masks as feet is unusual but effective, and the inner surfaces of the cabriole legs are carved. The name 'pier-table' arises from the custom of standing a handsome side-table against the area of wall called the pier, between the windows in a reception- or drawing-room. 'Pier glasses' are tall, narrow mirrors which hung above the pier tables (see p. 340a).

Another kind of side-table was the console; a table without back legs which was attached to the wall. Side-tables were usually fairly ornate, since they often formed part of a set for a formal reception room; both side and console tables could be used as pier-tables, and again were usually designed as a set with matching glasses. They were made in walnut, over-laid in silver, gilt (as the example above), mahogany, and painted wood. The tops were often of marble, or elaborately inlaid or painted wood.

b) Cabinet on stand, mahogany, c. 1730; ht. 92″ (233 cm.), wdth. 52¼″ (132 cm.), dpth. 26¼″ (66.6 cm.).

Although the style of this fine cabinet, probably by John Channon, puts it at about 1730, several details are ahead of that period. The inlays on the drawer fronts and on the mirrored doors are of engraved and gilded (or gold lacquered) brass, in the manner usually associated with Regency furniture. The splendid cast, chased and mercurial gilt mounts are of a quality usually associated with Boulton's work of c. 1780-90. The canted and reeded corners, adorned with gilt-brass flutes, bases and Corinthian capitals prevent any awkward break of outline between the cabriole legs and the upper section.

Matthew Boulton (1728–1802) was an English producer of ormolu mounts whose work was considered equal to the French makers. He enlarged his father's Birmingham toy factory, and made all kinds of metal ornaments; vases, candleabra, clock cases, etc. Many of his wares from 1762-1775 were made of 'blue john' (or Derbyshire Spar) mounted in ormolu.

a) Breakfast table, Chinese taste; c. 1730–40; ht. 28½″ (72.3 cm.), wdth. 22½″ (57.1 cm.), dpth. 23″ (58.4 cm.).

This table corresponds to a modern supper trolley. Plates and covered dishes for a light informal meal, not necessarily breakfast in our sense, could be wheeled near the fire or window of the morning room or bedroom. The drawer has fitted compartments for cutlery and the pierced lattice doors and sides are in Chippendale's Chinese manner. A very similar design is shown in the first edition of the *Director* (1755) and this elegant piece of functional furniture might well have come from the workshops of Chippendale and Rannie; Rannie was Thomas Chippendale's first partner.

b) Supper table, mahogany inlaid with brass; c. 1740; ht. 27⅜″ (69.7 cm.), dia. 26⅜″ (67.2 cm.).

No doubt our 18th-century forebears enjoyed impromptu fireside snacks, as this variation on the popular tripod table testifies. Of mahogany inlaid with gilded brass, it would have had ten suitably proportioned oval dishes, silver or porcelain, to occupy the outer spaces whilst the centre was probably occupied by either a salver for glasses surrounded by bottles or a silver tea or coffee 'équipage'. Known as supper tables, such pieces were obviously used for other light meals as well.

---

c) Side-tables; left: Carved walnut with marble top; ht. 31⅝″ (78.7 cm.), wdth. 50⅝″ (128 cm.); right: Mahogany, parcel-gilt; ht. 33″ (88.9 cm.), wdth. 48½″ (123 cm.).

That on the right is of the newly-fashionable mahogany with a plain wooden surface enclosed by a gadrooned border. The Greek key decoration on the frieze and the finely carved foliage on both pieces are very similar. The flowing cabriole legs of the walnut table on the left, terminating in claw and ball feet, are more pleasing to the eye than the rather stiff combination of cabriole, fluted stem and lions' paws of the mahogany table on the right, which has part of the central motif missing.

Furniture

English
MID–18TH CENTURY

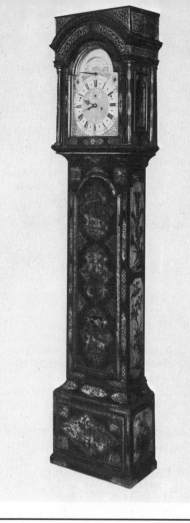

a) Long case clock, English japanned case, movement by Wm. Kipling, London, c. 1735; ht. 92" (233 cm.).

English imitations of oriental lacquer painting were generally gold on black; other background colours, less often seen, were dark blue, green and red. This clock's case has the less common arrangement of reserves, or cartouches of cream background set in the gold and black body, and containing the usual Chinoiserie scenes or figures. The clock has musical work as well as a quarter-chiming train and the subsidiary dial in the arch shows calendar indications and the 'equation of time' or daily variation between solar time and mean time.

Early long case clocks were in walnut, olivewood and ebony, and were often decorated with the marquetry so popular at that period (c. 1680–c. 1714). Japanned cases were fashionable from then until c. 1750. There was also a vogue for simpler cases, usually in oak veneered with finely-figured walnut, set off by restrained cross-banding—much like the small chest (p. 332a). For details of these clocks and their movements, p. 230d et seq.

b) left: Tripods; pair of painted and inlaid satinwood wine tables; centre—Chippendale style lamp or kettle stand, c. 1740.
c) right: Early Victorian amboyna wood centre table, ebonised, c. 1840.

These examples show the development of the popular tripod and pillar combination over about a century. In the centre of (b) the Chippendale style stand has typical features: pie-crust edge, fluted column, cabriole legs adorned with acanthus leaves and ending in bold claw and ball feet. The pair of wine or occasional tables have slender vase-shaped knops supporting the columns, and delicately shaped triple legs with spade feet.

The early Victorian centre table is of fine quality and the wood is handsome but the hexagonal column, lumpish trefoil base and heavy scroll feet compare unfavourably with the earlier tables.

Tripod bases were used for occasional and tea tables particularly during the second half of the 18th century, when tops were often of the tilt-top variety. They were usually of mahogany, although by the end of the century satinwood was used. Their design followed the fashionable trends and there are 'Chinese Chippendale', rococo and neo-classical examples. Sometimes circular wells in the top held cups and plates for tea, or light suppers.

a) Walnut arm-chair covered in original petit point floral needlework; c. 1730–40.

It was a compliment in the 18th century to say that so-and-so was 'a man of good bottom', or 'had a sound bottom', and the chairs of the period are clearly intended for the ample posteriors of men of bottom. The style and proportions suggest a date of about 1750, but the wood is walnut, not mahogany, so the date may be a little earlier. The subtle curves of the arm-rests enhance the functional seat and back, and the flowing cabriole legs not only please the eye but perform the engineering function of increasing stability by widening the base.

b) Bureau, walnut veneer and carved walnut base; c. 1740; ht. 44″ (111 cm.), wdth. 41½″ (105 cm.), dpth. 23½″ (59.6 cm.).

Bureaucracy has come a long way from the *bure* or coarse cloth used for covering writing boards. The traditional fall-front bureau started life as a box-desk on a stand, with the sloping lid hinged at the bottom, instead of the top, so that it could be held horizontal by sliding lopers. Two or three small drawers were added to the stand, and by 1700 the lower part became a complete chest of drawers. The one-piece structure appeared about 1710, but the original two-piece form survived until about 1740, as this example shows. The carved base is a rare feature.

---

c) Mahogany drawing-table; c. 1740; ht. 29″ (73.6 cm.), wdth. 22½″ (57.1 cm.), lgth. 33½″ (85.0 cm.).

Tables with rising slopes, adjustable by ratchet devices, and often with elaborately compartmented drawers, were used for writing or painting and for the display of pictures or prints in the drawing-room. They are often mis-called 'architects' tables, with little justification, as they were not primarily made for architects. This example is of solid mahogany, without veneer. The angled cabriole legs which still have a suggestion of hoof-shaped feet are interesting.

d) Inlaid and carved walnut sofa; c. 1740; ht. 42″ (106 cm.), lgth. 52″ (132 cm.).

Double or triple chair-back settees were popular throughout the 18th century. This example is of slightly later date than the pair of chairs on p. 331d. The principal difference is in the legs, which are not quite so elegantly curved, and in the feet. The 'goat's hoof', of the earlier example has given way to the 'claw and ball' which remained in fashion for fifty years. This type of foot represents a dragon's claw clasping a pearl. The delicate carving is enhanced by marquetry inlays of vases and flowers in the splats.

a) Pier-glass of architectural type; carved wood frame with gilt gesso, c. 1740; ht. 53″ (135 cm.), wdth 33″ (83.8 cm.).

From the late 17th century onwards furniture design was strongly influenced by the forms of Graeco-Roman architecture. In strictly architectural terms, the scrolls, shell and rosettes at the bottom of the frame bear no relationship to the frieze, cornice and pediment at the top; but the effect is harmonious and well-balanced. The looking-glass is not bevelled; bevelling, having been fashionable in the late 17th century, fell out of favour in the 18th (see p. 336a).

b) Carving-table, mahogany; c. 1750; ht. 34½″ (87.6 cm.), lgth. 58″ (147 cm.).

The sideboard started life as a simple table, high enough to make a convenient place for carving. In the 18th century, carving-tables were often flanked by pedestals enclosing in one, perhaps, slatted shelves with a 'heater' beneath for plate-warming and, in the companion piece, a lead-lined basin filled with warm water in which to wash cutlery between courses. Sideboards with the pedestal cupboards, cutlery drawers, etc. built in, evolved by 1750 but the plain carving-table remained popular into the 19th century. This example is a fine specimen of the 'Gothick Taste' so popular at this period.

c) Side cabinet, mahogany; c. 1750; ht. 33″ (99.0 cm.).

This small piece, described as a side cabinet, might well have been intended for bedside use, where the pretty galleried top would have prevented the user's watch or spectacles being accidentally swept overboard in the dark. However, in place of the large drawer shown here, most night tables had small cupboard doors which opened to reveal a compartment, sometimes marble- or lead-lined, for the chamber pot.

d) Triple-purpose mahogany table; c. 1750; ht. 27½″ (69.8 cm.), dia. 35″ (88.9 cm.).

Dual purpose furniture was often made and triple-function pieces, though rarer, are not uncommon. This half-round table opens on the gate-leg principle: turning over the first fold makes a circular table of polished wood suitable for breakfast or supper. If the second fold is turned back, ingeniously-designed hinges maintain the correct level, and a baize-lined surface, with shallow wells for money or counters, provides for card-playing. The last flap of all, secured by a lock, may also be opened to reveal a compartmented well for playing-cards, counters and similar oddments.

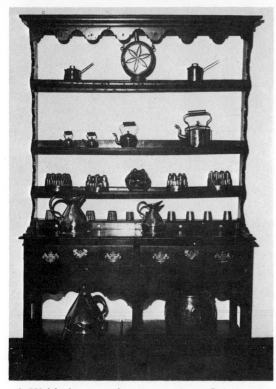

a) Welsh dresser, oak, c. 1750; ht. 79″ (200 cm.), wdth. 48″ (121 cm.), dpth. 20″ (50.8 cm.).

In many households where the kitchen was the principal living room, the dresser was more than a utility fitment. Made of oak, or less often elm, it was given a prettily shaped cornice, side supports, brass handles and lock escutcheons. Changing fashions scarcely affected cottage or farmhouse furniture and dressers are difficult to date. Bases and shelf rack were often separated, and 'marriages' must be looked for. Since the Welsh took particular pains to make pleasant, well proportioned dressers, many above-average examples are apt to be called Welsh whether or not they deserve the honour. This *is* an authentic Welsh example (see p. 354*b*).

b) Cabinet, carved mahogany; c. 1750–60; ht. 93$\frac{1}{2}$″ (236 cm.), wdth. 52″ (132 cm.), dpth. 21″ (533 cm.).

Thomas Chippendale claimed responsibility for all the designs he published, but many were 'cribbed' from Lock and Copland, another cabinet-making firm, and William Vile also influenced Chippendale. Vile (or Vile and Cobb), are less well-known than they deserve to be; the firm did a lot of work for George III, which made William Vile insufferably vain and pompous. This mahogany cabinet has many points in common with the famous 'jewell cabinet' Vile made for Queen Charlotte. The blind fret carving is a characteristic Chippendale feature which almost certainly originated with Vile. (For details about Thomas Chippendale, see pp. 343*c*, and 344*a*.)

---

c) Library table, mahogany, by William Vile, c. 1760; ht. 36″ (91.4 cm.), wdth. 60″ (152 cm.).

Perhaps Vile's patronym, or perhaps his excessive self-esteem, prevented his work becoming as well-known as Chippendale's. He died in 1767 and this fine table from Ashburnham Place may confidently be attributed to him. The carrying rings in the lions' mouths (now, alas, made redundant by 20th century castors) are a characteristic touch. In his definitive *Dictionary of Furniture* Edwardes wrote 'between 1750 and 1760 pride of place . . . must be assigned to Vile whose extant work has a distinction without parallel, and is unchallenged by anything known to have been produced by Chippendale whilst working in the rococo manner'. William Vile's partner was John Cobb (see previous example) and among the well-known houses they supplied with furniture are The Vyne in Hampshire, and Horace Walpole's house, Strawberry Hill, Twickenham.

Furniture

English

a) Chair in mahogany; Chinese Chippendale style, mid-18th century; ht. 36" (91.4 cm.), wdth. 22½" (57.1 cm.).

Furniture in the Chinese taste bears little relationship to anything made in China, but the rage for anything oriental ensured widespread use of Chippendale's Chinoiserie designs by cabinet-makers. The first wave of enthusiasm died away about 1775, only to re-appear at the end of the century largely because of the Prince Regent's use of Chinese style furniture and decoration in Carlton House and the Brighton Pavilion. The taste for Chinoiserie reached the point where Chinese copies of English copies of Chinese porcelain and other pieces were exported to England.

b) Early George III tripod table, mahogany; c. 1760; ht. 24" (60.9 cm.), dia. 11½" (29.2 cm.).

At first sight this tripod table seems out of proportion, but such tables were used as lamp or candelabrum stands, or for supporting large tea or coffee urns. With the top hamper in place, the proportions make sense. There is a foretaste of Victorian scrollwork in the legs but the curves are better balanced than those of most Victorian pieces. The knop is carved with stylized acanthus leaves and supports a fluted column.

c) Windsor chair, painted green; c. 1760; ht. 42½" (107 cm.), wdth. of top at back, 27½" (69.8 cm.).

Far from being a bad workman who bodges things, the bodger was a country craftsman who specialized in turning and bending the various parts of Windsor chairs. Whether made near Windsor or Wincanton, plain or fancy, the Windsor chair is characterized by the extensive use of turned work done in a primitive pole lathe, by curved members, softened for bending in a steam box and by solid wood saddle-seats. The example shown is unusually plain with no ornamental turning on the spindles and practically none on the legs.

Windsor chairs were made during the 18th century primarily for country inns and as garden chairs. The most common wood was beech, but they were made with elm seats and often the bow was yew-wood. When intended for outdoor use, they were often painted green and sometimes red and black. There are records of japanned and richly-carved mahogany examples, although these are quite rare. A very pleasant variation was the Gothic revival style, popular after 1750 (see p. 345*b*).

a) Card table, red walnut; c. 1760; ht. 28¾" (73 cm.), wdth. 36" (91.4 cm.), dpth. 17¾" (45.0 cm.).

The normal gate-leg action for supporting the flap of a fold-over table in the open position has the disadvantage that the legs are asymmetrical when the table is open, and the load in consequence unevenly distributed. The so-called concertina action, seen here, avoids the difficulty by hinging the frame in the centre so that the legs are symmetrically placed whether the top is open or closed. This example, with finely carved cabriole legs, has a damask-lined card-playing surface inset with four candle-stands and wells for money or counters.

b) Drawing table, mahogany; c. 1760; ht. 31½" (80.0 cm.), wdth. 36" (91.4 cm.), dpth. 22" (55.8 cm.).

Tables for the professional or amateur artist took various forms, and this type was popular. In addition to the adjustable slope (to the lower edge of which a wood slip could be pegged to hold papers in place), the whole front of the table slides forward, the L-shaped legs leaving the circular ones behind, to reveal a baize or leather-faced work surface. This in turn could be raised on hinges to disclose a multitude of fitments for paints, brushes, bottles and the like.

---

c) Settee, mahogany; c. 1760; ht. 39" (99.0 cm.), lgth. 50" (127 cm.).

The back-rests, legs and arms of this settee correspond very closely with one of the chair designs in the 1754 edition of Chippendale's *Director*, where he describes it as a 'chair with Ribband-back'. It is one of the most pleasing of Chippendale's rococo styles and one which calls for great skill in execution. In places the entwined ribbands look too delicate to bear any weight but the appearance of lightness is given by optical illusion and depends upon very clever interpretation of the design by the carver (*cf.* p. 347*c*).

Thomas Chippendale was born in Yorkshire (1718–79), but married and worked in London. His first partner was James Rannie (p. 337*a*), his second Thomas Haig. Chippendale has become a household name because of '*The Gentleman and Cabinet Makers' Director*'; the first large-scale publication devoted to furniture design. His book covered most types of furniture then in use, mainly in the three contemporary styles of rococo, Gothic and Chinese. The suggested materials were mahogany and japanned or gilded soft wood. (See pages 337*a*, 341*b*, 346*b*, 348*c*, 350*c*.) For comparison with an earlier chair-back settee see p. 339*d*.

Furniture

English
LATE 18TH CENTURY

a) Pier-glass frame, carved wood with gesso and gold leaf; c. 1760–75; ht. 69″ (175 cm.), wdth. 38″ (96.5 cm.).

Although Thomas Chippendale was not alone in publishing designs in the Chinese taste, his *Director* was most influential. In fact this large pier-glass frame displays a blend of French rococo and pseudo-oriental imagery. The blend is a happy one and the frivolity of the decoration enhances rather than detracts from the nice proportions. The little pagoda was doubtless once occupied by a prized Chinese vase or figure. See p. 340*a* for an earlier example of the pier-glass.

Chippendale's *Director* had 160 plates in the first two editions (1754, 1755), and 200 in the third (1762). However, although he continued to work in this rococo-influenced style, by 1762 neo-classical fashion was already making itself felt. His work at Harewood House, in Yorkshire is particularly interesting as his accounts (1772) show well-documented pieces, still there, and very much influenced by Robert Adam.

b) Secrétaire, mahogany; c. 1770; ht. 38″ (96.5 cm.), dpth. 20″ (55.0 cm.).

In the days when it was fashionable for the English to despise French terminology, the *secrétaire*, or *escritoire*, was content to be known as a secretary table or secretary drawer. Dummy drawers which were pulled out and the fronts let down to disclose fitments and a writing surface, were fitted into many pieces of furniture from small work-tables to large bookcases. The example shown is in a plain mahogany chest of drawers.

c) Wine cooler, mahogany, brass bound; c. 1770; ht. 26¾″ (68 cm.), wdth. 18¾″ (47.5 cm.).

Wine coolers or cisterns were made in many different forms, such as this plainly handsome hexagon. They were fitted with lead (later, zinc) liners in which the wine bottles stood in crushed ice, or 'freezing mixture' of ice and salt. The ice was imported from the Baltic or Newfoundland in winter and kept in well-insulated ice-houses which formed part of every country house of distinction. Town dwellers could buy their ice in small amounts from merchants or fishmongers.

a) Library table, mahogany; by William France, 1770; overall ht. 30″ (76.2 cm.), wdth. 25¾″, (65.4 cm.), dpth. 26″ (66.0 cm.).

Signed or stamped furniture is rare in England but it is known that this piece was made for the library of Kenwood House by William France in 1770. The adjustable slope was useful as a drawing rest or for use when consulting a large book or atlas. Tables of this type were sometimes fitted with rack-and-pinion devices for raising or tilting the upperworks. As this is a known, dated, genuine piece it is interesting to note the early Victorian flavour of the scrolled feet and the rather bulbous column with acanthus leaves carved on the knop.

b) Windsor chair, seat made of elm, the back and legs of yew; c. 1760–70; ht. 41⅜″ (104 cm.), wdth. of top, at back, 26½″ (67.3 cm.).

This fine example should be compared with p. 342c (the plainest sort of Windsor chair). Though elm and beech were the usual woods for Windsor chairs, only the seat of this one is elm, the rest being in yew, that most beautiful of woods. The use of steam-softened carved members is confined to the 'cow-horn' stretcher, the arm-rests and their supports. The well proportioned cabriole legs, with Gothic buttress brackets could have graced any drawing-room and the design of the chair as a whole shows that the 'Gothick Taste' reached far beyond Strawberry Hill, Walpole's house.

---

c) Wing-backed ('eared') easy chair; c. 1770; ht. 47″ (119 cm.), wdth. 33″ (83.8 cm.), dpth. of seat, 25½″ (64.7 cm.).

The photograph of this traditional easy chair says nearly all that needs to be said of it. Fitness of purpose combines so well with harmonious lines that it is easy to understand why modern reproductions of these or similar chairs are so popular.

d) Oval cellaret, mahogany; c. 1770; wdth. 24″ (61 cm.).

Wine cistern, wine cooler or cellaret are names given to this piece of essential dining room furniture (cf. p. 344c). This example may be lifted from its wheeled stand (note the early form of the trundles or castors) and contains the usual zinc (originally lead) liner in which to pack broken ice round the wine bottles. The use of ebony cock beads, projecting about ⅛″ (.32 cm.) is an alternative to the more usual flush stringing; the cock beads are more easily damaged. The decorative figure, or feather, of the pale mahogany may be seen in the photograph.

a) Brass chandelier, early 18th century; ht. $22\frac{3}{4}''$ (57.7 cm.).

The name chandelier has a long history; the first recorded use dates back to 1398. Nonetheless, it was not commonly used in England until the early Georgian period. Early examples were generally simple round hoops of iron, set with spikes for candles. In great palaces, the hoops were sometimes silver or gold. By the 16th century, brass and latten hoops appeared in the wealthier private homes. During the Stuart period, brass chandeliers 'in the Dutch fashion' were very popular; a round simple globe was the main stem ornament, onto which the arms were hooked. Later, the arms were bolted to the stem.

This lovely shape proved so popular that it has continued to be made up to the present day.

Most surviving 17th and 18th century examples were made for churches; there is often the dove of peace underneath the top hook, or other ecclesiastical motifs.

Furniture

English

18TH CENTURY

b) Chandelier of gilded wood with 8 arms; early 18th century (c. 1725); ht. 37" (93.9 cm.), wdth. $42\frac{1}{2}''$ (106 cm.).

Carved and gilded chandeliers became popular after the Restoration, partly no doubt because they could be made to imitate the enormously expensive examples in gold and silver which were used in the Royal houses.

The French influence was very strong, and many English makers followed the designs of Jean Bérain (see 317a) and Daniel Marot.

This beautifully carved chandelier makes it easy to understand Thomas Chippendale's plaintive report in the Directory (1762) that the majority of chandeliers then made were in glass or brass, which he thought was a pity, since wooden ones, burnished with gold, would be cheaper and more practical!

c) Glass chandelier of the Regency period (c. 1790); ht. 48" (121 cm.).

Rock crystal chandeliers had been made as early as 1667, but obviously for a few wealthy customers. With George Ravenscroft's 'glass of lead' (see p. 422) and the developing English glass industry, glass candlesticks and chandeliers became available to a much wider public. Early examples have plain arms set around a heavy central ball. Gradually they became more elaborate; towards the middle of the 18th century pendants and drops were used. By 1770, the neo-classical urn was the most popular main stem motif, the chains were longer, the arms notched and faceted, and the entire chandelier glittered with reflected candlelight.

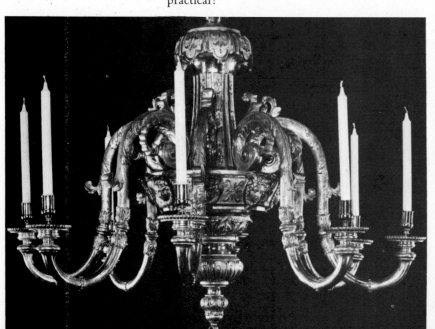

a) Drum table, mahogany; c. 1770; dia. 48" (121 cm.).

Another form of library table, usually with inset tooled leather top, is often called a drum table, for obvious reasons. The popularity and rising value of these tables has produced many fakes in recent years, with bases from plain tripod tables married to new upperworks on which an old plain top may serve again with a leather inset. The shape demands that alternate drawers be dummies; on this fine (and genuine) example, these alternative drawers are without the usual dummy keyholes. The ebony bands round the mahogany column add a nice touch and match ebony cock beads round the drawer fronts.

b) Chest of drawers, mahogany; c. 1775; ht. $31\frac{3}{4}''$ (81 cm.), overall wdth. 34" (86.4 cm.).

The chest of drawers varied from a plain functional piece of bedroom furniture to a splendidly decorated commode (not to be confused with the night-stool or close-chair for which 'commode' is a Victorian euphemism) for the reception room. Though fairly plain, this serpentine-fronted example in nicely figured mahogany represents a typical compromise between plain and fancy. The canted corners with carved reeding and acanthus leaf scrolls emphasize the lines. A pull-out writing slide is fitted and the chased and gilded handles are of fine quality.

c) Arm-chair, carved and gilded; c. 1775; ht. 41" (104 cm.).

This chair illustrates how old and new motifs could exist happily together provided the fundamental proportions were good. The shaped back rest with its knotted ribband is reminiscent of Chippendale's early style, but the laurel-surrounded bust and trailing flower sprays below the ribband are neo-classical.

Passing the acanthus leaf decoration on the arm-rests, we come to an Adam style classical frieze with an urn in the centre and smaller urns at either side. Wheat-ear decoration on the tapering front legs and the stylized acanthus toes complete an assembly which is rich but not gaudy.

Robert Adam (1728-92), architect and designer, believed that architects should concern themselves with everything, not only houses but interior decoration, carpets, furniture, silver, etc., even down to inkstands. His feeling for the classic revival was very strong, and his ideas revolutionized the homes of fashionable England. Straight lines and classical decorations mark his work, which was usually inlaid or painted with urns, swags, figures, etc. William France and Thomas Chippendale are two of the cabinet-makers known to have worked on Adam's designs (see p. 344a and p. 345a).

a) Two dining chairs, mahogany; probably country-made, c. 1775; ht. 36½″ (92.7 cm.).

Although much Georgian furniture was profusely decorated, it was rarely overdecorated and there was considerable demand for undecorated pieces such as these dining chairs from a set of 'twelve and two'. The only apparent concessions to adornment are in the Gothic trefoils where the hooped backs join the plain splats, and in the front legs which have a suggestion of Gothic buttress about them. Otherwise the pleasant effect is achieved by balanced proportions and the subtle curvature of the seat rails.

---

b) Hanging corner cupboard; c. 1780; ht. 43″ (109 cm.), wdth. 27½″ (69.8 cm.), dpth. 17¾″ (45.0 cm.).

A very wide variety of corner cupboards was made; large, small, medium, free-standing, hanging, open-fronted, solid-doored, glazed, bow- and serpentine-fronted, plain oak, lacquered, inlaid—the list is almost endless. This attractive hanging corner cupboard is perfectly plain except for the boxwood stringing and small inlaid panel of contrasting wood; it relies for its decorative effect upon the ingenious glazing bars arranged as a combination of a wide oval, half circles, elipses and Gothic arches.

c) Break-front bookcase, mahogany; c. 1780; wdth. (at top) 29½″ (74.9 cm.).

This small break-front bookcase is attributed to Chippendale Haig & Co. and shows that the firm, almost certainly responsible, supplied plain simple furniture as well as the more elaborate pieces associated with Chippendale's name. The central drawer is an elaborately-fitted secretaire and the appearance of fragility in the glazing bars was achieved by clever use of delicate boxwood stringing. Bookcases were originally considered the province of the architect as being 'built-in' the frame of the room. However, by the mid-18th century, bookcases were being designed by cabinet-makers and subjected to all the usual fashionable influences.

a) Two dumb-waiters; mahogany; c. 1770–80; hts. 39¼" (99.6 cm.) and 45" (114 cm.).

In American usage a dumb-waiter is what the English call a service-lift, but to the English, it is a three- or four-tiered arrangement of revolving trays on a tripod. As an adjunct to the informal meal, the dumb-waiter was a most useful piece of movable furniture on which condiments and other extras could be easily brought within everybody's reach. Like most other items, the dumb-waiter could be plain or decorated, as these show. Unfortunately, many have been dismantled and had the upper parts grafted on to new tripod bases to make individual tables.

b) Invalid's mechanical chair, mahogany, upholstered in red hide; c. 1780; ht. 48" (121 cm.).

Of all the special-purpose furniture shown, this George III propelling chair is the most ingenious. The detachable cranks rotate the brass fore-wheels (originally shod with leather) by bevel gearing, and the chair is much more easily moved and turned than the modern variety, which has propelling hoops attached to the wheels. The foot-rest with its supporting castors folds flat against the chair front when not required and the knob on the right side of the seat controls a catch which firmly locks the wheels. Rather smaller chairs on similar principles were made to fold up for travelling.

c) Three children's chairs; c. 1750–80.

The chairs to right and left of the photograph are miniatures of adults' chairs, with the proportions slightly out of scale, mounted on rockers like those of contemporary cradles. The rush-bottomed chair is typical of the ladder back style popular from about 1750 onwards, and the very primitive one in the centre is from Wales, probably made by a cottager and used, as shown, by being placed on a table or other support. The third chair, of oak, is of later date, probably c. 1780 (cf. p. 334a for earlier rush-bottomed chairs)

a) Four-poster bed with inlaid satinwood posts; c. 1780.

It was an article of faith to our forebears that the night air was dangerous. Having closed heavy shutters over the windows, drawn two or three layers of thick curtaining, arrayed themselves in long flannel nightgowns and padded nightcaps, they retired into a four-poster and drew the curtains to make, in effect, a draught-proof inner room. That most people survived on a straw mattress laid on the floor proved only that they were of inferior clay. This example is of Adam design with a pierced and gilded cornice round the canopy. The hangings are yellow silk taffeta.

b) Oval mirror frame in carved gilt-wood; c. 1785; max. ht. 82" (208 cm.), wdth. 38½" (97.8 cm.).

The slender swags and flowers of this mirror frame are too delicate to execute in carved wood. The technique of applying a thin coat of gesso over carved wood (see p. 330b) as a basis for the gold-leaf, was developed into moulding decorative detail in composition over wooden formers. To achieve the necessary slenderness, the swags and flowers of pieces such as this are moulded on iron wire cores or armatures, instead of wood. This example is probably one of a pair.

c) Library table, mahogany, c. 1780; ht. 32" (81.3 cm.), lgth. 61" (155 cm.).

The double-fronted library table, as it was called in the 18th century, was a logical development from the small knee-hole pedestal desk. The type was shown in Chippendale's *Director* and continued with little change into this century. This finely-figured mahogany example is unadorned except for the Gothic clustered-columns and the oval inlays of crossbanding between boxwood string lines in the end doors. The doors seen here are dummies, as the drawers behind them are real; in the matching pedestal the drawers are simulated but real doors not visible in this photograph open to reveal shelves big enough for folios.

d) Fold-over dressing-table, plain figured mahogany; c. 1785; ht. 29" (73.6 cm.).

Fold-over dressing-tables and washing-stands were made in great numbers in the last third of the 18th century and they display a wide variety of ingenious fitments. When opened, the lids made useful shelves for brushes, bottles and the like which could be stored in the interior compartments. In addition to being adjustable for angle, the looking-glass slides back or forward as required. The drawer is a dummy (because of the lidded compartments behind it) but many examples have one or more real drawers below the dummy.

a) *Pembroke table, satinwood with floral inlay; c. 1780;
ht. 29″ (73.6 cm.), lgth. 36″ (91.4 cm.), open.*

The Earl of Pembroke gave his name to a type
of drop-leaf table on which the leaves were not
supported by a gate-leg or concertina frame, but
by hinged fly brackets. The Pembroke table could
be rectangular, in plain mahogany or other wood,
or shaped to open to an oval, like this example,
with floral inlays of many woods. Pembroke tables
of later date and much less grandeur were stig-
matized by Dickens as being 'made of timber as
green as the trees in the park and just as certain to
shed their leaves before winter'.

b) *Writing desk, satinwood veneered; c. 1780;
ht. 40″ (101 cm.), lgth. 42″ (106 cm.).*

This magnificent tambour cylinder-topped
writing-desk is the ancestor of the roll-top desk
popular some seventy years ago. The pull-out
slides are an unusual and useful feature. The
structure is veneered with satinwood and the
delicate inlays are principally of harewood (green-
stained sycamore). The very slender tapering
fluted legs were much in evidence in Hepplewhite's
designs (see p. 359*d* for explanation of tambour).

---

c) *Lady's dressing-table, inlaid satinwood; c. 1780-90;
ht. 30″ (76.2 cm.), lgth. 48″ (121 cm.).*

The gracious curvature of late Georgian bow
windows was matched by correspondingly convex
chests of drawers, folding tables, and sideboards.
If this piece had a railed, curtained splash-back it
could be mistaken for a bow-front sideboard, but
it is a dressing-table, with ample clearance for a
woman with wide skirts to sit comfortably close
to it. The shape necessitates that drawers in the
sides would be wedge-shaped and as this is impracticable the side compartments are closed by
doors with dummy drawer-fronts.

d) *Chair in painted mock bamboo; Brighton Pavilion
taste; late 18th century; ht. 31⅜″ (80.0 cm.).*

The revival of interest in Chinoiserie between
approximately 1780 and 1810 was fostered by
George IV as Prince of Wales and Regent. Bamboo
was occasionally used for furniture, and mock
bamboo was widely used. The apogee of the taste
for the latter is probably represented by the pair
of cast iron 'bamboo' staircases in the Royal
Pavilion.

This chair is one of a set of seven. Though the
shape is pleasing, it shows the weakness of all
painted furniture which inevitably grows shabby
with use or misuse. A great deal of metal garden
furniture was made to resemble bamboo.

Furniture

English

LATE 18TH CENTURY

a) top: Commode, inlaid; Adam period, c. 1795; ht. 35" (89 cm.), max. wdth. 52" (132 cm.), max. dpth. 19½" (49.5 cm.); bottom: Detail of commode top.

Even if Robert Adam did not design this beautiful commode, it warrants attribution to him, representing as it does the best of English design in being splendid without being vulgar. The piece may have been one of a pair and if Adam was responsible, the decorative detail of the room for which it was designed was probably reproduced in the cabinet. The front panels are subtly curved where they swell into the buttresses. The tapered legs end in gilt metal caps of acanthus leaf form and the wreath-surrounded urns were almost an Adam hall-mark.

a) Sideboard and plate bucket, mahogany; late 18th century; ht. 33¾" (85.7 cm.), wdth. 62" (157 cm.), dpth. 19" (48.2 cm.); plate bucket ht. 16" (40.6 cm.), dia. 14" (36.8 cm.).

This sideboard is of an unusually plain and practical design. The delicately tapered legs and slight inlays on the splash-back suggest Sheraton influence. The brass-bound plate bucket is of the same period. The now-forgotten purpose of these buckets was to carry heated plates from kitchen to dining room; a flannel cover thrown over the bucket helped the wood to keep the heat in, and the slot down the front of the bucket allowed the plates to be lifted out easily. Apart from keeping heat in, the plate bucket provided a safe way to carry valuable porcelain.

b) Dining table, mahogany, banded with satinwood; c. 1790; ht. 29" (73.6 cm.), lgth. 138" (350 cm.).

Mediaeval dining tables were originally trestle affairs which were dismantled and hidden behind the arras when the meal was done, and the tradition of the 'disposable dining table' persisted into the 19th century. This example consists of a drop leaf 'breakfast table' linked to a pair of D-end side-tables, with extra leaves between the centre and tables, all clamped together with brass stirrups and sockets. The more elegant pedestal, or 'pillow and claw' tables were arranged to be similarly linked and are preferable as they give the diners more leg room.

Furniture

English

LATE 18TH CENTURY

c) Chest of drawers, figured mahogany, on 'French' feet with shaped apron; c. 1790; ht. 35" (88.9 cm.), wdth. 35½" (90.1 cm.), dpth. 19¾" (50.1 cm.).

The plain bow-fronted chest of drawers was a stand-by of the furniture trade for over a century. Varying in width from 60" (152 cm.) to less than 36" (91 cm.), the smaller ones are particularly sought after. Early in the 19th century, the bed-room night-stool was often disguised as a small chest of drawers, hence 'commode' became the Victorian euphemism for such a disguised piece. Many of these dummies have been given real drawers and the buyer should examine the inside carefully for traces of joints and hinges, which originally allowed the dummy chest to open along the centre line.

d) Two chairs in mahogany; c. 1790; ht. 35" (88.9 cm.), wdth. 21" (53.3 cm.).

Stark simplicity is not a new trend but 18th-century cabinet-makers usually managed to combine simple lines with harmonious proportions, to create a restrained elegant effect, which is more difficult to achieve than it would appear. These two examples from a set of 'six and two' are of mahogany, but very similar chairs with woven rush seats in place of the drop-in squabs, were made in oak, elm or beech by country joiners. The legs are chamfered and tapered to give an effect of lightness, whilst reeding of different widths emphasizes the vertical and horizontal lines.

a) Work-table, satinwood, Sheraton design; c. 1791–94; ht. 30" (76.2 cm.).

Thomas Sheraton (1751–1806) was born in Durham; by c. 1790 he was living in London. Although in his obituary he was called a journey-man cabinet-maker as well as an author and draughtsman, there is no evidence to suppose he ever had a workshop. Nonetheless, because of his design books a great deal of furniture, particularly satinwood, has been called 'Sheraton'. There is no doubt that his interpretation of the neo-classical style is distinctive, although he also designed many more elaborate Regency pieces.

Some of Sheraton's designs were very complex, particularly those involving mechanical disappearing fitments; some were downright ugly; some could not have been made at all and some of the text of his unfinished *Encyclopaedia* suggests that his mind was going. His first work, the *Cabinet-Maker and Upholsterer's Drawing Book* of 1791–94, contained designs of classic simplicity and elegance. This work-table is taken from the *Drawing Book* and the maker has been content with plain butt-joints for the tray-edges.

b) Welsh dresser, oak; c. 1790; ht. 81" (205 cm.), wdth. 68" (172 cm.), dpth. 20" (50.8 cm.).

This handsome and useful Welsh dresser would be equally at home in a well-to-do farmer's kitchen of the period or in a modern open-plan living room. The dresser as a piece of furniture, whether Welsh or not and whether made of oak, elm or deal was often partly built in or designed to fit a particular alcove. They were generally made by local carpenters rather than furniture makers as such, and could thus be varied to suit the customer—hence the manifold variations. (See p. 341a.)

c) below: Oval breakfast or supper table, mahogany cross-banded with satinwood and tulipwood; late 18th century; dia. 53" (135 cm.); right: Work-table, inlaid rosewood; Victorian; dia. 17" (43.2 cm.).

Toward the end of the 18th century, the pillar and tripod support was sometimes discarded in favour of a quadrupod (left). The four-legged base is handsome and suits large tables better than a tripod but, as every milkmaid knew, a three-legged affair will stand on an uneven surface without rocking. These handsome tables usually have tilting tops and can be stowed in a corner when not wanted.

The work-table (right), with rising top and fitted interior, shows how Victorian designers treated the quadrefoil base.

a) Commode in 'plum pudding' mahogany; c. 1790–1800; ht. 34" (86.4 cm.), wdth. 42" (107 cm.).

Like Sheraton, George Hepplewhite did not claim to have 'invented' any new style; not even the pretty shield or heart-shaped chair backs particularly associated with his name. However, the Hepplewhite design label can be put on this serpentine chest of drawers, one of a pair, and grand enough to be called a commode. It is cross-banded with satinwood, with a small band of box and ebony dentilation round the top, and ebony stringing to emphasize the canted corners. The splayed-out legs and shaped apron are often ascribed to Sheraton but the late 18th century cabinet trade simply called them French feet.

George Hepplewhite had been apprenticed to Gillow of Lancaster. His *Cabinet Makers' and Upholsterers' Guide* was published after his death in 1786, with around 300 drawings. Although his designs made no pretence of originality, they do give a good picture of prevailing taste at the end of the century.

b) Writing-table, rosewood; c. 1795; ht. 29½" (74.9 cm.), lgth. 92" (234 cm.).

When letter-writing was the only alternative to direct verbal communication, writing furniture assumed great importance and took a wide variety of shapes. Secrétaire drawers were let into book-cases, work-tables, chests of drawers and similar. This writing-table can also serve as a sofa-table. The fold-over end flaps, supported on concealed lopers when open, conceal compartments for pens, wax, paper and other writing utensils; the central surface is faced with leather. The severe plainness of the piece is relieved by plain but bold gilt-brass bands and mounts.

---

c) Commode, satinwood veneers; c. 1790–1800; ht. 34" (86.3 cm.), wdth. 42" (106 cm.).

The commode, in its original sense of a decorative chest of drawers, and/or cabinet enclosed by doors, was enthusiastically developed by English makers—usually without the superfluity of gilt-metal (ormolu) mounts which the French ébénistes tended to use in large amounts. This example combines a convex chest of three drawers with two concave-fronted cabinets, standing on tapering legs with spade feet typical of the period. The satin-wood veneers are emphasized by rosewood borders and adorned with flower paintings. The keyhole plates are made of ivory.

a) Dressing-table mirror on a Sheraton mahogany cylinder bureau; c. 1800; overall ht. 34″ (86.4 cm.), wdth. 17″ (43.2 cm.).

In the early 1700s dressing-table mirror bases were often made in the form of miniature bureaux with interior fitments which made good hidey-holes for trinkets. The fashion persisted alongside other types into the 19th century. This example has cross-banding of the lower drawer and cylinder in satinwood, bordered with box and ebony; the small drawers are fronted with satinwood, bordered with harewood and box, and cross-banded in mahogany. The mirrored central compartment reflects a tessellated floor of box and ebony; with the writing slide pushed back and the cylinder front closed, an inlaid shell motif appears.

b) Sofa-table in mahogany, cross-banded with satin-wood emphasized by ebony stringing; c. 1800; ht. 59″ (150 cm.), wdth. 27″ (68.6 cm.).

The sofa-table was originally placed in or near the centre of a room so that the light from a candel-abrum placed on it would benefit the occupants of a sofa (or chairs) placed with back-rest against it; it was also used as a writing-table. Because of its central position, both long sides were similarly decorated and the real drawers in one face were matched by dummies in the other. The hinged flaps were held up by fly brackets. Here, the elegantly curved supports are made to appear lighter by clever tapering of the reeding.

c) Two hall chairs, mahogany; c. 1800; ht. 32″ (86.3 cm.).

This pair from a set of six are typical examples of a type made, with appropriate variations, from the mid-18th century. The turned front legs and lattice work suggest the date and though not taken directly from his book, the design is in the Sheraton manner. Through all the variations of style two features remain constant: the reserves, carrying the owner's monogram or coat-of-arms and the un-comfortable flat wooden seats which were clearly thought good enough for the insensitive bottoms of those who might have to wait in the hall for their betters.

d) Two chairs, beech with cane-work backs and seats; Sheraton style, c. 1800; ht. 35″ (88.9 cm.).

Country-made chairs with woven rush seats were made throughout the 18th century, but cane-work backs and seats disappeared from 'polite' usage for almost a century. The contrast between these Sheraton-style chairs and those in p. 327a needs no emphasis. Whether caned or not, whether designed by Sheraton or Hepplewhite, whether made by Seddon or Gillow. the functional purity of such chairs as these could not be bettered. Painted black and gold with coloured flowers in the back rails, these chairs are strong, light, elegant *and* comfortable.

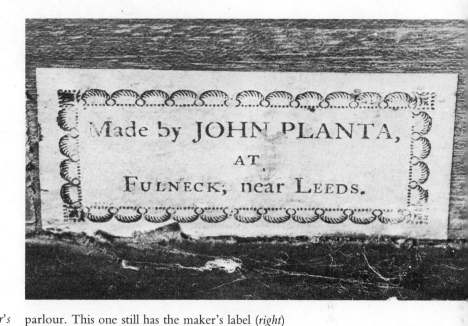

a) left: Spinning wheel, mahogany, and right: Maker's label; c. 1800; ht. 27″ (68.5 cm.) to table top.

The spinning wheel at which the cottager toiled long hours for meagre reward was a sturdy machine, usually of elm or beech. Prettified wheels such as this were made in mahogany or satinwood with ivory fitments, for the lady's boudoir or parlour. This one still has the maker's label (*right*) in the drawer, and for all its delicate appearance it is no ornamental toy but a perfectly operational machine. Spinning their own wool, possibly gathered from the quickset-hedgerows, became a fashionable pursuit for young ladies of Jane Austen's England.

---

b) Chair with scimitar legs, grisaille decoration on black background; c. 1800; ht. 36″ (90.0 cm.).

Scimitar legs, often mis-called sabre legs, were part of the neo-classical detail popularized by Adam, Sheraton and others, and inspired by the curved chair legs of classical Greece. Curved legs are desirable at the back of the chair as they help prevent overbalancing and the load on the seat-joint is taken in compression. Similarly curved front legs are less defensible mechanically, as they put the important joints between legs and side-rails in tension which tends to pull them apart. Nevertheless, the effect is so pleasing to the eye that its mechanical shortcomings must be forgiven. There is a cane seat below the squab.

Grisaille is a method of painting in greys to give the effect of sculptured relief. This kind of work was often done on stained glass.

c) Davenport, mahogany; early 19th century; ht. 37¼″ (95.2 cm.), wdth. 22¼″ (56.5 cm.), dpth. 20″ (50.8 cm.).

The original Davenport, it is believed, was made by Gillows for a Captain Davenport, who wanted a small but commodious desk-cum-chest of drawers to take to India. By 1800, the Davenport had become domesticated as this example shows. The desk slides forward on concealed runners over the user's knees, a large pull-out slide over the large drawers provides a shelf for papers, and the small drawers in the desk contain ink bottles, pen-tray and so forth. By 1840, the Davenport was further modified and had the desk permanently jutting forward, supported on scrolled brackets rising from a curved platform base (see p. 365b).

Furniture

English

EARLY 19TH CENTURY

a) *Carlton House writing-table, rosewood; c. 1805; ht. 39" (99.0 cm.), wdth. 68" (172 cm.).*

Advertised 'As supplied to H.R.H. the Prince of Wales at Carlton House', this type of writing-table is believed to have originated with George Seddon about 1780. Seddon's large firm—he employed over 400 men—was responsible for much fine late Georgian and Regency furniture. This particularly rich example, profusely mounted and inlaid with gilt brass, is attributed to the workshops of John McLean. The addition of gilt metal collars to the turned legs is interesting and uncommon.

George Seddon was born in 1727, and established his own firm around the middle of the century. He was very successful, and his firm is the largest known cabinet-making workshop of the period. He died in 1801, and his sons carried on the business until the mid-19th century.

Much less is known about John McLean, who worked in London (1774-1814). He was listed in Thomas Sheraton's *Cabinet Dictionary* as a master craftsman, and advertised that he specialized in 'elegant Parisian furniture'.

---

b) *Couch, in gilded beechwood; by Gillow of Lancaster, c. 1805; ht. 32½" (82.5 cm.), lgth. 80" (203 cm.), dpth. 31" (78 cm.).*

According to Cornelia Knight, when the Prince of Wales (later Prince Regent) learned of the death of Nelson he 'threw himself upon the sopha in a phrenzy' and later 'calmed his hystericks with a beaker of brandy'. It is on just such a couch, or 'sopha', as this that he might have thrown himself, since the gilded lion heads and paw feet suggest that it might well have been made in the year of

Trafalgar, 1805. With variations in the decorative motifs, the basic form remained popular throughout the 19th century.

The firm of Gillow had been established in Lancaster early in the 18th century. They opened premises in London in 1760, and continued, under various names, as cabinet makers and upholsterers. Late in the century (c. 1790) their name was sometimes stamped on their work as 'Gillows', or 'Gillows, Lancaster'. After 1820, almost all their work was so marked.

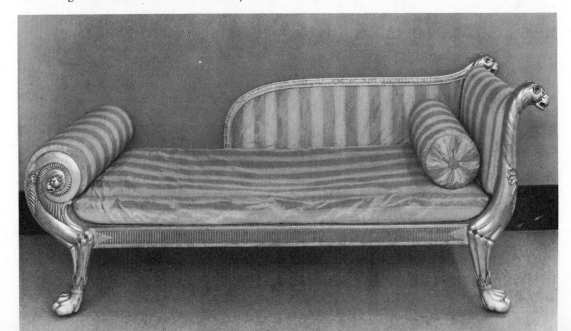

a) Pair of fold-over pedestal tables in rosewood with brass inlaid foliage borders; c. 1810; ht. 28″ (71.1 cm.), wdth. 36″ (91.4 cm.).

The principle of this type of table was evolved about 1730; the lower half of the 'fold' is pivoted slightly off-centre, so that when the top is turned through ninety degrees and opened, the centre of the extended surface is in line with the centre of the base. This elegant pair is baize-lined, for card-playing or writing, although sometimes they were veneered all over, and could then be used as tea or supper tables. The bases of fold-over tables, usually sold in pairs, illustrate a wide variety of fashions.

b) Porter's chair in panelled mahogany; early 19th century; ht. 65″ (165 cm.), wdth. 26″ (66.0 cm.).

In grand houses, two or more men-servants were permanently on duty in the hall to answer the front door, to hand visitors in or out of their carriages and otherwise attend them. The senior factotum, or hall porter, was allowed a chair (the lesser footmen had to stand) and, as even the grandest of halls could be draughty, the porter's chair was made rather like a sentry-box. A framed structure covered with leather and studded with brass-domed nails was usual, which makes this panelled example as unusual as it is imposing.

c) Canterbury in satinwood with turned legs; c. 1810; wdth. 20″ (50.8 cm.).

The original canterbury was designed as a portfolio rack for the Archbishop of Canterbury. On a smaller scale, it was soon considered a useful adjunct to the newly-fashionable pianoforte, as a holder for sheet-music. The lift-up table-top of this example is a rare feature. The canterbury took many forms, but the essential features of divisions above and a drawer in the base are common to all. The tapered legs and pillars of this example are made to appear hexagonal by the use of ebony stringing, which also emphasizes the side and end panels.

d) Writing-table with tambour shutter, mahogany; Sheraton style, c. 1810; ht. 38″ (96.5 cm.).

For no discernible etymological reason the type of folding cover enclosing this writing-table is known as a tambour shutter. It consists of a series of shaped slats glued to strong canvas, running in grooves at either side of the piece. When pushed up and back, the tambour shutter slides into a narrow compartment behind the pigeon holes inside the desk; the writing slide may then be pulled forward to reveal a well. The tambour shutter principle is particularly associated with early Sheraton and Hepplewhite designs and was used for cupboards and cabinets as well as for these roll-top desks (see p. 351*b*).

a) Centre table in pale mahogany, inlaid with ebony and silver; by Thomas Hope, c. 1807; ht. 28⅜″ (72.0 cm.), dia. 41⅝″ (106 cm.).

Thomas Hope (1770–1831), novelist, man of fashion and wealth, published his *Household Furniture and Interior Decoration* in which he gave a fillip to the Egyptian taste which came to the fore after the Battle of the Nile. This table was made for Hope's house near Guildford, where it remained until 1916. Not all his designs were so successful. Prince Pückler-Muskau (see p. 360c) visited Hope's town house and wrote: 'He is very rich and his house full of treasures. . . . His furniture theory, fashioned on the antique, I cannot praise in practice: the chairs are ungovernable . . . and the sophas have such sharp, salient points in all directions that an incautious sitter might hurt himself severely.'

b) 'Egyptian' bookcase in satinwood with ormolu mounts; c. 1810; ht. 100″ (254 cm.), wdth. 49⅛″ (124 cm.), dpth. 22⅜″ (57.1 cm.).

If the ancient Egyptians had bookcases, we may be tolerably certain they were nothing like this one which is said to be based on a drawing by Sheraton rather than Thomas Hope, as might have been expected. Like those of Chinese Chippendale, the Egyptian details were, in a sense, mere frippery, but in the hands of a master the style succeeded, as the basic forms were so good. The purist may note the busts surmounting the tapering terms or pilasters suggest Caesar's Rome, rather than Cleopatra's Egypt. The lion's paw feet remained popular long after the other Egyptian detail had gone out of favour.

c) Pair of tub chairs in mahogany with gilded lion masks and paw feet; Thomas Hope style, Regency; ht. 34″ (86.3 cm.), wdth. 30″ (76.2 cm.).

These arm-chairs in the Thomas Hope manner explain Prince Pückler-Muskau's choice of the word 'ungovernable' (cf. p. 360a); the lions do appear somewhat aggressive! The fundamental shape is both excellent and comfortable, the carved decoration on the rails and the gilded lions' heads and paws is admirable, and yet the effect is ponderous and unbalanced. The chairs therefore also illustrate that the lack of proportions, so evident in much Victorian furniture, started during the Regency. Prince Pückler-Muskau of Poland came to England to find a rich wife, which would enable him to support his extravagant mistress. One is happy to record that he succeeded!

a) Chair in painted wood; designed by Sir Astley Cooper, early 19th century; ht. 36¾" (93.3 cm.), wdth. 15" (38.1 cm.), seat only 7" (17.8 cm.) deep.

These curiously proportioned chairs with narrow seats were made in great numbers and were usually undecorated. They are now very useful as 'telephone' chairs in narrow hallways, and are called crofters' chairs, farthingale chairs, spinning chairs, or anything but the correct name, which is Astley Cooper chairs. They were designed to train children to sit correctly, avoiding curvature of the spine, by Sir Astley Cooper, a fashionable surgeon who was knighted by the Prince Regent after he had removed an unsightly wen from the Royal neck.

b) Lady's writing-table in rosewood, the top banded in satinwood and tulipwood; early 19th century; ht. 25½" (64.8 cm.), wdth. 21" (53.3 cm.).

This little drawing-room piece for dashing off the occasional scented missive is typical of 'Ladies Furniture' of the early 19th century. The drawer is pulled out to disclose a hinged leather-covered writing surface with compartments below for writing utensils; a subsidiary drawer slides out from the main one to bring the pen tray and ink bottles within reach. The sliding silk screen shields the writer's eyes from flickering fire-light, which is necessary in a candle-lit room. The familiar pole-screens served the same purpose, and were not primarily to shield complexions from the fire's heat, as is usually implied.

c) Chiffonier cabinet in satinwood, the top with a cross-banded border in rosewood; c. 1810; ht. 37½" (95.2 cm.), wdth. 50" (127 cm.), dpth. 19" (48.2 cm.).

The chiffonier was originally a small shelved bedroom cupboard for handkerchiefs, jabots, cravats, muslin shawls and other *chiffons*. It developed into a popular drawing-room cabinet during the Regency as this Egyptian-style example shows. Shorn of its period detail, with panelled doors in place of the gilt brass grilles and a heavily scrolled splash-back and mouldings, the chiffonier developed into a popular form of Victorian sideboard. By reversing the process, clever practitioners have been known to turn Victorian sideboards into Regency chiffoniers.

d) Two dining chairs in mahogany (from a set of 16) with scimitar legs; early 19th century; ht. 35" (88.9 cm.).

The curved legs of these chairs entitle them to the label Regency but some aspects of the broad top rails and acanthus centre rails suggest a slightly later period. It is difficult to be dogmatic; similar chairs to these but with turned Victorian legs are shown in George Smith's *A Collection of Designs for Household Furniture* of 1808, but some cabinet-makers were still making chairs with the more pleasing curved legs as late as 1845. Whether they were made in 1810 or 1830, these chairs are pleasing and practical.

a) Sideboard in rosewood with matching fitted knife-boxes; early 19th century; ht. 54½″ (138 cm.), wdth. 74″ (187 cm.), dpth. 30″ (76.2 cm.).

The carving-table flanked by pedestal cupboards, themselves surmounted by 'cutlery urns' or vase-shaped fitted knife-boxes, evolved into the one-piece sideboard, of which this is a Regency example. Some slight concession to the Egyptian taste is made in the shapes of the pedestals and cutlery boxes, which were soon to disappear in favour of fitted cutlery drawers. The six drawers and cupboards provide ample space for tablecloth, napkins, silver-mounted sauce or vinegar bottles, salt cellar and so on; originally, a matching lead-lined wine cistern probably stood between the pedestals.

b) Pembroke table in solid mahogany with butterfly flaps; Regency; ht. 28″ (71.1 cm.), wdth. 36″ (91.4 cm.), open.

This very plain Pembroke table has the serpentine edges to the flaps which entitle it to the rather fancy name of butterfly table. As butterfly tables are more valuable than plain ones, it is not unknown for rectangular flaps to go through a metamorphosis similar to that of the real butterfly. With veneered, cross-banded or inlaid tables the transformation is difficult and expensive; with unadorned solid wood flaps, such as these, it is easy and cheap. The collector must consider whether the serpentine edges are congruous with the style and proportions of the piece as a whole.

c) Table in mahogany, the top decorated with pen-and-ink drawing; signed and dated, Henzell Gooch, 1815; *ht. 28¼″ (71.8 cm.), lgth. 61¾″ (157 cm.), wdth. 25¾″ (65.4 cm.).*

This centre or sofa-table embodies several favoured Regency motifs such as the lyre-shaped end supports (see p. 363b), stylized rope-twist and acanthus leaf carving and cast brass lion's paw feet concealing castors. The decoration of the top, a landscape with a border of birds and flowers, is applied to the pale wood heavily enough to incise the surface slightly. A sheet of glass secured by a brass edge protects this decoration, but most pen-work pieces relied on the normal varnishing and polishing processes to preserve them.

d) Multiple-use table in rosewood with lacquered brass inlays, acanthus leaf mounts and brass lion's paw feet; c. 1820; ht. 28¾″ (72.0 cm.), dpth. 19⅝″ (50.1 cm.).

This Regency table has a sliding bag for needle-work materials, an adjustable slope for reading or writing, fitted drawers for silks, thimbles, pins, ink-bottles, etc. and a pull-out slide (originally with a little leather tongue to pull) inlaid as a chess board. The little gallery rails were to prevent candlesticks from being knocked over. It is as pleasant a little piece of furniture as one could wish for, and a good example of the ingenious way a variety of uses could be built into one small table.

a) *Plate rack, in mahogany; c. 1820 Regency; ht. 29″ (73.6 cm.).*

In the Regency household, the plate rack was a convenient wheeled table on which plates and dishes could be stacked for an impromptu snack, such as a 'devilled bone' or 'toasted pettitoes', eaten by the fireside. The column of this plate rack suggests the cabinet-makers were beginning to lose their eye for proportion. The rope-twist portion is needlessly stout, and perched rather incongruously on a fluted 'bun', which in turn sprouts from a rather coarse acanthus. Nevertheless the whole effect is still graceful.

b) *Sofa-table in mahogany, cross-banded with tulip-wood, enclosed in box and ebony stringing; c. 1825; wdth. 61″ (154 cm.).*

Together with dolphins, sphinxes, Egyptian terms or caryatids the lyre was a popular Regency —William IV—decorative motif. It is used here with splendid effect in the end supports of this sofa-table. The curved stretcher is an unusual feature: the lion's paw feet and *paterae* are of gilt brass. Lyre-end, sofa- and centre-tables were extremely popular and can be found in mahogany, rosewood, satinwood, lacquered and painted versions (see p. 362c).

Furniture

English

EARLY 19TH CENTURY

c) *Cheval glass in mahogany with ebony inlay; c. 1820; ht. 63″ (160 cm.), wdth. 29¼″ (74.9 cm.).*

This was also known as a horse glass, logically following the usage of clothes-horse, towel-horse, etc. In this case, the 'horse' was the four-legged frame on which the glass hung. The cheval glass came into being in the 18th century when making large sheets of mirror glass was difficult and expensive. Consequently, at first, half-length glasses were used which slid up and down like sash windows between hollow supports containing the counter-balance weights. Later they were made in one piece, as in this full-length example.

d) *Two arm-chairs japanned in black with gilt Chinoiserie decoration; Regency period; ht. 35″ (88.9 cm.), wdth. 21″ (53.3 cm.).*

Chinoiserie decoration appears on the back-rests of these black and gilt chairs. Apart from the little paintings on the back-centres and top-rails, the chairs are wholly English in style and the simulated festoons of drapery were used in many of George Hepplewhite's designs. Hepplewhite died in 1786 but his *Cabinet Maker and Upholster's Guide* was not published until after his death. His style therefore corresponds to the *Directoire* period in France. Hepplewhite did not necessarily invent all the various designs and motifs attributed to him, but codified and improved fashions already current.

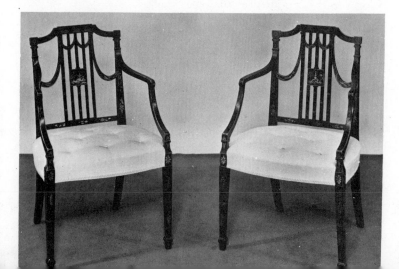

Furniture

English

a) What-not stand in rosewood; early 19th century; ht. 38″ (96.5 cm.), wdth. 19″ (48.2 cm.).

This most useful piece of furniture is still with us in the form of the multi-stage storage rack or room divider. At first (c. 1760) the wotnot, or what-not—both forms were used—was a tall tapering stand, often 84″ (213 cm.) high, for the display of *bibelots*. In its smaller form with all the tiers of equal size, it was used for almost any purpose from bedside table to book stand. A folding book-rest was often fitted into one of the upper stages and drawers were not always confined to the lowest shelf. Many 'wotnots' have been cut up to make pairs or sets of matching tables.

b) Card-table in rosewood on quadrefoil pedestal base; c. 1830–37; ht. 28½″ (72.3 cm.), wdth. 36″ (91.4 cm.).

This fold-over table was most probably made during the short reign of King William IV. Sometimes the period 1830–37 is referred to as the 'Adelaide Style' but Queen Adelaide's only known contributions to the domestic scene were Berlin wool-work (see p. 279a and d), and the Christmas tree. William IV disliked flummery, and wrote of the ·refurbishing of the private apartments at Buckingham Palace that he 'desires they may be plain and very little gilt', but he could not halt the trend towards over-decoration and heavy proportions.

---

c) Chair in papier mâché, c. 1840; ht. 33¼″ (84.4 cm.), wdth. 19¾″ (50.1 cm.), dpth. of seat 15¾″ (40.0 cm.).

18th century *papier mâché*, or more properly *carton pierre*, was made by glueing many sheets of strong paper together under pressure, dampening and moulding the resultant sheets of material and then decorating and finishing. Many splendid large trays with excellent flower or landscape paintings were made in this way. In the early 19th century, firms such as Clay, and also Jennens and Betteridge, improved the process by mixing and boiling cuttings of coarse paper in a solution of gum arabic. This pulped, or mâché, material could be moulded into elaborate shapes and was cheap, light and very strong. It was finished with many coats of black varnish, giving almost as durable a finish as stove enamelling.

d) Escritoire in white deal with mahogany veneers, c. 1845; ht. 43″ (109 cm.), wdth. 39″ (99.0 cm.).

Bonheur du jour is the French name for an English secretary table, although escritoire was also used. Though fundamentally a mid-18th century design, this one betrays its Victorian period by the unnecessarily robust structure of the clumsy scrolled end supports and feet, and the fussy brackets supporting the upper shelf. The feather mahogany veneers are nicely matched, but examination shows the piece to be a product of the machine age; the veneers are machine cut and paper thin and the 'carved' beading is cunningly-moulded plaster.

364

a) Gothic wardrobe; designed by Pugin, made by Crace of Wigmore Street, London, c. 1851.

Chippendale Gothic, Strawberry Hill Gothic and Regency Gothic styles were historically inaccurate or anachronistic yet continued to be pleasing and gay. Victorian Gothic was scholarly and accurate but rather forbidding. There were moral and religious overtones springing from the notion that the only 'true' religious architecture was Gothic. Augustus Welby Pugin, who was responsible for the Gothic detail in the new Houses of Parliament, approached the business with a zealot's fervour. This wardrobe was illustrated in the *Industrial Arts Journal* in 1851. One feels it would be incorrect to hang anything less than a chasuble and mitre in it.

b) Drawing-room davenport in yellowish walnut; c. 1850–70; wdth. 54″ (137 cm.).

Captain Davenport's ingenious travelling desk-cum-chest of drawers grew up into a stationary piece for the drawing-room (cf. p. 357c). The desk portion no longer had to slide back over the chest to save space in a ship's cabin, but could be larger and project permanently. In this form it was (apparently) supported by scrolled fly-brackets or, as in this example, by pillars rising from a shaped plateau. Many hundreds of these neat and useful small desks were made in the Victorian era, early ones of rosewood and mahogany, later ones—like this—of yellowish walnut. The barley-sugar twist legs and bun feet of late 17th century furniture staged a Victorian come-back but, inevitably, with the proportions sadly coarsened.

c) Two matching chairs in mahogany; by Henry Eyles of Bath, made for the 1851 Exhibition; ht. 44½″ (113 cm.), and 36″ (91.4 cm.), wdth. 44″ (112 cm.) and 20″ (50.8 cm.).

The every-picture-tells-a-story school of art influenced Victorian furniture design. These chairs have portraits of the Queen and Prince Albert on Worcester porcelain plaques. Apart from some fussiness of scrollwork round the portrait and rather clumsily proportioned front legs, the up- right chair is far from despicable. The arm-chair, however, shows many of the faults of later Victorian furniture. The exaggerated curves do nothing to hide the bloated proportions of the front legs, the gross scrolled curls below the arm-rests serve no purpose and, as a machine for sitting in, the piece fails because the seat is too deep from front to back and the back-rest too sharply raked; the occupant would be without lumbar support.

French Furniture Introduction

The evolution of French furniture is traditionally divided into periods. These periods, characterized by changes in style, sometimes have to be modified in terms of contemporary developments in other countries.

The Middle Ages describes, rather loosely, the Romanesque and Gothic periods, of which examples are very rare outside a few churches and museums. In mediaeval France, furniture reflected the successive phases of architectural decoration.

The Renaissance began much later in France than in Italy. In common with the rest of French art the decorative arts remained untouched till the beginning of the sixteenth century, when designs inspired by classical antiquity first appeared. The Renaissance style extends to the last years of the sixteenth century.

The Louis XIII style encompasses the reigns of Henri IV (1553–1610) and Louis XIII (1610–1643), a period characterized by a return to simple, rather geometric forms and to heavy woods. The most important influences came from Spain and the north, whereas the style of Louis XIV, which corresponds to the actual reign of the King (1660–1715), looks towards Italy with its taste for ostentation and for the figurative in art. However, the baroque, spreading rapidly across Europe at that time, left France relatively untouched. Only a few external features were used, without the adoption of fundamental principles.

The Régence (1715–1723) describes the transitional period between Louis XIV and Louis XV and in effect covers the first third of the eighteenth century.

The Louis XV style is contemporary with the rococo in Europe, but it is much less exaggerated in France than in Austria or Italy, for example. French rococo, even if it does subscribe to asymmetry and the sinuous line, is nevertheless characterized by a sense of what is fitting and by a dislike of exaggeration. The style became so popular that it continued for a very long time in the provinces, resisting the introduction of neo-classicism, already firmly established in England. During the years between 1760 and 1775 some features of the Louis XV style, curved legs for instance, were combined in a transitional style with the plain lines characteristic of Louis XVI.

European neo-classicism includes the Louis XVI and Empire styles, the first a forerunner of the second, but with more traditional features. Much gilt or painted wood was used for chairs, beds and consoles. The Empire period marks the introduction of an almost exclusive use of mahogany, a fashion imported from England, although in France it was everywhere enriched with bronze, even on chairs. The French Empire style, with some modifications, spread throughout Europe culminating in the Restoration in France, and Biedermeier in Germany and Austria. The eclectic Napoleon III style and a general lack of creative imagination prevailed in Europe throughout the second half of the nineteenth century.

On the whole France may be said to reflect European styles, either initiating a new style or borrowing from her neighbours, in which case she usually also imported a new technique: Italian joinery methods in the fifteenth century, for instance; Flemish or Italian inlay and marquetry during the seventeenth century; English mahogany in the latter part of the eighteenth century, or even today's techniques used for metal and plastics, originating in Germany or America.

French furniture owes its exceptional quality to the demand for perfection of execution and design expressed by an informed clientèle, and to the immense technical skill of the craftsmen, especially those in Paris, who were protected and controlled by the corporate guilds. The combined effect of an élite with a passion for decorating their houses, of creative designers on the lookout for anything new and of skilled craftsmen to carry out their demands has given French furniture those qualities of elegance and finish which are so eagerly sought by collectors throughout the world.

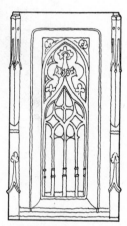

a) Cupboard at Aubazine; 13th century; ht. 60½″ (154 cm.).

This cupboard, one of the earliest surviving mediaeval pieces, shows that the first furniture-makers were really carpenters who adapted their own methods to a different purpose: thick planks hammered together for seating (benches, stools and chairs with backs), and plain joints for chests. The wooden carcass was then reinforced with iron bands to overcome any weakness in the jointing. The decoration is arcading reminiscent of the Romanesque style.

b) Gothic buffet; late 15th century; ht. 45″ (114 cm.).

Apart from chests, the commonest all-purpose design in the Middle Ages was the dresser or buffet, because it was used not only as a cupboard (if it had handles it could also be moved) but also as a seat and even a bed. Both dresser and buffet, being intended for the great hall, were more important than the chest. The dresser is made of shelves whereas the buffet is closed with two doors in the upper storey. It may also, as in the illustration, have two sliding drawers, showing the technical advance made by the joiners.

Detail of panel, Gothic buffet (b).

c) Gothic chest; 15th century; ht. 34½″ (87.6 cm.).

Comparison with *a* shows how methods had developed. Henceforward the woodworker's tools are distinct from those of the carpenter. Tenon and mortice joints with wooden dowels (and the later improvement of dove-tailing, which was used by the Egyptians and apparently re-discovered in Italy) eliminate the necessity for iron reinforcement. Now this method of assembly enabled tongued and grooved, carved panels to be inserted without glue, thus making the whole piece more flexible.

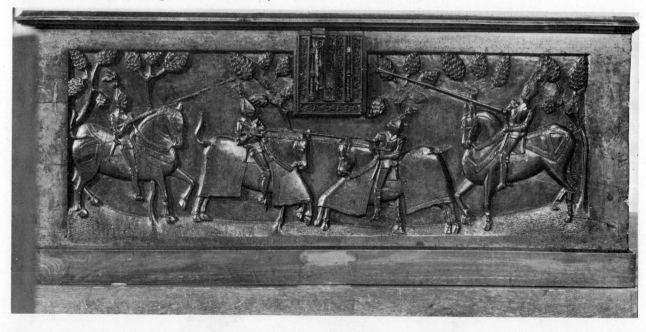

a) Bed from Château de Villeneuve-Lembron; 15th century; ht. 98″ (250 cm.), lgth. 81½″ (207 cm.).

This type of joinery bed, constructed either of side panels with two or, more often, four bed-posts, was the rule until the 17th century. The decoration is typical of the period. Linen-fold panelling for the lower part, with Gothic leaf-design and tracery on the tester. Carved ornament became general before the 15th century, without superseding painted decoration, which, owing to its fragile nature, has only rarely survived.

b) 'Chaire' with flamboyant decoration; late 15th century, ht. 78½″ (200 cm.), wdth. 30½″ (77 cm.).

Furniture of all kinds—chests, beds and seats— was constructed on the same principle, that is a framework filled in with ornamental panels. Of them all, the high-backed chair with arm-rests, reserved for the head of the household, has best withstood the test of time. The bottom was used for a chest and is decorated with linen-fold, while the motif on the back is arcading in the flamboyant style. Chairs sometimes have a canopy. The seat is usually rather high and varies in width, sometimes even in two places. A cushion, called *le carreau* overcame the discomfort of a hard wooden seat.

Furniture

French

15TH CENTURY

c) Table; late 15th century; ht. 29½″ (75 cm.).

The mediaeval table was normally a plain piece of wood laid on two trestles and covered with a cloth or precious fabric. There are some less crude examples: for instance, this small octagonal table, collapsible so that it can be easily moved. It shows just how far the joiners had advanced by the end of the Middle Ages. Another feature of this functional piece, the lectern, displays their ingenuity even further. It is a desk set on a movable pivot, enabling the clerk to read or write in a convenient position. The lectern has survived in the shape of the ecclesiastical pulpit.

*Opposite:
Dressing-table from the private apartments of the Empress Josephine, by the bronzier Thomire; France, 1809.*

Detail of profile medallion from chest (a).

a) Chest, said to be from Azay-le-Rideau; c. 1510–1515; ht. 41" (104 cm.), lgth. 79⅝" (202 cm.).

As new styles are foreshadowed in architecture by decoration, so also with furniture. Traditional shapes remain unchanged and the techniques are the same, but a whole new range of ornament (profile-medallions, scrolls, grotesques, candelabra, putti and ox-masks) appears on church façades and chests, proclaiming the discovery of the Italian Renaissance. New types of furniture, inspired by the study of classical buildings, do not make an appearance till later.

b) Fan-shaped table; mid-16th century; ht. 28" (71 cm.).

Imitation of classical antiquity is much more marked in this table—a replica in wood of the Roman *cartibulum*. The trestle-table was still in use, but a prestige table, or central console, now appeared. Many engravings of these tables (by Du Cerceau and Sambin) as well as the tables themselves (at Dijon, Besançon, Chantilly and Toulouse) have survived. They are usually made of walnut as if French joiners, abandoning the traditional oak in favour of walnut, wanted to acknowledge their debt to their Cisalpine colleagues.

Opposite:
Top: Small Louis XVI ormolu-mounted tulipwood cabinet stamped M. Carlin JME inset with four Sèvres plaques; France, c. 1775.
Bottom: Commode made by Gaudreaux for Henriette de France; France, 1740.

a) Sambin cabinet; 1574–1575; ht. 62¼″ (158 cm.).

Two different styles can be distinguished in these pieces, which are usually described as cabinets. The first, characterized by large figures in very high relief framing historical scenes, either painted or carved in low-relief, seems to derive directly from François I's designers at the first school of Fontainebleau. The fanciful, even preposterous French interpretations of Italian models are a good example of Mannerist taste for exaggerated form and effect. This tendency reveals the influence of the Dijon *ornemaniste*, Hugues Sambin, and pieces in this style are, perhaps all too readily, described as Burgundian or Sambin cabinets.

---

b) Cabinet; 1550–1600; ht. 71″ (180 cm.).

In the same way a certain kind of monumental furniture in which architectural themes—columns, pilasters, pediments, and cornices—predominate over relief-carving, is automatically attributed to the Ile-de-France. This refined style seems to have originated with the French designers trained in Italy (Philibert Delorme, Jacques Androuet Ducerceau), who absorbed the true principles of the Renaissance instead of reproducing only its external features. However, the two movements overlap so often that systematic classification is impossible.

Furniture

French
16TH CENTURY

a) Chair, the so-called 'caquetoire'; c. 1570; ht. 44¼″ (112 cm.), wdth. 22½″ (57 cm.).

The 16th century saw a fundamental change in chair construction. Immobile, heavy chairs and benches were replaced by chairs that can be described as conversation-furniture, because they were light enough to be moved about to suit an assembly. The most original design is seen in this nearly triangular seat with narrow back, many of which have survived, and which are usually (and probably inaccurately) described as *caquetoires*. This example is of exceptional quality with a finely-carved figure of Diana and arm-rests terminating in ram's heads.

b) Table, walnut carved with foliate designs, the legs of baluster form; late 16th century; ht. 33″ (84 cm.), wdth. 32″ (81 cm.).

The somewhat austere style of this table may be regarded as a strictly French contribution to the furniture of the period. On the other hand, the marquetry and polychrome decoration then popular show the effect of Italian—and especially Flemish—influence on the privileged workshops set up by Henri IV to instil new life into the artist-craftsmen. Because they were usually concealed by a cloth, tables were generally simple in design.

---

c) Ebony cabinet; early 17th century; ht. 83″ (211 cm.).

The influence of Italian, and especially Florentine, inlay work had long been the inspiration for the efforts of French woodcarvers to use expensive materials and woods, ivory, ebony or coloured wood. A few Renaissance cupboards were even inlaid with marble or porphyry plaques. Early in

the 17th century, the process of veneering produced a rather different result. The carcass of a piece was completely covered in ebony veneer, cut thickly enough to allow low-relief carving. Its form was very plain, relying on the scenes carved on the doors for decoration. Contemporary engravings supplied the subjects.

Furniture

French
16TH–17TH CENTURY

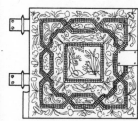

Detail of cabinet door (c).

a) Bed, said to have belonged to M. le Maréchal d'Effiat; 17th century; ht. 117½″ (298 cm.), lgth. 65″ (165 cm.).

Rich fabrics offset the austere effect of material (ebony and walnut) and form in the furniture of the period with textiles as important in decoration as they had been in the Middle Ages. High-warp tapestries, rich braiding, brocades or plain woollen material were all used for bed-curtains and wall-hangings to lend colour to interior furnishing. Post beds were still entirely surrounded with curtains as seen in this example. Engravings such as the famous interiors by Abraham Bosse (1602–1676) give the best impression of the period since very few genuine Louis XIII pieces have survived.

Furniture

French

17TH CENTURY

b) Fauteuil; Louis XIII (1610–1643); ht. 35½″ (90 cm.).

Chairs evolved according to the needs of comfort and social life. The first innovation came when the plain wooden seat and back were upholstered with horsehair and fabric; the second was the rising importance of turned wood and astragal moulding. The frame of the 'high-back' chair or the 'arm-chair' is the same: the legs have either an emblazoned stretcher (the blazon was a heavily-carved motif between the two front legs), or an H-shaped stretcher; the seat is square with a low, slightly sloping back.

c) Chair, Louis XIV; ht. 45¾″ (116 cm.).

Under Louis XIV, Italian influence made itself felt in a taste for expensive materials. It is well known that Louis XIV owned some solid silver furniture. Failing that, gilded wood became fashionable in France. The lines of this chair have a certain vitality. The four arms of the stretcher meet in a knot of foliage. The arms are fixed to the frame by means of a support in the shape of a reversed console. The plain crimson velvet formerly so popular is now sometimes replaced by vari-coloured Genoese velvet.

a) Guéridon; Louis XIV; ht. (of shorter) 28¾″ (73 cm.).

This type of table, several examples of which can be seen in the Royal collections, was intended to carry a branched candelabrum. It is reminiscent of the style of Le Brun, designer and official *ornemaniste* to the King for the greater part of his reign. The close collaboration between the King and his director of arts resulted in the majestic classic style which is found in every aspect of art at the time, architecture and interior decoration as well as furniture. The tall *guéridon* with narrow top later went out of fashion, though it survives in churches and many 18th century examples still exist.

b) Armoire by Boulle; early 18th century; ht. 86½″ (220 cm.), dpth. 23¾″ (60 cm.).

The surname of André-Charles Boulle is given to marquetry in copper or brass on ebony or tortoiseshell, proving his supremacy and the advances he made in this technique; and especially in his application of the method of *partie* and *contrepartie*, whereby sheets of tortoiseshell and brass were clamped together and cut in one operation. This produced two different and reversed compositions forming the inlaid designs for two pieces of furniture. Moreover it was Boulle who thought of applying bronze to furniture: masks, foliage, feet and handles, all of which served both to protect and decorate.

c) Commode attributed to Boulle; c. 1715; ht. 34″ (86 cm.), dpth. 27⅝″ (70 cm.).

Boulle's originality was not confined to decoration; he also created new shapes foreshadowing the 18th century style. The two 'bureaux en commode' which he made in 1708 for Louis XIV at Trianon later developed into the commode. This example, with two drawers, is still very broad and tall, but its curved legs and the violet-wood veneer proclaim the new style which dates from about 1715. Some work by Cressent and the first commodes by Gaudreaux belong to the same type of *Régence* commode.

b) Fauteuil; 1700–25; ht. 39½″ (100 cm.), dpth. 18½″ (47 cm.).

This example shows the transition from the Louis XIV chair, its back upholstered all over, to the *fauteuil* of Louis XV. The seat consists of a visible frame of carved wood, to which the curved legs are fixed. Technical progress, the study of the curve of the legs and of the stress at their joint soon led to the elimination of the stretcher. Then the back, too, was framed in wood. The seat lost its rigid, rectangular shape in favour of a trapezoid, sometimes curved in front; the arm-rests curve slightly outwards and are set back on the frame. Chairs of this transitional period show these changes to a more or less marked degree.

a) One of a pair of gilt Régence pliants, c. 1720; ht. 21″ (53 cm.).

The folding X-frames consist of conjoined C-scrolls carved with leaf and flame motifs and sunflowers at the intersections. The stretchers are of scrollwork, cabochons and acanthus leaves.

The *pliant*, which Madame de Sévigné (among others) mentions frequently for its habit of causing 'social difficulties' was used in the 18th century almost exclusively by the Court.

Furniture

French

EARLY 18TH CENTURY

c) Marquetry commode, stamped Fléchy; Louis XV; ht. 35⅛″ (89 cm.).

The period of the Régence saw a commode developed from the bureau, with two drawers and standing on tall legs. Another type, derived from the lower part of a cupboard (low-boy) with three or four drawers and very short legs, was called *en tombeau* or *à la Régence*. Both kinds were in use throughout the century. Under Louis XV the commode with two drawers took on a slightly bulbous outline with a motif called *cul-de-lampe* in the centre; legs are curved with bronze mounts. The front is veneered with marquetry in geometrical or, more often, floral designs. There were often one or two matching corner cupboards, usually surmounted with shelves.

a) Lacquer commode by B.V.R.B.; c. 1750–60; ht. 34″ (86.4 cm.).

The same type of commode could also be lacquered. In that case the drawers are completely concealed by the decoration covering the front. Lacquer was very fashionable in 18th century France. Whenever possible, Oriental panels from screens or chests were used and then they had to be adapted to the curved shapes of commodes or secrétaires. The fashion for lacquer naturally gave rise to imitations. Some lacquer-workers did no more than copy Oriental lacquer, others—the most famous being the Martin brothers—used the same methods of tracing and polishing while using French colours and designs. They created an original and colourful style in lacquer.

The mysterious initials 'B.V.R.B.' have been lately identified as the mark of three generations of Bernard van Risen Burgh. This family, natives of Holland, but settled in Paris, offers an 18th century example of the continuity common among craftsmen of former times, which enabled a son to follow in the steps of his master-craftsman father.

---

b & c) Bergère and veilleuse, both in carved and gilded wood and both by Tilliard; mid–18th century; ht. of bergère 45¼″ (115 cm.), ht. of veilleuse 42″ (107 cm.), lgth. 71″ (180 cm.).

These are examples of the rococo style at its height. Curves dominate with principally floral decorative motifs: garlands or bouquets. Some features—stylized foliage and wavy shells—are typically *rocaille*. Few pieces were left in the natural wood at this period, with gilding, as in these two examples, or painting preferred. The heart motif in the centre of the frame and on the back identifies these as the work of J-B Tilliard, the Elder.

Notice the arm-rests of the chair which are set far back to accommodate the wide, hooped dresses then fashionable, and form an unbroken, sinuous line with the frame, comparable with the line of the *veilleuse*. The latter bears the arms of the Marquise de Pompadour, which would have been added later.

a) *Bureau-plat, by G. Feilt; 1760s; ht. 30½″ (77.5 cm.).*

Different kinds of bureaux were popular under Louis XV: the sloping, fall-front desk, reserved mainly for women and the flat-topped desk, first created by Boulle, but less heavy in outline and with only three drawers. This example, with tooled leather top, marquetry decoration and ormolu mounts, is absolutely typical. The central drawer is set slightly back. Sometimes *bureaux-plats* had the addition of a set of shelves and pigeon-holes to hold papers.

b) *Small secrétaire en pente veneered on oak; 1760s; ht. 34″ (86.3 cm.).*

This small secrétaire is light and versatile enough to be moved at will. Many different kinds exist— writing tables, tables with a sloping front for reading, custom-built gaming tables, dumb-waiters with trays between the legs and bedside tables, often supplied with handles to enable them to be carried each evening from the dressing-room to the bedroom. This table has no signature. It is decorated with a pretty marquetry design of flowers, with bronze mounts on the lock and feet.

Furniture

French
MID–18TH CENTURY

c) *Marquetry dressing-table, stamped* J. Stumpff JME *and* J. L. Casson; *c. 1770; ht. 31″ (79 cm.), dpth. 19″ (48 cm.). Right: table open.*

This is another example of the kind of small table used to add a feeling of comfort and fantasy to a room. The top is slightly serpentine and inlaid in a variety of fruitwoods, partly green-stained, also ebony and mother-of-pearl and depicts a market scene.

The top slides back on a key-operated mechanism; the frieze drawer slides forward revealing three lidded compartments, the centre one rising on a spring and adjustable. Also on a spring plunger is the small drawer at the centre of the frieze—it is inlaid with a design showing a coffee pot, cups, a bottle and a ham. The elegant cabriole legs have scroll feet.

Born in Germany, Stumpff was received as a Master *ébéniste* in 1766, Casson in 1765.

a) Fauteuil by Heurtaut; c. 1770; seat ht. 17½" (44.5 cm.), wdth. 29⅛" (74.0 cm.).

The great craftsmen of this transition to the new, 'antique' style were the cabinet-makers Louis Delanois and Nicolas Heurtaut. The evolution took the form of a striving for geometrical outline; straight, often fluted legs, backs rectangular at the bottom and rounded at the top, with 'a return to the antique exemplified in specific motifs such as ribbons and laurel wreaths, friezes of Vitruvian scrolls and shells. Acanthus leaves replace the flowers and small rococo foliage. Survivals of the Louis XV style, especially cabriole legs, continued side by side with these new motifs throughout the transitional period.

b) Corner cupboard (encoignure) by J. F. Oeben, c. 1760-62; ht. 37" (94 cm.).

This example is one of a pair of corner cupboards stamped 'J. F. Oeben' and decorated with floral marquetry panels. Throughout the 18th century, the custom prevailed of using one or two commodes and their matching *encoignures* in a room.

Like Weisweiler, Riesener, Stockel and Benneman, Oeben was one of a large group of Germans trained in Paris, who were the most important *ébénistes* of the Louis XVI period.

c) Fire-screen by Georges Jacob, c. 1775-85; ht. 48" (122 cm.).

This screen in carved and gilded wood shows the new style quite clearly, with its mixture of classical detail (the sphinx, pointed arrows on the base of the columns, and cornucopias on the feet) and the attention to natural detail which was the inheritance from the previous period—the ribboned floral frieze is beautifully carved, as are the minute garlands on the top of the columns.

Georges Jacob (1739-1814) had come to Paris from his native Burgundy, and studied under a famous *menuisier*. He became a *maître menuisier* in 1765, and was soon one of the most important chair-makers in the capital; by the 1780s he had clients in England too, and was making beds, tables and other furniture (see p. 382).

Furniture

French
LATE 18TH CENTURY

b) Fauteuil with round back; by J. B. Lelarge; 1780s; ht. 35¾″ (90.8 cm.).

In a salon the furniture always comprised *canapés, bergères, fauteuils* and chairs, all en suite and upholstered to match. However, there was no limit to the number of pieces. The *canapé* could be designed for one or two seats, sometimes it also had extra seats added at the corners, when it was described as *à confidents*. The *bergère* was always supplied with a loose cushion, whereas those on *fauteuils* and chairs were fixtures. One also makes the distinction between seats called *à la Reine* (with straight backs and usually ranged against the walls) and *en cabriolet* (with a slightly curved back and normally set about the room at will).

a) Chair by Boulard; 1786; ht. 36½″ (92.7 cm.).

The floral ornament is accompanied by a rigorous, almost archaeological interest in antiquity exemplified in a type of chair which deliberately copies the classics (for instance the mahogany furniture created by Hubert Robert for the dairy at Rambouillet). The legs have vertical fluting but sometimes they 'are in spirals. The construction of the chair has not varied from the preceding style, only the forms have changed. The legs and seat supports are now sometimes turned.

c) Cartonnier by Dupin de Franceuil; late 18th century; ht. 61″ (155 cm.).

Development in cabinet-making was also characterized at this period by dominant straight lines softened by a predilection for delicate mounts. In this case, the only decoration is a veneer of geometrical design in which light lines are contrasted against a dark ground. The taste for light-coloured mahogany is characteristic of the period. The almost total absence of bronze mounts indicates that this is a simple piece despite its fine quality.

a) *Ormolu-mounted tulipwood cabinet with four plaques of Sèvres porcelain (dated 1774 and '75); stamped M. Carlin JME; c. 1775; ht. 33" (84 cm.), dpth. 17¾" (45 cm.).*

It became fashionable at this period to have porcelain inlaid on the tops or sides of tables. The idea came from merchants like Poirier (the *marchands-merciers* who sold trinkets and such to the ladies of fashion). Carlin may well have made this cabinet for *A la Couronne d'Or*, the shop and auction house run by Poirier and Daguerre, who nearly monopolized the Sèvres factory's output of porcelain furniture plaques.

This example displays superb craftsmanship and is of unusually small size and unusual shape. The top is of white marble bordered with chiselled ormolu cabochons and florettes. The two drawers are faced with ebony overlaid with scrolling ormolu leaves. Notice the female masks at the corners and the lion mask which divides the frieze. The Sèvres plaques, on the two doors and the sides, were painted by Méreaud and Levé—two of the highest paid of the factory's decorators. They are very accurate botanically, and depict spring flowers, among them lilac, tulips and carnations, on a white reserve within a narrow gilt border and wide apple-green border.

b) *Desk by Roentgen; late 18th century; ht. 46" (117 cm.).*

Apart from those foreigners who were trained in Parisian methods there were some *ébénistes*, like David Roentgen, who were content to apply their own style to the work they produced. In fact, Roentgen kept on his workshop at Neuwied and came to Paris only to sell his pieces, which were renowned for their superb marquetry and their smooth-working mechanisms. (He was entrusted by Vaucanson (see p. 685) with the building of one of his last automata, *The Dulcimer Player*). Comparison of this large *bureau à cylindre* with work done in Paris shows to what extent those foreigners who trained in the capital had absorbed a sense of line and proportion.

c) *Commode by Riesener; c. 1780, ht. 35" (88.9 cm.).*

In the furniture made by the *ébénistes*, evolution followed the same lines. The taste for lacquer and marquetry remained, but the treatment changed. The commode was no longer curved, but straight. Bronze consoles replaced the foliage mounts on the corners. In this transitional period a new type of commode was created by R.V.L.C. or Joubert as well as by B.V.R.B. The front panel is divided into three, with a central projecting section and the sides sloping sharply back. This division into panels encouraged the *ébénistes* to transform them into doors thus concealing the drawers of the commode.

In this example by Riesener, oak has been veneered with mahogany, and the lattice effect on the drawers achieved with veneers of ebony and light-coloured wood. The top is of marble, the mounts gilt-bronze.

Furniture

French
LATE 18TH CENTURY

a) *Chair by Georges Jacob, mahogany; c. 1785; ht. 33¼" (84 cm.).*
b) *Chair by Jacob Frères; c. 1796–1803; ht. 34" (86.4 cm.).*

With the establishment of the Directoire, things became a little more prosperous, and favoured an artistic revival. This explains why the style, actually lasting from the reign of Louis XVI to the beginning of the First Empire is known as *Directoire*. Georges Jacob and his two sons formed a partnership in 1796 which was to continue until 1803 under the name of Jacob Frères.
left: Jacob was one of the first French craftsmen to use mahogany extensively. He lightened the construction of the chair, as well as its design; this chair back with its pierced and carved strapwork design, and uprights in the form of columns, would fit happily into an English setting of the period. The fluted legs and in particular the rosettes, or marguerites which decorate the scrolls on the back, and the junctions of legs and seat rail, are Jacob characteristics.
right: Jacob Frères continued to make furniture of very fine quality. With the Revolution, the old guild system of dividing the *ébénistes* from the *menuisiers* vanished, and Jacob Frères produced every kind of furniture—tables, beds, etc. as well as chairs such as this whose pierced back design exhibits a strong influence carried over from the 'Etruscan' set Georges Jacob had made in 1787 for Marie Antoinette's dairy at Rambouillet.

---

c) *Bed for Queen Hortense, in mahogany and bronze; made by Jacob Frères; c. 1800; ht. 30" (76.2 cm.).*

This piece of furniture, not unlike the Roman day-bed, clearly shows the classical inclinations of the early Empire. The medallions have Roman heads, lamps, lyres and vases cast in low relief. The wood is mahogany, which indicates that gilded and painted woods were no longer fashionable, and considered too ornate even for the Palace.

Georges Jacob had retired officially in 1796, but with the new orders flowing in from the Bonapartes, he returned to work around 1800. His son Georges II died in 1803, but he continued in partnership with his other son as Jacob-Desmalter et Cie. After Jacob's death in 1814, the firm continued under his son, and then his grandson, until 1845.

Queen Hortense's library; château d'Arenenberg, Switzerland; after 1817.

Hortense de Beauharnais (1783–1837) was the wife of Louis Bonaparte (brother of Napoleon I) and mother of Napoleon III. Louis was King of Holland from 1806–10 but was forced into exile by his brother when he defied the latter's disastrous Continental System.

Expelled from Restoration France, Queen Hortense de Beauharnais acquired the château d'Arenenberg in 1817 (built in the 16th century by a Constance patrician) and turned it into a delightful small summer residence.

Filling the rooms with beautiful souvenirs from the glorious days of Napoleon I, she also added a part of her own life and personality, combining the sensitivity of the romantic with the classicism of the Empire.

The bureau-bookcase, illustrated here, was made for Queen Hortense. It is of mahogany and is a fine example of a type fairly common at this period, when the large number of different types of furniture seen in the 18th century was reduced, perhaps because the new society was more practical and less exacting. This type of bookcase with several doors and pilasters is of an essentially practical design—shelving with columns for books, above a cupboard for albums and valuable prints. Nevertheless, its functionalness does not detract from the purity of line and elegance of its architectural character. It stands 102″ high (258 cm.) is 140″ (354 cm.) long, and contains 1000 books.

Even when Napoleon III (who grew up at Arenenberg) had the château renovated and decorated in the style then fashionable, the rooms which had belonged to his mother were left respectfully in their original state.

After the second Empire fell, the Empress Eugénie occasionally stayed at the château which was again extended and modified. It has thus become a museum of living styles, with the monumental style of Napoleon I, the delicate romantic taste, that of the rich bourgeoisie at the advent of the second Empire and the neo-baroque splendour at its end uniting to give a vivid picture of the whole 19th century in French furniture.

a) *Cabinet, Egyptian influence; c. 1800; ht. 35½″ (90 cm.), dpth. 24″ (61 cm.).*
b) *Chair, Egyptian influence; c. 1802; ht. 38½″ (97.8 cm.).*

Apart from Greece and Rome, Egypt was another great source of inspiration. It is true that France had not awaited Bonaparte's expedition to introduce the sphinx and Egyptian motifs to

furniture, because many Louis XVI examples can be cited. However, the work of French scholars and Vivant Denon's *Description d'Egypte* were the main sources of faithful reproductions of hieroglyphs and Egyptian themes on furniture. Now the sphinx and the lotus flower appear on legs of consoles, on arm-rests and fire-dogs, or mounted on candelabra.

Furniture

French

EARLY 19TH CENTURY

c) *Empire low-boy; early 19th century; ht. 31″ (78.7 cm.).*

The Empire low-boy, like the commode, was usually of rather large dimensions. Its absolutely rectangular shape is only relieved by pilasters in relief or caryatids on the corners. The frame is mounted in bronze, as also the central part of the doors which conceal the drawers made after the English fashion. The finely-chiselled bronzes usually depict classical scenes, the head of Minerva, Apollo driving his chariot, or simpler motifs such as palmettes, stars and crowns of laurel or oak-leaves.

d) *Empire console; early 19th century; ht. 29½″ (75 cm.).*

The Empire console is different from that of the 18th century, which was always of carved, painted or gilded wood constructed to match the *boiseries* on the wall where it was fixed. In the Empire period the console, inspired by a style begun under Louis XVI, becomes an independent piece, standing on four legs. The only way it differs from the low-boy and the commode is that it is narrower and is not enclosed. It is, moreover, usually veneered with mahogany like most other furniture of the period. Painted wooden Empire consoles do exist, as do painted wooden chairs, but they are all rather commonplace.

a) Bed; early 19th century; ht. 50″ (127 cm.).

The Empire bed is always made of mahogany with bronze mounts, and stands against a wall. The head- and foot-board may be straight or circular (made in one with the side-piece and called *en bateau*—boat-shaped). Such beds were normally draped with complicated curtains, enhancing the importance of fabrics, the austerity of the mahogany countered by brilliant, usually contrasting colours. Seats and window-curtains were made to match.

This is a particularly elegant bed, with the swan motif often seen during the Empire period on arm-rests or supporting with its wings the basin of a tripod-stand.

Swan motif detail (see a).

b) Bergère by Marcion; early 19th century; ht. 35″ (89 cm.).

Side by side with the mahogany, all the rage at the beginning of the Empire, there existed, even in private houses, a type of gilt-wood furniture used for ceremonial occasions. This magnificent drawing-room suite made by the *ébéniste* Marcion —great rival of Jacob-Desmalter—for Marshal Mortier, is a rare example. Its rich and imposing appearance approaches the furnishings done at the same time for the Imperial palaces. After 1808 the continental blockade stopped all supplies of mahogany so the cabinet-makers were forced to use ordinary wood, either gilding or mounting it in bronze.

c) Fauteuil; early 19th century; ht. 43¼″ (110 cm.).

Chairs developed in the same fashion. The clear-cut lines of the Empire period disappeared in favour of curves which terminate, as on the arm-rests in this example, in heavy scrolls characteristic of the period 1830-1850. The type of chair called *en gondole*, with a wooden frame to the rounded back, an invention of the late 18th century, popular during the Empire and greatly favoured in the Restoration period, was still used along with straight-backed chairs. The complete furnishing of a room still comprised several *fauteuils*, chairs and *bergères*.

Furniture

French

b) Chair by Gaillard; c. 1900; ht. 38″ (96.5 cm.).

a) Bed, the so-called 'Madame de Maintenon'; Second Empire, c. 1850-60; lgth. 70½″ (179 cm.).

After 1830 furniture styles develop an almost archaeological tendency. Enthusiasm for the Middle Ages gave rise first of all to a pseudo-Gothic style called 'troubadour'. Then the *ornemanistes* were attracted by the bizarre themes of Renaissance decoration, and the revived rococo, which introduced once more the taste for woods, gilded or picked out in colour on a contrasting ground. This would-be Louis XIV bed shows what a mixture of styles resulted from the urge to reproduce historical settings.

Reaction against the imitations and over-decoration of the second part of the 19th century was expressed in a return to nature and to simplicity. In Paris the movement gathered round Bing and his *Art Nouveau* group. Grasset and Gaillard, the two leading theoreticians of this circle, sang the praises of nature: the study of plants and vegetables as subjects for linear design, respect for material, work in solid wood with neither veneering nor marquetry and functional designs for furniture. Gaillard added a social idea: the artist should supply models simple enough to be mass-produced without losing their artistic quality.

c) Water-lily table by Majorelle; c. 1900; ht. 27½″ (70 cm.), dia. 55¼″ (140 cm.).

The strong personality of Gallé drew the partisans of *Art Nouveau* in the province of Lorraine into the School of Nancy. In the same way as *Art Nouveau* in Paris, this school sought inspiration in nature, as witness this water-lily table. Majorelle is one of the few innovators of the new school who was trained as a cabinet-maker, which explains his taste for fine woods (in this case mahogany and polished tamarind) and for gilt bronze mounts. The exaggerated realism and distortion in the reproduction of plants, stalks and creepers soon reached fever-pitch with a positive reaction against it after the turn of the century.

Opposite:
Mahogany high chest with carved shell and fan motifs and quarter round fluted columns; Philadelphia, U.S.A., 1770-75.

American Furniture
Introduction

Difficulties in transportation and communication meant that the transmission to America of European styles was slow. During the seventeenth century, Jacobean design chiefly influenced furniture; joiners, trained in England, brought their experience and remembrance of pieces they had seen. Most surviving examples seem to date from c. 1650-1700.

During the seventeenth century, regional characteristics appeared as different areas developed individual interpretations. A group of chests made c. 1675-1725, characterized by carved stylized sunflowers and tulips on the three front panels, has been attributed to Peter Blin of Wethersfield, Connecticut. It can be contrasted with chests made in Hadley, Connecticut and Hatfield, Massachusetts, with decoration of much looser form, the latter group attributed to John Ellis and Samuel Belding.

In America, the William and Mary style lasted from c. 1700-25. One main innovation was the chest of drawers; sometimes a cabinet above formed a fall-front desk. Such pieces, with strong architectural overtones, remained standard forms of case furniture for most of the eighteenth century. Gate-leg and drop-leaf tables developed. The Spanish or paint-brush foot was sometimes used on the best of the upholstered arm chairs, which began to appear early in the eighteenth century, as did the typical Queen Anne vase-shape splat.

Philadelphia, Boston, and Newport, Rhode Island emerged as the leading cabinet-making centres during the Queen Anne period (1725-55). Elaborate high- and low-boys were often ornamented with japanning, and carved decoration was very important. The shell motif on the knees of cabriole legs is typical of this era. Individual treatments can be associated with specific areas, Newport, New York, Philadelphia, etc. The upholstered sofa and tea table were becoming increasingly popular. Stick construction furniture (popular in New England) continued to be made, although it became more delicate in feeling; such 'Windsor' furniture remained popular into the nineteenth century.

With the introduction of the Chippendale style (1755-85), regional characteristics became even more pronounced. This continuation of the rococo tradition was chiefly based on patterns from Thomas Chippendale's *Director*, which found its way to American cabinet shops shortly after the 1750s. Typical was the almost universal use of the ball-and-claw foot, and elaborately complex curved devices. The Goddard and Townsend families worked in Newport, Rhode Island, c. 1760-80. The successful development of the block front with its superb handling of rich Santo Domingo mahogany is attributed to them. Benjamin Randolph (active c. 1760-90) worked in Philadelphia using an elaborate statement of English rococo form. His famous attributed set of 'sample' chairs survives as one of the strongest statements of American Chippendale taste.

During the following early classical period, Baltimore, Maryland and Salem, Massachusetts had become important ports and schools of cabinet-making developed to supply the newly-rich merchant class. This period is often called 'Federal' because of the new government and federal political party.

New York was also an important centre; Duncan Phyfe (1768-1854), a Scottish born cabinet-maker who settled in New York, worked throughout an important period of transition. The factory method of production was successfully practised in his shop.

In Philadelphia, Henry Connelly and Ephraim Haines produced their own individual statement of Sheraton style furniture. Baltimore had become noted for the production of delicate high style furniture, often characterized by the use of inset *églomisé* panels.

About 1810-15, archaeological classicism became popular; it lasted, in relatively pure form, until c. 1835. Phyfe and Charles Honoré Lannuier, a Frenchman, worked in this style but a further debasement of the style took place after 1835. In 1840 John Hall published in Baltimore, *The Cabinetmaker's Assistant*, the first furniture design book published in the United States. Hall's designs were massive, heavy and dominated by 'S' and 'C' scrolls. Usually pine or poplar, such furniture was mahogany-veneered and was produced in great quantities.

The machine made many inroads on the time-honoured craft of hand production by 1825. By 1850, most parts of individual pieces of furniture could be machine-made; this greatly influenced furniture made c. 1850-1900 in the various revival styles. Whether Gothic, Louis XIV, Elizabethan, Saracenic, or some other revival style, nineteenth century designers most often turned to the past for inspiration.

As the various revival styles dominated design, their creators often combined one or more in a single piece. By the end of the century, it is often difficult to determine which style the designer had in mind. In revolt, certain designers inspired by the English Arts and Crafts Movement endeavoured to reform furniture design. Often architects, these reformers designed furniture for specific purposes. They brought a new vitality to lead the way out of the morass of eclecticism which engulfed design in the United States at the end of the nineteenth century.

Opposite:
Two bedrooms in Samuel McIntire's home, Pingree House,
Salem, Massachusetts; U.S.A., 1804.

Furniture

American

17TH CENTURY

a) 'Carver' arm-chair of stick construction, ashwood; New England, c. 1650–60; ht. 45" (114.3 cm.); wdth. 23½" (59.6 cm.).

The chair is made of ash which has been massively turned. Chairs of this type are generally called 'Carver' after Governor John Carver (died 1621) of Massachusetts Bay Colony who presumably owned a similar example. It is characterized by the use of spindles in the back with none under the seat. If spindles exist under the arms and seat, the chair is called 'Brewster' after Elder William Brewster (1567–1644) who traditionally owned one. Seats of these chairs were made of solid planks, splint, or rush; the latter is used in the present example.

b) Joint stool found in Maine; c. 1690–1700; ht. 21" (53.3 cm.); wdth. 15" (38.1 cm).

Stools of this kind were made of a variety of types of native wood, often with several combined into a single piece. This example has particularly well proportioned vase-and-ring turnings. This was the standard form of seat furniture in 17th century America. As in England oak was the favourite wood, with pine, poplar, ash and elm serving secondary purposes.

c) Press cupboard of oak and pine, probably made in Essex County, Massachusetts, c. 1680–1700; ht. 63" (160 cm.); wdth. 48" (122 cm.).

The surface of this piece is enriched by ebonization, strapwork carving, and applied split spindles and bosses. The heavy, turned baluster supports and flattened bun feet are all characteristic of American furniture made under the influence of Jacobean design. The similar court-cupboard familiar in English furniture of the Jacobean period (p. 323c), does not have drawers and compartments below. Press and court-cupboards were made only in the 17th century.

The name of Thomas Dennis, a cabinet-maker who worked in Ipswich, Massachusetts from about 1668 to the 1680s, has been previously associated with approximately one dozen pieces. However, a more careful appraisal reveals that very few of these examples can be attributed to Dennis with any sound documentation.

a) High chest (high-boy) made in greenwood, in the William and Mary style; New York, c. 1690; ht. 64" (162 cm.); wdth. 46" (116 cm.).

During the William and Mary period, early in the 18th century, walnut was the favourite wood in Pennsylvania with maple and pine, sometimes with veneered panels, popular in New England. The chest of drawers replaced the Jacobean chest during this period, as had already happened in England (see p. 327b).

Gumwood (bilsted) is the basic material used here; a small group of furniture survives made of the same wood with a New York history. This chest was made for the Mitchell family of Port Washington, Long Island. The spiral-twist legs are characteristic of New York treatment of baroque details. Simple tear-drop pulls are a type associated with this style.

b) Dressing-table (low-boy) probably made in New York, c. 1690–1720; ht. 27¼" (69.2 cm.); wdth. 32¼" (81.9 cm.).

In the William and Mary style, this piece is made of cherrywood. It has a particularly interesting base with baluster-turned legs and feet and curved stretchers. The stretcher remained associated with New England furniture longer than in any other area.

c) Table with drop leaves in the William and Mary style; New York, c. 1690; ht. 28¼" (71.8 cm.); wdth. 34" (86.3 cm.), open.

Tables with turned movable supports (gate-leg) and drop leaves developed during this period; the 'butterfly' table is probably a unique American form, its name derived from the sweep of the side of the solid support for the top, which resembles the wings of a butterfly; for the English butterfly table see p. 362b.

This table has a mahogany top and cherry base. The use of mahogany in this and another New York example, is virtually the earliest recorded in the American colonies. Made for the VanCortlandt family, this table has deep leaves and an elaborate gate-leg base with delicate vase-shape turnings.

d) Day-bed or couch of maple wood, made in Pennsylvania, c. 1710–40; lgth. 65" (165 cm.).

In the William and Mary style, day-beds with adjustable backs of this type were made in New England as early as 1690. The back can be let down with a ratchet and chain mechanism. The legs and stretchers are particularly well turned and proportioned. A laced-sacking bottom in the piece gives added comfort. Compare this day-bed with the walnut example (p. 325b), made in England some years before, and particularly the use of caning for the seat; the laced-sacking may well have been softer.

Furniture

American

EARLY 18TH CENTURY

a) *Queen Anne period desk and bookcase (secretary) of walnut, made in New England, c. 1730; ht. 91" (231 cm.); wdth. 38" (96.5 cm.).*

Probably made in the Boston area, this secretary is of walnut with fine star inlays in its front. It is highly reminiscent of English prototypes (see p. 332*b*). The broken-arch pediment is in the bonnet top form (closed) which is generally associated with New England. The ornamentation is particularly rich; the star inlays are in rosewood and satinwood, crotch veneer panels decorate the drawer fronts, drop lid and doors are surrounded with bands of mahogany, ebony and satinwood.

At this time (1725-55), Boston was one of the three cabinet-making centres in the colonies; the others were Philadelphia and Rhode Island.

---

b) *Card table with turret corners and needlework covering; Queen Anne style; Massachusetts (probably Boston), c. 1735; ht. 26¾" (67.9 cm.); wdth. 36¾" (93.3 cm.).*

The turret corners were designed to hold candlesticks with round bases. The needlework is original to the piece, a rare survival in American furniture. The top is shallow and the cabriole legs are extremely delicate; these are both characteristics of New England Queen Anne furniture. The table opens by concertina (accordion) action which affords greater comfort to the players than a swing-leg. American tables of this type are rare and are constructed with the back part of the frame hinged to fold inward so that the four legs of the table can be brought to corner position when extended.

c) *Dressing table (low-boy) japanned, made in the Queen Anne style; New England, c. 1735; ht. 28" (72.4 cm.); wdth. 33" (83.8 cm.).*

The japanned surface of this piece is elaborately decorated with Chinoiserie detail, angel heads, and flowers. It matches a high chest and both are thought to have been decorated by Thomas Johnston (or Johnson), who was working in Boston between 1732 and 1767. They were made for the Pickman family of Salem.

High-boys and low-boys were very important during this period; special pieces were often japanned, as this is, to imitate the Oriental lacquer panels which were very popular. John Pimm (died 1733) of Boston, was a cabinet-maker associated with the construction of this type of furniture, and Thomas Johnston's name is often linked with ornately decorated pieces.

a) Side chair in the Queen Anne style made in New York, c. 1742; ht. 41¾″ (106.0 cm.); wdth. 22½″ (57.1 cm.).

This is a particularly rare chair, for the set from which it comes, with a cypher carved in the back, is virtually unique in American furniture. The initials 'RML' stand for Robert Livingstone and Margaret Beekman who were married in New York in 1742. The vase-shaped splat associated with the Queen Anne style was introduced early in the 18th century. The cabriole legs terminate in ball-and-claw feet, a feature that had been adopted by New York cabinet-makers prior to 1750, and continued into the rococo period, when it came into fashion almost all over the country.

b) Sofa made in Philadelphia, c. 1740-50; ht. 36″ (91.4 cm.); lgth. 86¼″ (219.0 cm.).

The frame is of walnut which has been partially upholstered in leather. The curve to the back (camel back) is particularly successful and undoubtedly an early example. The cabriole legs terminate with carved web feet and the stretchers which are arrow-shape are quite unusual.

Curved lines were the chief ingredient of design, as carving was the chief decorative method.

Furniture

American

MID 18TH CENTURY

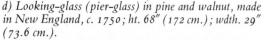

c) Wing arm-chair, probably made in Massachusetts, c. 1740-60; ht. 47″ (119 cm.); wdth. 34″ (86.3 cm.).

The base of the chair is made of walnut with blocked stretchers and angular cabriole legs which terminate in pad feet.

Chairs of greater comfort were first introduced into American furniture during the William and Mary period. This slightly later example shows the greater refinement which took place in the shape of the back.

d) Looking-glass (pier-glass) in pine and walnut, made in New England, c. 1750; ht. 68″ (172 cm.); wdth. 29″ (73.6 cm.).

This glass, which is one of a pair, is made of pine with walnut veneer and applied gilt ornaments in the rococo style. The source of inspiration was looking-glasses of the George I period. Mirror glass could be made only in small sections so it was not unusual to extend the length by the method shown here. Glasses of this type (pier-glasses) were most often hung over side-tables: for their derivation, see p. 336a.

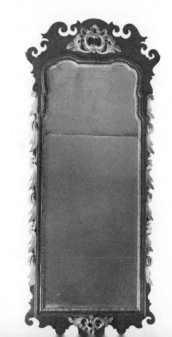

Furniture

American
MID–LATE 18TH CENTURY

a) Corner chair in the Queen Anne style, made in Philadelphia, c. 1750; ht. 36¼″ (92.0 cm.); wdth. 22″ (55.8 cm.).

Walnut was a favourite wood used in this city; this chair is of walnut and retains its original cowhide upholstery. The knuckles end in finely carved spirals and the vase-shape splats are inverted, an unusual feature. The delicate cabriole legs terminate in pointed web feet.

Another type of chair, with vase-shaped splat, curved cresting, bold arms and Spanish feet is associated with John Gains, a cabinet-maker who worked in Portsmouth, New Hampshire.

b) Tea-table with tripod base, mahogany, made in Philadelphia, c. 1750; ht. 28¼″ (71.7 cm.); wdth. 30″ (76.2 cm.).

The desk top with piecrust edge (see p. 338b) suggests the Chippendale period but other characteristics are Queen Anne. The bird-cage under the top makes it possible to revolve the top and to place it in a vertical position. The vase-shaped baluster is plain and the cabriole legs are carved with shells and terminate in elongated ball-and-claw feet.

The tea-table was a particularly successful design which first became prominent during the Queen Anne period, and here the Chippendale style (1755–85) is just beginning to influence the earlier designs.

---

c) Knee-hole desk or dressing-table, made in New York, c. 1760–70; ht. 33¼″ (84.4 cm.), wdth. 34″ (86.3 cm.).

Made of mahogany, this piece is typical of the refinement which New York cabinet-making reached in the Chippendale style. The type of vigorous squared ball-and-claw feet seen here are characteristic of the New York school. New York furniture seems to have always retained characteristics of the more Dutch baroque furniture of the 17th century (see p. 398c).

d) Basin stand of mahogany, made in Newport, Rhode Island, c. 1760–75; ht. 31⅞″ (80.9 cm.); wdth. 17½″ (44.4 cm.).

Of mahogany, this is attributed to John Townsend (see p. 395c). The fluted pillars and five-toe paw foot are all characteristic of this maker's work. Such a piece is illustrative of the type of specialized furniture form which became increasingly popular during the Chippendale era. Beginning with forms of furniture connected with tea drinking, this specialization became highly developed by the end of the 18th century.

*a) Fall-front desk, made in Massachusetts, c. 1760–70;
ht. 36″ (91.4 cm.); wdth. 45½″ (115 cm.).*

Of rich Santo Domingo mahogany, this desk is
in the rare Bombé (kettle-base) form. The piece is
constructed so that the sides of the drawers conform to the curves of the overall shape of the piece.
Bombé construction chiefly is associated with the
Boston area and it must have its source of inspiration in continental furniture as it was not an English
form. The brackets and pendants are particularly
elaborate on this example.

*b) Tall clock case, made in Newport, Rhode Island,
c. 1765–75; ht. 84″ (213 cm.).*

Typical of the work of the Goddard-Townsend
cabinet-makers, the case is of the rich Santo
Domingo mahogany so favoured in Newport.
This piece is representative of the finest work of the
Newport school. The fluted-urn finials and nine-
lobed shell as well as scrolls ending in flattened
rosettes, are all characteristic of Newport. The
name 'Wilson' is engraved on the English movement of the clock.

*c) Block front chest of drawers, of Santo Domingo
mahogany, by John Townsend (1732–1809); Newport, Rhode Island, c. 1765; ht. 33″ (83.8 cm.),
wdth. 34″ (86.3 cm.).*

This chest bears the label of John Townsend of
the Goddard and Townsend families who boasted
some 21 inter-related members, and dominated
Newport, Rhode Island cabinet-making during
the last three quarters of the 18th century. A typical
block-front chest has areas on the front which
extend forward on either side of a recessed panel.
The shells are carved in relief on the two outer
panels and intaglio on the centre. Such block-
fronts were usually carved from a single piece of
wood, although a few examples survive in which
the wood has been built up by glueing on pieces.

The very highly figured Santo Domingo
mahogany was beautifully adapted to the block-
front, and this piece shows how the tones and
contrasting raised and recessed surfaces reflected
the rich glow of the wood.

a) High chest (high-boy) of mahogany, made in Philadelphia, c. 1765-75; ht. 96¾″ (245.7 cm.); wdth. 45⅛″ (114.6 cm.).

This very elaborate piece was made for the Howe family. It represents the height of rococo style achieved in Philadelphia furniture. Vases of flowers, carved with great sculpturesque quality are used as finials. On the drawer at the base is a carving illustrating Aesop's fable of the fox and grapes. It is one of a very small number of Philadelphia case pieces with carvings illustrating the fables. Under the drawer front is a fanciful rococo carving and the short cabriole legs are ornamented at the knees with typical Philadelphia acanthus and scroll carving.

b) Looking-glass, mahogany frame, made in Philadelphia, c. 1768-76; ht. 45¾″ (116.2 cm.), wdth. 23¼″ (59.0 cm.).

The frame above has the simple type of scroll which continued in popularity from the Queen Anne through the Chippendale periods. The label of John Elliott (1713-91) is on this example, the third type of label which the maker used from 1768 to 1776. Most looking-glass makers were also importers; in some instances it is difficult to distinguish the imported from the native product as labels were affixed to both. This, however, is considered to be Elliott's work. Another Philadelphian cabinet-maker was William Savery (1721-88), a Quaker, who is chiefly remembered for his relatively simple labelled pieces in the Chippendale style.

c) Side chair with elaborate Chippendale carved detail, mahogany, made in Philadelphia, c. 1760-80; ht. 36½″ (92.7 cm.); wdth. 21⅛″ (84.0 cm.).

This side chair has the elaborate type of carving which typifies the Philadelphia school at the time of the American Revolution. It is one of a set of chairs which belonged to George Washington and were used in the Presidential Mansion in Philadelphia. The set was later owned by Colonel Frank M. Etting who was for many years the curator of Independence Hall.

d) Breakfast-table, mahogany, made in Philadelphia, c. 1770-90; ht. 28″ (71.1 cm.); wdth. 30″ (76.2 cm.).

The Pembroke type of table has short drop leaves which generally double the size of the top when extended. This form first became popular in the Chippendale era, of which this is an example, and reached its height of development as a classical form. Square legs of Marlborough type (popular in Philadelphia) are used and the gadrooned skirt with delicate brackets typifies the best type of this form. The stretcher is based on a design from Chippendale's *Director*.

b) Arm-chair made in New York, c. 1765–75; ht. 39¼″ (99.6 cm.); wdth. 31⅛″ (79.0 cm.).

The frame is of mahogany and the proportions of the chair demonstrate the holdover of baroque characteristics of boldness and breadth which characterize New York Chippendale furniture. The ruffle and tassel carved in the splat and eagles' head terminations of the arms are derived from George II design. The gadrooned border on the skirt as well as stringy acanthus leaf carving on the knees and type of ball-and-claw foot are all typical of the New York school. This chair was originally owned by Stephen Van Rensselaer who was the seventh lord of Rennselaerswyck, the family estate near Albany.

a) Card-table made in New York, c. 1760–80; ht. 27½″ (69.8 cm.); wdth. 33¾″ (85.7 cm.).

Characteristic New York attributes of this mahogany table are the five legs and deep gadrooning. The flat carving of acanthus scrolls on the knees is also typical of the New York school. The top of the present example is covered in green baize and contains pockets for counters as well as circular recesses for candlesticks.

c) Knife boxes, of mahogany, made in New York, c. 1770.

This form is quite rare in native American furniture and most of the examples seen in American houses are of English origin. These cases descended in the Stuyvesant family of New York. The silver mounts are by Lewis Fueter who was working in partnership with his father Daniel Christian Fueter, c. 1770. Knife boxes are particularly associated with the classical rather than the Chippendale period; the earliest phase of classicism in America lasted from c. 1785 to c. 1810.

d) Desk and bookcase (secretary) made in New York, c. 1775; ht. 98½″ (250.1 cm.), wdth. 47⅞″ (119.6 cm.).

The chief wood is mahogany with pine and tulip poplar as secondary woods. The broken-arch pediment is more unusual in New York furniture than the flat top. The frieze is carved with Chinese Chippendale fret. Glazed doors are relatively uncommon in American Chippendale furniture, their use becoming more standard during the classical period. This secretary has been attributed to Samuel Prince, a cabinet-maker who was active in New York from 1772 until 1776. It is representative of the finest type of case furniture made in New York during the Chippendale period.

a) Candle-stand of mahogany, made in Massachusetts, c. 1778; ht. 28" (71.1 cm.); dia. of top 9½" (24.1 cm.).

This type of tall candle-stand is rare in American furniture. An old inscription under the pedestal says that the table is the work of a British soldier who was captured at the Battle of Bennington in 1777 and that it was made at Charlestown the following year. His British training would explain the overlapping leaves on the knee and the parallel leaves around the rim which are unfamiliar American details.

b) Bed made in Connecticut, c. 1770–85; ht. 86" (218.4 cm.); wdth. 53½" (135.8 cm.).

Made of cherry, a wood popular in Connecticut, this bed has square bases on the foot posts which are derivative of Chinese Chippendale design. The bases are double-stepped and fluted and chamfered. The posts at the back and front are extremely delicate. This piece does not have any of the characteristics which are particularly unique to the Connecticut school, but it remains a lovely, elegant piece.

c) Kas, made in walnut; New Brunswick, New Jersey, c. 1785; ht. 97" (246 cm.); wdth. 74" (187 cm.).

Some pieces, such as this kas, often show the persistence of earlier forms in more rural furniture. It bears the label of Matthew Egerton, Jr., one of a family of cabinet-makers of northern New Jersey who worked from the mid-18th century until the early 19th. The kas is essentially a Dutch baroque form of the 17th century which was made chiefly in the Hudson River Valley, New Jersey, and Long Island. This example has scrolled bracket feet which are typical of Chippendale design, but it was made, of course, during the Federal period.

a) Chest-on-chest, mahogany, made in Salem, Massachusetts in 1776; ht. 92" (233 cm.); wdth. 45" (114 cm.).

Surely one of the great masterpieces of American furniture, this chest is made of mahogany. While the form remains basically Chippendale, all of the ornamentation is in the classical taste. A figure of Victory crowns the piece and is flanked by urns outside the broken-arch pediment. In the centre of the frieze below is a basket of fruit and on either side are putti holding floral garlands. It was made by William Lemon (active 1796) of Salem, with carving by Samuel McIntire, for Elizabeth Derby, the wife of Elias Hasket Derby. A bill of sale dated 22nd October, 1796 survives with this extraordinary piece.

During this period Salem developed rapidly as a cabinet-making centre, reflecting the change from Chippendale to the neo-classical styles of the Federal period (c. 1785-1810).

b) Side chair, mahogany, made in Salem, Massachusetts, c. 1795; ht. 39¾" (100 cm.).

Mahogany is used in this shield-back chair in the classical taste whose carving has been attributed to the Salem architect and carver, Samuel McIntire (1757-1811). The splat carved as an urn on pedestal with wheat issuing from its top, is typical of McIntire's work as is the grapevine device carved on the front legs. It originally belonged to the Salem merchant, Elias Hasket Derby (1739-99).

Classical or Federal furniture styles were based on the work of Robert Adam, interpreted by Hepplewhite and Sheraton. Samuel McIntire was an important exponent of the classical style; he created some of the most beautiful carved decorations of the period.

c) Arm-chair, probably made in Boston, c. 1795.

Of unusual shape, this arm-chair which is largely upholstered, has a mahogany frame. Also attributed to John and Thomas Seymour, this chair (one of a pair) descended in the Derby family of Salem. The type of classical carving on the arms and legs is indicative of the Seymours' work.

The Seymours produced masterpieces of craftsmanship, especially with tambour sections. Before 1812, Salem had six cabinet-makers producing excellent classical furniture.

b) Wine cooler, probably made in Boston, c. 1795; wdth. 29" (73.7 cm.).

Delicate, straight legs, square or round and tapering, were standard in the classical period. Classical devices were used in profusion for ornamentation and inlay and veneer became more popular than carving.

This is another piece of furniture which originally belonged to the Derby family of Salem. It is veneered with alternating vertical strips of mahogany and satinwood. The reeded, tapering legs are crowned with crisply carved acanthus leaves and terminate in brass casters. It has been attributed to John Seymour (1738–1818) and Thomas (1771–1848), his son, of Boston. Brass lions' head with handles have been affixed at each side.

a) Sideboard made in Baltimore, Maryland, c. 1790; ht. 39" (99.0 cm.); wdth. 69" (175 cm.).

This piece made of mahogany with inlay of light woods is typical of the Federal school of cabinet-making in Baltimore. The name William Moore is inscribed in old script on the reverse side of the bottle drawer. A cabinet-maker by this name is listed as working in Baltimore during the period in which the sideboard would have been made.

Furniture

American

LATE 18TH–
EARLY 19TH CENTURY

---

c) Sideboard of mahogany, made in Hartford, Connecticut in 1804; ht. 41¼" (104.7 cm.); wdth. 78½" (199.3 cm.).

Unlike most Connecticut furniture, the sideboard is made of mahogany rather than the usual cherry. The sideboard was a development of the classical era, and this one has particularly delicate square tapered legs. It was made by Aaron Chapin of Hartford for Frederick Robbins of Rocky Hill; a bill dated 22nd November, 1804 survives with the piece.

d) Lady's writing-desk of mahogany and satinwood, made in Baltimore, c. 1800; ht. 28" (71.1 cm.).

The chief decorative feature here is the inclusion of five oval glass panels with *eglomisé* paintings of allegorical figures. The use of glass panels of this type is typical of the Baltimore school during the classical period.

Baltimore cabinet-makers also excelled in painted furniture, much of it in the Sheraton manner, and mostly using seats and tables as the principal basic shape.

The front has a cylinder closing mechanism and a writing slide pulls forward from inside. It was originally owned by the Harris family of Mount Hill, Maryland.

a) Convex mirror, probably made in Boston, c. 1800-10; ht. 31" (78.6 cm.); wdth. 45" (114 cm.).

Of girandole form, this looking-glass has a gilt frame with pine base. It is crowned by an eagle standing on rocks; two dolphins are placed at either side. Chains with balls are suspended from the mouth of the eagle and the delicate candle arms have cut glass *bobèches* and prisms. The term 'girandole' was originally used to describe any wall light with a mirrored back.

b) Pair of side chairs made in New York, c. 1800, and attributed to Slover and Taylor; ht. 39" (99.0 cm.).

These mahogany chairs have carved details in their backs which are similar to that found on several documented pieces by that partnership of New York cabinet-makers, Slover and Taylor, who were active c. 1800. The Gothic arch is introduced in the present examples.

Furniture

American

EARLY 19TH CENTURY

c) Chest of drawers (commode), made in Boston, c. 1809; ht. 36" (91.4 cm.); wdth. 45" (114 cm.).

This is one of the most elaborate pieces of Boston classical furniture and mahogany, satinwood, rosewood and bird's-eye maple are all combined in its construction. The piece was billed to Elizabeth Derby, the daughter of Elias Hasket Derby, by Thomas Seymour in 1809. Lion mask pulls are effectively used for decorative purposes and the sides, which look like drawers, actually swing open to reveal cupboards. On the top at the back is a semi-circular painting of sea shells by John Ritto Penniman of Boston. This is documented by the bill which still exists. During this period, satinwood, boxwood and other exotic South American woods became favourites for inlay and veneer.

d) Sofa in mahogany; New York, c. 1810-20; ht. 33" (83.8 cm.), wdth. 86" (218 cm.).

Also attributed to Duncan Phyfe's workshop, this mahogany sofa with cane panels has a base in the Roman curule ('X' base) form. The beginnings of archaeological classicism can be seen in such a piece. Reeding on the base and delicate carving of drapery and tassels on the cresting piece are typical of Phyfe's best work. This style, which developed rapidly from c. 1810-c. 1835, sometimes called Empire, sprang from a desire to recreate the furniture of antiquity (compare with Thomas Hope's 'Egyptian' style around the same period—p. 360a).

a) *Piano case made in New York, c. 1810–20.*

The mahogany and satinwood case has been attributed to the workshop of Duncan Phyfe and the instrument is by Gibson and Davis who were active in New York from 1801 until 1820. Sheraton motifs are carved on the legs and stretcher and the delicate type is in the Empire taste.

The factory method of production was successfully practised in Duncan Phyfe's workshop. By 1805, New York was established as the United States' most influential city in setting style.

Furniture

American

EARLY 19TH CENTURY

b) *Combination writing- and work-table, satinwood; New York, c. 1800–10; ht. $31\frac{1}{4}''$ (79.3 cm.), wdth. $22\frac{1}{2}''$ (55.8 cm.).*

This highly sophisticated piece made of faded mahogany has been attributed to the New York workshop of Scottish-born Duncan Phyfe (1768–1854). The inlaid top opens to reveal a baize-lined adjustable writing flap with small compartments below. The lower section is reeded with a tambour door. The whole stands on four baluster-turned supports with leaf carving and these in turn are supported by four acanthus-carved legs which terminate in brass paw feet. Such a piece is of particular interest because of its incorporation of compartments for both writing and sewing.

Phyfe's first works were inspired by Sheraton, but because of his long career, his work extended through archaeological, or the revival, classicism and the debased classical forms of the 1840s.

c) *Dressing- or work-table of mahogany, made in New York, c. 1810; ht. 28'' (71.1 cm.).*

This highly inventive piece is another example which has been attributed to Duncan Phyfe's workshop. One of two known to exist, the piece opens in every conceivable manner to reveal a number of compartments, writing surfaces, etc. It is an early example of innovative furniture which was to become increasingly popular during the 19th century (cf. p. 362*d*).

a) Pier-table veneered in rosewood, made in New York, c. 1815; ht. 32″ (81.3 cm.).

This table, veneered with rosewood and having a marble top is embellished with gilded terracotta rosettes and ormolu mounts. It is one of nine pier-tables known to have been made by the French-born cabinet-maker Charles-Honoré Lannuier (1779-1819) and bears remains of three of his labels. Archaeological classicism is the most important influence in such a piece.

Lannuier worked in New York from approximately 1803 until his early death in 1819. He introduced the fashion for bronze and ormolu mounts.

b) Secretary, mahogany, painted and gilded, made in New York, c. 1825.

The elaborate stencilled and painted decoration in gilt on this piece is typical of New York and the piece has been tentatively attributed to the firm of Joseph Meeks and Sons. The basic wood is mahogany which has been darkened. Such massive pieces heralded another phase of classicism where only architectural proportion reminds one of the original source of inspiration, and relates directly to a similar trend in England (see p. 360*c*).

c) Desk and bookcase made in New York, c. 1836-50; ht. 88″ (223 cm.).

Another of the popular 19th century revival styles—the Gothic—is used for ornamentation in this rosewood piece. It bears the stencilled mark 'J. & J. W. Meeks Makers No. 14 Vesey St. New York'. The quality represented here is higher than is usually encountered. The Gothic architectural detail is delicately handled. The 'Victorian' Gothic revival has a long and respectable history, dating back to England in the mid-18th century, when many country houses were gothicized, *à la* Strawberry Hill (see p. 345*b*). It returned in force during the 19th century and American Gothic houses and furniture designs were very popular.

d) Centre table, rosewood, made in New York, c. 1850-60; ht. 30½″ (77.4 cm.).

The rococo revival style was the most popular of the century and rosewood was a favoured material for it. This centre table with marble top is of a type associated with the German cabinet-maker John Henry Belter (1804-63) who settled in New York City and succeeded Duncan Phyfe as the fashionable cabinet-maker. He used laminated panels of rosewood, walnut and oak which were built to the thickness required. These panels were steamed in cawls or moulds which shaped them. Belter patented his methods of furniture construction but there were cabinet-makers who infringed on his patents and imitated him.

403

a) *American cast iron settee, made c. 1870.*

Industrialization caused iron casting to become efficient and inexpensive. From the 1850s through the remainder of the century, a number of firms across the United States made furniture of this type often incorporating one or more of the popular revival styles. This particular piece has elements of both the rococo and Renaissance styles. Perhaps the most successful of these pieces were the ones which incorporated naturalistic details of leaves and branches into their forms.

Furniture

American

LATE 19TH–
EARLY 20TH CENTURY

b) *Side chair (one of a pair) in walnut, made in New York, c. 1869; ht. 37″ (93.9 cm.).*

This chair is stamped 'Hunzinger N.Y. Pat. March 30 1869'. George Hunzinger was a cabinet-maker of German origin who specialized in folding chairs. His work incorporated details from the vocabulary of Renaissance revival design but their combination is strictly his own.

c) *Cabinet, made in New York in 1884.*

This rosewood cabinet with exotic woods inlaid was made by Charles Tisch. It closely relates to 'art furniture' which had become popular in England. Orientalism is to be seen in a number of details. Although directly influenced by the English Aesthetic Movement, when Tisch presented the cabinet to The Metropolitan Museum in 1889, he called it a piece of 'purely American production'.

d) *Curio cabinet of mahogany, made in New York, c. 1910.*

This cabinet is a rare example of American Art Nouveau furniture. It bears a metal plaque which reads 'Trade FFF Mark Geo. C. Flint Co. West 23rd St. N.Y.'. While many small decorative objects were produced in the United States in the Art Nouveau taste, furniture was not so popular. This piece takes its inspiration from the work of such a French designer as Louis Majorelle.

Furniture Glossary

ACANTHUS: Ornament based on acanthus leaves used particularly for the knees of chair and table legs, etc.

AMBOYNA: Wood similar to maple but much harder.

APPLIED MOULDINGS: Carved, shaped edges to panels, etc.

APRON: Shaped piece below a chair's seat rail, or under the frieze, or base-rail between the legs of a cabinet.

ARCHITRAVE: Moulding around door frames.

ARMOIRE: Large, traditional two-door cupboard usually made by *menuisiers* (*q.v.*).

BALUSTER LEG: Turned and shaped leg in baluster form.

BARLEY SUGAR TWIST: Turned double twist for chair legs, etc. Also called rope or double rope twist.

BAS D'ARMOIRE: Low-boy, also called a *meuble d'appui* (*q.v.*) because it was convenient to lean on; has one or two doors.

BEAD, BEADING: Small, half-round moulding, also called astragal. It may be of wood or metal.

BEARER: Any horizontal member in joinery where it supports, or appears to support, any other member.

BERGERE: Seat lower than the *fauteuil* (*q.v.*), with a cushion and stuffed on the inner arm.

BEZEL: Metal rim framing a glass, often gilt.

BIRDCAGE: Device on early pillar or tripod tables to allow the top to be tilted and revolved.

BLOCK FRONT: See 'breakfront'.

BONHEUR-DU-JOUR: Small writing-table with a set of drawers or shelves closed with a door.

BONNET TOP: Form used with case furniture, the broken-arch pediment having a top extending to the back of the piece.

BREAKFRONT or BROKEN FRONT: Centre section projecting beyond the sides; or *block front* (Am.) recessed between them.

BUREAU-A-CYLINDRE: Writing-desk with a 'tambour' closure.

BUREAU PLAT: Large library table on four legs.

BUTTERFLY TABLE: Drop-leaf gate-leg table with top supports resembling butterfly wings.

CABRIOLE: Earlier, an arm-chair stuffed all over; now a chair or table leg with an upper convex curve merging via a concave portion into the foot.

CABRIOLET: Seat with a curved back.

CAMEL BACK: Arched back associated with Chippendale sofas.

CANAPE: Large upholstered settee with back and arm-rests.

CANTED: Furniture with wide chamfers at the junctions of front and sides would have 'canted' corners; see 'chamfer'.

CAQUETOIRE: Chair with narrow back, trapezoid seat, incurving arm-rests.

CARREAU: Large, horsehair or down-stuffed cushion.

CHAIRE: Solid wood seat with high back and arms.

CHAISE: Equivalent of *chaire* after the 16th century; *chaise à bras*, armchair; *chaise à dos*, with only a back; *chaise longue*, day-bed with a back.

CHAMFER: Surface of a bevelled angle; see 'canted'.

CHINESE CHIPPENDALE: Generic name for mid-18th century furniture in the Oriental taste.

CLUSTERED COLUMN: Three or four separate shafts linked together to form a leg or ornamental pillar.

COCK or COCKED-BEAD: Small bead (*q.v.*) projecting beyond an edge, often pinned around drawer fronts.

COMMODE: Particularly decorative chest of drawers.

CONFESSIONAL: *Bergère* (*q.v.*) with head-rest; i.e. wing-chair.

CONFIDENT: Corner seat, sometimes added to a *canapé*.

CONSOLE TABLE: Usually a shaped marble top, supported on a frame with decorative brackets, generally without back legs, to be screwed to the wall.

CONTREPARTIE: Technique invented by Boulle; after a design has been cut out of the layered material the part left is used as the opposing inlay, see p. 375*b*.

CORNICE: Projecting upper member of a bookcase, etc.

CORMANDEL (also CALAMANDER): Striped black and yellow ebony.

CURL: Feather-like markings in the grain of wood.

DEAL: Generic term—the wood of many coniferous trees.

DISTRESSED: A euphemism for surfaces deliberately rendered rough, stained or marked to simulate age.

DIVAN: Day-bed with neither back nor arms.

DOVETAILING: Cabinet-makers' method of joining wood by cutting wedge or fan-shaped projections in one piece and correspondingly shaped slots in the other.

DOWEL: Peg for locking a joint together; either solely as in early pieces, when they were called trenails, or to locate and reinforce glued joints.

DRESSER: Originally a board or table on which food was prepared, i.e. 'dressed'.

DUST BOARD: Thin board between adjacent drawer spaces.

EBENISTE: Almost the equivalent of cabinet-maker. Their work was distinguished from that of the *menuisier* by its fine inlay and veneering.

EMPIRE: French style with Egyptian motifs and lavish gilt metal mounts, fashionable under Napoleon I.

ENCOIGNURE: Corner-cupboard.

ESCUTCHEON or SCUTCHEON: Originally shield-shaped surround, or movable cover over a keyhole. Used for any metal keyhole plate and for inlaid, etc., keyhole surrounds.

FAUTEUIL: Chair with arms; used after c. 1675.

FIELDED PANEL: Panel with the large central area raised above the frame, generally separated from it by a chamfer.

FRENCH FOOT: Out-turned bracket foot.

FRET: Woodwork cut out as frets or trellis; *blind fret* carving resembles fretwork, with a solid wood backing.

Furniture
Glossary (contd.)

GADROON: See 'nulling'.

GRISAILLE: Painting in grey tones to simulate bas-reliefs.

HAREWOOD: Sycamore or maple stained a soft brownish grey.

HIGHBOY: Popular American name for high chest.

INTARSIA: Elaborate Italian inlay using pictorial scenes instead of patterns or floral design.

JOINT or JOYNED: Simple piece made by a joiner.

KETTLE-BASE: Swelling (*bombê*) form.

KINGWOOD: A dark almost purple hard wood (*dalbergia*).

LOO TABLE: Large, usually circular or octagonal table, on a central pillar; originally from the card game of 'lanterloo' or 'loo'.

LOPER: Sliding rail to support a flap.

LOWBOY: Popular American name for dressing table.

MARQUETRY: Elaborate inlay in arabesques, floral designs, etc.

MENUISIERS: Craftsmen responsible for interior woodwork, panelling, doors and seat-frames—nearly the same as the English joiner.

MEUBLE D'APPUI: See 'bas d'armoire'.

MITRE: The diagonal joint where two sides intersect at right angles.

MORTICE (or -ISE): A rectangular cavity cut in one member to receive a matching projection, the tenon, cut on another member.

MOUNT: Generic term for the metal attachments useful or ornamental, on furniture; see 'ormolu'.

NULLING (or 'GADROONING'): Alternating convex and concave flutes often on the edges of tables, etc.

ORMOLU: Literally 'ground gold'. Though French, the term is not used in France, as in England, to describe chased and gilded furniture mounts made of brass or bronze. The French call ormolu mounts *bronzes* and the ormolu workers *bronziers*.

ORNEMANISTE: Artist specializing in the design and execution of decorative ornament.

PARQUETRY: Similar to marquetry, but using geometric designs.

PARTIE: See 'contrepartie'; the first cut-out following Boulle's technique.

PATERA: An ornamental disc or boss lightly carved.

PATINA: The surface colour and finish of wood, etc. Product supposedly, of generations of use and polishing; contrary to popular belief it can be simulated.

PEDIMENT: Triangular or segmental feature on top of large bookcases, long-case clocks, etc. A broken pediment is one with central portion cut away and the space partly filled, usually with urn-shaped ornament; a swan-neck pediment, one with wavy or curved upper edges.

PEG: An early form of stout dowel, a trenail.

PIE CRUST: A carved scalloped raised rim round the surface of a table, dumb waiter, etc.

POLLARD OAK: Oak with a markedly wavy grain.

PRESS: Old name for any enclosed cupboard.

QUARTERING: Veneers (or boards) cut into quarters from the heart of a tree; the markings of pairs or fours of adjacent pieces make mirror-image patterns.

QUIRK: The groove cut by the side of a bead.

REBATE (RABBET, RABBIT): A continuous rectangular channel, to accommodate a panel, pane of glass, etc.

REGENCE, COMMODE A LA: A commode with drawers nearly to the ground and very short legs.

REINE, A LA: All chairs with straight backs are called *à la Reine*.

ROCAILLE: Motifs characteristic of the Louis XV style; foliage, scrolls, shells.

ROSEWOOD: Dark brown wood with a blackish figure.

SADDLE SEAT: Solid wood seat, often on 'Windsor' chairs, two shallow depressions separated by a ridge.

SATIN-WALNUT (American red gum): Soft yellow wood used for second grade Victorian furniture.

SATINWOOD: Rich golden-yellow wood, for veneers, inlays, etc.

SECRETAIRE EN PENTE: Secretary with sloping front (Louis XV).

SERPENTINE: Convex curve flanked by two concave curves.

SHOW WOOD: The visible wood of upholstered furniture.

SPLAT, SPLAD: The central upright member between the seat and the top rail of a chair back.

STOPPED CHANNEL FLUTING: Ornamental fluting or reeding, the hollows partly filled with convex ornamental device of carved wood or metal.

STRETCHER: The underbrace connecting furniture legs.

TOMBEAU, EN: Synonym for the *Régence* style.

UNDERCUT: Carving so deep that parts of the carved ornament are parted from the background.

VEILLEUSE: *Canapé* (*q.v.*) in which one side of the back is higher than the other, the lower side being placed near the fire.

WATER-GILDING: The most delicate and expensive method of applying gold-leaf to wood, gesso, etc. (not metal), used when it was desired to burnish the highlights; known also as 'burnish gold'. Metal was gilded by the mercurial or fire-gilding process until mid-19th century, since when it has been done electrically.

WINDSOR: Generic term for chairs, etc. of stick construction.

Repairs and Maintenance

Most furniture is made basically of wood. An examination of the back, sides, inner workings, and legs will help to determine whether repairs will be needed, in which case professional help will be required. If, however, the piece is sturdy and the joints firmly in place, attention should be paid to the wood itself. If possible, remove handles, metal fittings, and take out the drawers, if there are any. Rub the drawer runners with graphite or chalk if they stick slightly. Pine, walnut and beech are particularly prone to woodworm attack, although they may inhabit mahogany and oak as well. A careful inspection, with particular attention to the back and base (veneered furniture often had the cheaper, softer woods used for the parts which would not show) will reveal the presence of tiny holes. If fresh, there may be sawdust around the mouth of each tiny tunnel. Try tapping the wood if there are no obvious signs; sometimes the sawdust will fall out. Woodworm can be treated with a liquid insecticide, carefully and thoroughly brushed into all the holes. There are many good ones on the market, and follow directions carefully. If the infestation is strong, repeat after fourteen to sixteen days. At this time, minor repairs may be done, and the handles and other mounts cleaned.

Old furniture often. requires cleaning—use a mild solution of detergent and water, being careful to avoid any excess dampness. Above all, don't allow the water to soak into joints and crevices to loosen the glue or lift veneers. All newly-made furniture needs some protective coating and is usually treated with a medium which will help to seal the pores, yet allow the figure of the wood to be seen. The mellow, beautifully soft colour of much antique furniture is not entirely the result of hundreds of years of elbow-grease and bees-wax! Some artificial colour was almost always used in the first stages of finishing to darken the wood, and by sinking into the softer parts of the wood, throw up the harder grain into relief. To add lustre, the simplest form of polishing is rubbing with oil, but bees-wax dissolved in oil or turpentine is quicker and easier. This is still the best polish for solid wood furniture. Be sure and use real turpentine if you make the polish yourself—white spirit may damage old varnish. Many good wax polishes are available, but avoid silicone based products, which may cause a cloudy 'bloom' effect.

Oil-gilded furniture may be cleaned carefully with water, but water-gilding cannot be washed. If in any doubt, consult an expert before attempting treatment.

Refinishing is generally undesirable with antique furniture, since it will destroy the old patina; however, there are some cases where such drastic action is advisable. Remove the old varnish with a varnish stripper; you will need plenty of protection for the floor, and fresh air, since such products have a most penetrating smell. Leave on for about an hour, and remove the varnish with a brush. Wire (steel) wool may be used as a last resort, but try and do the job without it, if possible. Glass-paper or sand-paper can be used to remove any staining, but use a fine grade only, or you will roughen the surface of the wood. Such a procedure is also useful for removing layers of paint which have sometimes been used to coat the piece.

After stripping, wash off any residue very carefully, taking care not to soak the wood, and after it is thoroughly dry, stain if necessary, and polish. Remember that since there is no protective coating left, it will need careful and constant polishing for quite a while to build up a resistant surface.

Finally, the temperature of the room in which the furniture is kept will have its effect. Central heating is often drying and may cause wood to crack and split, and veneers to lift. And damp, stagnant air may lead to dry rot, with equally damaging results. An equable temperature is the best, with enough humidity to keep the wood from drying out. A bowl of water near the radiator is an easy way of ensuring this.

Furniture
Fakes and Forgeries

It has been remarked that there is more seventeenth to early nineteenth century furniture in the antique shops today than could have been made in those centuries; cynical perhaps, but not wholly unjust. Dishonesty is not always the cause; many fakes are good enough to deceive the non-specialist dealer and many more were done so long ago that they have genuine antiquity, even though they are false.

The dividing line between legitimate restoration and faking is very thin. Few would condemn a dealer who asks his usual cabinet-maker to make a complete drawer, replacing one which is missing from a fine seventeenth century chest; everybody would condemn the man who causes a complete chest to 'grow' round two genuine drawers and half a rotten plinth. The grey areas between must be searched by the buyer with as much expertise as he can muster, and with *caveat emptor* as his motto.

The construction of a completely spurious 'antique' from raw material can be done well enough to deceive the most expert; but such a fake may well cost as much as the real thing. The more common kinds of faking which the ordinary buyer should understand, involve 'improving' to make some piece appear older or more interesting, or 'marrying'. Examples of improving are manifold; Victorian dealers and amateur craftsmen were much given to adding 'Tudor' carving to plain oak chests, coffers or long-case clocks, and more recently, many a sound, but mediocre chest of drawers has doubled in value by having a full-width secretaire drawer put in place of the two small upper drawers.

The demand for small furniture leads to 'cutting and shutting' larger pieces, and unwanted ugly ducklings may be turned into swans; heavy mid-Victorian sideboards are stripped of their elaborate scrolled 'splashbacks' and recessed door panels and fitted with gilt-brass galleries, door-grilles and other adornments, so that they may pass muster as Regency chiffonniers—in the dark with the light behind them. Rather similarly, much of the fashionable 'country' stripped pine furniture started life as common painted deal. By removing the heavy Victorian or Edwardian top-mouldings and drawer knobs, together with the doughnut feet, and substituting reeded edges, a 'Sheraton' plinth and reproduction brass handles, an undistinguished cheap bedroom chest of drawers may be turned into an 'antique' of a sort which never really existed.

Mixed marriages are so prevalent that some practitioners seem to be conducting a sort of Gretna Green for runaway furniture. Tripods and upperworks of side- or card-tables are obvious victims and such tables should always be examined carefully; similarly the elegant bases of late Georgian cheval glasses (see p. 363c) can be married to suitable upperworks to become valuable sofa-tables.

Suitable hanging or standing bookcases or cabinets are obvious partners for bureaux, and the top and bottom parts of kitchen dressers must also be carefully examined for signs of forced cohabitation.

A profusion of gilt metal mounts of rather poor quality, or of brass inlays in otherwise undistinguished pieces, should be looked upon with suspicion. Similarly, carved 'knees' are worked on cabriole legs and 'pie-crust edges' are added to tripod tables or dumb-waiters which started life quite plain, and the relative shallowness of the decoration often gives the game away.

Advice in a brief article has to be confined to fundamentals. Study, and if possible handle, as many known genuine pieces as possible. Learn what kinds of woods were used in what periods—try to visualize what any decorated, carved or metal-mounted piece would look like without its adornments and study the progression of handles, foot shapes, etc. Look at drawer edges, etc., to gauge the thickness of veneers (see p. 300). Imagine that Georgian pedestal desk without its elaborately tooled leather top and its nice brass tear-drop handles and ask yourself whether it was once a Victorian dressing table; and was not the base of that delicate little wine table once a pole-screen stand?

The best advice of all is to make friends with reputable and expert dealers—there are many of them—buy from them when the opportunity offers and take advantage of the experience they are usually happy to share. Finally, if you can, also scrape acquaintance with an expert cabinet-maker who specializes in antique restoration work and study the technical aspects of furniture construction.

Further Reading

General

ARONSEN, J. *Encyclopaedia of Furniture.* London, 1966.
BOGER, L. A. *The Complete Guide to Furniture Styles.* New York, 1959.
HAYWARD, H. (ed.). *World Furniture.* London and New York, 1969.
HINCKLEY, F. L. *Directory of the Historic Cabinet Words.* New York, 1969.
JOY, E. *Furniture.* London, 1972.
PRAZ, M. *An Illustrated History of Interior Decoration.* London, 1964.

Continental

BODE, W. VON, and HERRICK, M. E. *Italian Renaissance Furniture.* New York, 1921.
BROSIO, V. *Mobili Italiani dell'Ottocento.* Milan, 1962.
Ambienti Italiani dell'Ottocento. Milan, 1963.
BURR, G. H. *Hispanic Furniture.* New York, 1941. (Enlarged ed. 1964).
DEL PUGLIA, R. *Mobili e ambienti italiani dal gotico al floreale,* 2 vols. Milan, 1963.
HENSCHEN, I., and BLOMBERG, S. *Svenskt Möbellexikon,* 3 vols. Malmö, 1961.
JONGE, C. H. DE, and VOGELSANG, W. *Holländische Möbel und Raumkunst von 1650-1780.* The Hague, 1922.
LASSEN, E. *Danske Møbler, Den Klassiske Periode.* Copenhagen, 1958.
MÖLLER, L. *Der Wrangelschrank und die verwandten sud-deutschen Intarsienmöbel des 16. Jahrhunderts.* Berlin, 1956.
MORAZZONI, G. *Il Mobile Neoclassico Italiano.* Milan, 1955.
Ambienti Italiani del Seicento e Settecento. Milan, 1964.
PIGNATTI, T. *Lo Stile dei Mobili.* Milan, 1951.
Mobili italiani del Rinascimento. Milan, 1961.
PINTO, A.C. *Cadeiras Portugueses.* Lisbon, 1952.
PLUYM, W. VAN DER. *Vijf eeuwen binnenhuis en meubels in Nederland, 1450-1950.* Amsterdam, 1954.
SCHMITZ, H. (ed.). *Deutsche Möbel des Barock und Rokoko.* Stuttgart, 1923.
SCHÖNEN, P. *Aachener und Lütticher Möbel des 18. Jahrhunderts.* Berlin, 1942.
SINGLETON, E. *Dutch and Flemish Furniture.* London, 1907.
STAVENOW-HIDEMARK, E. *Svensk Jugend.* Stockholm, 1964.

English

BIRD, A. *Early Victorian Furniture.* London, 1964.
English Furniture for the Private Collector. London, 1961.
COLERIDGE, A. *The Chippendale Period in English Furniture.* London, 1966.

EDWARDS, R. *Georgian Furniture* (Victoria and Albert Museum). 2nd ed., London, 1958.
(ed.). *Hepplewhite Furniture Designs.* Repr. with preface by Ralph Edwards. London, 1947.
Sheraton Furniture Designs. Repr. with preface by Ralph Edwards. London, 1949.
Thomas Chippendale: The Gentleman and Cabinet-maker's Director. Repr. of the 3rd ed., intro. by Ralph Edwards. Bonn, 1957.
The Shorter Dictionary of English Furniture from the Middle Ages to the late Georgian period. London, 1964.
English Chairs (Victoria and Albert Museum), 2nd ed., London, 1965.
EDWARDS, R., and JOURDAIN, M. *Georgian cabinet-makers c. 1700-1800—A New Revised Edition.* London, 1955.
FASTNEDGE, R. (ed.). *Sheraton Furniture.* London, 1962.
English Furniture Styles 1500-1830. London, 1955 and 1962.
GLOAG, J. *Georgian Grace. A Social History of Design from 1660-1830.* London, 1956.
The Englishman's Chair. Origins, design and social history of seat furniture in England. London, 1964.
English Furniture, 5th ed. London, 1965.
HARRIS, E. *The Furniture of Robert Adam.* London, 1963.
HARRIS, J. *Regency Furniture Designs from contemporary source books, 1803-1826.* London, 1961.
HAYWARD, H. *Thomas Johnson and English Rococo.* London, 1964.
HEAL, Sir A. *London furniture makers from the Restoration to the Victorian era.* London, 1953.
JERVIS, S. *Victorian Furniture.* London, 1968.
JOURDAIN, M., and R. F. *English Furniture: The Georgian Period, 1750-1830.* London, 1953.
JOY, E. T. *English Furniture. A.D. 43-1950.* London, 1962.
The Country Life book of English Furniture. London. 1964.
MACQUOID, P., and EDWARDS, R. *The Dictionary of English Furniture,* 2nd ed., rev. by Ralph Edwards, 3 vols. London, 1960.
MASSE, H. J. L. J. *The Art-Workers' Guild 1884-1934.* Oxford, 1935.
MOLESWORTH, H. D. (ed.). *A Treatise of Japanning and Varnishing, 1688 by John Stalker and George Parker.* Repr. with intro. by H. D. Molesworth. London, 1960.
MUSGRAVE, C. *Regency Furniture.* London, 1961.
PEVSNER, N. *High Victorian Design, a study of the exhibits of 1851.* London, 1951.
PUGIN, A. W. N. *Gothic Furniture in the Style of the 15th Century.* London, 1835.
SCHMUTZLER, R. *Art Nouveau.* London, 1954.
SELZ, P., and CONSTANTINE, M. (eds.). *Art Nouveau.* New York, 1959.

Furniture
Further Reading (contd.)

SYMONDS, R. W. *Furniture making in seventeenth and eighteenth century England*. London, 1955.

SYMONDS, R. W., and WHINERAY, B. B. *Victorian Furniture*. London, 1962.

WARD-JACKSON, P. *English Furniture designs of the eighteenth century*. London, 1958.

French

DEVINOY, P., and JANNEAU, G. *Le Meuble léger en France du Moyen-Age à nos jours*. Paris, 1952.

DEVINOY, P., JANNEAU, G. and JARRY, M. *Le siège en France du Moyen-Age à nos jours*. Paris, 1948.

GRANDJEAN, S. *Empire Furniture, 1800–1825*. London, 1966.

LEDOUX-LEBARD, D. *Les Ebénistes parisiens du XIXe siècle, leurs oeuvres et leurs marques*. Paris, 1965.
  Les Ebénistes français du XVIII°. Paris, 1963.

SOUCHAL. *French 18th Century Furniture*. London, 1961.

VERLET, P. *Les meubles du XVIIIe siècle*, 2 vols. Paris, 1956.
  French Furniture of the 18th century, trans. by G. Savage. London, 1967.

WATSON, F. J. B. *Louis XVI Furniture*. London, 1960; New York, 1961.

American

BJERKOE, E. H. *The Cabinetmakers of America*. New York, 1957.

BUTLER, J. T. *American Furniture, 1607–1914*. London, 1973.

COMSTOCK, H. *American Furniture: Seventeenth, Eighteenth, and Nineteenth Century Styles*. New York, 1962.

DOWNES, J. *American Furniture*. New York, 1962.

IVERSON, M. D. *The American Chair 1630–1890*. New York, 1957.

MONTGOMERY, C. F. *American Furniture of the Federal Period*. New York, 1966.

OTTO, C. *American Furniture of the 19th century*. New York, 1965.

RANDALL, R. JR. *American Furniture in the Museum of Fine Arts*. Boston, 1965.

Museum Collections

Great Britain

DURHAM: The Bowes Museum, Barnard Castle.

LANCASHIRE: The Towneley Hall Museum and Art Gallery, Burnley.

LONDON: The British Museum; The Geffrye Museum; The Victoria and Albert Museum; The Wallace Collection.

SOMERSET: The Holburne of Menstrie Museum of Art, Bath.

SUSSEX: The Brighton Art Gallery and Museum.

YORKSHIRE: Temple Newsam House, Halton, Leeds.

SCOTLAND: The Glasgow Art Galleries and Museum.

U.S.A.

CALIFORNIA: The M. H. De Young Memorial Museum; The Palace of the Legion of Honor, San Francisco.

CONNECTICUT: Wadsworth Atheneum, Hartford.

DELAWARE: The Henry Francis du Pont Winterthur Museum.

MARYLAND: The Historical Society, Baltimore.

MASSACHUSETTS: The Museum of Fine Arts, Boston.

NEW YORK: The Frick Collection, The Metropolitan Museum of Art, New York City.

PENNSYLVANIA: The Philadelphia Museum of Art.

WASHINGTON, D.C.: The Smithsonian Institution.

Index

Glass

Glass is an extraordinary material—brilliant, transparent, easily worked hot but brittle and fragile when cold.

We do not know how glass was invented, nor even when the first experiments took place. As far as research has been able to establish, glass objects were first made about 4,000 years ago, somewhere in the Middle East, or Western Asia. And that is all. Yet this very old craft has been strangely selective in its history. Even the most primitive societies had some form of pottery, and metalworking of various kinds, but not glass. This is perhaps understandable in one sense; to fuse the basic components, a temperature of over 2,500 degrees F. is needed, and few primitive kilns would be able to achieve the necessary heat. Pliny's apocryphal story of how glass was discovered is perhaps misleading; he reported that early Syrian traders built a fire on the beach, using blocks of soda they carried as merchandise to support the driftwood they used as fuel. The heat of the fire was enough, he wrote, to fuse the two basic components of glass (silica, which is usually sand of some kind, and soda or potash) and the surprised merchants found their fire swimming in a pool of liquid glass.

It is a delightful tale, but unlikely. A more probable explanation lies in the potter's kiln. A fairly simple kiln will reach such temperatures, and perhaps Mesopotamian potters, experimenting with glazes, found they had discovered a material of value and beauty in its own right.

It is perhaps strange that the potters who achieved the earliest, and perhaps the finest glazes ever made—the Chinese—have never exploited the potential of blown glass, but were content to use it as an imitation of porcelain or precious jade.

In any case, it was left to craftsmen farther to the West to make the first glass objects, and then to the Syrians and Alexandrians who probably invented glass blowing, and finally to the Romans who spread the craft throughout their empire, to make glass part of our everyday life.

Opposite:
Large standing cup, clear cristallo glass gilded and enamelled;
Venice, Italy, c.1500.

Glass
The Craft

In technical terms, glass is the result of heating various substances, which, when submitted to a temperature of over 2,500 degrees F., fuse together into a liquid. This liquid, ductile while hot, will become rigid as it cools, without reverting to its original crystallized structure. It has sometimes been called a super-cooled liquid, a name which seems quite appropriate when applied to a Regency chandelier whose showers of facet-cut drops seem more like icicles than glass.

The basic components of most glass formulae are silica, soda and lime. Silica, or sand, forms the glass, soda acts as a flux to allow the glass to melt at a lower temperature, and lime acts as a stabilizer.

This combination can of course, be modified; lead oxide used as a flux will make the glass less brittle, and more stable, but harder to work when hot. Various oxides will add colours, as will silicates, etc. and oxide of tin has been used to make the glass opaque, in the same way that glazes for pottery opaquified, by crystallizing the glass and destroying its transparency. For this reason, variations in glass formulae have usually been the work of chemists, such as George Ravenscroft, who worked with the glass-makers to perfect their products.

The interior of a glass-house has not changed much in the past centuries, and although today the source of heating will be electrical rather than an open fire, the furnace still keeps the temperature high, even on the coldest day. The glass metal is made in special pots which are set into the furnace filled with the mixture of raw materials, according to the formula being used. Meanwhile, the blow-pipe is set by the furnace to heat at one end—it must be hot for the molten glass to adhere to it properly.

The tools the glass-maker uses are comparatively simple. The blowpipe is a hollow tube, somewhat flared at the end, with a wooden mouthpiece. The pipe is dipped into the pot of molten metal, and a small 'gather' of glass will adhere to the end. Blowing through the tube will create a small bubble; this is known as the parison. By now the glass has cooled slightly, just enough to allow the workman to roll the parison over a heavy, flat metal or marble surface known as the marver. This distributes the glass forming a symmetrical shape which will expand evenly. The cooled glass will not adhere to the marver, and the bubble is given its first shape under pressure, as the pipe is rolled back and forth. The parison may be re-heated at the furnace mouth, possibly another gather added to thicken the glass wall, and the process repeated. When the parison is ready, the bubble is shaped, either by blowing free-hand, or expanding the glass in a mould. When the desired size is reached, a short solid iron rod (pontil rod) is used to take a small gather of glass from the furnace, and this is stuck onto the end of the

shaped bubble, and the required amount is cut off with a pair of shears. Rolling the blowpipe across the arm of his special chair, the gaffer, or master glass-blower, shapes the stem and foot with a pair of tongs, or calipers.

Patience and accuracy must, above all, be the attributes of the workers in this field since once the molten gathering has been collected from the furnace, adhering to the blowing rod, there can be no easing up. Whereas the potter has the advantage of having his clay upright in front of him and being able to revolve the wheel by treadle for working it, the glass-maker depends on his skill to keep the rod turning backwards and forwards with his hands whilst it is placed horizontally across the wide arms with enough momentum to fashion the 'gather' into a perfectly formed object.

Finally, the glass is attached to a clean pontil rod which is stuck on to the base of the foot. The glass is 'cracked off' the blowpipe with a wet metal file, and the bowl trimmed with a pair of shears while the worker holds the glass on the pontil. At this point he may widen or open the bowl with calipers, giving it its final shape. Another moment at the open furnace heats the rim enough to smooth out any sharp edges with a wooden clapper, and the glass is ready to be cracked off the pontil rod, and put into the annealing oven. Previously, the foot extended down past the pontil mark, left where the rod was cracked off, and the mark was rough. Since the late eighteenth century, the foot is flatter, and the mark is always ground down.

These processes are not the same in every glass-house, of course, but the general pattern is very similar. Traditionally glass-workers worked in teams, or 'chairs'; a footmaker, who begins the operation, a servitor who adds the stem and in fact fashions the foot, and the gaffer, the master craftsman who manipulates, moulds, and decorates the glass. Two apprentices will generally assist in the various operations.

Any moulded or applied decoration is put on during the time the glass is being made. Cutting, engraving, or painting on the glass is, of course, done only when the object has moved through the slowly-cooling annealing oven, or lehr, over a period of some hours. The annealing oven is perhaps the newest part of a glass-house; one of the problems of glass production is the inherent instability of the metal, often increased by the uneven cooling and re-heating processes which must be gone through to shape the desired object. Previously, glass set aside to cool at an uncontrolled temperature would shatter for no apparent reason. The annealing oven heats the entire glass, and then cools it down at a very even rate, so that the stresses and strains inside the glass metal will be eliminated. Once cooled, the glass is ready for any decorative process.

Roman and Venetian Glass Introduction

The early history of glass is at present unknown; hopefully new research and archaeological discoveries may one day trace the first glass-house to a particular area; at this time, the probability is that glass was first made in Western Asia. Certainly, by 2000 B.C., Egyptian craftsmen had developed a highly-skilled trade, with four main kinds of manufacture.

The first was almost a form of sculpture; the melted glass was cooled without further working: the raw glass was then carved and cut into the desired shape, and polished with a grinding·tool. The metal was often coloured to resemble semi-precious stones such as turquoise or jade; small pots of such glass are known, with rims mounted in gold. This technique was known for many centuries, but became fairly wide-spread by the eighth century B.C.

The second technique was the use of removable cores. First a core was moulded around the end of an iron rod. It was previously thought the cores were sand, but it is more likely they were mud, or mud and straw. This technique was in common use by the 18th dynasty (1567–1320 B.C.) and was mainly used for small perfume, oil, and cosmetic containers. *Amphorae* and *oenochoe* were vase-shaped, with stuck-on handles and tapering bases, usually with trailed, brightly coloured decoration, and were held upright by metal stands. The *alabastron* were similar to beakers, tall and cylindrical, with flat bases.

The third method involved the use of moulds, open and closed. Sometimes molten glass was poured in, but a variation was the use of ground glass as a paste; this was revived in France as *pâte de verre*.

A fourth technique was based on mosaic work, with small pieces of vari-coloured glass laid in a mould, and fused together during firing.

This pre-blown glass continued to be made throughout the Greek and Roman period, and Alexandria, in Egypt, became the centre of a thriving glass industry which concentrated on finely-made, carved, moulded and cut glass of the highest quality.

Sometime around the first century B.C., glass blowing was discovered, probably in Syria. Blown glass involved more than just a new technique: an almost entirely new material became possible; thin, transparent, and above all, infinitely flexible. With constant experimentation, it was soon discovered that production could be increased by the use of moulds into which the glass was blown. Moulded glass was made throughout the Roman world, and is a most fruitful field for the collector, comparatively easy to acquire.

During the Middle Ages, glass suffered along with most of the arts, but a new style developed in Northern Europe. This heavy, usually greenish glass was made in the Rhineland, France, Belgium, and England, and although it was often clumsy in shape and detail, the best of the cone beakers are beautifully elegant, and this Teutonic style has a charm of its own. For many centuries, European glass remained stagnant, until the growth of the Venetian Guild of glassmakers marked the beginning of a new era.

There are very few records of early Venetian manufacture, but the guild was formed by the thirteenth century, and when the industry was removed to the island of Murano, a great period of research and experimentation began. It may be that their experience in making glass mosaic for the Byzantine churches was a vital factor; in any case, from the fifteenth century they produced wonderful glowing colours, and jewelled and painted decoration of great elegance. These early glasses were usually coloured, but continual research and cooperation between scientist and craftsman led to the development of *cristallo*, a clear, transparent glass, extremely easy to work in its molten state. At first the decoration continued to be enamelled and painted, but soon the *cristallo* itself was used to create marvellous and delicate patterns.

During the sixteenth and seventeenth centuries, Venetian glass was exported all over Europe. In spite of severe penalties, workers left Murano to establish glass-houses in many other cities, such as Altare, Antwerp, Paris, and London. These thriving colonies produced glass originally entirely in the Venetian tradition, but gradually local markets and local craftsmen developed their own interpretations. *Façon de Venise*, as this glass is called, in turn influenced Venetian makers, who adapted many new shapes and ideas. An English trader sent drawings of the glasses his customers preferred, and complained about the quality and brittleness of previous imports. For the main disadvantage of *cristallo* was its extreme fragility, and the more elaborate its design, the more easily it was broken. English chemists worked to perfect a new and more sturdy formula, and their success, together with the growth of European expertise and styles, marked the end of Venetian supremacy.

Glass
Roman

Detail: the pattern cut in gold leaf, sandwiched between the two layers of a.

a) *Double-walled 'sandwich' bowl of gold-glass; made in colourless metal with gold-leaf decoration between the two walls; from the tomb at Canosa, near Apulia, Italy; late 3rd century B.C.; dia. 7¾" (19.6 cm.).*

The remarkable talents of pre-Roman glass-workers have never been more beautifully illustrated than by this double-walled bowl.

Two separate bowls were cast in two-piece moulds; the inner bowl was minimally smaller in circumference, with a lip that covers the rim of the outer bowl (see diagram). Both bowls were ground and polished until they fitted together perfectly. An acanthus leaf pattern, typical of early Greek art, was cut out of gold leaf, and applied to the inner bowl. The outer bowl was slipped on, and the two fused together lightly at the edges. Twenty centuries later, Bohemian glass-makers used similar methods to make their *Zwischengoldglas* (p. 453c).

---

b) *Set of 24 game pieces in opaque white, opaque blue, opaque yellow and translucent green—6 of each colour; the cane sections are white, green and wine. Found in Hertfordshire, England; late 1st century B.C.; dia. approximately 1" (2.5 cm.).*

The technique used in making these game pieces was refined and perfected in the manufacture of 19th century French *millefiori* paperweights. Rods of glass were worked together to make the pattern, which was then drawn out into a thin cane and left to cool. Round sections sliced off the ends were arranged on a blob of molten glass; this was then worked in an open mould to produce the required shape. All 24 pieces were found intact. For a fuller explanation of the *millefiori* technique, see p. 490.

c) *Mosaic bowl, in clear colours with opaque white; Rome; 1st century B.C.; dia. 2⅜" (6.00 cm.).*

This bowl is an interesting example of a very ancient technique. It seems to be blown glass, but in fact it is mould-pressed.

Glass canes were cut into sections, and the spiral-patterned sections were laid directly on a moulded base. They were lightly glued together with some sort of adhesive, the bowl was covered with a top mould, and the whole put into the kiln. During the firing, the sections would fuse together, and after the bowl had cooled the inside was ground to remove any flaws and the outside fire-polished.

These early bowls no doubt inspired later glass-makers in Venice (p. 418c) and France.

a) The Portland Vase; cobalt-blue glass with cameo relief in opaque white; Roman, late 1st century B.C., or 1st century A.D.; ht. 9⅝" (24.5 cm.).

Some time during the first period of glass-blowing, the Portland Vase was made. Legends have surrounded this work since its first known documentation in 1642, when it was in the Barberini Palace in Rome. One theory suggests that the vase was made as the funerary urn for the Emperor Alexander Severus. Its source, date and even the subject matter depicted in the reliefs are all a matter for speculation, but it is universally regarded as one of the highest achievements of cameo-glass carving.

Originally the vase probably tapered to a point, as do amphorae; at some unknown time this was damaged, and replaced with a new flat base, and additional cameo work.

The vase was blown in a mould, and then cased in opaque white. There are marks of wheel cutting, and the handles were attached after the white glass was applied.

In the 19th century, after the vase was broken, John Northwood made a copy which encouraged the fashion for cameo carving.

---

b) Jug of soft green glass, trailings nipped in diamond shapes, chain handle, trail around neck; 2nd–4th centuries A.D.; ht. 6½" (16.5 cm.).

During the great period of Roman glass simple everyday objects were made in many provinces. Those places which lacked raw materials or craftsmen imported household articles in huge quantities; enough fragments remain to assure us that the supply was cheap and plentiful. Over the centuries, buried glass deteriorates due to chemical reaction; the result is a flaky surface with an opaque, gleaming iridescent coat over the core of original glass.

c) Lion-prunt beaker of thin blown glass, applied prunts finely moulded into lion heads; Reims, France; 4th century A.D.; ht. 9" (22.9 cm.).

This large beaker marks a middle point between Roman and Northern styles; the thin glass is reminiscent of the typical Roman pieces still being used at that period, but the prominent prunts are linked to the evenly-spaced blobs and claws of the Rhenish beakers, roemers, and later the stangen-glasses popular in Northern Europe. These prunts were made from applied blobs of glass, which were then shaped with small, patterned moulds. The most similar glass yet found came from a 4th century grave in Holland, and raspberry prunts on drinking glasses were popular in Holland well into the 18th century.

Glass

Northern
Venetian

a) Cone-beaker of soft green glass, blown, with horizontal spiral trail below rim, vertical looped trail below; found Bedfordshire, England; c. 5th century; ht. $10\frac{1}{4}''$ (26.2 cm.).

With the gradual disappearance of the Roman Empire, most of the variety of glassware disappeared too. Painting, cutting, cameo-work and gilding ceased; almost the only decoration to survive was simple mould-blown shapes and trailing.

The glasses of pagan Anglo-Saxon and Northern European graves are remarkably similar; there are only 13 known types. Even up to mediaeval times the shapes gradually changed, but the number of types did not measurably increase.

b) Claw beaker of blown green glass; the trails at neck and base and the upper row of the hollow claws are royal blue; late 6th century A.D.; found County Durham, England; ht. $7\frac{1}{2}''$ (19.1 cm.).

The claw beaker required considerable dexterity to make, although the appearance is rather heavy. After it was made, and the trails applied, it was cooled while still held on the blow-pipe. Heated blobs of glass were applied; blowing through the pipe inflated only these still-molten spots which were drawn out and shaped with pincers. Finally the glass was transferred to the pontil, and finished in the usual way.

During the Dark Ages, the manufacture of glass in the Western world almost ceased, and most of the old craftsmanship was lost. It was not until the Venetian glass-houses were built, in the 11th and 12th centuries, that glass-making was renewed as an art again.

---

c) Goblet of blown clear glass, enamelled and gilt decoration on bowl with gadrooned base; hollow foot, trailed decoration; Venice; early 15th century, c. 1425; ht. $6\frac{3}{4}''$ (17.1 cm.).

By the 13th century, the Venetians were beginning to monopolize the newly-revived tradition of glassmaking. Soon the number of kilns in the city created a fire hazard, and the Venetian authorities removed all the glass-houses to the island of Murano. By isolating and controlling the workers, Venice gained a monopoly that endured for centuries. Their production depended on a very light, very clear and easily-worked metal called *cristallo*. Although too brittle for cutting, it could be worked into any kind of fantastic elaborate shape. Technical facility combined with artistry, and Venice developed an increasingly rich and ornate style that reigned supreme over European taste until the 18th century.

d) Goblet in turquoise blue glass, with enamelled dots in a fish-scale pattern of white, gilt and turquoise. Hollow foot with narrow folded rim, folded rim to bowl; Venice, Italy; c. 1500: ht. $5\frac{3}{4}''$ (13.5 cm.).

This kind of enamel decoration is typical of Venetian glass at the time; one could almost say the glass was jewelled—certainly when the gilt was fresh and the colours unworn, it must have seemed as if the glass had been set with tiny precious stones.

The Venetians also imitated precious and semi-precious stones in glass, such as agate, jasper and jade. Another technique is known today as 'ice-glass'; the hot glass was plunged into cold water; when the glass cooled, it had become opaque and crackled all over the surface.

Glass

Venetian
Façon de Venise

a) Small ewer (one of a pair) in millefiori clear glass, with silver-gilt mounts; Venice, Italy; 16th century; ht. 5″ (12.6 cm.).

Another Venetian technique presumably inspired by ancient Roman glass is shown in this miniature ewer. The appearance is very similar to that of the Roman bowl (416c) but the method used was slightly different.

The earlier piece was made with sections of canes lightly glued together, and then fired so that the canes fused. The Venetian technique used a base of clear glass, with the sections of canes imbedded into it. The appearance was much the same, although by this time the canes themselves were considerably more complicated, and were very similar to the canes used in French paper-weights of the 19th century.

b) Tazza, engraved in diamond point, on low, trumpet-shaped foot, with milled-thread and chain decoration; Venice, Italy; early 17th century; dia. 10⅝″ (26.9 cm.).

Although the *cristallo* was too thin to be carved or cut, it could be engraved with a sharp point; this particular technique is called diamond point, and it became very fashionable on Anglo-Venetian and early English glasses, and Dutch goblets later in the 18th century. An early reference was made in Germany (1562) to the 'all sorts of festooning and handsome lines drawn by diamond on the nice and bright Venetian glasses.'

As we can see in this dish, the heavier enamelled and painted decoration on often dark-coloured glass, began to give way to a much lighter effect emphasized by the clear glass and lacy engraving.

---

c) Jug of opaque white and clear glass; probably made in the Netherlands, mounted in England; the silver mounts hall-marked 1548-9; ht. 6″ (15 cm.).

In spite of all their attempts, the Venetians could not keep the glass industry entirely to themselves. Workmen from Venice did manage to get away from the restricted island of Murano, and they travelled to many parts of Europe.

Many of these travellers settled down in the Netherlands, setting up glass-houses, and teaching their apprentices Venetian methods and formulae. This jug, possibly belonging at one time to Queen Elizabeth I, is an interesting example of the cross-currents that helped craftsmen to learn from many different sources; the glass is Venetian in type, but probably made in the Netherlands, using a northern European pottery shape, with English silver mounts.

d) Goblet with winged stem; Netherlands; 17th century; ht. 8½″ (21.5 cm.).

The Netherlands glass-makers were particularly fond of the winged stem goblets which had been made in Venice since the end of the 16th century. They became more and more elaborate, using coiled and coloured ropes, twisted stems, and wings on either side (which have often suffered during the years since they were made). They were also occasionally made with covers, although the top of this octagonal bowl is obviously not intended for such a purpose. Such glasses were made in many districts, and are often difficult to attribute with any certainty. Generically, glass made in the Venetian tradition outside of Italy is referred to as *façon de Venise*.

Glass

Anglo-Venetian

a) *Verzelini goblet with hollow-knop ribbed stem, deep round bowl, engraved in diamond point; engraving attributed to Anthony de Lisle; English, 1581; ht. 8½″ (21.5 cm.).*

Jacope Verzelini (1522–1606) was born in Venice, where he learned his trade. He emigrated first to Antwerp, where he was married in 1555, and then in 1571 to England. Here he worked for Jean Carré, one of the French Protestant refugees from Lorraine who ran the Crutched Friars glass house. When Carré died in 1572, Verzelini took over. In 1575 he obtained a 21-year patent from Queen Elizabeth for the sole right to make Venetian glass in England, and forbidding its importation from abroad. At the end of that time, he retired to Kent, and died there in 1606, a rich and highly respected man. There are less than a dozen known glasses extant attributable to his glass-houses.

b) *Early glasses of lead metal, with Venetian and Northern influences; England, c. 1670; ht. 8½″ (21.5 cm.).*

On May 23, 1615, a 'Proclamation Touching Glasses' forbade the use of wood as fuel for glass-making. England depended on her trees for ship-building, housing, etc., and the forests were disappearing. Conservationists then, as now, saw the danger of continuing to burn up the nation's wealth. But in the glass industry panic was widespread; the pots then in use were not suitable for coal, and desperate attempts were made to build kilns in the new colonies of America, where raw materials were plentiful. All efforts failed for a variety of reasons (see American Glass).

In 1623 Sir Robert Mansell took over the glass monopoly and although he knew nothing about glass, he proceeded to organize the entire industry on a national level; new and stronger pots were designed that kept out the coal dust, new kilns were built, and sea-coal and pit coal mines were developed from Scotland to Wales. He also founded the first bottle-glass factory in England.

After Mansell, the Civil War disrupted trade for 20 years, but the Restoration gradually brought more indigenous styles and more durable metal; although merchants such as John Greene imported Venetian glass as late as 1676, George Ravenscroft and other chemists were evolving a formula for a heavier glowing metal more stable than the fragile Venetian *cristallo*. With his final success in the 1680s, English glass began.

420

Left: Vase of ribboned amethyst and white glass; Murano (Venice), Italy, 16th–17th century.
Below: Small Roman glass beaker; 2nd or 3rd century A.D.

English Glass Introduction

Drinking glasses were the most important product of the English glass-houses in the late seventeenth and eighteenth centuries. They are classified by stem, and further sub-divided by bowl and foot shape. There are five main stem groups, five minor groups, and the rudimentary stem which occurred throughout the period.

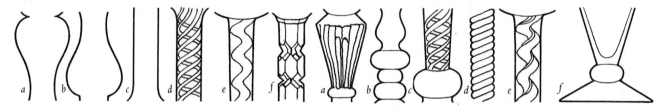

Major stem groups: *a and b)* Inverted and true baluster, c. 1685–1735; *c)* Plain, c. 1730–75; *d)* Air-twist, c. 1745–70; *e)* Opaque-twist, c. 1755–80, *f)* Faceted, c. 1760–1810.

Minor stem groups: *a)* Moulded pedestal, or Silesian, c. 1715–65; *b)* Balustroid, c. 1725–60; *c)* Composite, c. 1745–70, *d)* Incised-twist, c. 1745–70, *e)* Mixed and colour twists, c. 1755–75; *f)* Rudimentary.

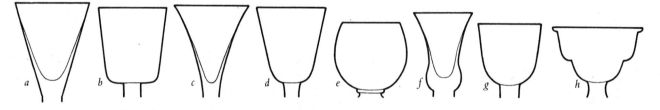

Bowl shapes: *a)* Funnel; *b)* Bucket; *c)* Trumpet; *d)* Round funnel; *e)* Cup; *f)* Bell; *g)* Ogee; *h)* Double ogee.

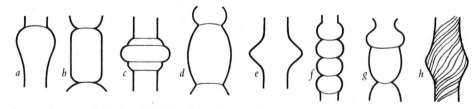

Some knop shapes: *a)* Drop; *b)* Cylinder; *c)* Annulated; *d)* Egg; *e)* Angular; *f)* Bobbin; *g)* Acorn; *h)* Swelling.

Basic foot shapes: *a)* Folded conical; *b)* Domed; *c)* Plain conical; *d)* Terraced; *e)* Flat (19th century).

Opposite:
Left: Green wineglass with round funnel bowl and centrally knopped incised stem.
Centre: Green wineglass with double knopped stem.
Right: Green wineglass, lower half fluted.
All English, late 18th, early 19th century.

Glass
English
LATE 17TH CENTURY

Finial of b; this type was often used on early American glass.

a) left: Decanter decorated with nipt diamond waies and 7 pincered and winged ribs, ribbed neck, trail collar and plain loop handle, on replacement gilt metal foot; the body highly crizzled; c. 1674-75; ht. 8" (20.3 cm.). b) right: Covered bowl of later Ravenscroft/Bishopp period, with gadrooned base and cover, chain trailing around centre and acorn finial; late 17th century; dia. 6⅛" (15.5 cm.).

These two fine pieces show clearly the difficulties encountered by George Ravenscroft, the analytical chemist, while perfecting 'a particular sort of Christalline Glass resembling Rock Crystall, not formerly exercised or used in this our kingdome'.

In April 1674 his new formula was presented to the Company of Glass-sellers who were so impressed that they offered him a glass-house at Henley-on-Thames to perfect his work in complete seclusion, and undertook to market his entire output, providing his glasses were made to the Company Clerk's designs and sizes. In May he received his 7-year privilege to make this glass. For 2 years he worked to eliminate the tiny cracks (crizzling) which appeared on completed pieces, because of imperfect stabilization in the glass metal, which can be seen in the decanter above. Gradually he improved production, discussing his work at intervals with fellow scientist, Dr. Plot, and Hawley Bishopp, a colleague at Henley. In April 1676 he was allowed to impress a seal on his glass and chose a raven's head.

In 1677 Ravenscroft guaranteed all his glasses against crizzling. However, most of his surviving sealed pieces show signs of this defect but possibly this appeared months or even years afterwards. Later examples, such as the bowl above, with clear uncrizzled metal were probably made in the Savoy Glass-house (c. 1680-85) under Ravenscroft's successor, Hawley Bishopp.

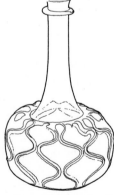

Ravenscroft decanter of purple glass.

c) Goblet with hollow stem; Ravenscroft/Bishopp, c. 1680; ht. 12 3/16" (31.5 cm.).

Many important goblets came from the London glass-houses once the production of Ravenscroft's *glass of lead* became firmly established. Numerous designs were made, and became extremely popular because of their strength, compared to the earlier European soda-glass-wares. The lack of competition ensured that by 1700 the output was vast; the craftsmen were completely free to use their artistic talents to explore this new medium, which required quite different handling, and new shapes.

This fine goblet is from the Ravenscroft/Bishopp transitional years. Raspberry prunts applied to a hollow stem is a difficult manipulative process and a rare feature.

d) Coin goblet with hollow knopped stem, nipt diamond waies and chain stringing on bowl; Ravenscroft/Bishopp period, c. 1680-85; ht. 7" (17.7 cm.).

This ceremonial goblet's round bowl has a moulded design at its base and delicate stringing above. The stem has a solid ball knop with a tear above a hollow knop containing a coin, and decorated with raspberry prunts, versions of earlier continental ornamentation (see p. 418*d*). The folded foot, a feature of early English glass, protected the rim from chipping. The clear metal indicates that Hawley Bishopp went on after Ravenscroft's death to perfect the formula, producing consistently clear glass without crizzling and thus ensuring English pre-eminence in the production of fine lead glass.

a) Short ale glass of the Anglo-Venetian period, c. 1690; ht. 5¼" (13.3 cm.).

The Venetians were particularly apt at expressing their artistic expertise through the medium of glass. Venetian ideas were still popular at the end of the 17th century and it is apparent on some of the early English pieces.

This ale glass shows Venetian influence in the wrythen (spiral) moulding terminating with a 'flammiform' border. Underneath the base of the tapered bowl is a 'winged' motif with a small flattened knop at the base; the well-made, high, conical foot has a folded edge.

This type of ale glass continued to be made in varying designs up to about 1750; later examples have short plain stems and are quite common.

b) Ale glass, the lower half of the flared bowl decorated with wrythen moulding, multi-knopped stem and folded foot; c. 1695; ht. 6" (15.2 cm.).

This early ale glass is even more rare than the preceding example; it shows clearly certain features which were to appear again and again throughout the next two centuries. The wrythen bowl gradually lost its flammiform edge and was moulded up to the rim (see p. 436d). The bobbin stem, allied in shape to bobbin-turned furniture, (see p. 326b) appeared in Newcastle glasses of the balustroid type, and even later in mid-19th century, on overlay glasses popular after c. 1851. An ale glass is characterized by its tall, somewhat narrow bowl.

---

c) Baluster mead glass with cup-shaped bowl narrowing towards the rim, and baluster stem; c. 1695; ht. 5⅛" (13.0 cm.).

The bowl has a gadrooned base and the double flattened knopped stem with an air tear, is over a basal knop and folded foot. This type of drinking vessel with a cup-shaped bowl, has been associated with the drinking of mead, an ancient concoction of fermented honey and water to which malt and yeast were added. It was very popular in the 17th and 18th centuries and until about 1830.

Early examples are usually found with baluster stems; later in the 18th century some were made with air or opaque twists which are very attractive and most still have the folded foot, a rare feature for that period.

d) Sweetmeat glass, well bowl with gadrooned base and flanged rim, simple baluster stem and collar over conical foot with narrow folded rim; c. 1700; ht. 4½" (11.4 cm.).

A charming example of an early sweetmeat glass in a rare design—showing the still-important Venetian influence.

Sweetmeats were made in a great variety of sizes and formations, for preserves and confectionery; all the stem groups are represented. They form a remarkably interesting section to collect. The beginning of the search is comparatively easy—as ambition grows, rare combinations of bowl, stem and foot take perseverance to find. There has always been some confusion between sweetmeat and champagne glasses; generally, the rim of a sweetmeat glass is obviously unsuitable for drinking.

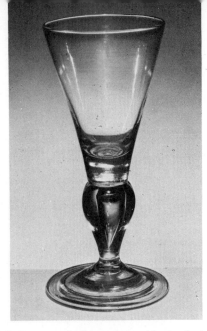

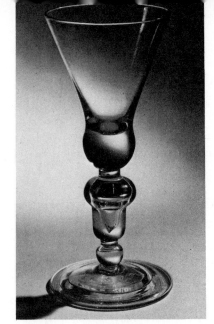

a) Baluster stem drinking glass with simple inverted baluster; c. 1695; ht. 8¼″ (20.9 cm.).

The name 'baluster', given to the stems of the first English series of drinking glasses and other tablewares (1690–1720), is an architectural one, the dictionary definition being 'one of a set of pear-shaped pillars that support a hand-rail'.

This is a splendid example of its period (in this case it is an inverted baluster), which marked the beginning of the great output of drinking vessels. The new heavy metal can be clearly seen from the fine funnel-shaped bowl with its heavy base and the wide folded foot. The massive knop contains a large air tear.

b) Goblet with acorn baluster and thistle-shaped bowl; heavy baluster period, c. 1690–1720; ht. 8½″ (21.5 cm.).

Of all the knop designs recorded during the heavy baluster period, a well-made acorn is perhaps the most pleasing and attractive. This particularly applies when it was the most important feature of the stem and also completely formed.

No finer specimen could ever have been made in any glass-house than the goblet in this illustration. Not only has the acorn been beautifully fashioned, with a large air-pocket of almost the same shape, but it dominates the glass, set off by a superb solid-based bowl and a small ball knop below showing perfect balance over a wide folded foot.

c) Baluster ale glass with central angular knop, ball knops above and below, with domed and folded foot; early 18th century; ht. 7½″ (19.0 cm.).

Following the first simple baluster stem knop, the glass-makers incorporated more than one type of knop in the same stem. Amongst the most popular was the angular knop, here centred in the stem of this fine ale glass. The angular knop was almost always made with other knops on the same stem, and served a useful purpose in its central position, giving poise and balance as well as being conveniently placed for holding and raising the glass. A flattened knop is similar but much shallower and often termed 'button', appearing throughout the 18th and well into the 19th centuries.

d) Baluster glass with teared egg knop, solid-based bowl with tear, folded foot; c. 1710; ht. 5¾″ (14.6 cm.).

The 'egg' or 'ovoid' knop has quite definitely become the rarest type. Really fine examples come on the market very infrequently. Perhaps it was difficult to make and therefore unpopular with the craftsmen, as several have been 'out of the time'; maybe they were not popular with the drinking fraternity—who knows?

The knop usually comprises the whole stem and here blends well with the bowl, both containing long air tears. This rare drinking glass is the most valuable in the heavy baluster series. As the century wore on the number of knops in a single stem increased.

a) Baluster stem goblet with cushion knop and wide folded foot; c. 1710; ht. 11¼″ (28.5 cm.).

This important baluster stem goblet is unusually formed with a massive ovoid bowl. The stem has an excellent cushion knop over a ball-shaped knop, with large air-pockets in the centre.

It is exceptionally tall for this period and would have been used at banquets or various festive occasions, probably passed round as a loving cup. Because of its unusually large size and the formation of the stem, great care must have been taken to keep the pontil iron turning evenly as the parts were joined. The craftsmen responsible for this beautiful goblet really excelled themselves.

b) Baluster stem candlesticks with multi-knopped stem, domed and corrugated foot; c. 1710; ht. 12½″ (31.7 cm.).

Early candlesticks are rare—no doubt many times the candle was allowed to burn down too low and the nozzle cracked. Sometimes the nozzle has been replaced at a later date and the darker early metal, full of grey tones, can quite clearly be distinguished from the clearer, more transparent glass used in the replacement. A pair of candlesticks is much rarer than a single one and a pair of baluster stemmed sticks would be very rare indeed.

---

c) left: Baluster stem glass with cylinder knop, short solid base trumpet bowl with air bead and domed and terraced foot; c. 1710; ht. 6⅝″ (16.8 cm.).

When attempting this knop the glass-maker had ample opportunity for displaying the really exceptional properties of glass in a concentrated form. The solid cylinder section shows the fine quality 'metal' which was being produced in England. The early glasses have a superb rich tone and almost liquid clarity; as the impurities were eliminated during the 18th century, the metal became much 'whiter' and more transparent. This gradual change in colour is one of the indications of the date of manufacture.

The bowl contains an air bead and joins the stem with a flattened ball knop and collar, with a smaller ball knop underneath.

d) centre: Baluster period drinking glass, bell bowl, plain foot; c. 1700–1710; ht. 7″ (17.7 cm.).

e) right: Wine glass with annulated knopped stem and trumpet-shaped bowl; c. 1715; ht. 6½″ (16.1 cm.).

Shown here is a bell bowl (extremely popular after c. 1705-10) on a semi-heavy baluster stem incorporating attractive flattened and true baluster knops successfully with a very short plain section, over a nicely proportioned conical foot. The next decade saw a wide variety of light baluster stems.

An annulated knop is a series of rings in the general shape of a swelling, or angular knop. They were made mostly during the light baluster period, usually accompanying bell-shaped bowls. The glass shown here on the right has a very rare combination of three sets of these rings or collars, with a trumpet-shaped bowl. Judging from the slightly smokey or yellowish metal it was probably made in Ireland (perhaps Cork).

a) Glass with moulded four-sided pedestal stem and letters GB on the stem, folded foot; c. 1714; ht. 6⅛″ (16.5 cm.).

This is the earliest and simplest of an attractive series akin to balusters in metal and weight, but with moulded stems. Only a very small number survive, contemporary with the ascension of George I of Hanover in 1714. They have an inscription in relief wording at the top of the stem, 'LONG LIVE KING GEORGE'.

This example bears the letters GB, which is even rarer. It has a typical funnel bowl with solid base, a large air tear in the stem, and a folded foot slightly flatter than usual for glasses of this period. Because of the continental influence this type of moulded pedestal stem is often called Silesian.

b) Glass with six-sided pedestal stem and folded foot; c. 1720; ht. 6⅜″ (16.1 cm.).

A few years later than the preceding glass, this shows a change in the stem design: an extremely graceful curve to the shoulder and concave hexagonal sides below, on a small plain section. The folded foot is unusually narrow for a glass of this period; most 18th century table pieces were made with wider bases in proportion to the diameter of the bowls.

However, there are always exceptions to the rule, and the quality and workmanship were features which only the English craftsmen achieved. For this reason they overcame all competitors connected with the art of glass-making during the 18th century.

c) Glass with deep funnel bowl and eight-sided pedestal stem, with star-studded shoulder and folded foot; engraved with coat of arms, c. 1725; ht. 7½″ (19.0 cm.).

This stem has the design nearer to a typical Silesian, although the moulded sides are still straight beneath the shoulder. The star-studded shoulder was a motif, which decorated some pedestal stems.

These somewhat lighter glasses with capacious deep bowls are often attributed to Newcastle, although the more usual stem formation there was a series of small knops on a tall stem (see p. 429b). This example was probably engraved by a Dutch artist, with the national coat of arms. There is a small flattened ball knop underneath the bowl. These points make an extremely graceful and well-proportioned drinking vessel.

d) Sweetmeat glass with Silesian stem and everted rim to the bowl, domed and folded foot, decorated with vertical rib moulding; c. 1740; ht. 6″ (15.2 cm.).

The slight wrythen pattern of the later pedestal stem is illustrated here; throughout the next 50 years this stem was usually adapted for sweetmeat glasses.

Other features of the glass-maker's art are a pronounced everted rim to the double ogee bowl, together with a domed and folded foot—always a pleasant combination. Joining the bowl to the stem and the stem to the foot are single and triple 'collars', which indicate a later date.

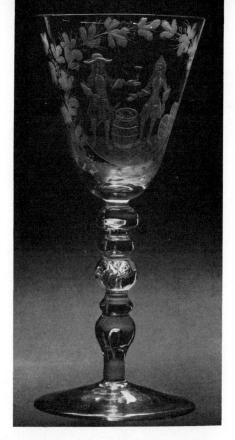

a) Goblet with light baluster stem formation; New-castle, c. 1730; ht. 8⅛″ (20.6 cm.).

This is an excellent example of the light baluster stem formation—illustrated here are the angular (top), annulated, drop and inverted baluster knops on a conical foot. The top of the bell-shaped bowl is finely wheel-engraved with an arabesque pattern. This type of Newcastle glass was sent across to Holland for decorating; the famous engraver, Jacob Sang, who signed some of his glasses, was one artist who worked on Newcastle goblets.

The round funnel shape of bowl on these elegant glasses is unusual. The engravings recorded depict coats of arms, crests, betrothal inscriptions, simple floral and bird designs, and many other emblems expertly executed.

b) Engraved wine glass, varied knops and plain conical foot; Newcastle, c. 1730-35; ht. 8½″ (21.5 cm.).

This splendid example shows one of the rarer subjects engraved by the wheel method—two figures, one with a wine glass, and wine barrels in the background. The detail in the garland of leaves is especially fine. The knops of the typical elegant stem are: mushroom (top), flattened, air beaded ball, drop, and inverted baluster with air tear.

These were the most elegant and well-proportioned drinking vessels ever made; their large capacity bowls are usually bell- or round funnel-shaped. The metal is brilliant and generally no other glasses from the English factories or any others, compare with them.

c) Light baluster period cordial glass with short trumpet bowl over collar; c. 1720; ht. 6¾″ (17.1 cm.).

Following the heavy baluster period, the formation of the air tears became lighter, the knops were smaller and less significant, but the glasses were still composed of fairly heavy metal. Later on the still lighter 'balustroid' series (see p. 430) appeared and were made up to the middle of the century.

This is a well-made cordial glass. The thick stem with a swelling knop contains a curious air tear formation over a plain conical foot. The swelling knop, usually centrally placed, creates a good balance for shape and use.

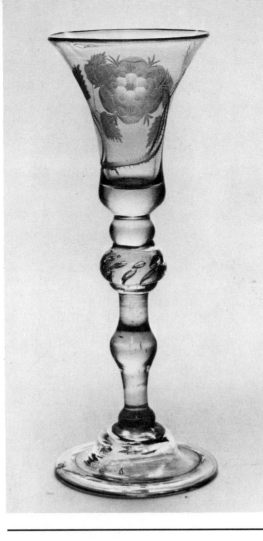

a) Jacobite wine glass of the balustroid period, folded foot; c. 1720–1740; ht. 7″ (17.7 cm.).

James II's son, John Francis Stuart, and his son, Charles Edward Stuart, stated that they had more right to the throne than the descendants of William of Orange. This caused one of the most intriguing situations in British history and a wealth of commemorative glass vessels were made. Bonnie Prince Charlie staged a series of battles with some success, but the main rebellions in 1715, by James, and in 1745 by Charles, were total failures for the Pretenders, owing to lack of organized support. The final defeat was in 1745 at the Battle of Culloden when Charles was beaten by the Duke of Cumberland and subsequently fled to Rome. He died in 1788.

Balustroid denotes a period when production of the early heavy baluster stems was ceasing. Although a lighter form, they were still of fine quality; the small version of the pure baluster knop was included sometimes. This glass is beautifully balanced, the stem combines a flattened ball, air beaded cushion knop and swelling knops on a good domed and folded foot.

---

b) Balustroid sweetmeat with lipped bowl decorated by vertical ribbed moulding, and domed foot; c. 1745; ht. 7½″ (19.0 cm.).

The outstanding feature of this fine sweetmeat is the perfect symmetry of outline, formed by the many knops, lipped bowl and domed foot. It clearly illustrates the expert and precise eye of the glass-maker; exact precision has to be maintained whilst twisting and blowing the metal rod, and about 10 pieces assembled and joined. The stem is composed of two sets of collars, air beaded ball knop and short baluster section. The ball knop was seldom used alone in a stem, but was included, sometimes flattened, in the majority of light balusters and often contained air beads.

c) Composite stemmed wine glass with heavy knop and base; c. 1730; ht. 5¾″ (14.6 cm.).

This is a most unusual example of a composite stemmed wine glass. Normally, very short glasses with heavy bases are called firing glasses: it was customary to knock them on the table instead of clapping, and this resembled the sound of musket-fire.

This glass is made of very fine metal, the graceful bell bowl drawn into a short plain section below which is a small, flattened and massive air beaded knop, in keeping with the heavy base. It would also be suitable for use on board a ship with appropriate decanters.

a) Goblet with large waisted bowl and plain stem, c. 1730; ht. 6″ (15.2 cm.).

This goblet illustrates the drastic change from the heavy and light knopped stem of the baluster period and the moulded decoration of the pedestal stem, to the plain straight stems made c. 1730-1750. The shapes of bowls began to vary—ogee, double ogee, waisted (as above), etc. During this phase, a popular type of glass was the drawn funnel wine glass (see following example) where the bowl was drawn into the stem in one operation, and was therefore a two-piece glass bowl-stem, and foot, instead of the more usual three or more piece.

b) Goblet with drawn trumpet bowl and plain stem; c. 1730; ht. 10″ (25.4 cm.).

This fine goblet is unusually large for this date; there were many copies made in the 19th century. The outline of the drawn trumpet bowl can be clearly appreciated in this photograph. The plain stem represents the second main period, c. 1730-45, terminating in a high conical and folded foot. After the baluster period the folded foot began to disappear and fewer glasses were made with it as the century progressed, although it is still possible to find them with every stem group up to 1790. In composite stems (those formed of different sorts) a plain section was usually included.

c) Wine glass with three piece flared bowl, plain stem and conical foot; c. 1730; ht. 6⅛″ (15.5 cm.).

This glass shows an interesting diversification from the usual drawn funnel bowl wine glass and is made in three pieces. The bowl is almost of thistle shape, but the solid base is less pronounced.

The full range of bowl shapes were fashionable by this date. Generally, the plain stemmed glasses had bowls in the following shapes: trumpet, funnel, round funnel, bell and ogee, cup and bucket. All remained popular until the end of the 18th century when the air spirals, white opaque spiral, and facet cut stems were introduced, although the trend was to make proportionately smaller bowls.

d) left: Plain stem cordial glass with small bowl; 18th century; ht. 6¾″ (17.1 cm.);
right: Plain stem champagne glass with double ogee bowl over an air beaded ball knop; c. 1730; ht. 6⅜″ (16.1 cm.).

The glass on the left is a typical cordial. The two main characteristics are a minimum height of 6″ (15.2 cm.) and a very small bowl (not necessarily on a plain stem), because of the strength of the cordial used. Gin was the staple spirit of the 18th century, but there were also a great variety of liqueurs and cordials, many of which could be purchased at two shillings per pint in 1703.

The champagne glass on the right is an excellent example both for quality and design. The bowl and beaded knop are over a plain shoulder knopped section and a very nice domed and corrugated foot.

a) Light baluster goblet with round funnel bowl and elongated air tears in the stem; c. 1735; ht. 6½″ (16.5 cm.).

An exceptional light baluster goblet; the stem has a flattened knop and short plain section containing elongated air tears. These clearly show the beginning of the idea which finally produced the air twist stems, brought to a fine art about 1740. This was followed by a large number of different air twist stems, perhaps the most attractive of the 18th century.

Eventually, the patterns developed from this interesting beginning were named by their appearance, e.g. mercury (which glows as if the air spiral was filled with mercury), corkscrew and close spiral, all in a variety of single and double series (one or two types of twists respectively in the same stem). Very occasionally one sees a triple series spiral with three separate components.

b) Wine glass with air twist stem and bell-shaped bowl; c. 1740; ht. 6¼″ (15.8 cm.).

This is a really attractive wine glass with a bell-shaped bowl engraved round the top with a fine diamond point floral design. The stem has a close air spiral and around the centre is an applied vermiform collar. The usual two types of this 'decoration' are the example shown here and double or triple plain rings. With these additions on the stem, the glasses were sometimes called 'drunkards' as it was easier to grip the stem.

Most of those recorded have air twist stems and bell-shaped bowls; a small number, however, are recorded with opaque twists and other types of bowls.

c) 'Amen' Jacobite glass with air beaded flattened ball knop over domed foot; c. 1740; ht. 6¼″ (15.8 cm.).

The drawn trumpet bowl wine glasses, formed in two sections, were the most useful and strongest types to be made; the plain and air spiral stems were the most common.

This glass is a rare variation, the bowl and stem being typical forms, but an air beaded flattened ball knop has been introduced over a domed foot; most stems were joined to a plain conical base. The rarest feature, however, is that this one belongs to a small historical group—the famous Jacobite 'Amen' glasses, (see p. 434*a*). They are diamond-point engraved with verses of the Jacobite anthems.

d) Air twist goblet with moulded hammered bowl and matching cover; c. 1740; ht. 12″ (30.4 cm.).

Comparatively few covered goblets have survived. They were used on festive occasions, and sometimes as loving cups, with or without handles. This is a particularly fine specimen of handsome proportions and fine quality; it has a moulded cover with an air beaded ball-shaped finial matching the base of the bowl below, which is an early triple air spiral stem and conical foot. Most other known examples are earlier but a certain number are later, with opaque and faceted stems. Usually they have lost their covers but very occasionally one comes to light with the original cover.

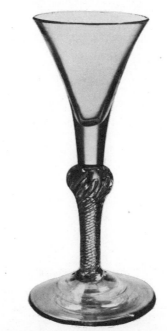

a) Green wine glass with vertical ribbed moulding on bowl, air spiral twist stem, conical plain foot; c. 1740; ht. 7¼″ (18.4 cm.).

Comparatively few coloured glasses were made before 1790. Green wine glasses and goblets are recorded in all five main stem groups, but are very rare. Also recorded are glasses with green or blue bowls and feet and opaque white stems. One set is known of mid-18th century glass with knopped stem. This glass from the air twist period is quite rare.

b) Three close air twist spiral glasses, all with plain conical feet; c. 1745; ht. of centre glass 6″ (15.2 cm.).

This photograph is a good example of different bowl shapes and a swelling knopped stem (centre). The tall elegant champagne glass (left) has a beautifully proportioned rectangular bell-shaped bowl on a simple close air spiral stem. The centre glass has a rare combination of the delightful double ogee bowl and a swelling knopped air spiral stem. The upper part of the bowl is wider than most of this type, sometimes called saucer or pan tops. The third wine glass has a round funnel bowl of generous capacity, decorated with moulded flutes at the base, on a close air spiral stem.

c) right: Cordial glass with double corkscrew air twist and engraved with a floral design; c. 1750; ht. 6¾″ (17.1 cm.); left: Wine glass with spiral cable stem and round funnel bowl; c. 1750; ht. 6⅝″ (16.8 cm.).

A cordial glass with typical small drawn trumpet bowl, this is engraved by the wheel method with a continuous floral design. The stem is composed of a fine double corkscrew air twist—a really fine technique which developed as glass-makers learned to introduce threads of air into a straight section of glass. The result was most effective and, as can be seen, graduated in size from top to base. Cordials were made in all stem groups.

The wine glass has a round funnel bowl engraved with an unusual figure subject and trees.

d) Wine glass with drawn trumpet bowl and composite stem; c. 1750; ht. 6¾″ (17.1 cm.).

An attractive wine glass which illustrates two types of formation in the same stem. The drawn trumpet bowl has a short plain section with a shoulder knopped air spiral stem below. It can be clearly seen how the lengthened air beads were eventually formed into the twist which had started the third main change in style about 1740-50. Composite stems were usually made with the major portion composed of an air twist section, but a smaller number comprised various formations of opaque twists, and to a lesser degree faceted knops, and a few even more unusual variations.

433

a) Jacobite goblet, close spiral stem with vermiform collar around the centre; c. 1750; ht. 6½″ (16.5 cm.).

This is one of the most important glass goblets made to commemorate the Jacobite rebellion. The large bucket bowl is engraved with a rose, two buds, star, the simple motto '*FIAT*' (may it be so) and one of the rarest inscriptions '*Turno Tempus Erit*' (literally, events will be changed) and on the foot '*Redeat*' (may he return) and a thistle.

Memories of the Jacobite rebellions of 1717 and 1745 linger on with emblems supporting the Jacobite cause engraved on drinking glasses, tumblers, jugs and other types of glasses. The most well-known phrase was the toast to the King over the water. The rose is the most portrayed symbol, usually with two buds, supposed to represent the Pretenders; also found are thistles, oak leaves, stars and other flowers, besides Latin mottoes and in rare instances a portrait of Prince Charles, or verses from the Jacobite anthem; these are called 'Amen' glasses (see p. 432c).

b) Goblet with incised twist stem and round funnel bowl; c. 1755; ht. 5½″ (13.9 cm.).

As a change from inside stem ornamentation, glass-workers evolved two methods of outside treatment in c. 1755–80: the incised twist and the faceted stems. The incised twist, a close wrythen pattern, either coarse or fine, has some Venetian influence. It was sometimes made in soda metal—usually with a bell-shaped bowl and folded foot.

This lead glass example is particularly good with a well formed round funnel bowl. Such glasses are fairly rare. The foot is nicely set (the sign of a genuine glass), and the centre of the foot is high, rising to meet the stem's base.

a) Three glasses with opaque twist stems; c. 1760; ht. of centre glass, 6″ (15.2 cm.).

This was the fourth main period of the 18th century glasses; the change from the air spirals took place about 1755-60, although one dated specimen has been recorded of 1747. The technique was very similar to 17th century Venetian *latticinio* work.

Different types of spirals were introduced into the same stem and are known as single, double series, etc. Canes of white enamel were placed around the inside of a cylindrical metal mould which was then filled with molten glass, After cooling, the glass cylinder was removed, reheated and drawn out and twisted by two men, into a thin cane; lengths of which were cut up for stems (see filigree canes p. 490).

Many glasses were made with opaque spirals sometimes known as cotton twists. The variety of twists is enormous; knopped stems are in the minority.

b) Sweetmeat glass with opaque twisted stem and decorated domed folded foot; c. 1775; ht. 6½″ (16.5 cm.).

Several rare features are incorporated in this glass. It has a lipped trellis-moulded double ogee bowl on a double series opaque spiral stem, and a similarly decorated domed and folded foot. The types of twist are a central multi-lace, and a double-entwined outside spiral.

All stem groups are represented in sweetmeats, the commonest being the faceted types (see pp. 437b and 446a). A series of short-stemmed sweetmeats were also made for 'dry' sweetmeats and are called comfit glasses; the rarest have a dentilated or looped edge (see p. 441b). Sweetmeats were also used to stand on a *tazza* surrounded by smaller glasses all holding candies and sweetmeats.

c) Jacobite ratafia glass, engraved with Jacobite emblems; c. 1755; ht. 6¾″ (17.1 cm.).

While most Jacobite glasses were produced during the air twist period, before Prince Charles' defeat at Culloden (see p. 430a), a smaller number of good specimens were made with opaque twist stems. This fine glass has a somewhat shorter bowl than those used for ale drinking—it was probably used for ratafia, a sweet cordial type drink popular in the 18th and 19th centuries and often drunk at tea time. The bowl is wheel-engraved with the Jacobite emblems of a rose and two buds and a butterfly. These glasses are now very difficult to find; the two rarest types are ratafias and ales.

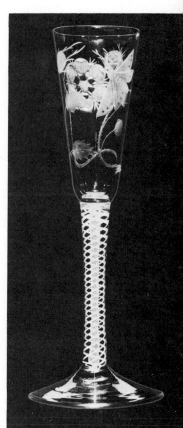

435

a) Cordial glass with long spiral stem and ogee bowl, on a plain conical foot; bowl and foot in green metal; c. 1770; ht. 8¼″ (20.9 cm.).

The typical height of a true cordial is 6″–7″, but a small number, including this glass, were made of exceptional dimensions and elegance. The superb workmanship can be clearly seen and the ogee bowl is perfectly formed; the close opaque spiral stem has a centre flattened knop.

Glasses of above average size and formation are sometimes known by the term 'Captain' but that is more often applied to sweetmeats placed in the centre of a *tazza* or salver.

b) Wine glass with mixed twist stem and trumpet bowl with double collar; c. 1770; ht. 7¼″ (18.4 cm.).

While there are 5 main groups of stem designs, other interesting variations were the results of the ingenuity of the glass-makers. One of these was the brilliant combination of the air and opaque spirals, known as the mixed twist.

This glass has a rare double collar, the stem is a well-formed multi-ply central opaque spiral, surrounded by a double air spiral. A great number of different combinations were made. Coloured twists were also made, sometimes with air threads, but usually with white opaque threads. Red and blue occur most frequently, yellow is the most unusual, although all are rare.

Glass

English

LATE 18TH CENTURY

c) Toastmaster's firing glass with deceptive bowl and opaque twist stem; c. 1770; ht. 4⅛″ (10.4 cm.).

Very often, as now, countless toasts were drunk at banquets and feasts. Some glasses were made especially for such events (e.g. the firing glass p. 430c); the toastmaster must have found it difficult to keep pace with continuous drinking to honour eminent guests. The glass-maker ingeniously solved his problem by making a small glass of suitable proportions but with an extra thick or 'deceptive' bowl. This left a very small capacity for the drink, although the glass looked full. It is most unusual to find the combination of a deceptive bowl and the firing foot on a double series opaque twist stem.

d) Ale glasses with wrythen decoration and short stems; 18th century; ht. 5″ (12.7 cm.).

There was a vast number of dwarf, or short ale glasses made with a variety of moulded wrythen decoration and short stems. These glasses show Venetian influence, as does the incised twist (see p. 434b). Because of the extreme strength and potency of the ale, small glasses were used. They are very useful nowadays for sherry or port; it can be most fascinating to collect a set with slight differences of decoration. These two glasses are good examples. Some dwarf ales have virtually no stems, others have knops and a short stem. Folded and plain feet were also made.

a) Wine glass with facet-cut stem (upright hexagonal), engraved with a bird and flowers; c. 1775; ht. 5½" (13.9 cm.).

The second method of decorating the stems on the outside was by facet cutting, between c. 1770–1790. The pattern was diamonds, hexagons, or vertical flutes. The latter is termed slice cutting, as it extends the whole length of the stem. The majority of glasses in this group have straight stems; it is rare to find examples with one knop and even a smaller number were made with double knops.

This glass has a well-formed ovoid bowl unusually engraved with a hovering bird and polished flowers. The cutting on the stem is carried on to the base of the bowl.

b) Sweetmeat glass with diamond cut stem, double ogee bowl and domed, scalloped base; c. 1780; ht. 12¼" (31.3 cm.).

This is one of the finest recorded examples of a facet-cut sweetmeat glass, bought for £35.00 in a Norwich sale many years ago. Of mammoth proportion, this glass has a double ogee bowl beautifully cut with geometric and flute designs, a Van Dyck edge and a fine domed and scalloped base. The stem is diamond cut and it is over 12" (30.4 cm.) high. No finer example of flat cutting could be found on a piece of this type.

c) Group of candlesticks, knopped with facet cutting, domed and folded foot; c. 1780; ht. of stick on right, 8½" (21.5 cm.).

Three of these candlesticks have their original loose savealls, the term used for the parts which fit into the sconces to catch the candle grease.

Candlelight would have been most effective with facet cut glass reflecting the glow from the fireplace and the table silver. Domed feet were particularly effective on candle and taper sticks giving a sense of balance when the candles were in place. Taper sticks were miniature candlesticks; supposedly they provided illuminations at tea parties in particular, and for writing. Many secretaires have slides which pull out to hold the taper sticks.

d) Pair of facet-stemmed goblets with large ogee bowls; c. 1780–1800; ht. 5¾" (14.6 cm.).

It is unusual to find good facet-stemmed glasses of goblet size such as these. The large ogee bowls are decorated with polished, engraved roses and buds, possibly a remembrance of Jacobite times. The stems show good examples of facet diamond cutting which also extends a short way into the base of the bowls; this reflects as an open flower formation inside. Facet-cut stems are found most often on small bowled cordial glasses and sweetmeats and candlesticks.

437

a) Two ale tankards; left: engraved with hops and barley, straight sides; ht. 5" (12.7 cm.); right: waisted tankard with gadrooned base, threading around the rim, engraved with a floral design; both mid-18th century.

Tankards and ale jugs were made throughout the century. Sometimes they were engraved with hops and barley, sometimes with flowers, a name and date, etc. The most usual shape is the waisted one on the right. The base was occasionally decorated with diamond moulding instead of gadrooning. Around the rim, just below the edge, a thin trailed decoration can be seen; this consisted of thin lines of applied trailed glass, circling the piece and was often used on tankards and bowls.

b) Jacobite loving cup; c. 1750; ht. 9" (22.9 cm.).

This is a fine example of a festal Jacobite (see p. 434a) loving cup. It is double handled, engraved with a large rose, has flattened knopped stem and a domed and folded foot. It was used by the more adventurous followers.

Decanters are also known with compass pointing. Other flowers connected with the Jacobite movement were: sunflower, carnation and daffodil (Welsh movement).

Loving cups also occur with other inscriptions, and were often used as ceremonial marriage goblets.

c) Group of 'label' club-shaped decanters; c. 1750; ht. of White Wine 14" (35.5 cm.).

Aside from the illustrated drinking glasses, there are some forms which recur throughout the period, usually for special uses. In addition to these 4 examples, there are patch stands, like miniature sweetmeats, jugs of varying kinds, flutes, sugar bowls, posset pots, etc.

Around the mid-18th century, a most attractive series of 'label' decanters was made, engraved with simulated silver wine labels and were either of club or mallet shape. Over 12 different names have been recorded, varying in rarity, the most uncommon being 'Calcavella' and the easiest to find 'White Wine'.

Opposite:
Double overlay glass with deep blue and white overlays on bowl and foot and hollow bobbin stem; England, 19th century.

Two cameo glass vases made by Frederick Carder at Stevens and Williams; England, 1880.

a) Coin goblet with funnel bowl, trailed and nipt chained waies, hollow ball knop with strawberry prunts and containing Queen Anne Maundy fourpenny pieces, over a folded foot; c. 1714; ht. 9″ (22.8 cm.).

There seems to be no particular reason for including a coin in a hollow stem; this technique was one of the most skilful in the glass-maker's repertoire. Usually the glass knop has remained clear and the coin can be easily identified. Although the date of this coin (1713) coincides with the fine goblet, it was the usual practice to include coins of an earlier date—this point should be borne in mind. Such pieces date from Ravenscroft's time. This particular goblet shows that Venetian influence was still strong, even at a comparatively late date.

b) Sweetmeat glass and cover with finial, the double ogee bowl with looped and prunted edge, over an inverted baluster stem; domed and folded foot, honeycomb moulded to match; c. 1740; ht. 10″ (25.4 cm.).

Another rare type of moulded decoration was the looped edge bowl, where most attractive separate sections were applied around the top of the bowl in a continuous 'croquet hoop' design; each junction was a separate seal or prunt. Some have survived without covers and with moulded Silesian stems. Many large drinking glasses would have been made with covers, which were easily lost. A great variety of sweetmeat glasses were made but generally the moulded design was the most popular.

c) Horizontally-moulded Lynn tumbler of clear glass; c. 1760; dia. 5″ (12.7 cm.).

Wine and ale glass decanters, jugs and finger bowls decorated with horizontal moulded ridges have always been attributed to the King's Lynn factory, since most early examples were found in East Anglia. Much Lynn glass was sold in Norwich, and blue drinking glasses etc. were also gilded by Absolom of Yarmouth. Blue Lynn finger bowls are rare but Lynn glasses have appeared, usually of wine glass size, and Lynn tumblers have also been found.

d) Wine bottle of cruciform design, with single anular neck; c. 1720; ht. 8⅛″ (20.6 cm.).

Following the early green wine bottles, clear examples were made in the shape of a cross, hence the term 'cruciform'. They are now comparatively rare. About the same time similar bottles were made with designs ranging from those moulded with additional indentations to others of mallet shape, the entire body being decorated with trellised design. Wine was usually served direct from these vessels at the table. They developed from the original clear decanter-jugs made by George Ravenscroft in the late 17th century.

a) Decanter of mallet shape, decorated with white enamelling by W. Beilby in vine-leaf and grape design; c. 1775; ht. 10½" (26.7 cm.).

Amongst some unknown enamellers of glass, both in white and colour, were the Beilbys of Newcastle, now well known to collectors as so much has been written about the simple, sporting, classical and other scenes they executed. William Beilby senior (1706-65) was born at Scarborough and later moved to Durham. He married Mary in 1733 and amongst his 7 children, William and Mary found their métier in enamelling on glass. Their first work is recorded c. 1762, of heraldic design; their subjects in coloured and white enamels covered a vast range.

The most important items are large goblets with Royal coats of arms bearing the signature 'V. Beilby'. One only has been found with the initial 'W'.

b) Faceted bottle in green glass, with gilt decoration, by James Giles; c. 1790; ht. 11" (29.2 cm.).

As well as decorating china, James Giles also worked on glass; he was one of the few business-men in London in the 18th century who decorated china. His favourite ground in glass was green and this bottle—one of a pair—would have been typical of his work.

Giles was always ambitious with his work and executed more complicated designs than any other artist in this field. Amongst his favourite motifs were stag's heads and paterae. His designs were always 'close', covering the whole item, usually an exquisite faceted scent bottle, or decanter, or other small pieces.

c) Pair of blue Bristol finger bowls, with gilt rims; signed I. Jacobs, c. 1790, dia. 5" (12.7 cm.).

Jacobs—father and son—were amongst the few individual craftsmen who recorded their work on glass. They were fond of geometrical designs, and the Greek key pattern border, as well as floral sprays of Adam style and other classical designs. Always of fine quality, their gilding appears only on coloured pieces. Lazarus' son, Isaac, was eventually appointed glass-maker to George III. Michael Edkins is another decorator in the city whose name is associated with painting on glass and porcelain.

In 1696 John Houghton mentioned three flint glass and ordinary manufacturers in Bristol and in 1725 Daniel Defoe recorded 'There are no less than 15 glass-houses in Bristol which is more than in the City of London'. Thus begins the history of this famous glass-making centre to which so much coloured glass, sometimes erroneously, has been attributed. Certainly blue, green, amethyst and sometimes red glass was made in Bristol, but typical pieces only represent a small group, e.g. decanters with gilded labels, finger bowls, plates, sauce bottles and certain opaque white items with enamelled flowers, etc. The peak period for Bristol glass of this kind was 1780-1820.

a) Portrait glass of Queen Mary, engraved in diamond point; 1695; ht. 9" (22.8 cm.).

There are commemorative glasses all through the history of English glass-making. They cover all sorts of subjects: loyalty to the Crown, as here and in the Williamite glasses, the Jacobite rebellion, sporting and family events, new bridges, etc.

On this glass a portrait of Queen Mary has been engraved, with the date, and the inscription 'Maria Regina' above a continuous hunting scene. It is made of 'glass of lead', but the shape of the bowl and the hollow knopped stem show the still potent Venetian influence. Some time ago a broken foot was replaced here with a wooden one.

b) Low tumbler with ribbed base, engraved The glorious Memory of King William III, Boyne July 1st; *c. 1780–1790; ht. 4" (10.1 cm.).*

This tumbler illustrates how engraving may commemorate a much earlier event; in this case the Battle of the Boyne, in 1690. It is obvious that the glass is much later, probably c. 1790, and perhaps it was a centennial celebration.

There are many kinds of Williamite glasses, including baluster stem cordials, with a cylinder knop, engraved with a portrait of William on a horse. These have been extensively copied and quite often faked.

Detail: a commemorative glass.

c) Goblet on annulated knopped stem; wheel engraved with two boxers; c. 1810; ht. 6½" (16.5 cm.).

There are more frivolous subjects as well, on commemorative glass, although no doubt many sportsmen would not like that appellation for the noble science.

This goblet is one of three in graduated sizes and may have depicted an actual fight, although there is no inscription. Other such goblets bore shooting, hunting and racing scenes; one is engraved with 'Rowton' a race horse and his rider, winner of the St. Leger in 1829.

d) centre: Detail from a frigate glass, with bucket bowl over an opaque twist stem, c. 1765. Right: Detail from an armorial engraving; c. 1790.

These frigate and privateer glasses are quite rare. They bear the names, and an engraving, of the ship in question.

It is generally accepted that these glasses were made in Bristol, one of the largest centres of shipping during the 18th century. They all follow the same pattern—a bucket bowl on an opaque twist stem, and usually bear names of ships registered in Bristol. 'Lyon' was one such name— other well-known examples are 'Eagle', 'Enterprise' and 'Renown'.

Armorial glasses were a speciality of Dutch engravers, particularly on tall Newcastle goblets.

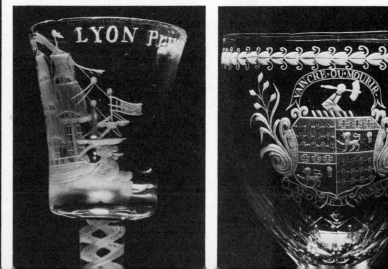

Detail of engraving on Buggen bowl.

a) Ravenscroft Butler Buggen bowl, with raven's head seal on the base, diamond point engraving; c. 1680s; dia. 7" (17.8 cm.).

This delightful bowl is one of Ravenscroft's more successful pieces with hardly any trace of crizzling.

Diamond point is one of the earliest methods of engraving, having been known from ancient times. In England some of the finest and earliest glass was decorated, and events recorded, in this manner. The technique differs from stipple engraving in that the surface of the glass was scratched by a splinter of diamond attached to a holder. As a result of this linear method, some scenes in glass have a slight amateurish appearance. In fact a great deal of detail, such as trees or animals, was portrayed.

b) Wine glass, stipple engraved and signed in Holland by Franz Greenwood; elegant triple knopped stem, folded foot; c. 1730; ht. 6¾" (17.1 cm.).

Stipple engraving was executed by a very small sharp-pointed tool, pressed to make a series of dots, eventually depicting a portrait or scene with delicate definition—the ultimate in glass decoration. Franz Greenwood (worked c. 1725-50) and David Wolff (worked c. 1750-1800) are two Dutch engravers expert in this method; they worked on glass shipped from Britain and became well known because they signed some of their pieces. David Wolff, whose work is found on glasses with faceted stems, was particularly expert in producing armorial crests, portraits and scenes with figures.

c) Punch bowl, pale green tint with white rim, wheel engraved with convivial drinking party and inscription; plinth base, c. 1750; dia. 8⅛" (20.6 cm.).

This type of engraving was widely used on all kinds of glass in the 18th and 19th centuries. A series of revolving wheels was used, similar to those used for cutting glass, but they were smaller in diameter and made of copper. This produced a bolder outline and in various scenes the actual surface of the glass was left to produce a polished effect in such motifs as flower petals, coats of arms, etc. This technique ranged from the simple festoons on decanters to the most intricate subjects.

d) Acid engraved goblet on a slice cut stem over a square base; c. 1820; ht. 6" (15.2 cm.).

Acid engraving was developed in Germany, but became quite popular during the early part of the 19th century. The glass was coated with wax, a design etched through the coating and the glass submerged in acid. After a sufficient time had elapsed, the glass was removed, washed, and the wax coating taken off; the result had a rather photographic effect. In America it was known as needle-etching, (see p. 475c).

a) left: Flat leaf design, with notch-cut edging; c. 1770–1780; centre: Double star motif within circle of leaves and swirl flutes; c. 1780; right: large diamond composed of smaller ones, with leaf patterns at each end; c. 1790.

To look upon a piece of cut glass, perhaps it would never occur to the casual observer that so much expertly thought-out work has been necessary to achieve the final result.

The peak period for the main output of cut table glass was the late 18th century, when many English manufacturers emigrated to Ireland. Duty had been imposed on glass in England in 1777, 1781, and 1787. Ireland remained free of taxation, and was granted free trade with England in 1780.

However, the glory of the art of cutting by no means belonged only to Ireland; records from the glass-houses of the English Midlands, especially the Brierly Hill district, show a prosperous glass industry, carried on despite the difficulties of taxation. Large numbers of really fine pieces were made there.

b) left: Flute cutting; in this instance, the flutes are concave, and the top edges curved; c. 1790–1810; centre: pillar flute cutting on the body of a decanter, with step cutting above; c. 1800–1825; right: simple diamonds, each composed of four triangular shapes, with a fan cut and scalloped edge; c. 1810.

The very vast variety of patterns carefully created by 18th and 19th century craftsmen included stars, diamonds of different formations, flutes, steps, ovals, etc. Every piece had to be made almost double the thickness necessary for the finished article, to allow for this treatment.

The conditions for working, and the methods used then have scarcely changed, except that any kind of machinery necessary, previously operated by foot treadle or steam, is now powered by electricity.

It is quite amazing to discover the number of different materials used in this type of ornamentation, either for the equipment actually used, or their effective employment: sandstone, cast tin, sheet iron, sand, water, copper, emery and oil, white wood, sometimes cork, putty (prepared from calcined tin), colcothar (the pink powder known as Jeweller's Rouge) and even Tripoli, a fine earth imported from Africa, near the town of Tripoli.

a) *Facet-stem sweetmeats, the first with shallow cutting on bowl and foot, both having a scalloped edge; the second with rib-moulded bowl and foot; both with facet-cut stems with swelling knop; c. 1770.*

As a general guide, the main styles and designs of cut glass are divided into three groups.

The first is flat smooth cutting, sometimes termed faceting, c. 1740–1790. This includes the early English glasses, often at first cut only on the stem (see p. 437a), and the first simply-cut sweetmeats and candlesticks, such as the two above. The patterns are usually large, and consist of shallow diamonds and ovals, with fairly simple cut edges.

This group also includes the early Irish cut glass, including the styles of the well-known Irish glasshouses at Waterford, Cork, Belfast, and Dublin.

Glass

English and Irish

CUT GLASS

b) *Strawberry diamond cutting; a variation of the diamond pattern, which was the most frequently used design, here cut into still smaller prisms instead of the central point; c. 1820.*

The process of cutting can be divided into 4 main stages:

1. Marking the design, usually with bright red paint.
2. First cutting, using an 18″ iron wheel, on to which falls a stream of wet sand.
3. Final cutting with a wetted sandstone wheel, adjusting the initial cuts, and smoothing out some of their roughness.
4. Final polishing with wooden wheels, with the aid of various powders which gradually increase in fineness, and thus eventually produce a perfectly-polished surface.

c) *Centrepiece, with detachable arms, the top tier holding hanging baskets, the lower tier with small attached trays; c. 1780.*

This centrepiece is an elaboration of the previous example's two sweetmeats; for the centre of the table, brilliant cut glass could well replace the traditional silver epergnes which were so popular at this time (see pp. 653a and 654b).

Such beautiful pieces are now quite rare. A metal arm plate is fixed into the centre with a rod placed in the hollow stem, which is secured with a small circular threaded screw. The top section also has a metal piece fixed on the end, which screws securely into the arm plate.

d) *Chandelier for 8 lights, with faceted notch-cut arms, chains of round and lozenge-shaped drops, cut in flat diamonds, and ornamented with stars and rings of cut glass; Adam period, c. 1780.*

The Adam brothers influenced every branch of domestic decoration, and glass was no exception. Chandeliers, superb pairs of candelabra, wall-lights—all followed the new classical designs.

Urns and festoons were particularly well adapted to lighting devices made of cut glass, as the hanging drops, swaying slightly with every current of air, would reflect and multiply the gleam of candle and firelight (see p. 346).

a) *Three Irish fruit bowls; left: an early, boat-shaped example with uncut stem and moulded square base, c. 1780; centre: slightly later type, boat-shaped, with more complicated cutting, and a beautifully cut Van Dyke edge; right: even later, a boat-shaped bowl with turned-over edge; bands of facet cutting over a short bobbin stem on a heavy, oval moulded pedestal base; ht. of first bowl, 9¾″ (24.7 cm.).*

These three bowls show how this typically Irish form developed. In the first example, star motifs have been used to make an uncomplicated design around the rim, which itself is simply cut in a straightforward scallop. The plain stem has a central, slightly flattened ball knop.

The second bowl is a little more elaborate; the band is made up of flat geometric diamonds, encased in circular flutes, with a band of leaf motifs running below. The short stem has a swelling knop, and the base, as always, is slightly small in proportion to the size of the bowl; here it has been moulded into scalloped edge flutes, not quite in line with the centre of the base.

On the third bowl, cutting has been concentrated on the turn-over rim, and a band of flutes beneath.

b) *Pair of quart size decanters, with thumb and broad flutes, and mushroom stoppers; c. 1810; ht. 15″ (38.1 cm.).*

The second period of cutting runs roughly from 1790 to 1810. It included the use of broad and narrow flutes, circular flutes, sometimes called thumb prunties, or thumb flutes, sharper diamond cutting, and close flute-cut bases.

The craftsman who cut this pair of decanters achieved a very interesting effect with his thumb flutes, which run in a thick band all around the bodies. As you can see in the photograph, the concave circles are reflected in a way which gives a 'hob-nail' effect when looking through the decanter to the other side. Broad flutes have been cut above and below this band, and the necks have three applied rings.

c) *Preserve jar and cover, showing change from flat cutting; middle period, c. 1810; ht. 6¾″ (17.1 cm.).*

This preserve jar, with its domed cover, is a good example of how cutting was changing in the early years of the 19th century.

The base has the sharper diamonds, more deeply cut, which gradually replaced the old flat cut style. A band of the fashionable broad flutes runs above the diamonds, and is repeated on the cover, much higher than usual on jars of this kind. The finial has been cut in triangles, and below is a matching band of diamonds. The pedestal base gives the piece a sense of proportion and the everted rim has a scalloped edge.

447

A nineteenth century glass, complete with its leather case (below).

a) Step-cut decanters; Ireland, c. 1815–20; ht. of right-hand decanter, 9¾″ (24.7 cm.).

The third main period of cut glass was a reflection of the Regency style, and its exhuberance was expressed in brilliant step cutting, sharp diamond cutting, strawberry cutting, and rosettes. In most cases, the whole of the surface of the article was cut. This period lasted from about 1810–30.

Step cutting was a popular Irish decoration, and when used over large portions of a piece, such as here, gives the impression of gleaming silver rather than transparent glass.

b) Bowl with central well, and candlestick; Regency period (c. 1820); ht. of bowl 6¹⁄₁₆″ (15.3 cm.).

The design of this bowl is rare; the centre well may have been used for ice to keep the fruit chilled. The diamonds and step-cut base are all sharply cut, with a brilliant effect.

Candlesticks were carefully made in a number of detachable parts, presumably to help the craftsman when he cut the pieces, and also to allow broken parts to be easily replaced. Several different kinds of drops were made; these have faceted buttons above triangular icicles.

---

c) Candlestick of ormolu, cut glass, and Wedgwood bases; Regency period; ht. 9⅜″ (23.8 cm.).

Another Regency design combined gilded bronze, pottery or porcelain and cut glass in the same piece. This was particularly the case with table light fittings. Here, the close diamond cut sconces and pans are made to fit on central ormolu shafts, the whole being mounted on blue and white Wedgwood fittings. The Wedgwood company made many such plaques, rings and medallions for use in glassware and furniture. They were also exported, and can be found on continental pieces as well as English ones (see p. 314b). Other examples used Derby and Worcester porcelain drums.

d) Cordial or liquor drinking glass; mid-19th century; ht. 5¼″ (13.3 cm.).

With the Great Exhibition of 1851, Bohemian coloured cut glass became very popular. Soon English manufacturers were producing Bohemian-style glass which often combined rich colours in one or two layers, cut away to see the transparent glass beneath. In most English examples elaborately-cut glass was colourless, and cutting was fairly simple on the cased glasses made in colour. But occasionally they combined a thin layer of coloured glass with the Regency close diamond cutting, as here; the bowl has been covered with a layer of blue, and cut away to leave panels of strawberry diamonds and stars in clear glass. The teared stem is notched.

a) Jar of white glass, decorated with Chinoiserie painting; c. 1775–1800; ht. 5″ (12.7 cm.).

During the 18th century, coloured glass was more or less restricted to blue, green, amethyst and opaque white. These white pieces resembled porcelain very closely, and were often decorated to make the resemblance even more striking. Opaque white glass was made at many factories, but the white Bristol glass was particularly fine, since it had a high proportion of lead. The addition of oxide of tin caused the glass to become opaque, the same technique that the potters of Delft used to coat their dishes and jars.

b) Green glass jug with opaque white loops, Nailsea type; early 19th century; ht. 6¼″ (13.9 cm.).

During the 19th century, the vogue for coloured glass became widespread. A large number of factories in England made it in varying forms, both in jugs, bowls, and other simple articles, and fanciful novelties, collectively known as friggers.

The Nailsea factory, near Bristol, was established in 1788, and in the first half of the 19th century made an enormous quantity of light-hearted glass objects, in a wide variety of designs and techniques, but perhaps the most typical Nailsea glass of this period is the type illustrated above—a heavy shape with white loopings.

---

c) Glass ship; c. 1830, ht. 10½″ (26.6 cm.).

Friggers were made at many of the Midland factories, and they included canes, walking sticks, rolling pins, pipes, etc.

Spun glass was a particularly appealing medium, and many unbelievably intricate objects were made, such as groups of birds of paradise, houses complete with gardens, and of course, the popular sailing ship.

The earlier models were of slightly better quality glass, and are often on a slightly smaller scale than the later, coarser examples. The details of the rigging, bulwarks, and in this case sailors working aloft, were all carefully observed. Meant for display under a glass dome, many of these delightful pieces have been broken, but occasionally intact examples can be found.

Glass

English
19TH CENTURY

a) *Commemorative paperweight with fine plaque of George IV; Apsley Pellat; 1820; ht. $3\frac{1}{4}$" (8.25 cm.).*

There were many more designs and techniques used in the 19th century than in previous periods; glass was painted, engraved, coloured, cut, applied, moulded, silvered, overlaid, pressed, and blown. The great period of English glass was in the 18th century, but some very fine and beautifully crafted pieces were made much later.

Sulphide glasses were one of the first 19th century innovations. Apsley Pellatt, at the Falcon Works in Southwark, London, experimented with white ceramic paste plaques embedded in clear glass. He called them Crystallo-Ceramics, but they are known today usually as Sulphides, or Cameo incrustations. They were often in the form of paperweights, jugs, small tumblers, scent bottles, etc.

b) *Pressed glass basket; Sowerby, marked with a peacock's head; last half of the 19th century; ht. $3\frac{3}{4}$" (9.52 cm.).*

Pressed glass was largely perfected in the United States, although hand presses had been used elsewhere for some time. Manufacturers in England, particularly in the North, copied the American techniques. At first they merely reproduced the popular but expensive fine Irish and English cut glass. After coloured and carved glass proved so successful at the 1851 Great Exhibition, pressed glass companies turned to moulded, coloured wares in solid colours as well as the richly marbled slag glass. Basket-weave and diamond-cut patterns were the most popular surface texture, although some more elaborate pieces were made.

c) *Plate in cameo carving, John Northwood; c. 1880s; dia. $9\frac{1}{2}$" (24.1 cm.).*

After the decline in popularity of cut glass, and the elaborate and highly decorative coloured glass of the mid-1860s and '70s, there was a return to more delicate work. Two techniques developed —intaglio, inspired by the carved rock-crystal designs of the 16th and 17th centuries, and cameo carving, largely influenced by Northwood's successful attempt to copy the Portland Vase (see p. 417a). The first, intaglio work, was a type of polished engraving, always done on clear glass, and later very much influenced by the Arts and Crafts movement and Art Nouveau. Cameo work was the re-creation of a very ancient technique, which required long hours of meticulous work to carve away the variously coloured layers. At first mainly classical, the designs also became influenced by the Art Nouveau line, and developed to a fine art. (See colour plate, p. 440). Some of the leading craftsmen were Northwood, Thomas Webb, and the Woodall Brothers. With the invention of an acid technique that made quickly-produced, cheap copies, carved glass lost its exclusive market, and production gradually stopped. Around the turn of the century, most English glass makers stopped experimenting with new ideas, and turned back to reproducing old patterns and reliable traditional shapes.

German and Bohemian Glass Introduction

Accepted concepts of 'Bohemian Glass' are traditionally synonymous with superb cutting and engraving techniques applied to coloured glass. This criterion is as valid today as it was several hundred years ago, and the industry's success and universal acclaim is the result of not only consistent artistic development and ingenuity, but also astute business acumen and brilliant commercial organization. Despite political and economic pressures, often precisely because of such setbacks, every period brought new achievements in glass-art techniques. Resourcefulness and skill resulted in artistic glass of almost unequalled individuality and diversity, and the generally very high standard was achieved by an approach to the glass material which was perhaps more academic than spontaneous.

The vast forests and mountain streams of Bohemia and her neighbours (and for political-geographical reasons the areas of Silesia, Slovakia, Moravia, Germany and Austria should be included), were ideally suited to the glass-makers' needs. Unstable economic conditions, over-exploitation of natural resources and the prevalent systems advocating apprenticeship in 'alien' glass-houses resulted in the frequent movement of glass-workers from one area to another, with beneficial interchange of ideas and know-how.

With the cessation of Roman influences, a native industry established itself more firmly. The blue-greenish or amber forest glass—*Waldglas*—fulfilled domestic requirements with small blown beakers applied with thorns or prunts—common to large areas of central Europe and windowglass. A tall, pipe-shaped beaker with applied warts appears to have been a typical product of Gothic Bohemia. Although Venetian influences are evident in the forms and decorative techniques of sixteenth and early seventeenth century drinking vessels, a rustic native style developed fairly quickly in thick, opaque enamelling. This pictorial type of decoration was frequently applied to large *Humpen* (also *Vilkum* = Welcome glasses) and represents a refreshingly original art practised widely. Usually inscribed and often dated, this group of glasses forms an exceptionally fascinating iconographic record of all spheres of society, and remained popular into the eighteenth century.

Cutting and engraving are perhaps the most aristocratic and skilful of all applied decorative glass techniques. The art-loving grandeur of ruling Renaissance and baroque princes provided a challenge for the finest artists and artisans of the day, who brought their native accomplishments to foreign courts. The rock-crystal style which developed in cut glass during the late seventeenth century was inspired by the work of Italian master lapidaries, and the revival of applying lapidary techniques to the medium of glass has always been associated with Caspar Lehman (1570-1622), lapidary to Rudolf II at Prague. Lehman's feat is the more admirable when we consider that the brittle Venetian *cristallo* was entirely unsuitable for such cutting techniques, and that a robust, sparkling glass metal, the Bohemian potash-lime glass, was not developed until about 1670. Lehman and his followers laid the foundation to a great school of glass engravers; the art spread to Nuremberg, Dresden, Frankfurt, Kassel and Potsdam, although some of the finest work in *Hoch und Tiefschnitt* (high relief and intaglio) was produced in Silesian workshops. The support of royalty and nobility who established glass-houses on their vast estates and attracted workers by the granting of special privileges, and the formation of glass decorators' Guilds as early as the seventeenth century, provided healthy encouragement for the industry. Home production of mirror glass and chandeliers ousted Venetian imports and the reputation of Bohemian glass became world-wide. At the end of the eighteenth century, when the native industry was severely threatened by the popularity of English lead crystal, new decorative techniques were created particularly in the field of colour glass. By the early to mid-nineteenth century Bohemian glass had become desired and eagerly copied all over the world. After the Napoleonic wars, the glass industry was mainly centred around the areas of Kreibitz (Chřibska), Steinschonau (Kamenický Senov), Haida (Nový Bor), Neuwelt (Nový Svět), Jablonc and Count Buquoy's factory in South Bohemia.

During the later nineteenth century, the industry experienced an artistic decline; the revival of a high quality glass art is largely due to Louis Lobmeyr, a Viennese glass designer and industrialist. Lobmeyr brought together some of the best Czech and Austrian artists to produce distinctive glass of high standard, and the success of Moser at Nove Dvory and Witwe Lotz (Loetz) at Klostermuhle confirmed these new ideals. The academic tradition of glass design was fully exploited and the industry re-established on an international scale. Today, Bohemia takes a leading role in the field of individual glass art, established as one of the world's most important manufacturers of fine table glass and chandeliers.

Glass

German
and Bohemian

16TH–17TH CENTURY

a) Krautstrunk (cabbage stalk) converted into reliquary; c. 1500; ht. 4⅛″ (10.4 cm.).

A popular drinking vessel in late mediaeval Germany, this converted specimen with black wax top and a red episcopal seal contains relics of a saint. The separately-applied foot has a crenellated rim, and there is a high kick-in base.

This vessel is of blown, pale green glass, the so-called *Waldglas* (Forest Glass). Produced in the forest regions from about the sixth century, its greenish colour varies slightly, depending on impurities present in the raw materials. The greenish tone was later deliberately produced. Smooth or thorny prunts applied to the outer wall facilitate handling of the filled glass (cf. p. 426c).

b) Roemer (Römer), globular bowl, hollow stem with applied prunts and conical threaded foot with kick-in base; Rhenish, 17th century; ht. 11½″ (29 cm.).

This Roemer (its name supposedly derived from the Dutch *roemen*, to praise) represents one of the most important forms of drinking vessels of the 17th and 18th centuries; widely produced throughout Northern Europe, it evolved from the earlier prunted beaker. Colours of pale green, greenish-yellow or greenish-blue were achieved by using metallic oxides. The bowl is globular or ovoid, and the stem and foot base are traditional Roemer features. The foot is produced by winding glass thread round a wooden conical mould. After removing the mould, the shaped threads are fused in the furnace and the foot applied to the stem.

---

c) Bohemian blue glass flask, in pistol form, enamelled, Christof Schurer, early 17th century; ht. 3½″ (34.3 cm.).

Towards the end of the 16th century, Christof Schurer rediscovered the difficult technique of producing blue translucent or transparent glass by adding cobalt. Brilliant enamelling in yellow and orange-red on the blue glass was very effective, and this rare flask, modelled closely on a Saxon wheel-lock ball butt pistol, and enamelled in opaque blue, yellow, green, brown and white, with applied gilded raspberry prunts, is a particularly fine example of this group. The Schurers, from Saxony, began to establish glass-houses from 1540 onwards, around Haida and Gablonz in Bohemia. These developed into the most important centres of the Bohemian glass industry.

d) Enamelled 'Ochsenkopf' Humpen from Fichtelgebirge (Franconia), dated 1668; ht. 7¾″ (19.5 cm.).

Venetian-inspired enamelling developed into a particularly successful and attractive decoration. The large *Humpen* was well suited to the rustic treatment and glowing opaque colours. Only fired enamelling is really durable; most early decoration was cold painted, and therefore survived badly. Popular pictorial subjects were allegories of the Holy Roman Empire (*Reichsadler Humpen*), its Electors (*Kurfursten Humpen*), armorial shields, guild insignia, family events, the Seven Ages of Man, scenes from the Old and New Testament. This *Humpen* represents the second highest mountain in Franconia, the Ochsenkopf.

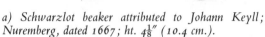

a) Schwarzlot beaker attributed to Johann Keyll; Nuremberg, dated 1667; ht. 4⅛″ (10.4 cm.).

Soon after the 1650s, a monochrome painting appeared, very different from the gay, 'peasant' style enamelling (cf. p. 138c). *Schwarzlot* had been used since mediaeval times for ornamenting stained-glass windows. Black, or sepia if applied thinly, it must be fired for permanent adherence. Its development is attributed to Nuremberg glass and porcelain painter Johann Schaper (1621–70). His favoured vessel, a small cylindrical beaker on three flattened ball feet, was painted with delicate landscapes, humorous and allegorical subjects, or portraits, perhaps the most sophisticated achievement in glass decoration. He often included his monogram 'J.S.', and the date (see p. 138c).

b) Covered goblet with hollow-blown stem; Nuremberg, late 17th century; ht. 17½″ (44.5 cm.).

During the Thirty Years War, Georg Schwanhardt (1601–67), a distinguished pupil of the famous Caspar Lehman, fled from Prague to Nuremberg, establishing there a distinctive school of glass-making. The unmistakable Venetian influence shows in the hollow-blown stem and folded foot, but the interspersed *mereses* (flat discs) of stem and finial are characteristic of the tall, elegant goblets produced in Nuremberg during the later 17th century.

c) Zwischengold and polychrome beaker, Bohemia, c. 1730; ht. 3⅜″ (8.5 cm.).

The most successful revival of ancient *Zwischengoldglas* took place in Bohemia from 1720–c. 1745. Such glasses are usually faceted beakers or goblets; an outer and inner vessel fit precisely into each other (see p. 416d). The outer base was removed to ensure the escape of air when the vessels are pushed into each other, and after decoration, replaced by a tight fitting glass disc. A rare type of *Zwischengoldglas* (c. 1690–1720) is an uncut beaker joined at the top of the rim. The decoration is frequently a marbled pattern covering the entire surface of the inner vessel; the interior may be gilded.

d) Covered goblet with frieze, aventurine and ruby inclusions in foot and finial; Potsdam, c. 1715–35; ht. 11½″ (20.3 cm.).

The Potsdam glass-house was established (1674) by the Elector of Brandenburg with one of the most able glass-makers of all time as chief chemist—Johann Kunckel (1630–1703). Kunckel experimented with many coloured and gold glass techniques. One of his greatest achievements was *Goldrubinglas* (gold-ruby glass) a marvellous deep red colour. Blue, emerald green, and milk glass were also successfully produced. Shapes were solid and rather heavy compared to the more elegant Bohemian glass. Potsdam employed many fine engraver-cutters. The pointed-leaf frieze in *Hochschnitt* (high relief) on this goblet's foot, base of bowl and cover was typical of its period.

Glass

German and Bohemian

18TH CENTURY

a) Covered goblet with rococo engraving; Bohemia, c. 1720; ht. 12¾" (32.4 cm.).

This covered goblet with its thistle-shaped bowl exemplifies all that is best in Bohemian 18th century glass. The fine rococo engraving and the knopped and faceted stem and matching finial complete a perfectly balanced specimen.

b) Covered goblet with Schwarzlot decoration; Silesia, c. 1725-30; ht. 10" (25.4 cm.).

Johann Schaper's delicate techniques were ably adapted by a number of later artists. Ignatz Preissler (c. 1676-1741), who specialized in *Schwarzlot* augmented by red enamel and gilding, worked at Count Kolovrat's North Bohemian factory of Rychnov, and in Breslau. Ignatz and his son evolved a distinctive rococo style with overall scroll-work, Chinoiseries and delightful vignettes of rural life.

The *Schwarzlot* decoration and gilding of this goblet is attributed to Preussler, a porcelain and faience painter who worked in Breslau around 1725-1750. He is frequently identified with the Preisslers; his finest *Schwarzlot* painting is found on imposing, well-cut and faceted goblets.

---

c) Wheel-engraved decanter with double-walled medallions of gold on red; Bohemia, c. 1725-50; ht. 12¼" (31 cm.).

Medallions such as Mildner's and later glass-makers', were based on a technique known since antiquity (p. 417). The most usual combination was goldleaf on a red/lacquered ground; a green or blue background is more rare, and occasionally the gold is picked out in silver, red and/or black.

The round, flattened body of this decanter is radially cut with ovals. The medallions on the front and reverse show respectively a bird and a small running dog. The ruby spiral inside the facet-cut stopper is another decorative feature, dating from the late 17th century.

d) Wine goblet, faceted stem with swelling knop, the bowl with gilt rim and cut in high relief; Silesia, c. 1750; ht. 6¾" (17 cm.).

Bohemian glass pedlars and decorators were not always warmly received on Silesian soil but the superior quality of their crystal glass provided a desirable raw material for Silesian cutter-engravers. At the Treaty of Breslau in 1742, Maria Theresa ceded Upper and Lower Silesia to Frederick II, who prohibited importation of Bohemian glass. Consequently, glass was frequently smuggled across the border; nonetheless, many Silesian craftsmen were forced to work in Bohemia.

The bowl of this finely proportioned glass, with a design of diamonds and roundels, has a constricted, facet-cut base, a characteristic feature in Silesian glass of this period.

a) Medaillonbecher; medallions with gilding on red ground, diamond engraved; signed Johann Joseph Mildner, *dated 1800; ht. 4" (10.2 cm.).*

These glasses were a most accomplished contribution to art. Mildner (1763–1808) lived and worked in Gutenbrunn (Lower Austria). By c. 1787, he perfected his special medallion technique, used mainly on smallish cylindrical milk or colourless crystal glass beakers. The double-walled inserts are decorated in gilt or silver and enamelling on a (usually) red ground. Fine portraits, attributed to Mildner, are often painted on parchment enclosed within roundels. The rim, and in particularly fine specimens, the base, are double-walled and decorated to match. Mildner signed the medallion's reverse, adding the date, the occasion or sitter's name and sometimes a naive little poem.

b) Biedermeier Ranftbecher with Transparentemail painting of the Palace of Schönbrunn, by Anton Kothgasser (1769–1851); Vienna, c. 1810–20; ht. 4½" (11.4 cm.).

After the Napoleonic wars, the glittering Empire style was succeeded by the Biedermeier (1815–1850)—restrained romanticism, comfort without opulence.

This large, typical beaker has a protruding circular base emphasized by cutting. The exquisite painting is in translucent coloured enamel. Kothgasser's range was unlimited: romantic emblems, nature, panoramic views, and portraits. Samuel Mohn (1761–1815) and his son Gottlob, had also used this technique; their portrait silhouettes are particularly attractive. These glasses are frequently signed.

---

c) Beaker, hexagonal, on 6 cone-shaped feet, engraved by Dominic Bieman; c. 1830; ht. 4⅞" (11.1 cm.).

An important aspect of Biedermeier life was a feeling for solid craftsmanship combined with artistic quality, admirably realized by Czech glass-engravers. Their industry centred mainly around Kamenicky Senov and Novy Bor, but many settled in Spas such as Karlsbad and Eger, decorating glass to order for visitors. Bieman (1800–1857) typifies Biedermeier glass engraving at its most accomplished and appealing. He specialized in superb portraits, usually showing the sitter in profile. This unusual wheel-engraved motif is in the form of a classical nude figure.

d) Hyalith scent bottle decorated with flowers and insects in fire-gilding, Buquoy factory, c. 1825; ht. 2½" (5.9 cm.).

Count Buquoy, a wealthy landowner, developed a black opaque glass which he patented in 1820. Perhaps he was influenced by the increasing popularity of Wedgwood's Black Basalt, but the black and gold *Style Egyptienne* was characteristic of Empire fashions. Hyalith is distinguished by excellent gilding of classical motifs, rococo Chinoiseries, flowers, insects. Later specimens, often by imitators, may have overall cut, gilt and enamelled decoration. Fine Hyalith was also made by Friedrich Egermann (1777–1864), a notable glass-maker and inventor of many ingenious colouring and staining techniques. He is best known for his marbled 'Lithyalin' glass (see p. 457).

a) left: Ruby overlay glass egg engraved with a forest scene including a fox in flight; mid-19th century; lgth. 2½" (6.4 cm.).
right: Opaque-white overlay beaker, cut, enamelled and gilded, c. 1840; ht. 4" (10.1 cm.).

The increasingly-popular Spas were responsible for the enormous quantities of souvenir wares, largely represented by coloured and engraved overlay (or cased) glass of variable quality but great charm. (See Glossary—*cased* and *overlay*.) Ruby overlay beakers and goblets predominated, but amber, blue and more rarely green, were applied with equally attractive results. During the 19th century, bone flour, used in the production of opaque-white glass, was replaced by stannic oxide, and the new, more gleaming white glass metal was quickly incorporated in colour overlay techniques.

b) Jug in opaque-white glass with enamelled decoration; Germany, c. 1840; ht. 5½" (14 cm.).

Opaque-white glass manufacture was attempted in a number of European glass-houses before 1700. Böttger's successful production of expensive hard-paste porcelain and the establishment of the Meissen factory in 1710 encouraged less costly imitations in opaque-white, or milk glass (*Milchglas*). This was entirely dominated by porcelain styles and frequently decorated by an artist specializing in porcelain painting. The above later specimen is German, the greyish-white metal not as successful as its Bohemian counterpart; the enamelling, in subdued shades of pink, green and blue, shows traces of gilding.

c) Vase in rococo style with Schwarzlot decoration and gilding; probably Lobmeyr factory, late 19th century; ht. 5" (12.8 cm.).

After the 1850s the Bohemian glass industry experienced a serious decline. Fortunately, a timely revitalization was achieved due to the efforts of Ludwig Lobmeyr of Vienna, who took charge of the family business in 1864. Employing the best technical and artistic assistants from the Bohemian and German glass industry, Lobmeyr revived quality glass-making not only with traditional techniques but also by creating artistic glass in contemporary style. Signatures may be present on important pieces.

Back row, left to right: 'Ranftbecher' amber cased and with partial enamelling in black, with floral engraving overall cut with polished ovals enclosing panoramic views; c. 1860.
'Ranftbecher' in blue opaline glass, cut and fire-gilded, with rococo ornamentation; c. 1830.
Massive goblet with interior gold-ruby stain and engraved hunting scene; c. 1835.

Footed beaker, amber stained and finely engraved with birds and plants; c. 1850.
Foreground left: Lithyalin box in red marbled glass showing cut decoration of superb quality; c. 1830.
Right: Egg-shaped paperweight in 'Annagrün' glass; c. 1840.

American Glass Introduction

The first attempt at glass-making was made when the London Company erected a glass-house in Jamestown, Virginia (1608). Eight glass-workers, probably Germans and Poles, were brought from Europe, but the venture ended unsuccessfully in 1609. In 1621 a second attempt, this time with Italian workmen, also failed. Seldom-substantiated tales of the workmen's extra-curricular activities, including marital conflicts and plotting with the Indians, are more prevalent than documentary evidence of glass production. No objects from these factories are known to exist; archaeological excavations have found small pieces of green bottle glass, suggesting that bottle production was intended. The previous theory that beads (for Indian trading) were actually made is now discounted. Until we have more definite information it seems advisable not to theorize further. Other glass-houses were built later in the century in Salem, Massachusetts and New Amsterdam, but little is known about them.

The first known successful glass-house was Casper Wistar's in Alloywaystown, southern New Jersey (1739). Although numerous 'South Jersey' pieces from the Wistarberg area may have originated in Wistar's factory, there is at present no positive documentation. Other local factories, established later, made similar wares, many showing Germanic influence.

The other most notable eighteenth century glass-makers were Henry William Stiegel and John Frederick Amelung. Stiegel's first Pennsylvania factory, near Shaeffersburg (1763), made bottles and window glass. Another (1765, in Manheim) added some tablewares to the range. His second in Manheim, the American Flint Glass Works (1769) was the first in America to specialize in fine tableware of clear 'flint' and coloured glass. This venture proved too ambitious; at its zenith, one hundred and thirty men were employed and his glass was sold as far away as Boston and New York, but costs far exceeded profits and the factory closed in May, 1774. Unless fully documented, today most pieces in his style are called Stiegel-*type*.

Amelung came from Bremen, Germany, to build the New Bremen Glass Manufactory in Maryland. For the first few years his fine quality glass seemed to ensure success, but by 1787 he was having financial difficulties which worsened after a disastrous fire on May 6, 1790. Despite energetic efforts to avert failure, he was forced to close (1795).

By 1800 about nine glass-factories were working mostly making bottles and window glass; by 1850 there were forty glass-houses in Pittsburgh alone.

Pittsburgh and the surrounding area (now Ohio and West Virginia) became an important glass-making centre, offering easy access to coal fuel and ample waterways for shipping the finished products. In terms of nineteenth century glass-making, this region is still called the Midwest.

The widespread use of blowing glass in full-size moulds to produce flasks, decanters and tablewares was reintroduced by American glass-makers to increase production and reduce costs. One important phase of these productions designed primarily to imitate contemporary cut glass is now generally called 'Blown-Three-Mould'. Many producers of flint glass-wares were operating in the early nineteenth century. All produced essentially similar wares: blown, pattern-moulded, blown-three-mould, and Anglo-Irish-influenced cut and pressed glass. From c. 1850 some factories produced Bohemian-style cased and coloured glass.

Partly because of improved technology, but largely due to the late nineteenth century desire for colourful and extravagant designs, Art Glass developed c. 1875-1900, especially in England, Bohemia and America.

Cut and engraved decorations kept pace with contemporary European designs. 'Brilliant' period cut glass (c. 1885 to c. 1915) was especially popular, giving employment to hundreds of glass cutters who worked in small independent cutting shops as well as in the larger factories.

About the same period the exotic *Art Nouveau* creations of Tiffany Furnaces, the Steuben Glass Works and factories including Quezal Art Glass, Union Glass Works and Honesdale Decorating Company, were being made.

In 1903, Frederick Carder came from England to found the Steuben Glass Works which at first concentrated on coloured glass, but afterwards continued to lead the development of high lead content crystal glass in America.

Some artist-craftsmen, accustomed to using kilns in firing their pottery, became interested in glass-making after World War II, turning away from the tradition of teamwork in a glass-house, to individual work in their studios. Experimentation with glass as an art medium has proved stimulating to many other craftsmen in America and has had a decided influence upon glass-blowing in England, Holland and Scandinavia. Nevertheless, the movement is still in its infancy and the permanent effect is yet to be seen.

Opposite:
Top: Pattern-moulded Stiegel-type tablewares; very few pieces can be specifically attributed to Stiegel except for the dark amethyst flask (far left); U.S.A.
Bottom: South Jersey type glass from southern New Jersey, New England, and New York State; U.S.A.

a) Group of Stiegel-type glass, possibly made in one of Henry William Stiegel's glass-houses; c. 1765–74; ht. of decanter 9⅞" (25 cm.).

Glass

American

LATE 18TH CENTURY

Stiegel, a colourful self-styled baron, established three glass factories in Pennsylvania with the profits from a successful iron works near Shaefferstown, Pennsylvania. He is thought to have made wares, enamelled and engraved with typical German folk motifs, for sale to his Pennsylvania Dutch neighbours, as well as more sophisticated pattern-moulded wares for the seaboard cities. The latter were much influenced by similar glass in England. So successful was he in imitating both English and continental glass that it is difficult today to distinguish between Stiegel's glass and that of his European competitors.

b) South Jersey type candle-holder and sugar bowl; perhaps made at Wistar's glass-house or Glassboro, New Jersey (founded by the Stangers); probably c. 1780 or later; ht. of sugar bowl 6⅛" (15.5 cm.).

Caspar Wistar emigrated to Philadelphia from Germany, became a successful button manufacturer and established his bottle and window factory in 1739. Craftsmen were imported from Rotterdam, Germany and Poland, to produce glass and teach others the trade. Thus the South Jersey tradition began—simple off-hand pieces produced in unrefined glass for local use with green, brown, and aquamarine tints. It shows strong Germanic influence dating back to the *Waldglas* of Northern Europe (see p. 452a). When Caspar Wistar died (1752), his son Richard continued the business until 1780. The Stangers, former employees of Wistar's, established their own factory in 1781.

c) left: Tobias and the Angel, engraved covered tumbler, made at John Frederick Amelung's New Bremen Glassmanufactory, Maryland; inscribed: Happy is he who is blessed with virtuous children Carolina Lucia Amelung, 1788; ht. 11⅞" (30.1 cm.). right: Detail of engraving.

Amelung arrived in America in August 1784 and he purchased land near Frederick, Maryland, built his factory, and then, houses for the workmen and their families. The New Bremen Glassmanufactory began making window glass, green and 'white' (probably clear, almost colourless glass) hollow-wares early in 1785. By 1787 the buildings were complete; accommodation for 135 'living souls', a large community house, which also served as a church, a German school and by 1789 a handsome Amelung mansion. This tumbler was presented by Amelung to his wife. The slightly

smokey, grey-greenish non-lead glass is characteristic of many of Amelung's table-wares.

Production at New Bremen included useful objects, table-wares; and non-lead glass in greyish blue, amethyst, and perhaps other colours. The influence of German traditions is apparent but Anglo-Irish characteristics predominate. A number of commemorative and presentation pieces with engraved designs and inscriptions have helped greatly in identifying Amelung pieces, the finest engraved glasses produced in America in the 18th century. However, many pattern-moulded and off-hand pieces, with and without engraved decorations, are so similar to those produced in other American and European factories at the time and later, that 'Amelung-type' and 'attributed to Amelung' are used for non-documented pieces.

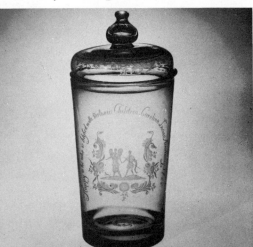

a) *Amelung glasses; made at New Bremen Glassmanufactory, Maryland, c. 1785-95; ht. of goblet 8¾" (22 cm.).*

A flask of greenish coloured glass and a salt are each patterned with a chequered diamond design. The large engraved goblet is one of a pair Amelung presented to his friend and merchant, George Trisler, dated 1793. The bottle or flask is engraved with a foliate wreath, a bottle, a plough, and a Masonic symbol on the obverse and 'F. Stanger 1791' and a simple wreath on the reverse. The goblet and flask are characteristic of about 30 presentation pieces made by Amelung. The pattern-moulded flask and salt are from his everyday production.

b) *Group of table-wares in the South Jersey style; late 18th-early 19th century; ht. of sugar bowl 4⅝" (14.2 cm.).*

These individual, often imperfect, pieces ornamented with threading, 'lily pad' (see p. 466d) rigarée, and other applied decorations, appealed to contemporary users, and later collectors. Simple beauty and applied ornamentation set a regional style in the 18th century and later for 19th century glass-makers in New York and New England as well.

The bowl and mug with applied threads date from the late 18th century; the sugar bowl, almost colourless lead glass, is attributed to a Milford, New Jersey glass-house of the early 19th century, and was made in a form characteristic of the earlier period. The swan-like finial has been broken.

Detail of Amelung glass (see a).

c) *left: Sugar-bowl and cover with swan finial, pale greenish-yellow glass, free-blown, applied handles; Amelung New Bremen Glassmanufactory, Maryland, or Albert Gallatin's factory; ht. 7¼" (18.4 cm.).*
right: Candlestick, green bottle glass, attributed to Gallatin's New Geneva or Greensboro factory; both late 18th-early 19th century; ht. 8" (20.3 cm.).

After Amelung's failure, his workmen dispersed. Some may have gone to the Philadelphia Glass Works or the New Geneva Glass Works in Pennsylvania, although this is doubted by some authorities. The New Geneva Glass Works was established in 1798 by a group of men headed by Albert Gallatin, Secretary of the U.S. Treasury from 1803-13. It moved to Greensburgh (or Greensboro), Pennsylvania in 1804 and continued, with a reorganization in 1830, until it burned down in 1847. The principal output was window glass and bottles but some hollow wares were made.

Glass

American

LATE 18TH–EARLY 19TH CENTURY

Swan finial typical of South Jersey style glass sugar bowls (see b).

461

Glass

American

EARLY 19TH CENTURY

a) Tablewares, plain and pattern moulded of olive amber, light green, aquamarine and green coloured glass; produced in Midwestern glass-houses, between c. 1800-1835; ht. of vase 6″ (15.2 cm.).

Pattern moulding had been practised since antiquity. The glass is blown into a dip, or open mould, removed, and then expanded into the desired shape. The pattern can be felt on the inside as well as the outside. Diamond, or honeycomb, patterns are common, as is ribbing of various kinds (16 rib, 24 rib, etc.). The diamond-daisy pattern is rare, and is attributed to Stiegel's glasshouses. Variations exist, although they have not been traced to any one factory.

The compote, pattern-moulded vase with applied handles and sugar bowl with double domed cover are characteristic of Zanesville, Ohio, glass-houses during the 1815-1835 era.

b) Flint glass-wares, undoubtedly made at the South Boston Flint Glass Works operated by Thomas Cains, or in his Phoenix Glass Works also located in South Boston; c. 1815-30; ht. of sugar bowl 11″ (27.9 cm.).

The sugar-bowl containing George III one shilling pieces, dated 1816 in the hollow knopped cover and stem, is almost identical to one owned by a great-great grandson of Thomas Cains, an Englishman who came from Bristol to America in 1811. He leased and operated the South Boston Flint Glass Works from 1812-20. This was the first New England production of flint glass; he then established his own Phoenix Glass Works which operated until 1870. Numerous forms of chain decorated glass (see p. 424d)—an English influence —were produced by this firm.

c) Cut glass in the Anglo-Irish style produced in Midwestern flint glass-houses; 1815-35; ht. of celery glass 8″ (20.3 cm.).

One of the largest flint glass manufactories in Pittsburgh was Bakewell & Co. founded by two Englishmen, Benjamin Bakewell and Edward Ensell in 1807. Ensell soon left the company and in 1809 the firm became B. Bakewell & Co. From then until 1882, when the factory closed, Bakewell and his descendants, with various partners, produced a wide range of all types of glass from bottles and flasks to fine tablewares. Between about 1815 and 1835 they were noted for their fine cut and engraved wares, which according to numerous

accounts in travellers' diaries were frequently 'copied from the latest London patterns' by workmen from both England and France.

The cut and engraved tumbler on the left bears a sulphide portrait of Washington in its base was produced, along with others bearing likenesses of Dewitt Clinton and Lafayette, by Bakewell, Page & Bakewell about 1824, in honour of Lafayette's visit to Pittsburgh that year. The decanter was also produced by this company and the pattern is very similar to that on two decanters which were awarded first prize at the second annual exhibition of the Franklin Institute in Philadelphia in 1825.

a) *Blown-three-mould decanter and two bottle-decanters; Mount Vernon Glass Works, New York, and the Keene (Marlborough St.) Glass Works in New Hampshire, c. 1815-30; ht. of centre bottle 10" (25.4 cm.).*

Blown-three-mould is a process which was developed largely to imitate the popular but expensive Anglo-Irish cut glass wares. A full-sized mould was used and the glass was blown into it and fully expanded. The mould itself might be made in 2, 3 or 4 parts, but the great majority were in 3, hence the name. The quality of blown-three-mould glass depended on the metal used and the skill of the craftsman in finishing off the piece. Though most blown-three-mould tablewares were made of colourless flint glass, moulds were used to produce bottles and decanters of bottle glass in varying hues of olive green and olive amber.

b) *Blown-three-mould glass, produced in Midwestern glass-houses; c. 1815-1840; ht. of decanter with stopper 9⅞" (25 cm.).*

The vase and two unmarked decanters are attributed to the glassworks in Kent, Ohio, 1823-1830. The decanter in the centre is marked 'Murdock & Cassel, Zanesville', the Ohio city where it was made c. 1832-c. 1840. Unlike these four pieces, which are of varying tonalities of green bottle glass, the covered sugar bowl was blown of light, brilliant amethyst glass in an unknown Midwestern factory between 1815 and 1830.

Although almost mass-produced by using full-size moulds to form a basic shape, all blown-three-mould glass required hand-finished tooling or manipulation, to complete each article.

---

c) *Pre-blown-three-mould dish, covered sugar bowl and salts; probably South Boston Flint Glass Works or the New England Glass Works, between 1815-1825; lgth. of bowl 8⅜" (21.5 cm.).*

The New England Glass Company was established in Cambridge near Boston (1818). It produced all kinds of glass; bottles and probably figured flasks, blown-three-mould glass, lacy pressed glass, pressed pattern glass, cut and engraved glass, and later, fine art glasses. It was very successful from its inception until shortly after the Civil War, when it had growing competition from Midwestern factories, where coal and gas for fuel were more readily available at lower costs. In 1888 a strike forced its owners to move to Toledo, Ohio, becoming the Libbey Glass Works. Pre-blown-three-mould glass is characterized by its thickness and the ground rims, which were required to finish the piece where it was blown over the top of the mould. The left-hand salt bears a fan decoration which meets the description in a New England Glass Company advertisement (1819) for 'fan-end salts'. The other salt is amethyst coloured. The diamond diapering, flutes, ribbing and fans copied from the Anglo-Irish cut glass are typical of this pre-blown-three-mould glass.

Glass

American

EARLY–MID 19TH CENTURY

a) Blown-three-mould tablewares and lamp attributed to various Eastern glass-houses; dia. of bowl $9\frac{7}{8}''$ (25 cm.).

The small cobalt-blue pitcher is attributed to the Boston and Sandwich Glass Works, on the basis of numerous fragments of this shell and ribbed pattern found there. Though best known for its lacy pressed glass, now known generically as 'Sandwich' glass, this company produced almost identical wares to those made by the New England Glass Company from the time of its inception until it closed in 1888, including vast quantities of many patterns of blown-three-mould glass. The large pitcher, tumbler and lamp were probably made in Cambridge near Boston c. 1818-40. The sugar bowl and shallow bowl cannot be attributed to a specific factory.

b) Flint glass whale oil lamps; made in New England and other eastern glass-houses, c. 1815-40; ht. of tallest lamp $13\frac{1}{2}''$ (34.2 cm.).

The tall cut glass lamp with elaborately pressed base may be attributed to the Union Flint Glass Works in Kensington, near Philadelphia, about 1835-1840. The small 'wine glass' lamp in the centre and the knopped stem saucer base lamp on the right, are among the earliest American glass lighting devices, made in New England glass-houses about 1815-30. The lamp on the left, with an elaborate pressed glass base, has a 'ground' font with painted decoration. The Union Flint Glass Works in Kensington was established by workers who left the New England Glass Company.

---

c) Flint glass lighting devices and table-wares, combining pressed glass bases and free-blown upper sections; c. 1827-c. 1845; total ht. of sugar-bowl $7\frac{1}{2}''$ (19 cm.).

The whale oil lamp in the foreground with an inverted cup plate as a base probably dates from between 1827 and 1830, and was undoubtedly made in a New England glass-house. The other pieces date from about 1830-45. The compote was probably made at the Boston & Sandwich Glass Works, the sugar-bowl at the right in a Midwestern, possibly Pittsburgh glass-house.

d) Pillar moulded glass, Midwestern; produced from c. 1830-70; ht. of bottle $9''$ (22.9 cm.).

Pillar moulded glass objects were made by Roman glass-makers from c. 50 B.C. and objects with such decoration are found in many periods and glass-making areas since that time. In the Pittsburgh, Pennsylvania area, heavy table-wares of this type, particularly decanters and pitchers, were called 'Riverboat' or 'Steamboat' glass because these heavy, wide-based objects were ideal for use on riverboats, where stability was a prime consideration.

The left-hand amethyst pitcher, above, has white vertical lines on the ribs and an applied handle. The other pitcher is light blue with swirled ribs and an applied handle.

a) *Early pre-lacy pressed glass tablewares; probably produced in Eastern glasshouses, c. 1825–1830; dia. of bowl at right 9″ (22.8 cm.).*

Like the earlier moulded glasswares, the first pressed glass also closely imitated the much more expensive Anglo-Irish cut glass.

Small hand presses, much like pliers with large jaws bearing a design in them, were not new; they had been used for the pressing of decanter stoppers and the feet of salts, goblets and compotes in Europe as early as 1785.

The first known patent for machine pressing was granted to John P. Bakewell at the Pittsburgh Glass Manufactory in 1825. That same year, Demming Jarves established the Boston & Sandwich Glass Company, and it was his company which is generally credited with developing pressed-glass production.

b) *Lacy pressed glass shell-form dish, and cake plate; both are attributed to the Boston & Sandwich Glass Works; probably c. 1830–40; wdth. of cake plate 11¾″ (29.8 cm.).*

This style of pressed glass continued in vogue until the 1840s. Machine pressing of glass was taken up by most factories producing flint glasswares and many varied patterns were produced in both eastern and Midwestern glass-houses. The rapid development of pressing technology may be seen in the open-work handles and border of the shell form and cake plates.

A characteristic of pressed glass is the smooth interior of hollow-ware pieces; since the glass is not blown against the mould the inside surface does not follow the curves and indentations of the outer surface (see diagram).

Glass

American
EARLY–MID 19TH CENTURY

---

c) *Lacy pressed glass table-wares, attributed to eastern factories; all c. 1830–50; dia. of large bowl 10″ (25.4 cm.).*

The covered sugar-bowl may have been made at the Providence Flint Glass Works between 1831–33. The cup plate in the foreground and the rose-thistle and sunflower plate at the right are attributed to the Boston & Sandwich Glass Works.

Pressed glass cup plates were in vogue in America from c. 1827 to the early 1860s. These small plates varied in diameter from about 2⅝″ (6.7 cm.) to about 3¾″ (9.5 cm.). Their purpose was to hold the cup after the hot tea was poured into the saucer to cool before drinking. They probably were first made at the Boston & Sandwich Glass Company in 1826 and soon after in many other eastern and Midwestern glass-houses.

Most cup plates were clear colourless glass but they are found also in amethyst, opaque white, blue, yellow-green, bluish-green, amber and a few other rare colours. Patterns range from lacy, geometric, floral and heart-shaped motifs to eagles, ships, and portraits of George Washington and Henry Clay.

Glass

American

a) *Group of pressed glass-wares, produced in Mid-western glass-houses, 1830–50; wdth. of octagonal plate 6⅛″ (15.5 cm.).*

The opaque white boat salt in the foreground is marked on the stern 'J.P. Robinson & Son Pittsburgh'. Midwestern lacy pressed glass is characterized in general by coarser stippling in the background and bolder decorative motifs around the rims of the plates, e.g. the 'bull's-eye' and alternating 'bull's-eye' and triangular motifs on the octagonal plate to the right. As both the boat salt and the plate to the right suggest, the recently invented steamboat was a popular decorative motif during this era.

b) *Lacy pressed glass toys; Boston & Sandwich Glass Works, c. 1830–50; lgth. of covered bowl 4″ (10 cm.).*

The cost of the elaborate moulds for lacy pressed glass was naturally high, and about 1840, partly as a result of the depression following the failure of the banks in 1837, and partly as a result of developing styles and technology, much simpler patterns were developed. This simpler type of glass, referred to as pressed pattern glass, resulted in almost complete services of pressed glass, and more than 1000 different patterns were developed in the 19th century.

c) *Cut and engraved table-wares and lamp showing the Anglo-Irish influences on eastern American glass-makers; ht. of tumbler 4⅜″ (11.1 cm.).*

The compote, or punch-bowl, and oval dish were acquired from the grandson of Phineas Dummer, one of the founders of the New Jersey Glass Works. They were made about 1840. The lamp and mug, acquired from a descendant of Richard Synar, who worked at the Union Flint Glass Works, Kensington (Philadelphia) were both made there in about 1826–40. These four pieces are among the few cut glass pieces which can be attributed to eastern glass-houses. The tumbler, depicting a group of buildings above the inscription 'WIDOWS AND ORPHANS ASYLUM in Philadelphia', may also have been made in the latter factory, about 1830.

d) *South Jersey type sugar-bowl and pitchers with applied lily-pad and threaded decoration; New York, c. 1835–50; ht. of tallest pitcher 8¹³⁄₁₆″ (22.3 cm.).*

Most 'South Jersey' decoration can be traced to English or continental sources; threading had been common on Rhenish glasses since mediaeval times (see p. 452b); the chain or guilloche is found on Venetian and English 17th-century glass (see pp. 419b and 424b). However, the lily-pad seems uniquely American. A 'blob' of glass is applied to the base of the parison and tooled and pulled up over the basic shape; the effect was as if the piece were cupped in a lily-pad, hence the name. These pitchers represent the highest development of the South Jersey style, which originated in bottle and window glass-houses about a century earlier (see p. 460b).

a) *Group of off-hand table-wares and candle-holder of varying shades of olive amber and olive green bottle glass; made in various Connecticut and New Hampshire bottle glass-houses; ht. of pitcher 7⅝" (19.3 cm.).*

The pitcher on the right with applied threading around the neck and superimposed 'lily-pad' decoration around the bowl is said to have been made by Matthew Johnson in a Stoddard, New Hampshire glass-house about 1850. These plainer, less decorated off-hand pieces are characteristic of the South Jersey style, as expressed in New England bottle and window glass-houses.

b) *South Jersey type glass with lily-pads or other applied decoration; 1850s–70s; overall ht. of sugar-bowl 10⅝" (26.9 cm.).*

The candle-holder and pitcher on a solid stem were probably made in the New London Glass Works, New London, Connecticut, which operated between 1856–70. The candle-holder contains a coin dated 1862, and has a scalloped foot. The other three pieces were made in New York State window glass-houses. The sugar-bowl has a chicken finial on a set-in cover; both cover and bowl have lily-pad decoration over a hollow stem.

Glass

American

MID–19TH CENTURY

c) *Loop-decorated glass vase; possibly South Jersey and the Pittsburgh area; 1830–70; ht. 9⅜" (23.8 cm.).*

The vase at the left is one of a pair blown by John Harrow, at Bakewell & Co's glass-house in Pittsburgh, Pennsylvania, about 1855–65. The candle-holder is also attributed to the Pittsburgh area, while the covered bowl and mug are products of South Jersey glass-houses. The origin of the powder horn is unknown, but it is probably from South Jersey. Prototypes of this loop-decorated glass are of English origin dating from the late 18th and early 19th century.

d) *Flint glass table-wares with broad, cut decoration characteristic of the mid-19th century; ht. of ewer 12⅛" (30.8 cm.).*

The compote and ewer are from Christian Dorflinger's Greenpoint Glass Works in Brooklyn and were both made about 1855. The decanter was made at the Union Flint Glass Works, Kensington.

Paralleling the trend of the plainer pattern glass, cut glass of the mid-19th century also became much bolder and broader in nature, and continued so until after the Centennial Exposition in Philadelphia in 1876. Much of it was cased, or overlaid, in layers (i.e. blue over white, on colourless glass) then cut in Bohemian style patterns. It was sometimes engraved or painted as well. The Bohemian influence was especially strong between 1850–1875.

b) Goblet and wine glass, clear colourless glass, Frosted Leaf pattern; light green toothpick holder, and light blue small dish—Tree of Life pattern; probably 1860s; Portland Glass Company, Portland, Maine; dia. of dish 3⅛″ (7.9 cm.).

a) Whale oil and fluid-burning lamps of pressed glass in various colours; probably New England Glass Co. or the Boston & Sandwich Glass Co., ç. 1840-60; ht. of right lamp 12¼″ (31.3 cm.).

Pressed pattern glass, made from about 1840–1900 (see p. 465a), is often called 'Victorian' or 'early American' pattern glass. It forms one of the largest and most varied chapters in 19th century American glass. Like the earlier blown-three-mould glass, the first pressed pattern glass attempted to copy the brilliantly-cut Anglo-Irish lead glass so much in vogue throughout the 19th century.

After the Civil War pressed glass novelties became very popular. Toothpick and match holders became miniature baskets, dog kennels, corsets, etc., and the ubiquitous hats and slippers were made in all patterns and colours.

Most pressed pattern glass pieces were made in clear, colourless or 'flint' glass, but colours used included blues, greens, and amethysts, milk-white, opalescent and marble glasses. Popular patterns were often copied, with minor variations or a different name to avoid legal complications. The Tree of Life pattern was made by several factories. Some authorities attribute this version to the Pittsburgh area.

---

c) Covered dish, Sawtooth pattern, possibly Boston & Sandwich Glass Company, c. 1865-85; covered dish, opaque white, so-called Atterbury Duck, Atterbury & Co., Pittsburgh, Pensylvania, patented 1887; candlestick, Caryatid, opalescent white glass, New England Glass Co., design patented 1870; candlestick, Dolphin, opaque white glass, Mount Washington Glass Co., or New Bedford Glass Works, c. 1869.

Opaque white and opalescent white glass, often

called milk glass, has long been a collector's favourite. Objects of this glass were usually pressed and covered a wide range of useful and decorative forms, including plates and bowls with pierced rims, as well as novelty items ranging from swan covered dishes and the Atterbury Duck (the head is purple and the eyes made separately and set in after annealing) to the battleship *Maine* and a bust of Admiral Dewey.

a) Butter dish and cover, comet (Horn of Plenty) pattern with Washington head knob (rare); about 1865. Goblet, comet pattern, late 1840s or early 1850s; ht. of goblet 6⅞″ (17.4 cm.).

In these wares, aside from the almost endless varieties of surface patterns, covered items seemed to particularly intrigue the customer. Covered butter dishes from the late 19th century appear in seemingly unrelated shapes and may be a stove, helmet, tomato or clock. The more unconventional shapes often had surprising knobs ranging from horse shoes and urns to George Washington's head. Other covered dishes included the 'farmyard assortment' of ducks, roosters, hens, swans and eagles, by Challinor, Taylor and Company.

---

b) Decanter, Honeycomb pattern; wine glass, Palace pattern, both New England Glass Company; water pitcher, Bellflower pattern, McKee Brothers, Pittsburgh, Pennsylvania, 1860-70.

The Midwestern glass-producing area, as including western Pennsylvania, West Virginia, Ohio and Indiana, vied with the eastern factories in the production of these wares. One reference book lists over 1000 patterns of goblets and most of these were items from table services sometimes containing as many as 25 different items. C. 1865-1900, water sets, also advertised as being for lemonade or cider, were popular items. These consisted of a pitcher and goblets or tumblers, sometimes with a waste bowl, all standing on a tray, which varied from a simple circle to irregular forms styled to fit the specific objects in the set.

Glass

American

a) Flint glass table-wares with engraved decoration; ht. of celery vase 9⅛" (23.1 cm.).

The celery vase second from the right is a characteristic Anglo-Irish form of the period about 1800–30, and may have been produced in a glasshouse in Philadelphia, Baltimore, or Pittsburgh. The decoration of the other three pieces is typical of the engraving produced in Midwestern glasshouses about 1815–35. The celery vase second from the left is also a rare example of Midwestern blown-three-mould glass. The base is gadrooned, with a swirling wave pattern above, and ribbing around the everted rim. All three stemmed pieces have the flattened central knop, which was so characteristic of early and mid-19th century stemmed glasses.

b) Tumblers in the Bohemian style, possibly Bohemian but quite likely made in one of several American glass-houses, c. 1850–1865; ht. of tallest tumbler 5⅛" (13 cm.).

These all bear views of scenes or buildings in America, *left to right:* Niagara Falls, Trenton Falls, N.Y., Union Hall, Saratoga Springs, N.Y., and the Female Seminary, Canandiagna, N.Y. From about 1850 onwards, Bohemian influence upon American cut glass craftsmen was quite strong, and probably more of this 'Americo-Bohemian' glass was produced in America than has been hitherto realized.

c) Vase, free blown, made and engraved in an unknown American factory, c. 1862; ht. 9⅞" (25.1 cm.).

This vase of non-lead colourless glass is engraved with a vignette depicting the engagement of the *Monitor* and the *Merrimack,* which took place in Hampton Roads, Virginia on March 9, 1862. The vine and grape motif surrounding the vignette and on the foot, together with the form of the vessel, especially the foot, are indications of Bohemian influence.

a) *left: Compote with cut and engraved decoration, Christian Dorflinger, Greenpoint Glass Works, Brooklyn, New York, c. 1861; dia. of bowl 9⅜″ (23.8 cm.); right: goblets, engraved design with inscription:* Mr. & Mrs. J. Hoare November 29, 1869; *goblet, engraved floral pattern with CD monogram of Clothilde Dorflinger; Christian Dorflinger & Sons, c. 1867.*

At the same time as pressed glass was being made for almost every kind of household necessity, fine free-blown and engraved or cut glass continued to be made in various glass-houses.

Christian Dorflinger was born in Alsace, France (1828) and learned his trade in the glass-houses of Lorraine. He emigrated with his family to America in 1846 and by 1852, he had established his first factory in Brooklyn N.Y. He became well known for the quality of his metal which was considered the finest crystal made in the United States. The firm continued after his death (1915) until it finally closed in 1921.

Left: This was part of a set of glass-ware ordered by Mary Todd Lincoln for the White House from A. P. Zimandy of Washington D.C., a dealer in glass-ware. His invoice of July 23, 1861 described the glass as 'one sett of glass ware rich cut and Engraved with a U.S. Coat of Arms'.

Detail of glass a (left).

---

b) *Silvered or mercury glass salt and lamp; salt marked N.E.G.Co.; date 1855–70.*

Thomas Leighton, an Englishman who came to America in 1826 and became superintendent of the New England Glass Company, was granted a patent for silvered glass door knobs in 1855. The two pieces on the right were said to have been obtained at the Boston & Sandwich Glass Works.

c) *Goblets, New England, Pineapple pattern, 1860s; Morning Glory pattern, 1860s–70s; footed salt, Petal and Loop pattern, 1850s; all Boston & Sandwich Glass Co. (salt possibly Pittsburgh area); pitcher, Ashburton pattern, probably New England Glass Co.*

Pressed pattern table-wares were supplemented with a generous variety of 'Victorian novelties' in the last third of the century. What many items may have lacked in aesthetic value is perhaps compensated for by their exploitation of the mould-maker's technical skill. The quality of these pieces depended on the designer and mould-maker more than on the actual workman 'at the fire'.

Ashburton was one of the earliest patterns; it was first made about 1840 and continued to be made for decades in New England and also at the Bakewell, Pears & Co., Pittsburgh.

Glass
American
LATE 19TH CENTURY

a) Cake dish with frosted cover, Westward Ho pattern, c. 1876; water pitcher, Classic pattern, Gillinder, Philadelphia, c. 1893; covered compote, with frosted stem, foot and knob, Three-Face pattern, Duncan Miller Glass Co., Washington, Pennsylvania, 1880s.

Ruth Webb Lee, one of the pioneer authorities on pressed pattern glass, lists the ten most popular patterns as follows: Bellflower, Horn of Plenty, Rose in Snow, Wildflower, Thousand Eye, Three Face, Lion, Westward Ho (all in clear, colourless glass), and in milk-white glass: Blackberry, Daisy and Button; this list represented collectors' favourites in the 1940s.

b) Platter, clear, colourless glass, Liberty Bell pattern, produced by Gillinder & Co.; Philadelphia, 1876; lgth 13½" (34.3 cm.).

The vogue for pressed pattern glass continued throughout the 19th century and into the 20th, the quality of both the glass and the designs deteriorating in general in these late years. Identification of these patterns is a never-ending task, and although origins of hundreds of these designs are known, many pieces appear which have not been identified to date. Reproductions of popular patterns have further complicated the verification of these objects. Books on these patterns (see bibliography) have helped materially, but all warn against reproductions, some of which are excellent copies of the earlier pieces.

---

c) Decorated art glass-wares, produced by the Mount Washington Glass Company; c. 1885-95; left to right: Crown Milano and Napoli cracker jars; ht. 8" (20.3 cm.).

Between about 1876 and 1895, the Mount Washington Glass Company, 'Headquarters in America for Art Glass', produced some of the finest and most varied types of Art Glass made in America. Among its products were Burmese glass, Peach Blow, Crown Milano, Albertine, and Royal Flemish glass, as well as Rose Amber. The latter was a transparent bipartite, or shaded, glass gradually going from amber to a deep fuchsia red, usually at the top. This company's Rose Amber,

or Rose Amberina, was the same glass as Amberina, patented by Joseph Locke of the New England Glass Company in July 1883. It proved to be a successful product for both firms.

Although the term 'Art Glass' has been more broadly used in recent years, the colourful, useful and ornamental glass c. 1880-1900s was designated as Art Glass by its manufacturers. Various companies from Indiana to New England used widely diversified techniques and colours. Often either ardently loved or passionately hated, they are admittedly an intriguing and often technically interesting phase of American glass-making.

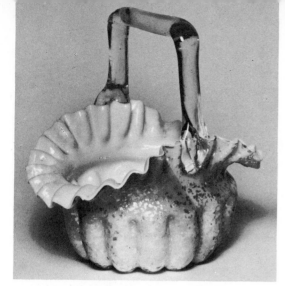

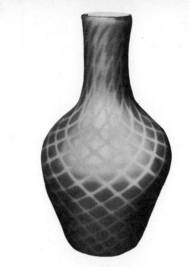

a) Basket, spangled glass, opaque white cased with shaded pink and clear colourless glass; unidentified, 1880s; ht. 7" (17.8 cm.).

'Spangled' is usually applied to late 19th century glass-ware ornamented by picking up assorted flakes of mica or bistite from the marver, on a parison of opaque white or coloured glass, and then 'locking in' these pieces with a layer of clear or tinted glass. Hobbs, Brockunier & Company was one of the principal producers in the 1880s.

'Splashed' or 'spatter' glass has no metallic flakes, but includes variegated flecks or blobs of glass picked up from the marver, sometimes encased, sometimes not. Both spangled and splashed glass were made in England and also on the Continent.

b) Vase, mother-of-pearl, satin glass, light blue over white glass; Phoenix Glass Company, Pennsylvania, c. 1888; ht. 14" (35.6 cm.).

The surface of 'satin' glass has been treated with acid, dulling the natural finish and producing a smooth satin or velvet texture. English and American glass-makers commercialized the finish around the 1880s. Art glass so treated was normally described by manufacturers as 'Pearl Satin Ware', 'Velvet' finish ware or 'Watered Silk'.

There were many variations, including mother-of-pearl. This was perfected c. 1885 by Joseph Webb, an Englishman associated with the Phoenix Glass Company. Locked-in air bubbles between two glass layers, usually in a diamond or other geometric or floral pattern, showed through the outer casing, greatly enhancing the satin effect.

---

c) Sugar and creamer, Pigeon Blood glass, plated silver mounts; National Glass Company, Bellaire, Ohio, c. 1890.

Silver-mounted pieces were very popular with Art Glass manufacturers. Indeed, the Mount Washington Glass Company had many of its pieces mounted by the Pairpoint Manufacturing Co., a neighbouring silver-plating firm. It is impossible to illustrate or describe all of the colours and varieties of Art Glass which have become collectors' items. Until about the mid-20th century there was little interest in many of these productions, and reliable information is still limited or unavailable on many types. Objects which have been neglected for decades are sought after as soon as a book or article appears which helps to identify them.

d) Dish, clear colourless glass, pressed decoration of United States coins dated 1892; Central Glass Co., Wheeling, West Virginia; lgth. 10" (25.4 cm.).

This rare coin glass pattern was produced in about 25 table-ware items for only a few months before production was stopped by the U.S. Government. Later 19th and 20th century coin patterns are not replicas of U.S. coins. A pattern produced by Fostoria Glass Company in the 1960s has the date 1887 on the 'coin'.

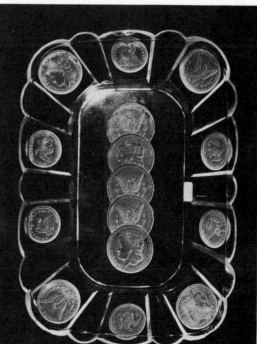

Pressed glass Amberina bowl and Rubina Verde bowl made at the Hobbs Brockunier Glass Works, Wheeling, West Virginia, about 1885-90; plated Amberina vase with pattern moulded decoration made at the New England Glass Company, 1886-88; and cranberry-coloured wine glass made in unknown American glass-house about 1850-60; ht. of wine glass 4¾″ (12.0 cm.).

Amberina has been one of the most popular collectors' items since it was first patented by Joseph Locke of the New England Glass Company in 1883. The shaded amber to red colour is produced by reheating the piece which causes the cooled, usually the top, portion to develop the red colouring. This process, called 'striking' is also employed in other shaded and opalescent glasses such as Burmese, Peach Blow, and Spanish Lace. The Mount Washington Glass Company produced a similar glass which they called 'Rose Amber'. Glass-ware of this type is still being made, often reproducing the original shapes. When carefully made they are practically impossible to identify positively as to age and origin.

The colours in the translucent shaded glasses shown in colour on p. 475, are produced by 'striking' as in the shaded transparent glasses like Amberina. Wheeling developed the original Peach Blow after the sale of a Chinese porcelain peach

bloom vase from the Morgan collection for $18,000 in 1886 attracted international attention. Wheeling Peach Blow was made in acid, matt, and the natural finish shown above. The New England Glass Company named its version of Peach Blow 'Wild Rose' to avoid legal complications. Wild Rose also was made in a matt finish. Mount Washington Peach Blow was bluish-grey shaded to rose-pink. This is one of the rarest colours in American Art Glass, made for only about 2 years, 1886-88.

Burmese glass, also shown on p. 475, delicately shading from lemon-yellow to a light plushy-pink, was another of Mount Washington's most successful Art Glasses, patented by Mr Shirley. He sent a present of this glass to Queen Victoria, who liked it so much she ordered a tea-service for twelve. Burmese glass was also made in England by Thomas Webb & Sons under Licence from the Mount Washington Glass Company and called 'Queen's Burmese'. Modern 'Burmese' pieces have been made in the United States and in Venice. These pieces vary in form from the originals, and in many instances are thicker and heavier; the character of the finish of the Italian Burmese is quite different from the 19th century productions.

Opposite:
Top: 'Lacy' pressed glass sander, curtain tie back, and various tablewares. Similar fragments have been found at the site of the Boston and Sandwich Glass Works, Sandwich, Massachusetts; U.S.A., c. 1830-50.
Bottom: Bi-partite, or shaded, art glasswares; U.S.A., all 1885-95.

a) Bowl, tortoiseshell glass, possibly Boston & Sandwich Glass Co., c. 1870–88; bowl, pink cased over opaque white glass with etched design, Mount Washington Glass Co., 1880s; bottle, Amberina glass, 1883–88 and vase, Pomona glass with cornflower decoration on first ground, both New England Glass Co., 1885–88.

Pomona glass was patented in April 1885 by Joseph Locke, then with the New England Glass Company. It is clear colourless glass with a border and other designs in bright pale amber stain often with various types of flowers, butterflies, berries, etc., usually in blue, but occasionally in red. These slightly iridescent patterns are on frosted backgrounds of two types. The first (often called 'first ground') has fine curlicue lines throughout the background and was made only from April 1885 to June 1886. The 'second ground' pieces, made from about July 1886 until 1888, have an evenly frosted ground with a slightly stippled effect, without the curlicue lines.

b) Butter dish and cover, opalescent glass, unknown origin; vase, clear yellow glass with opalescent Spanish lace pattern, possibly Beaumont Glass Company c. 1895–1905 or English manufacture; vase, ruby with opalescent hobnail pattern; patented June 1, 1886 by Hobbs, Brockunier & Company.

Opalescent glasses produced in both Europe and America in the 19th century and later, were produced by adding fluorite to the glass batch. The opalescent white colour is developed by cooling the raised portion of the moulded object immediately after removal from the mould before expanding the design. The reheating of this cooled portion produces the milky opalescent design in the transparent colour after the object is expanded and finished.

c) Bowl of opalescent art glass, sometimes called 'Foval', with green trim and silver deposit decoration; H. C. Fry Glass Co.; Rochester, Pa., c. 1900–1915; ht. 6″ (15.2 cm.).

Silver deposit, a decoration usually produced by electroplating the actual metal on the surface of the glass was another technique used in Europe and the United States in the late 19th and 20th centuries. In 1893 John H. Scharling of Newark, New Jersey, patented a method of laminating silver and gold on the glass surface and etching a design through these layers. The raised metallic pattern was then often embellished with engraved designs; this enhancing of the metallic surface by engraving was also done on other silver deposit wares.

Opposite:
Top: Glass designed by Louis Comfort Tiffany, produced at Tiffany Furnace (1902–20) and Louis C. Tiffany Furnaces Inc. (1920–24) at Corona, Long Island, New York, U.S.A.
Bottom: Glass designed by Frederick Carder, made at Steuben Glass Works (1903–18) and Steuben Division, Corning Glass Works (1918–33); Corning, New York, U.S.A.

Glass

American

LATE 19TH–EARLY 20TH CENTURY

a) Cut glass of the Brilliant period; left to right: Fry Glass Works; the Blackmer Cut Glass Co.; T. B. Clark Cut Glass Co.; ht. of pitcher 9″ (22.9 cm.).

After the Exposition in Philadelphia, and especially between 1885–c. 1915, Brilliant cut glass was in vogue. During this era, elaborate patterns were cut all over the surface of thick, brilliant lead glass blanks.

Some of this glass was made by glass manufacturing firms, but much was decorated by independent cutting and engraving companies who obtained their blanks from glass-houses in America and abroad. By 1900 more than 20 independent cutting shops existed in the small town of Corning, New York, alone.

b) Late 19th and early 20th century cut and engraved glass; left: decanter, ht. 7⅝″ (19.4 cm.).

These pieces illustrate the further influence of the Bohemian style on American glass-making. The decanter at the left is one of a pair cut and engraved by J. Hoare & Company, cut glass manufacturers in Corning, New York, on blanks made by Corning Glass Works, about 1890. The claret decanter was cut and engraved by H. P. Sinclaire & Company, Corning, New York, about 1910, and the pitcher engraved with floral decoration was blown at Christian Dorflinger's glass works about 1870–1880, and engraved there by Jacob Haar.

---

c) Vase, marked: Locke Art, and liqueur glass, produced by Joseph Locke, Toledo, Ohio, late 19th or early 20th century; goblet, clear colourless glass, unknown American factory, probably early 20th century; finger bowl plate, clear colourless glass, attributed to Dorflinger Glass Company, White Mills, Pennsylvania, early 20th century; dia. 6″ (15.2 cm.).

Glass pieces called 'needle-etched glass' were decorated with an acid-etched pattern, produced by mechanically controlled tools which traced the design through a wax coating. The object was then dipped in acid, or subjected to acid fumes, which etched the design on the glass surface where it was not covered by the wax. In England this is known as acid engraving and was very popular around the turn of the century, (see p. 444d).

d) Spill holder (or match holder), greenish yellow and white, Challinor Taylor & Co., Tarentum, Pennsylvania, late 19th century; bowl, pink shaded glass, inverted Fern and Feather pattern, probably Indiana Tumbler and Goblet Co., Greentown, Indiana, early 20th century; dia. 9½″ (24.1 cm.).

Pressed marble glass, also called slag glass, was patented in June 1886 by Challinor, Taylor & Co. Purple marble glass, a combination of shaded purple and white, was the most popular, but it was also produced in greens, blues, yellows and other colours. Slag glass was also made in England and in other American factories about the same time. Blown marbleized glass was made at Tiffany Furnaces, Quezal Art Glass and Decorating Works and elsewhere in the late 19th and 20th centuries.

This bowl is very rare and is not typical marble glass. The colours are fused into each other with a shaded effect rather than having sharp lines of demarcation.

a) *'Favrile' covered jar in light green with applied feather motif; Louis Comfort Tiffany, 1896; ht. 19½″ (49.5 cm.), dia. 11¼″ (28.6 cm.).*

Louis Comfort Tiffany (1848–1933), scion of the famous Tiffany family of New York jewellers, was the foremost proponent of the *Art Nouveau* style in America in the late 19th and early 20th century. His first company, Tiffany Glass Co. was founded in 1885 in New York. Tiffany was assisted by Arthur J. Nash, who developed many of the glass formulae, and they produced a wide variety of the finest glass made in America or Europe during the late 19th and early 20th century. His *Art Nouveau* forms have never been excelled and the glowing colours of his 'Favrile' and other colourful glasses are unsurpassed.

Louis Comfort Tiffany began producing objects in this manner about 1892. The style of his glass was based upon naturalistic motifs frequently expressed in the form of flowers, or of vessels decorated by highly stylized foliate designs. Tiffany was also influenced by the iridescence on ancient glasses, and successfully combined this iridescence with natural motifs in his creations. Not only his glass, but also some of his metal work and ceramics were termed by him 'Favrile' a word he coined based upon the Latin.

b) *left: Quezal vase, gold iridescent with trailed pale green lines and leaves, c. 1916–18, signed on base: Quezal; ht. 8¼″ (20.9 cm.), dia. 4¼″ (10.7 cm.); right: vase, clear colourless glass cased with green, acid-etched Art Nouveau design with gold accents on frosted ground: marked Honesdale in gold, Honesdale Decorating Company, c. 1917; ht. 14¾″ (37.4 cm.).*

The Quezal Art Glass and Decorating Company was established by Martin Bach, Sr., a former employee of Tiffany's who termed his company and his glass-ware 'Quezal', after a tropical bird noted for the iridescent greens and crimsons of its plumage. The quezal is also the national emblem of Guatemala.

Quezal glass-ware is quite rare; there were many shapes and colours, all similar to Louis Tiffany's Favrile glass.

The Honesdale Glass Decorating Company of Honesdale, Pennsylvania and the Imperial Glass Company of Bellaire, Ohio, also produced *Art Nouveau* glass.

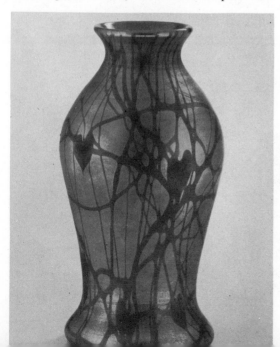

Glass

American

a) left: string holder, clear glass with blue and white filigree, or latticinio decoration; probably Nicholas Lutz, Boston and Sandwich Glass Co., c. 1869–88; centre: ewer, black, rib-handled sugar-bowl, light green; with aventurine effects in powdered gold in Venetian style; Union Glass Company, Somerville, Massachusetts, c. 1905; ht. of ewer 8¾″ (22.2 cm.), right: vase, hand-blown; Dorflinger & Sons, Inc., c. 1916; ht. 15″ (38.1 cm.).

Venetian glass forms and techniques inspired American glass-makers from time to time in the 19th and 20th centuries. Probably some of the best-known and least positively identified are the filigree or *latticinio* types made by Nicholas Lutz

at the Boston & Sandwich Glass Company in the 1880s. These pieces are so similar to those made in Murano, Italy, that it is often difficult to make a positive attribution either way without documentation. The aventurine effect was usually produced by adding iron or brass filings or mica flecks to the molten glass or picking them up on the parison from the marver. Gold flecks are also sometimes used.

The Venetian influence continued into the 20th century. Frederick Carder (see p. 481*a*) also produced many Venetian-style pieces in the first 20 years of the Steuben Glass Works.

---

b) Ribbed vase and pitcher, Grape pattern, purplish iridescent glass, Northwood Glass, Wheeling, West Virginia; mark: N in a circle. Low bowl, orange iridescent glass, Peacock pattern probably by Millersburg Glass Company; early 20th century; ht. of pitcher 8½″ (21.6 cm.).

Carnival Glass, sometimes called 'Taffeta Glass' was pressed moulded iridescent glass, mass-produced in at least eight or ten base colours including shades of blue, red, orange, yellow, green and purple. Purplish-blue and orange iridescent finishes were probably the most common. The

bulk of this glass was made during the first quarter of the 20th century by a number of companies in Western Pennsylvania, West Virginia and Ohio. The peak was from about 1910 to 1920 when carload lots of this glass were shipped to chain stores, mail order houses, such as Montgomery Ward, and other outlets. The name 'Carnival' probably derived from the use of these pieces as prizes in games of chance and other carnival concessions. Marked Northwood pieces such as the vase and the 'Northwood Grape' pitcher, illustrated, are highly prized by collectors of this type of glass.

b) Cased glass stem-ware with cut and engraved designs, late 1920s, early 1930s; left to right: champagne glass and goblet, gold ruby over crystal glass, cut and engraved; goblets, black over crystal with cut designs; champagne glass, green over crystal, cut and engraved; all designed by Frederick Carder, Steuben Division, Corning Glass Works.

a) Gazelle in pressed glass, designed by Frederick Carder at Steuben Glass Works; c. 1920; ht. 6½″ (16.5 cm.).

Frederick Carder was born in the Stourbridge glass-making district of England on September 18, 1863, and had been a designer and glass technician at Stevens & Williams (now Brierley Crystal) in Brierley Hill, Staffordshire, England from about 1880 until he left for America in 1903. The Steuben Glass Works, named for Steuben County in New York State where Corning is located, flourished under Carder's direction until 1918 when a shortage of materials due to World War I necessitated the sale of the factory to the Corning Glass Works. From then on it was called the Steuben Division of Corning Glass Works.

Frederick Carder continued as Art Director and/or manager of Steuben with the exception of a brief period following the end of the First World War, until 1932 when he was transferred from Steuben and made Art Director of Corning Glass Works.

The glass produced by the Steuben factory during Carder's regime included over one hundred colours, over 7,000 forms and dozens of production techniques ranging from variations of Ancient Egyptian and Roman processes to Carder's original Aurene, Tyrian and Intarsia pieces. During this period Carder designed the wares, including the cut, engraved and acid-etched decorations, formulated the glass batches, and supervised the production and sales.

c) right: Vase, 'Intarsia' glass, light amethyst pattern in clear colourless glass, designed by Frederick Carder, engraved facsimile signature: Fred'k Carder, c. 1930; ht. 7⅛″ (18.0 cm.); left: Puma, designed and cast by the lost wax method by Frederick Carder; signed on the base: F. Carder 1941; lgth. 7⅞″ (20.0 cm.).

After his transfer to the Corning Glass Works (1932-59) Carder experimented with lost wax casting of glass and carried this production to a greater degree of perfection than had heretofore been achieved. These *cire perdue* or lost wax pieces were entirely done by him in his office studio and only a limited number were produced each year. Carder retired in 1959 and died in Corning, December 10, 1963, nearly three months after his 100th birthday.

In the complicated intarsia technique, the pattern is a thin layer of coloured glass between two thin layers of clear colourless glass. Carder considered this one of his greatest achievements.

a) Wine glasses, goblets, and champagne glass made by the Libbey Glass Company, Toledo, Ohio, between 1932–39; ht. of goblet bearing United States coat of arms $8\frac{5}{8}$" (21.9 cm.).

In the late 1930s, as recovery from the depression progressed, some firms such as Steuben Glass, the Pairpoint Corporation and Libbey Glass Works, Toledo, Ohio, produced a number of fine quality lead glass-wares. The latter company produced a limited series of American glass designs. Following the war, however, they were not resumed. The Pairpoint Corporation, which went out of business in 1937, was reorganized in 1939 and operated under several names, among them the Gunderson Glass Works, the Gunderson-Pairpoint Glass Works. These firms produced a wide variety of colourless free-blown, cut and engraved glass and also revived the production of Peach Blow and Burmese, using the formulae developed in the 1880s.

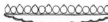

Detail of the Merry-Go-Round Bowl (see b).

b) The Merry-Go-Round bowl, designed by Sidney Waugh; ht. 10" (25.4 cm.).

This engraved crystal bowl was presented to H.R.H. The Princess Elizabeth on the occasion of her marriage, November 1947, by President and Mrs Harry S. Truman. The covered bowl, with plumed finial and ornamental base is elaborately engraved to depict a carousel in motion. Mr Waugh wrote of this theme: 'The country fair is the oldest and most unaffected of our festivals and the merry-go-round is the soul and symbol of that institution'.

Sidney Waugh, American sculptor and Steuben's chief associate designer, was largely responsible for the establishment of a distinctive style of engraved crystal as an art form in the United States. He designed other such celebrated Steuben pieces as the 'Zodiac Bowl' in the Victoria and Albert Museum, London, and the 'Gazelle Bowl' in the Metropolitan Museum of Art, New York.

a) left: Labyrinth, clear colourless glass, designed and made by Hans Frabel, Atlanta, Georgia, c. 1972, wdth. approx. 6″ (15.2 cm.).
Right: Vases, colourless glass with applied decorations in blue, amethyst and green and with roughened surface finish, designed and made by John Burton, Chatsworth, California, c. 1959; left: vase, ht. 8½″ (21.6 cm.).

Glass objects formed by reheating and melting glass rods, tubing or other glass pieces in a gas-oxygen flame have long intrigued the public. The skilled artist-craftsmen who fabricate these pieces are designated as being 'lamp workers' to differenti-ate them from the 'gaffers' or off-hand glass blowers who form their pieces directly from molten glass gathered from the glass furnace.

Lamp workers fabricate complicated pieces of scientific apparatus as well as decorative objects. Nearly everyone is familiar with the intricate ships, animals, birds, flowers and other whimsical novelties which lamp workers have produced for decades in Europe and America (see p. 490).

Since about the mid-20th century several talented lamp workers have revived this form of glass production and have achieved a degree of artistic excellence rivalling some of the best lamp work of the past.

---

b) left: Hot-glass sculpture, designed and made by Dominick Labino; signed Labino 4–1970; Grand Rapids, Ohio; ht. 7⅜″ (18.7 cm.).
centre: 'Unknown Glass Species' Group 3; designed and made by Andre Billeci, Alfred University, Alfred, New York; ht. 58″ (147 cm.).
right: 'Eye Form' designed and made by Harvey K. Littleton, Verona, Wisconsin.

The studio glass movement has become increasingly important since it embodies to most glass-workers a radical change from the traditional art of glass-making which required the cooperation of designs, a team of glass-makers, a huge furnace, etc.

Among the pioneers of this movement are Dominick Labino, Harvey K. Littleton of Wis-consin University and Andre Billeci.

Labino's work, above, is a free-blown form of pale blue glass, enclosing veilings of amethyst and blue shadings. The centre motif is of light blue with orange veilings, and two elongated bubbles. Labino is the Honorary Curator of Toledo's Museum of Art which has taken the lead in encouraging young artists to explore the world of glass.

Billeci's sculpture, of light greenish glass with applied coloured glass 'ribbons', is part of a glass 'environment' designed and made by the artist.

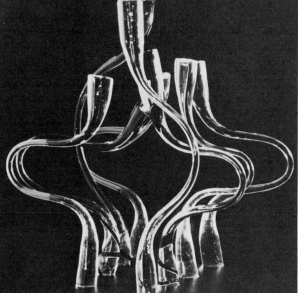

French Glass
Introduction

Glass-making in France begins with the establishment of workshops in Roman Gaul; the type of glass produced is consistent with specimens found over large areas of the Roman conquest. The Musée des Beaux Arts at Lyons displays the tombstone of one of the earliest glaziers to have worked on French soil—Julius Alexander, citizen of Carthage, 'opifex artis vitriae', who worked during the late second century A.D. Eastern influences introduced by Alexandrian and Syrian gaffers did not vanish entirely with successive Frankish and Merovingian styles. The early forest glass, *verre de fougère* of amber-greenish colour, remained popular for some centuries, with practical domestic forms persisting into mediaeval times. From the Rhône valley the industry spread to Lyons, north to Normandy and the Lorraine, along the regions of the Loire to Poitou, Amiens and Strasbourg. There is a controversial story that Normandy glass-makers emigrated to Altare, near Genoa in Italy, during the eleventh century, and that their descendants were amongst the first to leave the home industry and establish glass-making *à la façon de Venise* in sixteenth century France.

An interesting chapter is provided by the so-called *Gentilshommes verriers*. As early as 1399 certain privileges were granted to glass-makers of Poitou by Charles VI, and French craftsmen began to consider themselves as self-styled nobility. An attempt at clarification was a decree of the Cour des Aides, Paris, 1597: '. . . from the mere fact of working and trading in glass-ware the glass-makers could not claim to have acquired nobility or right of exemption; nor on the other hand, could the inhabitants of the locality assert that a nobleman was doing anything derogatory to his title by being a glass-maker'. Impoverished nobles leased or sold their forests to glass-making families, frequently establishing and working their own glass-houses. Dispossessed Huguenots eagerly turned to glass-making as a trade which would not disgrace their social status. From the diaries of the celebrated Huguenot glass-painter turned potter, Bernard Palissy, we learn of the industry's failure despite Royal interest and patronage. The most successful French achievements were stained and window glass; the broadsheet technique (cylinder or *manchon*) popular with the Lorraine glaziers, and the crown technique practised in Normandy. The production and huge export of window glass contributed greatly to the decline in hollow glass manufacture, and for well over two hundred years, until the late eighteenth century, table glass was imported from Venice, the Netherlands and Bohemia, precluding the development of an individual French glass style. One exception was finely enamelled glass of the early sixteenth century, including rare marriage cups with a characteristically wide conical bowl which may terminate in a flattened base; this represents a distinctive French design. The moulded glass created in the seventeenth century glass-houses of Bernard Perrot at Orléans was more practical. A mirror industry, hoping to oust the Venetian imports, was initiated in 1665 by Colbert, chief minister to Louis XIV. It proved disastrously costly, but a merger established a factory at the Château de Saint-Gobain under Louis Lucas de Nehou (1695) and today the Saint-Gobain industrial glass-works is among the largest in the world.

In retrospect, the French contribution is expressed rather by evaluation and exploitation of decorative glass-making than by development of form in any particular direction. The greatest period began in the late eighteenth century. Baccarat, established in 1764 under Royal patronage, developed superb crystal glass and highly accomplished cutting techniques augmented by gilding. St. Louis, founded in 1767, aimed at less ostentation, more refinement and clever colour effects. Clichy, established in 1848, joined the Sèvres porcelain factory in 1889. Choisy-Le-Roi produced interesting coloured glass during the 1820s under the direction of the able glass technician and designer, Georges Bontemps. Shortly before the 1850s the classic Empire style receded; a revival of ancient millefiori resulted in the creation of the fashionable paperweight.

By this time, however, a most exciting phase had begun, due to the marvellous achievements of individual research and studio work. French *Art Nouveau* represented by the Ecole de Nancy, which Emile Gallé established as an inspiring force, reached a supreme level of technical and aesthetic creation, including the revival of many ancient processes in entirely original form. The phenomenon of the glass artist was not coincidental; almost every one of the great innovators in this field had turned to glass-making from his primary chosen profession of painter, sculptor, designer or goldsmith.

a) The Four Seasons—verre filé de Nevers, greenish translucent glass overlaid in opaque white; late 17th century; ht. 5″ (12.7 cm.).

These locally-produced objects were made not only around Nevers but in many glass-making areas, including Marseilles and Paris. In 1605 the 'little dogs of glass and other animals made at Nevers' were favourite toys of little Louis XIII. They were still being made in the 19th century.

These lamp-worked, delightful miniatures include an astonishing variety of figurines, animals, classical, profane and religious characters. Complex tableaux and scenes were assembled and mounted. Glass-thread figurines were built on fine copper wire, but animal shapes are hollow-blown. The quality varies, but this set is a finely-modelled example of baroque art.

b) left: Typical Perrot beaker of greyish, crizzled glass, moulded with mythological figures and symbols; c. 1680; ht. 3½″ (9 cm.); right: Scent flacon, shell-shaped amber glass with opaque white glass threads and pewter screw cap; c. 1675; ht. 2½″ (6.3 cm.).

Bernard Perrot (d. 1709) came from a glass-making family originally of Altare. He worked first with his uncle, director of the Nevers glass-works. Perrot established his own factory at Orleans (1622) developing many new techniques which broke with the Venetian tradition, especially mould-blown glass with recurring symbols of fleurs-de-lis, hearts, crowns, etc. Perrot's methods for casting sheet glass for mirrors was invented in 1662. This drew the attention of the Royal Monopolists—privileges were lost or not renewed—he was forbidden to use his method, and the credit went to Louis Lucas de Nehou. Perrot apparently made fine milk glass and Venetian-inspired marbled and coloured glasses.

c) Goblet (chalice) and paten, soda glass, 18th century; goblet ht. 8⅝″ (21.9 cm.), paten dia. 6½″ (16.5 cm.).

This goblet with baluster stem and domed terraced foot differs very little in design from the Venetian inspired development of English drinking glasses of the period. Very light in weight, it is of soda glass with many impurities. The paten has a shallow well and wide, reeded rim. A similar chalice and paten at Sens Cathedral suggests the possibility of one of the Nivernais glass-houses as makers of these vessels.

Glass

French

Detail of opaline beaker, showing Napoleon in typical stance (see a).

a) left: White opaline beaker with gilt and polychrome decoration, c. 1820; ht. 3½″ (8.9 cm.).

At the close of the 18th century, French glass-makers began experimenting with coloured glass culminating in opaline, an opaque glass of varying degrees of translucency. The opalescence was created by calcium phosphate, later replaced by tin or arsenic for a non-reflective surface. Forms were based on the classical Empire period and complemented by the characteristic white or turquoise-blue colour. Gilding or ormulu mounts enhanced the most typical pieces. This beaker shows a defeated Napoleon within a floral garland.

b) centre: 'Vase Medicis', green glass body and cover, foot and finial white; perhaps Choisy-Le-Roi, c. 1825-30; ht. 7″ (17.8 cm.).

This Murano-influenced covered vase, although similar to factory catalogue designs of the 1830s, is probably a slightly earlier experimental piece. The metal is semi-opaque, of dulled surface texture; the green body and cover are decorated by deliberately arranged striations in a darker shade of green.

c) right: Milk jug in 'pâte de riz', with trace of gilding on body and handle; c. 1830, ht. 4″ (10.1 cm.).

From 1825-1850, and particularly after 1840, many factories, including St. Louis and Plaine-de-Walsch, made a cheaper opaline glass containing less lead. To imitate Bohemian 'alabaster' a new metal of coarse, greasy texture and grain-like consistency was developed. Due to its colour, which resembled rice water, it was called 'pâte de riz'. In spite of its greyish-white tint, this jug has a certain appeal, retaining much that is best in classic Empire design.

d) 'Gorge de Pigeon' opaline bottle with Gothic revival gilding; c. 1835-40; ht. 9½″ (24.2 cm.).

Paradoxically, the research between 1800-1848 involved in reproducing Bohemian and Venetian decorative techniques, resulted in the development of artistic glass of great ingenuity and originality. Opaline glass remained fashionable and from the mid-1830s it was also made in pale green, and a pretty rose-pink colour, frequently augmented by enamelling and gilding. Enamel surface decoration must fuse at a temperature low enough to ensure successful refiring without damaging the glass. This had been satisfactorily solved in Bohemia. In 1836 the Plaine-de-Walsch factory, under its enterprising director, Mr de Fontenay, successfully applied enamelled decoration to semi-crystal; in 1837 Joseph-François Robert, a porcelain painter at Sèvres, perfected his technique of surface-enamelling lead crystal. The even more complicated problem of gilded decoration had been successfully overcome by the mid-19th century, and this flask presents a fine example of gilding 'à la cathédrale'. The 'gorge de pigeon' opaline is the soft, pinky-grey shade of a pigeon's throat.

a) left: Millefiori wine glass; c. 1845; ht. 5⅜″ (13.7 cm.); centre: Shrine in pressed glass with sulphide incrustation on yellow-stained ground; after 1850; ht. 7¾″ (19.5 cm.); both by Baccarat.

By 1845, the revival of decorative techniques resulted not only in the colourful extravagance of paperweights made by many leading glass-houses, but also in a variety of objects decorated in millefiori and lace glass, which had been the special interest of Georges Bontemps at Choisy-Le-Roi (see p. 490).

Gros-Caillou in 1796, Mont-Cénis from 1818, La Villette from about 1827, Baccarat and St. Louis still as late as 1858, and Clichy, were all actively engaged in *cristallo-céramie* techniques (see p. 484). One of the earliest and best-known artists using this process was the sculptor Desprez.

b) right: Mosque lamp, blue and white enamel and gilded decoration; c. 1875; ht. 5¼″ (13.4 cm.).

Richly enamelled gilded glasses were produced in Syria from the 12th–14th centuries. At the 1867 Paris World Exhibition, Joseph Brocard exhibited a revival of Islamic enamelling techniques, applying his exquisite decoration to vessels of Syrian-inspired form. His experiments succeeded admirably, as illustrated above. The lotus blossoms, flowers and foliage design has been found on numerous ancient mosque lamps.

Similarly, exotic enamelling was used with far greater originality by André Fernand Thesmar (1843–1912) who particularly favoured *cloisonné* and *plique à jour*, the former usually applied to an opaque glass base. Here the Japanese influence in Art Nouveau design is most pronounced.

A sulphide medallion (cf. shrine in a).

---

c) left: Cameo glass vase, dark-green eucalyptus leaves on a pale green ground; c. 1890; ht. 6½″ (16.5 cm.); right: vase in Verre Double, c. 1880; ht. 4¾″ (12.1 cm.); both Emile Gallé, Nancy.

These vases represent several aspects of Emile Gallé's work, the great glass-maker and artist whose Ecole de Nancy was the centre of the 'naturalist' movement. The first is a fine example of cameo cutting, incorporating sandblasting, probably inspired by Gallé's study of oriental snuff-bottles. The leaves and buds are cut away from the pale background in a graceful rhythmic design which flows quite naturally. The smaller vase is far more subtle; orientalism, an essential facet of Art Nouveau, is clearly predominant, but the black rivulets imprisoned between two walls of amber, Vaseline-textured glass achieve an artistic result of great imagination and individuality.

d) Enamelled liqueur set by Emile Gallé; c. 1890; ht. 9¾″ (24.8 cm.) incl. stopper.

This decanter is a most impressive example of Gallé's supreme decorative enamelling. The delicate characteristic scrollwork of floral garlands is in perfect contrast to the grand 'lion rampant', a favoured heraldic motif which he also used on pottery. A bluish, mottled metallic film covers the stopper, handle and feet of both decanter and glasses. This interesting feature confirms that Gallé was familiar with a technique which was fully exploited by Tiffany (p. 521c) in America and the Austrian factory of Lotz (Loetz) Witwe. Gallé produced many liqueur sets; most decanters are of strangely awkward forms. The enamelling is always extremely fine.

Glass

French

a) left: Bowl in pâte de verre, luna moth design, by Gabriel Argy-Rousseau; c. 1925; ht. 3″ (7.6 cm.), dia. 4½″ (11.4 cm.).

The revival of *pâte de verre* was a most exciting development. This ancient process was practised by early Egyptian glass-makers (see p. 415). The semi-opaque material with a coarse-grained texture, was often lightly polished on the outer surface. *Pâte de verre* was ideally suited to Art Nouveau and Art Deco concepts and many outstanding artists achieved remarkable results. This bowl is typical of Argy-Rousseau's work; the frieze is marvellously subtle in tones of pale green, brown and pink on whitish-grey ground. Most *pâte de verre* pieces are signed.

b) right: Scent bottle, cased in amethyst, carved, acid-etched, gilded and enamelled; Daum, Nancy; c. 1900; ht. 2¾″ (7.0 cm.).

The Daum Brothers at Nancy produced work closest to Gallé's, but on a less elevated plane. Although Daum cameo glass, with its mottled base layer, falls short of the ideal, they made some very exceptional pieces such as this scent bottle, often collaborating with individual artists. Almeric Walter, for example, specialized in *pâte de verre*.

c) Moulded lamp of frosted glass, floral reliefs, traced in blue enamel; René Lalique, c. 1930; ht. 11½″ (29.1 cm.).

Lalique's characteristic subtly-frosted glass was one of several distinctive developments, another was clear crystal glass of milky opalescence. Sculptural forms frequently show stylized decorations. The female body was a favourite motif; inspired by Loïe Fuller and Isadora Duncan, he used repeatedly dancing figures in flowing, filmy garments. Lalique pioneered the modern architectural use of glass, designing and making doors, windows (St. Helier Church, Jersey), public fountains, etc. After his death the factory dropped the initial 'R', leaving only the signature *Lalique*.

d) 'Mask' vase, clear glass with gold-coloured bubbles, hot worked and acid etched; Maurice Marinot; Troyes, c. 1931; ht. 7¾″ (19.5 cm.).

The glass creations of Maurice Marinot (1882–1960) are the results of individual furnace work combined with expressionist artistic concepts. Marinot designed and produced every piece himself, and though his early work with enamelled decoration reminds us of his first-chosen vocation of painter, the abstract forms and deeply incised patterns of later glass specimens create a striking impact. Inlaid colours and air bubbles produce effects of compelling vitality and his work must be considered as the apex of modern French art glass.

Paperweights
Introduction

To the early nineteenth century archaeologists who opened the Roman tombs, to the collector-students of ancient glass like Heinrich von Minutoli, and to those whose vast and rambling collections were eventually acquired by the great museums of Europe, we owe the revival of interest in millefiori that was to find its highest expression in glass paperweights. (Millefiori—from the Italian *mille*, thousand, *fiori*, flowers.)

By the mid-1830s, experiments recreating ancient techniques were already under way in Eastern Europe. Silesian and Bohemian factories made a variety of objects—small vases, toilet bottles, drinking glasses, cutlery handles, earrings, buttons and other ornaments. Ten years later Venice had produced, among other things, an elaborate writer's companion in which the trivet-like tray, receptacles, and paper-knife handles were all of millefiori glass. All that was missing was a paperweight.

The invention of the glass paperweight seems the result of spontaneous generation in Bohemia-Silesia, Venice and France, with the first dated examples coming from France and Venice in 1845. These were European novelties produced in quantity at low cost, selling in stationers as accessories to the new interest in letter writing.

During the Classic period of high-quality production, lasting approximately from 1845-1855, France took the lead. English glass factories joined in about 1848, and the craze reached the United States after 1851 and continued through the 1870s.

A revival including three-dimensional forms began in France about 1878, reaching America at the turn of the century and lasting until the First World War. A revival of world-wide proportions began after World War II, continuing today wherever fine glass-making is still an art.

The most desirable collector's paperweights have always come from the 'Classic' French period. The three famous factories of Baccarat, Saint Louis, and Clichy competing fiercely with one another, made a greater number in a greater variety, and made them better than anyone else.

While other paperweights are generally of a lower order of inspiration and execution, superb examples from Bohemia, Belgium, England and the United States do exist, and are available, simply because they have been overlooked in favour of French workmanship. A growing appreciation of the best non-French paperweights is inevitable.

Bohemian weights, for example, include some attractive crowns; others are cased (overlaid), and some are topped by cased and cut vases. English paperweights include a well-constructed, exquisitely-coloured Bacchus concentric, or a Whitefriars chequer with coloured latticinio separations. Some of the best collector's opportunities lie in American

paperweights; the floral bouquets, spaced concentrics, and blown fruits from the New England Glass Co., the single flowers from Sandwich, the lovely Gillinder millefiori and the Mt. Washington and Millville flowers.

Happily for the collector, paperweights are not restricted to their country of origin—Venetian, Bohemian, French, Belgian, English and American paperweights turn up everywhere on both sides of the Atlantic.

Historical periods of paperweight making:
Classic Period in Continental Europe and England (1845-55)
Classic Period in The United States (1851-80)
French revival with three-dimensional forms (c. 1878 and after)
American revival with three-dimensional forms (c. 1900-14)
World-wide revival of Classic Period, three-dimensional and other forms (from c. 1950 and continuing)

Major glass factories making paperweights:

France

Baccàrat (Compagnie des Cristalleries de Baccarat, Baccarat, Alsace).
Saint Louis (Compagnie des Cristalleries de Saint Louis, Saint Louis, Lorraine).
Clichy (M. Maes, Clichy-la-Garenne, Paris).

England

Whitefriars (James Powell & Sons, London).
Bacchus (George Bacchus & Sons, Birmingham).

United States

New England (New England Glass Co., East Cambridge, Mass.).
Sandwich (Boston & Sandwich Glass Co., Sandwich, Mass.).
Gillinder (Gillinder & Bennet, later Gillinder & Sons, Philadelphia).
Millville (Whitall Tatum & Co., Millville, New Jersey).
Mount Washington (Mt. Washington Glass Works, New Bedford, Mass.).

Paperweights
The Craft

For the basic processes and tools of glass manufacture, see p. 414.

Millefiori Canes

Solid cylindrical glass sticks are made by using an iron pontil, either by dipping the pontil into pots of variously-coloured molten glass and shaping the resulting gathers freehand; or by plunging the pontil, with its gather of coloured glass, into a heated metal mould, shaping the glass into a long, thin rod. Then a layer of another colour is added, and the rod plunged again into another mould with a differently-shaped outline, and so on—much like the layers in a piece of English rock candy. While the hot cane is still ductile, a second pontil rod is attached to the other end. Two glass-workers, rods extended horizontally, back away from one another, stretching the cane like taffy (toffee) until it is many feet long, and thinner than a pencil. After cooling evenly on a track, the stretched cane is cut into hundreds of thin slices, each a cross-section of the same pattern.

Filigree Canes

Filigree canes are begun in a heated mould lined vertically with alternating rods of opaque-white, and clear glass. The pontil with a clear glass gather is worked into the mould and withdrawn, the upright rods adhering to the gather. Like millefiori, the filigree cane is then stretched, but also twisted to give the familiar spiral with a lacy effect. Sometimes a coloured rod is included in the arrangement in the mould; these are called colour twists. Filigree canes are usually cut in longer pieces and arranged more or less horizontally as grounds for the millefiori canes, which are usually arranged upright in designs.

A group or 'chair' of glass-workers, headed by a gaffer was undoubtedly required to make a complex paperweight. The tiny cane slices were painstakingly arranged upside down in a circular bed plate, or form. The gaffer lowered a pontil rod tipped with a gather of clear, viscous glass, and picked up the design, which adhered to the gather. A number of coatings of clear glass were added, and each shaped until the desired form and size were achieved. Then the weight was firepolished at the furnace to make the surface smooth and brilliant, 'cracked' (knocked) off the pontil rod, and placed in a lehr to cool slowly and evenly over many hours, to prevent fracture. When cold the glass-cutter ground out the rough pontil mark and perhaps cut an external design of flat facets or concave punties around the weight.

Lampwork

The lampwork process was used for designs of fruits, flowers, butterflies, birds and animals. A blow lamp or torch softened and coloured glass rods until they could be shaped, tooled, trailed onto and fused to one another to form the desired object, which could then be picked up in the same manner as the millefiori canes. Special care had to be taken to eliminate unwanted air bubbles, and still cover the fragile lampworked assembly without breaking it.

Crimping

The crimping process involved use of a metal tool (crimp) in the form of a rose, tulip, waterlily, umbrella shape, etc. After an original gather of clear glass had been shaped to receive the crimped design, a wad of coloured glass was fused to it by another worker holding a pontil rod. The gaffer then used the crimp to force the coloured wad up into the clear glass. As with the other processes the impressed gather was then given further coatings of clear glass, and frequently a foot was added.

While the crimping process is associated primarily with the Whitall Tatum factory of Millville New Jersey, in the early years of the 20th century, European and American paperweights of the 19th century frequently combined the millefiori, filigree, and lampwork processes within a single weight. A striking example is the Baccarat butterfly weight in which the body of the lampworked lepidopter is a filigree cane, while the insect hovers over a lampworked flower whose centre is a millefiori cane, and the whole design is framed in a circle of millefiori canes.

These basic processes involve only glass in the design and its manipulation. Sulphide paperweights include, as all or part of the design, the clay-silica paste cameos made from intaglio moulds and known to collectors as sulphides. Like the military and patriotic medals in metallic leaf, sulphide cameos are foreign matter as distinguished from the amalgam of worked glass within glass.

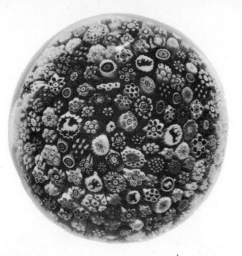

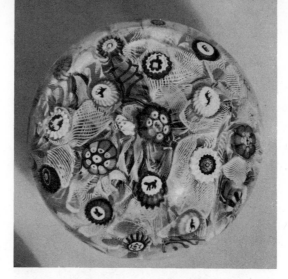

a) Baccarat close millefiori, dated 1847; dia. $2\frac{1}{2}''$ (6.35 cm.).

The variety of millefiori canes never ceases to fascinate. Every good collection should have at least one, (though not necessarily dated), example. Those dated B1848 are available, while the less common, dated 1846, '47 and '49, have grown more and more rare. The game is now to count figure canes, or to discover a rare cane such as the tiny pom-pom. Undated Clichy examples in stave baskets were also made. Bohemia millefiori closely resemble Baccarat.

b) Baccarat spaced millefiori, dated B1848; dia. $3\frac{3}{16}''$ (8.09 cm.).

Comparable to close millefiori, these are virtually standard in terms of high quality of execution, and without competition from other factories. Look for unreground examples in any size. The white lace ground is enlivened by brilliant blue and yellow figure canes, and also by random coloured filigree twists. Among spaced millefiori, only carpet ground examples are faceted.

c) Clichy spaced millefiori newel-post ornament; ht. $5\frac{1}{4}''$ (13.3 cm.).

At least this one uncommon, nearly spherical ornament retains the glass peg by which it was dowelled into the newel-post; others show the brass collar above the missing peg. But most have broken and been cut down, leaving the bottoms flat. The spaced concentric is sometimes of chequer design with filigree separations. A very few close millefiori newel ornaments are known from Baccarat.

d) Clichy chequer, dia. $2\frac{2}{3}''$ (6.71 cm.).

This successful solution to the problem of dramatizing spaced millefiori canes must have been difficult to achieve, for the quality range is broad. Most desirable are specimens with large (i.e. highly magnified) canes in brilliant contrasting colours. Avoid examples where the canes have sunk beneath, or are otherwise truncated by, the filigree separations. Other chequers feature coloured filigree or barber pole twists. Chequers were seldom if ever faceted.

e) Whitefriars chequer, dia. $3\frac{3}{4}''$ (9.52 cm.).

Though generally slipshod in execution, a few of these rare, usually magnum-sized, English weights are well made, showing a harmony of neatly spaced canes between dividing strands of pink, amber, or blue filigree. There are no known American chequers.

Glass
Paperweights

MILLEFIORI
CONCENTRICS

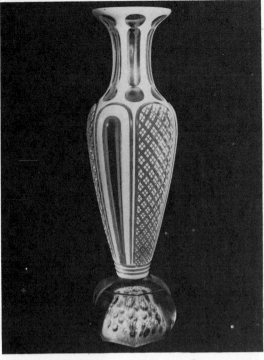

a) Bohemian paperweight vase; ht. 13⅞″ (35.3 cm.).

Several examples show this identical and typical Bohemian cutting, but sizes vary, this being tall. Other vases are cased (overlaid) white, or white over translucent red, and cut with thumbprint punties. The weights themselves are scattered millefiori on lace grounds, some with figure canes. One rare example is dated J 1848; and another is known to have been purchased in Paris in 1847—so these are unquestionably period.

b) Whitefriars miniature scent bottle dated 1848; ht. 3¾″ (9.52 cm.).

This miniature version of the well-known ink-well has a millefiori stopper only 1¼″ in diameter. Colour schemes for these concentric arrangements are usually attractive and sometimes unusual, with perhaps a dominant tonality of pale yellow, lilac, or lettuce green. An all-white example is rare. A collection of these tiny bottles is still a possibility.

---

c) Clichy concentric; dia. 2¼″ (5.71 cm.).

Unlike their Baccarat and Saint Louis counter-parts, these rich concentrics are contained in white and coloured stave baskets that hide the shortness of the canes and give the top view an opacity it would otherwise lack. Collectors like discovering occasional roses or even rows of roses. By contrast, New England concentrics show only two rows spaced apart over *latticinio*, but cane colours are sometimes finely orchestrated. Some French concentrics are pedestal weights.

d) Saint Louis concentric, dia. 3⅛″ (7.93 cm.).

A broad quality range here, with poorer examples showing uneven rows with one or two canes bulging into the next row, the colour schemes seeming unplanned. Look for evenly-spaced rows in felicitous colour combinations. Some concentrics are dated SL 1848, and these may contain a central and other figure canes, which increase the value considerably. The concentric arrangement also appears in mushrooms and pedestals from this factory.

---

e) Bacchus concentric, English; dia. 3½″ (8.89 cm.).

Limited in number, these solid magnums are extremely variable; the less desirable have wobbly rows of canes in uneven sizes and bland colour schemes, while the finer weights show perfectly even rows in breathtaking pastels, ranking with any of the best concentrics. With few exceptions these have been considered less desirable than their French equivalents.

Left: Candle holder in blue opalescent glass with milky translucent striations; France, c. 1815–20.

Right: Vase of gourd form in opaque pink and white latticinio glass; France, c. 1840.

a) Clichy garland; dia. 3¼″ (8.25 cm.).

Certainly one of the most attractive paper-weights of the Classic period, these garlands come in a wide variety of ingenious designs and brilliant colour schemes. The patient collector has unlimited opportunity to suit his particular fancy. Garlands were nearly all around 2¾″ to 3¼″ in diameter, so smaller examples are likely to have been ground down. Grinding frequently exposes the white underlay of a colour ground, distorts the outer canes, and lessens the value accordingly.

b) Clichy scent bottle; ht. 9⁹⁄₁₆″ (24.3 cm.).

Another collectable form in which the garland appears, this time on a blue ground. A bottle similar to this was shown at the Great Exhibition of 1851. Truly an integrated design, this delicate creation shows the glass inspiration of which France was capable.

---

c) Saint Louis panelled jasper; dia. 3⅛″ (7.93 cm.).

Although not common now, these have not been considered as fine as most other French weights. Usually, eight panels of rather coarse-grained jasper in alternating colours are separated by white spokes. The central hub is either a figure, or a miniature swirl cane. A peripheral coloured-twist torsade, not always apparent from the top, completes the design.

d) Baccarat double overlay; dia. 3″ (7.62 cm.).

Baccarat made both single translucent overlays and opaque double overlays in a variety of colours, usually with one top and six side punties, frequently with smaller punties beneath. Motifs are usually circular, or interlocked trefoil, garlands of canes,

but occasionally there are also mushrooms, with a torsade; a few show gilt decoration of the outer overlay. Translucent overlays are deep casings, *not flashed*, and can sometimes be reground if chipped, without penetrating to the clear glass.

e) Clichy colour double overlay; dia. 2¾″ (6.98 cm.).

Boxier than Baccarat, these brilliant overlays are usually cut with six flat or slightly concave side and top punties, to reveal a tightly packed concentric mushroom with stave sheath, but not torsade. Flat bases are crosshatched. Rows of roses add considerably to the value. There is likely to be a long bubble somewhere near the base, but this doesn't seem to bother collectors. Be suspicious of any fancy faceting, or trimming away of the overlay.

Opposite:
Top left: Clichy bouquet tied with ribbon. Right: Rare Baccarat snake on lace. Bottom left: Clichy entwined garlands in lace. Right: Rare butterfly hovering over red and white primrose.
All these paperweights were made in France.

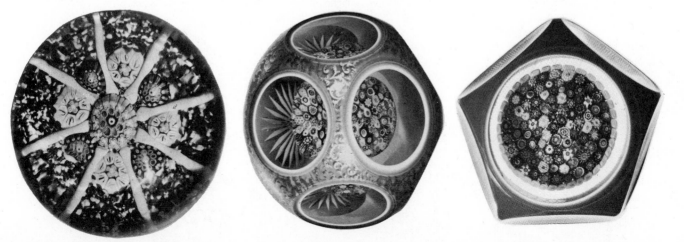

Glass
Paperweights

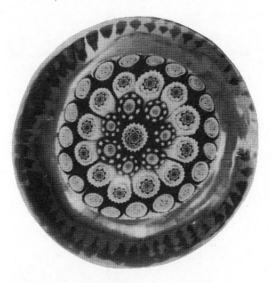

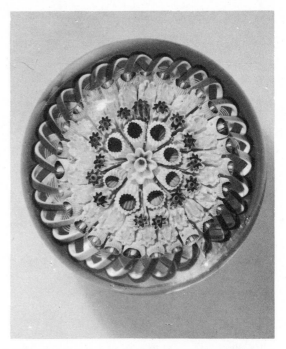

a) Baccarat mushroom; dia. 3″ (7.62 cm.).

Along with the pansy this is probably the most characteristic Baccarat paperweight. Hundreds of close millefiori mushrooms were made. More special are the beautifully-harmonised concentric mushrooms, while the all-white bridal bouquets are rare indeed, and close to perfection. Blue torsades are the rule, with occasional red or pink spirals. Large, mercury-like bubbles above the torsades are unintentional, and distracting. Numerous mushroom weights are attractively faceted, and some are overlays.

b) Bacchus mushroom, English; dia. 3¾″ (9.52 cm.).

These are rare, magnum-sized and impressive. A concentric mushroom of ruffled canes about a large central cane rises within a bold but finely wrought torsade in cobalt blue or, in this case, deep, fiery pink with white, the torsade lacking the bubble that plagues French mushrooms.

---

c) Saint Louis mushroom; dia. 3¹⁄₁₆″ (7.77 cm.).

Where most Baccarat mushrooms are close millefiori, Saint Louis mushrooms dated 1848 are usually concentrics. Earlier examples (1845) are close millefiori. Many undated concentrics show uneven rows and prosaic colouring, but fine workmanship and lovely colour combinations are likely to be valued accordingly. Torsades are usually blue, occasionally coral. Some weights are faceted and a few have amber-flashed bases.

d) Baccarat carpet ground; dia. 2¾″ (6.98 cm.).

In these nearly always well-done, and rather expensive weights, the spaced millefiori theme is carried out with a carpet of coloured canes as the filler in place of lace. Carpet colours include red, cobalt or aqua blue, green-white and the little-known *choufleur* (cauliflower) with its bent rods.

Panelled designs with honeycomb or stardust carpet filler set the Baccarat garland in the carpet ground. Garland specimens and those with spaced canes on white stardust carpet are eagerly sought-after, and very rare.

e) Saint Louis carpet ground; dia. 3⅛″ (7.93 cm.).

These lovely weights, with their carpets of evenly-packed, soft pink or green crimped canes are worth waiting for. Carpets of unusual mixed tonalities such as red, white and blue, and those weights with figure canes, are scarce, but the plain carpets are just as lovely to look at. Until 1970 the all-white carpet lined with red and blue was thought to be extremely rare; then five were discovered. Avoid weights cut down to under 2¾″— they cramp the design.

a) Gillinder carpet ground; dia. 2$\frac{15}{16}$" (7.46 cm.).

Unattributed until recently, these beautiful and rare weights were usually credited to Bacchus or to Saint Louis, but they were smaller than Bacchus, and much lighter in the hand than weights from either factory. Canes are generally crimped or ruffled; carpet colours are white or aqua blue in known examples, with large central canes in butter yellow, pink, or indigo blue. One has a central silhouette of Queen Victoria. The outer canes draw into the centre of the base and are usually speckled with black particles. Faceting is nearly always with deeply cut, long oval punties.

b) Clichy swirl, in three colours; dia. 3$\frac{1}{16}$" (7.77 cm.).

As much a Clichy trademark as the crown is a Saint Louis, the gay swirls come in two, and more rarely in three colours, as in this fine example with malachite green, amethyst and white swirls; the weight centres a Clichy rose. Quality is uneven, so look for closely-parallel colour strands spiralling out neatly from the centre without more than a sliver of clear glass, a good centre cane, and a minimum of bubbles.

c) Bohemian crown; dia. 2$\frac{3}{4}$" (6.98 cm.).

A cross between the Saint Louis crown and the Clichy swirl, these scarce, attractive weights centre a group of canes, including, perhaps, a figure cane or two, over the crown of red or blue and white rods. One pink and white crown is actually a swirl form. Virtually unknown, a Bohemian crown is an interesting and unusual addition to any collection.

d) Saint Louis crown; dia. 2$\frac{13}{16}$" (7.14 cm.).

In this characteristic Saint Louis form, two-colour twisted ribbons alternate with filigree twists. Less frequently, crowns show two differently coloured ribbons, or, rarely, amber *aventurine*

ribbons. Since all crowns are hollow, do not be put off by a small hole at the bottom; the pontil may have taken a bit of the base with it, which was then drilled to smooth out the perforation. Look for bright ribbons, evenly twisted and closely placed.

e) New England crown; dia. 2$\frac{1}{2}$" (6.35 cm.).

Representative of the best American crown work in Saint Louis style, this finely constructed example is attributed to gaffer François Pierre. Unusual pink filigree rods between alternately red-and-blue, and red-and-yellow twisted ribbons give off a rosy hue. The ample clear glass about the motif indicates that the weight has never been reground.

Glass
Paperweights

a) Baccarat anemone, dia. 2⅝″ (6.66 cm.).

Clichy for millefiori, Baccarat for flowers. The petals of this attractive red anemone are edged in white, tipped with a flamboyant gothic arch, and striped with three white-on-white bands. Proper faceting centres the flower neatly in each punty. A group of single flowers in various colours would make a fine collection.

b) New England Glass Co., pom-pom, dia. 3″ (7.62 cm.).

These American pom-poms over *latticinio* closely resemble the Saint Louis examples from which they were obviously copies, except that the petals are contained in an overlaid (cased) bowl, and the *latticinio* is generally less precise. The bud is small. The typical New England base is deeply concave; the basal rim usually uneven.

c) Saint Louis pom-pom, dia. 3″ (7.62 cm.).

Of these lovely flowers, the white blossom on pink *latticinio* is common; the pink on white uncommon; the white on tomato red *latticinio* ground unusual and very expensive. Flower petals may be precise or fuzzy; both are considered desirable. Baccarat pom-poms are scarcer and come in a variety of colours, set in clear glass, and usually surrounded by a ring of canes.

d) Baccarat butterfly over clematis, dia. 2⅞″ (7.30 cm.).

Here we see the well-known Baccarat clematis used as a foil for a hovering butterfly. As in other good examples the antennae are neatly attached, the wings colourful and white-edged, the flower well placed, with precise original faceting over a well-starcut base. Butterflies from Saint Louis, though extremely rare, are rather amateurish by comparison. Butterfly lightweight examples with flat, starcut bases are not Baccarat, but from an unknown source.

e) Mt Washington footed dahlia, dia. 3⅝″ (9.20 cm.).

All Mt Washington weights are scarce, but they do turn up. Known specimens are usually magnums, with roses or many-petalled dahlias in a variety of colours and petal treatments. The petals of this yellow-centred white dahlia are puckered and streaked with pink. Notice the three-dimensional effect; the flower is about half an inch thick. Rarity and attractiveness combine to make this an important weight in any collection.

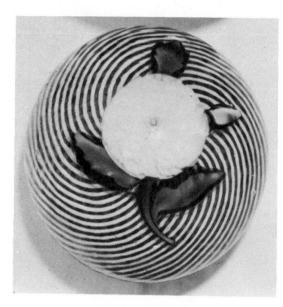

b) Millville pink rose, dia. 3¾″ (9.52 cm.).

These weights from the Whitall Tatum Co. of Millville, New Jersey show a tremendous range in type and quality. They come footed, unfooted, on pedestal, with and without leaves, with flat or concave bases. Some collectors look for opalescent-tipped petals, others for rarer colours such as rusty-red, or yellow. This weight has been often copied in America, China and Murano, but imitations are likely to be unfooted or poorly-footed, with a green or yellow cast in the glass, and the rose in baby blue or some garish colour.

a) Saint Louis dahlia, dia. 2⅞″ (7.30 cm.).

Desirable specimens of these full-blown flowers in pink, mauve, purple or yellow fill the dome of the weight with up to five rows of close-packed petals. Spaced green leaves peek from beneath the outer row. Avoid examples with numerous cracked petals, or heavily reground ones in which the outer petals appear blurred.

---

c) Sandwich pink flower, dia. 3″ (7.62 cm.).

There is no European equivalent for this American extravaganza with its inner row of goldstone petals. Sandwich profiles are generally low, glass usually clear and medium light in the hand. Some examples are magnums.

d) Clichy flat floral bouquet, dia. 3¹⁄₁₆″ (7.77 cm.).

These are so rare that they are sometimes improperly attributed at auction sales. Blossoms show so much variety, they may not be taken for Clichy; while leaves are often of various colours and shapes, some stamped with a waffle pattern. Arrangements appear casual, like a bunch of wildflowers just

picked. By contrast, the Saint Louis floral arrangements that seem casual are actually standardized.

e) Saint Louis flat bouquet, dia. 2¾″ (6.98 cm.).

A Saint Louis trademark is this small bouquet of canes and leaves over an amber flashed ground. It shows up to best advantage when elaborately faceted with concave punties, with a ring of canes about the flat bouquet, and the base cut with small diamonds. But if the base is scratched, some of the thin amber flash will have been removed, and cannot be replaced. Watch for occasional faking of amber flash with shellac.

Glass
Paperweights

FLORAL BOUQUETS

FRUITS

a) Baccarat floral bouquet, dia. $3\frac{5}{8}''$ *(9.20 cm.).*

These superb magnums, a few with facets, are carefully balanced arrangements, sometimes in cruciform, sometimes as a bouquet. Variety comes from the flowers running the Baccarat gamut in type and colouring—roses, pom-poms, buttercups, pansies, clematis all may appear. Advanced collectors look for three red pom-poms; somewhere there must be one with five red roses!

b) New England Glass Co. floral bouquet, dia. $3''$ *(7.62 cm.).*

Inspired by Saint Louis, these American weights place the upright bouquet in a *latticinio* funnel, or lay the floral sheaf across a *latticinio* bed. Upright bouquets are often attractively faceted in New England style with blazes between clover-cut punties. Large horizontal bouquets such as this are usually magnums, with finely formed leaves and flowers in bright canary yellow, blues and scarlet.

---

c) Saint Louis upright bouquet with torsade, dia. $3\frac{3}{16}''$ *(8.09 cm.).*

Encased overlays, scent bottles, handcoolers, vases from Saint Louis all feature the upright bouquet, but the form appears to best advantage encircled by a torsade under a brilliantly faceted dome. Whatever its colouring, blue or red with white, all-white, or the exceedingly rare yellow-and-white, the torsade frames the bouquet as lace frames a Victorian valentine. A starcut base completes the sparkle imparted by the faceting. Baccarat examples are very rare.

d) Saint Louis fruit, dia. $2\frac{1}{2}''$ *(6.35 cm.).*

Another Saint Louis speciality that set the pattern for American makers. Considerable variety is available, from the casual spill of fruits in *latticinio*

basket shown here, to the formally arranged turnips, single fruits, attractive strawberries with blossom, and the two cherries on a twig, faceted to look like fifty. Look for precisely interlaced, bright-white *latticinio*, and for leaves that show no white at the ends.

e) New England Glass Co. fruit, dia. $2\frac{7}{8}''$ *(7.30 cm.).*

Contrasted with casual Saint Louis placement of fruit, American work looks still and formal, the leaves like points of a star. Fruit and leaf colouring ranges from pale through brilliant to dark. *Latticinio* baskets are frequently pale and spidery, or distorted by bubbles. Weights average $2\frac{1}{2}''$ diameter, with deep basal concavities and sometimes a pontil mark.

a) *Millville ship, c. 1900, dia. $3\frac{5}{16}$" (8.41 cm.).*
This white, full-rigged ship riding the trans-lucent, royal blue seas was achieved by sweeping powdered white glass into the design engraved on a steel die. Though less common than the American motto weights, it also comes in clear glass, and on a translucent amber ground accompanied by the words *Rocked in the Cradle of the Deep.* Equally desirable are a variety of sail-boats with pennant, and/or lighthouse. Other subjects such as the hunter and god, horse, eagle are scarce and consequently prized.

b) *Clichy sulphide portrait, dia. $2\frac{1}{2}$" (6.35 cm.).*
Of all sulphides, Clichy are perhaps the most attractive, especially when framed in a ring of canes on rich colour grounds. Sulphides are under-collected compared with other weights of equal substance. Many subjects are uncatalogued, and all kinds from many factories are available, including attractive religious and pastoral scenes, unknown portraits, and commemorative subjects such as the Crystal Palace. Victorian sulphides often have a silvery look; whereas the modern ones look plaster white.

c) *Baccarat snake on upset muslin, dia. $3\frac{1}{4}$" (8.25 cm.).*
Though not everybody's dish, snakes are clearly somebody's, for these canapés in a variety of plain and mottled colours, on lace and sand grounds, are consistently highly valued. Baccarat archives indi-cate that in 1849 a few snakes were listed at ten francs. Snakes from Baccarat are sometimes elaborately faceted in the same style as the Baccarat sulphides of Joan of Arc and the hunter and dog.

Glass Paperweights

NOVELTIES

d) *Millville inkwell, c. 1900; ht. $9\frac{1}{4}$" (23.5 cm.).*
The umbrella-like form of the design was made with a crimp. These attractive 'lily' forms come in white, in custard-yellow speckled with many colours, and, as here, in alternately red, blue, and green stripes. A spherical bubble in both bottom and stopper floats above the 'lily' centre like a flower pistil. The glass is usually well formed and limpid.

e) *Saint Louis shotcup (penholder), ht. $5\frac{3}{16}$" (13.2 cm.).*
The cobalt-blue canes in the miniature paper-weight base complement the cobalt blue translucent overlay of the holder with its many printies, just as the filigree twist about the rim of the holder echoes the lace ground of the weight. Other holders may show red overlay, etching, *latticinio* swirl, or even twisted ribbons.

Glass
Glossary

ACID POLISHING: Restoring the polished surface to cut glass by immersion in an acid bath.

ANNEALING: Removal of strain in glass by controlled heating and slow cooling in an annealing oven, or lehr.

AVENTURINE: Coloured glass combined with flakes of gold (15th century), or crystals of copper (from 17th century) giving the glass a lustrous sheen.

BALUSTER: Stem of pure or inverted baluster form, sometimes with other knop motifs.

BASAL RIM: Bottom rim, in paperweights with concave base.

BASKET: General term covering vertical or funnel-shaped enclosures of paperweight designs.

BATCH: A mixture of raw materials prepared for melting.

CAMEO: Carved layers of glass to make design; also the moulded portrait in a sulphide glass.

CANE: The basic element of a millefiori design: a fused bundle of clear and coloured glass rods.

CARPET GROUND: Close-packed ground of identical canes used as a background or foil for a design.

CHAIR: A team of glass-makers.

CHEQUER (American CHECKER): 'Chequerboard' paperweight design with regularly spaced canes separated by a horizontal grid of filigree canes.

CLICHY ROSE: Rose-like cane favoured by the Clichy factory, but imitated by others.

COLOUR GROUND: Background of transparent or opaque colour on which designs are placed.

CONCENTRIC: Tightly packed or separated circles of canes about a common centre.

CORDS: Slight striae felt on the surface of flint-glass.

CRACKING OFF: Removal of moil by scoring and localized heating.

CRIZZLING: Loss of brilliance on the surface of the glass caused by a mass of tiny cracks.

CROWN WEIGHT: Hollow-blown paperweight.

CRUCIFORM: Term to describe early wine bottles made in the shape of a cross.

CRYSTAL, FULL, HALF LEAD: Full and lead crystal—potash glass containing about 30% of lead. Half crystal lead content—about half this amount.

CULLET: Broken glass scrap used in the mixed batch.

CUSP: A point at which two branches of a curve meet and stop. A centrally placed stem knop.

DECKELPOKAL; DECHELBECHER: Covered goblet; covered beaker—German term.

ENCASED OVERLAY: Single or double overlay design, further encased in clear glass.

FICHTELGEBIRGSGLAS: Glass made in the Franconian mountains of the Fichtelgebirge, of light greenish tint. Large output of enamelled Humpen and flasks.

FILIGREE (Common terms—LACE, MUSLIN): Clear glass cane containing twisted opaque white and/or coloured glass rods; American—COTTON TWIST.

FIRE-POLISHING: Reheating of finished ware to obliterate marks left by tools and produce a smooth brilliant surface.

FLAMMIFORM: A decorative effect usually at the termination of wrythen moulding.

FLAT BOUQUET: Design in which flowers and leaves (or canes representing flowers) have been placed flat, parallel to the base of the weight.

FLINT GLASS: Originally glass in which the silica was derived from calcined flints; glass in which lead oxide forms the flux. Lead crystal is the modern term.

FLUTE: A drinking-glass with a tall, deep bowl; also a vertical groove, cut or moulded.

GADROONING: Borders of moulded or cut deep convex flutes forming a decorative band.

GAFFER: Chief glass-maker.

GATHER: Blob of molten glass secured on the end of a blow-pipe, or pontil.

GIRANDOLE: Multi-branch candlestock.

GLORY-HOLE: Subsidiary furnace for reheating parts of worked glass.

GOBLET: A large stemmed drinking-glass.

GROUND: The flat or slightly domed background above, on, or in which the paperweight design rests.

HAND-BLOWN or FREE-BLOWN: Glass blown into shape without use of a mould.

HANDCOOLER: Egg-shaped paperweight, apocryphally used to cool the hands of over-anxious ladies in preparation for kissing; but actually occasionally used to darn socks.

HAND-PRESSED: Glass made in a hand operated press, as opposed to machine pressing.

HOLLOWED: Pontil scar, ground smooth.

INTAGLIO: Wheel-cut concave designs.

JASPER: Mottled ground composed of small particles of glass usually in two colours.

KALTMALEREI: (Ger.) cold-enamelling (much less durable than fired enamelling).

KICK: The pyramidical dent to be found in the base of early glass, especially bottles and decanters.

KNOP: A protuberance or knob, other than a baluster, breaking the line of the stem.

LATTICINIO: Lace glass, literally 'lattice' glass. Clear glass with embedded rods of opaque white glass forming a pattern.

LAUB UND BANDELWERK: Decorative pattern of leaf and floral garlands (German term).

MAGNUM: Paperweight over $3\frac{1}{4}''$ or 8.3 cm. diameter.

MERESE: A sharp-edged, flattened glass button connecting bowl and stem, or foot and stem.

METAL: Glass either molten or cold.

MINIATURE: Any paperweight not over 2″ or 5.1 cm. diameter.

MITRE CUT: Glass cut with V-edge abrasive wheel.

MOIL: Waste on blow-pipe.

MILLEFIORI: Term coined in the mid-19th century, first used in English in 1849 to describe the visual effect of a close grouping of many coloured glass canes of simulated floral design.

MOULDED GLASS: Blown glass ornamented or given its final body shape by the use of moulds.

MUSHROOM (TUFT): Vertical, spreading mushroom-shaped bundle of millefiori canes arranged in a close or concentric design, and nearly always encircled near the base by a spiral torsade.

NIPT DIAMOND WAIS: Diamond-shaped network made by pinching together vertical threads or ribs of glass.

OFFHAND: Entirely hand fabricated.

OPAQUE TWIST: See 'filigree'.

PASTE MOULD: Mould coated with carbonaceous paste.

PEDESTAL (French *piédouche*): A weight generally raised on a broad, cylindrical column, and having rings, flanges, or other basal orders.

PINCHBECK: Weight featuring a thin alloy plaque resembling gold or silver, modelled in relief and fixed to a clear glass crown by means of a tin, pewter, leather, or alabaster base.

PINCHED TRAILING: Applied bands of glass pinched into a wavy formation.

PONTIL OR PUNTY MARK: The scar left (usually on the base) on a glass when the punty rod is tapped off.

POT ARCH: Subsidiary furnace for pre-heating pot before transference to melting furnace.

POT SETTING: Transference of pots from pot arch to melting furnace.

POTASH GLASS: Glass fluxed with unrefined vegetable ashes.

PROFILE: Side elevation of a paperweight.

PRUNT: A glass blob or seal with surface plain or tooled, such as 'strawberry'.

PUNTY OR PONTIL ROD: Long solid iron used principally to hold a vessel during the finishing processes.

RETICULATED: Moulded pattern in network formation.

RIB or DIAMOND MOULD: Straight or twisted lines forming diamonds or other patterns and impressed on the surface of a bowl; honeycomb mould.

ROD: Solid, cylindrical stick of clear or coloured glass; the basic element from which canes, *latticinio*, or flora and fauna are created.

SCHMELZGLAS: (Ger.) Opaque marbled glass imitating stones, e.g. agate, chalcedony, etc.

SEEDS: Minute air bubbles in the metal indicating that the glass-house could not raise the furnace temperature high enough to eliminate all air bubbles trapped among the raw materials.

SODA GLASS: Glass in which the principal flux is carbonate of lime, usually the second alkaline base.

STAVE: Rectangular rod used as an enclosure for a design.

STONES: Red- and black specks within the fabric of early flint-glass, the result of imperfect fusion between oxide of lead and silica.

STRIAE: Apparent undulating markings within the metal, perfectly vitrified and transparent, showing the metal to be of uneven composition because insufficiently molten before working.

SWIRL: Paperweight in which rods of two or more colours radiate spirally downward from a top central cane.

SULPHIDE (CAMEO): Relief medallion, bust, or other design of clay-silica paste used in paperweights and a great variety of other glass objects.

TAKER IN: Workman who transfers ware to the lehr.

TEAR or AIR BEAD: A bubble of air enclosed in the metal.

THREAD: A thin trail of glass applied around the rim of the bowl or decorating the neck of a vessel.

TINT: A residual colour tinge inherent in the ingredients of which the metal is composed.

TORSADE: Filigree ring of opaque white and/or coloured threads, frequently of complicated pattern, used as a low set border for mushrooms and upright bouquets.

TRAILED ORNAMENT: Looped threads of glass applied to the surface of bowl or foot.

UPRIGHT BOUQUET: A vertically placed floral design.

VERMICULAR COLLAR: A wavy trail of glass encircling a stem; sometimes called 'vermicelli collar'.

VERRE CRAQUELE; BROCS A GLACES: French terms for the two Venetian techniques of 'ice glass', revived in 19th century.

VERRE EGLOMISE: So called after the 18th century French glazier Glomy. A technique of cold-painting behind glass, frequently augmented by application of metal foil and protected by a layer of glass or varnish. Related to the ancient technique of *fondi d'oro* and the *Zwischengoldglas* revival.

Glass
Repairs and Maintenance

Glass cannot look its best unless it is periodically washed and kept dusted. Warm water with a little liquid soap is the best medium after which it should be rinsed and then dried with a smooth cloth. Cut glass pieces should be finally brushed—soft bristles being used. Ammonia and methylated spirits in the water are good alternatives.

Decanters, vases, etc., should never be allowed to remain moist after use; they should always be dried thoroughly, otherwise a white, misty film will form and mark the surface. If this happens, only professional treatment will provide an effective remedy and even this only applies to glass of lead.

If the inside of a decanter has to be cleaned, tissue paper around a thick wire and twisted inside will remove excess moisture, followed by holding the decanter a short distance away from warm air provided by a heater or hair dryer. Dried brownish wine stains can be removed by vinegar before using the above method.

Small overhead lights in a show cabinet lined with black or dark grey velvet are effective methods of displaying all types of glass and are particularly useful in bringing out details of engraving.

Tissue paper should always be used first for wrapping and packing, filling out with several sheets around the necks of decanters, stems of glasses or insides of bowls—thus making an equal thickness before final wrapping. For post (mailing), plenty of newspaper in between the packages should be used without too much tightness, thus causing pressure. A carton within a carton with a layer of paper to cushion the first is advisable. For intricate or very valuable items—the advice of professional firms should be sought.

In order to preserve a glass, repair specialists can undertake remarkable work on a damaged piece. Chips can be smoothed and many other types of renovations can be successfully carried out.

Fakes and Forgeries

Fakes and forgeries can be described as definite copies of genuine antiques works of art. Certain pieces were copied more than others and almost always the same mistakes were made.

The tint of old glass is unmistakable. Under strong electric light on a low table is the best way for examination although good daylight is also effective. Looking down on a bowl or drinking glass a mellow greyish tint of varying shades will be seen especially around the rim and, next to a modern piece of glass, even though the design is copied from an antique, the difference will be more than apparent; i.e. in almost every instance, a colourless or white reaction—hence a copy or reproduction.

A piece of glass made over 100 years ago as with other works of art is subject to wear marks, and the genuine signs of age. On any piece of old glass, constant use will inevitably show on the part, whether narrow or wide, which comes into contact with the surface upon which it is placed, picked up and placed again. Through the years these marks become roughened and quite different from their original shiny surface. The forger has to try to simulate these marks, but the too-regular scratching, including straight lines, can be detected.

Mostly only rare and valuable items are copied—the following are typical examples:

1. Marked Irish decanters—usually too heavy and names too easily legible.
2. Commemorative Williamite glasses—made often from 1800 onwards—made of white metal.
3. 18th century wine glasses—bably proportioned with narrow and flat bases—striations (unequal marks caused through twisting during formation) either entirely absent or exaggerated.
4. Early glasses with modern historical engraving—latter too white and too well defined.

In most forgeries the underneath sharp centre of a glass (pontil mark) is absent, although this does not necessarily mean a forgery, as some later 18th century marks were polished off.

504

Paperweights
Repairs and Maintenance

Most dealers and collectors are disturbed by defects inflicted by ordinary wear and tear. So many weights are sent to glass-cutters for regrinding that fewer and fewer retain their original appearance. The irony is that regrinding may improve damaged weights, but in the long run, pristine examples may be more valuable.

Don't be deceived by the euphemistic term *repolished;* only the lightest scratches are removed by this final step in regrinding. An experienced craftsman may retain something of a weight's former beauty, but grinding removes a substantial fraction of the epidermis, alters the profile, and changes the relationship of the magnifying lens to the internal design. It may also expose the opaque white hem of a colour ground or eliminate part of the design—the outer row of a concentric may simply disappear from view!

Two easy tests can be made: (1) Place a thin tissue over the fingers of one upturned hand, hold the weight upside down over the tissue. Rotate slowly and evenly with the other hand; any slight wobbles, or flatness in the surface can usually be felt by the fingertips beneath the tissue. (2) Rotate the dome of the weight evenly, from side to side and back, under a good light. An uneven or wobbly flow of reflected light indicates regrinding.

An off-centre design may sometimes be recentred by regrinding. Submerge the weight in a bowl of room-temperature water; by eliminating the magnification factor, this shows the relationship of the design to the surrounding glass.

Caution to Collectors

Beware of weights without plenty of glass around the design, or low flattened crowns which distort or do not magnify the image—both have been poorly or heavily reground. Watch for faceting inappropriate to the factory or style, it has probably been added later to conceal major damage or defect of design. Chinese copies of the Baccarat pansy were mistakenly given the clover cutting of the New England Glass Co. Today anything goes.

Unless absolutely necessary, don't regrind a base as this removes a key to provenance.

An unfaceted weight should not be faceted. Refaceting should match the style of the original factory.

Bruised overlays and chipped pedestals should not be recut—a recut weight can never be restored. When in doubt, do nothing.

A few bubbles, stones or striae in the glass itself are not important; after all, paperweights were made to sell for a few francs, shillings or dollars.

Fakes and Forgeries

Each historical period has its own 'fingerprint'; the modern paperweight no more duplicates those of the nineteenth century, than the nineteenth century duplicates Roman millefiori. Mid-nineteenth century production, with its variable metal, its sense of design, pre-analine colour and forthright delineation of sentiment makes modern forgery virtually impossible. Most paperweight-makers do not even try.

Nevertheless, a certain amount of inadvertent or intentional imitation was inevitable. The Dupont-Baccarat millefiori weights of the early 1930s, previously attributed to Bristol even though they contained canes apparently made from old Baccarat moulds, are the most difficult to detect. Yet even so, the smallness of the canes, the spurious dating, the straighter sides and proportionately larger base distinguish these from classic Baccarat. The Dupont pansy, with gelatinous yellow petals and occasional false dates is easier to spot. Most obvious of all are the modern, Murano weights; millefiori etched on the flat base with a bogus Baccarat stamp; and spotted, flashed weights outrageously signed 'Tiffany'. Most makers using the Victorian style (including Baccarat and Saint Louis), have integrity and pride, inserting proper dates and signature canes.

The main deception occurs through the novice collector's unfamiliarity with the literature differentiating the various factories. The touchstone to successful collecting is thorough knowledge of historical provenance, range and characteristics.

Glass
Further Reading

General

BUCKLEY, W. *The Art of Glass*. London, 1939.
DILLON, E. *Glass*. London, 1907.
ELVILLE, E. M. *Collectors Dictionary of Glass*. Feltham, 1961.
GROS-GALLINER, G. *Glass: A Guide for Collectors*. London, 1970.
HAYNES, E. B. *Glass Through the Ages*. Harmondsworth, 1959. First published 1948.
HONEY, W. B. *Glass: A Handbook*. London, 1946.
JOKELSON, P. *Sulphides: The Art of Cameo Incrustation*. New York, 1968.
ROBERTSON, R. A. *Chats on Old Glass*. Revised; new chapter on American Glass by K. M. Wilson. New York, 1969.
WILKINSON, R. *The Hallmarks of Antique Glass*. London, 1968.
WILLS, G. *Antique Glass for Pleasure and Profit*. London, 1971.

Roman and Venetian

HAYNES, D. E. L. *The Portland Vase*. London, 1964.
MARIACHER, G. *Italian Blown Glass*. London, 1961.
PSINGS, C. *Roman Glass in Limberg*. New York, 1971.
VON SALDERN, A. *Ancient Glass in the MFA*. Boston, 1968.

Continental

AUVRAY, M. C. *Cristal de France*. Paris, 1967.
FROTHINGHAM, A. W. *Spanish Glass*. New York, 1964.
GROVER, R. and L. *European Art Glass Nouveau*. Rutland, Vt. and Tokyo, 1967.
MIDDLEMAS, K. *Continental Coloured Glass*. London and New York, 1970.
SAINT LOUIS (Factory). *Cristal de France 1767*. Paris, 1967.
VAVRA, J. R. *Das Glas*. Prague, 1954.
VON SALDERN, A. *German Enamelled Glass*. New York, 1971.

English

BICKERTON, L. M. *Eighteenth Century English Drinking Glasses*. London, 1971.
CROMPTON, S. (ed.). *English Glass*. London, 1967.
DAVIS, D. C. *English and Irish Antique Glass*. London, 1964.
DAVIS, D. C., and MIDDLEMAS, K. *Coloured Glass*. London, 1968.
ELVILLE, E. M. *English and Irish Cut Glass 1750–1950*. Feltham, 1953.
FRANCIS, G. R. *Old English Drinking Glasses, Their Chronology and Sequence, etc.* London, 1926.
HONEY, W. B. *English Glass*. London, 1946.
LLOYD, W. *Investing in Georgian Glass*. London, 1969.
WAKEFIELD, H. *Nineteenth-Century British Glass*. London, 1961.
WARREN, P. *Irish Glass: The Age of Exhuberance*. London, 1970.

WILKINSON, O. N. *Old Glass, Manufacture, Styles, Uses*. London, 1968.
WILLS, G. *English and Irish Glass*. London, 1970.

American

AMAYA, M. *Tiffany Glass*. 1971.
BARRET, R. C. *Blown and Pressed American Glass*. Manchester, Vt., 1966.
Identification of American Art Glass. Manchester, Vt., 1964.
GARDNER, P. V. *The Glass of Frederick Carder*. New York, 1971.
KOCH, R. *Louis C. Tiffany, Rebel in Glass*. New York, 1964.
LEE, R. W. *Antique Fakes and Reproductions*. Northborough, Mass., 1950.
Early American Pressed Glass. Wellesley Hills, Mass., 1960.
Sandwich Glass. Framingham Centre, Mass., 1939.
Victorian Glass. Northborough, Mass., 1944.
LINDSEY, B. M. *American Historical Glass*. Vermont, 1967.
MCKEARIN, G. S. and H. *American Glass*. New York, 1948.
Two Hundred Years of American Blown Glass. New York, 1962.
REVI, A. C. *American Pressed Glass and Figure Bottles*. New York, 1964.
WATKINS, L. W. *American Glass and Glassmaking*. New York, 1950.
Cambridge Glass 1818–1888. Boston, 1930.
WILSON, K. M. *New England Glass and Glassmaking*. New York and Toronto, 1972.

Paperweights

BEDFORD, J. *Paperweights*. New York, 1968.
BERGSTROM, E. H. *Old Glass Paperweights*. Chicago, 1940; London, 1947.
CLOAK, E. C. *Glass Paperweights of the Bergstrom Art Center*. New York, London, 1969.
ELVILLE, E. M. *Paperweights and Other Glass Curiosities*. Feltham, 1954.
HOLLISTER, P. *The Encyclopedia of Glass Paperweights*. London, 1970.
JOKELSON, P. *Antique French Paperweights*. Privately published, 1955.
MCCAWLEY, P. K. *Antique Glass Paperweights from France*. London, 1968.
MANHEIM, F. J. *A Garland of Weights*. New York, 1968.
MELVIN, J. S. *American Glass Paperweights and their Makers*. New York, 1967.

Museum Collections

Great Britain

LANCASHIRE: The Harris Museum and Art Gallery, Preston; The Towneley Hall Museum and Art Gallery, Burnley.

LONDON: The British Museum, The Victoria and Albert Museum.

NORTHUMBERLAND: The Laing Art Gallery and Museum, Newcastle.

SOMERSET: The Holburne of Menstrie Museum of Art, Bath.

IRELAND: Cork Public Museum; The Civic Museum, Dublin.

U.S.A.

KANSAS: The University of Kansas Museum of Art, Lawrence.

LOUISIANA: The Isaac Delgado Museum of Art, New Orleans.

NEW YORK: The Brooklyn Museum, The Metropolitan Museum of Art, New York City; The Corning Museum of Glass.

OHIO: The Cincinnati Art Museum; The Toledo Museum of Art.

VERMONT: The Bennington Museum.

WASHINGTON, D.C.: The Smithsonian Institution.

Index

Jewellery

The history of jewellery design is as much the history of techniques as of taste and fashion. The forms of fashionable or symbolic ornaments have, from the earliest times, been dictated by the special properties of the materials of the jeweller's art; the malleability and surface texture of gold and silver, the colour and shape of pearls, the natural fire and colour of precious stones, the effects obtained by polishing or carving hardstones and the many techniques of fusing colour with metal to produce enamelled decoration. The separate skills of the goldsmith, the gem-engraver, the enamellist and the lapidary or stone-cutter, have been employed in ways that have remained virtually unchanged in several thousand years, beyond the development of elaborate facet-cutting for precious stones (dating from the mid-seventeenth century) and the replacement of much hand work with machine production in very recent times.

Although ancient jewellery is very fragile, a surprisingly large amount has survived; beautiful Egyptian, Persian, Indian or Greek and Roman jewellery can still be bought by the collector. In theory it should still be possible to make a a collection of jewellery covering a period of nearly five thousand years, but in practice it is probably advisable to specialize. The jewellery of the earlier periods, notably Egyptian, Greek and Roman, mediaeval and Renaissance, was much copied—and faked—in the late eighteenth and the nineteenth centuries. Although it seems ludicrous to suggest that even a relatively inexperienced collector would be deceived by the fashionable 'Egyptian' or Etruscan jewels of the mid-nineteenth century, this certainly happened in the past, particularly with the best of the real fakes, a number of which may still be undetected.

A collection of jewellery from the period between the early eighteenth century and the first World War offers many advantages, the chief being that a reasonable number of pieces—some of no great intrinsic value—have survived in good condition, and many of these pieces are not only objects of interest for the collectors but they can be used for their original purpose, adornment.

Opposite:
Diamond and ruby necklace, English, c. 1860–70.

Jewellery
The Craft

Among the pieces of jewellery illustrated here, some are not even seventy-five years old, but owing to the late nineteenth century mania for the hand-made, the gulf which separates even those pieces from modern jewellery is almost as great as if they had been made a hundred and fifty years earlier. Until the 1880s, the spread of mass production, so constantly deplored by the Victorians, was confined to the production of the cheapest trinkets and to the completely basic tasks of rolling sheet gold, drawing wire, coiling chain and stamping or pressing ornamental and pierced links of regular size. The eighteenth century is regarded as the last age when these minor works of art were still uncontaminated by machine production, but in fact hand-finishing remained the rule even for pieces made partly by machine, for at least the next eighty years. Even today, the small amount of hand-made or hand-finished jewellery is made with tools and methods which differ very little from those used in the mid-eighteenth century, as can be seen from the illustrations in Diderot's famous *Encyclopédie* (published 1762).

The greatest alteration in the appearance of jewellery came with the development of facet-cutting for precious stones. The rose-cut and the brilliant-cut were both evolved in the seventeenth century, and by the early eighteenth century, precious stones, particularly diamonds, assumed a far greater importance in jewellery design than the gold-work or enamel which had dominated the jewels of the Middle Ages and the Renaissance.

By the end of the seventeenth century, enamel decoration of the settings of precious stones had been banished to the back; in the early eighteenth century even this was abandoned in favour of light foliate engraving which also disappeared after a few years, leaving the plain closed backs and settings cut down to reveal the greatest amount of stone; these were finally replaced over a long period of time by the open settings which were in fairly general use by 1800.

Many of these techniques of cutting and setting, which have come to be regarded as the most effective way to display the natural fire and colour of precious stones, were first used at the French Court in the mid-eighteenth century. During this period, French perfectionism and sense of style achieved a standard of design and craftsmanship which were to be the object of admiration and emulation for over a hundred and fifty years. The designs fashionable then have been revived continually; there is hardly a single decade until the end of the First War when diamond bows, stars, crescents or bouquets of flowers have not been made and worn. During this period, the complexities of brilliant-cutting were mastered and contemporary documents (i.e. inventories and jewellers' accounts) indicate that brilliant-cut stones were extensively used, but few pieces have survived. The brilliant-cut involves the greatest wastage of stone, and the high value of these stones made re-setting almost inevitable as fashion changed. Surviving mid-eighteenth century jewellery is usually made with foil-backed rose-cut stones in a closed setting, a situation which must already have existed in the nineteenth century since Victorian copies of eighteenth century styles are usually set like this.

Parallel with this development of elegant and expensive precious jewellery was the establishment of the trade in inexpensive novelties and fashionable trinkets which grew up to satisfy the demands of an expanding, and increasingly affluent middle-class public who were to influence the way in which Victorian design evolved. Middle-class taste, unhampered by the preconceived notions of taste of the hereditary aristocracy, favoured all kinds of experimental developments, including the widely deplored use of machine-processes to reproduce the laborious handcraftsmanship of the past.

With hindsight, at the distance of over half a century, one can see that too much emphasis was placed on the detrimental effects of mechanization, and too little praise lavished on the ingenuity of construction and impeccable technique of the best Victorian jewellery, virtues that may well have been taken for granted by people brought up in the tradition of eighteenth century French perfectionism.

Opposite:
Suite of jewellery consisting of a necklace, earrings and pair of bracelets in gold set with oval and round rose-cut, foiled, garnets in a closed setting; France, c. 1750-60.

English and Continental Jewellery Introduction

In Europe, after the Renaissance, the distinguishing features of regional jewellery design began to disappear, vanishing almost entirely in the nineteenth century. Although until then it remained possible to recognize the characteristic style of, say, Spanish or Portuguese work, or the Imperial Russian Court, even by the early eighteenth century the rich and powerful Court in France dictated the style of fashionable jewellery, a situation which continued almost without a break throughout the next two hundred years.

The cutting and setting of precious stones absorbed much of the creative energy of eighteenth century jewellers and, as the importance of the precious stone was increasingly emphasized, the enamelled decoration widely used for jewellery in the sixteenth and seventeenth centuries, the elaborately foliated engraving, repoussé work, the complex techniques of *quatre-couleurs* and *trois-couleurs* gold-work, inlaying of hardstones, gem-engraving and piqué work were confined almost exclusively to the decoration of boxes, vinaigrettes, *châtelaines*, cane heads and fan mounts. While these elegant little *objets de vertu* followed current artistic trends with some fidelity, jewellery design closely followed fashions in dress; indeed, many popular forms were very extravagant adaptations of fashionable accessories, originally carried out in embroidery, ribbon or braid. Currently fashionable styles used for furniture or interior decoration seem to appear first—if at all—in less valuable pieces. There is no true rococo diamond jewellery, though slightly asymmetrical, lightly-set bouquets and hair-ornaments of the 1760s are called rococo-style; there seems to be no true Chinoiserie, and neo-classicism—well established as a decorative style by the 1760s and 1770s—is hardly evident in jewellery until the turn of the century.

Precious stones and fine goldsmith's work were intended for—and enjoyed only by—the very rich; even in the eighteenth century there was a huge gulf between the grandest jewellery made for Royal or Imperial patrons and the comparatively modest commissions for affluent members of fashionable society. Though Marie-Antoinette's ear-rings by Boehmer were priced at 348,000 livres, surviving account books and inventories list diamond ear-rings at £170 (1741) and £73. 4s. 4½d. (c.1769). Even these relatively small sums were beyond any but the richest of the middle classes, so a range of inexpensive jewellery was designed.

Beautiful crystal and paste jewellery was made throughout the eighteenth century (the earliest colourless pastes seem to date from c. 1730). Towards 1800 there was a revival of interest in hardstones, either carved or engraved as cameos or intaglios, or inlaid in patterns and set in gold. Many of these were valued mainly for their geological interest. Wedgwood's Jasper cameos and Tassie's cast-glass gems, fine steel and marquisite jewellery and gold or pearl-framed enamel miniatures were fashionable in the eighties and nineties. Fine filigree, piqué, and seed-pearl work dates from early nineteenth century as does wrought or cast Berlin iron jewellery, but the quality deteriorated after about 1840, and these skills gradually died out towards the middle of the century.

The social changes caused by the Industrial Revolution prompted the mass production of cheap jewellery and greater mechanization led to indiscriminate use of half-misunderstood pattern-book designs, often pirated from the few firms who still maintained some kind of design studio. Many of the results were deplorably banal.

The 'Romantic' period, dating from the restoration of the monarchy in France until almost the mid-nineteenth century, saw the beginning of the historical revivals, perhaps the most interesting aspect of Victorian jewellery design. The aesthetic writers of the period saw these archaeological, neo-Renaissance or mediaevalized jewels as an acceptable alternative to the preoccupation with a lavish display of precious stones, supposedly characteristic of *nouveau riche* taste. Relentless criticism of fashionable jewellery by writers like Ruskin and Matthew Digby Wyatt encouraged the ideas of experimental, even semi-amateur, artist/jewellers of the late nineteenth century. Amongst much interesting, but technically unsophisticated work the French *avant-garde* designers stand out as being always rigorously professional. That the work of these artists connected with the Arts and Crafts Movement and the Art Nouveau style should ever have become acceptable to fashionable society is little short of a miracle; but the ideals of the handcraftsmen and the individual artists prevailed.

In spite of contemporary criticism and of twentieth century neglect, the elaborate Victorian diamond jewellery, the neo-classic jewellery of the Second Empire, the Renaissance-style enamelling of the seventies, and the 'Romantic' French and English Gothic jewellery as well as the bizarre and beautiful jewels of the turn of the century, have become valued and valuable collector's pieces.

Opposite:
Top: Necklace of Wedgwood blue jasper cameos showing signs of zodiac mounted in gold linked with gold chain and beads; England, 1789.
Bottom: Three bracelets in silver set with turquoises made by the Navajo Indians; the two lower bracelets date from the 1880s, the third is a modern version of the traditional design; U.S.A.

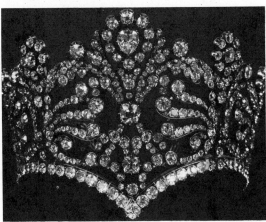

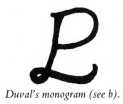

Duval's monogram (see b).

a) Front and back of a brooch, rubies and pearls set in gold, in the form of a bow, the back enamelled in a formal design of flowers and leaves; France or Holland, c. 1690.

This brooch, in the style of the French 17th century designer, Gilles Legaré, whose designs (published in 1663) were copied all over Europe, is typical of the taste of the late 17th and early 18th century. The enamelled decoration of the setting, already banished to the back, was to disappear completely in the early years of the 18th century, when the stone became a more important part of the design than the setting.

b) Brooch, diamonds set in silver, in the form of a flower spray; St. Petersburg, Russia, c. 1750–60.

Reputedly made for Catherine the Great, this brooch was probably one of a set of dress ornaments of the kind fashionable in Russia in the 18th century. Another nearly identical spray is described in the 1922 inventory of the Russian Imperial Jewellery as being close in style to the work of the Geneva-born jeweller Louis Duval, who was working in St. Petersburg from c. 1753; but the rather coarse workmanship suggests a Russian craftsman of the same period. The refining Parisian influence on Russian taste shows more clearly in the later part of the Catherine period— i.e. 1762 onwards.

c) Ear-rings, diamonds and precious stones set in silver, in a formal design of bows surrounded by leaves; Portugal, early 18th century.

Strongly influenced by French taste throughout the 18th century, both Portuguese and Spanish pieces have nonetheless an immediately recognizable style; this is characterized by formal foliate designs developed previously in the 17th century that were used almost unaltered throughout the 18th century. Many pieces incorporated a stiff bow shape, quite unlike the undulating ribbon-bows found in French and English designs of the same date—this is even true of pieces made in France for the Portuguese Royal Family.

d) Diadem, diamonds set in silver, France, c. 1800.

Once owned by the Empress Josephine, the diadem's box has her coat of arms on it. Documents prove that it dates back to at least 1800, and the characteristic Empire shape was just coming into fashion then. The recently published inventory of Josephine's possessions, from which some of her jewels have been identified, reveals that in the room next to her bedroom she kept about twenty complete parures, mostly of precious stones. Later this diadem was owned by the Empress Eugénie, much of whose jewellery was smuggled out of Paris by the Princess Metternich, when the Third Empire collapsed.

a) Shoe buckles, steel, silver and plated metal; England, 1750–1800.

Shoe buckles apparently became fashionable in England about 1660, being introduced from Europe by Charles II. They were widely worn by the end of the century in the form of large silver buckles in the Dutch style—one of the many fashions imported by the entourage of William of Orange. Popular for just over a hundred years, they were worn in every class of society, and made in every sort of material from the diamonds worn at Court to the Sheffield plate and polished steel of the working classes. The popularity of buckles, which by the 1770s and 1780s were worn on shoes,

on knee breeches, as bracelet clasps and as the centre of velvet ribbon necklaces worn choker-fashion, declined rapidly towards the end of the century. They were revived briefly in the 1860s when large 'Cromwellian' shoe buckles were worn by women, and at the end of the 19th century when shoe buckles in paste, marcasite and steel were worn in the evening. Buckle-making was one of the principal sources of employment in Birmingham in the 18th century, and when they went out of fashion many of the manufacturers turned to making the 'toys' and novelties for which Birmingham became famous in the 19th century.

b) Necklace, panels inlaid with coloured marbles in the form of butterflies, set in gold, linked by fine gold chain; Italy, c. 1810–20.

A fine example of the inlaid hardstone work, usually called 'Florentine' intarsia or mosaic, which, with Roman and Neapolitan mosaic work, was highly fashionable in the 1820s and 1830s. This was imitated in Derbyshire, England, where the background is usually the local black marble; the feldspar mines had been reopened at the end of the 18th century, and the production of ornaments continued during the first half of the 19th century, under the direction of the Duke of Devonshire. A few small pieces of jewellery were made in the form of crosses and round or oval brooches were decorated with flowers and insects.

c) Diadem, enamelled gold set with a cameo, diamonds and pearls; Italy, c. 1815.

The style of this finely-worked diadem, so unlike the Empress Josephine's (see p. 514*d*) is typical of the Italian neo-classical taste in jewellery popular throughout early 19th century Europe. Cameos were *de rigueur* for the woman of fashion (according to the *Journal des Dames*, 1805) worn in a necklace, a pair of bracelets, often on the upper arm, on a belt, and in the hair. Cameos remained fashionable, but were cut in much higher relief towards 1850 and the far more massive and elaborate settings contrast with earlier pieces made with light filigree or gold mesh chains, and delicate rope-work or beaded mounts.

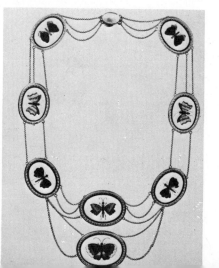

Jewellery

English and Continental

NATURALISTIC DESIGNS
CUT STEEL

AH

Hölmstrom's initials.

a) left: Brooch, diamonds set in silver, in the form of a spray of roses; France, c. 1790.

This very delicate French botanical jewellery set a standard of perfection for all the later work in this style. This technique of using pavé-set stones in a variety of sizes to create effects of light and shade in leaves and petals was developed in the late 18th century, and was used almost unaltered throughout the 19th century.

b) centre: Two brooches, diamonds set in silver in the form of a rose-spray; England, c. 1860; diamonds set in silver, in the form of a bee, England, c. 1870–80.

The romantic interest in botanical and other naturalistic forms for jewellery lasted from the end of the Empire period until the 1880s when the conscientiously realistic style gave way to the daring fantasy of *Art Nouveau* plant form.

c) right: Brooch, cabochon amethysts and diamonds set in silver and gold, in the form of the Russian Imperial Crown; made by August Wilhelm Holmström for Fabergé; St. Petersburg, Russia, c. 1890.

This beautiful little replica of Posier's crown, made for the coronation of Catherine the Great, is marked with the initials of Fabergé's chief jeweller, and with the St. Petersburg hall-mark of crossed anchors and a sceptre which puts the date before 1896. It was certainly made for a member of the Imperial family.

---

d) Tiara, cut steel set with Wedgwood jasper medallions and artificial pearls; England, early 19th century.

An unusually elaborate piece in faceted steel, the style of this tiara suggests a date around 1820. Steel jewellery, in the form of buttons, buckles, fine chain, small trinkets and sequins for sewing on dresses (c. 1780), had been made in Woodstock and Birmingham from the middle of the 18th century, when cut and polished steel was at its most fashionable and most expensive. A Birmingham pattern book dating from the 1760s illustrates a number of designs for steel jewellery, and the forms generally used follow diamond jewellery fashions fairly closely. Matthew Boulton (see p. 336b) himself the son of a buckle manufacturer, opened his Soho Manufactury in 1764, and a few years later combined with Josiah Wedgwood to produce the popular jewellery of jasper cameos set in faceted steel mounts. A fine sword-hilt of cut-steel set with Wedgwood medallions, traditionally said to have belonged to Beau Brummel, is now in the Nottingham Castle Museum. An elaborate *châtelaine* made of cut-steel was shown by a Mr Durham at the Great Exhibition in 1851, but in general, the quality of workmanship had declined after the turn of the century and steel jewellery went out of fashion long before the mid-19th century.

ФАБЕРЖЕ

Fabergé's signature in Cyrillic script (see c).

a) Filigree necklace, Berlin ironwork; probably Germany, early 19th century.

There is some evidence that cast or wrought iron jewellery was first made in Silesia in the late 18th century, and many of the early designs are close in style to the traditional filigree and wire-work jewellery worn by Silesian peasant women. The first factory in Berlin was opened in 1804, nearly ten years before the Prussian campaign against Napoleon I—1813-14—the date usually regarded as the beginning of the fashion for Berlin iron jewellery. Iron jewellery was made in Germany and France until the mid-19th century; some pieces by M. Deveranne of Berlin and Edward Schott of Ilsenburg-am-Harz were shown at the Great Exhibition in London in 1851.

---

b) Necklace with beads of piqué, tortoiseshell inlaid with gold and silver; England, early 19th century.

Piqué is made by inlaying tortoiseshell, ivory or papier mâché with points, stars, small flowers and leaves, birds, etc. in gold or silver. In the more elaborate designs the inlaid metal shapes may be engraved or chased; later pieces often have mother-of-pearl shapes incorporated into the pattern. True piqué jewellery on tortoiseshell or ivory was only made until about the 1850s and even the delicate early 19th century work is considered to be a very debased version of the 18th century piqué, which was mainly used to decorate snuff and patch boxes and étuis.

c) Brooch, gold set with scarabs; made by Castellani, Italy, c. 1870.

Fortunato Pio Castellani first began making jewellery in 1814. Between 1823 and 1827 he began the experiments in the revival of ancient techniques which eventually produced the much-copied 'Etruscan' style of decoration for gold-work. This consisted of patterns of very fine filigree and granules of gold soldered onto a gold surface which was itself textured by 'blooming' or engraving. Castellani's 'archaeological' jewellery was fashionable in France and England from the 1860s until the 1880s.

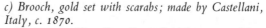

Castellani monogram (used by Fortunato Pio and his sons).

517

FROMENT MEURICE

Engraved signature used by François-Désiré Froment-Meurice and his son (see a, b).

a) Brooch, gold decorated with white enamel, set with a diamond, amethyst and emeralds; made by F. D. Froment-Meurice; France, c. 1855.

Froment-Meurice was famous for his Gothic and neo-Renaissance style jewellery. The pieces shown by him at the Great Exhibition in London, 1851, were enormously admired in England and had a considerable influence on the mediaevalizing jewellery of the mid-19th century.

b) Brooch, baroque pearl mounted in gold set with diamonds, in the form of a cuirasse and helmet; made by Emile Froment-Meurice; France, c. 1867.

Emile Froment-Meurice, son of F. D. Froment-Meurice, carried on the stylistic traditions of his father, specializing particularly in elaborate neo-Renaissance designs of which this is a typical example. He showed a number of pieces made of baroque pearls at the *Exposition Universelle* in Paris in 1867.

c) Brooch and bracelet, en suite, enamelled gold made by Carlo Giuliano, England, c. 1875.

Giuliano was born in Naples and came to England in the 1860s. He was apparently sponsored on his arrival by Robert Phillips, one of the first English jewellers to make jewellery in Castellani's 'archaeological' style, whose policy seems to have been to employ Italian craftsmen. He worked in the late sixties for Harry Emanuel (author of

Diamonds and Precious Stones, published 1860). He set up on his own in Piccadilly in about 1870. This very fine set in Giuliano's characteristic style is enamelled gold in a foliate design of almost filigree lightness. Giuliano also specialized in archaeological or 'Etruscan' style jewellery in the Castellani manner and in this work, as in the enamelled jewellery, his technical superiority is remarkable.

CG C.&A.G.

Carlo Giuliano's initials, used by him and his sons.

a) Necklace and pendant in the form of a dragon-fly, gold set with diamonds and decorated with plique a jour enamel; made by Lucien Gailliard; France, c. 1900.

Gailliard, who was originally a silversmith, was persuaded by René Lalique, his near-contemporary, to turn to jewellery-making. Around 1900, Gailliard began to employ Japanese workmen to perfect the Japanese mixed-metal and enamelling techniques, with which he had been experimenting in silver since the 1880s.

b) Necklace and pendant, silver set with moonstones, blister pearls and small precious stones; designed and made by Arthur Gaskin; England, c. 1908.

Arthur Gaskin and his wife were trained at the Birmingham School of Art, where they had both become ardent admirers of William Morris. They started making jewellery in 1899; some of their early work is in gold, but like much of the English artistic jewellery of the period, was mainly made of silver or silver-gilt and semi-precious or interestingly flawed stones in irregular shapes. For only one commission diamonds were used, causing a serious disruption in the workshop, where special precautions had to be taken.

Engraved or pricked initials of Arthur Gaskin.

c) Pendant, in the form of a ship, gold decorated with cloisonné enamel with five pendants of river pearls; England (?), c. 1910.

The use of *cloisonné* enamel for jewellery was revived in France in the 1860s by Alexis Falize, and was used for the Japanese style fashionable in the seventies and eighties. This pendant is more in the Russian or Norwegian *fin-de-siècle* taste, the enamel being used in the same way as the traditional Russian *skan* technique where some of the interstices in the pattern are left blank, but the ship motif, whether a galleon or a Viking ship, is also found in English enamel jewellery of the period, by designers like Henry Wilson, Edgar Simpson, and Nelson Dawson.

d) Pendant, in the form of a female head surrounded by sycamore leaves, gold decorated with opaque and translucent enamels; designed and made by René Lalique, France, c. 1900.

This design was repeated two or three times; one example, in the Kunstgewerbsmuseum in Berlin, was acquired in 1901, giving a good idea of the date of the piece, which is typical of Lalique's work in 1900. His reputation as the greatest designer of *Art Nouveau* jewellery has never seriously been questioned.

R. LALIQUE
LALIQUE
R.L.
Signatures and initials of René Lalique.

American Jewellery Introduction

Comparatively little jewellery was worn in the United States before the mid-nineteenth century, especially in the North. Some communities banned it altogether and others wore drab, unornamented clothes from choice. However, the Dutch settlers in New York provided a great contrast with their brightly coloured clothes and some ornamentation. A woman might own a few gold or silver pieces with diamonds, a silver chain and medallion, a silver belt or *châtelaine*, an étui, and shoe buckles; a man a gold-headed cane, signet ring and the inevitable shoe buckles. This was pitifully little compared to a moderately prosperous couple in Europe.

During the eighteenth century, England was the prevailing influence, until the War of Independence. Portraits show both the English style and the comparative absence of valuable jewellery. In Joseph Blackburn's painting, Mrs Jonathan Warner wears a simple hair ornament with a central pendant, a lace choker with a small pendant, and single-stone drop ear-rings. Mrs Ezekial Goldthwaite and Mrs Robinson both painted by John Singleton Copley in the 1770s, wear many-stranded pearl choker necklaces. Mrs Thomas Lea, painted by Gilbert Stuart in c. 1798, has a portrait miniature as a brooch; worn previously for sentimental reasons, miniatures became highly fashionable in the 1770s. News of the latest European fashions and the materials for the newest jewellery, were eagerly awaited. An advertisement in 1771 reads: 'Imported in the Neptune . . . an assortment of articles in the Goldsmith's and Jewellers Way, viz. brilliant and cypher'd Button and Earring stones of all Sorts, Locket Stones, cypher'd Ring Stones, Brilliant Ring Sparks, Buckle Stones, neat Stone Rings set in Gold, some with Diamond Sparks, Stone Buttons in Silver, by the Card, black ditto in Silver, best Sword Blades, Shoe and Knee Chapes of all sizes'.

After the Revolution, when patriotic women turned to France for inspiration, French taste became dominant; anything else was heartily despised. But by European standards, the women were still extremely modestly adorned. By the early 19th century, a number of firms were established in the principal American cities, but few relied solely on jewellery sales. The famous New York firm, Black, Starr and Frost, originally Marquand and Paulding, was founded in 1810 by Isaac Marquand, who had already owned a business in Savannah, Georgia, since 1801. The Prince of Wales bought some pearls at this 'Diamond Palace of Broadway' in 1861, but that year they still advertised 'Ball's American Camp Cooking Range and Boiler'.

Charles Lewis Tiffany opened a fancy goods store in New York in 1837. He imported Parisian jewellery from 1841, but stocked glass, porcelain, clocks, cutlery and the original bric-à-brac and stationery, only concentrating on silverware and jewellery after the 1850s.

Significantly, the United States' exhibit at London's Great Exhibition of 1851 contained no jewellery, although there were thirteen displays of artificial teeth. The following is from the introduction to the American Section in the Official Catalogue: 'The absence . . . of those vast accumulations of wealth which favour the expenditure of large sums on articles of mere luxury . . . impart to American industry a character distinct from that of many other countries. The expenditure of months or years of labour upon a single article . . . (an object of *virtu*) is not common in the United States. On the contrary, both manual and mechanical labour are applied . . . to increasing the number or the quantity of articles to the wants of the whole people, . . .'.

Nonetheless, an enormous change was to take place in American society. The 'Victorian bible of the parlour', *Godey's Lady's Book and Magazine* (first issued 1837), in February 1857 printed its first article on jewellery, recommending the currently fashionable French style. Louis Godey sent artists to Paris to collect material for the fashion plates and possibly for the jewellery designs. Godey's editor, Sara Josepha Hale wanted to concentrate on improving the servile position of married women, but in spite of much serious material, it is best remembered as an excellent fashion guide. Its wide circulation enabled women to follow the latest styles. By 1872, James McCabe Jr. was writing: 'Extravagance is the besetting sin of New York society. Money is absolutely thrown away. Fortunes are spent every year in dress and all sorts of follies . . .'.

By this date wealthy American businessmen had largely replaced the impoverished European aristocracy as the most important customers of the great jewellery houses in Paris, Boucheron, Cartier and Van Cleef and Arpels all opened branches in New York for their new clientele, but by 1900 jewellery designed and made by Louis Comfort Tiffany was being sold at the shop *L'Art Nouveau*, opened by Samuel Bing in 1895. In just over a century the wheel had come a full circle.

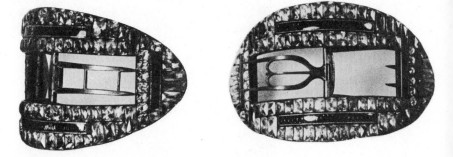

a) Miniature, oil on ivory with seed-pearls, mother-of-pearl, hair mounted in gold, oval portrait of Catherine Clinton Taylor Van Cortlandt; by John Ramage; New York City (1791-1794), c. 1748-1802.

This mourning jewel is in the neo-classical style fashionable in England from the 1770s. The miniature shows Catherine Clinton, who later became the first wife of Pierre Van Cortlandt II, mourning the death, in 1791, of Captain John Taylor of the British army, to whom she had been clandestinely married. The English influence lingered on in America in spite of the War of Independence on account of the Napoleonic Wars in France.

b) Shoe buckles, blue and colourless pastes set in silver; probably originating in England, c. 1790.

This pair of buckles may have been the property of Pierre Van Cortlandt I (1721-1814). It is apparent from 18th century advertisements and inventories of ship cargoes that small pieces of personal jewellery like knee and shoe buckles were imported ready-made from England (see the 'Shoe and Knee Chapes of all sizes' mentioned in the advertisement, p. 520). The earliest colourless paste jewellery dates from the 1730s; though it was not intended solely as an imitation of diamond jewellery, the styles used are similar to currently fashionable diamond pieces.

c) Print of a brooch, in the form of a feather in diamonds, by Tiffany, New York, 1877.

The feather brooch, a revival of an 18th century form, was popular in Paris in the sixties and seventies. This brooch by Tiffany is very much in the Boucheron style, and must have stood up well to the inevitable comparisons which were possible at this exhibition where Boucheron—probably one of the best known French firms in the United States with a number of important and wealthy American customers—also showed jewellery. Tiffany's sold jewellery made by Boucheron in their shop in New York.

d) Print of pendant, amethyst set in gold decorated with enamel surrounded by a border of leaves in wrought gold, with berries of pearls; 'Godey's Lady's Book and Magazine', February, 1857, p. 163.

This pendant, which is very Parisian in taste, has the 'waterfall' or *pampilles* setting, which with the similar articulated gold fringe decoration became very fashionable at the end of the forties. The jewellery designs for Godey's magazine appear to have come from French sources, like the fashions and accessories, such as lace and embroidery designs. Whether these designs came directly from Paris as Godey claimed, or from contemporary French fashion magazines, as the slight time lag in fashion suggests, it is difficult to say.

a) Angelica van Buren, painted in 1842, by Henry Inman; The White House, Washington, D.C.

Mrs van Buren, who acted as hostess for her father-in-law, Martin van Buren, the eighth president, was married in 1838 after which she went to Europe on a 'Grand Tour'. She was in England at the time of Queen Victoria's coronation which she attended, an event which deeply impressed her. Her style of dress is based very much on that of the young Queen, quite an unusual taste in America at this date when Parisian fashion was so much more admired than English.

b) Demi-parure, consisting of a brooch and a pair of ear-rings, in jet and gold; c. 1870–80.

Jet was used for mourning jewellery from about 1820–30 until the end of the 19th century. It was the only material permitted for jewellery to be worn with crepe, the dead black material worn during the deepest periods of mourning. In the later stages, and with half-mourning, it was often combined with gold or pearls. In spite of its melancholy associations, jet became fashionable in the sixties and seventies and was extensively used for trimming and embroidering the elaborate dresses of the period.

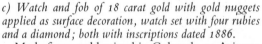

c) Watch and fob of 18 carat gold with gold nuggets applied as surface decoration, watch set with four rubies and a diamond; both with inscriptions dated 1886.

Made from gold mined in Colorado or Arizona by Anson W. Callen who served as a guide to expeditions going to Colorado and Arizona in search of gold. The watch is inscribed inside the case 'A.W. Callen to his daughter E.E. Callen on the 16th Anniversary of her birth April 19th, 1886'. The fob, consisting of 18 heavy links and a swivel, is engraved on the back, 'J.B. Callen on the 27th Anniversary of his Birth with love from his father *Old Grizzly* Junction City, Kansas, September 22, 1886'.

d) Watch and brooch pin, gold set with diamonds in the form of a coiled snake, made by Tiffany and Co.; c. 1890.

Charles Lewis Tiffany (1812–1902) opened his first shop in New York, selling fancy goods and stationery, in 1837. From 1841 he imported and sold Parisian jewellery, then in about 1848, having profited by the political unrest in Europe which enabled him to acquire a stock of diamonds at a very low price, he began manufacturing jewellery on his own account. By the mid-seventies C. L. Tiffany's was the most famous jewellery store in the United States with the largest single collection of gems in the world.

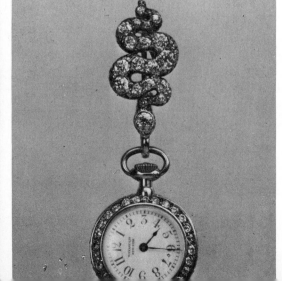

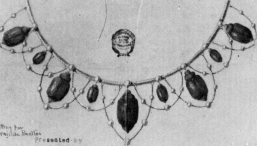

a) *Design for a necklace in the Etruscan style, set with Brazilian beetles; anonymous; c. 1900.*

L. C. Tiffany made two necklaces in the same archaeological style, with beetles set in the same manner as the scarab-set jewellery fashionable in the mid-19th century. One was set with real beetles, the other with the Favrile glass beetles which he made and sold for use in jewellery (see p. 479a for Tiffany glass).

b) *Design for a necklace by Charles Boleschka (1857-1939); c. 1700-10.*

This design for a necklace set with faceted stones in swags of chains with pearls and a pendant drop-shaped pearl is in a modified *Art Nouveau* style, closer really to Liberty's than the bolder and richer French and Belgian designs of the period. Compare with the design for the necklace set with beetles. (see p. 523a).

TIFFANY & CO
550 BROADWAY

Impressed mark of Tiffany & Co.

c) *Brooch, gold set with a sapphire, emeralds and pearls with a drop shaped emerald pendant, designed and made by Florence Koehler (1861-1944), c. 1910.*

Florence Koehler was a leading designer and craftswoman in the American craft revival movement, who lived and worked in Chicago. The Arts and Crafts movement in the United States had been growing in influence throughout the eighties and nineties and both the Boston and Chicago Arts and Crafts societies were formed in 1897. Craft work and hand-made jewellery were much admired in intellectual circles after the turn of the century and were in great contrast, both in design and material, to the vast quantity of mass-produced metalwork which had been flooding the market in America since the 1870s.

d) *Necklace, Alexandrite topazes, other semi-precious stones and gold; designed by Louis C. Tiffany, hand-made by Tiffany & Co., c. 1914.*

Tiffany Studios started making metalwork and jewellery in 1900, and L. C. Tiffany established a separate artistic jewellery department when he became vice-president of Tiffany and Company at the time of his father's death in 1902. Tiffany's work, with its combination of English and Continental *Art Nouveau* ideas, as well as an extra dimension of originality in the use of curiously-shaped semi-precious stones, and the rich palette of rather Egyptian or Byzantine colours characteristic of American *Art Nouveau* taste, bears comparison with that of any of the great jewellery designers of the turn of the century.

Jewellery Glossary

BAGUETTE: Small rectangular-cut stone.

BATON: Stone similar to, but larger than a baguette.

BRILLIANT: Now the most widely used cut: the perfect brilliant has 58 facets, 33 above the girdle, 25 below.

BRIOLETTE: Oval or drop-shaped stone faceted all over, often pierced at the top to hang as a pendant.

CABOCHON: Dome-shaped cut, much used in 19th century antique revival jewellery.

CAMEO: Gem or shell cut in relief; treated banded stones are used for two-colour profile cameos.

CARBUNCLE: Garnet cut *en cabochon*.

CHASING: See p. 678.

COLOURED GOLD: See p. 71 (*quatrecouleur*).

ENGRAVING: See p. 678.

ENGINE TURNING: Chasing or engraving with a machine, introduced c. 1750. Translucent enamel over engine-turned decoration is called *tour-à-guillocher*, a technique used by Fabergé in much of his work.

GRANULATION: Technique of decorating the surface of a jewel with thousands of minute grains of gold in patterns.

INTAGLIO: Engraving on a gem-stone; reverse of 'cameo'.

MARQUISE: A pointed oval shape, fashionable for rings, brooches, etc., at the end of the 18th century.

PAVE-SETTING: Method of covering the surface of the jewel in a 'paving' of stones, which are held in place by minute grains of metal.

PENDOLOQUE: Drop-shaped stone very like the 'briolette', but cut with a table on the upper surface.

PINCHBECK: Alloy of zinc and copper used to imitate gold, invented in the early 18th century by the clockmaker, Christopher Pinchbeck.

PIQUE: See p. 71.

REPOUSSE: See p. 541.

ROSE-CUTTING: The stone has a flat base and the upper surface is faceted, all over, rising to a point in the centre. This method pre-dates brilliant-cutting. The earliest record of facet-cutting, c. 1640, is of cutting with 16 surfaces which was increased to 24 facets (called a Dutch Rose), then to 36 (Rose Recoupée).

STRASS: Name given to fine glass-paste, after the 18th century French jeweller Georges Frédéric Stras (b. 1701).

Fakes and Forgeries

As with most collectable antiques, a number of pieces now classified as fakes actually started life as perfectly respectable reproductions of earlier pieces, and were only sold as antiquities at some later time, but in the late eighteenth and nineteenth centuries a number of pieces of jewellery were made in imitation of ancient Egyptian, Greek, Roman and Etruscan jewellery, some of which were certainly deliberate (and excellent) fakes. Later, with 'Gothic' and neo-Renaissance jewellery these archaeological pieces became fashionable, a large number were made and some may well have found their way into contemporary collections of antique jewellery. Now as their value as genuine nineteenth century pieces certainly equals or exceeds that of rather suspect classical or mediaeval pieces, the temptation to sell pieces made by the Castellanis, Melillo, Giuliano or the mediaevalizing designers as anything but their own work has greatly diminished.

The danger with jewellery of the period covered here is not so much of buying a fake (though there are innumerable copies of eighteenth century pieces which get wrongly dated, these are generally recognizable from the cutting of the stones or the workmanship), but that the stones may not be genuine. The best of the faked stones are really hard to detect (see *Diamonds are for Glamour*, by Bevis Hillier, The Times Review (London), Saturday, 8th July, 1972), unless the stone is removed from its setting. As well as the ingenious 'doublets' and 'triplets' (i.e. a paste or other colourless stone covered by, or sandwiched between, layers of real stones) other substitutes for precious stones include colourless zircons, rock-crystal—the Portuguese jewellery made with the beautiful *minas novas* crystals is truly deceptive—and pastes; amethyst-coloured paste is particularly good and was widely used. The 'off the cuff' tests for hardness and coldness seem to be completely unreliable; even the classic 'black spot' test for pastes has been discredited since a number of eighteenth century stones, which have been tested and found to be genuine, show the black spot on the point below the girdle which was once regarded as an infallible indication that the stones were paste.

Hardly any of the substitutes like pastes, imitation pearls or pinchbeck were used for making fakes; in the eighteenth century and more rarely, in the nineteenth, imitation stones were even used mixed with real stones if the design required a colour that was not available, but since the price of jewellery depends so much on the value of the materials, it is only reasonable to ensure that they are genuine. The greatest safeguard against buying something that is worth only a quarter of its price is to go to a reputable and highly expert dealer.

Repairs and Maintenance

For superficial dirt only, pure soap and warm water is the best cleaning material for antique jewellery, with the exception of any pieces with foil-backed stones, and Berlin iron jewellery. Use a worn toothbrush to get into the crevices and cracks—a shaving brush is a little too soft, and a new toothbrush too hard.

Silver jewellery may be cleaned with silver polish, but it should never be immersed in one of the new solvents; this will give the piece a bright colour quite out of character with antique examples.

Never attempt to remove embedded dirt or repair a damaged piece; take it to a well-qualified professional.

Further Reading

D'ALLEMAGNE, H. R. *Les accessoires du costume et du mobilier depuis le XIII jusqu'au XIX siècle.* Paris, 1928.
BRADFORD, E. D. S. *English Victorian Jewellery.* London, 1959.
CLIFFORD, A. *Cut-steel and Berlin Iron Jewellery.* Bath, 1971.
CLIFFORD-SMITH, H. *Jewellery.* London, 1908.
CURRAN, M. *Collecting Antique Jewelry.* New York.
EVANS, J. *History of Jewellery, 1100-1870,* revised edition, London, 1971.
FLOWER, M. *Victorian Jewellery,* revised ed. London, 1967.
FREGNAC, C. *Jewellery, from the Renaissance to Art Nouveau.* London, 1965.
GERLACH, M. (ed.). *Primitive and Folk Jewellery.* New York, 1970.

HUGHES, G. *Jewellery.* London, 1966.
LEWIS, M. D. S. *Antique Paste Jewellery.* London, 1970.
MCCLELLAN, E. *Historic Dress in America 1607-1800.* Philadelphia, 1904.
Historic Dress in America, 1800-1870. Philadelphia, 1910.
RAINWATER, D. T. *American Silver Manufacturers, Their Marks, Trademarks and History.* Hanover, Pa., 1966.
SAVAGE, G. *Forgeries, Fakes and Reproductions, a handbook for the collector.* London, 1963.
STEINGRABER, E. *Antique Jewellery, its history in Europe from 800-1900.* Munich, 1956; London, 1957.
VEVER, H. *La Bijouterie Francaise au XIXième Siècle,* 3 vols., Paris, 1906-1908.

Museum Collections

Great Britain

DURHAM: The Bowes Museum, Barnard Castle.
LANCASHIRE: Liverpool City Museum.
LONDON: The British Museum; The Geological Museum; Goldsmiths' Hall; The London Museum; The Victoria and Albert Museum.

U.S.A.

MARYLAND: Historical Society, Baltimore.
NEW YORK: The Cooper-Hewitt Museum of Design; The Metropolitan Museum of Art.
PENNSYLVANIA: The Philadelphia Museum of Art.
WASHINGTON, D.C.: The Smithsonian Institution.

Index

Metalwork

Metalworking is among the oldest crafts, and basically some of its techniques have remained unaltered since biblical times. Despite refinements introduced over the centuries, if it were possible to resurrect a metalworker from 3000 years ago and put him in a workshop, he could with little adjustment begin work at once.

But this continuity of method has in no way restricted the proliferation of applications or the development of design. There are, on the one hand, tiny artefacts like finger-rings and snuffboxes, and, on the other, large architectural works like choir-screens, gates and aqueducts, with every passing phase of fashion reflected in their designs.

Apart from objects of pure metalwork, metals have sometimes been used in conjunction with other materials. Iron has been used for decorating and strengthening wooden doors; iron and brass have provided decoration for much furniture (such as brass inlay in boulle cabinet-work), in addition to providing such working parts and details as hinges, handles, locks and escutcheons. These embellishments can provide a reliable guide for dating a piece.

It is difficult to think of any artefact that has not at some time, or in some way, been affected by metalworking. In the old metalworkers' legends, much emphasis was placed on the way in which other trades relied on their products—the carpenter for his tools, the tailor for his scissors, the butcher for his knives. Indeed our lives would be very different without metals.

Other human activities also have been much affected by metalwork: architecture would be unimaginable without ironwork; the home would be unimaginable without at least a few utensils in brass or copper, and without metalworking there would be no coins or medals, no jewellery, no machinery, nor many other objects in long-familiar forms.

Opposite:
Wrought-iron garden arbour, 'the birdcage', Melbourne Hall, Derby, England.

Metalwork
The Craft

There are four main divisions in the shaping of metal, each subdivided into various processes, and all of which are sometimes used on the same object. They are forging, bench-work, casting and sheet-metalwork.

Forging is generally restricted to ironworking, although it is on rare occasions used on copper. It is the shaping of heated metal by hammering. Forging is particularly suitable for shaping wrought iron, as the heating and hammering help to consolidate the laminae of its fibrous structure. It is never used on brass, which disintegrates if heated and hammered. The main forging processes are drawing-out, jumping-up or upsetting, perforating, welding, bending and twisting.

In drawing-out, a bar of heated metal is lengthened and its shape modified by hammering. In jumping-up or upsetting, the heated bar is shortened and its shape modified by hammering. Drawing-out produces such things as knobs and swellings. Perforations are made by hammering a punch or drift through the heated metal; they are never, in pure forged work, made by drilling. In welding, two pieces of metal are upset on their ends to form interlocking knobs (this process is known as scarfing), heated to the point of fusion, and vigorously hammered into one piece. (Apart from welding, the metal may be joined together by rivets, collars, pins, screws or bolts.) Bending and twisting are self-explanatory: the bar of metal is heated and bent or twisted into the required shape by hammering or wrenching, sometimes using a form. The scroll, the most ubiquitous motif in architectural ironwork, is made in this way.

In bench-work, sometimes called locksmithery, as it is used in making locks and keys, the metal is worked cold by filing, chiselling or drilling. It gives sharper detail than forging. Forging and locksmithery are often used on the same piece, as on the gates of the chapels of Bishop Alcock and Bishop West in Ely Cathedral. But generally locksmithery appears to best advantage on small work.

In casting, the metal is melted and poured into a mould, which may be a simple depression in the foundry floor, or an elaborately-made sand mould in a box or, in large work, one reinforced with clay or firebricks. Usually a wooden pattern is required and if the casting is to be hollow, a second pattern, the shape of the interior of the casting, is needed for making a core. In a simple casting, the pattern is placed in a covered box, sand is rammed around it and after it has been removed, two holes are made from the top of the mould to the cavity: the sprue, for introducing the molten metal, and the riser, to allow the displaced air to escape, and to show when the mould is full, the rising metal in it giving it its name.

There are many variations and refinements of casting; such is the intricate 'lost wax' process by which statuary and other complicated shapes are cast.

In sheet-metalwork a development is first made of the shape of the object required; that is to say, it is reduced geometrically to a plane area, which is marked on the surface of the metal to be used. This is cut out and hammered, rolled, pressed or drawn into three-dimensional form. Joints are made by riveting, soldering or brazing.

The surface of sheet-metal may be decorated by etching, engraving, chasing, perforation or by raised patterns hammered into its surface. One of the most important forms of raised decoration is repoussé, in which the most refined shapes are made by hammering and punching the underside of the metal. Repoussé was much used in the eighteenth century in decorating ironwork, when leaves, masks, flowers, swags, heraldic devices and cloths of estate were used to embellish structure of forged work. The greatest master of repoussé in iron was the Frenchman Jean Tijou (see p. 531b).

British Metalwork Introduction

Metalworking has been practised in England since pre-historic times; it flourished during the Roman occupation and during Anglo-Saxon times. But, coinage apart, examples from such early periods are of great rarity.

Mediaeval metalwork is nearly as rare, but there is a certain amount in museums and some of it, especially locksmithery, occasionally comes on to the market. Until the fifteenth century, copper was the most plentiful metal especially in its alloys of brass and bronze and their sub-divisions, particularly latten (flat, or plate brass), dinanderie (cast or beaten brass), and bell metal (used for casting bells). Latten was the alloy used in memorial brasses and much church plate.

Early English mediaeval ironwork is usually pure forged work. It was much used in the great meandering scrolled hinges on church doors that served not only as pivots, but also to strengthen the doors and to hold their planks together. Some work, like the late thirteenth century lattice grille before the tomb of Humphry, Duke of Gloucester, in St. Albans Cathedral, show oriental influence, perhaps brought back from the Crusades.

The thirteenth century saw a great upsurge in brilliant locksmithery, which did not lose its impetus until Jacobean times. This too, may have been influenced by work seen by Crusaders in Asia Minor. Such work reached its culmination in the late fifteenth century Gothic gates and screen in St. George's Chapel, Windsor, by Master John Tresilian, a vast work 11′ 6″ (3.51 m.) wide by 9′ 0″ (2.74 m.) high, made from tiny sculptured components.

While such brilliant work was being made, the technique of casting was being developed, especially in the Weald of Kent, where iron grave-slabs, fire-backs, fire-dogs, ordnance and, later, hollow-ware were cast. Simultaneously, small household artefacts were made in many parts of the country. Thus, in several ways, a firm foundation was laid for the later expansion of the metalworking industry.

The next big development occurred at the end of the seventeenth century when the French smith, Jean Tijou, came to England. He worked under Wren at St Paul's Cathedral, where his ironwork is still in place. He employed many assistant smiths, and these in time formed the core of English blacksmithery in its golden age, during the first half of the 18th century. Among these smiths was Thomas Robinson, maker of the screen at New College, Oxford. (See p. 532a).

The eighteenth century witnessed the first architectural use in England of cast iron; for example on the railings around St Paul's Cathedral (1710-1714) and the Senate House, Cambridge (c. 1730). In little more than a century its use became widespread, for in the nineteenth century everything imaginable was made of it, ranging from the Crystal Palace and bandstands, down to tea-pots and money-boxes.

During the whole of this time, smaller items of brass and copper were made, some of them purely utilitarian, but many highly decorative, and reflecting the styles of the times in which they were made—sheet metal warming pans and chestnut-roasters, with repoussé or pierced decoration, and sometimes wrought iron handles; brass candlesticks conceived with the refinement of silver; brass chandeliers showing the influence of Dutch fashions introduced by William and Mary. Many similar things were made in wrought and cast iron.

Design in the nineteenth century, in both domestic and architectural metalwork, was less consistent than hitherto, for there was a romantic yearning for every kind of exotic and historical escapism. Mediaeval influence was particularly evident on architectural wrought ironwork, as in that on the Law Courts in the Strand. But cast iron, which could with ease be laden with all kinds of decoration, showed every twist and turn of this escapism, so that it was no uncommon thing for an object to be made with a decorative mixture of baroque, rococo, gothic and classical styles. Nevertheless, much of it had charm and a certain grandeur of conception, sadly missing from much disciplined design.

Metalwork

British

a) Cast iron fire-back; 15th century; wdth. 36″ (91.4 cm.), ht. 21″ (53.3 cm.).

Fire-backs protected brick or stonework, and radiated the fire's heat. This primitive type was moulded in the sand floor of the foundry; swords and rope were pressed into the surface for decoration. The melted iron, drawn off into a crucible, was poured into the mould via small channels. Simple fire-backs are not necessarily the earliest; they were sometimes made by later foundrymen who had no elaborate moulds.

b) Cast iron fire-dogs; 16th century; ht. 44″ (111.8 cm.).

Fire-dogs (andirons, brand irons, or cob irons) were made in both cast and wrought iron from the mid-16th century onwards. The horizontal billet bar supported the logs; the decorated front upright, or stauke, prevented the logs from falling into the room. Later ones were more elaborate, in brass, bronze, and even silver.

---

c) Copper curfew, 17th century; ht. 21″ (53.3 cm.).

The curfew (French *couvre-feu*, fire cover) was used from the Middle Ages until the 19th century to cover the fire overnight, so that it continued to burn without wasting fuel. Shaped like a half-dome, it was pushed against the fireplace's back wall, over the embers; when removed in the morning, the fire should have been glowing sufficiently to make a fresh start, after adding fuel. Curfews, usually of beaten sheet brass or copper, were often decorated with repoussé, as here.

d) Brass lectern; Church of Wiggenhall, St. Mary the Virgin, Norfolk, 1518.

Lecterns are among the most notable examples of early brasswork. They were usually made by a combination of casting and bench-work. Their most characteristic feature is the great eagle with spread wings on which the Bible is placed—probably a representation of the emblem of St John the Evangelist. They are often inscribed and this

one exhorts the reader, in Latin, to pray for the soul of Brother Robert Barnard of Walsingham. Lecterns were made by the same craftsmen who made monumental brasses and effigies and who would also have made such utensils as ewers, jugs and cauldrons.

e) Brass candlestick; 16th century; ht. 13½″ (34.3 cm.).

There are hundreds of shapes, sizes and patterns of brass candlesticks, and every branch of metal-working technique was used in making them; the one illustrated was cast. They became popular at the time of the Restoration and, particularly during the reign of William and Mary, were much influenced by Dutch designs. Some are fitted with a slide and button to adjust the position of the candle as it burns away; some are fitted with glass shades and some with snuffers. Others imitate patterns used for silver candlesticks. Cast, engraved and perforated decorations are all known. Modern reproductions are common.

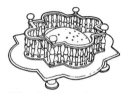

a) Copper warming pan; 17th century; lgth. (handle) 36½" (92.7 cm.).

Warming pans are usually made of copper, but brass ones are not unknown and Samuel Pepys, in 1669, recorded one of silver. They were much used from Tudor times onwards; the earliest specimens often have wrought iron handles and are frequently inscribed with a motto or rhyme. The pan itself is made of sheet metal. Filled with hot embers or cinders, it was used to iron the bed either under the sheets, or with the sheets turned back. Similar in form, but smaller, were chestnut roasters, although these almost invariably had metal handles. Sometimes, however, chestnuts were roasted in warming pans.

b) A panel from the Fountain Screen at Hampton Court Palace, by Jean Tijou, c. 1700.

Jean Tijou was one of the world's supreme smiths, and the Fountain Screen is his masterpiece. Its basic structure of forged ironwork is remarkable, but more impressive is its magnificent repoussé work, a difficult technique in any metal, but especially so in iron. Yet Tijou has succeeded in giving three-dimensional form to the foliage, birds, heraldic devices, and above all the masks. Little is known of him personally but there are records of his activities in the building accounts of St Paul's Cathedral, and he published in 1693 *A New Booke of Drawings* for ironwork.

Wrought and cast iron brazier, made in 1702 and still in Trinity College, Cambridge.

---

c) Brass chandelier in the nave of St. Helen's Church, Abingdon, Berkshire, 1710.

Brass chandeliers are almost always English or Dutch; the latter are commoner, as in Holland they were used both in public buildings and private houses, whereas in England they were used mainly in public buildings, particularly churches. Normally these chandeliers had a bulbous centrepiece with scrolled arms radiating from it. In this example, the dove finial (a representation of the Holy Ghost) will be noted; it was the most usual, but among others were winged cherubs and flame tufts. Decorative motifs, of which there are many different kinds, were often used to fill in any spaces between the arms.

d) Latten and steel rim lock with key and matching hinges; early 18th century.

This group, signed *Johannes Wilkes de Birmingham Fecit*, illustrates the refinement to which locksmithery could be taken. The decorated parts are made of engraved and pierced latten riveted to blue steel plates and the effect of the colouring, which is obtained by heating the steel on sand, is brilliant. The detailing is exquisite, and the pair of unusual daffodils in the centre of the lock are especially attractive. John Wilkes of Birmingham was a well-known locksmith, noted for fine work of this kind. He also invented a detector lock that recorded the number of times a door had been opened.

a) Wrought iron gate and screen at New College, Oxford, by Thomas Robinson; 1711.

This, among the finest wrought ironwork in England, was made by 'that ingenious Artist, *Mr. Thos. Robinson* at Hide-Park Corner', as the historian John Ayliffe described him in 1714. Robinson worked at St. Paul's Cathedral, 1697–1715, where he came under Tijou's influence. His work there must have been intermittent, for the New College work was erected in 1711. In his own work, as here, Robinson transformed Tijou's continental magnificence into something restrained and essentially English with the emphasis on splendid scrollwork, rather than on repoussé. The transom panel is one of the happiest examples of scroll infilling extant.

b) Wrought iron lantern frame and cast iron railings at the Senate House, Cambridge, by Thomas Goff, c. 1730.

The railings on James Gibbs's Senate House were made about 1730 by the founder, Thomas Goff. The cast iron balusters alternate with slender wrought iron uprights; the frame and leaves of the lantern frame are also wrought iron. The standards are placed at regular intervals, and they act also as gate piers. The alternation of wrought and cast iron cleverly prevents a feeling of heaviness, such as would be given by cast iron alone. The bronze and copper lantern is modern. Gibbs had used this type of railing around the church of St. Martin-in-the-Fields, London (1710–1714).

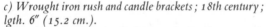

c) Wrought iron rush and candle brackets; 18th century; lgth. 6″ (15.2 cm.).

Rushlights, first used during the 17th century, were tapers made by dipping rushes in fat. They gave a feeble light, but were much used by poor people after the Candle Tax was introduced in 1709; they continued in use even after it was repealed in 1831. William Cobbett gave instructions for making them in *Cottage Economy* (1822). The holders, usually made by jobbing blacksmiths, had loose plier-like jaws, in which the taper was moved along as it burned. The handle was weighted to make the jaws grip firmly—in this case by a candlestick—giving the holder a dual purpose.

d) Wrought iron chimney cranes; 18th century.

Chimney cranes or gantries (called sways in Scotland) were used for lifting heavy stew-pans and cauldrons. Some, especially early examples, are simple pivoted brackets with chains. Others, like these three specimens, are elaborately decorated with scrolls and leaves. Specimens in cold-worked iron exist, but are scarcer. They are operated by a fulcrum which is hooked behind knobs giving various vertical positions. Pots were often suspended from these cranes by pot hooks, also variously known as jib hooks, cotralls, hangers or tramells. Another type of crane allowed a kettle to be tilted without removing it from the fire.

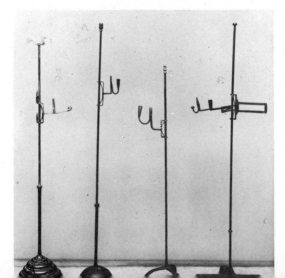

a) The white gates and part of the screen, Leeswood Hall, Mold, Flintshire, by Robert Davies of Croes Foel, Bersham, Wales, c. 1739; lgth. 100' (30.5 m.), ht. 17' (5.18 m.).

The huge work shows considerable continental influence. The broken pediments, the short moulded balusters in the overthrow, much of the detailing of the scrollwork and interlacing panels, and the vases of flowers on the piers, combine to give an effect of rococo typical of much contemporary continental work, particularly in Germany. The Welsh smith, Robert Davies, made work which was installed over a wide area. Among it are gates at Chirk Castle, at Newnham Paddox in Leicestershire and at Wrexham Parish Church.

b) Wrought iron inn sign; 18th century.

This sign belonged to the Fox Inn, Huntingdon. It is a successful though unsophisticated exploitation of the possibilities of scrollwork by an unknown country blacksmith. Even the division between red and white on the fox's pelt seems to be suggested by the double scroll in its body, and the problem of showing its ears, eye and brush has been overcome brilliantly. Doubtless, it was cheap —even today it would not be very expensive to make—illustrating the charm that so often belongs to simple ironwork, made in village smithies between shoeing horses and repairing agricultural implements.

c) Brass tobacco stoppers; 18th century.

Cast brass and bronze tobacco stoppers of many different designs were made during the 17th and 18th centuries, and in smaller numbers during the first half of the 19th century; some are still made, either as fakes or souvenirs. They were used to push down and consolidate the burning tobacco in a pipe. Although brass and bronze ones are commonest, they were also made in silver, lead and pewter. Other smokers' utensils, sometimes made of brass, include tobacco and pipe-boxes, spill stands and pipe-tongs (for holding a cinder to light the pipe). 'Churchwarden' pipes were occasionally cast in brass.

Metalwork

British

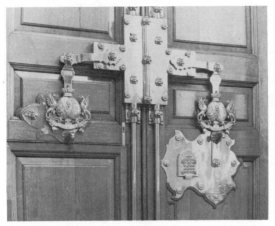

b) Cast iron wall grille or clairvoyée at Portmeirion, Merionethshire; 19th century.

A delightful example of cast iron decoration, this combination of mermaid, tridents, shells and dolphins is one of a group of grilles taken from the Old Seamen's Home, Liverpool, now at Portmeirion. Cast iron was for long popular as a decorative medium at the seaside, being more resistant than any other metal to the effect of salt water. So, at many seaside resorts, especially Brighton, splendid examples of architectural cast ironwork may still be seen—bandstands, piers, shelters, railings and shop fronts. In Brighton Pavilion there are stanchions in the shape of cast iron palm trees with sheet-metal leaves.

a) Brass lock at Blenheim Palace; c. 1780.

This magnificent and complicated system of lock and bolts must be one of the finest in England. It combines successfully the crafts of the locksmith and the foundryman, and uses a utilitarian security device as a vehicle for demonstrating pomp and estate. The inscription reads 'C. Smith & Son 25 Gt. Charles St. Birmingham, Inventors and Makers Locksmith, Bellhangers Whitesmiths &c&c'. The lock was copied from one of the gates of Warsaw, for the 4th Duke of Marlborough by permission of the King of Poland.

c) Cast iron London coal plate, 19th century.

Coal plates—pavement covers of coal chutes in the cellars of old houses—are still quite common, but it is nevertheless only a matter of time before they disappear entirely. Their heyday was the 1860s and at that time their design proliferated into hundreds of patterns, embracing everything from Gothic to Japanese. Some are ugly, some delicately beautiful, like magnified snow crystals or engine-turning; some are inlaid with brass or glass. But the most attractive have functional non-slip patterns. One of the best ways to collect them is to take rubbings, like those taken from church brasses.

d) Cast iron door-stop in the form of a hound, c. 1810.

It is not known when cast iron door-stops or door porters were first made, but this specimen must have been one of the earliest. Their subjects varied enormously, and included Punch, Judy, Highlanders, Wellington, horses, Aesop's fables, dogs, woodmen, rabbits, fox masks, horseshoes, and very many more. They are made in bas-relief, with flat backs so that they stand firmly against the door. Sometimes, at the base, there is a little lip to push under the door, so that the stop does not fall over. Bronze and brass specimens are known, but are more unusual.

a) Horse-brasses; 19th century.

Horse-brasses were used for decorating harness from the middle of the 18th century; they are still being made, as fakes, souvenirs and curiosities. The earliest form was the 'sun-flash', a polished dome which sparkled in the sun's rays. It was the usual type until about 1800, after which many others appeared. By the 1860s the designs were legion, varying from simple abstract discs to portraits of soldiers and politicians. Several grades of brass were used, and methods of manufacture included casting, stamping and finishing by bench-work. Specimens made before 1860 are uncommon; really early examples are rare.

b) Brass powder folders; 19th century.

These are typical of the elegant small tools and machines made of brass during the 19th century. Powder folders were used by chemists to make neat wrappings around powders, which were much prescribed in those days. The paper containing the powder was folded by hand, and then, to sharpen the folds, it was passed through the two plates or tongues; these were sometimes adjustable, sometimes in fixed positions, and sometimes there was only one of them. They were made by a combination of casting and bench-work. During the 19th century, brass was also used for making chemists' scales and weights.

c) Copper jelly mould; 19th century; lgth. 8" (20.3 cm.); wdth. 4⅝" (11.7 cm.); dpth. 5⅝" (14.3 cm.).

Jelly moulds of various materials have been in use at least since the Middle Ages. They have been made in beaten and raised copper since the early 19th century. Because of the risk of poisoning from verdigris, they were tinned inside, and the tinning was sometimes burnished, because a rough surface would have hindered the clean ejection of the jelly. The sizes and shapes vary enormously from tiny containers for aspic delicacies, to large spired designs for fruit jellies, charlottes russes, and rings for cakes. The lion design illustrated is unusual: abstract patterns were more popular.

Money box, English, c. 1875—good specimen of 'folk art' as it was originally a lock.

a) Cast iron seat in the Gothic taste; English, c. 1850; lgth. 48" (122 cm.).

In the mid-19th century, Gothic taste was applied to ironwork, as to most other things. Frequently the results were charming, as with this little garden seat, just wide enough to accommodate two people.

For easy moulding and manufacture, it was made in flat sections, which were all bolted together upon completion.

Such construction was much used for iron furniture, particularly by Mr. Mallet of Dublin, who used cast iron interchangeable units to provide a variety of design and many different kinds of furniture especially for the garden and the summer-house.

Some of Mr. Mallet's designs were published in J. C. Louden's *Encyclopedia of Cottage . . . Architecture and Furniture* published in 1833.

Seats and tables such as this have recently been copied in modern materials, and this particular seat has been copied in aluminium.

b) Beaten copper sconce in the Art Nouveau style by Margaret and Frances Macdonald; Scotland, 1896.

The curvaceous, slightly sinister line of Art Nouveau lent itself superbly to metalwork. Margaret Macdonald was the wife of Charles Rennie Macintosh (1868–1928), the great Scottish exponent of the Art Nouveau style, and architect of the Glasgow Art School; Frances was her sister. This wall-sconce was made by a combination of bench-work, sheet-metalwork and repoussé, which was used for the decoration in the panel. Specimens of Art Nouveau architectural metalwork are to be seen in many places, among them the Glasgow Art School, the Wellington Pier Pavilion at Gt. Yarmouth (England), and on certain Métro entrances in Paris.

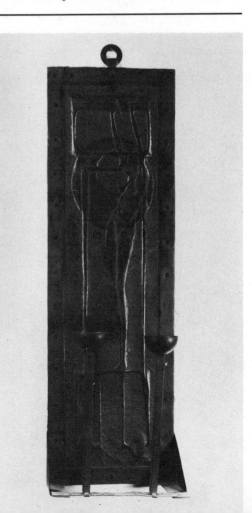

Continental Metalwork
Introduction

The early development of continental metalworking was in many ways parallel to that in England. But one important difference was the immediacy of Middle Eastern influence after the fall of Rome and with the spread of Islam. Great centres of Arab influence in the arts arose, especially in Spain and Sicily. In Spain, during the Caliphate of Cordova, the Arabs founded a school of metalworking noted for its fine ironwork. Its influence spread throughout Europe, from the Baltic to Southern Spain, and by the eighth century metalworking was being practised everywhere.

For long, most European ironwork was dominated by the crafts of the armourer and swordsmith. But simple forged artefacts were made also, from door-hinges and handles to horseshoes. Among other metalwork were sheet-metal bells although, from about A.D. 900, these were usually cast in bronze.

Another great contribution to the development of European metalworking was fostered by Charlemagne, Emperor of the West from A.D. 800. He had found a shortage of metalworkers when he ascended the throne and to overcome this, ordered that smiths should be procured and that each manor should obtain metal tools and equipment including brass kettles, cauldrons and other hollow-ware.

Between the eighth and eleventh centuries, metalworking was also spread by Norsemen who were among the most skilled and advanced ironsmiths in the world.

Brasswork and ironwork were much used from the Middle Ages onwards, especially in churches. Mediaeval bronze effigies are impressive: fine examples are in the Church of our Lady at Bruges, those of Charles the Bold and his daughter, Mary of Burgundy. The latter was by the fifteenth century Brussels metalworker, P. de Beckere, who paid his workmen 40 florins apiece for the loss of teeth caused by the action of the mercury used in gilding the effigies. Smaller objects including door-knockers, crucifixes and portable effigies, were also cast during the same period.

Much ironwork—especially in Spain—was spectacular, like the vast screens in the cathedrals of Seville (1529) and Burgos (1523), with their magnificently forged balusters and lush detailing. But some of the most pleasing of all mediaeval European ironwork is French locksmithery which, apart from locks and keys, was used to make furniture mountings, knockers, candlesticks, lecterns, statuettes, seals, scent bottles, jewellery, bag frames, tools and, above all, delightful miniature caskets.

As with its origins, so with its development. Metalwork on the Continent evolved much as it did in England, but reflecting the national taste of the country in which it was made. Thus, in France, there was a tendency to use elaborately detailed repoussé ornament which reached its apotheosis in the ironwork made by Jean Lamour for the Place Stanislas at Nancy (1751-1759). French nationalism was reflected in the seventeenth century ironwork around Versailles, French imperialism in that at Malmaison. Italian ironwork, especially in Venetia, has elaborate grace and even a dramatic element, like the Italian character. German ironwork is elaborate also, but in a Germanic style, as in gates at the Church of the Franciscans, Salzburg, with their winged putti and sprays of flowers; and in the screen in Constance Cathedral, constructed on a scheme of false, almost *trompe l'oeil* perspectives (both eighteenth century).

The use of cast iron spread, especially after 1664 when the fountains and waterfalls at Versailles were provided with cast iron supply pipes. Delightful cast iron fire-backs and stoves were made in Germany and Holland, some of which were imported into England. In nineteenth century Germany, such tiny objects as cast iron chessmen were made; even cast iron jewellery was made during the Franco-Prussian War, to be given to patriots in exchange for precious jewellery presented for the war effort (cf. p. 517a).

Brass and bronze work was made on the Continent as in England. In addition to domestic brassware, small castings and bench-worked pieces were made for decorating carriages and furniture; these may still be seen today on Venetian gondolas, some representing sea monsters.

Metalwork

Continental

FRENCH
SPANISH
ITALIAN

a) Wrought iron key; France, 17th century.

Keys, elaborately cut with Gothic or Renaissance patterns, illustrate the lengths to which the minuteness of the locksmith's technique may be taken. This example is comparable with the elaborate carving of a Chinese ivory chessman. The whole of the handle and ring is hollowed out, leaving a thickness of a little over 1/32″; the masks on each side of the ring are riveted in place. The bit, as usual with keys of this type, is divided into layers as thin as the teeth of a comb, and it is thus that such keys obtain their French name: *clefs à peigne.*

b) Wrought iron shop sign; France, 18th century.

Shop signs, being comparatively small and therefore less costly than large architectural work, allowed the blacksmith's imagination and craftsmanship full rein. This example is overlaid with elaborate repoussé work as brilliant and sensitive as that made a little earlier by Jean Tijou, who designed and published in his book engravings of such signs. Shop signs were an important and ubiquitous feature of the urban scene in most parts of Europe until well into the 19th century; they helped the mass of illiterate people to identify the trades of the shopkeepers. This example was obviously made for a locksmith.

---

c) Wrought iron window-grille; Salamanca, Spain, 16th century.

A *tour-de-force* of blacksmithery combined with locksmithery. The scallop shells, arms and castles and the horizontal semicircles were all made in cold iron; the remainder, including the pleasing twisted uprights, were forged. The rhythm of the design, with the three half-cylinders swelling out from a plane framework, shows wrought iron design at its most imaginative, with the development of many variations. The twists in the upright bars add strength as well as decoration. Grilles provided a favourite medium for Spanish blacksmiths. Sometimes they are quite small, as here, but some Spanish cathedral grilles are vast monumental works.

d) Wrought iron tabernacle door; Italy, 17th century.

It is difficult to decide on exactly what plant the motifs in this delightful little door and frame are based, but it nevertheless affords a lively example of the vitality which an imaginative smith can obtain from an apparently hard and unyielding material. The formalism of the scrollwork in the border shows the same sense of inherent life. Although, in contrast, the flat vase and the almost roughly constructed framework are naive, the total effect is as brilliant as a page from an illuminated manuscript.

a) Decorated hack-saw frames, the first two of iron, the third of steel; Italy; the first and third, 17th century; the centre frame c. 1732; lgth. of first frame 20¼″ (51.4 cm.).

This group illustrates the variety of designs that a metalworker can obtain from a simple shape, from the scrolled motifs of the top example, through the looped bar of that in the centre, to the simple decoration of the bottom one. The different devices on the eye through which the screw passes will also be noticed. It is interesting that, the elaborate designs apart, these hack-saw frames are of basically the same designs as those used to-day—thus illustrating that once a logical and functional design for a tool has been achieved, it will remain in that form so long as there is use for it.

b) Gondola prow of iron; Italy, 17th century.

A most unusual design for a gondola prow, this was probably made for a special patron, and some of the devices used may have been taken from his arms. The perforated disc forming the main part of the design was made in two separate pieces, the central part, a disc, fitting inside an outer ring. The two parts are joined together by a number of riveted links. It is difficult to decide why it should have been constructed in this way, as it would have been as easy to cut it from a complete piece of metal. The limited use of engraving is pleasing.

c) Wrought iron well crane; Capodilista Emo Palace, Padova, Italy, 18th century.

Well cranes have often allowed the blacksmith to combine function with pleasing decoration. Here the motifs of scroll, simple twisted leaves, and circles provide the decorative elements on the functional arch and serve also to support the repoussé arms and coronet. The craftsmanship is so simple that it might have originated anywhere in western Europe, although its scale is larger than usual on English examples. It is doubtful, also, that an English smith would have upset the verticals of the arch quite so elaborately. Interesting well cranes in England are at Old Hall, Langham, Rutland, and Castle Ashby, Northamptonshire.

Metalwork

Continental

DUTCH
GERMAN
RUSSIAN

a) Warming pan of pierced and engraved brass; Holland, c. 1602; lgth. of entire pan and handle 41" (104 cm.), dia. of pan 13½" (34.3 cm.).

This is an elaborate example of Dutch brass work, showing an interesting combination of pierced work with engraving. The design, which shows Italian influence, has strongly erotic elements, particularly in the centre group with Cupid's hand on the genitals of the ambiguous main figure. The remainder of the design is strongly reminiscent of the decoration in Italian illuminated manuscripts of the 16th century. Despite its elaboration and the diversity of its motifs it has been cleverly worked into a cohesive design, fitting well into the circular framework.

The little rhyme around the circumference can be translated: 'This pan is nice for women who prefer to get into a warm bed and have no one to warm it for them—then they must heat the bed with this pan if they have no man to warm their feet.'

b) Brass miniature casket; South Germany, c. 1600.

Caskets have been a favourite product of fine metalworking for at least 600 years, although the earliest specimens are usually made of ivory with brass fittings. As they were used for the protection of jewellery, illuminated manuscripts and other precious objects, it is not surprising that the strength of metal was considered necessary in their construction. They were made in many parts of Europe, particularly in the Low Countries, Germany, France and Spain, and the metals used varied between brass, iron and copper, and sometimes two or three combined. Enamel, gilding, engraving and etching were among the surface decorations used.

c) Wrought iron snuffbox, inlaid with gold; probably German, 18th century; lgth. 2" (5.08 cm.), wdth. 1¼" (3.18 cm.), dpth. ½" (1.27 cm.).

This little box is decorated with damascening, a process that originated in Asia Minor and took its name from Damascus, where it was practised. Dovetailed furrows were cut in the surface of the iron, and gold (or more rarely, copper) wire was placed in them and hammered so as to fill them out. The surface of the gold was sometimes subsequently engraved, as here. Damascening was much used in the Middle Ages for decorating armour and weapons. Many small objects, like this box, were made by bench-work; among them seals, jewels and *bonbonnières* (sweet-boxes). They were often gilded.

d) Brass military button; Russia, 19th century; dia. ⅞" (22.2 cm.).

Metal buttons are one of the cheapest and most varied subjects for the collector of metal artefacts. They were made by stamping or casting and include in addition to military buttons, those used on servants' liveries, on railway uniforms, on club, hunting and racing coats, and elsewhere. They were made in brass, iron, silver, pewter and copper, and the range of design is infinite. Finishes include gilding, enamelling, engraving, engine turning, and embossing. They were made in many parts of Europe, but the biggest centres of production were Birmingham and Sheffield (England). The trade gradually declined after the 1840s.

Metalwork Glossary

ANTHEMION: A decorative motif, derived from the honey-suckle flower; popular c. 1775–1825.

ARCADE: A repetitive horizontal motif, often a series of arches.

ARMOUR BRIGHT: A bright finish on ironwork, obtained by a combination of special forging and scraping.

BEAD: A swelling or knob, or a series of such, obtained by upsetting.

BENCH-WORK: Work on cold metal usually carried out at a bench.

BLOCKING: A widened portion of a rail, swelled out by upsetting, so that it may be perforated to allow another bar to pass through it without loss of strength; also called a lockett.

BLOOM: A mass of smelted wrought iron, before it is made into bars.

BLOWHOLES: Holes in a casting caused by excess gas during pouring.

BOLT: (a) A screwed, headed pin; (b) a short, stout piece of round bar.

BUTTON POINT: A termination, in the shape of a berry, much used in wrought ironwork.

CASTING ON: A method of attaching ornaments to wrought bars, by pouring the molten cast metal around them in a mould.

CHARGE: The mixture of metal, fuel and flux in a cupola.

CLAPPING BAR: A vertical bar attached to the front bar of one gate in a pair, to form a rebate into which the other gate may close.

COLLAR: A ring or clamp of metal, used for joining two or more bars together. There are many forms.

CORE: The part of a mould by which cavities, apertures, etc. are made in a casting.

COTTER PIN: A tapered or wedge-shaped pin, usually headed.

CUPOLA: The furnace, once called a 'hell', in which cast iron is melted; hence 'cupolette', a small cupola.

DAMASCENING: Surface decoration of iron or steel by in-laying with another metal, usually gold.

DINANDERIE: Cast or beaten brass.

DOWEL PIN: A cylindrical, parallel-sided pin; also called a charlin or stick-in-piece.

DRAWING OUT or DRAWING DOWN: The reduction to shape of a piece of hot metal by hammering its heated part.

DRESSING: Removal of surface defects, etc. from a new casting.

FETTLING: The removal of sand runners and risers from a new casting.

FLAME TUFT: A finial consisting of a number of upright twisted motifs resembling a flame.

FLASK: A moulding box; the upper part is the cope, the lower the drag.

FORGING: (a) The act of shaping metal by heating and hammering; (b) a piece of metal shaped by forging.

FOUNDER: A craftsman skilled in making castings.

HAMMERMAN: The blacksmith's assistant who wields a heavy hammer; also called a striker.

LATEN or LATTEN: Flat, or plate, brass.

LID GATE: A gate pivoted horizontally instead of vertically.

LOCK RAIL: The two horizontal rails of a gate, between which the lock is fitted; the remainder of the space thus enclosed, which is often decorated, is called a lock panel.

LORINER or LORIMER: A craftsman skilled in making the metal parts of horse harness.

LUNETTE: A half-moon shaped decorative motif.

MOULDER: A craftsman skilled in making moulds.

OVERTHROW: The stationary decorative arch above a gate-way.

PAKTONG: An amalgam of copper, nickel and zinc, it resembles polished steel; also called 'tutenag'.

PIN: A short piece of metal used for joining two other pieces of metal together.

PINKING: In sheet metalwork, the cutting of the edge of the metal into indented scallops, waves or other patterns.

POUNCING: Embossing sheet metal by applying blows to its underside, as in repoussé.

PUNCHING or DRIFTING: The perforation of hot metal by hammering a punch or drift through it.

REPOUSSE: The art of raising patterns on sheet metalwork by blows administered on the underside.

RISER: In a mould, a vertical hole between the cavity and the top surface. It allows gases to escape from the mould, indicates when the mould is full, and acts as a reservoir from which gaps or holes in the cavity are filled.

RIVET: A headed pin used for joining together two pieces of metal.

RUNNER: In a mould, a vertical hole between the cavity and the top surface, through which the molten metal is introduced.

SCREEN: A tall or grand balustrade, usually considerably decorated.

SCANTLING: The section of a piece of metal, e.g. 1″ square, ½″ round.

SCARFING: The process of preparing the ends of two pieces of iron prior to welding; hence 'scarf' for the prepared end.

SCROLL: A piece of metal forged into a convolute spiral; there are many types, named after their terminations, e.g. bolt end, snub end, leaf end, ribbon end, etc.; groups of scrolls are sometimes named after their combined shapes, e.g. C-scroll, G-scroll, S-scroll, etc.

SHUTTING TOGETHER or SHUTTING UP: Same as welding.

SOW: The large ingot at the centre of a piece of smelted

Metalwork
Glossary (contd.)

iron; smaller ingots are joined to it at each side, called 'pigs' (hence 'pig iron').

SPRUE: In casting, a channel leading from the runner to the mould.

STAIR RAMP: A curved or raked hand-rail or balustrade, as for a staircase.

STANDARD: A large upright in a balustrade or screen usually placed at regular intervals as a support; also a vertical bar in a grille.

STAY or STAYBAR: A bar, usually shaped or curved, placed behind a standard to strengthen it; also a horizontal bar in a grille.

STIDDY or STITHY: A smith's workshop; also his anvil.

TENON: A projection forged on the end of a bar, to be put through a corresponding hole and riveted in position.

THUNDER AND LIGHTNING: Fencing with alternate straight and wavy balusters.

TOE: The bottom end of a vertical bar; also the lower pivet of the hinge bar of a gate.

TRANSOM BAR: A horizontal bar at the top of a gate or screen, or in an overthrow.

UPSETTING: Increasing or modifying the girth or shape of a piece of heated metal by applying hammer blows to its end; also called 'staving' and 'jumping-up'.

VANE: A flag-shaped or similar motif pivoted on an upright to swivel in the wind and indicate its direction; the term should not be applied to a weathercock.

WASTER: A spoilt casting.

WELDING: Joining together two pieces of iron by heating them to the point of fusion and hammering them together; also called 'shutting together' or 'shutting up'.

YETT: A gate used to protect a doorway when the door is left open.

Repairs and Maintenance

Generally speaking, repairs are best left to the expert, for metalworking is exacting and demands years of practice. Nevertheless, care should be taken in deciding to which craftsman a repair or restoration should be entrusted.

In any case it should be ensured that the restorer understands what is wanted. Present-day techniques may be out of place. Electric welding should never be used on wrought iron, as it damages the laminae of the metal, and thereby encourages rust. If riveted or collared joints are to be remade, the surfaces should be cleaned and painted. If dents are to be removed from brass, one must be careful in applying heat or hammering it, in case it crumbles. Indeed with brass it is often best not to attempt a repair. Copper is less delicate but is also best left to the expert.

If their use permits—and once a good polish has been obtained—brass and copper objects are best lacquered. This is especially true if they have decorated surfaces which might be damaged or obliterated by constant polishing.

Cast iron is little affected by rust. It is best preserved by painting but it easily breaks if dropped or hit.

In wrought iron architectural pieces, the best form of protection is to burn off the old paint, spray the surface with zinc, and then repaint it. If subsequently the paint is kept in repair, little further attention should be necessary. Small domestic pieces require little attention if in constant use, but any sign of rust should be cleaned off by gently heating and brushing the surface, or, if that is impracticable, by rubbing it with Vaseline. They may be painted, but are best with their natural surface showing; this may be preserved by brushing them with linseed oil and applying a gentle heat.

Fakes and Forgeries

There are few fakes and forgeries in metalwork, but there is a considerable amount of modern work made to old patterns, which is sometimes offered as antique.

The main things to watch are the surface texture and the technique used. In wrought iron, one should remember that electric and oxy-acetylene welding are modern, though they may appear on a badly repaired antique. Their presence should always be treated with suspicion. So, also, should hexagon-headed bolts and screws, or screws with a modern thread. Excessively light sections are nearly always modern. Scrolls are another guide. In old work they are sturdily made, correctly voluted and with proper terminations; generally, too, they have some structural significance. In modern copies they are often carelessly made, irregularly

Fakes and Forgeries (contd.)

voluted, and have rough terminations.

In cast iron, the best test is to examine the surface. On modern work the rust is of a brighter colour than on old work. Black-leading may also provide a test: applied over the years and mixed with soot, as on fire-backs and fire-dogs, it becomes hard and tenacious; new black-leading is soft and easily rubbed off. Many objects once made in cast iron are now made in cast aluminium from the original patterns; but as aluminium was not thus used until recent years and as it is so much lighter than cast iron, there should be no confusion.

Brass and copper are likewise best tested by their surfaces, although there are also points of technique that may, with experience, be applied. Any surface that is more or less free of wear should arouse suspicion. If it is a standing object, like a candlestick or a tray, the condition of the under surface should give a clue to its age. But really no test can replace experience and a trained eye.

Further Reading

General

ALBERT, L. S., and KENT, K. *The Complete Button Book.* 1949.

ARYTON, M., and SILCOCK, A. *Wrought Iron and its Decorative Uses.* London and New York, 1929.

BURGESS, F. W. *Chats on Household Curios.* London, 1914.

BUTTER, F. J. *Locks and Lockmaking,* 2nd ed. London and New York, 1931.

FFOULKES, C. J. *Decorative Ironwork from the XIth to the XVIIIth Century.* London, 1913.

GARDNER, J. S. *Ironwork,* Parts I, II, and III, revised 1927, 1930 and 1922.

GEERLINGS, C. K. *Wrought Iron in Architecture.* New York, 1929.

GLOAG, J. E., and BRIDGEWATER, D. L. *A History of Cast Iron in Architecture.* London, 1948.

JEKYLL, G., and HUSSEY, C. *Garden Ornament,* 2nd ed. London, 1927.

LILLICO, J. W. *Blacksmith's Manual Illustrated.* London, 1930.

SQUIRE, G. *Buttons.* 1972.

TIJOU. J. *A New Book of Drawings.* Reproduced with English descriptions by J. S. Gardner. London, 1896.

English

BROWN, R. A. *The History and Origins of Horse Brasses.* 1952.

GARDNER, J. S. *English Ironwork of XVIIth and XVIIIth Centuries.* London, 1911.

GOODWIN-SMITH, R. *English Domestic Metalwork.* Leigh-on-Sea, 1937.

HARRIS, J. *English Decorative Ironwork from Contemporary Source Books, 1610–1836.* London, 1960.

LARWOOD, J., and HOTTEN, J. C. *English Inn Signs.* London, 1951. Revised version of *History of Signboards,* London, 1866, with chapter on modern signs by Gerald Miller.

LINDSAY, J. S. *Iron and Brass Implements of the English House.* 1927; revised ed. London, 1970.

LISTER, R. *The Craftsman in Metal.* London, 1966; Toronto and Cranbury N.J., 1968.
Decorative Cast Ironwork in Great Britain. London, 1960.
Decorative Wrought Ironwork in Great Britain. Newton Abbot (repr.) and Rutland Vt., 1970; repr. Newton Abbot, 1972.
Great Works of Craftsmanship. London and Cranbury, N.J., 1967.
Hammer and Hand. An Essay on the Ironwork of Cambridge. Cambridge, 1969.

MURPHY, B. S. *English and Scottish Wrought Ironwork.* London, 1904.

NEEDHAM, A. *English Weather Vanes.* Haywards Heath, 1953.

PUGIN, A. W. N. *Fifteenth and Sixteenth Century Ornaments Part II, Iron and Brass Work Designs.* Edinburgh, 1904.

SMALL, T., and WOODBRIDGE, C. *English Wrought Ironwork, Mediaeval and Early Renaissance.* London, 1931.
English Wrought Ironwork of the late 17th and early 18th Centuries. London, 1930.

STRAKER, E. *Wealden Iron.* London, 1931.

Continental

ARTINANO, P. M. de *El Tesoro Artistico de España.* Barcelona, n.d.

BYRNE, A., and STAPLEY, M. *Spanish Ironwork.* New York, 1915.

FRANK, E. B. *Old French Ironwork.* Cambridge, Mass., 1960.

HARVARD, H. *Les arts de l'ameublement: la serrurerie.* Paris, 1892.

KIPPENGERGER, A. *Die deutschen Meister des Eisengusses im 16 Jahrhundert.* Marburg, 1931.

KUHN, F. *Wrought Iron* (tr. from German). London, 1965.

PREECE, J. *Gates of Veneto.* London, 1968; New York, 1969.

Metalwork
Museum Collections

Index

Opposite:
Wrought iron 'ram's head' fire-dogs; France, 17th century.

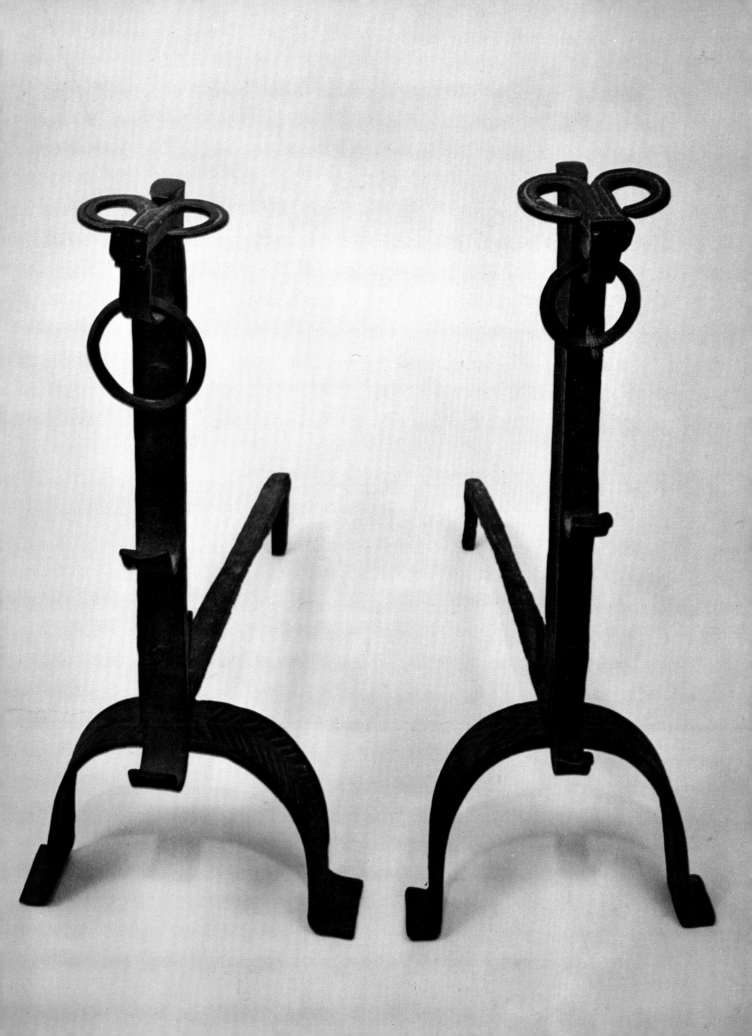

Musical Instruments

Musical instruments are precision tools producing a wide range of highly complex sounds—in short, functional works of art. Their construction and development involved craftsmen in the applied and decorative arts; scientists, mathematicians, philosophers and, naturally, executant musicians and composers. This unique co-operation resulted in instruments of striking elegance, long collected for appearance alone, and with little regard for their inherent function.

In recent years, this attitude has changed to an interest in playable instruments, or those which can be restored to playing order. This has revived the co-operation between science and art, bringing early instruments to such excellent condition that knowledge about the correct performance of early music has gained incalculable benefits.

A principal aim will be to guide collectors towards an evaluation of sound potential.

There is no 'best' period for any one class of musical instrument. The earliest and simplest Italian harpsichords were triumphs of precision and elegance. By the same standard, there are no 'primitive' instruments in the sense of being faulty or inadequate. But there are instruments of deceptively *simple* appearance—like a cornett or a recorder—which, although difficult to play well, fulfil their function admirably.

Change in structure and sound was not necessarily a sign of dissatisfaction. Often, it was dictated by fashion, with a result that the history of instruments reflects the rise and fall of empires (musical automata were considered suitable gifts even for Royalty), the variety of architectural enclosures (brass for the high-domed, galleried cathedrals and virginals in tapestry-hung boudoirs), and clothes (the pochette would be too big for anyone's pocket today). To some extent, the pace and sounds of life in the past can be re-created; in the cloister dormitory nuns could play the quiet-voiced clavichord without disturbing their sisters. Even more precisely, the *nature* of that environment can be defined by the materials used, whilst embellishments in precious metals and stones indicate wealth, trade and commerce generally. To give one obvious example, the start and development of the Industrial Revolution is clearly marked when mass production took over from the skilled craftsman and quality deteriorated. By about 1870, the collectors' interest in early instruments began in earnest, but ironically enough, at the same time and with some exceptions, the period over which instruments are worth collecting comes to an end.

Opposite:
Harpsichord inscribed Fait par Pascal Taskin a Paris, 1786, *probably made for a child; Paris, France, 1786.*

Musical Instruments
The Craft and its History

Keyboards

There are three types of stringed keyboards, classed according to the manner in which the string is made to vibrate. Harpsichords, virginals and spinets have a plucking mechanism; a jack armed with a small projection of quill or leather is flung up when the key is depressed, flicks the string in passing and falls back under its own weight. In pianos the string is attacked by a hammer which falls back immediately it has hit the string. In the clavichord the string is struck by a metal tangent at the end of the key and does not fall back until the key is released; thus the player retains control over the sounding string and by an up and down movement can produce various degrees of vibrato, like a singer.

The clavichord is the earliest and smallest stringed keyboard, dating back to the eleventh century at least. Its origin can only be traced in pictorial representations. It is also the quietest of all musical instruments and among the frailest. Very few early examples have survived and these, as well as the later ones of the eighteenth century, are already in museums.

The plucked stringed keyboards—harpsichords, virginals, and spinets—were surprisingly robust and the number dating from the sixteenth century onwards is very satisfactory, making possible profound studies of their development. Nevertheless, one great mystery is unsolved: when and by whom was the sophisticated plucking mechanism invented? The oblong virginal pre-dates the harpsichord. The date of the first harpsichord is unknown, but it cannot have emerged until the technique of wire drawing had developed sufficiently to produce the longer lengths needed for stringing. The spinet co-existed with the harpsichord.

The name spinet is frequently misapplied to a number of keyboard instruments, particularly the square piano (which was, in any case, a rectangle). Spinets are generally wing-shaped. The early grand piano is sometimes called a forte-piano. This is a little misleading, as the *forte*-piano and the piano*forte* are one and the same early grand piano, which looked like a harpsichord!

Covering little more than a hundred years, the history of piano making is one of frenetic competition characterized by a constant flow of refinements designed to improve the tone and the action. For the connoisseur, interest dwindles soon after 1850. Before this, square, upright and grand pianos with their leather covered hammers, light stringing, and cased in fine, carefully weathered· woods, had notable personal voices which, when played in ensembles, blended perfectly with those of singers, fiddlers and flutes. This softer blending diminished in direct ratio to the increased tension from below 7 tons to the 30 tons carried by the cast iron frames of the latter part of the

nineteenth century.

Some makers indulged in appealing dashes of fantasy and produced instruments whose musical function is cleverly concealed. There have been writing-case spinets and walking-stick flutes. Some pianos—notably by Pape—look like ordinary tables or consoles.

Bowed and Plucked Strings

The unbroken tradition of making, restoring and conserving these is hundreds of years older than that of keyboards. There is also plentiful evidence from recordings made in the Middle East (where a major proportion of European instruments originated), and isolated districts of Europe and the Balkans, of how some of these were originally strung, tuned, bowed or plucked and how they sounded.

A very few of the earliest harps survive—those low-standing and sometimes bejewelled instruments with which the minstrels of the fifteenth and early sixteenth centuries accompanied their songs. Their sound was probably strong and bell-like, similar to that of the triple harp (often called Welsh harp). Originally the strings were struck with the ends of the finger or plucked with long nails. The technique of pulling the strings and producing the familiar harp sound of today probably originated somewhere in the eighteenth century with the introduction of the pedal harp.

Curiously enough, whilst this category of bowed and plucked stringed instruments offers an untold wealth to the performer, it also provides the collector with the richest selection of mute objets d'art; craftsmen, as far back as the sixteenth century, with hundreds of years of tradition behind them, achieved a pinnacle of virtuosity in their work. This resulted in instruments of such spectacular, even extravagant, beauty that even to *handle* them, with eager and probably sweating hand, is dangerous, let alone to attempt to play them. These instruments with their incredible decorations, inlay and carvings—made sometimes of such thin materials that the light shines through them—have dried out so much that it would be little short of madness to ask them to sing again.

Woodwinds

Names and numbers have somewhat dominated the collector's choice of woodwind instruments largely because, in comparison with the highly mechanized woodwinds of the twentieth century orchestra, they are exceedingly difficult to play and few have the courage or time to try.

All woodwind instruments have their origins in unrecorded time, but the bulk of those that survive are from the seventeenth and eighteenth centuries. The earliest Renaissance flutes were cylindrical and keyless. They became conical and jointed, and an increasing number of keys were added. Fashions in tone quality varied and so did the material; besides a variety of woods they were made in glass, china, crystal, ivory and silver. Oboes and clarinets also, and at the same time, started with open holes and then, in order to facilitate intonation and fingering, more keys were added. Not only were the bore and the bell enlarged or reduced in order to suit the tonal taste of the time, but the type and cut of the reed were experimented with. It is not difficult to find the right embouchure (shape of the lips) for an early flute, but it is exceedingly difficult to find the right reed for an early clarinet, bassoon or oboe.

Brass

Because of the exciting glint and glow of the metal—often seductively curved—brass instruments are popular objects of decoration in anything from humble inns to stately homes; the meanest junk shop has some dented and tarnished example on the premises—probably without the mouthpiece. Their sound is more often imagined than heard, since the bands and functions for which they were designed became successively obsolete. We are, unfortunately, a long way away from the lightly carried hunting horns, straight trumpets and keyless bugles, and today in brass bands lighter, modern instruments have tended to supersede the old brass instruments.

Percussion

The history of European percussion instruments is exceedingly curious in that it shows the minimum of imagination on the part of the makers and composers alike. All over the world and throughout time, percussion instruments have been used to accompany dance and ritual and to pass messages—even some animals communicate by taps and thumps! Slit log drums, square drums, double ended drums, hour-glass shaped drums, friction drums, chromatic drums, with or without jingles or snares, were often played with breath-taking virtuosity with the fingers, hands or a variety of beaters of different shapes and materials. Sophisticated European music makes use of roughly only three types: kettle, side and bass. For the collector, the most attractive are the mounted and military drums of the eighteenth and nineteenth centuries, because they are emblazoned with coats of arms.

Automata

In the course of time, at least one of the instruments in all the foregoing categories has come in for automation. Many of these musical automata were 'fun' instruments, but some were not. The chamber barrel organ of the eighteenth century, for example—often constructed by the finest cathedral organ builders—played better than some village organists and was sometimes considered preferable.

Although musical automata date back to classical antiquity, European survivals are found from the sixteenth century onwards, the pinned barrel mechanism already being the usual one for setting off bells, strings and pipes. Much later the barrel is still used for pianos and fair-ground organs. The tuned comb, activated by a pinned cylinder and then in the nineteenth century by a perforated disc, originated in the eighteenth century, and examples of these two systems have survived in their hundreds.

The 'fun' side of musical automata should not, however, be exaggerated; they were made with wonderful precision with a particular regard for what—at the moment of making—was the correct performance of the music. Proof of this can be heard in the best bird boxes. The songs of these automated singers, if compared with that of the live creatures of the same breed, reveal a similitude of pitch and pattern that is truly astounding.

The only form of musical automata that is not designed to imitate any other instrument is the music box. Polyphons, reginas, and symphoniums, all plucking their notes from a tuned steel comb, are in this category. Techniques of restoration of these instruments are now so advanced that unless the cabinet is badly worm-riddled and warped and the brass and steel mechanism rotted with rust and ground down by neglect and carelessness, they can be successfully restored.

Finally, wherever or however you discover an instrument slumbering in a dark attic or barn, or covered with dust in a country auction, remember that though it may be decorative and delightful to look at, it is a precision tool designed to conduct sounds, *not* as a silent object without a voice, without music.

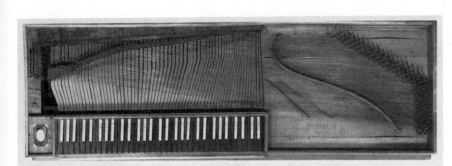

a) *Clavichord, Barthold Fritz; Germany, 1751; lgth. 5' 10½" (179 cm.), wdth. 1' 10½" (57 cm.), dpth. 6½" (16.5 cm.).*

By the time this example was made, the clavichord was out of fashion and, because of its small voice, is rarely heard even today in recitals or broadcasts.

This Fritz is larger than earlier examples, and its voice—silvery in the treble and bold and rounded in the bass—can be heard comfortably at a distance of between 20 and 30 feet (18-27 m.). Most clavichords are best heard at a distance of 2-3 feet. It is the domestic instrument par excellence and the one for which Bach wrote his 48 Preludes and Fugues.

b) *Harpsichord with outer case; Vito Trasuntino, Italy, 1571.*

Note the length and sweep of the tapering in relation to the shallowness of the cabinet on this typical Italian harpsichord.

In common with many harpsichords and virginals of this period, the instrument has an outer case and can be slid out and placed on a table. This outer casing protected the delicate instrument from bruising and also created a layer of air which insulated it against atmospheric changes that normally cause havoc to the tuning. Some virginal cases were lined in costly velvet for added protection, later, when stronger instruments were made, this outer case became obsolete.

Musical Instruments
KEYBOARDS

---

c) *Square piano, Zumpe; England, 1763; lgth. 4' 3¾" (130 cm.), wdth. 1' 6½" (47 cm.), dpth. 6½" (16.5 cm.).*

This instrument is by one of the first makers in Britain. It represents the beginning of a hundred years of feverish activity on the part of manufacturers headed by firms such as Stoddart, Broadwood, Wornum, Stein, Erard, Pape, Pleyel and even Clementi. Their improvements were chiefly concerned with obtaining a more reliable action and more expressive voice.

This Zumpe has a small, domestic voice and narrow dynamic range. It should be played with the lid down, but with the small flap (the 'swell') on the right of the player open; otherwise the sound of the mechanism is intrusive.

d) *Grand piano; Schneider, Vienna, 1851; lgth. 8' (243.8 cm.), wdth. 4' 6" (137.1 cm.).*

A peak in grand piano making. The case, of American bird's-eye maple has inlaid banding of fine wood mosaic. The frame is of wood—as in all early pianos—but there are steel braces and a wrought-iron hitch pin block. The soundboard is not varnished. The hammers are leather covered—in this case, with deerskin.

The tone of the very first grand pianos—made by Backers in the 1770s—derived from that of the harpsichord, but this Schneider has the true, hammered-string voice. Besides having notable carrying power, the sound is limpid and the relationship between bass and treble perfectly balanced.

*a) Violin; Ventura Linarol; Venice, Italy, 1581;
lgth. 22" (55.5 cm.), body 13⅝" (34.5 cm.).*

This seemingly ordinary violin is really very
rare. The majority made by the great makers, from
Amati and Gasparo onwards, have been altered in
numerous details: a lengthened neck, the curved
bridge replaced by one more curved, the original
tail-piece exchanged for a new one and gut
instead of wire stringing—all to conform with
changing performance techniques. This Linarol is
in its original condition.

Too rare to play, the sound of these untouched
fiddles remains a matter for speculation. It can,
however, be assumed with some confidence that
double-stopping was far easier with the less curved
bridge.

*b) Bass viol, painted with purfled trellis patterns, and
the Somerset coat of arms; England, late 16th century;
lgth. 51¼" (130 cm.), dpth. 4¾" (12.0 cm.).*

The virtuoso-made instrument could not be
used for daily practice and performance. The
festooned decoration includes floral designs done
with a hot needle.

Viols—bass, tenor and treble—emerged around
1450-1500, and the variations in their shapes over
the next 300 years is a study in itself. They are
played with the body held downwards, the curved
bow held with the wrist facing outwards. This
exerts less pressure on the gut strings than does the
normally-held bow, drawn across wire. The
voice, sweet and subdued, frequently resembles the
ideal human singing voice, which was then
considered the most perfect sound.

---

c) Pochette; England, 18th century.

Measuring but some 1' 2⅝" (37 cm.) long, this is
not to be confused with a toy or miniature violin.
Also known as dancing master's kits, these were
designed to be carried in the pockets of the 19th
century dancing masters. Many were boat shaped.
All were played with a small curved bow.

In spite of the size, the somewhat harsh, nasal
voice has surprising carrying power and can be
heard well at about 32 feet (10 m.); presumably it
would have cut through the squeals and chatter of
the young dancers.

d) Triple harp; Italy, 17th century; ht. 76" (193 cm.).

During the early 17th century—perhaps before
—some unknown person devised a harp with
three ranks of strings. The outer ranks provided
the 'white' notes, the inner, the 'black'.

Vivaldi and Handel composed for this harp.
Mysteriously it reached south-west Britain,
becoming known as the 'Welsh harp'.

The hook harp (with tuning blades for each
string), the two-pedal harp, and the modern
orchestral seven-pedal harp, have not been proved
to be developments of this triple harp.

The tradition of playing the triple harp now
rests in the hands of one old woman. When she
goes, the glorious, bell-like voice of incomparable
clarity and vivacity will not be heard again.

551

a) Deep rose in early guitar with mother-of-pearl inlay.

One particular feature characterizes a whole range of instruments that includes lutes and arch-lutes, citterns and arch-citterns, guitars and harp-guitars, pandoras, mandoras, theorbos, mandolins, balalaikas and various types of lyre: the rose.

Apart from being a decorative device in the belly of the instrument (and also, incidentally, found in the sound-boards of harpsichords, virginals and spinets), the rose has other functions. Makers often incorporated their initials into the design as a form of signature. The rose was part of the accoustic design of an instrument and, in a manner not yet fully understood, encouraged the body to vibrate more eagerly. Finally, since it is comparatively easily lifted out, it provides a sort of spy-hole through which the maker or restorer can peer at makers' labels and sound-posts, and in keyboards particularly, insert a hand and remove rubbish such as shavings or forgotten tools.

b) left: Guitar, Vihuela; Spain, 16th century.
c) centre   uitar, José Pages; Cadiz, Spain, 1798; lgth 38½″ (98 cm.), body 17¾″ (45 cm.), dpth. 3 11/16″ (9.4 cm.).
d) right: Guitar, Altimira; Barcelona, Spain, 1840; lgth. 37½″ (95 cm), body 17¾″ (45 cm.), dpth. 3¾″ (9.5 cm.).

These three Spanish guitars demonstrate two facts. First, that the earlier the guitar the less waisted, and second that the rose as a decorative device was eventually dropped—although in some cases, it simply dropped out and was never replaced.

Guitars and lutes are fretted. That is to say, the fingerboard is marked off by slightly projecting metal strips and enables the player to find his notes more easily.

a) Early boxwood oboe; England; lgth. overall 1' 11½" (59.6 cm.).

The modern oboe is the result of centuries of house training of a wild Arabian breed used for open-air music. Earlier models were of light woods, such as box and maple. Later, heavier woods (such as cocus) made it possible to add more holes for tuning and for the little screws of the key mechanism, without cracking or splitting the wood.

The tone of double reeds such as the oboe and bassoon and single reeds such as the clarinet, depends greatly on the choice of the right reed cut in the appropriate manner.

b) Flute; England; lgth. overall 2' 0¾" (63.1 cm.).

The history of flute making and playing is well documented, since there were a number of distinguished performers (Frederick the Great, for one), writer-composers (Quantz) and practical musical theorists and gossips (Boehm and Rockstro).

The delicate voice of the early light wooden models fulfils a romantic notion of the pastoral. Those with few or no keys are more expressive, for with a well-adjusted embouchure (the hole into which the player blows is also called the embouchure, and is small on early models) and subtle fingering, the flautist has more control over intonation and can make use of passing microtones.

c) Recorders, the Bressans consort; made in England; late 17th/early 18th century.

This fine consort of recorders was made by the man known as the 'Stradivarius of the recorder'. Unfortunately, the pitch and tuning have been altered and 'brought up to date'.

In the hands of a good player, the recorder can be made to produce a whole range of delicious sounds. But, because it is easy to get a note from, the recorder is given to children to play and they, producing the most dismal sounds, have given it a bad name as a musical instrument.

d) Concertina, 48-keyed English system, amboyna wood; made by C. Wheatstone; London, England, 1848.

The concertina dates from the middle of the 17th century. It belongs to the class of free reed instruments, activated by bellows.

Until the early part of this century, concertinas were beautifully made with rare woods and using tortoiseshell, ivory, silver and mother-of-pearl for embellishment. Fine morocco leather was used for the bellows and these were embossed with gold leaf decorations. The instruments were supplied in velvet-lined cases, sometimes of rosewood and sometimes of leather. Good instruments originally cost up to £20. Wheatstone and Lachenal were the most celebrated makers, and they stamped individual serial numbers on every wooden part.

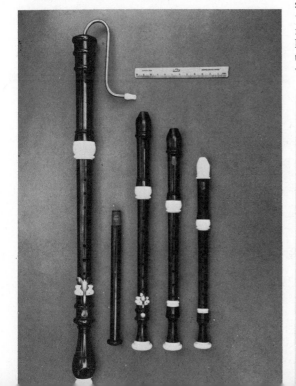

a) top: Horn, J. Chrétien; France, c. 1700; overall lgth. 2′ 2″ (66 cm.).
b) above: Orchesterhorn, Carl Gottlieb Schuster; Germany, c. 1800; loop dia. $11\frac{1}{16}$″ (28 cm.), bell dia. $11\frac{7}{8}$″ (30 cm.).
c) right: Ballad horn, Rudall, Rose & Carte; England, c. 1870; max dia. across coils $9\frac{5}{8}$″ (24.5 cm.), ext. bell dia. 6 15/16″ (17.6 cm.).

Visually, brass instruments—which are roughly divided into horns, trumpets and trombones, keyed, and lastly valved instruments—give an unusually clear picture of the history of their development.

The earliest instruments are straight or slightly curved. These could only sound the basic harmonic series. The need for more notes led to an ever increasing number of loops, coils, crooks (different lengths of detachable coils) and eventually keys and valves.

A large proportion of this class of instruments was used in orchestras, bands and ensembles of a composition that it is impossible to recreate today. Moreover, the functions for which some brass instruments were used are obscure or, if known, are obsolete. For these reasons their various voices are not properly known and the joy of collecting them may ever remain visual rather than musical.

---

d) Bass drum from Royal Anglesey Light Infantry Militia; England, 1870.

Emblazoned with the Royal coat of arms, this is a dream-drum for the collector.

The role of the drummer in Royal, military and ceremonial bands is intended to be spectacular and therefore the drums are spectacular. The sedentary, orchestral percussionist in early symphonic music was to be heard but not necessarily seen and therefore his '*batterie de cuisine*' was as plain as the kitchen sink.

Side and military drums are shallower than this bass drum and have snares (lengths of thin, coiled wire) running underneath the batter head: these can be tightened and brought to bear against the skin to produce the characteristic rattle of the drum, or slacked off to make the sound duller.

Paired kettle drums (timpani) of, for example, the Beethoven orchestra, are shallower than those of the 20th century and visually not particularly thrilling. But the mounted kettle drums used by cavalry regiments—with their embossed bowls and trappings worked in silks, gold and silver—have incomparable martial splendour.

a) Mechanical spinet; Samuel Bidermann, Germany, c. 1575.

This little 36-note spinet works off a clockwork driven pinned barrel that sounds but 20 of the notes. It is one of the few surviving automata of this period.

The small sound is 'boxey', but not displeasing and for the musicologist the tuning, tempi, ornamentation and harmonization of the Renaissance dances it plays provide a guide to the manner in which humans performed similar music.

b) Barrel organ, Flight & Robson; England, 18th century.

These instruments were made by the best organ builders. The barrels were pinned with both sacred and profane music, and could be used in churches to accompany the choir and in the home for dancing.

When out of tune, with pins on the barrel bent or missing, with leaky bellows, the sound is horrible. Because many survived to be played in this poor condition, they were considered 'joke' instruments. When well preserved the sounds are equal to a good chamber organ, speaking in clear, silvery voice. It is quite difficult to keep turning the handle at a steady pace, often in counter rhythm to the music.

c) Steel comb from large box; Switzerland, late 19th century; lgth. 1' 3½" (39.4 cm.).

Tuned steel combs were used in a variety of automata with a serious musical purpose. Bigger boxes played favourite classical pieces and the current 'hits'. The translation of orchestral or piano scores on to the pinned cylinder was done by anonymous craftsmen known as 'musical engineers'. In a good box, all the tunes sparkle with embellishments, and in some, the mounting complexity of the variations on a simple tune is very exciting.

Many famous composers have written music especially for musical automata, from Mozart to Stravinsky, Haydn to Saint Saens, and this gives sufficient proof of their importance as serious musical instruments.

d) Regina; U.S.A. (made under licence), late 19th century; dia. of disc 1' 3½" (39.4 cm).

Reginas, polyphons and symphoniums also produced music from tuned steel combs, but instead of these being plucked by the passage of a pinned barrel, a perforated metal disc with small plucking tongues at the back of each hole, rotated slowly over the comb. Unlike the pinned barrel, which carries up to six tunes, each disc carries only one tune.

Called the precursor of the 'juke box', reginas reached a wider audience than music boxes and their repertoire was also wider, including Wagner, Verdi and Puccini. The cabinets were designed as a form of amplifier. Regina boxes, with their excellent cabinets, produced a strong, rich bass which balanced nicely with a clear, shiny treble.

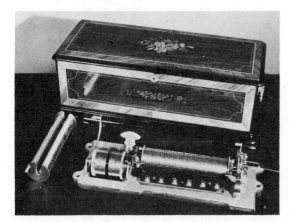

Musical Instruments Glossary

BATTER HEAD: Skin stretched over a drum shell.

BRIDGE: In violin family, arched piece of wood over which strings pass from tuning pegs to tailpiece.

CORNETT: Simple horn of cowhorn or wood with open finger-holes, blown through a cupped mouthpiece.

CITTERN: Early pear-shaped guitar; French form—Pandora.

DOUBLE STOPPING: On stringed instruments, two strings played simultaneously.

FELTS: Material with which later piano hammers and dampers were covered.

HARMONIC SERIES: Series of overtones present in almost every note from every instrument. Each note can be sounded separately on wind instruments by overblowing i.e. increasing the wind pressure.

HITCH PIN BLOCK: Plate (generally metal) to which strings in a piano are attached or hitched.

JACK: A plectrum in harpsichords; small, wooden oblong device with sprung slat armed with quill or leather which leaps up and twangs key in passing.

MANDORA: Form of lute, pre-dating the mandolin.

MICROTONE: Less than a semitone.

MOUTHPIECE: Detachable cup through which all brass instruments are blown.

NAMEBOARD: Vertical plank of wood running parallel to the keyboard bearing maker's name and sometimes date of instrument and his address.

PAD: Skin-covered underside of metal keys on all wood-wind and brass instruments.

PINNED BARREL: Musical automaton. Cylinder studded with metal pins, set so that, when cylinder revolves, the pipes or strings speak.

REED: Slivers of reed are specially trimmed to fit mouth-pieces of woodwinds or be incorporated into instruments of the concertina family.

ROSE: Equivalent of sound or 'f' holes in fiddle. In non-bowed and keyed stringed instruments it is circular and slotted with delicate and very elaborately designed decorations in wood or parchment.

SNARE: Coiled wire run under batter head of some drums.

SOUND POST: Cylindrical pillar or peg within body of instruments of violin family which both prevents the body from caving in and acts as conductor of sound.

SWELL: In square pianos right hand flap which, when open, increases volume of sound.

TAILPIECE: V-shaped piece to which strings are hitched on violins, cellos, etc.

TANGENT: Small metal tongue on end of clavichord key.

THÉORBO: Form of lute.

WREST PINS AND PLANK: Tuning pins and wooden part into which they are screwed, in keyboards.

Fakes and Forgeries

Fortunately the faking and forging of musical instruments has proved too difficult and unprofitable to constitute a serious menace to the collector, but there are one or two dodges worth mentioning.

Makers of bowed and plucked stringed instruments, including harps, stuck their labels inside the body of the instrument and these can be seen through the rose or 'f' holes. Often enough these labels have been forged and stuck into worthless fiddles, guitars, and so on.

Keyboard makers inscribed their names on the vertical plank running above the keyboard, sometimes incor-porated their initials or trade mark in the rose or, more rarely, signed their name within the instrument—under the bass keys or behind the name board. Disreputable makers and dealers made a habit of exchanging name boards or forging them.

Brass instrument makers always engraved or stamped their name on the bell and likewise woodwind makers stamped each joint with their name and, generally, a number.

Any collector should, for his own protection, always keep a photograph of his instrument, a note of the maker, number, dimensions, materials as well as the history (where purchased and from whom). The rising tide of interest in early instruments has created a tendency for them to 'disappear' unexpectedly and without this information they can be impossible to trace.

Above all, however, collectors should view with deep suspicion and a strong microscope any instrument that has an 'as new' appearance with glittering strings, wrest and hitch pins and glowing cabinet or body from which all traces of wear marks have been effaced. These are signs of destruction rather than restoration and in most cases are irreversible.

Repairs and Maintenance

An instrument made playable is not necessarily one restored to its original condition. In the first instance, little or no attempt is made to discover its true voice; modern techniques and materials are used only to bring back a sound. This can lead to the destruction of its musical value, and eventually to its physical destruction.

Restoration is a long and delicate job requiring not only a considerable knowledge of ancient techniques and modern equivalents, but a working knowledge of early music and its performance. Laden with dust, cracked, warped, full of tangled strings and loose parts, an instrument is less dismaying than one 'got at' by a commercial restorer with his frightening bagful of plastic tricks. There are not many fine craftsmen-restorers and they all work exceedingly slowly, but the need to find them and wait patiently for the benefit of their advice and skills cannot be too strongly emphasized.

All the amateur needs is clean dusters and some labels. A little dusting is harmless, but proprietary cleaning materials can destroy the original varnish, as well as the wear marks which every used instrument bears; these are of the greatest importance in determining how the instrument functioned. Suction cleaning may whisk away minute fragments of original materials of vital importance. Any dismantling is to be discouraged, but any part that must be removed should be labelled and its precise position noted.

Never attempt to bring any instrument up to modern pitch—that is, A 440; never wind up fully any musical automata; these are two strict rules. Finally, do not keep instruments in centrally-heated rooms without compensating humidification.

Besides being a semi-tone or more lower in pitch than those of today, most early instruments had much quieter voices. An instrument, unplayed for any length of time, will have lost its true voice; it may take up to a year to recover its original tone colour. Success also depends on using the correct technique of performance. Modern techniques applied to any early instrument will distort the voice.

Keyboards have been amongst the most misunderstood and ill-treated of all early instruments. Harpsichords have been chopped down or converted to pianos. Thousands of early pianos have suffered wanton destruction or conversion into furniture. Always sit down to play an early keyboard and use only delicate finger weight on the keys. Excessive weight can produce an extremely ugly sound, especially if the instrument is out of tune.

Broken strings, moth-eaten felts, missing jacks, strings or hammers and so on are not fatal. Nor is a warped cabinet. It is a badly cracked sound-board that may defy restoration, and only an expert craftsman can decide what can be done.

But any bracing that impedes the free vibrating area of the sound-board is not recommended. Whether or not a sound-board should be varnished is also a matter for the expert.

Many of the solemn warnings issued above apply also to bowed and plucked stringed instruments, including harps—only more so because these are less robust. They have also, down the years, been better treated and conversions been less savage.

A cracked sound-board is fatal to a harp. Even the slightest warping must be viewed with gloom. If the full complement of strings is eased up to even an uncomfortably low pitch, it is unlikely that a warped sound-board will be able to sustain the tension for long. Such instruments are best preserved as mute objets d'art.

There is nothing more dull to look at than cases full of woodwind instruments. They are after all, mere tubes. And whereas keyboards, stringed and brass instruments are always decorative and can inspire an idea—however inaccurate—of what they sounded like, rows of pipes inspire no more than confused fantasies about inefficient plumbing. In this category, specialists in restoration are as few as are good performers.

A crack in any of these pipes can be fatal to the tone. Faulty springs, pads or joints can be easily repaired. None of these wooden instruments should be blown into before the proper steps have been taken to restore the humidity content of the material. A sudden gust of hot air would warm up the instrument too suddenly, produce excessive condensation and might crack the wood.

For brasses, the correct mouthpiece is all-important. Whereas techniques of cleaning and of smoothing out bruises are today sophisticated and successful, the instrument will still not sound well with an alien mouthpiece.

The skin or batter head of percussion instruments should be treated with respect and the original vellum should never be replaced with plastic. Not only does the plastic look very plain (the delicate graining and shading of the real skin being absent), but it is less responsive and the sound lacks a number of harmonics.

Musical Instruments
Further Reading

General

BAINES, A. *European and American Musical Instruments.* London and San Francisco, 1966.

BERNER, A., VAN DER MEER, J. H., THIBAULT, G., and BROMMELLE, N. *Preservation and Restoration of Musical Instruments.* London, 1967.

BUCHNER, A. *Mechanical Musical Instruments.* London, n.d.

GROVE, SIR G. *Dictionary of Music and Musicians.* London, 1889.

HARRISON, F., and RIMMER, J. *European Musical Instruments.* London, 1964.

JENKINS, JEAN (ed.). *Ethnic Musical Instruments—Identification and Conservation.* London, 1970.
Larousse de la Musique. Paris, 1957.

MARCUSE, S. *Musical Instruments, A Comprehensive Dictionary.* New York and Toronto, 1964.

SACHS, C. *The History of Musical Instruments.* New York, 1940; London, 1942.

Keyboards

BOALCH, D. H. *Makers of the Harpsichord and Clavichord to 1840.* London, 1956.

BRINSMEAD, E. *The History of the Pianoforte.* London, 1889.

HARDING, E. M. *The Pianoforte.* London and New York, 1933.

HUBBARD, F. *Three Centuries of Harpsichord Making.* Cambridge, Mass., 1965 (repr. 1970); London, 1965.

RIPIN, E. M. (ed.). *Keyboard Instruments.* Edinburgh and Chicago, 1971.

RUSSELL, R. *Harpsichord and Clavichord; an Introductory Study.* London and New York, 1959.

Stringed Instruments

BACHMANN, A. *An Encyclopedia of the Violin.* New York, 1966.

GRUNFELD, F. V. *The Art and Times of the Guitar.* New York, 1969; London, 1970.

HILL, W. H., A. F., and A. E. *Antonio Stradivari: His Life and Work.* New York, 1963.
The Violin-makers of the Guarneri Family (1626-1762). London, 1931.

PANUM, H. *The Stringed Instruments of the Middle Ages.*

RIMMER, J. *The Irish Harp.* Cork, 1969.

Woodwind Instruments

BAINES, A. *Woodwind Instruments and their History.* London and New York, 1966.

BATE, P. *The Flute.* London, 1969. *The Oboe.* London and New York, 1956.

HUNT, E. *The Recorder and its Music.* London, 1962.

LANGWILL, L. G. *The Bassoon and Contra-bassoon.* London and New York, 1965.
An Index of Musical Wind Instrument Makers (2nd edit.). Edinburgh, 1962.

RENDALL, F. G. *The Clarinet.* London and New York, 1954.

Brass

BATE, P. *The Trumpet and Trombone.* London and New York, 1966.

FITZPATRICK H. *The Horn and Horn Playing.* London and New York, 1970.

MENKE, W. (tr. G. Abraham). *History of the Trumpet of Bach and Handel.* London, 1934.

MORLEY-PEGGE, R. *The French Horn.* London and New York, 1960.

Percussion

BLADES, J. *Percussion Instruments and their History.* New York, 1971; London, 1972.

Museum Collections

Great Britain

KENT: The Colt Clavier Collection, Bethersden (Nr. Ashford).

LONDON: The British Piano Museum and Musical Museum; William E. Hill; Horniman Museum; Royal College of Music; Royal Military School of Music; The Victoria and Albert Museum.

OXFORD: Ashmolean Museum; Philip Bate Collection, Faculty of Music; Pitt Rivers Museum.

SURREY: The Dolmetsch Collection, Hazlemere.

SCOTLAND: The Raymond Russell Collection, St. Cecilia's Hall, Edinburgh.

WALES: National Museum of Wales, Cardiff; Welsh Folk Museum, St. Fagan's.

U.S.A.

MASSACHUSETTS: The Museum of Fine Arts, Boston.

MICHIGAN: The Stearns Collection of Musical Instruments, The University of Michigan, Ann Arbor.

NEW YORK: The Metropolitan Museum of Art.

WASHINGTON, D.C.: Smithsonian Institution, The Library of Congress.

Index

Netsuke and Inro

Netsuke is a charming form of miniature sculpture, cherished for its artistic and imaginative qualities: it is both an article of apparel and an *objet d'art*. To appreciate netsuke fully, one must understand its use. The kimono is a loose cloak tied with an *obi* (sash); in lieu of pockets a toggle or netsuke was devised to facilitate carrying personal belongings. It is attached by cords to any one of a variety of *sagemono* (hanging things): *inro* (compartmented case for medicines), *kinchaku* (money purse), *kagi* (keys), etc. The connecting cord, passed under the *obi*, allows the *sagemono* to hang below, with the netsuke above acting as a stop. A sliding bead (*ojime*) on the cord is used, pushed up towards the netsuke to open the *inro*, down to keep the *inro* closed. In the generic sense of toggle, netsuke were not limited to Japan, but have been used wherever native dress also comprised a cloak and sash, as in China, Tibet, Mongolia, and Hungary.

The art of lacquer developed in both China and Japan, first for use as a preservative and hardener, then as decoration. As usual, China originated and taught, while Japan adapted and improved. Lacquer-decorated objects range from the huge screens and elaborate cabinets of China to the exquisite Japanese inro and other small boxes which are considered the greatest achievement of the lacquer craft.

The economics and conditions that permitted the development of superb netsuke and art lacquer no longer exist, and fine examples face a progressive scarcity.

Opposite:
Left: Inro; black lacquer with gold and silver map, signed 'Inaba' saku'. Ojime; gold bird on a peony bush. Netsuke; wood, showing the good luck god Fukurokuju.
Centre: Inro; powdered gold lacquer, signed 'Yoshitsura at the age of 69'. Ojime; iron, an owl and (reverse) the moon. Netsuke; wood, a kylin signed 'Tametaka'.
Right: Inro; raised gold lacquer with enrichment of cut sheet gold, signed 'Kajikawa saku'. Ojime; silver with inlays. Netsuke; ivory, signed 'Ikkosai'.

Netsuke and Inro
The Craft

The most popular netsuke carving is three-dimensional *katabori* or carving-in-the-round, especially those which avoid reliance on a base for support of figures and objects, thereby meriting greater approval. *Anabori* (interior carving) is a specialized form of *katabori* with micro-miniature carving deeply recessed, as in a cave. The *manju* is a round flat cake giving its name to netsuke of this shape, whether a solid block or two mated sections; it is always carved in relief, either inlaid, incised, raised or sunken. A variation is the *ryusa*, named after its creator, comprising two mated, hollowed-out sections with a perforated or cut-out design. The elongated *sashi* netsuke is thrust deep into the *obi* for security and support; the similar *obi-hasami* has a hook at one end to catch on the lower edge of the *obi* for additional safety. Often, a netsuke had a secondary function, doubling as a seal, a compass, a sundial, an abacus, etc.

'Souvenir' netsuke were made in various localities; for example, in the Uji tea district it was a tea-picker carved in painted wood of the local tea bush; in Nara the Noh actor, and in Hida Takayama the animals of the zodiac and others, in local yew-wood. The carving technique used was *ittobori*; 'single knife carving', but actually a technique of carving in angular surfaces, giving the effect of hammered silver, but with much larger planes.

About three-quarters of all netsuke are wood or ivory. Boxwood (*tsuge*) is the principal material, dense and close-grained, it shows the most minute details. Other popular indigenous and imported woods were ebony, red sandal-wood, ironwood, teak and all the fruit woods—especially cherry and black persimmon.

In addition to elephant ivory, marine ivories were also used, including narwhale, walrus tusk, and the tooth of the sperm whale. An exotic material found occasionally is hornbill ivory. Stag antler, a domestic material, was relatively cheap and plentiful. In no way inferior to ivory, it is even more durable. The difficulty was to find sufficiently large solid pieces.

The balance are bamboo, metal, lacquer, porcelain, jet, coral, tortoise shell, buffalo horn, etc. No list of materials seems to be complete; there is always a horse bone or a petrified egg netsuke to be added!

The sap of *Rhus vernifica*, the lacquer tree, is first sticky and transparent; after exposure to air and sunlight, it turns blackish. Objects coated with this resinous varnish are known as lacquerware.

The base of most lacquered objects is wood, which for a small inro may be no thicker than a playing card. The perfectly dry base, free from sap or oil, was made by a specialist, his diligence evident in the compartments of an inro, or the lid of an incense box, fitting without a trace of play or warp.

An astonishing division of labour followed; the basic lacquering was by the *nuri-shi* and his assistants, who primed, sealed, smoothed and hardened in various processes, using rice paste, paper, astringents, and lacquer. The *nuri-shi* finished with successive coats of clear and black lacquers, meticulously polished with leaves, grass, different grades of charcoal, and finally with incredibly fine, soft powdered deer horn. Only this laborious polishing created the mirror-black ground, a background for the gold lacquer craftsman the *makie-shi*, employing a huge assortment of tools, brushes, and materials. His special palette included gold and silver powders, flakes and foils in numerous sizes and grades, various lacquers, colouring ingredients, and shells and other materials for inlay. Red and black were the most common lacquer colours, but green, yellow, and very rarely, white, were also used.

The main techniques were *hira-makie*, *taka-makie*, *togi-dashi*, *raden*, and carving. *Hira-makie* are decorations in flat lacquer, *taka-makie* are in slightly-raised low relief. *Togi-dashi* are pictures covered over with clear lacquer, which was rubbed down until the pictures reappear; the effect is like a water-colour painting. *Raden* designs were made of inlaid mother-of-pearl and iridescent shells, often with gold and silver foil. Built-up layers of lacquer were made sufficiently thick for carving, usually in red (*tsuishu*) or black (*tsuikoku*) lacquer. Sometimes the red and black layers were painted on alternatively, then carved in scroll patterns (*guri*). Other techniques imitated metals (*sabiji*), cloth or material, (*nunome*) and wood grain (*mokume*). A design engraved in hair-lines, which were then filled with gold or coloured lacquer, was called *chinkin-bori*.

Opposite:
Japanese netsukes, left to right: Boxwood, Bukan Zenshi, his tiger and apprentices; ivory, Chinese temple pavilion and bridge; stag antler, long-nosed mask wrapped in a cloth; ivory, grazing deer; painted wood, female entertainer; ivory, resting goat; pearl octopus with coral eyes; wood, monkey and tiger; boxwood, Kwanyu, the famous Chinese Han general.

Netsuke
Introduction

The Japanese prototype (pre-seventeenth century) was probably quite similar to its contemporary Chinese toggle; a stone, shell, root, burl, bamboo node or other natural material was selected for its suitable size, shape, and magical, medicinal and symbolic properties. A minimum amount of carving and polishing would emphasize these properties and enhance the texture. The simple decorations were messages and symbols of felicity, success, long life, etc.

The Japanese authorities claim netsuke as their exclusive art, a claim with some validity if those produced during the Tokugawa and Meiji periods (1603-1912) are compared with their Chinese counterparts. The function was identical, but the attitude and goals of the Chinese toggle-maker and the Japanese *netsuke-shi* (netsuke craftsman) diverged radically. The Chinese continued to select his toggle for curative and medicinal benefits, efficacy as a charm, auspicious markings, or for sensual and tactile pleasure as a fingering piece. The importance of his toggle was its symbolism; for example, stag antler, pine tree and turtle for longevity, and lotus pod, pomegranate or gourd for a numerous family. The Japanese selected his netsuke for its subject, the suitability of the material and artistic considerations of form, balance, contrast and composition. The Chinese ultimate was the toggle with the richest meaning; the Japanese ultimate was the most beautiful creation.

By the end of the eighteenth century the *netsuke-shi* was supported by an integrated organization of importers, wholesalers and retailers. The craft employed countless materials and a vast range of styles, techniques, and subjects exhibiting great virtuosity and artistry. In 1781 the *Soken Kisho* was published (the first book with a section on netsuke) containing the names of 54 *netsuke-shi*. The Chinese toggle-maker had remained a peasant artisan repeating his conventionalized but meaningful designs; in Japan netsuke became big business as well as great art, and remained so until the early twentieth century.

Certain types were made by other craftsmen, as adjuncts to their main professions. Metal artists made the special *kagami-buta* (mirror-lid), with a metal disc fitted into a bowl of ivory, wood, or other material. They used gold, silver, copper, *shibuichi* (silver bronze) and *shakudo* (gold bronze) for the lids, applying their remarkable swordsmith techniques of inlay, chasing and overlay. The mask carver had only to reduce the size of his product to Lilliputian proportions, and provide holes for the cord, in order to have a perfectly shaped netsuke. Lacquerers frequently made complementary or harmonious netsuke for use with their *inro*. The ceramist made netsuke in porcelain and in pottery; at least one kiln, the Hirado, produced them in quantity.

The practice of signing developed with the carvers who produced only netsuke. About half of all netsuke are signed; the earlier ones the least frequently. Like the Chinese toggle, the Japanese prototype is customarily unsigned. No conclusion regarding quality based on signature alone is justified.

The demise of netsuke as an article of wear is attributed to changing styles. The old custom of carrying a pipe case (*tsutsu*) and tobacco pouch (*tonkotsu*) suspended from a single netsuke was replaced by the fashion of thrusting the *tsutsu* directly into the folds of the *obi*. Western clothing was introduced following the Meiji Restoration (1868) and slowly but surely, pockets and handbags became part of everyday wear.

Today the netsuke is no longer subject to the whims of fashion. It lives on as a collector's item—perhaps more alive than ever before. This esteem was at first largely fostered by foreigners who recognized the importance of netsuke as an expression of the Japanese artistic genius, wrote about it extensively in periodicals and books, and above all, acquired and preserved fine examples. Many of the greatest collections are in Europe and the United States, both in private hands and in museums. Nonetheless, growing appreciation has led to a new interest and Japanese collectors are beginning to bring many of these intriguing little carvings home to their native land.

Opposite: Japanese inro.
Tonkotsu simulating an inro, inlaid in ivory, lacquers, various stones; chrysanthemum-shaped netsuke.
Four case inro of coloured togidashi; kagamibuta netsuke, ivory case and shibuichi lid.
Four case inro, paulownia wood (kiri) ground with ivory, (raised) gold lacquer; manju netsuke, pottery inlay.
Four case inro, basket weave with black, silver and gold lacquer.

a) Taoist saint in wood, unsigned; probably 17th century; ht. 3 15/16″ (10.0 cm.).

The Taoist pantheon is peopled with strange gods who, though saintly and ascetic, look like fiends, live with weird beasts and make their homes in bare caves. The figure illustrated is an example. He holds a metaphysical jewel (*tama*) but he has the visage and clawed hands and feet of a dragon. He is mounted on a *baku*, a benign beast, with an elephant-like trunk, that feeds on bad dreams and on evil.

The netsuke is an engraved seal which reads 'Daimin' (Great Ming Period—1368-1661).

b) Karyobinga in ivory, unsigned, 18th century; ht. 2 3/8″ (6.0 cm.).

The *Karyobinga* is a creature of Indian mythology, half woman and half bird. Her bearing is regal, with human head and torso, the wings of a bird and a tail of feathers. She stands on bird legs and talons. Rarely represented in Japanese art, she is extremely popular in Thailand and Indonesia. In netsuke, she is a rare bird indeed and recognized as an exotic import.

The idea of a creature half woman and half bird is not so strange to devout Buddhists, who believe in the transmigration of souls and the reincarnation of one life-form from another.

Signature of Gechu carved on the base of c.

c) left: Shishi (lion) in ivory, signed Gechu, 18th century; ht. 2 5/16″ (5.8 cm.).

Shishi is translated as 'lion' because no fauna exists which it more nearly resembles. It is also known as the Chinese lion and Korean dog, appearing wherever Buddhism prevails. In male and female pairs, one with open maw, one with closed, *shishi* guard the entrances of temples and shrines, exhibiting the sculptural characteristics of their countries of origin.

The *netsuke-shi* have created a remarkable range and variety of *shishi*. A most satisfying collection might be made of this one subject. Gechu is one of the 54 *netsuke-shi* listed in the *Soken Kisho*.

d) centre: Kaibutsu (imaginary animal), with young, wood, signed Tomin; 18th century; wdth. 1 3/8″ (3.5 cm.).

This animal and young are unidentified. The head shape is somewhat lengthened with a heavy beard; it has a little, nub-like tail, and the paws have three pronounced claws like the predatory talons of a hawk. *Kaibutsu* is a term which covers all animals of fantasy, *dobutsu* includes all real ones.

e) right: Pigeon-hawk in ivory, signed Rangyoku; dated by Ueda to the 18th century; lgth. 1 7/8″ (4.8 cm.).

Rangyoku stretched his artistic licence considerably in carving the tail and wings of this strange bird like a pigeon, and the head and beak like a bird of prey. Should an artist be concerned with identification when his goal is a lovely functional figure? This netsuke, all hawk or half pigeon, is the ideal weight and size for use with a lacquer inro.

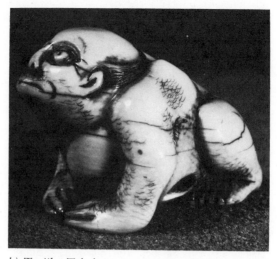

a) Saishi, one of the twenty-four paragons of filial devotion (Nijushi Ko), ivory, signed Miura shi *(of good family)* Yoshinaga; *probably 18th century; ht.* $2\frac{5}{16}''$ *(5.8 cm.).*

Under the Confucian ethic, an orderly society depended upon fixed relationships and obligations. Filial obedience and sacrifice were cardinal virtues. Confucius himself is credited with writing an account of the hardships and sacrifices bravely endured by these devoted children for their aged, diseased or dying parents. Adopted by the Japanese, the *netsuke-shi* often represented the Nijushi Ko.

This netsuke is of Saishi, and her aged, toothless mother-in-law, who was unable to eat solids. Saishi fed her with milk from her breasts until the old woman died. The artist is not one of the Yoshinagas listed in *The Netsuke Handbook*.

b) Tenjiku Tokubei in ivory, unsigned; probably 18th century: wdth. $1\frac{9}{16}''$ *(4.0 cm.), ht.* $\frac{1}{2}''$ *(1.2 cm.).*

Tokubei is a semi-legendary 17th century character, a bold robber who repeatedly escaped his pursuers by using magic and disguise. A Noh drama bears his name, depicting him as a master of Frog Magic (*Gama Yojitsu*) living among a numerous band of frogs, disguising himself as one of them at will.

The subject is commonly portrayed with a man in relationship to a frog that identifies him as Tokubei. However, the carver of this piece attacked the problem with a more complex approach, designing a creature with body and expression that is half human and half frog.

---

c) Grazing horse in stag antler, unsigned; probably 18th century; ht. $3\frac{1}{16}''$ *(7.7 cm.).*

The horse is one of the twelve animals of the Oriental zodiac, and a preferred netsuke of the man born in the Year of the Horse. The zodiac animals occur in fixed order beginning with the rat and ending with the wild boar. When a Japanese tells his 'animal' this sequence will give his exact age—excluding the possibility of a 12-year error! The horse is often combined with the rat, since the seventh year following the birth year is expected to be lucky. This netsuke has been made from a particularly large specimen of stag antler.

d) Wolf and whelp in ivory, unsigned; probably 18th century; ht. $1\frac{3}{4}''$ *(4.5 cm.).*

The fox and dog are common in Japanese art, unlike their canine relative, the wolf. Indeed, the wolf is not mentioned in Volker's *The Animal in Far Eastern Art*. Nevertheless, he is a menace in some mountain areas where shrines are erected to his spirit and farmers pray for his forbearance.

The unknown carver has created an interesting composition; the vulpine ferocity of the beast is augmented by contrast with the sleepy helplessness of the cub. Perhaps there is also a philosophical or moral aspect; the wolf's rapacity is concentrated on defence of her young—not predatory attack.

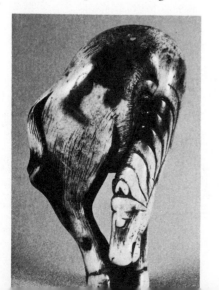

a) Man holding pipe with lower lip—wood, signed Masayuki and kakihan; early 19th century; ht. 1⅜″ (3.5 cm.).

The ordinary city dweller (*chonin*) tries to hold his long-stemmed pipe (*kiseru*) with the pressure of his lower lip, his palm open to catch the pipe should it drop. It was an amusing game and so was the carver's choice of subject. Many believe that one of the *netsuke-shi's* goals was to amuse; the *chonin* displaying this netsuke when smoking with his friends would have found it a delightful 'conversation piece', while the samurai needing medicine or a philter from his inro must have experienced a lift to his spirits from the *chonin's* ridiculous activity.

b) Swan 'gourd' in ivory, signed Mitsuhiro; mid-19th century; wdth. 1⁵⁄₁₆″ (3.4 cm.), ht. 1⅛″ (2.8 cm.).

The gourd in its numerous varieties and shapes has always fascinated the Japanese and is frequently represented in art; the natural gourd was one of the most common prototype netsuke. Large specimens held water or *saké* for the traveller; smaller ones contained scent or a philter. Gourds were sometimes forced into artistic shapes by wires tied on the growing plant. The *netsuke-shi* were so entranced with their loveliness that they imitated them in a variety of materials, including glass and agate. Here, Mitsuhiro has designed an utterly simple gourd that conveys the impression of a graceful swan.

---

c) Oni mask in hornbill ivory, signed Shounsai and kakihan; probably mid-19th century; ht. 1⁷⁄₁₆″ (3.7 cm.).

The *oni* (devil), common in Japanese art, is easily identified by horns and clawed hands and feet. Not very intimidating, he is often shown as a dwarfish ogre fleeing from Shoki, the gigantic demon-queller.

Most collectors want a good specimen in this rare, ivory-like material, its source being the helmeted hornbill, found only in the inaccessible mountains of Borneo, and parts of Indonesia. The skin is brilliant orange-red, the inside pale-to-canary yellow. Here, the red is used for horns, curly hair and cheeks, taking the greatest advantage of the colour contrast.

d) Kaiba (sea-horse) in wood, signed Masayoshi; mid-19th century; ht. 1¼″ (3.1 cm.).

The Oriental mediaeval natural histories describe many wondrous beasts, such as the unicorn, of which the *kirin* is the most popular for netsuke. Other varieties are rarer; this example, for instance, does not quite match the species described by Joly in drawings and descriptions. It has a goat's head and beard, the unicorn's single horn, the *shishi's* thick curly tail, and a carapace turtle-back. It is quite like a woodblock print by Eitaku (1843–1890), reproduced by Katherine Ball and there called a *kaiba* (sea-horse).

a) Tadamori and the oil thief (abura bozu) in ivory, signed Shunkosai; *mid/late 19th century; dia.* 2⅜″ *(6.0 cm.).*

Tadamori, a 12th century warrior hero, rescued the Yasaka Temple, Kyoto, from a fiery dragon seen on rainy nights. Ambushing the 'monster', Tadamori found a servant blowing on his oil lamp to keep it alight: the culprit had regularly been stealing oil when protected by obscuring rain.

This solid Manju netsuke is carved in deep relief.

b) Fox in bamboo, unsigned; probably late 19th century; ht. 2 1/16″ *(5.2 cm.).*

This example, although made much later, typifies the pre-17th century prototype netsuke, when the first artistic strivings consisted of a discriminating choice of attractive material, needing the minimum shaping. Here, the bamboo was already a satisfactory toggle, suggesting a lean, feral body and tail—a suggestion enhanced by shaping the head, smoking to improve the colour, and polishing.

This netsuke doubles as a seal, probably made by a seal engraver. He would customarily carve the handle but leave the base untouched. The purchaser chose a handle from stock and the seal maker would engrave his name or design on the bottom.

Signature of Shunkosai, on a.

---

c) Stylized Mandarin duck in ivory, signed Fuji Masanobu *and kakihan; mid/late 19th century; wdth.* 1⅝″ *(4.1 cm.).*

This duck is a fine example of *anabori*, recessed behind the opening in the shape of half a cherry blossom. The interior carving comprises numerous people, structures and activities. In the foreground there is a bridge with pedestrians and a *palanquin*, in the middle ground a boat under sail, and in the far background a *torii* and shrine.

Masanobu, a retainer of the Owari clan, was one of the foremost practitioners of *anabori*. The stylized Mandarin duck is frequently represented in Far Eastern Art where it is considered a symbol of conjugal happiness and fidelity.

d) Senkyo in wood, signed Ryosai; *probably 19th century; ht.* 1 13/16″ *(4.7 cm.), wdth.* 1⅞″ *(4.8 cm.).*

Chinese art and literature is full of legendary wonders: fantastic men and animals of mythological lands, seas and mountains—men with only one eye, one arm and one leg, who had to walk in pairs for balance, animals that resulted from the union of the cow and the dragon, etc. Some of these inspired the *netsuke-shi*.

The Senkyo were normal men except for the neat round holes in their chests; a long pole could be run through the hole of a tired Senkyo enabling his companions to carry him, as in this example of an amusing netsuke.

The supreme symbol of congratulations: Kotobuki, a popular decorative motif.

Netsuke

a) *Actor in Noh drama, Dojoji (Dojo Temple), made in Tsuishu, signed* Horan; *probably late 19th century; ht. 2¼″ (5.7 cm.).*

This depicts the main character in *Dojoji* performing the dance which is the climax of the play. Anchin was a dedicated young priest, Kiyohime a young woman whose love for him grew more impetuous with each gentle rebuff, until Anchin took refuge under the huge bronze bell of the temple. Love turned Kiyohime to fury, and her face became a she-devil, her body a serpent. Enveloping the bell, she incinerated poor Anchin.

The actor wears the mask of Hannya, the She-Devil, and holds the hammer to strike the bell. As in Kabuki, all the actors and dancers are men.

b) *Shozuka Baba in wood, signed* Soshin to *(carved); probably 19th century; ht. 4⅛″ (10.5 cm.).*

Shozuka Baba is the only female official of the Buddhist Hell (*Jigoku*) where the tortures of the damned make Dante's Inferno a pleasure palace by comparison. She is keeper of the river which the wicked dead cross, on the way to their destination of eternal spasms and convulsions. Shozuka Baba steals their garments which she hangs on dead trees along the banks. She puts the children-dead to the everlasting task of building rock piles, which she knocks down every night. She is recognized by her immense height of sixteen feet and by her pendulous breasts and belly.

---

c) *Abstract crab (kani) in whale tooth, signed* Ono Ryomin *and kakihan; late 19th century; ht. 9/16″ (1.5 cm.), wdth. 15/16″ (2.3 cm.).*

The species of crab, upon which this abstract netsuke is based, is called *Heike-gani*. The Heike clan was decimated by the Genji at the Battle of Dannoura in the 12th century. Consistent with a belief in transmigration, the souls of Heike warriors are thought to inhabit the bodies of the local crabs. The fighting faces of samurai are imagined in the folds and markings of the crab's shell, and the red colour reflects the colour of the Heike standard.

The complete inscription reads, 'Using the tooth of the whale, abstract Heike crab Ono Ryomin'.

d) *Elephant in stag antler, signea* Koku(sai); *late Tokugawa/early Meiji (19th century); lgth. 4⅝″ (11.8 cm.).*

Kokusai was a rare artist of whimsey, humour and originality working mainly in stag antler, an intractable medium owing to its branching shape, spongy interior and limited size. Kokusai's genius was the ability to find an embryonic and artistic design in the most unlikely shapes. This netsuke is the elongated type known as *obi-hasami*.

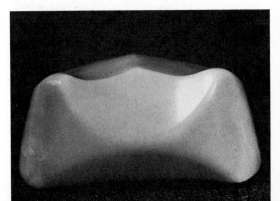

Inro
Introduction

Lacquer (*urushi*) is the exuded sap of several varieties of the ash tree, which grow only in the Orient.

Lacquer developed first in China, but by the tenth-twelfth centuries, the craft was practised in Japan. There is evidence of an interchange of information between China and Japan during the Sung, Yüan and Ming Periods (960-1644), but there are nevertheless certain differences between their lacquers: the Japanese is of better quality, having no additives; the Chinese is adulterated with pig blood and with glue residues from fish, deer horn and ox hides. Chinese subjects are comparatively limited, with highly conventionalized and repetitive designs and patterns; the Japanese found original decorative motifs in legend, history, nature, fantasy and everyday life. The Chinese lacquerer considered the practical use of the object, finishing the inside, back and bottom with fewer coats and with less care than the open or facing sides. The Japanese craftsman was motivated by a desire for perfection, finishing every surface with uniform concern and dedication. The Chinese tended to specialize in both carved and inlaid lacquer which was often heavier and bolder than the Japanese. The Japanese output was concentrated in gold lacquer.

The Tokugawa (1614-1867) was a period very conducive to the development of lacquer. The *daimyo* (lords) had to maintain residence in Edo (Tokyo), the new capital, as well as in their provincial capitals. Travel between Edo and the castle towns was continuous. Seclusion and leisure encouraged sophisticated games, gift exchanges and elegant furnishings; the demand for fine lacquer for these purposes was so great that the *daimyo* sponsored and retained individual lacquerers. In this respect, the *makie-shi* (gold-lacquer craftsman) fared much better than the *netsuke-shi*. Gold lacquer objects included cabinets, incense burners, tea containers, hair ornaments, saddles, boxes for letters, incense games, cakes, cosmetics, medicines, writing sets and tables. Usually only the smaller articles were signed, as they might be given as gifts; the larger articles were made by craftsmen-retainers for their lords.

Inro represent the greatest flowering, the jewel of the art of the *makie-shi*. Within the tiny area at his disposal, he applied the finest concentration of skill and originality of techniques and treatments. He was faced with the additional problem of cutting the completed inro along the borders of the compartments without marring the design.

Much has been said about the years required to produce fine gold lacquer. While it is true that some lacquerers spent over ten years on a single object, the apparent conclusion that he produced only a few articles in his lifetime is false. Lacquer dries slowly and only in naturally moist air. It cannot be dried artificially or scientifically. Thus, after the application of each coat the object must be put aside to dry. It is this protracted drying process that lengthens inordinately the time required to produce a single article, and a lacquerer would work on numerous objects at the same time, although any one might take years to complete.

Lacquer had become so popular in the West that during the eighteenth and nineteenth centuries most European countries attempted to copy the Japanese artists, especially on larger pieces of furniture which were so difficult to ship out and back from the Orient. However, the real lacquer tree, which contained the basic ingredient, and the centuries of traditional skill, were both missing.

a) Chinese cosmetic box in red lacquer; late Sung dynasty (960-1279 AD); dia. 7½" (19.0 cm.), ht. 6⅞" (17.4 cm.).

This octagonal box consists of two sections and a lid. It is in red lacquer with an all-over design of peonies in hairline engraving filled with gold lacquer. The Japanese call this technique *chinkin-bori*. The lower edge is decorated in the same technique with a sawtooth design.

b) Chinese lacquer table; Ming dynasty, 1637; dia. 1' ⅝" (32 cm.), ht. 1' 8½" (52 cm.).

This fine five-legged table is decorated in red and green lacquer, the top with a dragon design in gold lacquer, and flowers and butterflies on the panels, shoulders and legs. An engraved, gold-filled inscription on the back of one leg (see detail) reads *Ta Ming Ch'ung Ching Ting Ch'ou Nien Chih* indicating that the table was made in the year 1637 of the Ming Dynasty.

---

c) Four-case lacquer inro, signed this year 85 years old, Tsuchida Soetsu and kakihan; late 17th century; ht. 2⁵⁄₁₆" (5.8 cm.), wdth. 2" (5.0 cm.).

A stag in raised dull gold lacquer and a sleeping doe in raised pewter compose the design against a black ground. The reverse side is decorated with a pine tree in gold lacquer and a *torii* inlaid in pewter and pearl. The inside of the compartments is black lacquer with the edges rimmed in gold.

d) Four-case lacquer inro, signed Masanobu; early 18th century; ht. 3⅛" (8.0 cm.), wdth. 2½" (6.3 cm.).

Black-on-black is a difficult lacquer technique, known as *yami-makie*. The design is made visible by contrasting the dull black decoration against the bright black of the ground, or vice versa.

On the reverse, two boatmen in harness on the shore pull the ferry upstream. Note that the design continues without interruption around the ends or cord channels of the inro. The inside compartments are in black lacquer with rims in dull gold (*fundame*). The flat-polished red lacquer signature is in seal form characters. Masanobu is an 'art name' (*go*) of Shiomi Masanari.

a) Four-case inro with carved crawfish and matching netsuke, signed Tachibana Gyokuzan; late 18th or early 19th century; ht. 3¼" (8.3 cm.), wdth. 2 1/16" (5.2 cm.).

A Japanese crawfish carved in red lacquer high relief (*tsuishu*) lies on the mirror black ground (*roiro*) of this inro, complete with its matching netsuke and ojime. The technique of *tsuishu* requires the successive application of numerous coats of red lacquer until a sufficient thickness for carving is built up. The compartments are in black lacquer and dull gold (*fundame*), the ojime and netsuke in harmonious carved lacquers. The *manju* netsuke is adorned by circles of peony, plum and chrysanthemum.

b) Five-case inro in Somada, signed Somada Hisa-mitsu and kakihan; early 19th century; ht. 3¾" (9.5 cm.), wdth. 2⅜" (6.0 cm.).

The Somada technique, named after its originator, has imbedded sections of iridescent green, blue and reddish-purple shell (*aogai*) and cut gold and silver foil (*kanagai*). The compartments are decorated inside with *nashiji*.

Jurojin, the God of Wisdom, stands under a pine branch, offering grain to a crane. On the reverse, the young attendant's branch is hung with the attributes of the Seven Happy Gods. The complementary netsuke bears Jurojin's fan and scrolls of knowledge, so that the total design comprises a symbolic wish for success, good fortune, long life and numerous descendants.

---

c) Four-case lacquer inro, signed Moei and Tomi (or Fu); early 19th century; ht. 3" (7.6 cm.), wdth. 2 3/16" (5.6 cm.).

A swallow (*tsubame*) flies in the rain; the bird is in raised bright black lacquer with dark grey and red markings, the rain is represented by diagonal lines of gold and silver. An unusually heavy under-coating of black lacquer darkens the gold ground, which has sprinkled gold particles scattered on it in cloud patterns (*mura nashiji*). The lacquerer's signature is visible on the illustrated side. The obverse has two swallows in flight. The inside of the compartments has *nashiji* ground embellished with *gyobu*, irregular gold-lacquer flakes.

The signature is *Moei* (and seal) *Tomi*; an alternative reading, *Fu*.

d) Three-case lacquer inro, signed Shueisai Yuzan; probably early 19th century; ht. 2 15/16" (7.5 cm.), wdth. 2⅛" (5.4 cm.).

The design on the upper side of this lacquer inro represents the silk brocade bag for the tea jar, in raised brown lacquer on the reverse. The bag is in *taka-makie* with a repeated family crest in *nashiji*; the tea jar simulates Seto pottery. The ground is mirror black (*roiro*). The compartments are decorated with *nashiji*.

The artist is unknown. Though obviously an accomplished lacquerer, Yuzan does not appear to be recorded, nor does his work suggest association with a particular family school.

Signature of Moei and (on seal) Tomi—on c.

Inro

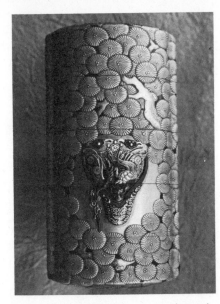

Signatures on a.

a) Four-case inro of gold lacquer and metal, signed Kajikawa and hogen Haruaki; 19th century; ht. 4″ (10.2 cm.), wdth. 2⅟₁₆″ (5.3 cm.).

An all-over design of pine needles in raised gold lacquer (*taka-makie*) almost covers the mirror-black ground. The metal inlay, set against a bright gold lacquer (*kinji*) sun, is Jurojin holding a turtle and a branch of plum blossoms. It uses gold, silver, silver bronze (*shibuichi*) and gold bronze (*shakudo*), in various metalcraft techniques. The reverse inlays are a crane in silver and a nest of young in gold. Each design symbolized longevity. Inside the compartments is a rich mosaic of *gyobu*.

The signatures are *Kajikawa* and seal for the lacquer, and *hogen Haruaki* for the metal.

b) Lacquer tonkotsu, signed Zeshin; ivory netsuke, signed Mitsuhiro; 19th century; ht. 1¹⁵⁄₁₆″ (5.0 cm.), wdth. 2⅟₁₆″ (5.2 cm.).

The *tonkotsu*, which is used for loose tobacco, has only one compartment. This example with a wooden lid imitates glazed Seto pottery, simulating the thick drip-glaze and the naked clay body revealed at the foot of the tea bowl (*chawan*). The tonkotsu is signed in this master's characteristic hairline strokes, reputedly etched with a rat's tooth. Zeshin was a great original and versatile lacquerer, whose technical perfection was so great that copies rarely succeed in deception.

The ivory netsuke signed *Mitsuhiro* continues the tea ceremony theme with a simulated tea bowl and tea whisk.

c) Three-case Awaji pottery inro, unsigned; probably 19th century; ht. 3¼″ (8.2 cm.), wdth. 2³⁄₁₆″ (5.6 cm.).

This is an unusual example of *Awaji-yaki* (pottery made on the Island of Awaji), in leopard-skin glaze with a very fine crackle; the colours are yellow and a deep brownish purple. Unusual in pottery, the risers securing the compartments are extremely tall, measuring 1.4 cm. in height. The glaze on the reverse side is identical. *Awaji-yaki* imitated Chinese porcelain of the K'ang-hsi period.

d) Four-case lacquer inro, signed Kajikawa saku; probably 19th century; ht. 3⁷⁄₁₆″ (8.8 cm.), wdth. 2⁷⁄₁₆″ (6.2 cm.).

This type of inro fits snugly into a slip case, through which the cord channels pass. The case has cherry blossoms of gold, silver and red. The inro itself is in coloured *togidashi*, with a Mandarin duck on a river bank; on the reverse, his mate is swimming. Tiny flecks of coloured shell (*aogai*) on the path are separately inlaid with a long bamboo needle. The compartments are adorned with the identical rich *nashiji* that lines the case.

The Kajikawa family school is very extensive in time and membership; dating must be based on intrinsic elements, such as style and technique.

Netsuke and Inro Glossary

ANABORI: deeply recessed and minuscule carving.

AOGAI: inlay of thin iridescent shells of green, blue and reddish purple.

AWAJI-YAKI: pottery made on the island of Awaji, between Honshu and Shikoku.

CHINKIN-BORI: hair-line engravings on lacquer filled with gold or contrasting colours.

EDO: the name of Tokyo until the Meiji Restoration.

FUNDAME: a dull gold finish.

GO: art name, or pseudonym.

GURI: successive coats of lacquer carved in scroll patterns.

GYOBU: irregular large gold flakes imbedded in a lacquer ground.

HIDA TAKAYAMA: a rural area near Gifu where the Tokugawa and Meiji arts and crafts are preserved.

HIMOTOSHI: holes or channels in netsuke and inro through which the cords are passed.

HIRADO: an island off Kyushu which produced a fine porcelain.

HIRA-MAKIE: flat lacquer designs almost level with the ground.

HIRAME: irregular gold and silver particles individually imbedded in a lacquer ground.

HOGEN: an art title, conferred for excellence in painting and sculpture.

ISU: a prunus wood; some species were imported from China.

ITTOBORI: literally, single knife carving in large angular planes producing a characteristic effect somewhat similar to hammered silver.

KAGAMIBUTA: netsuke with a metal lid fitted into a bowl of ivory, wood or other material; the metal work is the important part of the kagamibuta.

KAKIHAN: a carved or written personal seal as opposed to the usual stamped or impressed seal.

KANAGAI: inlay of sections of gold and silver foil.

KATABORI: three-dimensional carving in the round.

KINJI: bright gold finish.

KIRI: paulownia, wood often used for netsuke cabinets.

KIRIGANE: literally, cut metal; tiny geometric shapes of gold foil inlaid in lacquer.

KOTOBUKI: a character signifying congratulations and felicitations.

MAKIE-SHI: gold lacquer craftsman who applies the final gold and coloured decorations.

MANJU: a round flat cake or filled pastry; the name used for netsuke of similar shape.

MEIJI PERIOD: from the Restoration of Meiji Dynasty in 1868 until 1912.

MOKUME: lacquer technique imitating wood grain.

MON: an heraldic or emblematic design; the Japanese family crest.

MURA NASHIJI: nashiji strewn in cloud patterns.

NASHIJI: a coating or design in strewn gold particles.

NUNOME: lacquer technique imitating woven materials.

NURI-SHI: the lacquer craftsman who strengthens, seals, hardens the foundation and applies first basic coats.

OBI: a sash worn with the kimono.

OBI-HASAMI: type of netsuke similar to sashi, but secured additionally by a curve or hook which catches on the obi.

OJIME: a sliding bead for tightening the cords of the inro, pouch or purse.

RADEN: mother-of-pearl inlay.

ROIRO: a mirror-black ground with highly smooth and reflective surface.

RYUSA: similar to manju netsuke but hollowed out with a perforated or cut-out design.

SABIJI: simulating metal surfaces in lacquer.

SAKU: made, as in 'Zeshin saku'—made by Zeshin.

SASHI: elongated netsuke thrust deep into the obi.

SETO: a famous pottery kiln site near Nagoya.

SHAKUDO: gold-bronze alloy.

SHI: of good family.

SHIBUICHI: silver-bronze alloy.

TAGAYASAN: Indonesian ironwood.

TAKA-MAKIE: raised lacquer decoration in low relief.

TAKE: the sacred jewel, an emblem found in Taoism and Buddhism.

TANSU: a cabinet of any shape or size made of wood.

TO: carved.

TOGIDASHI: decorations coated with clear lacquer and then polished level with the background imparting a water-colour painting effect.

TOKUGAWA PERIOD: also known as Edo Period; 1603-1867 one of the great periods of Japanese art.

TORII: the Shinto gate comprising two uprights and a single or double cross beam.

TSUGE: boxwood; the most popular wood of the netsuke-shi.

TSUISHU: red lacquer applied in numerous coats and carved.

UJI: a district near Kyoto famous for its fine tea.

UMIMATSU: literally, sea pine; but actually a coral; black or brown in colour.

UMOREGI: jet; a semi-petrified wood.

URUSHI: a raw lacquer, as tapped from the tree.

YAMI-MAKIE: black lacquer design on a black lacquer ground.

ZO: made.

Netsuke and Inro Repairs and Maintenance

When not on display, netsuke and inro are best kept in special Japanese cabinets (*tansu*), with silk or velvet-lined compartmented drawers. Many collectors separate the inro from their attached netsuke, to prevent chipping the delicate lacquer.

The great dangers are dryness, heat and sudden change of temperature; do not wrap or pack tightly, or store for long periods in hot dry places. Wrap loosely and keep in a slightly damp, cool place, with a bowl of water nearby to ensure sufficient humidity. Even if displayed there should be a tumbler of water inside the cabinet. Treasured ivories may crack almost like pistol shots on sudden exposure to cool air after a long period of hot, dry storage.

Satisfactory netsuke repairs depend upon the extent and type of damage; well-matched wood is more easily disguised, but ivory is extremely difficult; a fresh repair may match closely, but after a few months it will change colour. Generally, defects are regarded with a leniency proportionate to age; old damage can be preferable to the new repair.

Clean wood netsuke with a badger-hair brush for delicate parts, a horse-hair brush for more solid parts, and finally polish with a silk cloth. Patient use of brush and silk on dull examples will restore most of the original lustre without oils or chemicals. Above all, *never* wash wood netsuke in soap and water, or you destroy the original polish and patina. For those who must use a preservative, botanists recommend a solution of natural bees'-wax in rectified spirits of turpentine. Particularly dirty ivory netsuke may be soaked for a few minutes in soapy warm water, then dried thoroughly, brushed and rubbed. Whether wood or ivory, if the original surface has been obliterated (disregarding deeper defacement by erosion) it may be recoloured or restained, but it will appear as new. Cracked and even split ivories can sometimes be repaired by tieing tightly with a damp cloth, exerting pressure against the crack for a day or two.

Chips and cracks in old lacquer can never be repaired perfectly, since shades and textures are almost impossible to duplicate. Protect lacquer with soft wrapping, but for displayed pieces, blow off accumulated dust and wipe the surface several times with a soft dry cloth. Remove any remaining dust with warm water, then dry thoroughly and wipe with a silk cloth. For caked or greasy dust, use warm soapy water or a weak alcohol solution sparingly. Never rub harshly or vigorously.

Loose inlays of metal or shell are not serious flaws, provided the surround is not warped or chipped. The Japanese boast that no scientific cement is more durable than their traditional clear glue, although adding that even this does not last forever. After a life span of sixty-five years the vestiges of the old bond must be removed and the inlays reimbedded anew—a repair best done in Japan.

Fakes and Forgeries

For the greater part of their existence, netsuke were simply not important enough to fake. The bare dozen most-frequently forged names are of carvers in the *Soken Kisho*, together with a few others; Tomotada, Masanao of Kyoto, Okatomo, Kaigyokusai, Mitsuhiro and Gyokuzan, and their favourite subjects are very popular, so treat the Tomotada cow, the Masanao sparrow, the Okatomo quail, the Kaigyokusai monkey, the Mitsuhiro loquat and the Gyokuzan skull, with special caution.

Remember that a forgery is always a commercial venture revealing hasty, slipshod workmanship, lack of detail and an absence of careful finish. Some cheap, mass-produced models bearing well-known names have flooded the market during the last two decades. Unworn and thickly stained, they have misplaced cord holes and inappropriate signatures.

Genuine family-school signatures appear repeatedly, such as Masanao (of Yamada), Tomochika and Shugetsu in netsuke, and Koma, Kajikawa, Shibayama for inro. The output of a 'family' included many generations and individuals, usually blood relatives or adopted apprentices, with an enormous range in quality. Never accept a name as an indication of quality; quality is intrinsic, not external, and a signature is only confirmation.

As prices rise we will find more expert copies of the best craftsmen; nineteenth century forgeries of Korin (1658-1716), Ritsuo (Haritsu), 1662-1747, and Hanzan (d. 1790) are already abundant. Detection is helped by reasonably accurate dating, since age alone will easily separate the vast majority of recent forgeries from the genuine.

The best protection—an eye for quality—can be developed by study, examination of collections, and talking to dealers and fellow enthusiasts; in the words of the wise collector 'buy the book before the antique'.

Further Reading

General

BALL, KATHERINE, *Decorative Motives in Oriental Art*.
EDMUNDS, WILL H., *Pointers and Clues to the Subjects of Chinese and Japanese Art*, London, 1934.
HOKUSAI, KATSUSHIKA, *Hokusai Manga* (Caricatures by Hokusai) 15 volumes, 1814-1878.
JOYA, MOCK, *Things Japanese*, Tokyo, 1960.
VOLKER, T., *The Animal in Far Eastern Art*, Leiden, 1950.
WEBER, V. F., *Koji Hoten*, Paris, 1923.

Netsuke

BEHRENS, W. L., *Collection, Catalogue of the*, edited by Henry L. Joly, London, 1913-14 (reissued 1966).
BROCKHAUS, ALBERT, *Netsuke, Third Edition*, Leipzig, 1925.
BUSHELL, RAYMOND, *Bitten by the Netsuke Bug*, Orientations, Hong Kong, October 1970.
Collectors' Netsuke, New York and Tokyo, 1971.
The Netsuke Handbook of Ueda Reikichi; Vermont and Tokyo, 1961.
The Wonderful World of Netsuke, Vermont and Tokyo, 1964, one hundred illustrations.
Yoshimura Shuzan, Orientations, Hong Kong, June 1971.
CAMMAN, SCHUYLER, *Substance and Symbol in Chinese Toggles*, Philadelphia, 1962.

HILLIER, MARY, *Kagetoshi and His Netsuke*, Oriental Art, 1964.
INABA, TSURYU, *Soken Kisho*, Volume 7, 1781
JOLY, HENRY L., *Legend in Japanese Art*, London, 1908, (reissued 1967).
JONAS, F. M., *Netsuke*, London and Japan, 1928, (reissued 1960).
MEINERTZHAGEN, FREDERICK, *The Art of the Netsuke Carver*, London, 1956.
O'BRIEN, MARY LOUISE, *Netsuke, A Guide for Collectors*, Vermont and Tokyo, 1965.
RYERSON, EGERTON, *The Netsuke of Japan*, London, 1958.

Inro and Lacquer

BOYER, MARTHA, *The Walters Art Gallery, Catalogue of Japanese Lacquers*, Baltimore, Maryland, 1970.
CASAL, U. A., *Japanese Art Lacquers*, Sophia University, Tokyo, 1961.
HERBERTS, K., *Oriental Lacquer, Art and Technique*, Harry N. Abrams Inc., New York.
JAHSS, MELVIN and BETTY, *Inro and Other Miniature Forms of Japanese Lacquer Art*, Vermont and Tokyo, 1971.
LEE, YU-KUAN, *Oriental Lacquer Art*, New York and Tokyo, 1972.

Museum Collections

Great Britain

CAMBRIDGESHIRE: Fitzwilliam Museum, Cambridge.
LONDON: The British Museum; The Victoria and Albert Museum.

U.S.A.

CALIFORNIA: De Jong Museum, San Francisco.
NEW YORK: The Metropolitan Museum of Art.
WASHINGTON, D.C.: The Freer Gallery.

Index

Pewter

With the exception of sporadic references to tin, or *stannum*, in early Roman literature, the first written records of pewter in more modern Europe are of the ninth century A.D. in France; slightly later, but much more specific records have been found in England, in ecclesiastical visitation lists, where such things as processional candlesticks, chrismatories and cruets were frequently mentioned. However, the history of pewter in England goes back to the Roman invaders when, in the third and fourth centuries A.D., plates, small cups and ewers in particular were made.

The Anglo-Saxons made small articles including brooches and beads of a poor quality pewter and there were possibly other uses of this period as yet undiscovered.

Various small plates, of from 4″ (10.2 cm.) to 5″ (12.7 cm.) diameter have come to light in excavations, one from a site securely dated in the period 1290–1300. Of the same date, or perhaps slightly later, are two relief-decorated pewter cruets, one of which is shown here.

Pewter spoons have been made at least from the thirteenth century. There is comparatively little extant pewterware of British origin of the period before the end of the sixteenth century, and this is mainly in the form of small plates or spoons, and very little hollow-ware; a far larger quantity of mediaeval items of all descriptions seem to have survived elsewhere, in Holland and the Netherlands in particular, due, no doubt, to its safe preservation in the soft mud of the dykes and waterways, and its discovery during later and extensive drainage operations.

In Britain the 'Golden Age' of pewter, when some of the finest examples were produced, was in the sixteenth and seventeenth centuries, and on the Continent perhaps a century earlier; even up to about the third quarter of the eighteenth century, much excellent quality pewterware was still produced. About this time, however, the guilds both in England and elsewhere began to lose control of their members and, as a result, the quality of the products often declined. Pewter, which had been a virtual necessity in the home, was being superseded by pottery, porcelain and even silver.

Despite the decrease in the home trade, an expanding market was opening in the colonies; not only was pewterware exported in large quantities but pewterers themselves, because of the local decline in trade, emigrated to the new countries, taking their moulds and skills with them.

Opposite:
Tall coffee pot by Colonel William Will of Philadelphia; U.S.A., c.1775.

Pewter
The Craft

Pewter is an alloy, composed principally of tin to which other metals such as copper or lead are added in varying proportions, according to the quality required. In its original state, tin is in the form of cassiterite, or tin dioxide, and appears as yellowish-brown crystal, found in veins and stratae of granite rocks in certain areas only. The cassiterite must pass through various stages of refinement before the tin is obtained. No doubt, in its first application, tin was used to harden copper for use in tools and only later, perhaps even accidentally, was it found that by increasing the proportion of tin and reducing the copper, a good malleable alloy would result. Such an alloy would have comprised up to 75% or 80% of pure tin to a remainder of copper; for the finest pewter, a small proportion of antimony might be added.

A less costly and lower grade pewter was also made by including lead instead of copper or with lead and copper together with the tin. These combinations produced a substantially harder alloy than the mixture of tin and copper alone though it had a lower melting point, and was thereby much easier for use in castings.

Pewter comprising at least 60% of tin was made and used by the Romans in Britain during the third and fourth centuries A.D. Pewter of a sort, with an even higher proportion of lead, was in use by the Anglo-Saxon community for small ornamental objects in the seventh and eighth centuries A.D. It is possible to date the earliest of the known examples of pewterware, other than that of the Romano-British or Anglo-Saxons, in the late twelfth century, c. 1190, as small plates of pewter, in combination with a pewter chalice, have been found in the coffins of priests and ecclesiastics—placed there, presumably, as symbols of their status.

At least as early as the fourteenth century it was realized that the lead content of pewter could produce deleterious effects when in contact with certain foodstuffs, and about this time the guilds and organizations which had been set up to assist and control the pewter craft began to lay down precise regulations as to the alloys to be used for particular commodities and purposes. In England, for example in 1348, the Ordinances of the Craft of Pewterers of London decreed that porringers, saucers, platters, square pitchers and chrismatories should be 'made of fine pewter with the proportion of copper to the tin, as much as by its own nature it will take'.

The largest amount of copper which could be absorbed was found to be approximately 26 lbs. (11.8 kilos) to 112 lbs. (50.8 kilos) of tin. Other items, i.e. 'rounded vessels' such as pots, cruets and candlesticks, were to be wrought of tin alloyed with lead 'in reasonable proportions'; the proportions were stated to be 22 lbs. (10 kilos) lead to 112

lbs. (50.8 kilos) tin. These two specifications became more or less the standards for flatware and hollow-ware respectively for the next three hundred years, until towards the end of the seventeenth century, when classifications were laid down. On the Continent, especially in German-speaking areas, an alloy known as 'test pewter' was widely used; this varied in composition from place to place, but appears to have compared favourably with the English standard for lead content. The local guilds set standards of workmanship which had to be observed by pewterers within their jurisdiction; if their wares were found to be faulty in either quality of alloy or method of production, they could be confiscated and the offender punished by fine or, for persistent offences, debarred the craft entirely. Plates and dishes were to be hammered in the booge (i.e. the curve of the well), and sometimes all over, to add strength; the ears of the porringers were to be 'burned on' (i.e. cast on to the body by placing the ear mould against the already cast bowl) and not 'run on with pale' (soldered on with inferior metal).

At certain periods, injunctions required that spoons be hammered in the bowl or stem, and all wares were to bear the maker's own touchmark. The methods employed by the ancient pewterers have often remained virtually unchanged throughout the centuries; in some modern pewtering centres, old moulds which had already served perhaps for two or three centuries are still producing good castings.

Probably one of the largest tin producing areas today is the far East, with some good pewterware produced in Malaya and elsewhere, but there has recently been something of a revival of Cornish tin mining and both English and imported tin is being used in the production of modern pewterware—thus there has been, in England at least, a continuous use of pewter for commercial purposes for upwards of seventeen centuries.

British and Continental Pewter Introduction

Pewter was known and used in ancient China and other parts of the far East and in Egypt, more than two thousand years ago but extant examples and written references of such early application are too rare to enable any really useful data relative to its composition to be established. It is probable that the small brooches and ornamental objects from Egyptian tombs, for example, were composed of almost pure tin—a substance which, in later years, was found to be far too soft in unalloyed form to serve any of the practical purposes to which true pewter was eventually put.

In Europe, pewter was well known to the Romans before the fourth century A.D., although there is no evidence of its actual manufacture on the Continent prior to that period. It is more than probable that the few examples of early Roman pewterware which have been excavated in France and Holland originated in England where the invading Romans had access to the Devonshire and Cornish tin mines, which districts were also able to produce the requisite copper. Lead, the other and at that time, the more usually employed hardening agent, was available in vast quantities in various nearby districts. It is more generally accepted that the earliest European domestic pewter, in the forms of small plates (paterae), dishes and ewers, was that made by the Romano-British craftsmen, and that there were several more or less concentrated areas in which it was made, mainly in the south-western counties but ranging north-eastwards towards East Anglia and the fenlands; such information is based on the areas in which concentrated finds of Romano-British ware have been made—some of the largest hoards around Somerset and Wiltshire, and others in Cambridge, Suffolk and Lincoln.

References have already been made to Anglo-Saxon ornamental objects although, if one may judge from the lack of actual finds, they failed to continue its usage into the domestic field. It is, in fact, not until the first quarter of the ninth century that we find any actual records, at which time, at the Council of Rheims (803–813 A.D.) the poorer churches were allowed to use pewter chalices; this edict was confirmed at the Council of Tribur (895 A.D.) and on several later occasions.

There is evidence that at least one foreign pewterers' guild was inaugurated in the middle of the thirteenth century but others, in Germany, Holland, Belgium and even Spain, were known to have craftsmen working in the early fourteenth century, and there can be no doubt that the trade was well established in most European centres by the year 1400.

It is not known at what date the craft was first organized in England; it is evident, however, that it was well-founded by the year 1348, at which time the London guild produced ordinances for the protection of its members and to ensure a standard quality for the wares they produced. The first Charter of Incorporation as a City Livery Company followed many years later, in 1473.

In France the main, and earliest centre was Paris; in Germany, Nuremberg and Augsburg; in the Netherlands and Flanders, Brussels, Antwerp, Bruges and Ghent; in Holland, Breda and Amsterdam; Italy, Bologna, and Sweden, Gothenburg.

It would seem, from examples illustrated in published literature, that some of the earliest foreign specimens hail from the largest producing countries, i.e. the Netherlands, Germany and France, in that order, but needless to say, the precise dating of such specimens must be somewhat conjectural. Although Italy and Spain are known to have been producing pewterware in the early fifteenth century, no closely datable examples from these countries are known. Sweden was a comparably late comer to the field but nevertheless has a tradition of high quality workmanship from the mid-eighteenth century to a quite late date.

Broadly speaking—for there will always be found exceptions—the quality of alloys allowed to be used for specific purposes in England has, throughout the centuries, remained at a consistently higher level than elsewhere, although in other respects the main guild regulations in all countries seem to have been closely allied to those in Britain.

In modern times, the quality of alloy used in pewterware has become higher; some excellent wares are produced today by Belgian, Dutch, Swedish and German manufacturers in particular.

There is, too, a revival of the trade in England and it is gratifying to record that steps are being taken by the ancient Pewterers' Company in conjunction with the newly formed Association of British Pewter Craftsmen, to require exceedingly high standards of design and quality, and to ensure adherence to these by the use of specific marks. Such examples will, in the course of time, become collectors' items in their own right.

b) A group of small Anglo-Saxon items; 7th to 10th centuries A.D.

Pewter

British

ROMANO-BRITISH
ELIZABETHAN

a) Romano-British pewterware; 3rd and 4th century A.D.

At top, a narrow-rimmed plate with intaglio decoration in the centre medallion, found at Stamford, Lincs.; from left to right, a vase of inverted bi-conical form (compare with the handled vessel at right), site of finding unknown; a small wrythen decorated bowl, from Cirencester, Glos.; a bowl with concave-flanged rim, on hollow foot, from Havillick, Cornwall; an oval patera with central depression, from Lakenheath, Suffolk, and a bi-conical ewer or flagon, from Selsey, Suffolk.

An amazing variety of small circular brooches, buckle-loops, rings and beads, mostly with highly ornamental relief-cast decoration, were made and used during the 7th to the 10th centuries A.D., indicating that the skills of the Romans in Britain had not been forgotten. Such things would have been produced in clay or chalk moulds which were not intended to last (the ring at left is of twisted silver wire). The brooches range from about $\frac{3}{4}''$ (1.9 cm.) to $1\frac{3}{4}''$ (4.4 cm.) diameter, and the beads up to $1''$ (2.54 cm.) in length. This particular hoard, of some 40 or more examples, was excavated in Cheapside, London.

c) Mediaeval relief-cast cruet; 13th–14th century; ht. $4\frac{1}{2}''$ (11.4 cm.).

Although pewterware for ecclesiastical purposes is mentioned frequently in early records there are comparatively few examples still extant. This cruet was found in the moat at Weoley Castle, near Birmingham. An almost identical cruet, but cast from a different mould, was found at Ludlow Castle, in Shropshire (and is now in the British Museum). There are one or two isolated instances of domestic pewterware, such as small plates, and perhaps one or two equally early lidded vessels, which have been excavated in London and elsewhere, but these are mainly in exceedingly frail or incomplete condition and difficult to date precisely.

d) Spoons, c. 1500–c. 1675.

English pewter spoons are known from the 12th century onwards, the earliest with slender plain stems, sometimes with a single ball knop at centre or top, and all with a shallow pear-shaped bowl. Examples shown here include some of the more ornamental knops; the first, an Apostle, c. 1600; another Apostle, c. 1675; in centre, the Chanticleer, c. 1575; the Woodwose (Wildman), exceedingly rare, c. 1500, and lastly, the Lion Sejant, c. 1600. Others, with plainer knops include the Diamond Point, the Baluster, the Acorn, the Wrythen Ball; many, but not all of these types had silver prototypes.

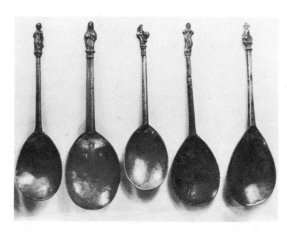

1) Porringer; c. 1575–1600; dia. of bowl 6⅛″ (15.6 cm.), overall diameter across ears 8¾″ (22.3 cm.).

Porringers of this period appear always to have had two ears, and the London Pewterers' Company insisted, in 1556, that they should be cast in one piece with the bowl—not attached with inferior metal. This example is one of about six excavated in or near London; almost identical specimens have been found in Germany and Holland. From c. 1600, porringers with only one ear came into general use. Pewterers of France and some other continental countries continued the use of two ears until a much later date. Often, the design of the ears is the only guide to nationality and dating.

b) Porringer with shallow straight-sided bowl and fretted ear; c. 1650; bowl dia. 5¼″ (13.3 cm.).

This bowl form, with only slight variations in contour, came into use at the beginning of the 17th century, and continued to about 1660. The ear forms used were smaller and of simpler design than those on later types. Specimens in good condition are rare, most of the extant examples having been discovered in excavations in London. American pewterers in the mid-18th century and later, adopted ears of similar patterns on their own porringers, which were more usually of the curved, or 'booged' bowl shape.

c) Porringer with relief-cast and hammered ornamentation; Queen Anne period, c. 1700–10; dia. of bowl 5¼″ (13.4 cm.).

The band of running 'grapevine' around the upper edge is of the same general character as that on an earlier group of relief-cast ware (p. 582b), and similar bands sometimes adorn the wide flanged foot of either salts or candlesticks of the late Stuart period. The wrythen flutes around the curved bowl are typical of those used by silversmiths of the period, and are occasionally seen on two-handled caudle-cups and lidless tavern pots. In other respects the form of the bowl is similar to those of the majority of pewter porringers from c. 1675–1740, and that of the fretted ear identical to that on many normal curved bowl porringers of c. 1700.

d) Dish with punched ornamentation around the rim; dated 1585; dia. 16¾″ (42.5 cm.).

Coevally with relief-cast decoration, pewterers throughout Europe used individual letter punches to achieve the effect so well illustrated here; in general, punched decoration ceased to be used by about the middle of the 17th century, but isolated examples (see p. 584b) are sometimes found where punches have been used to augment some other feature.

Mark on c.

*a) Plate with 'wriggled' decoration; c. 1680; dia. 8⅜"
(21.3 cm.).*

This method of ornamentation, contrived by
pushing and rocking a narrow blade across the
surface, and thereby removing shallow furrows of
metal, was used prolifically by pewterers on both
plates and tankards from the last quarter of the
17th century to c. 1730. Wriggled plates of this
character are frequently found in pairs, and are
known to collectors as 'marriage plates'. This
particular plate is of narrow-rimmed type, with
a multiple-reeded edge; the majority of wriggled
plates are of later style, with a single reeding on the
border.

*b) An alms dish ornamented with both punched and
hammered motifs; c. 1720–30; dia. 11⅝" (29.5 cm.).*

The wrythen, petalled feature of the central
decoration is an extension of that used at least two
centuries earlier on brass alms dishes made in
Nuremberg. Large pewter plates and dishes,
originally of normal domestic style, were ornamented in this fashion and used, occasionally in
pairs, for embellishment of the altar in some
English churches, and could also serve the function
of alms dishes; in private houses they might also
grace the banqueting table as rosewater dishes.

*c) Charles I period 'muffin lidded' flagon; c. 1630;
overall ht. 12¾" (32.4 cm.).*

It was not until 1603 that pewter was allowed
to be used for consecrated vessels for use in Holy
Communion, although an occasional specimen,
perhaps domestic, of earlier date is found. Types of
church flagons followed closely the forms of those
in silver from c. 1575 onwards. In the Cromwellian
period flagons became broader, with wide, hollow
foot, and a 'Beefeater's Hat' shaped cover; in
Charles II period, c. 1680, the body was of plainer
form, with a flat cover, such as is seen on the
following tankard.

*d) Charles II flat-lidded tankard; c. 1685; overall ht.
6⅝" (16.8 cm.).*

This is a form which came into vogue shortly
after the mid-17th century and remained constant
until c. 1700, sometimes found with the drum
entirely plain, but the majority of specimens bearing wriggled ornamentation of the character
shown here. The designs of the thumb-pieces
varied; some were of ramshorn form, others of
twin love-bird motif, and the handles, too, show
some variety. On this particular specimen the
handle terminal is in the form of a scroll; others
may have a splayed or shield terminal. From c. 1690
similar plain drum tankards were made with
domed covers, the earlier examples still displaying
the denticulations at front.

Maker's mark on b.

a) Queen Anne period domed-lid tankard; c. 1705–15; overall ht. 7¼″ (18.5 cm.).

This lidded form remained in vogue during the first half of the 18th century with only minor variations, such as changes in the styles of the thumb-piece to a broader scroll, or a chair-back form and with handle terminal of fishtail or ball formation. About 1740 an incurved, or tulip-shaped body evolved, and became popular during the remaining 25 years or so. Unlidded tavern mugs came into use from c. 1680, the earlier forms tall and slim, but the body eventually more closely resembled that of the lidded example shown here, and it remained a popular shape, especially from c. 1775 to 1800.

b) Flagon of flared base type; c. 1725; overall ht. 12¾″ (32.4 cm.).

This style of body remained constant throughout the first three quarters of the 18th century, it is, however, more usually found with a double curved handle, and later examples were often fitted with a pouring spout. The single curved handle seen on this example appears to have been used on this type by only one maker, John Newham, of London, whose mark is shown in the margin alongside.

c) An early wine measure; late 16th century.

This slim baluster form is known to have been in use from the mid-16th century onwards to c. 1670, and is found with hammerhead thumb-piece (as shown), or with one likened to a 'ball on wedge'. In the last quarter of the 17th century the body became broader and of more squat shape, and the handle terminal was separated from the body by a short strut. Various new forms of thumb-pieces adorned the later specimens, firstly the bud (c. 1680–1725), secondly, the double volute (c. 1720–80). On the latest examples the handle terminated with a ball finial. The later form of body was also made and used in Scotland, sometimes in unlidded form.

d) A Scottish 'pot-bellied' measure; c. 1725; overall ht. 9¾″ (24.8 cm.).

The earliest known form of Scottish measure, some of which date from c. 1650, the type remained in vogue until about the middle of the 18th century—some lidded and others lidless. There can be no doubt that this bellied form evolved from an earlier and closely similar Dutch model, with a long free-standing spout, known as a Jan Steen flagon from the fact that it was frequently portrayed by that artist. The Scottish form was made in several sizes, from the Scots pint (three pints Imperial or 1.7 litres) to the Scots gill, or half mutchkin.

585

a) Scottish tappit-hen measures; late 18th and early 19th centuries.

The term 'tappit-hen' can be applied only to this form of Scots measure; the plain domed lid form first appeared in the late 17th century and continued in use until the first quarter of the 19th, and may be found in a long range of capacities, both Scottish and Imperial, whereas the crested type (i.e. with knopped cover) was made in three Scottish sizes only, from c. 1790 to c. 1830. The unlidded form is attributed to the Aberdeen district, and these were made to Imperial standard measure only, after 1826. Of those shown, the first two are of chopin capacity (1½ Imperial pints or .85 litres) and the third, Imperial quart (1.14 litres).

Pewter
British

b) An Irish haystack-shaped spirit measure; c. 1830.

This is the well-known Irish form, in use generally from c. 1825 to 1860, and in some isolated areas of Ireland used to a quite recent date. The only other essentially Irish measures are of slim baluster shape, without a handle, and found generally in four small sizes only, from the ½-pint (.28 litres) to the ¼-gill (.036 litres). There is one firm, Joseph Austen & Son, of Cork, whose marks appear on the majority of Irish measures; this factory later became known as the Munster Iron Works.

c) Channel Islands measure—the Jersey type; c. 1790.

The Channel Islands have consistently resisted the introduction of Imperial measure and have used, until the present century, a liquid measure indigenous to the Islands. The form of vessel is quite distinct from any in use elsewhere in the British Isles or on the Continent, although the twin acorn thumb-piece itself is a French heritage. Examples of this plain squat type may be found both lidded and lidless, and in at least six sizes, the largest known as the pot holding a capacity of 69.50 fluid ozs. (or approx. 3½ Imperial pints = 1.97 litres). The lid is slightly convex, and is heart-shaped.

d) Britannia metal.

Towards the end of the 18th century some manufacturers employed the process of making articles from thin sheet pewter, which were then seamed and shaped and finished by lathe-turning. This required a far harder alloy, and either bismuth or antimony, perhaps both, were added to the high grade pewter alloy. The illustration shows a large variety of objects produced in this medium, which might include also tea-pots, candlesticks and a host of other domestic ware.

There appears to be no evidence of the production of pewter for domestic purposes on the European continent prior to the ninth century, and it is doubtful if many such pieces, of a period before the eleventh or twelfth century are in existence today. Ludwig Mory, in his *Schönes Zinn*, illustrates two amphorae, one of which he attributes to the fourth century, and the other to the sixth or seventh; these, however, would doubtless have had ecclesiastical use. It is a fact that fairly considerable numbers of early specimens have been preserved in foreign museums such as the Boymans at Rotterdam, now the repository for the well-known Verster collection, and of many of the pieces excavated from the ruins following the bombing of Rotterdam in 1940. Here will be found several well authenticated examples of the fourteenth century, and many more of a period prior to the sixteenth century. The Rijksmuseum at the Hague owns several more and here, too, is housed the hoard of sixteenth century pewterware recovered from the ill-fated Dutch expedition which foundered at Nova Zembla in 1596.

---

a) North German or Scandinavian tankard, dated 1561; ht. to top of cover 5¼″ (13.4 cm.).

This fine squat tankard displays three typical processes of adornment indicative of its period of manufacture—the body is line-engraved all over with arabesques, human faces, animals, birds and flowers; the hinged cover bears repeated punched ornamentation around the edge and on the knop, and the handle is cast with a panel in low relief—a feature more commonly employed in Scandinavia than elsewhere. In this example, on the inside of the base, there is a domed and pierced 'mound' which screws into position, to hold nutmeg or spices.

b) Frontal view of the same piece as (a), showing the engraved merchant's mark, and the twice repeated date.

The additional date at the back of the handle is struck from individual numeral punches. Note the strong five-piece hinge and the finely cast thumb-piece. The three ball feet, in this instance, are sensibly placed on the solid foot rim, and have considerable aesthetic appeal, whereas, on many German pieces in particular, these are set on an insecure flange and are a source of weakness. This tankard is of excellent metal, form and construction, showing the high degree of skill and workmanship attainable in the 16th century.

a) A Dutch candlestick with central drip-catcher, of the late 16th century; ht. 8⅛″ (20.2 cm.).

This came from a hoard of pewterware found in Nova Zembla in 1871-75, and left there by a Dutch ship in 1596; the expedition was under the command of one Jacob van Heemskerk and Willem Barentz, and this particular form has become known as the 'Heemskerk' type. Two other forms of pewter candlesticks, with bell-shaped bases, and many other items, including steeple salts and large ewers were found, and all are now to be seen in one museum collection.

b) A Dutch or Flemish chalice of unusual form; dated 1684; ht. 8¼″ (21 cm.).

A noticeable feature of most continental chalices is the smallness of the bowl in relation to the overall height of the object, whereas in this example the bowl is well-proportioned to the knopped stem and domed foot. It is engraved at the front 'KIRCHE LAASS, 1684', but made probably some 30 years earlier.

c) A French relief-cast dish, from a model by François Briot; 17th century; dia. 18 1/16″ (45.8 cm.).

This type of all-over decoration, cast in high relief from deeply engraved moulds, was brought to perfection by François Briot in the early 17th century, and examples continued to be made over the centuries by successive pewterers. In Germany such work is known as *Edelzinn*. This dish depicts, in centre, Adam and Eve, surrounded by medallions representing Minerva and the Arts and Sciences and, on the outer edge, twelve medallions of Roman emperors on horseback.

d) Austrian engraved beaker; mid-18th century; ht. 4⅞″ (12.4 cm.).

This is one of several closely similar beakers, some of which are accompanied by a domed cover, said to be engraved with a nail by the notorious Baron Friedrich von Trenck whilst he was imprisoned in Magdeburg in 1754-63, and to which he refers in his autobiography. The engraving and lettering in German text is exceedingly well executed. Another almost identical specimen, with its cover, is in the possession of the Tiroler Landesmuseum, Innsbruck.

a) Saxon guild flagon of the Thum Lacemakers; dated 1680; overall ht. 18" (45.7 cm.).

This example, finely engraved with floriate scrolls and the names of guild officers, was made by Christoph Dürr of Annaberg, (floriate 1650–82). The shield on the hinged, domed cover bears the title of the guild and the date and would, originally, have been held by a model of an armoured warrior (now missing). German guild flagons were frequently in the form of large standing cups and covers, known as *Hanaps*.

b) A German pegged flagon or tankard; mid–17th century; overall ht. 12" (30.5 cm.).

A representative example of the general type of German flagons of the mid-17th century, this is, however, finely line-engraved with huntsmen and hounds harassing a stag, bears and a boar in the three landscape panels, and has a gilt medallion inset in the cover. Around the inside of the drum, pegs have been set at regular intervals to enable a drinker's ability to quaff the contents to be judged.

---

c) A Flemish bulbous measure or flagon; c. 1750.

This example has a distinctive form, representative of a large series of closely similar bulbous flagons peculiar to the Netherlands and Belgium, and datable from c. 1725 to the end of the century. The hinged cover of the Flemish examples is always domed, and the thumb-pieces are usually of the cockle-shell pattern, as seen here. Somewhat similarly shaped flagons, of coeval date, but with flat-topped covers, and any one of a variety of other types of thumb-piece were made in the northern regions of France.

d) A French (Normandy) measure, c. 1775.

This form of measure is loosely associated with Normandy, and of a general character in common use in France throughout the 18th century. There are numerous local variations, measures from each district having their own peculiar characteristics. This particular specimen bears the mark of a Caen maker. Variations will be found mainly in the shapes of the thumb-pieces, the majority of which will be made with the twin acorn form; in some others it may be erect.

American Pewter
Introduction

Among the first settlers of the American Colonies in the seventeenth century were pewterers trained in England. From the beginning these craftsmen laboured under difficult business conditions. The principal source of tin, the main ingredient of pewter, was Cornwall. The English, desiring to keep the American pewter trade for themselves, put such a high tariff on tin that Colonial makers could not afford to buy it and compete successfully against their English rivals. Faced with this formidable disadvantage, local craftsmen had to use worn pieces as raw material, often trading new for old and allowing 50 to 60% of the cost to obtain it. It is small wonder, therefore, that most of the pewter found today in America is English. It is nonetheless satisfying to know that there is enough American pewter available to interest a collector, and yet not too much to make it common! Except for German and Swedish forms of Pennsylvania, the dominating influence was English. Without a guild such as the London Company, Colonial pewterers were not required to mark their wares, but every pewterer of any consequence had at least two sets of marks—one for large surfaces which included his name, frequently the town where he worked, and sometimes a set of hall-marks; the other for small surfaces, usually containing his initials. Sometimes the pewterers would stamp the name of their sales agent on the pieces sold by him.

Most of the marks before the Revolution were derived from English symbols, the rose and crown, the rampant lion, the full-rigged ship, etc. Shortly after the beginning of the war, however, these were replaced by the eagle, symbolizing the New Republic. One can, therefore, date marked pieces with a fair degree of accuracy. One of the intriguing, unsolved mysteries is who designed and cut the dies of the marks. The variety of individual designs achieved in the touches is delightful and pewter collectors never cease to hope these die-makers will be identified some day.

In the Massachusetts Bay area at least fifty pewterers worked before 1825, a dozen of these before 1700. Very early pieces are rare. Although there is a relative abundance of flatware dating from 1760–1810, surprisingly few pieces of hollow-ware survive. After 1815, many pewterers in the smaller towns near Boston produced a variety of forms.

In Rhode Island the first craftsmen worked in the cosmopolitan port of Newport around 1730–50, the earliest being Lawrence Langworthy who worked from 1731–39. Only a few early examples survive; baluster measures, a few tankards and porringers. Although the variety of hollow-ware was limited, Rhode Island pewterers were skilful craftsmen who produced fine metal.

It was not until 1733 when Thomas Danforth I moved to Norwich that pewter was made in Connecticut Valley. The Danforths and Boardmans remain an essential part of American pewter, producing an extraordinary amount of the existing pieces.

The pewterers of New York and Albany have left us the most important group of great hollow-ware that have survived. The beautiful chalices produced by Peter Young, a completely American design with no prototype in European pewter, and the sugar bowl with 'neat' engraving by George Coldwell should not go unmentioned. This period in New York was a golden era; after 1800 many of the later makers produced many good pieces in the new forms.

Unlike the other largely Anglo-Saxon colonies, Pennsylvania had a cosmopolitan population. It is not surprising, therefore, to find Swedish and German influence in the products of some of the pewterers. This is shown notably in the forms made by Johann Christopher Heyne of Lancaster. The products of Heyne and Colonel William Will add lustre to Pennsylvania pewter in the eighteenth century. John A. Brunstrom, and later Parks Boyd, were excellent craftsmen. Many other pewterers followed, to give a relatively large and varied inheritance.

The earliest marked American pewter is a spoon by Joseph Copeland of Chuckstuck, Virginia (c. 1675), yet very little was produced in the south before 1800. The few known examples dated before then are some plates. The dearth of southern pewter is due to the fact there was not a good accessible market. Overland communication was difficult; the wealthy planters of Maryland and Virginia could buy their pewter in London where they had large credits, duty free and shipping free, the competition for their tobacco being so keen. It was not until the nineteenth century when Connecticut makers migrated to the South that any great amount of pewter was made. Nineteenth century production consisted of plates, dishes and basins. Lightner and Kilbourne of Baltimore are the only pewterers who produced any hollow-ware that has so far survived.

a) Quart cylindrical tankard with flat cover and crenate lip, ram's horn pattern thumb-piece, hollow cast handle and dolphin terminal; John Bassett, New York City (working 1720–61); ht. 6″ (15.2 cm.), dia. of top 4⅜″ (11.1 cm.).

This type of tankard was made by several New York pewterers. This is one of three known surviving tankards by John Bassett. Tankards must have been prized possessions in New York in those days because so many fine examples from at least ten different shops have survived. These splendid vessels varied in design of cover, handle, thumb-piece and handle terminal. The crenate (cut out) lip of the cover and the dolphin terminal of the handle are unique features in New York tankards. The capacity range covers the giant 2 quart, 3½ pint, quart (1.14 litres) and pint (.568 litres) tankards.

b) Fluted and engraved presentation plate, by Francis Bassett I; New York City, 1732; dia. 8½″ (21.5 cm.).

This example is one of the earliest surviving dated pieces of American pewter. Another example, dated 1728, is unmarked. Its lovely flower and foliage design and fluted rim recall the strawberry dishes of a century earlier in Great Britain. New York was one of the great centres of American pewterware, the craftsmen created marvellous pieces of every description, and the eighty years between 1720–1800 were a particularly fertile period.

---

c) Oval globular footed tea-pot with pine free finial, engraved decoration and wood handle; Frederick Bassett, New York City, (working 1761–1800); ht. 7″ (17.7 cm.), dia. of base 3″ (7.62 cm.).

Another similar tea-pot by Frances Bassett I is the earliest surviving American tea-pot recorded to date, c. 1718–1758.

This tea-pot is one of three marked examples of this form and the only one with engraved decoration. Frederick Bassett, grandson of John Bassett, was the last of the great group of New York pewterers. For a short period during the Revolutionary War (1781–1786) he moved to Hartford, Connecticut, returning thereafter to New York where he worked until his death in 1800. The fine surviving examples of his work place him in the first rank of American pewterers.

d) Quart tankard with double-dome cover and boot heel terminal; John Carnes, Boston, Massachusetts (working 1720–60); ht. 6½″ (16.5 cm.).

In Massachusetts pewter had been made since 1635, when Samuel Graves of Salem advertised his wares, but little has survived. 17th and 18th century known hollow-ware consists of plates, dishes, basins, a few porringers, mugs with strap handles, beakers, and this one tankard. It is only in recent years that a few 17th century hammered dishes and plates with smooth or multiple reeded rims ascribed to John and Edmund Dolbeare and John Baker, have been found. In contrast, considerable flatware exists dating from 1760–1810, generally of superior quality and workmanship; they range in size from 8″ (20.3 cm.) to 15″ (38.1 cm.) diameter.

Pewter

American

a) *left: Porringer with solid handle; David Melville, Newport, Rhode Island (working 1775-94); dia. 5½" (13.9 cm.).*

b) *centre: Porringer with crown handle; Joseph Belcher, Newport, Rhode Island (working 1769-86); dia. 5" (12.7 cm.).*

c) *right: Porringer with Rhode Island type handle; Samuel Hamlin, Providence, Rhode Island (working 1771-1801); dia. 5¼" (13.3 cm.).*

The handle design of a) *left* is only found on porringers by the Newport pewterers and by Thomas Danforth III of Stepney, Connecticut and Philadelphia, Pennsylvania. Ten pewterers working in Newport and Providence from c. 1770–1830 have left a large number of pieces, although relatively limited in form. A wide variety of flatware, some quart and pint mugs with hollow cast and double handles survive along with beakers and sugar bowls, but above all, there are porringers—more porringers by Rhode Island pewterers than in all other areas combined! These had distinctive solid and pierced handles.

The handles and bowls of most American porringers were cast separately and soldered together being reinforced with a bracket under the handle. The solid handle porringers made in Pennsylvania were cast in a single mould.

---

d) *left: Large shaker; Thomas Danforth III, Stepney, Connecticut and Philadelphia, Pennsylvania, c. 1790; ht. 6½" (16.5 cm.). right: Fine globular tea-pot with acorn finial and wood handle; Thomas D. Boardman, Hartford, Connecticut, c. 1805; ht. 6¼" (15.8 cm.).*

The history of pewter in the Connecticut Valley largely consists of the story of five generations of one remarkable, prolific family. Fourteen Danforths were pewterers, in addition to Thomas, Sherman and Luther Boardman, and Otis Williams, whose mothers were Danforths. In their shops were trained so many apprentices that they fanned out in eight of the thirteen states: Rhode Island, Massachusetts, Vermont, Pennsylvania, Maryland, Virginia, North Carolina and Georgia.

e) *Tall flagon with double-dome cover and pine tree finial, reverse double C handle and bud terminal; Samuel Danforth, Hartford, Connecticut, (1795–1816); ht. to top of finial 13½" (39.3 cm.).*

Approximately 75% of American pewter existing today is the product of Connecticut pewterers and 50% of this is the work of the Boardmans. The Connecticut makers were great merchandisers. Thomas Danforth II was the first to send out salesmen with carts, the travelling salesmen of their days and his grandsons Thomas D. and Sherman Boardman developed the first chain store operation, having branches in New York City, Troy, New York and Philadelphia, Pennsylvania. For the most part, the pewter produced in the 18th century was good.

a) *Pair of candlesticks, Johann Christopher Heyne, Lancaster, Pennsylvania (working 1756–80); ht. 22¼″ (56.5 cm.).*

Heyne received his training in Saxony and Sweden before coming to Pennsylvania in 1742. In his earlier years he was a minister, teacher and missionary. His early interest in church affairs may be the reason for the fact that most of his surviving pieces were made for use in churches. With the exception of one example by John Bassett of New York, two pairs of tall altar candlesticks by Heyne are the only 18th century candlesticks that have come to light. The raised decoration of religious symbols and their design most probably makes them unique. His flagons, chalices, sugar bowls and other forms place him among the top American pewterers.

b) *Quart tankards by John Andrew Brunstrom, Philadelphia, Pennsylvania, 1781–1793; left: Quart tulip shape with double-dome cover, hollow cast handle and bud terminal; ht. 7⅞″ (18.7 cm.), dia. of base 4 1/16″ (10.3 cm.); right: Quart cylindrical with beaded, flattened double-dome cover, hollow cast handle and bud terminal; ht. 6¾″ (17.1 cm.), dia. of base 4¾″ (12.0 cm.).*

Brunstrom marked most of his pewter with a London scroll, a crowned X quality mark, together with two love birds facing each other over the word 'love'. This is known as the 'Love Bird Touch'.

c) *Round tea-pot with beading and wood handle of the Federal period by Colonel William Will; Philadelphia, Pennsylvania, c. 1790; ht. 6½″ (16.5 cm.), bottom dia. 4 11/16″ (11.9 cm.).*

d) *Covered sugar bowl with finial, fine beading and trifoot, pear-shaped creamer with crenate rim; products of the shop of Colonel William Will, Philadelphia (working 1764–98); ht. of sugar bowl 4⅝″ (11.7 cm.), ht. of creamer 4 1/16″ (10.3 cm.).*

Colonel William Will, patriot and statesman, came to Philadelphia after serving as an apprentice in the shop of his father John and older brother, Henry, in New York. The Will family had come from Germany to New York in 1752. Leslie I. Laughlin has well expressed the feeling of most students of American pewter about this craftsman: 'William Will typifies all that is best in the history of American pewter. The surviving examples of his work are of a standard of quality as high as our pewterers ever attained'.

Pewter Glossary

ACORN-KNOPPED: spoons bearing an acorn at the end of the stem.

ANTIMONY: a metal used to harden the alloy known as Britannia Metal (*q.v.*).

APOSTLE SPOONS: spoons with knops representing the Apostles; they are extremely rare in pewter.

BALL-KNOPPED: spoons having a small ball at the top end of the stem.

BALUSTER-KNOP: a type of knop on spoons having a small button on the stem end of the baluster (16th century).

BALUSTER MEASURE: a type of pewter measure with the body of this shape and with a flat, hinged cover, used specifically for wine.

BISMUTH: a metal which is added to pewter to harden it.

BOOGE or BOUGE: the curved part of a plate or bowl between the rim and the flat bottom.

BRITANNIA METAL: a varying alloy of tin, antimony, copper, and bismuth.

CHOPIN: a Scottish measure containing $1\frac{1}{2}$ pints (Imperial measure), or four Scots. gills.

CHRISMATORY: a vessel for the oil for Extreme Unction.

COSTREL: a harvest or pilgrim's bottle, usually of wood, or earthenware, but sometimes of pewter.

CRI: the name for the sound given by tin, and by the best pewter when bent backwards and forwards.

CRUETS: small sacramental vessels on feet, with lids, usually found in pairs, one marked 'A' for aqua, and the other 'V' for vinum.

DIAMOND-POINTED KNOP: a name for an early type of spoon (15th century).

EAR-DISH: a shallow dish with one or two flat projecting handles.

ECUELLES: bowls and porringers (French).

GARNISH: the old name for a complete set of vessels in pewter, consisting of 12 platters, 12 dishes or flat bowls, and 12 saucers, (i.e. small flat plates).

HEXAGONAL KNOP: a common type of knop found on spoons (16th century).

HIND'S FOOT: (see 'pied-de-biche'). The shaped end of the flat stem of a spoon.

HOLLOW-WARE: the generic name given to large pots, measures, tankards, and flagons.

HORNED HEAD-DRESS: a type of knop found on spoons (15th century).

HORSE-HOOF KNOP: a rare type of knop found on spoons (16th century).

LAY (LEY): tin mixed with lead so as to be of lower quality.

LAY-(LEY)MEN: men who worked in such metal.

LION SEJANT KNOP: a form of knop in which the lion is sejant, or sitting (16th century).

LOGGERHEADS: circular inkstands, usually with a flat disc for a base.

MAIDENHEAD: a type of knop in the form of a female bust, found on spoons (15th century).

MONK'S HEAD: a very rare type of knop found on spoons (16th century).

MUTCHKIN: a Scottish measure holding $\frac{3}{4}$ pint (Imperial), or two Scots gills.

PALE: the pewterers' name for solder of inferior quality.

PEAK: the old pewterers' name for lead.

PEG-TANKARD: a tankard with pegs on the inside, at regular intervals.

PIED-DE-BICHE: a type of spoon so called because the end is split like a deer's foot.

PLATE-METAL: pewter of good quality.

POINTILLÉ: ornament produced by stabbing the metal with a pointed tool.

PORRINGER: a porridge dish.

POUNCE-BOX: see 'sand-box'.

PRICKET: a candlestick with a spike to hold the candle.

QUAIGH: a word used for a shallow circular drinking vessel, somewhat like a deep saucer, with two handles (Scottish).

SADWARE: the trade name for the flat heavier articles, e.g. plates, trenchers, dishes, and chargers.

SALER: a salt container.

SAND-BOX: a box with a perforated lid, by means of which fine sand was sprinkled on documents to dry the ink.

SCOURING: the proper name for the cleaning of pewter.

SEAL: a mark impressed on a measure by an inspector, to indicate that the vessel had been checked for capacity, and conformed to the standard then in force.

SEAL TOP: a type of knop found on spoons.

SILVORUM: a sham-silver alloy of the 17th century.

SLIPPED IN THE STALK: a variety of spoons in which the stem is cut (or slipped) on the slant (16th century).

SPINNING: process by which a thin plate of metal in a lathe is forced to take the shape of a solid or built-up wooden core.

STIPPLED: ornament produced by marking or pricking the surface with small dots.

STUMP-END, or STUMP-TOP: a rare type of spoon (16th century).

TAPPIT-HENS: Scottish vessels of a certain form, and of three pints capacity. Other sizes in the same shape are said to be of tappit-hen shape.

TEMPER: tin when alloyed with copper.

THUMB-PIECE: the lever by which the lid of a jug or tankard is raised. It is often called a purchase.

TOKENS: small pieces of pewter formerly issued in Scotland to intending Communicants. They might be circular, square, octagonal, or oval.

TOUCH: a private mark (or trade mark) impressed on pewter ware by the pewterer.

Glossary (contd.)

TOUCHPLATES: five plates of pewter preserved at Pewterers' Hall, on which all the touches or private marks of pewterers were supposed to be stamped. (London).

TRIFLE: pewter of common quality is usually called trifle.

TRIFLERS: the trade name for the men who made spoons, forks, buckles, buttons and toys.

VOIDER (VOYDER): a large dish.

WRIGGLED: see p. 678.

WRITHEN-KNOP: a very rare form of knop found on spoons (16th century).

Repairs and Maintenance

Most pewter, according to the density of its tin content, and perhaps of its other ingredients, and certainly if it has been exposed for long periods in cold, damp conditions, will have deteriorated in colour and become duller and darker by the formation of an oxide on the surface.

This condition may often be only slight and may be cleaned off easily with ordinary metal polish, but more frequently if a piece has been stored away, unhandled for many years, it can form a hard, dark and ugly 'scale' of oxide which is difficult to remove except by drastic treatment with one or another process of chemical application, followed by continual hard polishing, to restore it to its pristine condition.

However, there are many instances in which any radical cleaning would be unwise, in particular in the cases of early and rare examples such as are shown in the first few illustrations. All that should be done there is to carefully wash off all dirt and easily removed incrustation in warm soapy water and dry thoroughly; a thin coating of wax furniture polish will preserve them from further deterioration, and they will need only an occasional polish with a cotton duster.

In less rare examples some intermediate condition may be desirable, but *overcleaning* should be avoided. In all cases, even if some of the hard scale is to be removed it is advisable to leave some traces of it in the grooves and not easily accessible crevices at the points of handle fixture, or in the depths of engraving or ornamentation. It should be appreciated that a faker cannot truly imitate natural oxidation and the patina of age, and so if all traces are removed there will always remain doubts as to whether the piece is, in fact, old or a reproduction.

Fakes and Forgeries

As in most other spheres of antique collecting, when the supply of the old exceeds demands and prices begin to rise, the faker has entered the field, and there are some serious pitfalls for the beginner collector to avoid. Reproductions of pewterware may be classed in at least two categories, (i) those pieces made in exact replica of old and rare examples, artificially aged to deceive—many also bearing copies of marks used by known makers, and (ii) examples not necessarily of old form, but some parts of which have been cast from old moulds, the complete item produced purely as an ornamental reproduction for decorative purposes. In both cases some of these pieces have now acquired up to forty years of age in their own right, and will become increasingly difficult to recognize as time progresses. Pewter collecting in England reached a popular peak in the early 1930s, and most of the faked examples date from about then but there are, even today, some modern pewtering firms producing good reproductions which they sell as such, though some unscrupulous persons are still prepared to add the spurious touch of age by battering, scratching and discolouring.

In 1969, an exhibition was held at Reading Museum as a warning to the uninitiated. It featured only faked examples of supposedly rare pieces, collected together by members of the Pewter Society of Great Britain, and included a collection of 'Billie and Charlie' faked mediaeval Pilgrims' Badges, etc. some of which, at the end of the nineteenth century, fooled many of the experts of the day, but which have now become of collectors' interest in their own right.

Pewter
Further Reading

General

BELL, M. *Old Pewter*. London 1905; rev. ed. 1913.
COTTERELL, H. H. *Old Pewter, Its Makers and Marks*. London, 1929, repr. 1963.
   National Types of Old Pewter. Boston, Mass., 1925.
   Pewter Down the Ages. London, 1932.
MASSE, H. J. L. J. *Pewter Plate*. London, 1904; rev. ed. 1911.
   Chats on Old Pewter. London, 1911.
   The Pewter Collector. London, 1921.
MICHAELIS, R. F. *Chats on Old Pewter* (original Massé ed., 1911, revised). London, 1949; 2nd rev. ed. (with new section on American pewter by Henry Kauffman), New York, 1971.
   The Pewter Collector (original Massé ed., 1921, completely revised). London, 1971.
PRICE, F. G. H. *Old Base Metal Spoons*. London, 1908.
ULLYET, K. *Pewter Collecting for Amateurs*. London, 1967.

British

BURNS, REV. T. *Old Scottish Communion Plate*. Edinburgh, 1892.
DE NAVARRO, A. *Causeries on English Pewter*. London, 1911. New York, 1912.
INGLEBY WOOD, L. *Scottish Pewter-ware and Pewterers*. Edinburgh, 1905.
MICHAELIS, R. F. *Antique Pewter of the British Isles*. London, 1955. 2nd ed., New York, 1971.

A Short History of the Worshipful Company of Pewterers of London. London, 1968.
British Pewter. London, 1969; New York, 1970.
PEAL, C. A. *British Pewter and Britannia Metal*. London, 1971.
WELCH, C. *History of the Worshipful Company of Pewterers*. London, 1902.

Continental

BERTRAM, F., and ZIMMERMAN, H. *Begegnungen mit Zinn*. Prague, 1967.
BOUCOUD, C. *Les Pichets d'Etain*. Paris, 1958.
BRUZELLI, B. *Tenngjutare I Sverige*. Stockholm, 1967.
DUBBE, B. *Tin en tinnegieters in Nederland*. N.V. Zeist, 1965.
HINTZE, E. *Die deutschen Zinngiesser und ihre Marken*, 7 vols. Leipzig, 1921–31.
MORY, L. *Schönes Zinn*. Munich, 1961; 2nd ed. (revised), 1964.
SCHNEIDER, H. *Zinn*. (Catalogue of pewterware in the Swiss National Museum.) Olten, 1970.
TARDY. *Les étains français*. Paris, 1964.
VERSTER, A. J. G. *Das Buch vom Zinn* (revised and enlarged by R. M. Vetter). Hanover, 1963.
VETTER, R. M. *Linzer Zinngiesser*. Munich, 1967.

American

LAUGHLIN, L. I. *Pewter in America: Its Makers and Their Marks*, vols. 1, 2, and 3. Barre, Mass., 1969.

Museum Collections

Great Britain

BIRMINGHAM: Art Gallery; Weoley Castle.
CORNWALL: Truro Museum.
LONDON: The Pewterer's Hall (viewing by arrangement); The Victoria and Albert Museum.
IRELAND: National Museum of Dublin.
SCOTLAND: Royal Scottish Museum, National Museum of Antiquities of Scotland, Edinburgh; Art Gallery and Museum, Glasgow.

U.S.A.

DELAWARE: The Henry Francis du Pont Winterthur Museum.
MICHIGAN: Henry Ford Museum, Dearborn.
NEW YORK: The Brooklyn Museum; The Metropolitan Museum of Art.
NORTH CAROLINA: Museum of Early Southern Decorative Arts, Winston-Salem.
WASHINGTON, D.C.: The Smithsonian Institution.

Index

Broad-rimmed charger; England, c. 1660.
Foreground left: James I flagon; England, c. 1610.
Centre: Porringer, William and Mary; England, 1690.
Right: Charles I bun-lid flagon; England, c. 1630.

Scientific Instruments

As modern science in the western world began to develop there was a growing realization of the necessity for careful examination of natural phenomena. As a result, instruments were developed to assist Man's unaided senses and the craft of scientific instrument-making slowly evolved, drawing on and developing the skills of workers in wood, metal and glass. Permeating all activities was a new spirit of enquiry, spreading from the active groups of savants to the wider realms of society. By the early eighteenth century, the sciences had become, to quote Edmund Stone in 1723, 'a popular study . . . a part of the education of almost every Gentleman. . . . They are so useful so entertaining and extensive a branch of knowledge, that it is no wonder they should gain ground'. Many teachers found that the didactic potential of the instruments provided the key 'by which those sciences are rendered useful in the Affairs of Life. By their Assistance it is that subtile and abstract Speculation is reduced to Act. They connect as it were, the Theory to the Practice, and turn what was bare Contemplation to the most Substantial uses'. Equally, those whose interest in science was somewhat dilettante found that the approach to science through the medium of its apparatus was not only readily comprehensible, but also delightfully entertaining. Such an attitude encouraged the plethora of ingenious improvements and inventions with which the instrument-makers amused the growing number of their amateur customers.

There had always been those whose interest was only marginally 'scientific'. Libraries of wealthy Renaissance patrons of the arts were graced by devices that were not merely advanced pieces of scientifically designed mechanical technology but—and equally important—objects of considerable beauty, made by skilful craftsmen of high repute. Today's collector may quite properly follow the historical example for there is no doubt that many instruments have, intentionally, an overt aesthetic appeal.

Some highly utilitarian instruments have little or no applied decoration; their visual appeal may be less obvious, but the purity of unadorned, functional form has a strong attraction. Other collectors may be motivated solely by antiquarianism, the contemporary technical and scientific significance of an instrument being the important feature.

Thus, as the instrument-makers sought to please both the scientist and the dilettante, so the collecting of scientific instruments can satisfy the search for knowledge and the sense of beauty.

Opposite:
Helio chronometer of brass, engraved and decorated with foliate designs; England, 1715.

Scientific Instruments
The Craft

The field of activity for the collector of early scientific instruments is very wide, extending in time from before 1400 to beyond 1900 and covering subjects as diverse as alchemy, gnomics, medical electricity and geodetic surveying. With such a diversity of subject matter within what is in itself a specialist area, the central problems of identification and dating are especially difficult. A knowledge of the history of the separate sciences can provide only a *terminus post que*, for many instruments continued to be made to more or less their original specifications for one hundred and fifty to two hundred years.

Artistic patterns, methods and materials of manufacture provide useful pointers but require experience in interpretation. If the instrument is signed with the maker's name the scale of the problem is immediately reduced. Most signatures tend to be in obvious places, but this is not always the case. The key to the identification of a strange instrument lies in an intelligent appraisal of the probable function of the device followed by a search of the scattered literature. To those with a feeling for things mechanical, this appraisal should not be too difficult.

Probably the most informed approach to collecting early instruments is through an interest in the history of the separate sciences and their related technological artifacts; but such an approach may lead to frustrations. The overwhelming majority of surviving instruments are manifestly not the devices used in epoch-making discoveries by the great scientists of the past. Such prototypes rarely survive. In contrast, the commercial products of the instrument-makers' workshops do. There are many examples of the well made, well tried and workmanlike instruments made for the large group of men that the late Professor Eva Taylor has aptly called the 'Mathematical Practitioners'—men whose professions ranged from architect to excise officer and from land surveyor to navigator.

Another of the instrument-makers' important customers was the teacher, who required standard apparatus to demonstrate and explain old and new scientific principles and discoveries. In addition there was the eighteenth century equivalent of the Renaissance patron, the educated gentleman of leisure. He required what Maurice Daumas has called 'instruments for the salon', in order to be—and to show himself to be—conversant with science and its practical applications that were so manifestly advancing the age in which he lived.

A comment should be made on the survival rate of particular classes of instruments. This—while an irrelevant aside to the purist—is of some importance to the collector, for it defines and limits the areas of potential interest and activity. Survival is a function of a number of complex and inter-related features. The most significant are time, material of manufacture, original use, and contemporary practice. Hard and fast statements cannot be made on the effect of these features, only general indications of tendencies. Thus, in general both the ravages of time and an overall increase in output dictates that more nineteenth century instruments survive than those made in the preceding century.

In particular cases, however, this comment has to be substantially modified. There is for example a pronounced survival peak for European astrolabes made from 1550-1600, followed by a very rapid decline in seventeenth century examples, for the instrument became obsolete. The other survival factors are more closely inter-related. For example, chemical glass-ware, made to designs that altered little from the sixteenth to the nineteenth century, rarely survives. This is partly because a fragile, delicate material like glass is inherently susceptible to breakage; however, the mode of use in the laboratory is very significant. An alembic is an alembic, regardless of its age. The chemist used it for a host of routine operations and when it broke, replaced it.

Utilitarian items were used by their original purchaser and any subsequent owners until they wore out or were superseded by an improved design. Either way, neither the scientist nor the professional practitioner of the scientific arts would habitually keep redundant apparatus. At best the instrument might be delegated for the instruction of novices or stripped and the separate parts utilized.

In direct contrast many of the instruments acquired for the salon by virtuosi scientists and gentlemen of leisure have a greater potential for survival. They were frequently purchased as examples of the ingenuity and technical prowess of the instrument-maker and these gimcrack and quasi-educational diversions survive because successive owners continued to be attracted by their original mechanical and visual allurements.

Introduction

The first scientific instruments to be made in Europe were the work of Islamic craftsmen who had settled in southern Spain. A number of eleventh century Hispano-Moorish astrolabes survive, but even at that date the Muslim conquerors were losing their hold on the Peninsula. In the twelfth century, Toledo became a centre of intellectual activity when Alfonso VII of Castile encouraged the translation of Arabic, Jewish and Greek works into Latin. Astronomical writings were included in this translation programme and they had a strong influence in Europe, so that by the fourteenth century the leading scholars of Paris and Oxford were designing and making astronomical instruments.

However, it was not until the fifteenth century that a separate and distinct craft of scientific instrument-making evolved. The City State of Nuremberg was the scene of this activity. It has a well organized guild structure and many craftsmen skilled in metalwork. John Müller (Regiomontanus) settled in Nuremberg in 1471, 'because I find there all the peculiar instruments necessary for astronomy', and his activities greatly stimulated the new workshops. Nuremberg and the neighbouring town of Augsburg rapidly became famous for their scientific craftsmen; they maintained this reputation until overtaken by the disruptions of the Thirty Years War (1618–48).

Interest in instruments spread with interest in science, and by the end of the sixteenth century craftsmen making scientific instruments were established in Italy, the Low Countries, France and England, in addition to Germany. The Scientific Revolution of the seventeenth century placed increasing emphasis on qualitative and quantitative observation. Of major importance were the new optical instruments, the microscope and telescope, which added unseen and unimagined dimensions to the natural world.

In Italy, Rome was the main centre of activity, though by the early seventeenth century Galileo's workman, Mazzoleni, was making sectors on a commercial scale in Padua, while later in the century isolated craftsmen have been recorded working in Genoa, Modena and Livorno. In France, Paris became a major European centre of instrument-making; and with the exception of Dieppe it was not until the eighteenth century that there is evidence of any significant provincial activity. In England, London held a similar position, and while the eighteenth century saw the development of the instrument-making trade outside the capital, it also saw London makers exporting their wares across Europe and to markets further afield. London's professional skills were in demand at this time, instrument-makers being encouraged to emigrate and set up workshops in Russia, and Swedish journeymen sent to London to learn the finer arts of the trade. The English colonists in

North America tended to rely on imports from London, though the roots of the nineteenth century independent manufacturing capability were established during the previous hundred years.

The important Flemish workshops of the sixteenth century, which centred round the Arsenius family in Louvain, did not maintain their high reputation. The position in the Low Countries in the seventeenth and eighteenth centuries contrasts strongly with that in England and France in that the trade was not confined to one city but distributed among small groups of craftsmen active in a number of centres—notably Antwerp, Louvain, Brussels, Amsterdam, Leyden, Rotterdam and Utrecht. In the German City States a similar wide geographical distribution existed, Nuremberg and Augsburg being joined in the seventeenth century by Aachen, Danzig, Dresden, Munich and Vienna. The nineteenth century saw the development and growth of precision mechanics in Germany, with London's position as the leading centre of instrument-making in the world challenged, and in many areas passed by German workshops re-emerging to a position of eminence.

The nineteenth century also saw the widespread adoption of machine tools, the growth of mass production techniques and the new science of electricity playing an increasingly dominant role. The instrument-making trade was closely involved in furthering all these innovations so that the inexorable decline of the craftsmanship and tradition that took place during the nineteenth century can only be seen as laudable progress. Inevitably, and understandably, this great step forward created a barrier that few collectors have attempted to cross. The late nineteenth century is too recent to have a nostalgic appeal to the antiquarian. The gentleman amateur scientist is gone and the practical, mass-production of useful engineering design has triumphed. The new instruments of the period have little aesthetic connection with those of the previous two or three hundred years.

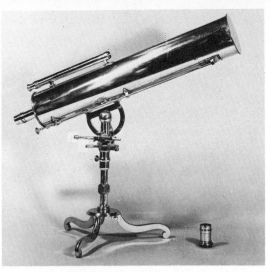

a) Prospect- or perspective-glass, paste-board covered with gold-tooled vellum, by G. Campani; Rome, Italy, c. 1670.

Giuseppe Campani of Rome constructed the large telescopes with which J. D. Cassini of Paris Observatory made important astronomical discoveries. He also made this small telescope or perspective-glass, which has vellum-covered paste-board tubes. Though Galileo's epoch-making observations of 1610 were made with only a small instrument of low magnification, later small telescopes were not intended for serious astronomical work: *vide* Samuel Pepys in 1667, 'I did entertain myself with my perspective-glass, up and down the church, gazing at a great many fine women, and so I passed away the time till sermon was done'.

b) Gregorian reflecting telescope, brass, by J. Short; London, England, c. 1745.

17th-century improvements in magnification and image quality of the telescope were achieved by using very long instruments, often over 100 feet long. Gregory (1663), Newton (1668) and Cassegrain (1672) proposed reflecting telescopes, with mirrors forming the magnified image; the potential advantage of the reflector was its significantly smaller size for a given magnification. However, only in the 18th century did opticians fully master the intricacies of polishing curved mirrors. The leading maker was Edinburgh-born James Short; astronomers throughout the world used his instruments. Short only made reflecting telescopes, over 1,300 between 1734 and 1768, all signed and numbered (see p. 611b).

c) Achromatic telescopes, in wood and brass, by P. Dollond; London, England, c. 1765.

Radical improvement in the telescope's performance followed John Dollond's 1758 announcement that an object-glass composed of a flint and crown glass doublet gave an image relatively free from colour fringes. While not an independent invention, the discovery was protected by a patent and, after his father's death in 1761, Peter Dollond took legal action to enforce his monopoly. In partnership with his brother John, Peter continued as a leading maker of achromatic doublet and triplet objectives after the patent lapsed in 1772. The firm's fine reputation encouraged the sale (c. 1800) of telescopes signed 'Dolland', obviously intended to mislead unwary buyers.

d) Achromatic telescope, wood and brass, by Utzschneider and Fraunhofer; Munich, Germany, c. 1825.

For many years continental workshops could not acquire good flint glass and so compete with the London opticians in producing achromatic telescope objectives. However, by 1800, a Swiss glass-maker, P. L. Guinand, was manufacturing high quality optical flint glass. In 1806 Guinand joined the instrument-making firm financed by J. Utzschneider, and English opticians lost their pre-eminence. This telescope has a wooden barrel, five feet long, with brass fittings. The sturdy wooden tripod and the telescopic stabilizers are typical of the workmanlike astronomical telescopes of the period, made for use in the observatories of amateur and professional astronomers.

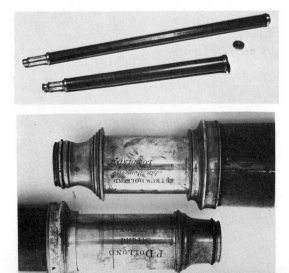

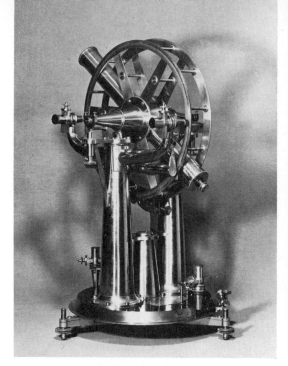

a) Alt-azimuth circle, brass with silver inlay, by E. Troughton; London, England, c. 1806.

When the astronomer requires quantitative measurement of stellar positions his telescope must be set on a suitable stand. The design of the mounting is determined by the particular measurements to be made, but sturdiness combined with a facility for delicate adjustment in orientation and accurately divided scales are essential. This instrument is made to Edward Troughton's 1792 design. The 18-inch vertical circle measures altitudes. The 15-inch horizontal circle, on which the rest of the instrument may revolve, measures the azimuth bearings. The finely divided scales are marked out on silver, let into the brass. They are read with micrometer microscopes.

b) Copernican armillary sphere, in cardboard, by G. Pigeon; Paris, France, c. 1780.

The armillary sphere was used in teaching astronomy and cosmography. The earliest 15th century spheres are models of the earth surrounded by rings (Latin, *armillae*) depicting the celestial equator, the tropics, the solstitial and equinoctial colures and the ecliptic. From the late 16th century the instrument was elaborated to present the whole solar system incorporating rings for the sun, moon and planets. Frequently these spheres were made in pairs to demonstrate the Ptolemaic (earth-centered) and Copernican (sun-centered) universes. Late 18th century spheres, made in France with cardboard rings, are considerably less rare than the impressive silver and brass Renaissance examples.

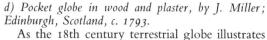

c) Orrery in brass with ivory fittings, by G. Adams Jnr.; London, England, c. 1788.

The orrery is a mechanical model of the solar system, and was named after the Earl of Orrery for whom John Rowley made an early example in 1713. This table model probably dates from 1788, since the planetarium fitting shows William Herschell's discovery of the planet Uranus (1781) and two of its satellites (1787). Herschell also discovered two satellites of Saturn (1789) adding to the five known since the 17th century, and four further satellites of Uranus (1794). Next to the stand is a Tellurian apparatus, which illustrates the diurnal and annual motions of the earth and moon.

d) Pocket globe in wood and plaster, by J. Miller; Edinburgh, Scotland, c. 1793.

As the 18th century terrestrial globe illustrates the era's discoveries by circumnavigation, so the celestial globe records the many newly-mapped stars. The plates for the printing of the paper gores were cut by the specialist map-engravers. Most globes were sold in pairs and are still found together; detailed comparison of the title cartouche will indicate recently paired separate editions. Pocket terrestrial globes, in a case lined with celestial gores, date from the early 18th century. The celestial gores often have no cartouche; occasionally they are reprints of gores for a celestial globe, without re-engraving to adapt to a concave surface.

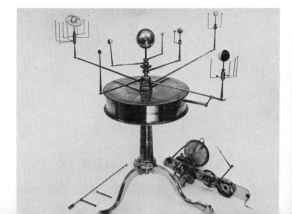

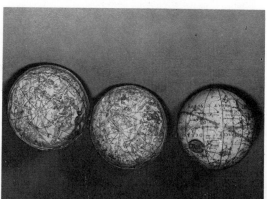

a) Astrolabe, brass, by Muhammed b. as-Saffar; Cordova, Spain, 1026-27 AD.

Known from the 2nd century AD, the astrolabe is essentially an astronomical calculating device allowing the observation of solar and stellar altitudes. Most are of brass, although silver, gilt-metal and even cardboard instruments are known.

This, the earliest known European-made dated astrolabe was made by a Syrian. Obsolete in Europe by the 18th century, Islamic manufacture continued for another two centuries. Beneath the pierced rête, whose pointers represent important stars, are normally a series of thin brass discs, each engraved for use at a particular latitude. 20th century Islamic reproductions, not uncommon, have poor rêtes that lack star pointers.

b) Dutch- or Holland-circle, brass, by J. de Steur; Leidon, Holland, c. 1675.

After 1533 and the enunciation of the principle of triangulation (which eliminated all distance measurement except for the base-line), the primary surveying instruments recorded angular bearings. During the next two centuries specialist instruments evolved, the earliest directly related to the geometric divisions on the reverse face of the astrolabe. This type was designed by J. P. Dou in 1612. There are two pairs of fixed 'slit-and-window' sights and a further pair on the alidade which turns round the fixed compass-box. The circle may be suspended vertically to read angles of elevation or set on a tripod for taking horizontal bearings.

c) Circumferentor, by Thomas Heath, London, with theodolite attachment by Heath & Wing, London, England, c. 1760.

The circumferentor has only two pairs of sights; one pair fixed, the other pair set on the alidade. It also differs from the Dutch-circle in that the compass box rotates with the alidade. Thomas Heath was a leading English maker of the period. The vertical semi-circle with telescopic sight was added after 1758, when Heath took Tycho Wing into partnership. It converts the instrument to a theodolite and allows horizontal bearings and angles of elevation to be measured simultaneously. The combined circumferentor and theodolite is a typical 18th century English surveying instrument; the parallel-plate levelling head and the tripod seldom survive.

d) Graphometer in brass, with engraved flowered and leaf motif, by J. Baradelle; Paris, France, c. 1780.

Neither the Dutch-circle nor the circumferentor was popular with French surveyors, who preferred the semi-circular graphometer. In P. Danfrie's original 1597 design both the fixed sight-line and the alidade extended well beyond the circumference of the semi-circle. However, on the instrument as made in France and Germany from the late 17th century and throughout the 18th century, these parts were substantially the same radius as the divided circle. On this graphometer is seen the typical pierced centre section. In earlier examples, the decoration tends to be more extensive and detailed.

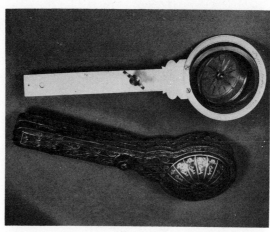

a) Surveyor's compass in wood, by J. Halsy; Boston, Massachusetts, U.S.A., c. 1750.

The American instrument-making trade shows a high incidence of instruments constructed in wood, where European makers preferred brass. These wooden instruments were all made in New England; the commonest survival being the surveyor's compass, like this example 'Made and sold by James Halsy near ye Draw Bridge in Boston'. This was probably the most essential instrument in America, as settlers staked out their newly acquired land. New England makers also constructed brass instruments, but the local native woods (cherry, apple, oak and laurel) provided an excellent alternative for cheap and tolerably accurate instruments for the non-professional surveyor.

b) Plane-table compass, in brass with gold-tooled leather covered case, by P. Baillou; Milan, Italy, c. 1760.

Plane-tabling is a method of surveying that by-passes the need to observe with a theodolite or circumferentor, where readings are logged in a book and later plotted to produce a map. The plane-table procedure of direct plotting is inaccurate but exceedingly rapid. The instrument shown here is an accessory used to orientate a wooden plane-table. The design, with the compass mounted in gimbals, follows that recorded by Sangiovanni in 1759. The case is paste-board. Up to the mid-18th century, decorated cases are not unusual, though shaped or moulded cases like this are less common.

c) Theodolite in brass, by G. F. Brander; Augsburg, Germany, c. 1780.

George Brander first made this type of theodolite in 1777 naming it 'Observatorium Portatile'. The auxiliary telescope gives increased accuracy by maintaining a permanent back-sight. Bearings are read from the micrometer-screws that mesh into the rack cut into the circumference of the circles. A similar mechanism was used as a 'slow-motion' device on telescope stands of this period, but divided instruments were usually read with a traditional Vernier. Brander, and his son-in-law and successor, Hoeschel, were among the few makers commercially producing the micrometer-type slow-motion device. Most workshops were unable to cut accurate lead-screws to the necessary fine tolerance (cf. 236c, d).

d) Garden sundial in slate, by R. Melville; Glasgow, Scotland, c. 1845.

Portable and fixed sundials, popular from the 15th to the mid-19th centuries, were often used to regulate unreliable watches. Then, cheaper and better pocket watches, the development of the railway network, and the subsequent adoption of standard time, relegated the sundial to the status of a garden ornament.

Most garden pedestal dials were topped with brass plates; those that have stood for centuries are heavily weathered. Richard Melville's weather-resisting slate dials are as finely engraved as earlier brass instruments. Coarse engraving, or calibrations cast in the metal, betray dials made in London and Birmingham during the 20th century, sometimes with spurious 17th century dates.

a) Diptych dial in ivory, by P. Reinman; Nuremberg, Germany, c. 1602.

Pedestal dials only operate at the latitude for which they are designed. Pocket dials are intended to be of use over a range of latitudes. On this dial, the string gnomon is adjustable for use between latitudes 39° and 54°N. The magnetic compass is used to orientate the dial on a north-south axis. As with most German dials of this period, there are a multiplicity of secondary hour scales with pin-gnomons giving the time in Jewish, Babylonian and Italian hours. Diptych dials were made in Germany until the early 19th century. Later pine-wood examples were covered with hand-coloured paper scales.

b) Butterfield dial, with 'bird' gnomon, by Michael Butterfield; Paris, France, c. 1700.

This English instrument-maker worked in Paris from about 1670 until his death in 1724. A highly reputable craftsman, he attracted imitators whose sub-standard work bears his often mis-spelt name. Butterfield's best known design was the Butterfield dial, made in Parisian workshops until the late 18th century. Of silver or brass, normally with an octagonal base, there are two distinguishing features, the four hour scales engraved on the plate for use between latitudes 52° and 43°N., and the 'bird' gnomon which is adjustable for latitude. As commonly found on portable dials, major towns and their latitudes are listed on the base.

c) Equatorial dial, in silver, engraved with heavy foliage and dog design, by J. G. Vogler; Augsburg, Germany, c. 1750.

This portable dial is a typical 18th century design from Augsburg, a town renowned for its instruments since the 15th century (see p. 236c). Technically it is an equatorial dial, because in use the hour-ring is set parallel to the equator. The hour-ring is set against the latitude arc and may be a complete or a broken circle or formed of alternate concave and convex segments. The brass-plate is normally octagonal or square and heavily decorated. The maker's instruction sheet is occasionally printed in French or Spanish, in addition to German; it is a rare survival.

d) Equatorial ring dial, brass, by W. Collier, London, England, c. 1715.

This dial is self-orientating. The sliding suspension ring is set for the local latitude making the hour circle lie parallel to the equator. On the diametrical bridge the sliding pin-hole-gnomon is adjusted to the date, and the dial suspended and turned until sun shining through the pin-hole falls on the hour-ring, so indicating the time. The bridge may be calibrated in months on one face and the zodiacal signs on the other. English instruments made before 1752 can be distinguished by the first day of Aries being March 9, rather than March 20; in 1752 England adopted the Gregorian calendar already in use elsewhere in Europe.

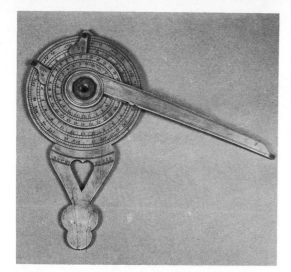

*b) Back-staff, by B. King; Salem, Massachusetts,
U.S.A., c. 1775.*

a) Nocturnal, boxwood, London, England, c. 1740.

The nocturnal was developed during the 16th
century to determine the time at night by observing
the circumpolar rotation of the stars, usually the
'guards' of the Great Bear or the 'bright star' of the
Little Bear. This nocturnal is designed for 'BOTH
BEARS' and is the design favoured by English
navigators. 16th and 17th century examples,
French, German and Italian in origin, are made of
brass and survive in greater numbers than the
utilitarian boxwood instruments. On these metal
nocturnals the inner disc often has pronounced
'hour' teeth so that the time can be read in the dark.

An essential navigational observation is the
measurement of the sun's mid-day altitude, taken
to compute the observer's latitude. The astrolabe
and other instruments, notably the cross-staff,
originally used for this observation, were superseded in 1594 by John Davis's invention of the
back-staff. With this instrument the observer
turned his back to the sun and observed the angle
cast by the shadow of the sight vane. Rosewood,
mahogany or ebony frames with boxwood arcs
are normal on English and American instruments.
A maker's name plate is often found on the brace
while serial numbers are stamped on both signed
and unsigned back-staffs.

*c) Octant, wood and brass, engraved flower and scroll
design, by J. C. V. Vüer; Holland, c. 1775.*

John Hadley's quadrant was invented in 1731.
It measures solar altitude by reflection. Because
there is a double-reflection, the 90° range is contained within an arc of 45°; so the frame of the
instrument subtends an eighth of a circle; hence
octant. Octants usually have mahogany or ebony
frames, rarely brass. On early examples the arc is
of boxwood, divided, as here, by transversals.
Later instruments have ivory scales read with a
Vernier. Ivory maker's name plates on the brace are
common. An ivory-topped pencil slotting into the
brace is an unusual survival[1]

*d) Sextant, of brass with silver inlay, by E. Troughton;
London, England, c. 1802.*

In its principle of operation the sextant is
identical to the octant; the greater arc allows larger
angles to be observed. Generally sextants are better
constructed and their scales more finely divided to
enable more accurate measurement; brass frames
and fittings are usual. High quality 19th century
instruments may be divided on silver, platinum or
even gold. Though introduced by Campbell in
1758, the sextant did not totally replace the cheaper
octant until late in the 19th century. The sextant
shown here is made with a pillar and plate frame,
a construction style patented by Edward
Troughton in 1788.

Scientific
Instruments
NAVIGATIONAL
INSTRUMENTS
DEMONSTRATION
APPARATUS

b) Azimuth compass, wood and brass, signed Rich; Glynne, Londini Fecit; *London, England, c. 1706.*

a) Mariner's dry-card compass, by F. W. Lincoln Jnr. & Co.; Boston, Massachusetts, U.S.A., c. 1850.

The exact origin of the magnetic compass remains a matter for speculation; however, it is certain that such an instrument was being used by European navigators in the early 13th century. Surviving examples of this very utilitarian device earlier than the 18th century in origin are rare. This mid-19th century example pivots in a gimbal-mounted brass bowl (wood was used in the previous century) set in a binnacle lit by paraffin lamps. On the underside of the compass card handwritten repair dates and signatures may occasionally be found.

The azimuth compass, a specialised adaptation of the magnetic compass, was designed following 16th century observations of the phenomenon of magnetic variation and used to compare the true bearing of the sun with its magnetic bearing, and so calculate the variation. This nicety is unnecessary for short sea voyages, but on long trans-oceanic passages it is essential.

Although signed by Richard Glynne, the compass card, printed from an engraved plate, provides clear evidence of sub-contracting. It is marked: 'Made by I: Sellars & C. Price Hydrographers to ye Queen Compass Makers to Navy Royall, Waping' and separately signed: 'R. Spofforth Sculp'.

c) Inclined plane, mahogany with brass fittings, by J. Kley; Rotterdam, Holland, c. 1757.

During the 18th and early 19th centuries, a wide range of mechanical instruments, apparatus and models, were made as teaching aids. University professors, schoolmasters and itinerant lecturers in experimental philosophy, whose popular expositions were a feature of contemporary scientific education, all found them useful. Remarkably few of these didactic pieces survive, possibly because they are still not recognized for what they are. This inclined plane was used to observe the forces acting on a body on a slope. The equilibrium conditions deduced from the principle of the triangle of forces can be clearly demonstrated.

d) 'Newton's cradle', mahogany frame on iron tripod base; Dutch, 19th century.

Fashionable as a prestige toy for tired business executives, 'Newton's cradle' was originally a 17th century piece of demonstration apparatus, illustrating the phenomenon of compound collision between elastic and inelastic bodies. The experiment dates from the 1670s and the theoretical analysis of the French scientist Edme Mariotte. The balls are ivory; soft clay would be used to simulate inelastic collisions.

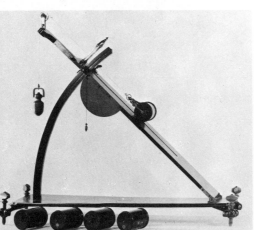

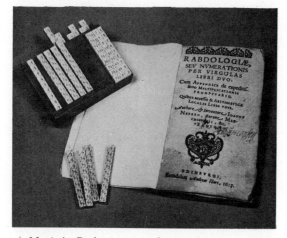

a) Napier's Rods, ivory in boxwood case; London, England, c. 1680.

Anyone who has struggled to learn the multi-plication table will appreciate why Napier's Rods were so highly valued in an age when relatively few educated men had the mathematical skills to proceed beyond simple arithmetic. Named after their inventor, John Napier of Merchiston, they were also called Napier's 'Bones', since many early examples were made from ivory. Sets of four-sided rods in ivory, boxwood or softwood covered with paper scales, and double-sided strips of boxwood or brass, were made and sold in Europe throughout the 17th century. By the mid-18th century, as mathematical education improved, their popularity declined.

b) Two-foot Gunter's rule, boxwood, by Belcher Bros.; New York, U.S.A., c. 1830.

In 1614 John Napier's publication of his great invention of logarithms provided a rapid and powerful means of computing. Books of tables intimidated many practical men, and in 1623 Edmund Gunter showed how Napier's 'artificial numbers' could be set out on a scale and used for navigational calculations with the assistance of a pair of dividers. Gunter's rule remained exceed-ingly popular with navigators until the late 19th century. Normally it was two feet long and made of boxwood. The scales marked out on both faces of the rule rarely depart from the pattern illustrated here.

c) Sectors, in brass, by Gilbert; London, England, and Clerget; Paris, France, c. 1730.

The sector evolved during the late 16th century; the year 1598 and the names of Galileo and Hood being traditionally and separately given priority of invention. The sector rather than the slide-rule was the widely used instrument of calculation until the late 19th century. Particular arrangements of the scales are associated with English, French and Italian instruments. Boxwood, brass, silver and ivory were all used for the limbs, six inches being a common size. Note the typical slight decoration and the scrolled leaf on the hinge of the French instrument. The English sector has a folding friction leaf, an unusual addition.

d) Gauger's slide-rule, boxwood, by E. Roberts; London, England, c. 1790.

William Oughtred invented the sliding rulers some time before 1630. The true slide-rule, with fixed stock and moving slide, was published by Partridge in 1661. However, not until the mid-19th century was the slide-rule in general use. Before that date, it was rare outside Britain and even then confined to a few specialist applications. This is an example of Verie's Rule, used by Excise Officers to calculate (gauge) the content and capacity of barrels and vats when levying tax on ale, wines and spirits. Verie's pattern is distin-guished by having a slider on each of the four faces of the stock.

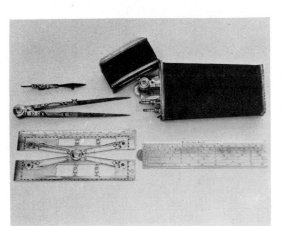

a) Shagreen pocket case of silver mathematical instruments, by Richard Glynne; London, England, c. 1715.

Boxed sets of mathematical drawing instruments have been made and sold from the 17th century to the present. In the 18th and early 19th centuries pocket-cases were very popular in England and France. The most expensive contained silver instruments and, as here, each piece was exquisitely decorated. Leather, and polished, stained shagreen (see *c* below) are common coverings on 18th century sets—the less expensive, coarse, unpolished black shagreen is more frequent in the later period. Typical contents include compasses, dividers and drawing pens with interchangeable points. There is always a sector, a parallel ruler and a protractor, here combined in one instrument.

b) Marshall-type compound microscope, paste-board, leather and brass; London, England, c. 1715.

For the layman the microscope has long been the archetypal scientific instrument. Though it was invented in the second decade of the 17th century we can still echo Henry Power's 1661 comment that it is the instrument 'by whose augmenting power we now see more than all the world has ever done before'. This example, though unsigned, is probably the work of John Marshall and follows his 1693 design for a 'great double microscope'. The paste-board tube is covered with gold-tooled leather, a form of decoration found on English, French and Italian optical instruments of 1650–1750 (p. 605*b*).

c) Culpeper-type compound microscope, wood and paste-board with brass fittings, by Edmund Culpeper; London, England, c. 1725.

Culpeper's microscope design, of which this is an early example, superseded the Marshall-type instrument. One of its major innovations was the introduction of a mirror beneath the stage, giving improved illumination of the object. The barrel is covered with polished shagreen (the skin of shark or dogfish), Culpeper's trade card is stuck in the box; the drawer beneath houses the accessories. The Culpeper-type instrument exists in a number of variant forms. The all-brass variety dates from 1750 and was made for over 100 years; the later models have rack and pinion focusing.

d) above: Compass microscope, ivory and brass; London, England, c. 1750; below: Simple ivory screw-barrel microscope; London, England, c. 1720.

It was the simple microscope with the single magnifying lens that provided the major biological discoveries during the years 1670–1720. Anton van Leeuwenhoek of Delft did important work with his own home-made instruments giving high magnification and excellent resolution. The optical instrument-makers also produced simple microscopes; this 'compass' microscope has the lens set in a light-catching mirror, or *Lieberkühn*, invented in 1738 by the German physician, J. N. Lieberkühn. The 'screw-barrel' microscope is made to James Wilson's 1702 design, itself an unacknowledged modification of a 1694 design by the Dutch scientist and optician, Nicklaas Hartsoeker.

a) Compound microscope, brass, by L. F. Dellebarre; The Hague, Holland, c. 1785.

For a century following the death of Leeuwenhoek (1723) the optical properties of the microscope were unchanged. The problems of achromatic and spherical aberration remained largely unsolved. Meanwhile, the microscope underwent extensive mechanical development by Dutch, English, French and German makers. L. F. Dellebarre, the French-born instrument-maker, who spent much of his working life in Holland, made his first model of the microscope shown here in 1762. In 1777 his work was commended by the *Académie des Sciences* in Paris. Design features seen on the Dellebarre microscope are also found on most large compound microscopes of the period 1770–1830.

b) Reflecting microscope, brass, by G. B. Amici; Modena, Italy, c. 1830.

During the early 19th century microscopists and opticians attempted to construct compound achromatic objective lenses. Initially, their performance was disappointing and in 1827 the young Italian scientist, Amici, returned to an idea proposed by Newton in 1679. Amici made reflecting microscopes in which the objective lens was replaced by an ellipsoidal mirror. His instruments attracted considerable attention but their optical performance was not outstanding. The potential of the design was exploited with more success by skilled opticians, notably Cuthbert and Tulley in London, and Chevalier in Paris. Following the introduction of the successful achromatic objective lens, the reflecting microscope was abandoned.

c) Achromatic compound microscope, brass, by Powell and Lealand; London, England, 1856.

Following J. J. Lister's pioneering studies of the theoretical principles governing the performance of compound objective lenses, the microscopical sciences experienced a virtual rebirth. From 1830 instruments of sound optical and improved mechanical design were made by skilled workmen like Ploessel of Vienna, Pistor of Berlin, Oberhauser and Nachet of Paris, Powell and Ross of London. The firm of Powell and Lealand, established in 1841, achieved great renown for their craftsmanship. This is their 'Number 4' stand introduced in 1847.

d) Inverted microscope, by Nachet & Fils; Paris, France, c. 1886.

In the later decades of the 19th century, English microscopes lost their pre-eminence as both the makers and the English microscopists clung to traditional ideas. The theoretician, Ernst Abbe, stimulated the work of Zeiss of Jena, and other European firms continued to adapt and innovate. The instrument shown here is described in Nachet's 1886 catalogue as *Nouveau microscope renversé*. It is one of a number of specialist adaptations to conventional microscope design for the particular purpose of studying '*éléments anatomiques dans les milieux gazeux*' and facilitating observations of '*culture des ferments, d' absorbtion de gaz . . .*'

Scientific Instruments Glossary

ACHROMAT: The achromat, or achromatic lens eliminates colour fringes distorting the image formed by the optical system of both microscope and telescope. In the telescope, crown and flint glass objectives, either as doublet or triplet combinations, were common by the last quarter of the 18th century. In the microscope the truly achromatic multi-cell objective was not being manufactured until the third decade of the 19th century.

ALIDADE: A sighting device pivoted at the centre of a circular or semi-circular instrument. It extends over the complete diameter with pin-hole or slit and window sights at the opposite ends.

CARTOUCHE: That part of a globe, normally surrounded by a border, and containing such information as the title, name of maker, engraver, authorities consulted and date of publication. In subsequent editions these imprimature details may be altered whilst the existence of updating information may be recorded outside the border.

DIAGONAL SCALE: See 'transversals'.

GOLD TOOLING: Decoration of the leather and vellum-covered bodies of microscopes and telescopes. Distinct styles of tooling permit instruments to be assigned to particular periods but recent research has shown that in London at least, tooling is *not* an acceptable guide to a particular maker.

GNOMON: The art of designing and making sundials was formerly called *dialing* or *gnomics*. The term gnomon is generally applied to the shadow casting part of the sundial. More specifically it is possible to distinguish between a *style*, which is an edge whose shadow cuts the hour scales, and a *gnomon*, the term reserved for dials in which the position of the tip of the shadow marks the time.

INDEX: A measuring device pivoted at the centre of a divided instrument and extending over the complete radius. At the tip of the index is placed the scale reading device—for example a Vernier. Only rarely is the index equipped directly with sights, though it must be linked to and activated by the sighting mechanism (see also 'alidade').

MICROMETER: A mechanism for measuring distances or reading scales to a high accuracy. On astronomical instruments the micrometer often takes the form of a calibrated tangent screw *q.v.*; whereby each complete turn of the tangent screw moves the index *q.v.* through a known proportion of the scale. Thus fractional parts are directly represented by fractional parts of a complete turn of the calibrated head of the tangent screw. (See 'Vernier' and 'transversals'.)

NONIUS: A precursor of the Vernier (*q.v.*) designed by P. Nuñez. The Vernier is often incorrectly called a Nonius.

QUADRANT: A sector of one quarter of a circle. Normally fitted with pinhole sights and a plumb line—occasionally with an index arm (*q.v.*). Quadrants may be calibrated variously: The *Simple* quadrant has a scale of degrees on its circumference. The *Sinical* quadrant has the addition of a rectilinear grid of lines. The *Horary* quadrant is designed to be used as an altitude sundial and includes many varieties from the rare medieval *quadrans vetus* to the *Gunter's* quadrant so popular from the 17th century onwards.

REFLECTING TELESCOPE: Has mirrors of polished metal (the specula) which produce the magnified image. There are three basic designs: the *Gregorian* and *Cassegrain* have a concave primary mirror pierced by a central orifice; the secondary mirror is either concave (Gregorian) or convex (Cassegrain). In the *Newtonian* the primary mirror is not pierced and the image is viewed from the side; the secondary mirror is an optical flat.

ROTULA: See 'volvelle'.

STYLE: See 'gnomon'.

TANGENT SCREW: A device which assists the accurate alignment of an index (*q.v.*) or alidade (*q.v.*). The latter is clamped in position at an approximate position on the scale and then finely adjusted by the turning of the tangent screw (see 'micrometer').

TRANSVERSALS or DIAGONAL SCALE: A geometric method used to estimate fractional parts of a scale. The principle was proposed in the 14th century. Transversals may be recognized by the network of diagonals crossing a series of lines placed close to and parallel to the main scale. (See also 'Vernier'.)

VERNIER: A device for measuring fractional parts of a scale. Invented in 1631 by Pierre Vernier. Normally the Vernier is placed on the index (*q.v.*) or alidade (*q.v.*) adjacent to the scale. The Vernier has one more or less part than the scale over a similar arc or distance. (See also 'Nonius', 'micrometer' and 'transversals'.)

VOLVELLE: Often found on the underside of 17th century sundials. It consists of one or more calibrated discs and graduated circles, so as, for example, to facilitate the conversion of lunar hours to solar hours or compute the age of the moon. Complex paper volvelles, usually called 'rotulas' were made in the 18th century. They function as a form of anologue computer.

Fakes and Forgeries

With the exception of the astrolabe, it is only in recent decades that antique scientific instruments have attracted the wide interest and spiralling prices that are a necessary concomitant of forgery. Restoration of incomplete specimens is acceptable when it is acknowledged and undertaken with skill. Refabrication, copying and the production of replicas by the electrotype process is not objectionable *unless* there is an unwitting or intentional attempt to deceive, and to perpetuate a fake or a forgery. Regrettably, deception has occurred and no doubt will continue to occur. It is little consolation to the collector to be told that most major museums have more than one drawer full of disreputable instruments of suspect authenticity. Spectrographic analysis of the metal can provide an objective test where there is suspicion but such facilities are not readily available. Fortunately overt forgery is still uncommon and in an historic context may be of some interest, like the 'degenerate' astrolabe forgeries made in the 18th century by a group of Persian craftsmen 'copying' the finest products of Isfahan as produced by the renowned 'Abd al-A'imma', which flourished 1678–1722.

The unacknowledged 'restoration' whereby an acceptable instrument is made up from the pieces of two or three incomplete or broken items is difficult for the inexperienced collector to detect. In contrast, the creation of a 'pair' of globes is usually patently obvious from a comparison of the publication details printed on each globe. The making good of missing accessories by robbing an even more depleted item seldom escapes the practised eye. However, the very nature of accessories encouraged contemporary losses and subsequent replacement, so that absolute originality should not be expected. Neither should a full but disparate complement of accessories necessarily indicate a recent and knowing deception.

Signatures like *Doland* and *Buterfield* are of interest; providing that today's collector appreciates their significance as contemporary 'near-forgeries' designed to mislead the original purchaser. Spurious datings are more likely to be of a recent origin; the most frequently found instance is the 1930s brass garden sundial with a 17th century date, but this example could only deceive the over-enthusiastic and the naïve. Attributions to particular and well-known makers should be treated with a healthy scepticism; the existence of the original box with a trade label or bill of sale stuck in the lid is one of the few reliable pointers, though even here there are traps for the unwary.

Dating of instruments is seldom straightforward. The collector must exercise his judgement balancing the seller's natural inclination to date pieces earlier, rather than later, with his own knowledge that the 19th century saw the prolific production of many instruments made to basic designs that had been unchanged for decades. Of course, incorrect attribution, whether to a particular maker or to a particular era, only marginally constitutes fakery, and in a subject so poorly covered by readily available secondary literature such attributions are more often born of ignorance than of deliberate intention to deceive.

In direct contrast to the outright fake and the careful forgery is the ill-conceived and uninformed restoration. A frequent example is the painstaking removal of the black or blue-green oxidized finish applied to many instruments manufactured in the latter part of the 19th century. Such a practice is to be deplored. He who polishes up the base metal originally protected by the oxidizing paint also exposes his own ignorance. Such buffed-up pieces are an obvious anachronism and are best left to the machinations of smart interior decorators.

Further Reading

BEDINI, S. A. *Early American Scientific Instruments and their Makers.* Washington, 1964.

BRADBURY, S. *The Evolution of the Microscope.* Oxford, 1967.

BRADBURY, S., and TURNER, G. L'E. *Historical Aspects of Microscopy.* Cambridge, 1967.

BRYDEN, D. J. *Scottish Scientific Instrument Makers 1600–1900.* Edinburgh, 1972.

CAJORI, F. *A History of the Logarithmic Slide Rule.* London and New York, 1909.

DANSON, A., and COUDER, A. *Lunettes et Télescopes.* Paris, 1939.

DAUMAS, M. *Scientific Instruments from the 17th–18th centuries* (Paris, 1953). Eng. trans. Holbrook, M. London, 1972.

GUNTHER, R. T. *Astrolabes of the World.* Oxford, 1932.

KIELY, E. R. *Surveying Instruments.* New York, 1947.

KING, H. C. *The History of the Telescope.* London, 1955.

MADDISON, F. R. *Early Astronomical and Mathematical Instruments.* Cambridge, 1963.

MICHEL, H. *Traité de l'astrolabe.* Paris, 1947.
Instruments des sciences dans l'art et l'histoire. Paris, 1966, Eng. trans. by R. E. W. and F. R. Maddison, London, 1967.

REPSOLD, J. A. *Zur Geschichte der astronomischen Messwerkzeuge.* Leipzig, 1908.

ROHR, R. R. J. *Les cadrans solaires.* Paris, 1965.

Scientific Instruments
Further Reading (contd.)

ROOSEBOOM, M. *Bijdrage tot de Geschiendenis der Instrument Makerskunst in de Noordelijke Nederlanden.* Leiden, 1950.

SMART, C. E. *The Makers of Surveying Instruments in America since 1700.* New York, Vol. I 1962, Vol. II 1967.

STEVENSON, E. L. *Terrestrial and Celestial Globes.* New Haven, 1921.

TAYLOR, E. G. R. *The Mathematical Practitioners of Tudor and Stuart England.* Cambridge, 1954; *The Mathematical Practitioners of Hanoverian England.* Cambridge, 1966.

TAYLOR, E. G. R., and RICHEY, M. W. *The Geometrical Seaman.* London, 1962.

WEBSTER, R. S., and M. H. *An Index of Western Scientific Instrument-Makers to 1850.* Winnetka, Illinois, A–B, 1968, C–F, 1971.

ZINNER, E. *Deutsche und niederländische astronomishe Instrumente des 11–18 Jahrhunderts.* Munich, 1956.

Museum Collections

Great Britain

CAMBRIDGESHIRE: Whipple Museum of the History of Science, Cambridge.
LONDON: Science Museum; National Maritime Museum, Greenwich.
OXFORD: Museum of the History of Science.
SCOTLAND: Royal Scottish Museum, Edinburgh.

U.S.A.

MASSACHUSETTS: Peabody Museum (Navigating Instruments), Salem.
NEW YORK: Metropolitan Museum of Art (Sundials), New York City.
WASHINGTON, D.C.: Museum of History and Technology of the Smithsonian Institution; Medical Museum of the Armed Forces Institute of Pathology (Microscopes).

Index

Navigational compass in wooden case ; Portugal.

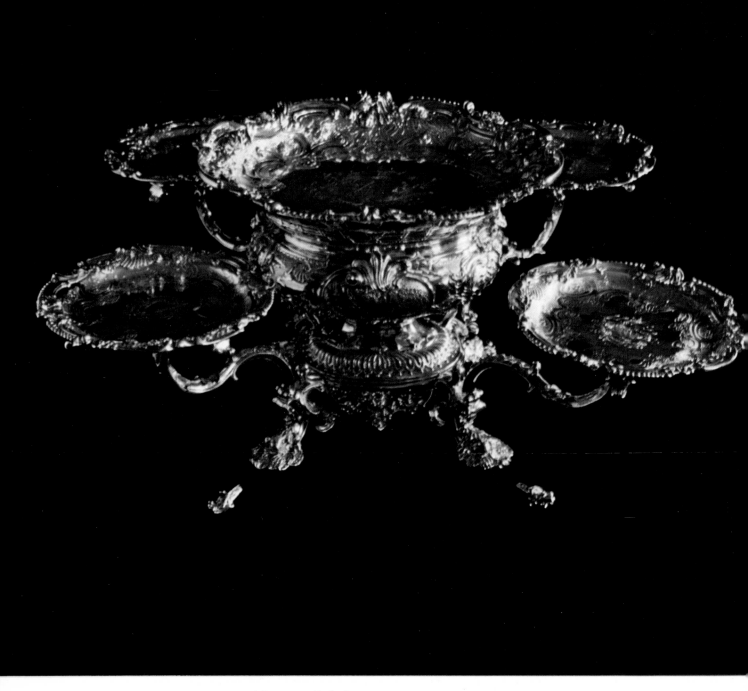

Epergne by Paul de Lamerie; England, 1743-44.

Silver

The relative scarcity of silver always accorded to it an inherent value, which accounts for its use in coinage. This alone explains why wrought silver objects were personally or corporately owned and enjoyed, usually by the more privileged members of a given society. The distinctive visual and material properties of silver have been recognized from the remotest antiquity and in combination with its value on the one hand and its limitation as a metal on the other, have governed the use of silver in a way that has remained surprisingly constant over several thousand years.

Silver objects fall broadly into five categories: first, those concerned with the service and consumption of food and drink; second, articles used in religious ceremonies and for the adornment of the church; third, items of personal toilette; fourth, for jewellery and items of personal adornment; and fifth, for furnishings and weapons, mostly as inlays or decorative plaques and sheathings. In all cases silver is an expression of the owner's status, since most silver objects existed in other less costly materials—wood, leather, ceramics, stone, copper, etc.

Surviving antique silver must be recognized as only a small percentage of what was actually produced. One cause of its disappearance lies in the relatively soft nature of the material itself; denting, tearing, breaking and general weakening are all the natural result of constant wear and tear on objects. There comes a time when a weak hinge, an open seam, a missing finial, a dent, a hole or a worn edge make it unwelcome to the sight and unsuitable for further use. Such pieces are candidates for the melting pot since, unlike most other possessions that have outlived their usefulness, they can be readily sold for their value by weight.

Indeed, by far the larger quantity of vanished silver—even religious objects such as communion vessels—has been melted down deliberately by the owners, either because of obsolescence or because of its value as a financial asset. This unsentimental liquidation of silver, no matter how superbly wrought, has often applied equally to a few pieces from modestly prosperous homes, as well as to vast collections of ceremonial and semi-official plate owned by great princes and ruling dynasties.

Despite these enormous losses, a considerable body of antique silver has survived and it is safe to say that it is not likely to be further reduced; the value of such ware is now far beyond its value as a mere commodity. Today we have enough to supply a broad idea of the progress of the craft of the goldsmith over three and a half centuries.

Silver
The Craft

Even today, the finest silver is still chiefly hand-made. Some parts, and even entire small objects, are often cast, and each component of a piece—spout, handle sockets, finial and so on—must be carefully soldered together before the piece is ready for the finishing processes, the planishing that removes the coarser hammer marks, the polishing that brings up the lustre, and the various decorative processes. Mechanization has, in fact, very little touched the silver trade, though nowadays most silversmiths buy their metal ready rolled or cast into ingots of the required standard. Some wares, usually of rather thin gauge, are stamped and a good many are spun on the lathe—though neither of these processes is very new: stamping was much used in the Midlands trade in the second half of the eighteenth century and spinning has its origins in ancient Egypt. It is in detail rather than in general that the manufacture of silver has changed with the times.

In raising a piece of silver by hand—that is, using a series of hammers to shape it from the sheet—the craftsman works over it meticulously row by row, forming first a dish-like shape and then inverting the piece over a stake to produce deeper, narrower forms, such as the bodies of jugs or tea-pots. Frequently he has to stop and anneal his work, heating it to a dull red over the hearth and then cooling it to make it malleable again, and always he must ensure that the hammer blows are even and that his ware is also of the correct thickness. Apart from the calipers, his only gauges are his eyes and his sense of touch.

For straight-sided coffee-pots and other fairly simple tall objects, a flat section of silver is turned up into a cone and then soldered along its length—an old process that sometimes betrays itself by close inspection of the interior of a pot or tankard where a slight solder-line can often be detected, usually under the line of the handle. Other pieces may be shaped by spinning over a wooden chuck cut to the required shape, the operator pressing against the metal with a long tool held under his arm and, as in raising, working the metal row by row until he reaches the top. Silver made by this process sometimes shows slightly curving lines, though, as with the hand-raised pieces which are planished (a sort of polishing under a special hammer to get out the original hammer marks) the craftsman tries to make sure that all such minor blemishes are removed in the finishing process.

Silver can, of course, be left rigorously plain and unadorned, though since earliest times the silversmith has been both craftsman and artist, and fine decoration has always been at a premium, even at periods—such as during the first quarter of the eighteenth century—when taste veered towards simplicity.

The chief tool of the silver decorator is the chasing punch, with which the craftsman coaxes the metal into relief. Chasing worked from the front, known as flat chasing, produces a very shallow ornament that, after some years of wear, can even be confused with engraving, though in fact the edges are softer because the metal is pushed, not cut away. Bolder chasing, at its best a combination of embossing and repoussé work, is done by producing the main outlines by working up bosses from the back. This is the simplest form of chasing, but to give it detail and definition, the craftsman works on the metal from the front, using perhaps hundreds of different punches for producing different depths and types of surface, such as stipple-like matting, which must be very evenly done or the effect will be 'spotty'. Similar repoussé chasing is used to sharpen up the fluted and other patterns produced by casting—the scroll ornament popular at the base of coffee-pot spouts for instance.

Two types of decoration remove metal for ornamental effect: engraving and piercing. Engraving is certainly the oldest of all decorative techniques, and on silver two variants are usual. In the oldest type, a sharp graver draws the design—lettering, coat of arms, ornament or even a picture—on the surface of the metal, cutting away fine slivers. A variation, known as bright-cut engraving was especially fashionable between about 1770 and 1800. Here the back of the tool is highly polished, so that as the cuts are made, often deeper and sometimes by 'wriggling' as opposed to ordinary engraving, the edges are given a brilliant polish.

Piercing, often used in conjunction with both engraving and chasing, is achieved by two methods. Until about 1760, it was done with hammer and chisel, the cutting tool being used with such skill that very fine and delicate pierced work was not unusual and in the hands of the finest piercers, the tools achieved even better results than that of the piercing saw. The piercing saw, a fine blade held in a frame, remains the hand-piercer's chief tool today, and is used not only for cutting intricate designs but also for shaping some of the attractive foliate and scroll motifs of cut-card work (see Glossary).

Continental Silver Introduction

As a result of regional and historical factors there is a great variety in continental silver and this makes its appreciation as much a delight for the eye as an exercise for the perception. Foremost of the historical factors is the supply of raw material. Goldsmiths were not involved in the mining or refining of the necessary metals, and depended on general market conditions. In the Middle Ages the mines of Spain, Hungary and Germany supplied new metal, and constant re-meltings, either for monetary value or in part exchange, made a good supply available. This changed dramatically at the end of the fifteenth century when quantities of new silver came into the Iberian Peninsula from the Orient and the New World, to be dispersed all over Europe in the course of trade. So much was used that a universal shortage of silver developed which brought forth various remedial efforts. Sumptuary laws were passed in Spain, since the shortage was blamed on extravagant use by the Church and nobility. Elsewhere the resulting rise in cost encouraged the production of thinner-walled vessels, and surface decoration was favoured as an alternative to the many cast details that used up so much extra metal. Throughout the seventeenth century, simpler forms were introduced; some elaborate pieces continued to be made but in diminished quantities. By the beginning of the eighteenth century new mining operations came into production and were ultimately able to supply the demand for coinage and for the goldsmiths.

Another historical factor was the guild system which was in general use by c. 1450. Each guild was an independent confraternity of goldsmiths, yet their authority and institutions were surprisingly similar throughout Europe; a guild house was used for meetings and the safe keeping of records, etc., and often their workshops were concentrated nearby, either by preference or by order. This proximity fostered the sharing of new ideas and influences and was one way that the rapid adoption of new styles was possible. The guilds ensured high standards by their power to forbid the production of gold and silver wares by non-members and membership required a strict examination. The young goldsmith served a seven to eight year apprenticeship and had additional training as a journeyman for a master goldsmith. Many guilds required a 'masterpiece' or test piece of the applicant's own design, to be executed unaided under the eye of the wardens within a stipulated time. Once a member, a goldsmith enjoyed a high social standing.

There were also responsibilities. The guild officers were charged with ascertaining that members did not use metal with a higher percentage of copper alloy than that permitted by statute. The elaborate hall-marks system, a remarkable feature of European and English silver, originated with this concern. The earliest marks required were the goldsmith's—at first a symbol, later initials and/or a symbol. A second mark identifying the town was a universal practice by the sixteenth century. Later elaborations included the use of wardens' or assayers' marks and a letter code, dating the actual year of manufacture. France had the most rigorous marking system of all (see p. 50).

The power of the guilds was not used to restrict the movement of member goldsmiths, but was occasionally employed, usually without success, to curb the activities of qualified strangers coming into the town; new arrivals were often encouraged by the reigning prince and frequently excused from membership in the guild. Nor did the guild system restrict the flow of new ideas. These travelled in three ways. First, migrating goldsmiths, travelling for personal, political or religious reasons, often implanted new uses of old methods in the host country, or influenced design. The persecution of the French Huguenots scattered goldsmiths into a number of countries including Holland, Switzerland and England.

A second source of new ideas was the actual importation of foreign pieces of silver, such as German sixteenth century silver, into the neighbouring countries. The third and most constant means by which new styles and decorative schemes travelled was by the circulation of commercially printed designs, constantly produced from c. 1550 onwards.

Many labour-saving machines developed in England c. 1750–1850 and these travelled rapidly over Europe. Within a short period hundreds of craftsmen had been taught how to use the new devices and machine-made silver was produced and bought in enormous quantities in the nineteenth century.

Finally, continental silver retained strong regional characteristics often affected by social rather than strictly historical factors—for example, the ubiquitous tankard of northern beer-drinking countries is completely non-existent in the wine producing areas of Italy, France and Iberia. This too helped to give continental silver its enormous diversity during a period from c.1450 to the close of the eighteenth century.

Silver

Continental
PORTUGUESE
SPANISH

a) Dish on low foot, silver-gilt with applied circular plaque of enamelled copper in the manner of Limoges; Iberia, probably end of 15th or early 16th century; dia. 12″ (30.4 cm.).

Highly ornamental dishes of this type were the most characteristic domestic plate in Portugal and Spain during the late 15th and the 16th centuries. Marks, already introduced in Oporto and Lisbon, are missing here—unfortunately true of much Iberian silver. The quantity of silver devoted purely to ornamentation is indicative of Portugal's wealth derived from its position as Europe's first 15th century colonizing power and its continued prosperity under Manuelo I, 'the Fortunate'. A multitude of figures in high relief tell the story of Judith in frames round the border, and Faith, Hope, Temperance and Fortitude in the well of the dish.

b) Dish on low foot with border of relief decoration, and centred with an enamelled coat of arms, silver-gilt; Portugal, c. 1500-50; dia. 12¼″ (31.1 cm.).

The border tells the story of Noah in a continuous series of stylized figures. The coat of arms was possibly for Vasco da Gama (1469-1524) or his son. Although goldsmiths were recorded in Lisbon from the 14th century, craft regulations were not recorded until 1460; by 1537 there were 430 craftsmen. The over-elaboration of this and the previous example is characteristic of the golden age of Portuguese silver. The vast supply of precious metals encouraged a certain profligacy. Artisans flocked to Portugal from all over Europe but this dish maintains a definite Portuguese style, including the polychrome armorial.

c) Custodia, parcel-gilt with lapis lazuli base, by Cristobal Becerril; Cuenca, Spain, 1585; ht. 37″ (93.9 cm.).

This custodia was commissioned by the Bishop of Cuenca for the Parish Church of San Juan, Alarcon. Cristobal was a member of the famous Becerril family whose combined talents made Cuenca important among contemporary centres of goldsmithing. Small, compared to towering cathedral custodias, its 62 small religious sculptured figures, its classical organization into two storeys, with entablatures carried on Corinthian and Ionic columns, and its three-tiered cupola, make it significant both in design and execution. A variety of techniques are apparent: repoussé, chasing and engraving. The matching *viril*, or monstrance, now missing, fitted on the small first platform.

d) Chalice, silver-gilt, with applied shaped panels of enamelled silver-gilt; inscribed: Hic est enim calix sanguinis mei novi, *and marked* Luis; *probably Cordoba, Spain, c. 1600-50; ht. 11″ (27.9 cm.).*

The guild at Cordoba enforced strict standards of workmanship, although it was not a long established centre, such as Toledo, Seville and Burgos. The raised enamel areas are deep pink translucent enamel painted with small animals and birds such as rabbits and eagles in opaque white enamel. Polychromy was a marked feature of the mediaeval period which continued after Renaissance designs and Italian and German goldsmiths arrived in Spain. Other archaizing features are the pierced-edge foot, the ogival outlines to the stepped base and the form of the inscribed letters. Nothing is known of Luis, the maker.

Cordoba city mark.

Barcelona city marks.

Dish, silver-gilt with applied plaques of translucent polychrome enamel in arabesque designs; Spain c. 1620–30; dia. 26″ (66.0 cm.).

The fondness for polychromy which was so marked a taste in goldsmiths' work in the mediaeval period survived longest in Spain, and is illustrated by this dish. Possibly a Royal gift to an ecclesiastical foundation, the dish bears in the centre a shield enamelled with the arms of Castile, France and Leon. The workmanship is on a broader scale than was seen in the preceding century.

a) Processional cross, silver and silver-gilt on wood core, with 20 niello plaques engraved by Baccio Baldini after collaborative designs by Maso Finiguerra (1426–64) and Antonio Pollaiuolo (born c. 1433, d. 1498); Florence, Italy, c. 1465; ht. 21¾″ (55.2 cm.).

The cypher 'ABL' for Baccio Baldini (working mid-15th century, d. 1487), the goldsmith responsible for the niello plaques, appears on one of them. One of the most exquisite achievements of the Italian Renaissance goldsmiths was their conversion of the ancient decorative technique of niello to the production of pictorial compositions of great emotional power. Small plaques were used; parts of the design were excavated and filled with a powdered substance containing silver, lead, copper and sulphur. Under heat this was fused; when cool it was a level, hard, black inlay which adhered well to the silver. The art was practised intensively from c. 1460–1500.

---

b) Tazza, silver-gilt; Italy, c. 1570–85; ht. 15½″ (39.4 cm.).

The figure represents the Roman Emperor Caligula and is surrounded in the shallow bowl of the tazza with scenes depicting high points of his life. The tazza is one part of a service of twelve, each bearing the figure of one of the twelve Caesars and each bowl chased with scenes relating to that particular Emperor. This service is one of the very few to have survived, though it has been dispersed to various collections. Probably the service was for ceremonial and decorative purposes rather than for use. Pope Clement VII is thought to have been the original owner.

c) Ewer, silver-gilt, Rome, Italy, c. 1600; ht. 18¼″ (46.4 cm.).

The size and weight of this object places it among the group of valuable sideboard articles that were meant more for show than for use. The decorative scheme is highly sculptural in concept, particularly in the design of the handle which consists of a figure of victory and a rampant lion. The continuous band of relief decoration round the middle of the ewer represents the Triumph of Caesar. Such large pieces, which were made in some numbers for the embellishment of noble rooms have not survived in great part, and tend to be better known from contemporary paintings.

Detail: base of a tazza.

a) *Rosewater basin, silver-gilt, (a companion to the preceding ewer), Rome, Italy, c. 1600; dia. 24⅝″ (64.6 cm.).*

The boss is vacant and probably contained a coat of arms or inscription. While not in use the foot of the ewer was accommodated perfectly within the circumference of the boss. The decoration is largely achieved through the use of casting, the plaques of the rim being made separately and fixed with bolts from the under-side. The subjects of the border are of stories from the Apocrypha and ancient history, Judith, Darius, Paris and Alexander.

Rome City mark.

b) *Frame for a relic of St. John the Baptist, silver-gilt, Italy, probably Florence; mid-17th century, ht. 36″ (91.4 cm.).*

In an interesting reversal of earlier practice the anonymous maker of this reliquary relied on the concepts and methods of sculpture rather than goldsmithing for this large work, the greater part of it being achieved by cast elements assembled together. The base supports a relief plaque depicting the beheading of St. John while angels at the corners bear salvers holding symbols of his martyrdom. A figure of the Baptist surmounts the entire composition.

c) *Statuette, Christ at the Column; by Alessandro Algardi (1595-1654); Rome, Italy; c. 1640-50; ht. 8¾″ (22.2 cm.).*

Algardi, an architect and sculptor, also carved ivory and modelled small subjects for casting in bronze and silver. This figure recalls the central figure of his bronze Flagellation group and may have been intended for a member of the Colonna family, whose emblem, a column crowned, related to this subject. Neither goldsmiths nor sculptors were averse to repeating a successful work in a different medium or smaller scale if there was a prospective client.

a) Incense burner in the form of a covered bowl; Upper Rhine, Germany, c. 1450–1500; ht. 32″ (81.2 cm.).

In contrast to contemporary Italian goldsmiths, so many of whom practised other arts with distinction, German goldsmiths were generally active only within their own sphere.

Their greatest patron was still the Church, not only with major commissions for important new articles, but also for such standard items as incense burners, a necessary adjunct to all masses. This example, with four chains for swinging the censor and a fifth to raise the lid, has the architectural form of two superimposed orders of Gothic gables and towers, and a tile-engraved roof. The Gothic style gave way to the Renaissance in the following century.

b) Covered cup of silver-gilt; Germany, perhaps Ingoldstadt; c. 1450–1500; ht. 11¼″ (28.5 cm.).

This important cup traditionally belonged to an Ingoldstadt angling club which met for convivial dinners in the 16th century, although it was probably made a century earlier. Entirely Gothic in design and conception, this ample beaker with gently flaring sides rests on an attached stand supported by three jesters blowing flutes. The cover is surmounted by a child holding a fruit and a bird. The leaf curling round a branch on the stand is a repeated ragged thistle, a religious symbol frequently found on Gothic silver. This cup was one of many silver pieces confiscated in 1813; somehow it escaped the melting pot.

Silver

Continental

GERMAN

c) Tankard, silver-gilt and silver filigree, Augsburg, Germany; c. 1550; ht. 8″ (20.3 cm.).

This unusual tankard has mounts of the finest workmanship above and below the deep band of silver filigree, which forms the body of the vessel. Undoubtedly there was originally an inner vessel of glass or crystal and a disc of similar material mounted in the cover, the purpose of which, according to a sincerely held belief, was to detect the presence of poison in the drink by either breaking asunder or discolouring. A small number of similar filigree mounted tankards which have retained their glass or crystal linings are known dating from the same epoch. The use of the silver filigree which may be of Italian origin, brings the tankard into the large group of objects made of unusual or exotic materials which were completed by the addition of silver or silver-gilt mounts, a combination for which the Germans seem to have had a special fondness. At the time this tankard was made, Augsburg was second only to Nuremberg in wealth and commercial activity. The power and influence of its great family, the Fugger, rivalled that of the Medici of Florence and was similarly powerful far beyond the limits of its home base.

a) *Cup, partly gilt, Strasbourg, Germany (now France), c. 1560–67; ht. 3⅝" (9.21 cm.).*

This cup, engraved with a figure representing Virgo, a symbol for August, is flanked by scenes representing harvesting, and is probably from a set of twelve, one for each month. Thierry de Bry, a member of the Strasbourg guild, whose mark appears on this cup is better known for his designs printed from engraved copper plates and widely distributed. Until the formal connection of Strasbourg with France after 1697, silver of this town is more German in character. The decoration of the lower part of the cup evokes the familiar stem with prunts or 'cabbage stalk' of German popular glass. (See p. 452a.)

b) *Frame, silver-gilt; by Wenzel Jamnitzer (b. 1508), Nuremberg, Germany, c. 1568–70; ht. 11⅝" (29.5 cm.).*

This frame's design is taken from the title page of Jamnitzer's book, *Perspectiva Corporum Regularum* (Nuremberg, 1568). The main features are four female figures, Architecture, Geometry, Arithmetic and Perspective, and two armorini, Inclination and Diligence. In addition to the raised repoussé figures and other parts, matting, engraving, and chasing give depth and clarity to and emphasize the pictorial quality, testifying to Jamnitzer's contemporary fame as a superb craftsman.

Born in Vienna, he migrated to Nuremberg, enrolling in the goldsmiths' guild in 1534. Other Jamnitzers were active in Nuremberg in the second half of the 16th century; Albrecht was master of the guild in 1550.

Strasbourg city mark (1567–1681).

c) *Covered cup of silver, silver-gilt and niello; Augsburg, Germany, probably c. 1576–1585; ht. 11¾" (28.9 cm.).*

This cup is in the form of a great acorn, cut with part of its woody stem and carried over the shoulder of a striding woodsman. The decoration consists, however, of arabesques of silver against a black ground of niello. Such designs were available to goldsmiths in the later 16th century in printed pattern sheets that were available commercially all over Europe, and Augsburg was itself a principal centre of such activity. Drinking vessels form the most numerous category of the objects made in the two South German goldsmithing centres of Augsburg and Nuremberg, and there appears to have been a continual extension of ideas for new forms. Even now, drinking vessels of one kind or another of German manufacture from the 16th to the mid-17th centuries are the single most numerous class of antique European silver objects to have survived, and illustrate dramatically how large must have been the original production and how wide must have been their commercial dispersal.

Nuremberg city mark.

Silver

Continental
GERMAN

Hamburg city mark.

Detail: inside lid of casket, design attributed to Mores.

a) Covered beaker on a pedestal stem, silver-gilt; by Eberwein Kossman, Nuremberg, Germany, c. 1575–84; ht. 21⅝″ (54.9 cm.).

This cup can be dated after Kossman became a master goldsmith in 1575. (He died in 1584.) Its unusual size suggests a company cup for public use on festive occasions when such large cups were customary. The busts, fruit and strapwork are repoussé, chased and engraved, and seem to shine against a finely matted dull background. Round the lip, deftly engraved in a style of interrupted lines, is a continuous hare hunt. Formalized leaves are acid-etched on the foot, a technique of mediaeval armourers that was adopted by a number of German goldsmiths in the 16th century for decorating silver.

b) Covered cup decorated with scenes from Ovid's Metamorphoses; silver-gilt in the style of H. Jamnitzer (working 1561–1603); Nuremberg, Germany, late 16th century; ht. 11⅝″ (29.5 cm.).

This exquisite cup, undoubtedly the personal property of an individual of wealth and education, is an example of the extreme elaboration that was possible in goldsmiths' work. The compositions on the bosses and lobes of the bowl are taken from the woodcuts by Bernard Salomon in a 1559 edition of the *Metamorphoses*. The workmanship of the relief decoration, on an unusually small scale, upholds the reputation of the Jamnitzer family (see p. 625b). A flat printed composition has been translated into a three dimensional work, literally and with great clarity, representing a tour de force of sculptural, as well as a goldsmith's skill.

c) Double cup; 2 cups fitting together, the upper reversed, wrythen stems, silver-gilt and silver; by Caspar Beutmüller the elder, Nuremberg, Germany, late 16th century; ht. 20¾″ (52.7 cm.).

The double cup is a characteristic German form. 15th century examples usually have a smaller upper cup; later, equal-sized cups were preferred. The rounded bosses, and cut thistle leaves on wires round the stem, are earlier Gothic features, but its size and the finely engraved band on each lip indicate its actual date. This stylistic mixture was common at this period when Nuremberg had been, for over a century, the most important German commercial and artistic centre.

On the major trade route to northern Europe, its wealth and culture were famous, and its goldsmiths' work was exported throughout Europe.

d) Casket, silver and bronze-gilt; probably after a design by the Hamburg goldsmith Jacob Mores; Germany, 16th–17th century; ht. 9¾″ (24.8 cm.).

The casket is designed on an architectural plan, the main emphasis being on the scenes in relief under the rounded arches. These refer to the Passion of Christ; in front, from left to right, the Last Supper, the agony in the garden and the taking of Christ. The reliefs are of silver and the frame of bronze-gilt. Variants of this casket are known. The production of highly worked caskets and jewel boxes in silver is an especial German characteristic of the 16th and 17th centuries.

a) Automaton, silver, silver-gilt and jewels; by Joachim Friess; Augsburg, Germany, c. 1605–10, ht. 14¾″ (37.5 cm.).

The clockwork mechanism concealed within the six-sided base of this object enables it to move about on small wheels underneath. The maker is recorded as the originator of several other automata of this kind and it may well have been his speciality. The head of the stag is removable and presumably served as a cup, the hollow body of the stag serving as a reservoir of wine. Less elaborate cups were made in Augsburg which consisted simply of figures of birds or animals with removable heads and hollow bodies but without the elaborate clockwork in the base. The general development of such novelty cups was one aspect of the enormous output of vessels for drinking, many of very original design, which characterized German production in the 16th and early 17th centuries.

b) Tankard, silver-gilt and amber; maker of the mounts, Andreas Meyer, (active 1606–1647), Konigsberg, Germany, ht. 9½″ (30 cm.).

Konigsberg was in the region of the principal finds of amber by the sea coast of East Prussia. There were several guilds of amber=turners in the region and tankards of amber mounted by local goldsmiths were a characteristic reflection of the taste for mounting rare or unusual materials into drinking vessels. Other such materials were Venetian *latticinio* glass, ostrich eggs, coconuts, Turkish pottery and semi-precious stones such as jasper and serpentine. The tall straight-sided form of the tankard is the so-called 'Baltic' type.

c) Nef, partly gilt, by Esaias zur Linden; Nuremberg, Germany, early 17th century; ht. 19⅝″ (49.7 cm.).

Used as a drinking vessel, while humorously representing a sailing ship with six figures and two cannon on deck and two more figures climbing the rigging, the exterior of the hull is repoussé and chased to suggest waves and dolphins. At the time this ship was made the ceremony and high solemnity that had attended the use of the nef in mediaeval times at the tables of princes and nobles had largely evaporated. In its earlier phase the nef was often of gold and of some size and was used for salt or rare spices at the tables of Kings and Popes. It was also used in coronation ceremonies.

627

a) Wager cup, silver-gilt and enamel, possibly by Hieronimus Imhof; Augsburg, Germany; early 17th century; ht. 8″ (20.3 cm.).

Imhof of Bamberg was active as a goldsmith in Augsburg. The skirt of the lady forms a conical drinking vessel when inverted and a smaller more obvious cup is held on pivots above her head. The purpose of the cup provided for a certain round of hilarity at the expense of selected individuals who attempted to quaff the contents of the larger cup without spilling the contents of the smaller cup. Such vessels originated in Germany and do not appear to have been fabricated elsewhere with certain notable exceptions, such as one of English manufacture belonging to the Vintners' Company. A number were made, in a sentimentalizing vein, in England in the 19th century.

b) Clock-case, partly gilt, Augsburg, Germany, c. 1700. ht. 31¾″ (80.6 cm.).

The elaborate mount is composed of four highly wrought silver plaques united by gilt swags and borders. The subjects are the toilet of Venus, Venus and Vulcan, Venus and Diana, Venus and Mars, carried out in repoussé and casting for those parts of the compositions that are totally disengaged from the background. Three of the mounts are signed by Johann Andreas Thelot, 1655–1734, whose principal output was decorative plaques. The clock movement is the work of Franz Xavieri Gegenreiner, also of Augsburg, while the tortoiseshell veneer of the base is the work of a third craftsman. The use of tortoiseshell for an object large enough to be considered a furnishing is typical of the period.

a) Coconut cup; stand, cover and mounts are of silver-gilt in combination with a carved coconut; possibly by Aert van Muers of s'Hertogenbosch, Netherlands; early 17th century; ht. 11" (27.9 cm.).

The cup itself is of polished coconut carved with three scenes illustrating episodes in the stories of Lot, Samson and David. Inscriptions in Latin on the coconut give Bible references by chapter and verse and on the metal mounts encourage the user to quaff the contents handily but to beware of drinking immoderately. Coconut cups were originally a German invention but were made outside Germany in Holland, Austria and occasionally England.

b) Sauce-boat or ewer, silver-gilt, by Adam Van Vianen (1565-1627); Utrecht, Netherlands; dated 1621; ht. 4½" (11.4 cm.).

This container equipped with a handle, spout and cover nevertheless provides scope for a depiction of the Rape of Proserpine by Pluto whose horses are represented fording the river Cyane. Even if the maker's signature were not present on this piece, the grotesque mask of a sea monster and other convoluted decoration on the sides would proclaim it as the work of Adam Van Vianen, one of the most original goldsmiths of the 17th century.

---

c) Beaker; Enkhuizen, Netherlands, c. 1630; ht. 7¼" (18.4 cm.).

The beaker rather than the standing cup was the characteristic Dutch drinking vessel in the 16th and 17th centuries, and after the Reformation also replaced the chalice as a vessel for sharing the Sacrament of wine in communion services. Religious decoration was frequently introduced on these latter, as on this example which has scenes from the Story of Tobit, finely engraved. The foot is strengthened with bands of stamped and moulded silver.

d) Cup, in the form of a prancing horse, silver-gilt; Amsterdam, Netherlands, 1637; ht. 7¾" (19.7 cm.).

Like the coconut cup the wine cup in the form of a hollow animal with a detachable head is a German rather than a Dutch form which was occasionally reproduced in the more northern country. The direct and simple realism of this model is particularly appealing, while the base is a conventional one with repoussé decoration and a stamped edging.

Silver

Continental
DUTCH

Amsterdam city mark.

a) *Plate, by Sigismund Zachammer; Amsterdam, Netherlands; 1685, dia. 14¼″ (36.2 cm.).*

The style of the decoration of the plate is characteristic of Dutch work of the second half of the 17th century. It consists of closely placed natural motifs such as flowers, fruit and leaves and living figures among them, but on a much diminished scale. Sometimes the figures are of animals, sometimes, as here, children representing the five senses. Such decoration is carried out in repoussé with details added in chasing, engraving and matting. The effect was imitated in London contemporaneously.

Sigismund Zachammer originally came from Joachimstad in Bohemia. He migrated to Amsterdam.

b) *Coffee-urn by Tijomon Suyk, Amsterdam, Netherlands; 1733. ht. 15″ (38.1 cm.).*

In contrast to the lightness and grace of silver made in The Hague, Amsterdam silver shows more weighty forms and decoration that recalls Huguenot work of the early part of the century. Large areas of the vessels were left undecorated. The urn illustrated here is equipped with no fewer than three spiggots and two large swing handles attached at the lip.

c) *Ewer, silver-gilt, by Christoffel Radijs, The Hague, Netherlands; c. 1740-50; ht. 9¼″ (23.5 cm.).*

The use of the shared rosewater dish and ewer which descended from mediaeval times, continued into the 18th century but was gradually replaced by vessels for private ablutions. The gay, cosmopolitan tone of life in The Hague, already a centre of European diplomacy, is reflected in the choice of silver-gilt, a feature rarely seen in Dutch silver, and the engraved and chased rock, shell and lattice work which were fundamentals in the contemporary international rococo style.

The Hague city mark.

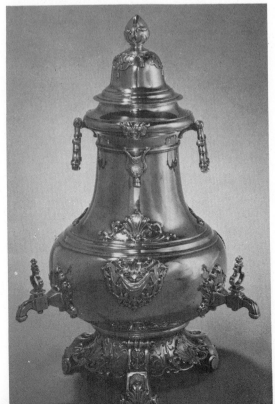

a) Candlestick, maker identified only by his initials, I.D; Paris, France; 1690-91; ht. 9¼″ (23.5 cm.).

This stately candlestick is of a formality that is associated with the manner of furnishing interiors in the reign of Louis XIV. It could only be achieved by the use of a two part casting, a technique that was very much employed at the end of the 17th century not only for making small items such as candlesticks but also for the larger pieces of furniture for which the period was noted. It exhibits the clarity and superb sense of definition that characterized the use of decoration on French silver in the later 17th century continuing into the early 19th century.

b) Wine taster; probably by Jean Charles Bataille; Paris, France, 1724-25; dia. 4½″ (11.4 cm.).

These small cups usually with thick walls and rounded at the bottom edge were customarily owned by all who had any professional contact with wine, such as butlers and vintners. A number of genuine ones have survived to the present, including one in gold, and suggest that the wine taster was a very common object, in daily use. The single flat handle and ring handle beneath it is customary, as is the spray of leaves engraved round the side.

Paris duty mark, registered 1681.

c) Bowl, silver-gilt; Strasbourg, France, c. 1725-28; ht. 2¾″ (6.9 cm.).

Strasbourg silver is distinguished from other French silver of the 18th century in its frequent use of gilt. After passing under the sway of France in 1697, however, the silver of this city is distinctly French in its decoration and form. The vertical straps seen on this bowl are a regular development of the cut-card innovation introduced in Paris in the late 17th century. The shaped field against which the straps are set and the engraving upon them is of extraordinary fineness, as is the quality of the cast handles.

d) Ecuelle by Eloi Guerin; Paris, France, 1749-50; wdth. across handles 12½″ (31.8 cm.).

The wide, fairly shallow bowl with flat horizontal handles and a domed cover is a form so typically French that it is known by its French name although it was also made in Germany and Russia, and occasionally in other countries. The form was taken up in France by the pewterers, faienciers and porcelain factories. Ecuelles were made in great numbers which probably explains the apparent anomaly of cast features such as handles and finials from the same model appearing on pieces by different makers. There was a trade among themselves by the goldsmiths for stock items such as these.

Paris duty mark, registered 1703.

b) Ewer and basin, by Louis Samson; Toulouse, France, 1761–62. Made for Etienne Bernard de Sapt, Lord of Villelisse and his wife Catherine Thérèse de Catelan; lgth. 15½" (39.4 cm.).

The small ewer and narrow basin was a typically French pair, not made elsewhere in Europe except in Spain and Portugal. It was also made in less precious materials such as porcelain and faience. These small ewers and basins were for private ablutions before a meal, and replaced the large ceremonial objects which, during the Middle Ages and onwards into the 16th century, were carried around from guest to guest at the table—an interesting point of social history. The retention of the rococo style in Toulouse is notable in that very southern city, where goldsmiths were conservative about stylistic fashions, although execution and skill in craftmanship were of a standard equal to Paris.

a) Tureen and plateau, by François Thomas Germain; France; mid–18th century; lgth. 23" (58.4 cm.).

Silver

Continental

FRENCH

Part of a large dinner service bearing the Royal arms of Portugal made for the Portuguese Court. This commission, which Germain executed with the aid of several other goldsmiths, is an indication of the high regard in which French silver was held in the 18th century. The Russian court was also supplied with silver services. The plateau was a customary companion to the grand soup tureen.

c) Coffee-pot, silver-gilt; by Martin Guillaume Biennais; Paris, France, c. 1794–1814; ht. 13" (33.0 cm.).

This coffee pot is from a large service in silver-gilt that the Emperor Napoleon is said to have presented to his sister Pauline and her husband Prince Camillo Borghese, but the precise details of the occasion and the date are not known. Biennais was Napoleon's favourite goldsmith and executed a large number of commissions for the Emperor. The partners Charles Percier and Pierre Fontaine, who were principally architects, supplied many of the designs from which Biennais worked, and his silver, as in the example here, exhibits the severe classicism for which the firm was noted.

Toulouse duty mark (various dates).

Bruges city mark (post 17th century).

Louis XVI oval soup tureen and stand from the Orloff Service by Jacques Nicholas Roettiers; France, 1770.

a) Chalice, silver-gilt with translucent enamel panels, decorated with symbolic vine and grape design in silver gilt wire; Hungary (Bohemia), early 16th century; ht. 9½" (24.1 cm.).

The goldsmith's art was an ancient one in Hungary; records date from the 13th century. When King Matthias Corvinus died in 1490 (whose policy had been to enrich his realm) all the churches were richly furnished. Though Corvinus himself was artistically progressive, the goldsmiths retained traditional Gothic styles until well into the 16th century, especially for ecclesiastical works, such as this chalice, which suggests a simple palm-cup resting in a richly decorated stand with a tall stem. A Latin inscription indicates it belonged to Dom John of Breslau. Translucent enamel and twisted wire techniques were due to the influence of Venetian craftsmen.

b) Tea-pot, by Braun; Basle, Switzerland; c. 1720–30; ht. 5½" (13.9 cm.).

In the 16th, 17th and 18th centuries Basle was an important centre of goldsmithing but Swiss silver generally is scarce today, and silver from the late mediaeval to early Renaissance period is almost non-existent, although much must have been made. This tea-pot of low pear shape is exquisitely decorated with a formal design of interlacing straps, shells and leaves carried out in fine matting and engraving. The spout has a hinged cover.

Basle city mark.

Budapest city mark.

c) Tea and coffee service, partly-gilt, by Johan Henrik Blohm; St. Petersburg, Russia, c. 1773; ht. 10¼" (26 cm.).

Following Peter the Great's forced Westernization of the country, Russian silver design began to reflect European models. Blohm was a Court goldsmith. Borrowed from Germany was the practice of having both a tea and coffee-pot to accompany a creamer, bowl and sugar-box in one matching service. This set is said to have been the gift of Catherine the Great to Count Peter Rumiantzeff for his victories in the war against the Turks. The principal decoration of enamel portraits of Russian rulers is suitably framed by raised and gilt rococo 'shellwork and military trophies.

Opposite:
Two fine silver beakers of almost matching designs engraved with three apostles with formalized scroll and strapwork borders; Breda, Holland, 1645 and 1653. Foreground: Two-handled bowl; Rennes, France, 1725.

Silver

Continental
RUSSIAN
POLISH
NORWEGIAN

a) Kovsh, partly gilt; Russia, 1691; lgth. 11⅞″ (30.2 cm.).

The boat-shaped *kovsh* was the standard drinking vessel in Russia until the deliberate Westernization of the country under Peter the Great. In aristocratic and well-to-do circles it was gradually superseded by cups of the usual form, but among the poorer classes it continued in use in both wood and silver.

The inscription in Cyrillic script explains that the *kovsh* was presented to Pyotr Ivanov of a well-known Kazan Tartar family of Lebedev for having paid his share at a levy of taxes at Sevsk.

b) Beaker, probably Poland; about 1720; ht. 5½″ (13.9 cm.).

This beaker with slightly flaring sides is a good example of the connection between silver money and silver of coin standard being used for items of domestic application, for they are combined in this piece. The use of coin to decorate a piece of silver is characteristic of the more northerly European countries. Between the coins are leaves engraved in outline and less polished against a matted ground.

c) Tankard, by Isack Andersen Feldthus; Stavanger, Norway, 1812; ht. 8¼″ (20.9 cm.).

The seven silver pegs set above each other at equal distances against the inner wall is a peculiarity of Scandinavian tankards and indicated each guest's due 'portion' at a convivial gathering. The delicate 'bright cut' decoration is a contemporary note on an object that is otherwise very traditional in form. The simple hoop handle set with a shield at the end, the lion thumb-piece and mask decorating the hinge of the lid, the drum-shaped body itself and the three ball and claw feet are all features already found at the end of the 17th century.

Moscow city mark (after 1747).

636

English Silver
Introduction

English silver holds rather a special place among the minor applied arts, for not only is it durable and usually beautiful in appearance, but it provides a readily datable key to the development of styles in many aspects of domestic decoration. From earliest times, the London silversmiths were quick to follow the newest styles, usually originating abroad; this was especially true in times of expansion, such as the Elizabethan period, and from the Restoration onwards into the Victorian era. The wealthy were far from purse-proud when it came to making their homes fashionable. Sometimes old or worn plate was sent to the silversmith to be remade in the latest manner, or into a novelty for the table, the toilet or the drawing-room. Often, however, they merely relegated the out-dated silver to the strongroom, a source of extra money (for it was sterling like the coinage) should it be needed for personal or political reasons. A surprising amount of old plate has therefore survived, despite the depredations of wars and tax-gatherers and the vicissitudes of taste.

Changing ideas and evanescent fashions have perhaps wrought more havoc than hard wear or the incessant polishing by over-zealous butlers has ever done. With only a cursory glance at the form and decoration, and without so much as checking the important (though not always all-revealing) hall-marks, even a relatively novice collector can soon come to spot later ornament, whether it is overall chasing in style out of keeping with the original period, or an addition such as a monogram or a later coat of arms.

English silver styles, both London and provincial and even more spectacularly, Scottish and Irish styles, have a distinctive air appropriate to their period. Even when careful reproductions are made in later years they betray their anachronistic origin. A Tudor standing cup is undeniably sixteenth century in form and ornament, just as an imitation of it made a century later looks as though it were made a century later. A Regency essay in the rococo, however finely worked, always manages to look like an early nineteenth century copy of a piece made fifty or sixty years before.

For every silver collector and for the newcomer especially, the hall-marks are, of course, an important guide. They are there, primarily to protect the buyer by assuring him that the silver is of the purported standard—usually sterling, which is 92.5 per cent pure silver, on which the Assay Offices strike a lion *passant* (except in Ireland, where the mark is the crowned harp, and since 1758 in Scotland, where the thistle denotes the standard mark). Sometimes the higher Britannia standard, made obligatory from 1697 until 1720, and occasionally used since, shows the metal to contain 95.8 per cent pure silver. In addition to the standard marks, each Assay Office, of which only four remain in Great Britain and one in Ireland, struck its own local mark and a letter to denote the year of assay. The variations of these marks and of the various local marks, some of them still not definitely identified, provide an absorbing and rewarding study in themselves, though they are not, *per se*, the be-all and end-all of antique silver studies. Antique silver and modern silver as well, should be considered on its merits as a design, well made and suitably decorated, a piece for use or for display that is right for its period and good of its kind, whether it is a rare and fine *tour-de-force* of a famous maker or the functional, down-to-earth, product of a lesser silversmith or a large workshop.

a) Mazer, maple wood with silver gilt mount; engraved: Benedicam Dominum in Omni Tempore, umarked, c. 1460; dia. 4¾″ (12.1 cm.).

Although only about 80 English mazers have survived, with a few Scottish examples, these drinking bowls must have been relatively plentiful during the Middle Ages. One Church text book, the *Rites of Durham*, states 'every monk had his mazer severally by himself to drink in . . . largely and finely edged with silver double-gilt.' The most usual wood was spotted maple; the mounts, usually gilt, were often inscribed in Latin or the vernacular. Some had central bosses or prints, often enamelled; Scottish mazers had a foot, rare in England. The earliest appear to date c. 1350; a few were made as late as c. 1620.

b) The Cressener cup, font-shaped; maker's mark a crossbow, London, 1503; ht. 6⅜″ (16.2 cm.).

The font-shaped cup was a not unusual form during the first half of the 16th century, before the Renaissance styles invaded English workshops. Like the contemporary mazers, many were inscribed, and some were richly embossed and chased. Of those with covers, the disc-like finial is sometimes flat and inlaid with an enamelled print—in this instance the arms of the family in whose possession it remained until 1722. Similar cups include the Campion Cup (1500), an elaborate version of 1515 at Corpus Christi College, Cambridge, and several in English church collections. The style was out of fashion by around 1550.

Coat of arms detail (see b).

c) Gourd cup and cover, silver-gilt; maker's mark HW; London, 1563; ht. 10½″ (26.6 cm.).

The Renaissance brought with it ingenious and exotic designs as well as fostering the use of rare or unusual materials. The gourd-inspired cup illustrated is one of ten such recorded cups, all of them dating from the reign of Elizabeth I. Other unusual forms include the acorn. Very occasionally one finds nautilus shells, ostrich eggs and even more rarely, cups formed in the German manner as birds or animals. These were table ornaments, essentially, rather than drinking cups. Similarly exotic forms were also used for the important standing salts of the period.

d) German stoneware jug with silver-gilt mounts; Maker IC; London 1565; ht. 7⅞″ (18.7 cm.).

Many jugs or tankards in reddish-brown mottled 'tigerware' appear to have been exported to England, especially the West Country. They were often mounted with silver or silver-gilt foot, neck and handle mounts, a fashion lasting from about 1550 to c. 1610. This example is rare for its relatively small size, for being fully marked, and for the deep engraved neck mount with its foliate and strapwork motifs in contrast to the more usual and often coarsely embossed mounts. Box hinges were usual, and covers almost always embossed and chased, with a finial, which like the thumbpiece was often cast.

Standing mazer of the Barber's Company (1523); Pepys drank from it in 1663.

a) Gilt standing salt; London, 1569; maker's mark a bird; ht. 12" (30.5 cm.).

One of the best-known Tudor architectural salts, this example shows the inter-European styles then fashionable: the chased panels bear the Cardinal Virtues embossed after Virgil Solis of Nuremberg (1514-62) whose designs for goldsmiths were widely copied. The standing salt was a focal point of the high table from the Middle Ages until c. 1650, with few made subsequently.

The quadrangular and drum-shaped Elizabethan salts were invariably in high Renaissance style, often richly embossed and chased with classical scenes, decorated with swags of fruit and foliage, sphinxes (as here), vase finials, and often surmounted by the figure of a warrior or deity.

b) Tankard and cover, parcel-gilt; maker IC, eagle's head between; London, 1579; ht. 7¼" (18.4 cm.).

The tapering drum-shaped tankard was another showpiece of the Tudor period. Boldly projecting mouldings usually partition the various parts of the body, with either engraved strapwork and scrolls or embossed chasing filling the areas between, and often including small applied masks or other ornament in relief. The foot and domed cover were usually chased with strapwork, scrolls, fruit or foliage, and the finial and thumb-piece often cast. In a taller and larger form, the drum-shaped tankard became the flagon or livery-pot; many were used for replenishing the Communion cup in churches.

---

c) Bell salt, parcel-gilt; maker's mark ER, 1599; ht. 9" (22.9 cm.).

By the end of the 16th century, a new version of the great standing salt was introduced, also accommodating spices such as pepper and nutmeg. Bell salts were less extravagant in design than the architectural salts, usually with engraved or flat-chased decoration, standing simply on three shell or ball-and-claw feet. The 'bell' divides into three sections, with wells for the salt and spices and sometimes, as here, with a caster in the top of the cover. A few are actually formed as bells. In about 1619, they were superseded by spool- or capstan-shaped salts.

d) Beaker, with spreading foot; maker IA, London, 1602; ht. 6½" (16.5 cm.).

Probably the oldest form of man-made drinking vessel, the beaker remains a basically simple piece derived, no doubt, from a truncated horn. The Elizabethan silver beaker in England and on the Continent was a relatively tall cup, its spreading foot usually decorated with an ovolo or other simple border. The tapering slightly everted sides also had quite simple decoration, the most common type having a strapwork band enclosing scrolls or foliage with depending motifs of flowers, leaves and fruit. About 1660, rim-footed beakers only 3 or 4" (7-10 cm.) high replaced the taller type.

Silver

English

a) Shell-shaped box for sugar or spice; maker's mark TI, a mullet below; London, 1619; lgth. 5″ (12.7 cm.).

Between about 1598 and 1628, there was a fashion for table boxes mounted on either shell or snail feet with the cover tooled realistically as a scallop shell. There is a tradition that these were used for spice or sugar (both expensive luxuries at the period), which seems likely: a late example of 1627 is accompanied by a contemporary, though unmarked spoon, small and hoof-shaped (not uncommon at the period). Not only does it fit perfectly into the box but its shape is ideal for roughly cut sugar.

b) Wine cup, maker I.H.; London, 1631; ht. 8¼″ (21 cm.).

The graceful plain wine cup with tapering baluster stem, plain circular foot and bell-shaped bowl is one of the most attractive survivals of early Carolean plate, so much of which was lost during the Civil Wars and the subsequent frugal years of the Commonwealth. Later to be closely imitated in the new flint glass, these must once have been far more plentiful than the few survivors suggest. This example, pricked with the words 'God Tries the Truth' and the initials 'DB', also bears the name Edmund Hamond and the date 1631 engraved later with the family's coat of arms.

Charles I wine taster (1638).

c) 'Sawcer' dish, of thin gauge silver; maker IG over a covered cup; 1634; lgth. 7″ (17.8 cm.).

Light, shallow dishes, sometimes called sweet-meat dishes but contemporarily listed as 'sawcers', presumably for mixing or serving sauces, have curiously survived in some numbers. Of the 17th century type, most date between 1629 and 1640, with a few being made between then and 1681. The great majority are circular, fluted into eight or more panels and decorated with punchwork, beaded fruits and simple scroll motifs. Most have a pair of shell-shaped handles, and though most conform in style and many were made by a maker identified as William Maundy, few pairs exist.

d) Scroll salt, silver-gilt; maker FC monogram; 1638; ht. 6½″ (16.5 cm.).

Early in the 17th century, when the high table was becoming a less important aspect of ceremonial and the dining saloon began to supersede the great hall, the great salt also became less formal. Those few that were made were the property chiefly of corporations and city companies, like this example presented to the Mercers' Company in 1638. Known as a scroll, or capstan, salt this spool-shaped type—round, square or octagonal in outline, featured scroll supports, probably accommodating a flat dish-cover or napkin to keep the salt covered.

'Sawcer' dish of 1638 (see c).

a) Porringer on spreading foot, almost straight-sided bowl decorated with punchwork, matted rondels, with cast scroll handles; Commonwealth period, maker RN: London, 1655; dia. 4⅜″ (11.1 cm.).

Tankards and porringers are perhaps the most typical of all silverware made from 1640–90. Covered and open porringers were made in every size; the earliest were often very similar to this example. Contemporary, more bulbous examples were repoussé chased with large flowers, foliage, animals and birds; other were severely plain, perhaps lobed into panels or with applied cut-card ornament round the base. The foot might have a ropework, plain or stepped rim. Handles, usually cast, were plain scrolls, foliate scrolls and often featured stylized caryatids. Covers were usually slightly domed following the cup's style and outline.

b) Saucepan or skillet on three feet; maker's mark RF; London, 1657.

Pans for heating sauces and hot drinks, such as posset and caudle, were advisedly of silver to prevent contamination from acid ingredients. The earlier type was a skillet on three short legs, the body straight-sided, with a scroll side-handle. The stop for the shallow domed cover (which could be used as a stand or a porringer) frequently bore the owner's initials or crest engraved. Otherwise saucepans were plain and functional. By the 18th century the usual silver pan was a small baluster or tapering cylindrical shape with a straight rising side-handle; it was used for warming brandy or cream.

---

c) Straight-sided tankard and cover, with finely matted body, flat domed cap cover and scroll handle with double thumb-piece; maker Henry Greenway; London, 1661; ht. 7¾″ (19.7 cm.).

This type, often very large, was standard from the Commonwealth until the end of the 17th century. Plain examples had simple armorials in a plumed mantling, others were chased with borders of acanthus foliage, flat-chased with Chinoiseries or, very rarely, encased in cagework pierced sleeves. A few tankards had Scandinavian-style pegs and these followed the northern style for straight-sided cylinders with pomegranate or lion feet and thumb-pieces. Holes at the base of the handle allowed steam to escape when it was soldered on and were not designed as whistles, as is sometimes suggested.

d) Rare early tea-pot of 'wine-pot' form; maker's mark a crowned S, probably Robert Smythier, London, c. 1675; ht. 6¼″ (15.8 cm.).

While the earliest known tea-pot looks exactly like a coffee-pot, the styles soon diverged, and the Chinese 'wine-pot' style was adopted. This oviform example is the plainest of the three earliest known. For about a century after its introduction in England (about 1650), tea was very expensive and pots consequently small. By the beginning of the 18th century, the oviform had given way to the pear-shaped pot, with high domed cover, the spout usually at right angles to the handle. Occasionally they were provided with stands and braziers, or their own small waiters or tea-pot stands.

Commonwealth tankard of 1654 with 'skirt' foot (see c).

Silver

English

Small beaker of 1665 (compare a).

a) Small beaker with embossed and chased decoration; maker's mark AR, London, 1681; ht. 4″ (10.2 cm.).

The small handleless beaker, along with the half-pint mug and the tumbler cup, was one of the most popular and plentiful of late Stuart drinking vessels. Its slightly flared cylindrical body was sometimes left plain, sometimes engraved with a few pendant flowers and strapwork, flat-chased with Chinoiseries, or, as here, embossed and chased with bold, naturalistic flowers and foliage. Many of these little beakers are engraved or pricked with initials and sometimes also the date: this one has the pricked date 1682 and the owner's initials above the ropework band below the lip.

b) Pair of trencher salts, both on spreading octagonal bases; 1684; dia. 3¼″ (8.25 cm.) at widest.

Not all Restoration period silver was grand, though many a merchant and householder sought, like Samuel Pepys, to have a fine collection of silver and it was their patronage, as much as that of the noble houses, that kept the silversmith busy and introduced the new era of truly domestic silver. The great standing salt was now replaced by individual trencher salts like these, engraved with the initials 'L' over 'H' and 'E'—no doubt, for an owner and his wife not entitled to bear arms. They weight 2.55 oz. The maker's mark, somewhat eroded by the salt, is 'TH', as yet unidentifed.

c) Pair of baluster form cast candlesticks on moulded octagonal bases by Pierre Harache; London, 1685; ht. 6¾″ (17.1 cm.).

Even before Louis XIV had revoked the Edict of Nantes in 1685, many Protestants were finding life in France intolerable, and they fled in large numbers to England, Germany, Switzerland, Ireland and America. A few managed to establish themselves in England, despite the objections of the London craftsmen, and among the first to be allowed to work in London was a fine Huguenot silversmith from Rouen, Pierre Harache, who was made Freeman of the Goldsmiths' Company in 1682. One trait of Huguenot design was the sturdy baluster form and the use of heavy gauge metal, as in these cast candlesticks weighing 23.65 oz.

d) Chinoiserie punch bowl or monteith, with notched rim and applied foliate border, by George Garthorne; London, 1688; dia. 10″ (25.4 cm.).

One curious and charming style deriving from the extensive overseas trade of the later 17th century was Chinoiserie. In silver, plants, birds, temples, warriors and mandarins were flat-chased (or rarely, engraved) on a variety of wares between c. 1685-90. The similarities of the scenes and motifs suggest that possibly many were decorated by the same hand for different silversmiths, but it is more likely that they were derived from one or two pattern-books and then copied. Many appear on otherwise typical silverwares, such as this with matted vertical panels, seven enclosing Chinese figures, the eighth, a contemporary coat of arms.

a) Sugar caster by Christopher Canner; 1690; ht. 7″ (17.8 cm.).

Trade with the West Indies was as lively as with the East, and casters for sugar began to appear on fashionable tables about 1670. Straight-sided, their rather coarsely-pierced covers were secured by slip-locks or bayonet fastenings. In this example, the foot is heavily gadrooned, matching the gadrooned border and fluted calyx on the cover. Others had plain stepped bases, or had the foot pierced with stars, hearts or crescents to match the piercing on the covers. Sets of three, one about 7″ high, the pair 5½″ (14 cm.) high, were also made.

b) Footed salver by Robert Cooper; 1691; dia. 11½″ (29.2 cm.).

Another mid-17th century newcomer to the English home was the footed salver, very often quite plain except for the armorials in the centre, though some were chased with Chinoiseries or occasionally engraved with flower and foliate designs. This example with its bold gadrooned rim and gadrooned trumpet foot corresponds closely to the William and Mary period furniture.

c) 'Monument' candlestick; maker's mark RS; 1691; approx. ht. 9½″ (24.1 cm.).

Despite the growing taste for 'Huguenot' styles, there was still much demand during the 1690s for the traditional fluted column candlesticks that had been so popular for some ten years. Bold gadrooning above the octagonal base was repeated on the knop of this 'Monument' candlestick which is of the large size that went out of fashion by the end of the century and was not revived for another 50 years.

d) Helmet-shaped ewer, by Pierre Harache; 1697; ht. 12″ (30.5 cm.).

The elegance of the Huguenot style is seen to advantage here. The English style of ewer had a straight top, here given height with a high moulded lip above an applied mask and shell—a favourite Harache motif. The cast caryatid handle rising from a foliate scroll shows the fine modelling achieved by the immigrant craftsmen and their skilful handling of ornament and fantasy. The body and foot of the ewer are formal and restrained, with an applied beaded moulding encircling the upper part, a gadrooned foot and knop and a calyx of fine cut-card work. The armorials are later.

Silver

English

*a) left: Punch bowl by Isaac Dighton; 1699; dia. 11"
(27.9 cm.).*
*b) right: Punch bowl by William Andrews; 1701;
dia. 10½" (26.7 cm.).*

The punch bowl or monteith (the latter usually
so called from its notched, often removable rim
after a Scotsman who chose to wear a scalloped
cloak) was an important piece of silver at the turn
of the century, the centre of many a drinking
party. Most were the work of English-born
silversmiths and were not in the new French style.
Chased and scrolling panels, further elaborated
with foliage and husks, were almost reminiscent of
the fluid Van Vianen styles of the early Carolean
age, while baroque cherub masks and scrolls were
almost standard decoration around the rim and
drop handles depended from lion masks. Most
bowls were about 11" in diameter, and weighed
upwards of 55 oz. Many were the work of Isaac
Dighton, who made the fine panelled example
(*left*). In more formal style, William Andrews
made the heavy 68.3 oz. fluted punch bowl (*right*)
in 1701, though in the same year such bowls, at
least when used without the rim, might be as
plain as those fashionable a quarter of a century
later.

c) Tankard by George Lewis, 1701; ht. 8⅜" (21.3 cm.).

The straight-sided Stuart tankard had changed
little for half a century but about 1700 the new
formal styles began to change even that practical
and simple shape. The flat cap cover was raised and
domed, as in this gadrooned example, while a
finely modelled and decorative thumb-piece was
also sometimes used, as the lion *couchant* here.
Capacities remained generally large; this tankard is
tall and weighs a massive 40 oz.

*d) Sugar and spice casters, by Henry Greene; 1704;
hts. 8½" and 6¾" (21.6 and 17.1 cm.).*

Sugar and spice casters, frequently made in sets
of three, were by Queen Anne's reign invariably
of baluster shape, and generally the piercing on the
covers, attached by bayonet fastenings, was much
finer than a few years earlier. In this set, a moulded
rib around the bodies is echoed by another on the
covers, dividing them and allowing the piercer to
vary the design with intricate scrollwork below
and simple diapers above the ribs. One of the
smaller casters is fitted with a 'blind' sleeve so that
it cannot pour, and was perhaps used for dry
mustard.

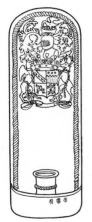

*William III silver wall
light, 1698.*

a) Mug by Thomas Atkinson; 1707; ht. 3½" (8.9 cm.).

Sturdiness was not only typical of immigrant silversmithing in the early years of the 18th century. This little tapering cylindrical mug of 1707 was made by Thomas Atkinson and weighs 7.8 oz. although only 3½" high. It is not, however, in the fashionable baluster shape that was beginning to oust the straight-sided style for tankards and mugs, and even the heart-shaped terminal to the scroll handle more properly belongs to the previous century.

b) Set of casters in cruet frame by Edmund Pearce, 1709; ht. of small pair 5" (12.7 cm.).

An early instance of the octagonal form used for a set of casters contained in a five-ring cruet frame. The silver-mounted glass bottles are later, probably a mid-18th century replacement. Note the alternate designs used for the pierced covers, following the outline of the octagonal form. The covers are secured by slip-locks.

c) Chocolate pot, plain but with engraved armorials on the reverse; by Gabriel Sleath, 1709; ht. 10¼" (26 cm.).

The popularity of coffee and chocolate rose to a crescendo in the early years of the 18th century, and despite the trend towards the baluster shape, pots for these drinks remained straight-sided and practical. For chocolate, a hinged or sliding aperture in the domed cover allowed for the insertion of a stirrer stick, known as a molinet, to mix the thick hot chocolate, while a small hinged flap ensured that even in the spout the drink remained hot. Wood was generally used for the side handle, at right angles to the spout, while discs or applied cut-card work helped to strengthen the body.

d) Coffee-pot by Anthony Nelme, 1714; ht. 10" (25.4 cm.).

The coffee-pot varied little from the contemporary chocolate pot except that there was no additional hinged cover, and the chained hinge was not used. Spouts, sometimes simple curves, sometimes faceted, were still set at right angles to the turned wood handle, but by the second decade of the century the hinged spout flap was replaced by the 'duck's head' terminal integral to the spout. The high domed cover remained in fashion until the 1720s, gradually becoming shallower, however, until by about 1730 it had been superseded by the cap cover.

Candlestick from a pair by Robert Kempkin, 1711.

645

Snuffer stand and pair of snuffers, by Simon Pantin, 1716.

Octagonal spice dredger, by Glover Johnson, 1718 (compare d).

a) *Tea kettle on stand with lamp; chocolate pot and stand; tea-pot and stand; by Joseph Ward, 1719.*

The second decade of the century was the decade of the octagon, and here a rare matching tea and chocolate set, complete with stands, shows its application to the tea-table silver. The squat pear-shaped tea-pot and the tall cylindrical chocolate pot retained the domed cover, but by now spouts were set opposite the handle. Heavy cast scroll supports are typical of the kettle lamp-stand, but the kettle is a 'duty dodger', the silversmith having inserted a mark from a less weighty piece and so avoided the duty on 85 oz. of silver.

b) *Jug by Augustine Courtauld; 1718; ht. 6¾" (17.1 cm.).*

Perhaps the happiest use of the baluster form was that for the jug, whether covered or, as here, plain and elegant. Probably used chiefly for beer and ale, a few such jugs are recorded with the names engraved on them, but most had no other orna-ment—at least until the age of the rococo—than engraved armorials. The rim was strengthened with a plain wire, the lip was almost vestigial, while a bold scroll handle with scroll thumb-piece and stepped moulded foot gave these jugs a good balance. This example is one of a pair by the Huguenot silversmith, Augustine Courtauld.

c) *One of two matching sets of casters by Paul de Lamerie, London, 1723; ht. of tallest 8½" (21.6 cm.), ht. of smaller pairs just over 6" (15.2 cm.).*

Of octagonal vase shape, these casters' most unusual features are the incurved angles and the gadrooned borders. Engraved with medallion heads, the covers are most intricately pierced with flowerheads and interlaced strapwork in alter-native panels: a most painstaking process achieved by hammer and chisel in an age before the inven-tion of the piercing saw. The casters bear the arms of John Harvey, 1st Earl of Bristol.

d) *Square waiter with engraved armorials of George Treby; by Paul de Lamerie; 1723; wdth. 6" (15.2 cm.).*

Though not without his peers, Paul de Lamerie's work is always unmistakably fine. Mouldings are of heavy quality, even if they are absolutely simple as here; ornament, whether engraved, chased or cast, is unexceptionally of superb standard. The finely engraved armorials of George Treby, enclosed within a most elaborate baroque cartouche incorporating masks, shells and medal-lion heads amid diaperwork, husk festoons, birds and other devices is typical of his skill and this is but one of many pieces made for Treby during the 1720s.

a) Octafoil salver, by Gabriel Sleath; 1724; dia. 11″ (27.9 cm.).

The making of salvers and waiters is one of the most skilled of the silversmith's tasks, and square, oblong and multifoil shapes are the most difficult. This fine plain salver has its shaped moulded rim deeply up-curved; the salver rests on panel feet. In the centre is a coat of arms in a typical baroque cartouche of the period. Note the maker's mark, which is put on by the silversmith, distant from the three hall-marks.

b) Single-eared shallow bowl with pricked date 1725; by John Elsten, Exeter, 1720; dia. 5¼″ (13.3 cm.).

Commonly called a bleeding bowl, though more probably used as a porringer, the single-eared shallow bowl made its appearance during the 17th century, often inverted as the cover of a skillet or pan for warming the drink or food that would subsequently be taken from it. The flat pierced handle was often intricately designed, and frequently bore the owner's initials and the date. This suggests that perhaps these bowls were used in childbirth, much as the similar two-handled bowl or *écuelle* was presented to mothers. This is a relatively late example.

Bullet tea-pot of 1731, ht. 3¾″ (9.5 cm.).

Bullet tea-pot of 1738, showing rococo influence (cf. c).

c) Tea-pot with unusual 9-sided spout; by Humphrey Payne, 1726.

By the mid-1720s, the pear-shaped tea-pot was giving way to the bullet shape on a rim foot, the handle opposite an almost straight spout. Tea was still very expensive and sizes were still small, with rather diminutive lids, sometimes hinged, sometimes loose. A band of flat-chased or of engraved ornament decorated the shoulders and lids of many of these pots, but collectors should beware of remade bullet pots, as many received hard wear during their busy lives.

d) Oblong inkstand by John White; London, 1726; lgth. 11½″ (29.2 cm.).

The standish, or inkstand, was an important piece of library or writing-table furniture throughout the 18th century. Many were elegantly simple oblong dishes, fitted with ink-pot, sand caster and either bell or taperstick or both. Here, the cover of the pounce or sand-pot is intricately pierced, in contrast to the simple aperture for the ink-pot (of which the cover is missing). Though some inkstands were later to be elaborate in design, even during the rococo period many were functionally simple.

Silver

English

a) Silver-gilt service of 28 pieces, by Isaac Liger; London, 1728.

'A fyne sett of dressing plate', as Paul de Lamerie's account described his 28-piece set made in 1724 for the Rt. Hon. Sir George Treby, had been a favourite present for the bride ever since the Restoration, and indeed it was between about 1670 and 1690 that most of the great toilet services were made. However, a few superb sets were executed during the 18th century, among them this elaborate silver-gilt service of 28 pieces made by Isaac Liger in 1728—though in design many of the canisters and caskets are derived from a late 17th century pattern book, the candlesticks, covered bowls and stands and the snuffers and tray are in the current style of the period. The mirror could easily have been found in a Charles II service, perhaps an indication of how outmoded the toilet service had become by the 1720s. This example, which weighs a massive 581.7 ounces, was made for Lady Mary Booth, heiress of the wealthy patron, the Second Earl of Warrington, or for her mother.

Double-lipped sauce-boat by Peter Archambo, 1724 (compare b).

b) Pair of sauce-boats by Pezé Pilleau, 1730; lgth. 8½″ (21.6 cm.).

The dining room became an important aspect of English social life and new silverwares made their appearance: chief was the sauce-boat, the earliest apparently a pair of 1717. The double-lipped sauce-boat was popular from then until c. 1730, usually made in pairs, with handles on either side and shaped moulded rims and lips. These, by the Huguenot Pezé Pilleau, have a shell chased beneath each lip, in keeping with the shell terminals to the scroll handles. Because of their shape, it was usual to engrave the owner's armorials to one side of the handle.

c) Oval basket with fixed handle, by John White; London, 1731; lgth. 12½″ (31.8 cm.).

One of the most satisfying of all the varied designs made during the first half of the 18th century must be the table basket, its sides worked to simulate natural basket-work, its base often richly flat-chased or engraved with scales and shells around a coat of arms. This fine basket features trellis-work sides below the everted rims which have ropework edges. At the same period, Paul de Lamerie made a number of very similar style baskets but with end handles instead of a fixed or swing handle.

a) Set of three casters, by Charles Kandler; London, 1731; ht. 8½" (21.6 cm.), and 7" (17.8 cm.).

Though dating from two years earlier, this set of casters indicate how very elaborate English rococo design was soon to become. The pierced covers with their baluster finials seem almost restrained in contrast to the vase-shaped bodies overlaid with finely and boldly modelled straps from which depend female masks in high relief and festoons of fruit and foliage. The set together weigh 55 oz., an indication of the grandeur and heavy gauge of the silver during the rococo period.

b) Pair of covered jugs, by Charles Kandler; London, 1733; ht. 10½" (26.7 cm.).

In the early years of the century, applied ornament and other detail was used sparingly except on the most opulent Royal and ceremonial silver. By the second quarter of the century, however, taste generally was turning to more decorative silver, and applied strapwork often became elaborate with intricately pierced and chased masks and scrolls alternating with foliate motifs, as in this fine pair of jugs which bear the contemporary arms of the 2nd Earl of Breadalbane. Such jugs were probably used for wine or beer.

c) Coffee-pot by Pezé Pilleau, London, c. 1738; ht. 10" (25.4 cm.).

During the 1730s, the straight-sided coffee-pot tended to go out of fashion, being replaced by the slightly tapering pot with a tuck-in base and flatter domed cover. Spouts, still gracefully curved, were often faceted and always set opposite the scroll-shaped handle. For greater decorative appeal, scrolling shells, diaper work and other rococo motifs were flat-chased on the bodies and some-times, as here, the body itself would be fluted into a melon style, which was also favoured for tea-pots of the period. Soon afterwards, the fine flat-chased ornament gave way to bolder relief-chased scrolls, flowers and shells—motifs much copied in the 19th century in imitation of the original rococo period.

d) Pair of sauce-boats, by Lewis Pantin; 1739; lgth. 9" (22.9 cm.).

Rococo depended for its decorative inspiration on natural shapes, especially rocks, shells, foliage, various animals, fish such as the dolphin, and even the serpent, butterflies and insects. The flowing form of the shell was the rococo equivalent of the truncated horn that served as a basis for most vessels.

These sauce-boats emphasize their shell shape with the central oval foot cast and chased with shells, and the applied moulded rim with shells at intervals. Like most good work of the period, they are heavy, the pair weighing over 40 oz. Pantin was a member of a Huguenot family of silversmiths.

Coffee-pot by Richard Bayler, 1728 (compare c).

Silver

English

MID-18TH CENTURY

Dublin marks.

Pierced basket of 1750 by Paul Crespin, London (compare b).

a) Salver by Joseph Sanders; 1741; dia. 18" (45.7 cm.).

The moulded border of salvers gradually became more decorative with profuse use of shells and masks and more shaping than earlier in the century. Further detail was added by flat chasing an inner border. The flat-chasing pushed the metal into patterns, not removing it as in engraving: this can be seen by comparing the chased border with the engraved armorials. Many plain salvers and other wares were, however, chased up in later periods, and the discriminating collector should beware of such pieces. This example shows how the contemporary chasing is in the same 'key' as the border, echoing the style and outline.

b) Bread or cake basket, by John Hamilton; Dublin, c. 1745; lgth. 14" (35.6 cm.).

Wealthy Irish patrons in the mid-18th century were quick to emulate the latest London designs, as in this fine example by one of the leading Dublin makers. Apart from the Irish armorials and the Dublin marks of about 1745, there is really nothing that differentiates this fine pierced basket with its applied cast and chased border from a London-made example. The alternate quatrefoil and scroll pierced motifs were favourite rococo period pierced-work themes, a contrast to the formal wickerwork motifs of the 1730s. The caryatid terminals, here a sketchy head with leaf-scroll body, were often very elaborate.

c) Snuffers tray, by William Hunter; 1748; lgth. 8" (20.3 cm.).

Incorporating the characteristics of the mid-18th century—even in so apparently ordinary a piece as a snuffers tray—was typical of the craftsman's approach to design. Here William Hunter gives even the shell corners and fluted moulded rim a rococo air in this back-handled example. The handle, like most scroll handles, is leaf-capped, while hoof feet, heavy and bold, support the shapely little tray. It weighs a good 10 oz. and reminds one of its rococo age by its engraved armorials as well.

d) Rococo caddies and sugar vase, by William Cripps; 1750; ht. of vase 4" (10.2 cm.).

Fantasy at the tea-table: here the favourite ingredients of rococo ornament combine. Bases are enriched with curvaceous marine monsters, the vase-shaped bodies chased with flowers and fruit within scroll cartouches above a band of shells while, in a sort of decorative logic, butterflies perch on the covers. Made at the height of the rococo period, they also show the importance of the tea ceremony and the stress laid on the proper blending of teas—undertaken at the tea-table—one caddy usually containing green, the other black tea. In some caddy sets, the central bowl was used for mixing rather than for sugar.

Opposite·
Silver three-piece tea-set by Godbehere, Wigin, Bult and Fox; England, 1802.

a) *left: Circular epergne by Benjamin Godfrey; 1753; ht. 6½" (16.5 cm.), dia. of central dish 9½" (24.1 cm.).*

The curiously named epergne, or centrepiece for the table, provided the silversmith with an opportunity to produce silver that was both spectacular and functional. Around a central pierced frame he could arrange dishes and baskets, to be piled high with desserts, fruit or sweetmeats. Until about 1760, most were of relatively low height, usually with shallow fluted dishes. This fine example by a maker noted for his basket and other pierced work has a cast frame, chased and pierced with flowers and masks, while the swirl-fluted dishes are flat-chased with flowers.

b) *centre: Candelabrum from a pair by William Cripps; 1750; ht. 16" (40.6 cm.).*

Gradually during the century, the cast candle-stick became taller and taller, and also more elaborate, though always retaining the intrinsic baluster shape. For the grandest houses, sets of as many as a dozen were not uncommon, many of them fitted with branches, generally at this period for two lights, with either an ornamental central feature or another socket.

c) *right: Salver by William Cripps; 1754; dia. 27½" (70 cm.).*

Waiters or salvers were made in every size and shape from a few inches in diameter, probably used for tea-pot or coffee-pot stands, to massive versions such as this one with its cast and pierced vine border applied with chased shell and mask motifs above the cast vine-pattern feet. This salver shows a typical finely engraved contemporary coat of arms in a rococo cartouche.

d) *Richly chased coffee-pot by Samuel Courtauld; 1757; ht. 10½" (26.7 cm.).*

Chasing, whether flat or repoussé, might be considered the great art of the rococo—a skill to be copied, though often without its original aplomb, during the early years of the 19th century. Indeed, so much damage was done to plain coffee-pots by the 19th century 'improvers' that even fine examples such as this are often eschewed by collectors. However, the pot shows how the mid-century chasing achieved a freedom and fluency in the scrolls and foliage motifs chased in high relief—attributes often lacking in later copies.

e) *Soup tureen by Francis Butty and Lewis Herne; 1758; wdth. 12½" (31.8 cm.).*

Not all patrons of the rococo period liked—or could afford—the highly ornamental. But even simple designs owed something to the rococo style —as this example shows. The basic oval shape was used whether the piece was to be relatively plain or much decorated, and gadrooned borders remained as popular as they had been half a century before. There is almost a baroque touch about the lion mask and paw supports and the cast bud finial, but the makers have added swirling rococo touches in the shells and foliage applied to the cover and the applied rococo cartouche for the owner's arms.

Opposite:
Bowl, embossed silver in leaf design by C. R. Ashbee; England, c. 1893.

653

b) Epergne by Emick Romer; London, 1770; overall ht. 14¼" (36.2 cm.).

a) Tall baluster coffee-pot by Walter Brind; 1761; ht. 11" (28 cm.).

Almost ascetic in contrast to the elaborate silver of the period, this coffee-pot is nonetheless typical of much silver made during the 1760s. Tea and coffee drinking were as popular among the richer middle classes as among those who could afford the most opulent silver, and many may well have preferred the relatively simple styles to the contortions of the rococo. This pot has a gracefulness which is accentuated by the applied foliage work on the spout, the flame finial and the flowery cartouche for the owner's coat of arms.

Even after the advent of the formal neo-classical styles, the rococo lingered on, as in this fine large epergne by Romer, a Norwegian silversmith who settled in London and who specialized in making baskets and other pierced silverwares. The pierced shell and scroll footed stand supports an apron pierced with quatrefoils from which rise four scrolling branches supporting fluted dishes and four others from which hang circular pierced baskets. In the centre is a large boat-shaped basket. Many such epergnes weighed well over 100 oz., but this much-pierced example weighs just under 84 oz.

c) Candlesticks by John Carter; 1769; ht. 10¼" (26 cm.).

Even before Adam, some patrons were already tiring of the rococo style and there was a trend towards greater formality. Some silversmiths looked once again across the Channel for inspiration, others had already turned to the classical forms that had for centuries provided Europe with most of her best designs. By the end of the 1760s, the trend to neo-classicism was well under way, as in these tall gadrooned, but still basically baluster, candlesticks by John Carter, who was apparently one of the craftsmen employed from time to time by Adam.

d) Pair of oval sauce-boats, by John Darwall; 1773; lgth. 8" (20.3 cm.).

In the intermediate style between the rococo and the classical, these sauce-boats have gadrooned rims and leaf-capped scroll handles. The central foot is also gadrooned, and given added interest by fluting and the shaped outline. Other contemporary sauce-boats, notably a series by the Royal goldsmith Thomas Heming, hesitated halfway between the boat and the tureen, but most veered definitely towards simpler styles with very little applied ornament.

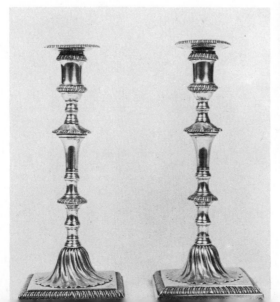

a) left and right: Sauce tureens by James Young and Orlando Jackson; 1773. centre: Laurel-festooned soup tureen by Henry Greenway; 1778; ht. of tureen 6" (15.2 cm.).

The Roman urn, excavated in large numbers, did suggest a suitable shape for many table-wares: These sauce tureens are from a set of four; of oval vase shape, applied with formal paterae and pierced festoons rising to lion mask and ring handles, they have a formality an age away from the rococo.

Within a few years, silversmiths seemed generally to be a little less strict in their classicism, as this soup tureen shows. Fan-fluting appeared frequently and beading, or pearling as it was then known, became almost a trade mark of the period, along with rising threaded or reeded handles.

b) Tripod jug, by Henry Greenaway; 1775; ht. 11⅛" (28.3 cm.).

One of the difficulties the classicists encountered was finding suitably shaped Greek and Roman vessels for turning into tureens and coffee-pots, punch bowls and other practical pieces for the English dining saloon and drawing-room. On occasion, original classical forms were adapted to modern use, as this jug, probably for chocolate or perhaps hot water. Slender-footed, it is given stability by an incurved base, while drapes, paterae, acanthus foliage and satyrs' masks introduce the elegant motifs of the Adam period in English design and decoration.

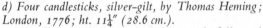

c) Vase-shaped coffee-pot by John Robins; 1776; ht. 12½" (31.8 cm.).

Most frequently, the silversmiths catered for their patrons' wish to be in the neo-classical fashion by using classical motifs for decorations and only half acknowledging classical forms. This tall coffee-pot adapts the vase to the pot and then gives it the required functionalness and capacity by adding a long neck and curved spout. The leaf-crowned satyr's masks on either side are set between drapery festoons above a crisp and formal leaf border, but although classical in inspiration, few would mistake this for anything other than an English design.

d) Four candlesticks, silver-gilt, by Thomas Heming; London, 1776; ht. 11¼" (28.6 cm.).

Not all the leading London silversmiths followed the new classicism at once, and Thomas Heming in particular seems to have found inspiration in French patterns. France, like England, had tired of the sinuous rococo by the 1770s, but their reaction towards formality was only partly classical. Heming interpreted this in this superb set of candlesticks, four from an original set of 38 made for Count Toulski of Russia in 1776. The circular bases are chased with laurel wreath borders with paterae at intervals. The stems rise from bases enriched with acanthus foliage and pendant husks, a theme repeated at the shoulders.

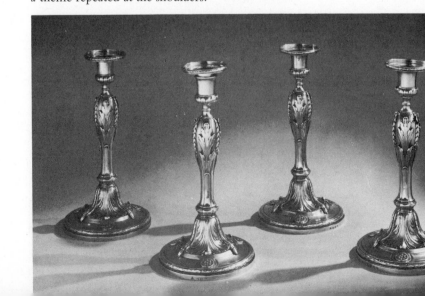

a) Baluster-shaped argyle with flame finial and beaded base, by John Rowe; 1777; ht. 10″ (25.4 cm.).

Dining table silver in the later part of the century was often extremely practical, and even at times suggested a universal interest in gadgetry. Among newcomers to the table silver were the biggin, or coffee percolator, and the argyle, a jacketed pot used for keeping gravy hot. Various versions were made, some holding a heated iron in the base but the most usual had a liner with an aperture, usually near the top of the handle, into which hot water could be poured. Spouts, often set at right angles to the handle for easy serving, were usually rather steeply curved and narrow.

b) Pair of candelabra, the bases by Robert Makepeace and Richard Carter, the branches by Henry Hallsworth; London, 1778; ht. 12″ (30.5 cm.).

The vase and the urn were even adapted to the candelabrum—a style far more fashionable at the period than the single 'stick', though often, as here, candlesticks and branches were by different makers and sometimes of different dates. Others were made in Sheffield and then overstruck by London makers who would add the branches if required.

The circular bases of this pair are chased with a band of paterae, with fluted motifs above and a band of foliage at the bases of the vase-shaped stems. Wide bead-edge drip pans are set below the matching sconces, while a classical urn is set in the centres.

c) Punch bowl made for Chester Races by William Cox; 1779; dia. 13½″ (34.3 cm.).

In many fields, tradition died hard, even after so distinct a change of style. For many years, a city prize at Chester Races had been a punch bowl, and the plain ogee-shaped bowl (along with the gold tumbler cup given by the Earls of Grosvenor) appeared on race cards for many years. In this example, the city arms still appear in an engraved shell and flower rococo cartouche, with the name of the Mayor and the date, 1780, circumventing the bowl.

d) Oval tea caddy by Hester Bateman; 1782; ht. 5½″ (14 cm.).

For many people, the 1780s mean Hester Bateman, whose workshop in Bunhill Row produced a variety of tea-table wares—goblets, wine labels and other silver, often prettily designed and engraved with bright-cut festoons, foliate borders. Beaded rims were much used in the Bateman workshops, and this tea caddy perhaps unites all the characteristics of the silver bearing her mark; the oval shape with a beaded edge, the step-domed cover with a neat finial, and the festoons of bright-cut husk and floral swags intertwined around the oval ribbon-tied cartouche.

Standard and London assay office marks 1776–96 (bottom rt. from 1786 only).

656

a) Tea-pot on matching stand, by Barrak Mewburn; 1784; overall ht. 4½″ (11.4 cm.).

One of the most delightful ornamental techniques of the period was the style of deep-cut engraving known as bright-cut, giving wrigglework, foliate and other simple borders a brilliance and crispness that, in the finest examples, has not faded with time and use. The classic tea-pot of the period was oval or round, often of shaped outline, but almost always with a flat base, necessitating a footed stand. Since tea-drinking had become a national obsession, tea-pots were made in huge numbers, many for families not entitled to bear arms, so that initials are often found in the engraved medallion cartouches.

b) Set of four salts with blue glass liners, by Robert Hennell; London, 1788; lgth. 2¼″ (5.7 cm.).

By the second half of the century, the specialist maker of such things as candlesticks, casters and salts, was fairly prevalent in the London trade. One firm which had for many years been masters of making small salts were the Hennells, by the 1770s run by Robert, grandson of the founder. The familiar round-bellied salt of the mid-century now gave way to the boat shape, made more graceful with pierced and engraved ornament. In this fine set, Hennell breaks the leaf-pierced borders with engraved ovals for initials, and uses beaded claw-and-ball feet, echoing the beaded rims.

Pedestal salt of c. 1730.

---

c) Standish by Robert Hennell; London, 1788; overall ht. 2½″ (6.4 cm.).

For everyday silverwares, the oval and the boat shape were adaptable for a host of objects, from pen trays and sauce tureens to cake baskets and toast racks. Here Robert Hennell uses a simple oval stand with upcurved scroll handles and four panel feet to take three detachable frames for silver-mounted glass ink-well, sand-box and pounce-pot. Glass was widely used at the period, not only for liners, but mounted for tea caddies, sugar bowls, preserve pots and ink-wells.

d) Sauce tureen, by John Robins; 1790; ht. 5¾″ (14.6 cm.).

Stern simplicity in silver table-wares complemented the simple lines of Sheraton and Hepplewhite furniture, and many pieces relied entirely on their line for appeal, with perhaps a simple baluster or urn-shaped finial to the domed cover, and a couple of lines of reeding to the loop handles, as in this sauce tureen, a sturdy 18 oz. piece.

Salt of c. 1750 (compare both of these with b).

Silver

English

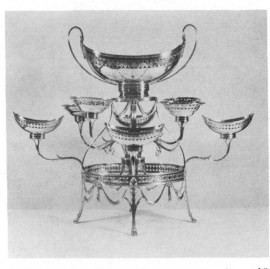

a) Epergne, by Henry Chawner; 1791; ht. 21¼″ (53.9 cm.).

The 'pretty, fragile look' that was castigated by opponents of the Adam style is perhaps best seen in the graceful and light-looking epergnes of the 1790s. Here, Henry Chawner uses the boat shape for the large central baskets and four of the smaller dishes, interspersing them with four round baskets, all suspended high above the pierced and festooned frame. Though in a light and graceful style, and seemingly balanced on slender reeded paw feet, the epergne weighs no less than 126.75 oz.

b) Tea urn, by John Denzilon; 1792; ht. 13¾″ (34.9 cm.).

Even tea-table silver, which during the rococo and early Adam periods had been among the most decorative made, seemed surprisingly plain in the 1790s and many wares, like this, had an almost angular design, accentuated by the fluting and the shaped plinth. Even the bright-cut border is more formal than usual, though this is somewhat marred by the wreathed cartouches on either side.

Sugar basket by Wakelin & Taylor, 1790.

c) Globe inkstand, by John Robins; London, 1792; ht. 6″ (15.2 cm.).

Between about 1791 and 1804, the plateworker John Robins made a series of charming and unusual globe inkstands, a style that no doubt appealed to many a lady penning letters or accounts at her desk. Basically, he made two styles, one on scroll feet, rather like a library globe, the other on a circular foot, into which he sometimes incorporated a revolving perpetual calendar, as here. Held in a beaded frame with shell terminals and festoons between, the inkstand itself has a fall-front and contains a small rack with miniature ink and sand bottles, an ivory tablet, pen and pencil.

d) Honey-pot by Paul Storr; London, 1798; ht. 4¾″ (12.1 cm.).

A charming conceit of the turn of the century was the honey-pot made in the shape of a straw skep. This example, one of several by Paul Storr, has a typical reed and tie bordered stand. The ring handle was sometimes replaced by a model of a bee. A glass liner fits inside the dome. While many of these pots were made by Storr, a few by other makers, including Sheffield silversmiths, are recorded.

b) Vase inscribed to Thomas Lavie Esqr., Captain of H.M.S. 'Blanche' for Skill and Bravery in the Capture of the French Frigate 'La Guerrière'; by Scott and Smith, 1805; ht. 15¼" (38.7 cm.).

The Napoleonic War provided more opportunities for the silversmith to create impressive silver, a piece of plate being considered a suitable reward for bravery and loyalty. Some 66 vases were commissioned by the Patriotic Fund at Lloyd's and presented to sea captains during 1805 to 1807. Made by Scott and Smith, the form was standard: a crater-shaped vase with a lion finial to the cover between vertical incurving handles decorated with chased paterae. Between running bands of rosettes and foliage were depicted in low relief Hercules slaying the Hydra on one side and Britannia, seated, on the other.

a) Salt from a set of six, gilded; by Digby Scott and Benjamin Smith; 1803.

The simple lines and delicate engraved decoration of the later neo-classical period gave way by 1800 to a bolder and more ornamental style, with the emphasis on chasing and casting rather than on engraving and piercing. This salt shows the new grand approach. The part-fluted circular bodies are each on three heavy lion and paw feet with applied shields, the rims have boldly patterned borders matching the border of the plinths. Gilded for greater effect, the six weigh no less than 97 oz.

---

c) Centrepiece, probably by Philip Cornman; 1806; ht. 18½" (47 cm.).

Great centrepieces were a magnificent feature of the banqueting tables before and during the Regency, a period usually extended backwards to about 1800 to include the years of the Prince of Wales's influence on fashion and the arts. Here the Graeco-Egyptian style is represented by the sphinxes supporting the triform base with panels in low relief above, and superbly modelled palmettes and anthemion motifs—in fact a masterpiece of the art of the caster and the chaser. Cornman, who was commissioned by Rundell & Bridge in 1806, is known to have made several similar centrepieces in this style.

d) Soup tureen by Paul Storr; 1808; dia. 12" (30.5 cm.).

The return to formality did not swing away from classical ornament, but often revived the original themes and detail promoted in the first years of Adam neo-classicism. Styles were perhaps a little heavier, gilding was more usual but here, such details as the lion masks below the short reeded and foliage handles, the rich anthemion border, the gadrooned rim and fluted foot might well have been borrowed from a predecessor of c. 1775. However, this tureen is circular with more contrast in the plain and decorated surfaces. Its maker was himself trained by Andrew Fogelburg, a leading exponent of Adam neo-classical design.

a) Wine cooler, silver-gilt; by Paul Storr; 1809; ht. 14" (35.6 cm.).

Regency classicism was somewhat more ponderous than earlier pieces, and there was an even stronger trend towards imitating classical vase and urn shapes and translating carved marble into metal. This fine cooler is one of a pair which with their paw-supported stands, weigh a massive 467 oz. They are enriched with bacchanalian processions in relief, a design repeated on several other wine coolers of the period. Others show variations in the vine and grape frieze above and the oak-leaf and flower-cornucopiae below. The design was modelled by William Theed, who prepared several silver designs for Rundell, Bridge & Rundell.

b) Dessert stand, silver-gilt; by Paul Storr, 1810; ht. 13¾" (34.9 cm.).

In its own genre, the early 19th century was quite strong and despite the multitude of different details from figure-work to festoons and lion masks to naturalistic basketwork, it managed to amalgamate them all into a majestic entity. This stand is in itself a grand centrepiece, made en suite with other silver-gilt table appointments for the ambassadorial service issued to the Duke of Wellington in 1810. Other examples made to similar designs were presumably put out by the Court goldsmiths, Rundell & Bridge, to whichever workshop was free at the time to undertake the work.

---

c) Warwick vase from a pair by Paul Storr; 1814.

Epitome of the essays in classicism was the Warwick Vase in silver, copied from the original marble now at Warwick Castle. As an example of modelling, casting and chasing, the vase presented the silversmith with considerable problems, and it is a tribute to the skills of the Regency craftsmen that they were able to interpret the carving so well. This example, along with many others, was made in Paul Storr's workshop. A liner and collar allows its use as a fruit cooler. It was part of the plate issued to Baron Berwick. The fashion for the Warwick Vase continued until the 1830s (see p. 677c).

d) Six-light candelabrum by Paul Storr; 1815; ht. 32" (81.3 cm.).

The grouped figurework and massive candelabra and centrepieces that one tends to associate with the mid-Victorian period were, in fact, a product of the Regency, as this six-light candelabrum clearly shows. The central section can be removed to accommodate a large circular fruit dish, replacing the candle-branches. The candelabrum-centrepiece weighs 565 oz. Similar sculpture-work in silver is recorded in another fine Storr candelabrum and in dessert stands in the Royal Collection.

York marks.

a) Four-piece tea service; by Paul Storr; 1815/16.

The feminine delicacy of the bright-cut oval or fluted tea service vanished with the Regency, and the grand service was as much part of the tea-table as the dining table. This fine service shows the development of the compressed circular pot, the base half-fluted, the upper part of the vase-shaped bodies decorated with formal anthemion and husk chasing on matted grounds—a motif repeated along the short curved spout of the tea-pot. Snake handles were another fashionable feature on jugs and bowls of the second decade of the century, while the tripod lampstand was almost a trade mark of Storr hot water and coffee jugs.

b) Decanter stand; one of a pair, by Paul Storr, 1818.

Vines and bunches of grapes provided an obvious but nonetheless most effective theme for decanter stands or wine coasters, which were usually made in sets of two, four or six. The slightly everted style was abandoned in the early years of the 19th century for the deeper straight-sided variety, which in the hands of craftsmen such as Benjamin and James Smith or Paul Storr was made a vehicle for superb casting, chasing and piercing. This is from a fine pair with reed-and-tie rims which match a set of four made by Benjamin Smith in 1807.

Bristol mark.

c) left: Oval tray; by Philip Rundell, 1822; wdth. 22½" (57.2 cm.).

After Benjamin Smith and Paul Storr had both left Rundell's to work on their own, Philip Rundell registered his own mark, which appears on this massive tray which is supported on four large feet chased with lion masks and foliage. At either end double serpents are intertwined to form the handles, while the wide border is pierced and chased.

d) centre: Entree dish, from a pair; by Paul Storr; London, 1824; dia. 11" (27.9 cm.).

Even the functional entree dish acquired its portion of grandeur during and immediately after the Regency. Gadroon, shell and foliate borders, matching those on meat and fish dishes and plates, soup and sauce tureens, were probably the most favoured pattern; this is dated some five years after Storr parted with Rundell Bridge & Rundell and began work on his own in the West End.

e) right: Sideboard dish, silver-gilt; from a pair by Edward Farrell, 1824; dia. 15" (38.1 cm.).

One of the most skilled casters and chasers of the Regency and reign of George IV was Edward Farrell, whose work ranges from wine labels and snuff-boxes in the manner of Teniers to great dessert services and massive centrepieces. This sideboard dish is chased in high relief with fruit within shaped reserves.

a) *Tea service, by Paul Storr; 1827.*

About 1820, the revived rococo had made its influence fully felt, and silversmiths began to create a 19th century decorative style drawing motifs from nature—roses, foliage, thistles, shells and so on being especially popular. Naturalistic finials included flowers, birds and butterflies and there was also a tendency to make tea-pot and coffee-pot handles of silver, inserting slivers of ivory or bone near the sockets for insulation. This four-piece service heralds almost a century of similar flower-chased patterns in an age when silver tea services were considered among the most important possessions of the middle-class family.

b) *Pitcher in green glass with silver vine and grape motif mounts and handle; by J. W. Figg, 1840.*

The design-books of the first half of the 19th century were almost wholly dependent on the drawings of archaeological finds, to which were engrafted whatever decorative details the craftsmen approved. The Pompeian-style pitcher, or ascos, for instance, was a favourite theme much used by Storr towards the end of his life, executed wholly in silver with miniature models of goats reclining along the rim. This more unusual version is a pre-cursor of the dozens of silver-mounted claret and lemonade jugs in decorative glass made throughout the century.

Silver

English

MID–LATE 19TH CENTURY

c) *Hexagonal entree dish, cover and stand; by Robert Garrard, 1852.*

The inevitable Victorian taste for novelty meant that designs appeared with shape borrowed from one style, detail from another, the whole mixed and intermixed to create the style called 'high Victorian'. Many of the best examples were interpreted with great craftsmanship and painstaking detail, as here. The Gothic shape is decorated with finely chased scrollwork, foliage and masks on a matted ground in the manner of the early 18th century, though the fluted acorn feet to the gilt-metal stand and the finial seem out of period with both the chasing and the shape.

d) *left: Churn-shaped cream pot, cat with cream decoration; by George Angell, 1868.*
right: Japanese inspired vase by Frederick Elkington, 1881.

As an antidote to Victorian solidity, silver table 'toys' found ready buyers throughout the second half of the century. Most of them featured domestic animals—chicken condiments, kangaroo claret jugs, monkey inkwells, and of course a multitude of cats, such as this one on a cream pot (*left*) of 1868.

The creation of the Japanese Empire in the 1860s and the opening up of trade with the West gave rise to a new artistic influence, quickly put to decorative use by the English silversmiths, especially firms such as Barnards and Elkingtons, who used Japonaiseries to delicate effect, as *right*.

Sheffield mark.

662

a) Baluster-bodied vase, intertwined handles and hammered finish; by Ramsden and Carr; London, 1902.

In 1898 two young Sheffield artists, Omar Ramsden and Alwyn Carr decided to go into partnership and seek their fortunes in London. Impressed by the skills of the mediaeval goldsmiths, whose surviving works were much in demand among collectors, they were equally inspired by the need for reviving the arts and crafts of Britain, and the European *Art Nouveau* movement soon brought their modern-style silver into the limelight. This vase typifies their style, continued by Ramsden alone after the partnership was dissolved in 1918. In the following decade, he was at the forefront in promoting the skills of the modern silversmith.

b) Condiment set made by Leslie Durbin for presentation to Corpus Christi College.

One of Ramsden's most skilled silversmiths, Durbin later set up on his own and has been responsible for much of the most elegant modern silver of the years since World War II. This condiment set incorporates the college crest of a pelican in the cast and chased supports for the simple containers.

Silver
English
20TH CENTURY

---

c) Milk jug with contrasting plain and textured surface; by Gerald Benney.

Strictly unadorned silver has the disadvantage that the surface rapidly becomes finger-marked, tarnished, and with time, scratched. A leading designer of pieces with textured surfaces is Gerald Benney. His sense of form and function, allied with a lively sense of publicity, has done much to promote contemporary silver.

d) Tumbler with gilt filigree over silver body; by Stuart Devlin.

If Gerald Benney deserves the title of Master of Texturing, Stuart Devlin has won his as Master of Filigree, but filigree in a new manner, with intricate twiggy patterns overlaying basic simple shapes or even creating openwork silver and gilt frames as though they were glass. This tumbler is a 20th century interpretation of the cagework fashionable 300 years ago.

e) Candlestick by Alex Styles.

Though hand-craftsmanship is still an extremely important aspect of modern silversmithing, new techniques are by no means eschewed by contemporary designers. In this unusual candlestick (one of a pair) Styles has used the electro-forming process to create an unusual turbine-like decoration on the silver.

a) Old Sheffield plate covered vegetable (or entree) dish; c. 1810; lgth. 11½″ (29.2 cm.).

Today very much a collector's item in its own right, old Sheffield plate has often been wrongly dismissed as a mere substitute for silver. Yet for about a century, from some time before 1750 to soon after 1840, it was the basis of a highly skilled industry centred on the cutlery city of Sheffield and at Boulton's Soho works in Birmingham.

Sheffield plating is a method by which a thin sheet of sterling silver is fused to a core of copper. In the earliest examples, only one side was plated but about 1763, double-plating was invented and a host of domestic wares appeared—plain, pierced or engraved. The Sheffield platers were not only skilled at their own craft, but were as skilled as the silversmiths of the period at engraving and other decorative work, and when duty of 6d. an ounce was reimposed on silverwares in 1784, the trade progressed and prospered.

b) Old Sheffield tea service; including tea-pot with wooden handle, sugar basin and creamer; c. 1825.

New developments included plated shields hard-soldered in for engraved armorials and filled silver mounts, both in use about 1790, followed in the next twenty years or so by rubbed-in silver shields and fancy mounts. Not all Sheffield plate was, of course, of the best quality and some—especially in the early 19th century—had only a relatively thin layer of silver. Meanwhile, further innovations in plating processes culminating first in 'magnetic plate' and then in electro-plating of pure silver on to base metal finally killed the craft in the 1850s.

American Silver Introduction

The art of the goldsmith in the United States began in the colony of Massachusetts, for the earlier artisans to be found in Virginia were prospectors for metals. The earliest whose work survives was London-trained Robert Sanderson, who arrived in the Boston area around 1630 as did the child, John Hull. Hull learned the mystery from his half-brother, and held many important offices in the colony; he also kept partly retrospective diaries: 'Some passages of God's Providence about myself and in relation to myself; penned down that I may be more mindful of, and thankful for all God's dispensations towards me'. Appointed Mint-master by the General Court in 1652, he records taking his friend Sanderson as his partner, 'to which the Court consented'.

Hull's diary records a number of their apprentices. A Boston ordinance of 1660, following a preamble about insufficient training, concludes: 'It is therefore ordered that no person shall henceforth open a shop in this Towne, nor occupy any manufacture or science, till hee hath compleated 21 years of age, nor except hee hath served seven years Apprenticeship'. Sanderson trained three of his sons, but only Benjamin's work is identified. Hull's only child to reach maturity was a daughter, who married another diarist of considerable repute, Judge Samuel Sewall.

The first native-born New England goldsmith whose work is known was Jeremiah Dummer (1645-1718). New York's first goldsmiths were Dummer's contemporaries and, as their names suggest, were largely of Dutch or Huguenot origin.

Nowhere in the colonies was there supervision of the craft which was regulated in Boston by a Town Meeting of 1677 (repeated in 1679): 'That care be taken all ware made of pewter or silver whether brought to the countrie or made here ... be of ye just alloy'.

Although goldsmiths usually marked their wares, it is unfortunate that today, unmarked pieces are sometimes given fraudulent marks. In the absence of the English dated hallmark system, knowledge of the goldsmith's time and style is a safer criterion than engraving. Proof of this is in the will of Daniel Gookin who, in 1685, left his wife Hannah 'a piece of plate either a Cupp or Tankard to be made new mark'd D^{G}H'.

In the last decade of the seventeenth century Huguenot goldsmiths worked in Philadelphia, and spread the craft throughout the colonies. By this time, English influence was predominant, but each of the centres continued to have its local flavour. Virginia gentlemen usually ordered their plate from England until shortly before the Revolution when the most famous, George Washington, made important purchases in New York and Philadelphia.

During the eighteenth century, goldsmiths were practis-

ing in many other centres: Newburyport and Salem in Massachusetts, Portsmouth and Exeter in New Hampshire, New Haven and Hartford in Connecticut. Rhode Island's first craftsman was in Newport; Samuel Casey was the best known of a small group in Little Rest, and Providence, beginning later, is still a centre of silver manufacture.

We have concentrated on domestic silver, hoping that ecclesiastical silver will remain largely in its churches. In the 1960s, an octogenerian member of the church which owns Edward Winslow's great baptismal 'bason' (1706), succeeded in having its sale blocked through Court action, a thoughtfulness which continues to influence other congregations in the attempt to save such pieces for posterity.

English influence was of primary importance in many aspects of American silver; comparison between this section and that on English silver is of interest.

Engraved silver tankard by Thomas Hammersly.

a) Caudle cup pricked with initials B.B., by Robert Sanderson (1608–93) and John Hull (1624–83); Boston, Massachusetts, 1660–70; ht. 3 3/16" (8.1 cm.).

Initialled for Beriah Bright (born 1649), this chased panelled caudle cup reflects the flat-carved furniture of the period, though others are plain or embossed with a girdle of flowers, one even showing a turkey. These and other early vessels survive partly because they were used in churches. Among Hull and Sanderson's pieces even those with one partner's mark were made during the partnership. Sanderson also fashioned an exceptionally large tankard for Isaac and Mary Vergoose, the only one to survive without an added spout, or other indignities. The partners made numerous standing cups, some domestic, others for the churches which have treasured them.

b) Tankard, by Jeremiah Dummer (1645–1718); Boston, Massachusetts, c. 1690; ht. 6 3/4" (17.1 cm.).

John Hull's pious request in noting Dummer's 8-year apprenticeship that 'The Lord make me faithful in discharge of this new trust committed to me', was amply fulfilled. Dummer's monumental candlesticks are indubitably his most imposing work. He is thought to have introduced cut-card decoration, and gadrooning on church cups (dating from 1700). This tankard has Sanderson's double-spiral thumb-piece. Some of Dummer's caudle cups have handles cast from those of *a* and he was named an 'overseer' of Sanderson's will. He vied with John Coney for variety of porringer handle designs, and both made 'great basons', later used for baptisms.

---

c) Covered cup by Jurian Blanck, Jnr. (c. 1645–1714); New York, c. 1691; ht. 5 5/8" (14.3 cm.).

This acanthus ornament appears of Dutch derivation, but the cup's form is more English than continental. Probably a marriage cup for Jacobus and Eve VanCortlandt, it bears the bride's family coat of arms in a typical New York cartouche. Gerrit Onckelbag (1670–1732) made two similar cups, one with its lady's arms correctly in a lozenge, its feathery cartouche surmounted by a marriage chaplet. Tinctures of armorial engraving, often copied from Guillim's *Display of Heraldry*, were neither fully understood, nor followed. These covers, inverted and used as servers, were multi-footed earlier than the salvers made for the purpose.

d) Salver by Timothy Dwight (1654–91); Boston, Massachusetts, c. 1685; dia. 11 5/16" (28.7 cm.).

A documented apprentice of the partners, 'Tim' appears in Sewall's diary. He is known in 1972 only for a tankard and this salver: its original decoration was the trefoil cartouche of prick-work for its first owners' initials. The East India—if not Chinoiserie—animal design was probably engraved by John Coney for Thomas and Mary Barton whose initials are superimposed: he made a number of pieces for them.

Dwight's tankard also has a lion sejant thumb-piece of great charm. Coney mounted Governor Belcher's standish on lions and a contemporary tankard by Dummer recently published bears a lion thumb-piece.

a) Beaker by Cornelius Van Der Burch (1653-99); New York, 1685; ht. 8" (20.3 cm.).

This beaker is by the only New York goldsmith known to have worked entirely in the 17th century. The largest of the 'Dutch' type, its rarity is in the engraved designs after Adrian Van Der Venne. Although characteristic of New York, at least three are known by Hull and Sanderson, reflecting a Dutch one (1637) bearing the initials of Robert and Elizabeth Sanderson. Mrs Sanderson's will, typical of a well-to-do colonial, disposed of rings, silver spoons, wine cup, bowl and caudle cup, her greater and lesser silver tankards, 'bigger and little silver basons', 'my other great Silver bason', bigger and small silver porringers, silver bowl.

b) Bowl or grace cup, engraved with the Stoughton arms, by John Coney (1656-1722); Boston, Massachusetts, c. 1701; ht. 10" (25.4 cm.).

John Coney left the greatest variety and quantity of plate of any of his contemporaries. William Stoughton presented this cup to Harvard College, when Judge Sewall recorded: 'he order'd us to present this Bowl. After Dinner and singing, I took it, and had it fill'd up, and drunk to the president saying that I presented the Grace-cup *pro more Academiaram in Anglia.*' Stoughton left his niece in 1701 'as a particular remembrance of me, twelve pounds to buy a piece of Plate'. Her chocolate pot in Oriental form is by Coney, the first New Englander known to have made tea and chocolate-pots.

c) Sugar-box by Edward Winslow (1699-1753); Boston, Massachusetts, 1702; ht. 5" (12.7 cm.).

Winslow was probably trained as Dummer's apprentice; they made similar standing salts; for his chafing-dishes, he used all-over rather than banded, pierced ornamentation. Two of his four known sugar-boxes were sent to England, one (with a snake handle) when new, the other during the American Revolution. Both are dated 1702. The third remained in the Winslow family; another bears the initials of Governor and Mrs Saltonstall (of Connecticut). The Winslow family had a tradition of public service; Winslow himself held so many public offices, one wonders how he had time for his craft.

d) Panelled bowl by Jacob Boelen (1657-1729); New York, 1700-20; dia. 7¾" (19.7 cm.).

Jacob Boelen's parents emigrated from Amsterdam when he was two. Later, he held town offices; a son and a grandson followed his craft and he probably trained his nephew, Koenraet TenEyck of Albany. His daughter married Philip Goelet, the New York goldsmith.

This typical New York bowl has Boelen's mark over-stamped by Simeon Soumain (c. 1685-c. 1750); such re-marking happened occasionally.

Boelen used more elaborate handles for some work (though not as intricate as John Coney's). Those illustrated are repeated on a similar bowl. In 1733 Peter Lefferts advertised as stolen, 'made by Mr Jacob Boelen, stamp'd IB. One large Cup with two cast Ears, with Heads . . .'.

a) Caudle cup by John Edwards (1671–1746) and John Allen (1671–1760); Boston, c. 1700; wdth. overall 6¾″ (17.1 cm.).

Edwards (London-born) and Allen, native Bostonian, were both apprenticed to Dummer. About 1700 they worked as partners and made the third known American standing salt. This cup is similar to some by the first partners. Although these plain vessels were once identified only with New England, rare examples are now known by Onckelbag and Van der Burch of New York. Jacob Hurd made the latest known in this form (1744). Handles could be elaborate; many cups now have bases reinforced with a band of moulding. Coney's earliest dated piece (1676) was a caudle cup and he is the only known maker of a covered one.

b) Porringer, by Johannis Nys (1671–1734); Philadelphia, 1700–25; dia. 5″ (12.7 cm.).

Countless inventories and the few surviving day books show clearly that this shallow bowl was a colonial porringer. Pairs were frequent, and children's were in small sizes.

This has an early geometric handle; the first New York design was simple but very intricate cutting soon developed. Around 1725 so-called 'keyhole' handles, at first with arched cuttings near the bowl, evolved in New England. New Yorkers preferred a relatively solid, flat trefoil handle with three piercings, circular at the tip and shaped ones below. Nys also made chafing dishes with spaced fleur-de-lis below the rim, and parallel scrolls rising for supports.

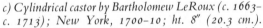

c) Cylindrical castor by Bartholomew LeRoux (c. 1663–c. 1713); New York, 1700–10; ht. 8″ (20.3 cm.).

New York's earliest Huguenot goldsmith, LeRoux, was supposedly London-born. He trained his two sons—Charles (1689–1745) who left outstanding English pieces, and John (b. 1695) lesser known, but competent. Bartholomew's daughter married Peter Van Dyck, the most remarkable goldsmith of his time. His Stoutenburgh nephews were presumably his apprentices; Lucas became one of South Carolina's first goldsmiths.

Cylindrical castors became fashionable, perhaps after one by Gamble (London, 1700) was imported into Boston. Early castor sets of three (sugar, pepper and mustard) were recorded; very few remain, notably by grandson Bartholomew LeRoux II (1717–58) and Adrian Bancker (1703–72), both in vase form.

d) Tankard, by Peter van Dyck (1684–1751); New York, 1705–15; ht. 7³⁄₁₆″ (18.3 cm.).

This tankard has a characteristic stamped base moulding, double spiral purchase and applied design on the handle and tip; the slightly domed lid with gadrooning and rayed embossing is unique among published pieces. The Wendell arms and crest are in an acanthus-scrolled cartouche, similar to LeRoux's.

Van Dyck's three tea-pots show a wide scope of design; his known repertoire includes a castor similar to LeRoux's, beakers, a chafing dish, the only known American mustard pots of his period, a rare covered porringer, a pepper box, sauce-boat, snuff box and a marked clasp for gold beads.

Opposite:
Silver tankard by Philip Syng Jr. of Philadelphia; U.S.A., 1703–89.

*Background, left to right: Silver porringers; by Joseph M.
Moulton of Newbury Port, Massachusetts, c. 1765; by
William Jones of Marblehead, Massachusetts; and by John
Brevoort of New York City, 1738.*
*Foreground: A combination of 'teether' and rattle and whistle
by Richard Pitts of Philadelphia, c. 1745.*

a) Tankard with dolphin and mask thumb-piece by Samuel Vernon (1683-1737); Newport, Rhode Island, c. 1710; ht. 7⅝" (19.4 cm.).

The thumb-piece, favoured in New England around 1700, is slightly higher than usual on this tankard. Traditionally, dolphins symbolized power, the mask, gaiety; today so much symbolism is read into all ornamentation that one wonders how the goldsmith himself would react! Perhaps Vernon was apprenticed to Coney, although some of his tankards have New York characteristics; he was probably Newport's second, and probably best known, goldsmith. Tankards were made everywhere throughout the 18th century for ladies, gentlemen, married couples, even for children and dolls! In the 19th century, many tankards were given pouring spouts.

b) Punch bowl by John Coney (1656-1722); Boston, c. 1718; dia. 9⅝" (24.4 cm.).

In 1718 the Harvard students of Tutor Flynt gave him a Coney grace cup. This bowl has the same foot and engraved cartouche, here with the Riddell arms. Owned by a British naval officer, it only returned to Boston in 1972. The same rim moulding appears on the Livingston bowl (made with a removable monteith rim).

Coney excelled in engraving (p. 667b); one plate has flowers and cherubs with a feather cartouche; many of his tankards are armorial. Cherubs were embossed amid flowers on two large caudle cups, were cast on some tankard handle-tips, and rimmed his monteith bowl for the Colman family.

---

c) Salver, by John Burt (1693-1745); Boston, 1720-30; dia. 5¾" (14.6 cm.).

John Burt was another apprentice of Coney, succeeding him as plate supplier for pupils' gifts of plate to Harvard College tutors; for Nicholas Sever he made candlesticks, chafing dishes, salvers, a cann and a globular tea-pot. This charming hexafoil salver is still unique. Coney's inventory listed two candlestick moulds, Burt had '6 pr flasks for casting' of unspecified form. He made two candlestick styles, one with a snuffer and stand, but colonial silver candlesticks were never common. A superb wrought pair, with Chinoiserie engraving and matching upright snuffer and stand, by New York's Cornelius Kierstede (1675-1757) is now happily reassembled.

d) Tea-pot, by Henricus Boelen II (1697-1755); New York, 1725-40; ht. 7" (17.8 cm.).

This was New York's favourite tea-pot shape from 1725-1750, used by Van Dyck and Bancker amongst others. The general outline is not unlike the Mascarens and Dudley family tea-pot bodies made in one piece by Coney and John Allen respectively. Although Allen's had a moulded, hinged cover, Jacob Boelen's almost globular tea-pot had a straight spout and a baseband very like his bowl (p. 667d); the unattached domed cover has a slight flange. New England's globular tea-pots had cast curved spouts and usually invisible hinged flat lids with partly wooden finials. This 'pyriform' shape was becoming inverted by the 1750s.

Silver

American
MID–18TH CENTURY

a) *Tankard, by Jacob Hurd (1703-54); Boston, 1730-50; ht. 8" (20.3 cm.).*

Hurd, succeeding in his generation as Coney had in his, made impressive grace cups, numerous comfortable globular tea-pots (one with a sugar bowl, the first tea service!), chafing dishes, several sizes of trumpet and multiple footed salvers and the usual output of tankards, canns, castors, salts and porringers.

This tankard is typical of New England; Coney inaugurated the so-called midband and simple domed cover with small finial. These, and this thumb-piece, continued throughout the century. The bulbous drop of this upper handle joining disappeared; the handle tip was sometimes fashioned of a coin, or was a cast mask.

b) *Pepper-box by Jacob Hurd (1703-54); Boston, 1725-50; ht. 3¾" (9.5 cm.).*

Since English writers relegate these to 'kitchen peppers' it seems desirable to give them their proper standing in the colonies. Nathaniel (1729-77) and Benjamin (1739-81) Hurd, Jacob's sons, were goldsmiths. Nathaniel became better recognized as an engraver, known today from his portraits by John Singleton Copley. One clearly shows Guillim's *Display of Heraldry*, and probably Samuel Sympson's *Book of Cyphers*, 1726 edition. Nathaniel left fine silver to prove his training. He engraved (signing with his initials and a calligraphic bird) the monteith made by his brother-in-law, Daniel Henchman, for the office of the President of Dartmouth College.

c) *Chafing dish, by Thomas Dane (1726-c. 1795); Boston, c. 1750; lgth. 13⅜" (34 cm.).*

Dane's work is rare. Born in Ipswich, Massachusetts, he was probably apprenticed in Boston, where he married. Doubtless this was one of the customary pair, the other of his two known chafing dishes has hoof feet. More chafing dishes are known by Jacob Hurd than any other goldsmith. Coney's are the earliest, with claw feet grasping wooden balls. Perhaps some attachment made Dane's equally practical. All these dishes distinctly resemble each other with the exception of Winslow's, and Nys', and the younger Philip Syng's (its bowl unpierced). Their successor was the dish ring, now known in only one example by Myer Myers.

d) *Tankard with double-scroll handle by Nicholas Roosevelt (1715-1769); New York, c. 1750; ht. 7¼" (18.4 cm.).*

This mid-century New York tankard is typically sturdy with simple baseband, scroll thumb-piece, and flanged flat cover. The handle retains the heavy drop from the hinge but not at the upper joining. New York tankards often had coins in the cover or in the base. Nicholas, the nephew of Johannes and Jacobus, ancestors of Presidents Theodore and Franklin Delano Roosevelt respectively, was probably apprenticed to Cornelius Wynkoop. Between 1753-1765 he made six gold boxes for presentation by the city government.

a) Candlesticks, by Myer Myers (1723-95); New York, 1759; ht. 10″ (25.4 cm.).

Myers' *rimonim*, or scroll bells for synagogues were the impetus for his biography. He worked mainly in New York and also made simple pieces for churches. Samuel and Susannah Cornell commissioned the previously mentioned dish ring, a bread basket in similar pierced work, a coffee-pot and cann. A recently-found pierced mustard pot reflects his successful use of this decoration. These two cast candlesticks were separated from a matching pair by Catherine Livingston Lawrence's will (1811). Any colonial silver candlesticks are unusual: the only other set of four was made by Thomas Dane.

b) Pear-form tea-pot engraved with Bayard coat-of-arms, by Philip Syng Jnr. (1703-1789); Philadelphia, c. 1760; ht. 5½″ (14 cm.).

Syng and his father emigrated from Ireland in 1717. His standish for the Philadelphia Assembly (made 1752) was later used at the signing of the Declaration of Independence. Syng became Colonial Treasurer of Philadelphia, and with his friend, Benjamin Franklin, was co-founder of the Library Company of Philadelphia, the University of Pennsylvania, the American Philosophical Society, and Warden of the first American Masonic Lodge. He made handsome salvers in varied styles, and impressively large bulbous tankards. He left Philadelphia in 1772, recommending Richard Humphreys to his customers. This tea-pot exemplifies a favourite form in the last years of the colonies.

c) Cann, by Joseph Richardson (1711-84); Philadelphia, 1750-80; ht. 3⅞″ (9.8 cm.).

Canns appear in inventories and day-books in pairs and singly, succeeding the straight-sided strap-handled mug around 1710-1720. Joseph, son of Francis Richardson, trained his sons Joseph Jr. and Nathaniel, the third generation of craftsmen. Joseph's richly embossed tea-kettle on stand is still unique; his more restrained coffee-pot and matching sugar bowl (1754) are as rare as they are charming. By 1793, Joseph Jr. was apparently the last smith of his family when he began making his famous 'Peace Medals' which President Washington presented to Indian chiefs. He was Assayer of the Mint (1795-1831) until his death.

d) Chocolate-pot by Zachariah Brigden (1734-1787); Boston, c. 1755; ht. 9⅞″ (25.1 cm.).

This example, with its chained, removable finial, is in the earliest known coffee-pot shape. It was *raised* in the best tradition, although seaming had already been introduced in New York. Its coat of arms appealed to Ebenezer Storer, and was on much of his silver; he married the daughter of John Edwards and was a lavish patron of her brothers, Thomas and Samuel. Brigden, apprenticed to Thomas, married *his* daughter. Samuel Edwards fashioned a pair of plates (c. 1730), almost 6″ in diameter, rare in the colonies, and inventoried in 1757 as 'a pr. butter 9 oz. 2 dwt. 8 gr.'!

a) Sugar-bowl and cream-pot, pear-form, attributed to Jacob Gerritse Lansing II (1736-1803); Albany, c. 1760; sugar-bowl ht. $4\frac{5}{8}''$ (11.7 cm.), cream-pot ht. $4\frac{1}{2}''$ (11.4 cm.).

Kiliaen Van Rensselaer, apprenticed to Dummer in Boston, was first of several Albany goldsmiths. A mark without letters, apparently unique in the colonies, has recently been attributed to him. Jacob Gerritse Lansing (1681-1767) worked in Albany with his grandson of the same name. The latter neglected to mark this bowl though later added his family initials; his mother-in-law's are on the cream-pot. In Albany the surname initial was sometimes at the lower right, that of the wife's given name in the triangle's apex. Embossed pear-form tea pieces are found from the three centres of the craft, mostly around 1750-1775.

b) Salver, by Paul Revere II (1735-1818); Boston, 1760; dia. $12\frac{7}{8}''$ (32.7 cm.).

Revere was a son of the Huguenot lad, Apollos Rivoire, who came to Boston to be apprenticed to John Coney. 'Paul Rivoire' was named in Coney's will (1722); by 1729, when he married, his name was entirely anglicized. The young Revere's service to his country began in 1756 when he went to Crown Point; he was noted as a patriot before his silver received particular attention. This is his first known dated piece of domestic silver. Two similar salvers exist but without the inner chased border, both were fashioned and one dated, in 1761 when Revere began keeping, very desultorily, day-books.

c) Coffee-pot, by Daniel Henchman (1730-1775); Boston, c. 1760; ht. $11\frac{1}{8}''$ (28.3 cm.).

This coffee-pot is more full-blown than the earliest curvaceous ones. Henchman was a son of the minister who in 1737 commissioned a globular tea-pot and sugar bowl, apparently the earliest dated pieces toward a silver tea-set in the colonies, and made by Jacob Hurd to whom Henchman was apprenticed. The latter is known for his plaintive 1773 advertisement:

'And as his work has hitherto met with the Approbation of the most curious, he flatters himself that he shall have the Preference . . . to those Strangers . . . who import and sell English Plate to the great Hurt and Prejudice of the Townsmen . . . bred to the Business . . .'.

d) Double-bellied coffee-pot with salver, by William Hackle (working 1763-1772); Baltimore, c. 1770; ht. $13\frac{1}{4}''$ (33.7 cm.), dia. $6\frac{1}{8}''$ (15.6 cm.).

Coffee-pots in this form were stylish along the entire eastern seaboard; the salver's gallery shows how this Philadelphia style spread. Hackle, one of Baltimore's earliest goldsmiths, either left town or died around 1772. His small 'camp cup' may be the first of the type Richard Humphrey made for George Washington; Hackle's other pieces include a double-bellied tripod cream-pot and an unusual tea-pot whose cover hinge, fastened to the body, places the upper handle socket lower than usual. This coffee-pot is similar to Richard Humphreys' work; he moved from Delaware to Philadelphia in 1772, sponsored there by Philip Syng.

a) Cream-pot by Elias Pelletreau (1726–1810); Southampton, Long Island, 1770–80; ht. 5½" (14 cm.).

Elias, of Huguenot origin, was apprenticed in 1742 to Simeon Soumain, the New York master goldsmith. Although made a Freeman of the city (1750) he returned to his native Southampton where he worked primarily, excepting the time during the Revolution when he and his family were based in Connecticut.

A one-man exhibition at the Brooklyn Museum in 1959 showed this style of cream-pot, an imposing grace cup bearing the VanCortlandt family arms, cylindrical and octagonal pepper-boxes (unusual for the era), keyhole-handled porringers, a tripod cream-pot, a silver-hilted sword, a child's 'whistle and bells', among other pieces.

b) Tea-pot, drum form, by John David (1736–94); Philadelphia, c. 1780; ht. 5¼" (13.3 cm.).

John, son of the goldsmith Peter David (1707–55) and namesake of his Huguenot grandfather, advertised in Philadelphia in 1763:

'Having opened shop. . . . Makes and sells all manner of Gold and Silver Work, in the neatest manner. . . . Those who are pleased to favour him with their custom, may depend on being faithfully served, and at the most Reasonable rates . . .'

His son John Jr. began working about 1785.

A drum-form tea-pot is virtually a Philadelphia goldsmith's signature although Revere made some in the early 1780s. This example has the galleried rail around the rim which seemingly originated in Philadelphia and spread southward only.

---

c) Tea-pot and candlesticks by Joseph and Nathaniel Richardson (working 1785–91); c. 1785; pot ht. 5" (12.7 cm.), sticks ht. 5½" (14 cm.).

This raised tea-pot is one example of the brothers' skill; another in the Virginia Museum has an acorn finial; one at Yale University has similar beading but a domed top with turned finial. All three have loose lids and delicate shoulder engraving.

The neo-classic fluted candlesticks are unique in published American silver. The shaped edge of the loose bobeche (drip pan) matches the ornament on the base. Dummer's monumental candlesticks and Coney's wrought ones have flanges rimming their sockets, but Coney's and Burt's candlesticks lacked bobeches. They reappeared as separate parts on rococo candlesticks and are useful adjuncts today.

d) Tea-set by Benjamin Burt (1729–1805); Boston, 1790–1795; sugar-bowl ht. 9½" (24.1 cm.).

Fluted tea-sets in this style are generally attributed to Paul Revere II, who charged a rare covered 'cream-jug' to James Swan (1784) while still making raised drum-form tea-pots. His day-books record an elliptical and seamed tea-pot in 1785; panelled ones in 1787 and 1789; fluted and engraved in the 1790s.

Benjamin, John Burt's youngest son, trained by his brothers Samuel and William, rivalled Revere. He was chosen leader of the goldsmiths in the Boston procession (1800) in memory of George Washington. This service by Burt is unusual in New England in having no owners' initials, although its history is known.

a) Tea-set, by William G. Forbes (1751–1840); New York, c. 1800.

William G. was a grandson of a Scots immigrant, and was made a Freeman in 1773. Of his four sons, three were silversmiths (Colin, John and Garret). The family is said to have dominated the craft in New York at the turn of the century.

Forbes' first tea-pots were straight-sided, accompanied by urn-form pieces. Of his later tea-pots, one similar to this has an urn-form sugar bowl and barrel cream-pot by Joel Sayre, also of New York. John W. Forbes made two of the few known American plateaux; George Washington's plated one had come from France in 1790.

b) Pitcher, by Paul Revere II (1735–1818); Boston, c. 1800; ht. 7″ (17.8 cm.).

Having given up work for five years of the Revolution, Revere resumed goldsmithing in 1786, only one complete tea-set is recorded in 1764; not again until the 1790s did he charge a tea-pot, sugar-bowl and cream-pot simultaneously. Having borrowed other pottery forms for his sauce-boats, he was the first to realize the useful shape of imported Liverpool pottery pitchers. This is one, among several, made for his own use; a presentation pitcher in this form is his last dated piece (1806). His Bell and Cannon foundry pioneered the manufacture of copper bolts, spikes, and rolled sheet.

c) Tea-set, by John McMullin (1765–1843); Philadelphia, 1805–15.

The proliferation of tea-set pieces extended in Philadelphia and Baltimore to a pair of tea-pots (perhaps one for hot water?) which this service may well have had. Contemporary tea-pots in New York and New England were sometimes flat, often with a simple base-band, and needing an insulating stand, or set on four ball feet, with matching sugar bowl and cream pot. The reversed flutes flanking spouts and handles recall the panelled elliptical pots of the late '80s. Flat-based tea-pots accompany urn-form coffee and other pieces in the well-known galleried service by Joseph Richardson Jr.

d) Panelled slop-bowl by Charles Louis Boehme (1774–1868): Baltimore, c. 1805; dia. 3¾″ (9.5 cm.).

Born, and presumably trained in Philadelphia, Boehme went to Baltimore in 1799. He started to advertise in 1802, the year his mark apparently first incorporated his middle initial. In 1805 he announced that he employed 'several of the best workmen, some of whom have worked in the first Manufactories in London'. For sale he had an 'elegant assortment of London jewelery' and of his own manufacture, 'coffee and tea-pots, sugar dishes, slop basons, and cream ewers in sets'.

This basin has the same panel engravings—a floral basket and rondels—as the Van Bibber tea-set (1804), but is on a lower foot.

a) Small tureen, with wrought leaves, c. 1810; Lewis & Smith (listed in Philadelphia Directories, 1805–11); ht. 6⁷⁄₈″ (17.5 cm.).

Tureens are rare in early American silver, becoming more popular in the 19th century. Hugh Wishart (working 1784–1825) of New York, for example, made at least four. This fine example has leaves around the lower body, with matching attachments for its everted handles and loop finial. Harvey Lewis, presumably the senior partner, worked from 1811–1828, living on the same street as this firm. Smith is not identified; hopefully more research will increase our knowledge of Philadelphia goldsmiths. Lewis's two known 'French Empire' inkstands have been traced by Graham Hood to silver designs by Martin Guillaume Biennais of Paris (see p. 632c).

b) Pitcher with domed and dolphin cover, by Fletcher and Gardiner; Philadelphia, c. 1815; ht. 16″ (40.6 cm.).

This firm began in Boston (1808), moving to Philadelphia in 1811, where Fletcher and Gardiner began making monumental pieces which have only recently attracted attention. Thomas Fletcher is said to have been the firm's designer, especially notable for his sword designs. Gardiner died in 1827 although the firm mark, or Fletcher's alone, continued to be used. Their sculptural presentation vases for DeWitt Clinton show considerable indebtedness to the Warwick Vase (p. 660c). The delicate panels and handling of this piece, and the popular dolphin finial, are overshadowed by the strange dog's head entwined by an interrupted snake handle.

---

c) Sugar basket with chamfered handle, by Obadiah Rich (1809–88); Boston, c. 1830; ht. at ends 5³⁄₁₆″ (13.7 cm.).

Moses Morse's apprentice, Obadiah Rich, appears to be a pupil who outshone his master. Rich belonged to the Massachusetts Charitable Mechanic Association (founded 1795), whose first president was Paul Revere. They exhibited his version of the Warwick Vase given by the Citizens of Boston to Daniel Webster, statesman and orator. Two small ink-wells have recently been attributed to a design by the Boston sculptor, Horatio Greenhough; Rich is the only American goldsmith suggested to have had such a collaborator. This simple basket reflects the traditional forms to which he gave his own interpretation.

d) Coffee-pot by S. Kirk & Son (1846–61); Baltimore, 1854; ht. 11¼″ (28.6 cm.).

Samuel Kirk (1793–1872), apprenticed in Philadelphia, moved to Baltimore in 1815. The previous year that city had established the only hall-marking system in the nation, although it was apparently enforced only until 1830.

This is a presentation piece, one of many by this firm, whose elaborate cast flatware and floral embossed hollow-ware is well-known. Note the characteristic flowers on its foot, and exuberant landscapes surpassing those which John Angell of London had made for the Salisbury family in 1818–9. A reserve on one side shows the Pratt crest; the dated inscription for Isaac Pratt Jr. and the donor company is under the foot.

Silver Glossary

ALLOY: Mixture of metals (though originally the standard of gold or silver). Silver is alloyed with another metal, usually copper, to harden it.

ANTHEMION: Stylized honeysuckle flower motif, popular in classical architecture and thus frequently found on silver articles of the Greek revival period (late 18th century).

BALUSTER: Turned or faceted pillar of decorative outline, particularly popular in the early 18th century.

BEADING: Band of half spheres frequently used as an edging ornament.

BRIGHT CUT: Form of engraving where cuts of varying styles are employed, the 'brightness' achieved by the cuts being burnished by the polished back edges of the graver. Popular in the late 18th century

BRITANNIA STANDARD: Higher standard (958 parts per 1,000). Compulsory from 1697-1720, and used occasionally thereafter. Distinguished by a hall-mark punch depicting Britannia.

CASTING: Shaping of silver in the molten state in moulds—usually used for smaller ornamental parts.

CHASING (may be 'embossed', 'flat' or 'cast'): Decoration by means of punches, producing high or low relief by pushing the metal surface into patterns. No metal is removed.

CUT-CARD DECORATION: One of several types of applied ornament. Introduced c. 1650, it is a thin sheet of silver soldered onto a piece, perhaps as a strengthening at a handle socket but more often as decoration, e.g. round the base of a porringer or the cover of a caster (see 'Strapwork').

EMBOSSING: Relief decoration worked from the back. Further definition is usually given by chasing (q.v.).

ENGRAVING: Cutting of lines or grooves with various types of tool; used for inscriptions, etc.

FLATWARE: Table-wares such as spoons and forks, which have no cutting edge.

FLUTING: Decoration of semi-circular parallel channels, usually embossed.

GADROONING: Lobed border of fluting in reverse, usually used for banded decoration and edges, embossed or cast.

GILDING: Process used for protection against tarnishing and for effect; old gilding was done by the mercurial process (see 'parcel gilding').

GOLD PLATE: Term used in old inventories, almost always refers to gilt plate, as opposed to 'white' or ungilded silver.

MATTING: Type of chasing of fine punched dots covering a surface to give a matt texture.

NUMERAL 13: Mark most frequently seen on antique European silver, alone or as part of a more elaborate mark. An indicator of quality, it shows that the silver is of a fineness expressed as 13 parts silver to three of alloy. This quality was used in the German state, Austria, Hungary, Poland, Czechoslovakia and Strasbourg (when under German or Austrian rule). In the same areas, a lower quality, expressed by the number 12, was permitted and higher quality silver, expressed by the numbers 14 and 15 was also sometimes made. However, these were rare in comparison. Fine silver was expressed by the number 16.

PARCEL GILDING (or 'part gilding'): Process especially popular in 16th century, an effective method of 'picking out' decorative detail (see 'gilding').

PATERA: Round or oval raised ornament of flower head or fluted design, popular on plate of the Classical revival period.

PIERCING: See page 618.

RAISING: Shaping of metal by hammering.

REEDING: Moulding of half flutes or reeds, commonly used for an edge ornament.

SCORPER: Chisel for engraving.

STAKE: Polished steel anvil of suitable shape upon which an article is placed for hammering.

STERLING: Usual standards for British silver (925 parts per 1,000).

STRAPWORK: Decoration which replaced 'cut-card' by the end of the 17th century; it might be cast, chased or pierced (see 'cut-card decoration', 'piercing').

SWAG: Applied or embossed ornament in the form of festoons or garlands of fruit, foliage or flowers.

WRIGGLEWORK: Series of lines and designs made with a fine punch.

Repairs and Maintenance

It is only reasonable that over the centuries and through numerous changes of ownership, many articles of antique silver have been damaged, repaired or changed in other ways, so that while acceptable as an expression of the art of the goldsmith in former times, they do not now appear precisely as they were when new. Damage and loss are most likely to occur at vulnerable points such as finials and the extremities of figures cast in the round or in high relief. It is a sound plan to examine these areas to see if a repair is needed or has been effected or if a replacement has been supplied—e.g. on the covered cup by Hans Jamnitzer (p. 626b) the finial, a figure of Zeus, is a gold replacement and a wing of one angel and one entire figure of another have been broken off and re-attached elsewhere. The glass or crystal lining for p. 624c is missing and has been replaced by a metal one. Enamel and to a lesser extent niello are very liable to chipping and repairs have sometimes been made with a matching paste which does not however have the translucence or sheen of the original. There are numerous chips on the enamel plaques applied to the various pieces of p. 635c.

A common form of renovation is re-gilding. The same Hans Jamnitzer covered cup has been very sensitively re-gilt but often re-gilding offends by being too bright and new-looking. The silver-gilt mounts of the coconut cup (p. 629a) are very worn and the gilt surface has faded to the palest suggestion of a lemon gold colour. It is this condition that invites re-gilding although it is not unattractive to the eye of a connoisseur.

Sometimes the original appearance of an antique silver object is changed by the addition of later marks of ownership or by inscriptions recording it as a gift. For instance, the ornate monogram of p. 630a was added at least a hundred years after the dish was made. Occasionally a fine piece is found which is made from several old pieces which did not originally belong together, and which only appear to harmonize well before close considerations and scrutiny. For instance, some of the *tazze* of the service to which p. 622b belongs were at some point in the last century equipped with much more ornate stands and bases. These are thought to be Spanish, but of the sixteenth century.

Signs of genuine wear are still one of the best first guides to the authenticity of a piece of antique silver, a reassuring note on which to begin a more careful examination of the marks, the subject, the technique and the artistic integrity of the whole.

Fakes and Forgeries

The largest, though fortunately not very extensive, group of forgeries are those to which genuine marks have been transposed. A genuine group of marks is cut from a smaller or damaged piece and soldered into the body of a modern copy, usually of substandard silver. Many of these fakes are themselves poor things, and the tell-tale line of solder usually quickly reveals the forgery to the practised eye as does the position of the marks, which is frequently wrong. The marks themselves, having been taken from another piece, also sometimes betray the fake, since they may become distorted in transposition or they may equally be misleading in that, say, a coffee-pot appears to have been made by a man who specialized in, perhaps, spoons or casters.

Other forgeries are made by copying original antiques by casting or, more recently, by electro-typing. Here care should be taken, especially with objects such as small trencher salts or candlesticks, that the marks do not appear soft-edged or pitted, and that marks on second or third pieces are not identically placed and worn—until the nineteenth century, marks on English pieces were always individually struck at the Assay Offices, and those on, say, a set of spoons, would appear differently spaced.

Fake marks are another hazard, though often the forger's greed precludes him from making fine punches such as are used at the Assay Offices, and his copper imitations leave nothing like the crisp impression of the genuine steel dies.

Illegally altered silver is sometimes quite cleverly done, and again knowledge of makers, marks and styles is the collector's chief safeguard. Silver of small value or not particularly saleable, such as small mugs, damaged coasters and the like, is sometimes found having been converted into casters, salts, and so on—while ordinary spoons acquire rat-tails and other decoration to make them more expensive.

One other aspect of illegal hall-marking is perhaps less culpable than those outlined above: duty-dodging. When a duty of 6d per ounce was imposed in 1719, many English silversmiths were naturally loath to pay heavily at the time of assay on larger wares, and not a few practised duty-dodging, sending a small piece of silver for assay and then incorporating the marks in their new and larger ware. Like later fakers, they often placed these marks in the wrong place —usually between the foot and the body of a cup, kettle or wine-fountain—but though these pieces may not legally be offered for sale, most are of the correct standard of silver, unlike most of the other and later fakes and forgeries.

Silver
Further Reading

General

ABBEY, S. *The Goldsmiths' and Silversmiths' Handbook.* London, 1952, Princeton, N.J., 1953.

BRUNNER, *Old Table Silver: Handbook for Collectors and Amateurs.* London, 1967.

CELLINI, B. *Treatise on Goldsmithing*, trans. by Ashbee. London, 1898; New York, 1966.

CHAFFERS, W. *Handbook to Hallmarks in Gold and Silver plate*, 9th ed. London, 1966; Alhambra, Calif., 1967.

DICKINSON, H.W. *Matthew Boulton.* London and New York, 1937.

DELIEB, E. *Investing in Silver.* London, 1967.

HACKENBROCH, Y. *English and Other Silver.* London, 1964.

HAYDEN, A. *Chats on Old Silver.* London, 1970.

HENDERSON, J. *Silver Collecting for Amateurs.* London, 1965.

HUGHES, G. B. *Small Antique Silverware.* London, 1957.

JONES, E. *Old Silver of Europe and America.* London and New York, 1928.

MACDONALD-TAYLOR, M. A. *A Dictionary of Marks.* London and New York, 1962.

NATAN, A. *Renaissance Silver.* London, 1961.

PENZLER, N. M. *The Book of the Wine Table.* London, 1947. New York, 1948.

TAYLOR, G. *Art in Silver and Gold.* London, 1964.
Silver. Harmondsworth, 1956; rev. ed. Baltimore, 1964.

WILLIAMS, G. R. *Collecting Silver and Plate.* London, 1971.

WILLS, G. *Silver for Pleasure and Investment.* New York, 1970.

WYLER, S. B. *The Book of Old Silver.* New York, 1937.

Continental

ASH, D. *Dutch Silver.* Cambridge, 1965.

CADUCCI, C. *Antique Italian Gold and Silver.* London, n.d.

DAVIES, F. *French Silver 1450–1825.* London, 1970.

DENNIS, K. *Three Centuries of French Domestic Silver*, 2 vols. New York, 1960.

GANS, M. H., and KLINKHAMER, T. M. D. de W. *Dutch Silver.* London, 1961.

TAYLOR, G. *Continental Gold and Silver.* London, 1967.

VICTORIA AND ALBERT MUSEUM. *French Domestic Silver.* London.
The Golden Age of Hispanic Silver 1406–1665. London.

English

ASH, D. *How to Identify English Silver Drinking Vessels 1600–1830.* London, n.d.

BANISTER, J. *English Silver.* London, 1965.
Old English Silver. London, 1965.
Late Georgian and Regency Silver. London, 1971.

BRADBURY, F. *British and Irish Silver Assay Office Marks 1544–1968.* Sheffield, 1968.
Guide to Marks of Origin on British and Irish Silver Plate, various editions.
History of Old Sheffield Plate. London and New York, 1912.

CURRAN, M. *Collecting English Silver.* London, 1963.

DENNIS, J. M. *English Silver.* London, 1970.

EVANS, J. *The Great Goldsmiths of London.* London, 1936.

FINLAY, I. *Scottish Gold and Silver Work.* London, 1956.

GILCHRIST, REV. J. *Anglican Church Plate.* London, 1967.

HAYWARD, J. F. *Huguenot Silver in England 1688–1727.* London, 1959.

HEAL, A. *The London Goldsmiths: 1200–1800.* London and New York, 1935.

HUGHES, G. B. and HUGHES, T. *Three Centuries of English Domestic Silver.* Woking, Surrey, 1952.

JACKSON, C. *English Goldsmiths and their Marks.* London, 1921. 2nd ed., London and New York, 1964.
An Illustrated History of English plate, 2 vols. London, 1911.

OMAN C. C. *English Domestic Silver*, 6th ed. New York, 1965. 7th ed., London, 1968.
The English Silver in the Kremlin. London, 1961.
Caroline Silver. London, 1971.

PEACOCK, P. *Hall Marks on British and Irish Silver.* Bristol, 1970.

RAMSEY, L. G. G. (ed.). *Antique English Silver and Plate.* London, 1962.

ROWE, R. *Adam Silver.* London, 1965.

STONE, J. *English Silver of the 18th Century.* London, 1965; New York, 1966.

VICTORIA AND ALBERT MUSEUM. *English Mediaeval Silver.* London.
Tudor Domestic Silver. London.
Charles II Domestic Silver. London.
Queen Anne Domestic Silver. London.
Adam Silver. London.

WARDLE, P. *Victorian Silver and Silver-plate.* London and Camden N.J., 1963.

Museum Collections

Great Britain

BIRMINGHAM: The City Museum and Art Gallery.
LONDON: The British Museum; Goldsmiths' Hall; The Victoria and Albert Museum; The Wellington Museum.
NORTHUMBERLAND: The Laing Art Gallery and Museum, Newcastle.
OXFORD: The Ashmolean Museum.
SOMERSET: The Holburne of Menstrie Museum of Arts, Bath.
IRELAND: Cork Public Museum; The Civic Museum, Dublin.
SCOTLAND: The Glasgow Art Galleries and Museum.

U.S.A.

DELAWARE: The Henry Francis Dupont Winterthur Museum.
ILLINOIS: The Art Institute of Chicago.
MASSACHUSETTS: The Museum of Fine Arts, Boston.
NEW YORK: The Brooklyn Museum; The Metropolitan Museum of Art, New York City.
OHIO: The Cincinatti Art Museum.
PENNSYLVANIA: The Philadelphia Museum of Art.
WASHINGTON, D.C.: The Smithsonian Institution.

Index

Toys
and Automata

Playthings have at long last come into their own as collector's pieces, and the discarded toy, even the broken toy, is eagerly sought to add to a proudly-displayed group. The most desirable are those from the eighteenth and nineteenth centuries; as these become scarce, the attics, cellars, and bottom drawers are searched for forgotten treasures played with by our grandparents, or great-grandparents.

Toys can be divided into groups; the period in which they were made, the material they are made of, hand-made or mechanically-produced, or the various countries of origin. Indeed, in few other spheres is the variety so great or the history so concerned with the lives of everyday people; many toys are, after all, faithful replicas in miniature of objects long extant.

Ancient toys may be seen in museums; the manuscripts of the Middle Ages often show children at play, and later paintings occasionally included a toy in family groups or scenes. Gradually folk museums are devoting more space to the playthings of the past.

Some will have been purchased from bazaars now vanished, others from the private addresses of toy makers. The toy shop itself did not appear until about the mid-nineteenth century, and it also provided a variety of knick-knacks, souvenirs and haberdashery. The village post office sold toys and 'improving' games; many card games were instructional, with historic events, capitals of the world, or wild and garden flowers. Some astronomy cards were pricked with holes, which, when held up to the light, gave the illusion of the sky at night. Educational playthings are not new, but were encouraged in Victorian and Edwardian homes.

From the cradle toys of babies to the expensive automata of the rich, all in their own manner provide an endless source of wonder and amusement to the present generation.

Opposite:
Animated scene under a dome, English, 19th century.

Toys and Automata
The Craft

The Gröden carvers of traditional toys used cembra wood and the better figures were carved from limewood at Oberammergau where most toys were painted. The wooden ring method of carving animals was evolved by a Seiffen turner about 1814. By 1870 the use of the mechanical lathe led to mass production.

Small, flat metal figures standing on a 'plate' were invented by Andreas Hilpert; by 1780 he was famous for toy soldiers, animals and foliage. These were made of tin or pewter and were cast in slate moulds, the front being in one half and the back in the other; the resulting animals were about $2\frac{3}{4}''$ (6.9 cm.) high when their left and right sides were joined.

Filigree metal, cut like lace, was used in 1780. It was so thin it could be bent to form minute tables, etc. for dolls' houses and garden seats and hedges for pastoral scenes. Painted dark green or brown, it was usually sold flat to bend into shape at home.

Pressed tin-plate was used for toys in France in 1815. This led to the many tin-plate toys and pull-alongs with cast-iron wheels and spokes cut in a 'daisy pattern' fashion. The U.S.A. toys were famous for their variety, while in Europe the iron toys were mostly of kitchen-ware type.

Metal trains were hand-coloured but later the thin brittle colouring was done by varnished paint applied by heat. Early steam locomotives had hand-rolled and soldered tubes but on later models, after about 1850, the metal rods were drawn through a series of holes of graduated size.

Rubber toys were of gutta percha soaked and moulded, then pressed into prepared moulds, two sides for an animal, a front and back for a doll. The two halves were later pressed together and the toys were hollow. In 1840 they often contained squeakers.

Celluloid, highly inflammable and latterly banned for use in toys, was used for German dolls. About 1908 these were painted by gifted Italian girls brought to Germany for the purpose. The first kewpies were of celluloid as were the ping-pong balls from the U.S.A. Bath toys, such as swans and goldfish, were beautiful.

Toys made from pulp in 1740 had a mixture of kaolin added to the papier mâché thus making them much stronger. This recipe by Friedrich Müller of Sonneberg had been known in the furniture trade for some while. By 1781 there were dolls with elaborate hair-do's, often used as fashion models, galloping horses, soldiers with guns, and dolls' heads coated with wax.

Dolls' bodies, little more than leather bags, were at first stuffed with bran, later with animal hair or seaweed, and later still with wood shavings. Coarse leather gave way to thin sheepskin. A beautiful wax head and yoke would be joined by two tapes to a coarse calico body and the upper legs stuffed with straw. The moulds for wax heads were in sections tied together; the hot wax was then poured in and allowed to cool. A similar process was used for the lower arms and legs.

The hair was inserted with a sharp knife cutting into the wax. This was confirmed by the widow of C. E. Pierotti and by Miss A. M. Pierotti, of a famous doll-making family. Both stated that they had never seen hot needles used for this work, as had sometimes been assumed.

Unglazed china made from a kaolin mixture is known to potters as biscuit and to doll collectors as bisque. Artists made the plaster moulds for a variety of heads. Early Jumeau heads were pressed into moulds; later on the mixture was poured into moulds and fired. He added the ears to his larger heads after they had been in moulds; colouring was done with flesh-tinted stains and the heads rebaked to fix the colours.

Hollow bodies were made partly for lightness and partly for inserting mechanisms for speaking and walking, and of course for re-threading. Joins on animals could be hidden by real fur or hairy fabric.

Introduction

All over the world, children have played with toys or used their imagination where there were none. Balls and skipping-ropes came from grasses, dolls from bones and rags, pots and animals from clay and marbles from stones. Traditional toys in the Middle Ages were mostly of wood; hoops, balls, tops, windmills, ninepins and hobby horses.

Cup and ball was played by the Eskimos in the spring to hasten the return of the sun, the American Indians carved katchinas to help the crops and bring the rains, the Japanese offered prayers to their tumbler dolls, and wax dolls were said to be made by magicians.

Toys were given as presents to queens, princes and princesses: precious toys of silver, exotic birds covered with real feathers. 'Costly and ingenious dolls which display *actiones* by means of concealed clockwork' were made in Augsburg and Nuremberg and were shown on the streets of France in 1716, and in Italy, Thomas de Francini had peopled grottoes with automata before designing the fountains at Versailles.

In the eighteenth century, puppets were not allowed to speak with natural voices, hence the raucous noises of Mr Punch and his followers.

Jacques de Vaucanson of Grenoble amazed the world with his working models; his 'movable anatomies', the flute player, the duck and the drummer, became famous in 1738. Pierre Jaquet-Droz (see p. 222b et seq.) in 1758 made some extraordinary clocks and his writer, draughtsman, and musician models made with the help of his son and Jean-Frédéric Leschot, are still in working order at Neuchâtel.

While craftsmen and inventors perfected their complicated ideas, the pedlar with his pack toured the countryside bringing carved animals and dolls to the children of Europe and America. Soon it was almost obligatory for merchants with goods to have illustrated sheets as catalogues, and G. H. Bestelmeier of Nuremberg issued a catalogue with four hundred drawings of toys between 1798-1807. In Europe, Nuremberg was the centre for toy-making, while in the New World it was Pennsylvania and New England.

The pecking chickens of Russia, the bear and hammer toy, the monkey on a stick, and the jumping-jack, all had movements which were utilized down through the centuries. Italy became known for the crèche (miniature figures that make up a Nativity scene) and for marionettes, the Netherlands for doll houses, Germany for toy soldiers, England for paper cut-outs, and the U.S.A. for cast iron toys. The Swiss were famous for their automata which gradually became more intricate and more expensive, leading to complicated affairs under glass domes. These eventually led to the cheaper clockwork toys said to be evolved by a Frenchman named Cruchet, and which were perfected by the Germans.

Spring-powered cannons came about 1800, and by 1815 pressed tin-plate was used for toys in France. During the middle of the nineteenth century metal toys became rivals to those of wood.

In 1806, Merlin's Mechanical Museum in London had on show an artificial bat, a cruising frigate, and a juggler playing with cups and balls. Later came the walking toys of Rouillet, the automata of Durand, and the clown figures of G. Descamps in the 1880s.

Electric trolley-cars were made by Carette of Nuremberg in 1893, and by Carlisle and Finch of the U.S.A. in 1897 at Cincinnati. Steam locomotives came late in the century. By the 1900s all the gadgets for railways had arrived including Victorian railway stations looking rather like metal conservatories. By 1903, the Basset-Lowke trains ran by clockwork.

Games can be revived years later; diabolo in 1910 was a revival of the French *diable* of a hundred years before, the yo-yo of forty years ago has returned today, and was known in the Far East in ancient times. History too, has played its part; the building of the Thames Tunnel led to pretty paper panoramas in 1843, and the toy dump-trucks of the U.S.A. were inspired by the building of the Panama Canal, opened to commercial traffic in 1914.

a) left: Model chariot, terracotta, pole and axle restored; Sūmerian, from Ur, c. 21st century B.C.; wdth. 3" (7.62 cm.). above: Woman in an ox cart, terracotta, wheels and cord restored; north Syrian, 9th–8th centuries B.C.; ht. 3" (7.62 cm.), lgth. 3" (7.62 cm.).

Little carts and chariots with thick solid wheels have been unearthed from Mesopotamia, Egypt, and later on from India. Other pull-along toys are of animals with four wheels, or birds with two, the latter swaying up and down as they go along. Usually reddish or pale brown, they are of baked earth (terracotta) and were made by the Sūmerians about 3000–2750 B.C.

The Indo-Europeans introduced spoked wheels to lighten their chariots for sport and warfare. Later, wheeled toys had spokes indicated with paint, to imitate this practical development.

b) Rocking horse; Scotland, c. 1775; lgth. 44½" (113 cm.), ht. to seat 21" (53.3 cm.).

A genuine, unrestored 18th century wooden rocking horse is hard to find; this one belonged to Sir Walter Scott when a child. These heavy, cumbersome toys had carved heads, real horse-hair tails, foot rests and holsters for pistols, and were often made by estate carpenters.

Legs were sometimes painted on the boards. The gap between was later carved away, till the almost complete horse was placed on rockers. Some had painted eyes, others had inset glass eyes. In 1785, William Long from London arrived in the U.S.A., where he advertised rocking horses as being made 'in the neatest and best manner'.

c) top: Coach and horses, carved and painted wood; England, c. 1835; lgth. 13½" (34.2 cm.); bottom: Coal-cart and horse, carved and painted wood; England, c. 1913; lgth. 11½" (29.2 cm.).

Dappled-grey horses were much in favour in the mid-19th century and large pull-alongs were popular, made of wood, and painted. They were copies of the vehicles of the day: brewer's drays, fire engines, dust carts, and hay-wains in England, ox teams, covered wagons with pioneer figures in the U.S.A.

Sets of iron wheels could be purchased for home-made toys, harnesses were made from real leather, cheaper toys having varnished paper, and many appropriate articles were added. By the 1870s lithographed paper replaced many of the painted details.

d) Governess cart, Bronderslev, Jutland, Denmark, c. 1870; cart lgth. 15" (38 cm.), shackles lgth. 13⅞" (35 cm.), ht. 9½" (24 cm.).

Many home-made toys paid great attention to detail and this original governess cart of about 1870 is no exception. The seats are padded leather, the wooden horse is partly covered with hide, and has the original harness made by the coachbuilder's son.

The platform on which the horse stands is curved at the front with a painted edge, and is typical of the Bohemian toys of the 1880s, as also are the small iron wheels with four spokes. In the photograph, two French dolls recline on the seat.

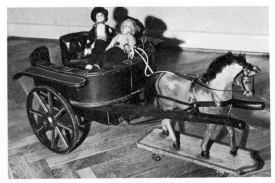

Toy pedlar's cart marked H.C. Wolven; U.S.A.

Interior of doll's house; England, 19th century.

a) *Tricycle in the form of a horse, painted wood on a metal frame; England, c. 1875–1880; lgth. 31″ (78.7 cm.).*

This is a dappled horse for a child to ride which jogs up and down as he moves along. Bicycles with horse's heads and tails had been played with by the royal children on the top floors of Buckingham Palace in 1871—toys which had belonged to their uncles. The Prince (b.1856) also had an elaborate horse tricycle with harness, but they were most popular about 1878; any kind of horse toy had been popular since the 14th century.

In 1822 a patent was granted in Europe for a three-wheeled toy horse to be ridden by a child.

b) *Hunting cheetah; Desnoor, India, 19th century; lgth. 17½″ (44.4 cm.).*

Eastern toys have a distinct charm of their own with their highly coloured and varnished paints. This is a carved and painted wooden toy; many are of exotic birds and humped cattle.

Toys were brought home by travellers and army relatives when Queen Victoria was Empress of India. From China and Japan come toys of papier mâché, such as tigers with nodding heads and the Daruma tumbler figures. Elephants, horses and camel pull-alongs are made today in Rajasthan, Southern India, and also native vehicles such as tongas, jatkas, shikaras, carts and houseboats.

c) *Ferry-boat, wood and printed paper; W. S. Reed & Co.; Massachusetts, U.S.A., 1877; lgth 20″ (50.8 cm.).*

This wooden pull-along toy ferry-boat is covered with lithographed printed and varnished paper. Between 1875 and 1900, Reeds of Massachusetts were one of the largest toy manufacturers in the world and the lower deck shows toys and crates marked with their name.

Recently, these pull-alongs have been given the name of carpet toys, that is, toys to pull along indoors. The term is used especially in the case of boats which would normally float in water, and many Noah's arks with flat bottoms. In the U.S.A. they are known as parlor toys.

d) *Terracotta doll; Egypt, 15th–13th centuries B.C.; ht. 9″ (27 cm.).*

This well-made doll from Egypt has a hair socket at the top of her head, and brush marks to indicate clothing. The hair could have been stiff grass, or grey beads threaded on a cord. She is a typical female figure, perhaps a child's plaything. If she is a grave figure or a concubine, then the legs are close together to prevent her from running away.

Clay dolls have been found in districts near rivers such as the Nile, Euphrates and Ganges, the proportion of female dolls to males is about 100 to 12, presumably since the females are also fertility symbols.

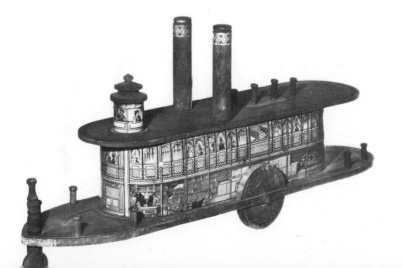

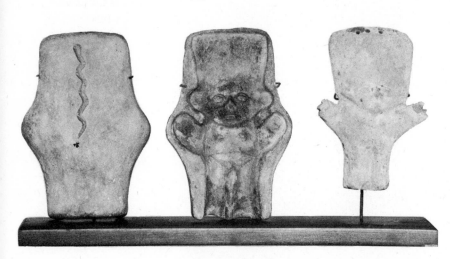

a) Ancient Peruvian doll in mould; South America; mould ht. 6½" (16.5 cm.), doll ht. 5½" (139 cm.).

The outside and the inside of the ochre coloured mould are both shown, together with the clay doll, which when dry will be coloured, using browns, reds, ochre and black. These dolls from ancient Peru are found in graves and may be seen in their coloured finished state in the British Museum. Some are from Ancon and others from Chancey.

The more familiar ancient Greek dolls were made in the same manner, but these often had separate limbs joined to the bodies by cords, thus making them articulated. Similar Roman dolls belong to about the first century A.D.

b) Nigerian clay dolls, painted; traditional; hts. 7" (17.7 cm.), and 9" (228 cm.).

These curious dolls are from Fika, Nigeria, and are made by the Kanuri children. Both have incised ornament; the larger is of light brown clay, the other dark brown.

All over the world native dolls are made from local materials and in some parts the features are deliberately omitted, for if a doll should become too lifelike a spirit might enter into it! In the Moslem countries it is rare for children to have dolls because of religious stricture, but in other parts a doll might be considered lucky, and a help in child-bearing. Folk-lore and superstitions abound even to the present day.

Toys and Automata
DOLLS

c) 'Queen Anne' wooden doll; England, mid–18th century; ht. 17" (43.1 cm.).

A fine doll, with well-carved head, painted inset black enamel eyes and nailed hair wig. She wears a blue silk ribbon lace cap, several petticoats, hooped skirt, rose silk dress trimmed with silver braid, kid mittens, muslin apron, handkerchief, pocket, pin-cushion, pink knitted silk stockings with white clocks and blue-trimmed pink bootees. She is a typical 'Queen Anne' doll, both valuable and rare. The plump rounded face and leading reins denote a child doll. The English were noted for these; one named Letitia was taken to America in 1699 by William Penn and given to a child in Philadelphia.

d) Black pedlar doll with tray; England, first half of 19th century; ht. 10½" (26.6 cm.).

Early pedlar dolls had wooden or wax faces and mere stumps for bodies. In 1810, the licence could be seen pinned to their cloaks or their baskets and trays, and some dolls at this time had faces of chicken skin. Young girls wore wide straw hats, old women wore straw bonnets covered with the hood of the cloak, sometimes scarlet, sometimes black, and all wore aprons.

In England pedlars carried their goods on foot, and hawkers by cart. American 'pedlars' used carts and wagons as their business increased. Today, pedlar dolls are of more value when under glass domes.

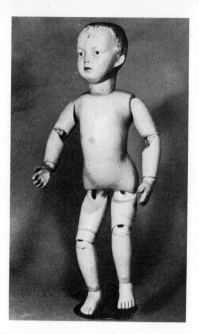

a) Bisque child doll with cloth body; German, c. 1887; ht. 17″ (43.1 cm.).

An unmarked German child doll represents the many bisques (the American Tariff Act of 1890 made it compulsory for all dolls to be marked with their country of origin). She has fixed eyes, a well-waisted cloth body, cloth upper arms and thighs, china forearms and lower legs. She wears a Victorian chemise, drawers, dress and pinky-red buttoned jacket.

Later, their makers' signs were impressed in the bisque, usually just under the hair-line at the back. Such firms as Armand Marseille, Handwerke, Heubach, Kestner, Kammer & Reinhardt, Schoen-hau & Hoffmeister, Simon & Halbig, all marked their products.

b) Wooden doll; by Albert Schoenhut; Philadelphia, U.S.A., 1911; ht. 16″ (40.6 cm.).

This all-wooden doll made by Albert Schoenhut of Philadelphia, is without clothes in order to show the joint device, a combination of steel springs and swivels which enable all the limbs to be put in a natural position. Under the foot are two circular holes in a straight line, one slanting, one vertical, thus making the doll capable of standing easily on a flat disc which has two pins—a speciality of the Schoenhut dolls, in addition to the painted head and carved hair. Her back is marked 'Schoenhut doll, pat. Jan 17'11. U.S.A. & Foreign Countries'.

c) Peep show with hand-coloured engravings; Augsburg, Germany, c. 1740; 6″ (15.4 cm.) square.

A peep-show had cut-out pictures and figures as on a stage; in this case hand-coloured engravings by Martin Engelbrecht (1684-1766). These were made in Augsburg, and are beautifully coloured with much detail.

In this example, the box contained slots to take four cut-out scenes, the front of the box had another cut-out, and the back was painted with a landscape, making six 'curtains' in all. These led to the toy theatres published by Green in 1834, and to panoramas of the Great Exhibition, and eventually to pop-up books and many novelties.

d) La Poupée Modèle, cut-out figure with 5 day dresses and 4 head dresses in original box, hand coloured; published by R. Ackermann Junior, 191 Regent Street, London, c. 1833; ht. 8½″ (21.5 cm.).

La Poupée Modèle, a paper cut-out, was made possibly for the French market. The enormous sleeves with tight cuffs and the elaborate hair styles were fashionable in 1833. From 1809 Rudolph Ackermann issued several books, including some on costume, with hand-coloured prints from etched or aquatinted plates. The cut-out paper dolls were similar to the fashion plates of the 1770s; they were primarily for children, such as the 'History of Little Fanny' (1810), a book in which the heroine could change her ready-cut outfits.

Ackermann died in 1834 and La Poupée Modèle was published by Ackermann Junior.

a) Jigsaw puzzle, hand-coloured lithograph; England, c. 1860; 8¼" (20.9 cm.) by 11¼" (28.5 cm.).

Jigsaw puzzles were descended from the dissected maps invented by John Spilsbury in the 1760s. The first were made of mahogany, later ones were of whitewood. Only the border interlocks in this fine jigsaw called 'My Birthday Presents' which include a wooden horse on wheels, a wooden Noah's ark, a dressed doll, this jigsaw, a toy elephant and a peacock with outstretched tail. On the ground is a large ball and a battledore and shuttlecock.

The picture is cut haphazardly except for the border. Earlier jigsaws would have followed the design, later ones would have all the pieces interlocking.

b) Victorian picture bricks; probably German, 1870–1880; largest ht. 6" (15.2 cm.).

These pictorial bricks are five-sided each one fitting inside another, the largest one is the box sometimes with a lid. This one is of chipwood, covered with varnished paper, and a small child will pile one above the other. The five sides were usually related, such as the seasons down one face, animals down another and often included the alphabet. This toy lasted well into the 1900s.

The nested wooden dolls of Russia are traditional as are their highly polished wooden eggs. From Madagascar came nested baskets, and nested blocks were made in the U.S.A. by Jesse Crandall about 1870.

c) Building blocks; U.S.A., late 19th century.

Picture blocks, usually cubes, appeared in the 1840s, sometimes in boxes complete with six pictures as a simple puzzle to copy. These American picture-making blocks show a circus procession when laid out correctly, and on the reverse is an Atlantic-Pacific Line Express train. They are printed by chromo-lithography on paper and stuck to rectangular wooden blocks, a most unusual shape. Others came in wooden boxes with sliding lids.

C. M. Crandall was famous for his interlocking building blocks in 1867. In Germany, blocks of different shapes and sizes made by Richter, and called *Anker-Steinbaukasten*, won medals at the Paris Exhibition of 1900.

d) Straw-covered wooden ark made by French prisoners-of-war; c. 1820; lgth. 16" (40.6 cm.).

At first, the toy ark and animals were sold together in chipwood boxes; later the ark became the container. Wooden arks are usually sturdy, with a house on deck, a lift-off sloping roof, or sliding doors in the side walls.

Their great period was between 1825–1875, when they were made in Saxony, Germany, beautifully coloured and decorated with windows, porches and patterns. The dove was usually painted on the roof with the olive branch in its beak. Hallbach, near Olbernhau, specialized in making arks from c. 1850. Many are of pinewood, decorated with straw work; other variations come from Pennsylvania and Japan.

a) Two hand carved wooden cows from Switzerland; c. 1920; ht. of larger cow 8″ (20.2 cm.).

Wooden animals in the Noah's arks were made by the 'ring' method from about 1815, but it was not until 1875 that it was decided to try and adjust their sizes to one another, i.e. the ladybird should be smaller than the elephant.

In Pennsylvania (U.S.A.) a Swiss named Huguenin, and a German named Schimmel, carried on their traditions of making hand-carved wooden animals, in the mid-19th century.

Animals covered with natural skin do not come out of the ark; perfect on their own, some pull carts, and sheep and mountain goats are complete with bells.

b) A game of 'Amusement and Instruction of Youth of Both Sexes'; by E. Wallis, 42 Skinner St., Snow Hill, London, England, c. 1825; wdth. 5½″ (12.5 cm.).

The mid-18th century was a great period for mixing a little amusement with the dull routine of instruction; the forerunners were pictorial cards issued during Queen Anne's reign. Historical cards depicting the history of England were published by Wallis just after 1760, ending with the death of George II.

Instructional games were played at Windsor Castle and therefore became popular. At first they were hand-coloured but about 1768 aquatint plates were used. The game shown here is tinted in pale colours. Many board games were provided with tee-to-tums, for the tossing of dice was considered wicked.

---

c) left: The old town-gate in Ziestal, Switzerland, paper; ht. 9⅞″ (25 cm.), lgth. 7⅛″ (18 cm.); right: Swiss chalet, wood; c. 1900; ht. 11¹³⁄₁₆″ (30 cm.), wdth. 13¾″ (34 cm.).

It is but a short step from building bricks to building houses, and the possibilities with cut-paper printed sheets were endless—from elaborate stage scenes to the surprise picture books of the 1840s.

In the 1830s and '40s the chromolithograph was in vogue and by 1850, printed sheets appeared as toys to be cut up and erected. There were dolls to dress for the girls, vast armies of soldiers for the boys, and many board games. Most durable were the wooden construction toys, such as this intricately carved Swiss chalet or the log cabins produced in the U.S.A. c. 1866.

d) The brownstone doll's house has three storeys with a central staircase—note the variety of wooden chairs; American, 1846.

A doll's house becomes a cupboard holding all the miniature articles which a child has collected; originally, elaborate cabinets had been made for grown-ups to display their miniature reproductions and their 'silver toys'. Between these extremes are the many dolls' houses with elaborate façades, opening to reveal rooms furnished correctly in their periods.

In the 16th century they were made in Germany, in the 17th century in France and Holland, and in the 18th century in England and Italy; all showed the characteristic architecture of the country of origin. The *Puppenhuizen* of Holland were considered the most magnificent.

a) Pieces of tin-ware and iron for a toy kitchen and a 'Little Fanny' iron stove; made by the Philadelphia (U.S.A.) Stove Works; mid- to late 19th century; wdth. (of stove) 6″ (15.2 cm.).

America is noted for early tin toys and by 1850 there were as many tin as wooden toys. There were sad-irons which would hold hot coals, silver toys reminiscent of the Dutch, and cast-iron stoves complete with many utensils. Some of these were decorated with paint rather in a bargeman's style.

The Philadelphia Tin Toy Manufactory made pull-alongs, furniture for doll's houses, and metal animals with large wheels, but the toy kitchen utensils for domestic use surpassed most others. Another company was that of George W. Brown, with his wind-up toys, gigs and fancy buggys of 1872.

Toys and Automata
MODELS

b) Tin soldiers; mid-19th century; ht. $3\frac{3}{4}$″ (9.52 cm.); 3″ (7.62 cm.).

The Hilperts of Nuremberg concentrated on the casting in tin of little flat figures, Andreas Hilpert sometimes signing his with 'A.H.'. They made animals of all kinds and produced tin soldiers in great quantities, followed later by Gottschalk and Wehrli of Switzerland. By the middle of the 19th century, Heinrichsen of Nuremberg and Allgeyer of Furth, both well known for their toy soldiers, decided on a standard height of 33 cm. ($1\frac{1}{3}$″) for their grown men.

These examples of knights are what are known as 'flats', fixed into stands and painted.

---

c) Foot soldiers in lead by William Britain; England, c. 1900; guardsmen ht. $2\frac{1}{2}$″ (6.4 cm.), bandsmen ht. $2\frac{3}{8}$″ (6.0 cm.).

By making his soldiers hollow instead of solid lead as before, William Britain cornered the market which previously had belonged to Germany.

Britain made his first set in 1893, some mounted soldiers of the 1st Life Guards, and by 1914 was even exporting to Germany. Every war was commemorated by his toy soldiers and he prided himself on the accuracy of his uniforms and equipment.

The soldiers were marketed in boxed sets, including all the Imperial soldiers of Queen Victoria's Empire, and they were coveted by both boys and men.

The fort here is of printed and varnished paper.

d) Game in which little balls contained in a sack in the tower are thrown from the roof—the holes (cellar level) are numbered to show the score; probably German; date unknown; ht. overall 38″ (96.5 cm.).

Games of chance go back to the beginnings of the history of mankind: natives played with nuts, soldiers with marbles, princes and nobles with cards and since then many games have been devised with winning as their main object.

Games such as E & O, Pope Joan, backgammon and tablan have resulted in the design of many beautiful boards and playing pieces such as dicing-cups, precious chess men, racing jockeys, Chinese counters and Indian squails. In later Victorian days, many games of skill had a moral or instructive element added.

a) *Mechanical figures of painted bonework made by French prisoners-of-war for Captain Lincoln Barker, last Governor of Norman Cross Barracks, near Peterborough, England in 1816, c. 1800; ht. 7½″ (19.0 cm.).*

Becalmed sailors often made fascinating toys with bones, such as intricate boats and cribbage boards with inlay, fans etc. In England the French prisoners-of-war between 1797 and 1815 made most elaborate models, many of the guillotine, all in bone, with a little colour on the French flag or on a banner. Other toys, like those shown here, were prettier, with women wearing poke bonnets and shawls, and soldiers in uniform. All were working models, many with musical accompaniment, and at times the bone work was so thin it was translucent. Many bone models—particularly ships—were intended for display rather than playthings.

b) *left: 'Smoking' man with cigarette holder, moves head, raises stick; probably H. Vichy, Paris; c. 1900; ht. 24″ (60.9 cm.). right: Spanish dancer, taps foot, rotates, shakes tambourine, flirts eyes from side to side; head probably by Schoenhau & Hoffmeister, Germany; c. 1900; ht. 20″ (50.8 cm.). Both on musical box base.*

Many performing figures are by Jean Roullet who won a bronze medal at the Paris Exhibition of 1867, and by the 1800s was working with Ernest Descamps. They made smoking, drinking, conjuring and dancing dolls, some on wheels to pull along, others on musical boxes, all being well dressed and typically French. To save time, they used bisque heads made by Jumeau and others.

Vichy patented an automatic doll in 1862, smoking figures were patented in the U.S.A. in 1874, and flirting eyes in Germany in 1890. The Descamps catalogue, 1880, includes smoking figures.

c) *Wooden toy musical boxes; left: The base showing label; France; ht. 3 1/16″ (7.7 cm.); right: Showing picture and handle; ht. 4 3/16″ (10.6 cm.).*
d) *Schoenhut piano, marked* Pat, Sept. 18. 1900 *on paper panel, U.S.A.; lgth. 15¾″ (40 cm.).*

Toy musical boxes are usually turned on by a hand-crank. They were made in Switzerland and Germany in the late 18th century. Kensington Palace state apartments have one which belonged to the little Princess Victoria where a doll walks between trees, going in and out of a pagoda.

Toy pianos were made by Schoenhut & Co. from 1872 onwards. This upright cottage type, with the black 'notes' painted on the white keys, had sounding pieces of steel plates, tuned with the utmost care.

*a) Clockwork peacock, metal; 19th century; ht. 9"
(22.8 cm.)—10" (25.4 cm.).*

This wonderful peacock has a metal body
adorned with real feathers. When wound up and
placed on the ground, the bird turns its head to left
and right, takes a few steps forward, repeats this,
pauses and then lifts its tail and spreads it out in the
shape of a fan. It closes realistically then the tail
feathers drop and again sweep the ground as it
moves majestically forward a few steps before
repeating the performance.

Crocodiles which crept forward and tigers
which sprang, opening and shutting their jaws,
were other novelties made in realistic manner.

*b) Walking doll dressed in yellow silk, black lace, with
papier mâché head, cardboard body, kid hands; U.S.A.,
1862; ht. 10" (25.4 cm.).*

The *Autoperipatetikos* is a curious name for this
now famous walking doll, patented in the U.S.A.
in July, 1862 and in Europe in December the same
year. Names on the original boxes can be Joseph
Lyon & Co., Martin & Runyon, or Munn & Cobb.

Examples are usually 10" high, with head in
papier mâché, parian, china or bisque, fair or dark
hair often in a snood, kid arms and elaborately
trimmed clothes with a wide skirt over cumbersome feet. This doll must not be confused with the
'Toy Automaton' walking doll patented a year
later in the U.S.A. by J. S. Brown.

*c) Clockwork porter with bisque head, brown hair,
metal body and blue uniform; c. 1876; ht. 12½"
(31.7 cm.).*

Walking figures were patented by William F.
Goodwin in the U.S.A. in 1866. The legs wound
up and the cart prevented the figure from falling.
Boys on tricycles were patented by A. M. Allen
in 1870.

Here a porter wheels a yellow barrow with red
wheels. 'Hotel Metropole' is painted on either side
of the cart. The clockwork mechanism is underneath and connected to the porter by two rods.
When wound, he turns his head from side to side,
while striding forward to keep up with the moving
cart. Such a toy with the initials R D is the sign of
Rouillet and Descamps.

*d) Clockwork engine with tender, in painted metal;
Germany, 1910; lgth. 13" (33.8 cm.), without tender.*

Clockwork engines without rails were made in
France in the early 1860s, and train sets with rails
and painted tin-plate engines in Germany in 1865.

The train makers of Bavaria were Marklin in
1859, who marked the initials G M C on their toys,
Bing in 1865, marking his with G B N, and Carette
marking his with G C & CO. Clockwork trains
in England were by Basset-Lowke in 1903, and
later on by Hornby.

In the early 1900s, electric trains in the U.S.A.
were built by Ives, Lionels and later by the American Flyer factory in Chicago.

Toys and Automata Glossary

BABY DOLL: In England, a doll dressed as a baby; in France, a child, as opposed to a grown-up, doll.

BARTHOLOMEW BABIES: Small carved wooden dolls first sold at English fairs in 1721, held on the Feast of St. Bartholomew.

BATH METAL TOYS: Made from zinc and copper alloy.

BILDERBOGE: Cut-paper toys sold in sheets, German.

BIMBELOTERIE: The toy-trade, French. A *bimbelot* is a plaything, a *bimbelotier* a toyman.

BISQUE: China dolls with a flesh-colour matt surface, i.e. unglazed.

BONNET DOLLS: Dolls with bonnets or hats made in one piece with the head; mostly American usage.

BOSTON ROCKER: Two curved pieces side by side, with a seat between them at one end, and a horse's head at the other.

BREATH MOTIVATION: Movement of toys by blowing.

BRISTOL PENNY TOYS: c. 1800, mostly wheeled toys, wooden, glued and painted; by 1850 made in London and sold in the streets.

CHECKERS: American name for draughts.

CLOCKWORK: Spring-operated toys; these were made as early as 1672 by Hans and Gottfried Hautsch of Nuremberg.

CRAZED: Applied to lines in 'crackled' pottery and on wax dolls' faces.

DANCING JACKS OR PANTINS (French): Flat cardboard figures with limbs joined to the bodies by strings.

DECAL: A transfer, American.

DUTCH DOLLS: Possibly imported from Germany, Czechoslovakia, Bohemia, or perhaps Holland. In Holland these dolls are called *Duitse poppen, Duit* being the Dutch for German; hence the confusion.

ESCAPEMENT: See p 267.

FLANDERS BABY: A name given to the 'Dutch Dolls' from Europe.

FLIRTING EYES: Name for the doll's eyes which move from side to side, American.

FRENCH FASHIONS: Beautifully dressed dolls made in the 1860s as playthings for the luxury classes.

FROZEN CHARLOTTES: Unjointed little dolls from an American poem in which 'Charlotte' was frozen to death.

GONGBELL TOYS: Made in the U.S.A. in the 1880s.

HEINRICHSEN OR NUREMBERG SCALE: Applied to soldiers; adults 30 mm. high, horsemen 40 mm. high.

JACKSTRAWS: American name for the English spillicans.

JACKS: Jack-on-strings, merry jacks, jumping jacks, traditional wooden folk toys, sometimes painted.

JACK-IN-THE-BOX: American jump-ups.

KATCHINA: Little dolls of the American south-western Indians, given to children after religious rites.

KELLYS: Tumbler toys, American.

KEWPIE: A small doll designed by Rose O'Neill, the most popular being those made of celluloid, 1911 and 1912. American; copied in bisque in Germany.

MACHÉS OR MASH: American name for papier mâché dolls.

NEST TOYS: Wooden toys of many sizes fitting into one another, which originated in Russia.

O GAUGE: $1\frac{1}{4}''$ between the rails for trains.

OO GAUGE: Double O, half the width of O gauge; schoolboy nickname Dublo, became trade name.

PANDORAS: Large French fashion dolls, c. 1700; for showing dresses and hairstyles; discontinued after the arrival of ladies' fashion magazines.

PANORAMAS: Paper scenes, one behind the other and viewed from the front.

PAPERWEIGHT EYES: Those in which the iris is threaded.

PARIAN: Name given to dolls with heads and usually hair of fine white china-clay (see p. 204b).

PEG DOLLS: Small wooden dolls, often for dolls' houses.

PENNY-WOODENS: 'Dutch dolls', American.

PENNSYLVANIA BABIES: Late 18th century dolls of carved and painted pinewood, American.

POUPARDS: A doll which can be twirled around on a stick.

PUMPKIN HEADS: Composition dolls heads—the head and hair thinly coated with wax. The eyes usually without pupils, the cheek colouring underneath the wax.

SAND TOYS: Trickling sand is used to activate the movement.

SCISSORS TOYS OR LAZY TONGS: Traditional wooden toys from Saxony, criss-cross wooden pieces with soldiers standing on the cross pieces to give a marching effect, or girls driving geese.

SHOO-FLY: Two horse-shaped boards on rockers joined by a seat; patented 1859 in U.S.A.

SLIT-HEADS: Wax doll heads with the hair inserted in a deep central cut, simulating a parting, American.

SPOON-HANDS: Wooden, with scooped-out palms, the thumb showing, the fingers sometimes indicated but joined together.

TEDDY-BEARS: Named after American President Theodore Roosevelt.

THREE FACES: One head with a crying, smiling, sleeping or frowning face; the two faces not showing covered with a bonnet-shaped hood.

WIND TOYS: Toys motivated by the wind as early as 1875.

YOKE: Doll's shoulders when made of same material as the head.

697

Toys and Automata
Repairs and Maintenance

Tiny pots of enamel paint are useful when one needs only a small amount of many colours. They include authentic colours of racing cars, railways and military uniforms.

Transparent lacquer keeps miniature objects free from tarnish. Non-yellowing, it is suitable for brass, copper and silver.

Dolls must be looked after and, especially bisque, should not be kept in a strong sunlight. Wax dolls must not be in airtight bags or near an electric light. It is wiser to lay them flat in tissue paper rather than standing continually; never hang by the neck in case it breaks.

Use a warmed modelling tool on cracked wax faces, gently following the direction of the crack and not across it. Cracks in bisque can be rectified with filler lightly tinted with oil-colour dimmed down with a touch of black and wipe away any excess from the surface before it sets. Fingers can also be mended with this, carved to the correct shape, rubbed with sand-paper and painted.

Jumeau used sawdust for stuffing towards the end of the nineteenth century, though many makers had already replaced this material with horsehair. Composition bodies can be painted with matched oil paint and then varnished.

When renewing a wig there are many patents with helpful diagrams. Lengths of hair, imitation or real, knotted over a piece of string tied between two chair legs, make a 'fringe'. Cover the head with muslin, and wind the 'fringe' around the head beginning at the nape of the neck and continue in a spiral till the crown is reached, sticking it with adhesive as you go. Do not go too near the forehead as a fringe will probably be cut later. If an old doll's hair is faded, good quality hair-dye may restore the colour.

Before 1806 sewing thread was made of silk and sometimes of wool and flax. A smooth cotton yarn was used up to 1826, when cotton thread was invented. Machine-made lace and embroidery had been used on clothes since the eighteenth century.

Up to 1850 everything was stitched by hand; by the 1860s there were several sewing machines. Even then it is unlikely that a bulky machine was used for dolls' clothes. Much would be done by the child as a sewing exercise or as a treat instead of plain hemming.

Cleaning is a vital question with dolls' clothes; use only pure soap flakes and not a detergent.

Fakes and Forgeries

Many toys can be mended, repainted and refurbished; eventually, how much of the original is left? The only really authentic dolls and toys are those handed down through the years in the same family. Well-used rocking horses have been renovated for succeeding generations, and modern dappled markings look as if they have been done through a stencil of wire-netting.

Early 19th century moulds for soldiers, zoo animals, etc. still exist. Anyone may use these, and although some fine detail may be lost, the models are neither fakes nor forgeries unless falsely dated.

Separate parts for train sets, such as couplings, were supplied by rival firms, making it more difficult now to state the actual maker. Individual items (locomotives, coaches, etc.) are cheaper than complete sets.

A doll will have been redressed many times for the same little owner or succeeding children. A new wheel and a fresh coat of paint on a toy makes a better gift. Most playthings have been refurbished, and in the world of antiques a really genuine untouched toy is rare; very old ones have hand-made nails.

Reproduction 'Dutch' dolls are poorly made and finished compared to the originals, which had smoothed-down wood, symmetrically painted features and spoon-shaped hands. Many of this type are sold today as early Victorian.

On labelled dolls beware of newly-stamped maker's names, even the faded brown signatures on wax doll bodies have been imitated. A descendant of the Pierottis stated that as far as he knew their wax dolls had never been signed, yet a scratched signature has been found just under the back hair; a peculiar place to mark a wax doll.

However, moulds of some well-known bisque makes, including Bru heads and marked bisques, have been found and used; and sewn to old bodies, these apparent deceptions are sold at antique prices. Collectors must study bodies very carefully, the sewing, stuffing, eyelet holes, every little detail. Where possible, compare with an original article. There may even be two right legs or arms so take off the shoes and socks and look.

Beware of the perfect smooth finish, poorly-painted or badly matched details of eyebrows and lips; the yoke may not be well modelled, and the eyes may not be in exact focus. This is never the case with a well-bred doll, in spite of carrying a lorgnette. Lastly, no true collector would be fooled by a nylon wig!

Further Reading

BOEHN, M. U. VON *Dolls and Puppets.* Tr. Josephine Nicoll. London, 1932.

CHAPIUS, A., and D. E. *Les Automates, Figures Artificielles d'Hommes et des Animaux.* Paris, 1949.

COLEMAN, D. S. et al. *Collector's Encyclopedia of Dolls.* New York, 1968.

DAIKEN, L. *Children's Toys throughout the Ages.* London, 1963. *World of Toys,* Sidcup, Kent, 1963.

DESMOND, K. *Dolls.* London, 1973.

FLICK, P. *Discovering Toys.* Tring, Hertfordshire, 1971.

FRASER, A. *A History of Toys.* London and New York, 1966.

FREEMAN, G. L. and S. *Yesterday's Toys.* New York, 1962.

FRITZSCH and BACHMANN. *An Illustrated History of Toys.* Leipzig, 1965.

GARRATT, J. C. *Model Soldiers,* London, 1959.

GERKEN, J. E. *Wonderful Dolls of Wax.* Nebraska, 1964.

GIBSON, C. *A History of British Dinky Toys 1934-1964.* Hemel Hempstead, Hertfordshire, 1966.

GREENE, V. *English Dolls' Houses of the 18th and 19th centuries.* London, 1955.

HANNAS, L. *The English Jigsaw Puzzle, 1760-1890.* 1972.

HARRIS, E. D. *Model Soldiers,* New York and London, 1962.

HASKELL, A. and LEWIS, M. *Infantilia, or the Archaeology of the nursery,* London, 1972.

HERTZ, L. H. *Handbook of Old American Toys.* New York, 1947.

HILLIER, M. *Pageant of Toys.* London, 1965.

HOPKINSON, W. P. *Toys and Banks.* Concord, Conn., 1970.

JACOBS, F. G. and FAURHOLT, E. F. *A book of dolls and doll houses,* Rutland Vt. 1967.

JOHNSON, A. *How to Repair and Dress Old Dolls.* London, 1967.

LATHAM, J. *Dolls' Houses.* London, 1969.

MCCLINTOCK, I. and M. *Toys in America.* Washington D.C., 1961.

MURRAY, P. *Toys.* London, 1968.

NOBEL, J. *Dolls.* London, 1967.

HEARD, J. *Pollock's World of Toys.* London, 1969.

REMISE, J., and FONDIN, J. *The Golden Age of Toys.* Tr. by D. B. Tubbs, London, 1967.

SPEAIGHT, G. *History of the English Toy Theatre.* London, 1968.

WHITE, G. *A Picture Book of Ancient and Modern Dolls.* London, 1926. *A Book of Toys.* Harmondsworth and New York, 1946. *A Book of Dolls.* London, 1956. *Dolls of the World.* London, 1962. *European and American Dolls and their marks and patents.* London and New York, 1966. *Toys and their Background.* London, 1971.

Museum Collections

Great Britain

BRISTOL: City Museum, Blaise Castle, Henbury.

DURHAM: Bowes Museum, Barnard Castle.

KENT: Royal Museum, Tunbridge Wells.

LONDON: Bethnal Green Museum; Horniman Museum; London Museum and Kensington Palace; Pollock's Toy Museum.

WARWICKSHIRE: Doll Museum, Warwick.

YORKSHIRE: Abbey House Museum, Kirkstall (Leeds)

SCOTLAND: Museum of Childhood, Edinburgh.

WALES: Welsh Folk Museum, St. Fagan's (Cardiff).

U.S.A.

CONNECTICUT: Connecticut Historical Society, Hartford.

MASSACHUSETTS: Essex Institute, Salem.

MICHIGAN: Children's Museum, Detroit.

NEW YORK: Brooklyn Children's Museum, New York City; City of New York Museum; New York Historical Society, New York City.

PENNSYLVANIA: Bucks County Historical Society Museum, Doylestown; Pennsylvania State Farm Museum, Lancaster.

Index

Index